The Foundations of Rock

THE FOUNDATIONS OF ROCK

From "Blue Suede Shoes" to "Suite: Judy Blue Eyes"

Walter Everett

UNIVERSITY PRESS
2009

OXFORD
UNIVERSITY PRESS

Oxford University Press, Inc., publishes works that further
Oxford University's objective of excellence
in research, scholarship, and education.

Oxford   New York
Auckland   Cape Town   Dar es Salaam   Hong Kong   Karachi
Kuala Lumpur   Madrid   Melbourne   Mexico City   Nairobi
New Delhi   Shanghai   Taipei   Toronto

With offices in
Argentina   Austria   Brazil   Chile   Czech Republic   France   Greece
Guatemala   Hungary   Italy   Japan   Poland   Portugal   Singapore
South Korea   Switzerland   Thailand   Turkey   Ukraine   Vietnam

Published by Oxford University Press, Inc.
198 Madison Avenue, New York, New York 10016
www.oup.com

Oxford is a registered trademark of Oxford University Press

Library of Congress Cataloging-in-Publication Data
Everett, Walter, 1954–
The foundations of rock : from Blue suede shoes to Suite : Judy blue eyes / Walter Everett.
    p. cm.
Includes bibliographical references (p.) and index.
ISBN: 978-0-19-531023-8; 978-0-19-531024-5 (pbk.)
1. Rock music—Analysis, appreciation.   I. Title.
MT146.E96 2009
781.66'09046–dc22   2008006415

Recorded audio tracks are available online at http://www.oup.com/us/thefoundationsofrock/

9 8 7 6 5 4 3 2 1

Printed in the United States of America
on acid-free paper

Preface

How does Hendrix get those sounds from his guitar in "The Star Spangled Banner"? What is that weird instrument at the beginning of "Strawberry Fields Forever"? How do both James Brown's "I Got the Feeling" and The Who's "I'm Free" put me so far off balance? Why are Brian Wilson, Frank Zappa, and Eric Clapton considered geniuses? What is the fastest rock song of the 1960s? What makes Janis Ian's "Society's Child" sound so profoundly sad? This book, which will address these sorts of questions and lead the reader to consider many more, was written to bring a richly detailed understanding of popular music, particularly rock music, to everyone who enjoys it, whether as a casual listener, a loyal fan, or a performing musician. Even the professional composer, performer, or educator is bound to improve their musical experience by reading this volume because even though the book assumes no prior musical knowledge, it explores every domain of rock and pop recordings in greater depth than experienced anywhere else.

Our focus is on the period 1955–69. This, after all, is the golden age of rock music—of Elvis Presley, the Beatles, the Rolling Stones, Ray Charles, the Beach Boys, the Supremes, the Temptations, Stevie Wonder, Aretha Franklin, The Doors, the Grateful Dead, James Brown, Janis Joplin, Chuck Berry, the

Mothers, the Platters, Buddy Holly, Sly and the Family Stone, The Who, the Yardbirds, and the early Led Zeppelin. That this is considered the greatest rock music of all time is argued in major polls and critics' lists appearing right to the present day. The actual music researched for this study occupies a broad and deep range of popular and critically acclaimed recordings. Over the better part of a year, I did little other than listen (*really* listen) to all 2,459 records that appeared among the top twenty positions of *Billboard*'s weekly "Hot 100" singles chart, plus hundreds of notable lesser hits and more than three hundred full albums released in the same fifteen-year period, for a total sample of well over sixty-five hundred songs. (Modern jazz, existing in more of a hermetic environment, while by most accounts a type of popular music, had little impact on top album and single sales, and so is not a focus of this study.) All of this music represents the cauldron out of which rock was born, so this book is defined as covering the "Foundations of Rock Music" in reference to stylistic parentage, in reference to the embryonic nature of the era of repertoire covered, and, most importantly, in reference to the elemental materials—color, pitch, rhythm, form, lyrics, and engineering—that form the building blocks of rock music. Although the surfaces have changed greatly over the intervening years, right through the likes of the Red Hot Chili Peppers, Radiohead, and Dr. Dre, the fundamentals have not.

The early history of rock unfolded in an era that witnessed an increasing role of artistic experimentation in what had originally been a very direct means of expression. Despite this once-direct connection between artist and listener, the dominant method of musical reproduction—the transferring of data from plastic disc to loudspeakers—has tended to dehumanize and mystify the nature of musical sound. And because most of today's listeners are far less aware of the qualities of music's elements than were preceding generations, the most devoted and imaginative fan still misses out on a lot of what is conveyed, even from a good seat at a live performance. Only when listeners become consciously aware of their reactions to the despairing cry of a wah-wah pedal, the acerbic bite of off-the-string bowing, the physicality of the vocal purr, the tension underlying the anticipation of a returning harmony, the emotional release of the consonant resolution of a phrase ending, the dynamic nature of an altered scale degree, the expressive value of a particular harmonic digression, the complacency or discomfort brought on by contrasting rhythms, the intimacy or wide-open public space created by the recording engineer, and the tone and phraseology of the lyric—only then can the complete musical message come through; only then can one who has heard a familiar song for perhaps the five-hundredth time over a span of several decades fully appreciate that experience once again as if for the first time. Thus, depending on musical preferences, the newly informed listener will have a more vivid fantasy, a more exciting catharsis, a more compelling romance, a more successful rebellion—or simply a stronger distraction from the pain of the Stairmaster—while at the same time rehumanizing all those good vibrations.

Although this book's subject matter—the elements of this music and their meanings—is investigated in all possible thoroughness, there are several topics and approaches that will not be found here. We are deeply interested in what is heard from the record's groove and the CD's track, but not so much in the personalities or the creative procedures by which that material got there— that's all great stuff, but it's covered elsewhere. So for convenience's sake, we will often refer to the singer or guitarist as the song's agent of communication without acknowledging that it could well have been a faceless composer, producer, arranger, or even a bass player who was responsible for creating the effect of interest to us at any given time. We'll refer to Judy Collins's "Both Sides Now," with full unspoken knowledge that Joni Mitchell wrote the song, Joshua Rifkin arranged it, and Mark Abramson produced it, simply for the sake of the reader who needs only to know what recording we're discussing. Similarly, although we may seem to be ignoring the larger intertextual picture by which the listener contextualizes any given passage of a song into a life rich with potential personal, cultural, and literary references, we wish to make no claims here as to the musical or other life experiences held by the average or even the ideal reader-listener—that is for every individual to work through on their own. Nor are we here interested in the potential place of this or that musical phrase within this or any other society's cultural experience—we thank sociologists for addressing this as they wish. There's enough on our plate—plenty happens within a song and many are the potential meanings of its structures. We'll happily leave it to others to explain how best to muse on its social, political, and cultural contexts.

I have kept terminology as jargon-free as possible. Whereas music scholars have labored in the opposite direction, developing a rich vocabulary for achieving maximum clarity, I have sacrificed a great many academically useful words and approaches in hopes of satisfying a general audience with a more streamlined text. This will not be the place, for instance, for the reader to discover the differences among the concepts of pitch, pitch class, and note. It is hoped that the context of the discussion, despite any informality of language, will at all times contribute sufficiently to a clear understanding, and that little if any nuance of thought has been sacrificed in such a direct approach. Needless to say, concepts that have no bearing on this music will not be referred to here, no matter how central they may be to Beethoven or Brahms. Rest assured that if a topic commonly discussed in regard to other repertoires does not appear in these pages, it probably doesn't happen in this music. Otherwise, for example, complexes such as the German and French sixths so key to eighteenth- and nineteenth-century voice leading have their analogues in our repertoire, but they function here so differently, these terms never need appear again. Perhaps a reader who discovers here the joys that can be had in focused listening will then go on to more formal reading in music theory and musicology as well as to a broader listening and thinking experience with many styles of music, ultimately learning about the German sixth while studying Mozart or Tchaikovsky. Those interested in continuing their reading but in a rock-only context are directed to the list of further readings found on the other side of the book's chapters.

Many readers will have some literacy in music, and can perhaps even read musical notation. Some may play an instrument. Some may know what is meant by the key of B-flat, or a G-minor scale, or an E-major chord, or "an F-sharp in the bass." These designations are necessary for the professional musician, and are used by all sorts of practicing players, but they are unnecessary for those who just listen to music—particularly the vast majority who do not know what key a song may be in. Instead of referring to pitches by name, all pitch relations discussed in this book will be in terms of scale degree, and therefore reliance only on the numbers from 1 to 7 will simplify the reader's task in learning what is essentially for many a new language. Scale degrees will be expressed as Arabic numbers (1, 2, 3 . . .) when referring to individual pitches and as Roman numerals (I, ii, iii . . .) when referring to chords. For those familiar with letter-name pitch spelling, initial discussion will relate briefly to this system through the depiction of a piano keyboard, and the Appendix will provide note-name spellings of every single chord mentioned in the book. This might be a good place to explain the slash notation that is used later in the book to indicate interactions of melodic and chordal materials: the label 5/I/3, for instance, indicates that the main melody features the fifth scale degree, which is supported by the I chord with the third scale degree in the bass, owing to the ordering of Arabic and Roman numerals as separated by slashes. From a different label, 4/V, the reader should infer that the melody has 4 over the V chord, which is presented with its root in the bass (the default position that need not be routinely indicated as 4/V/5). All of these concepts will be explained in due course, but the system's mechanics are introduced here for ease of reference.

Musical events in a particular song will often be cued for the reader by keying them to timings programmed into digital recordings, whether taken from commercial compact discs or downloaded from online files. At other times, brief quotations of lyrics will allow the reader to identify the exact spot at which a musical event appears. For instance, read the following cue, taken from Neil Sedaka's "Calendar Girl": "[IV] yeah, yeah, my [i°⁷] heart's in a whirl, I [I] love, I love, I love my little [VI^{m7}] calendar girl every [II^{m7}] day (every day), every [V^{m7}] day (every day) of the [I] year (every) [IV] (day of the) [I] (year)." The lead vocal line is given within quotations, and backing vocal lyrics are parenthesized. This quote focuses on harmonic events, so that the IV chord is seen as sustaining through the words "yeah, yeah, my," at which point the chord changes to $i°^7$. The Appendix shows that the IV chord contains scale degrees 4, 6, and 1 (a fact that will be covered in many ways through the course of the book), and that in the key of C such a chord is made by combining F, A, and C.

Instead of relying on musical notation, we will illustrate many concepts with recorded examples. Callouts in the text marked "Web audio example" refer to specific examples among some 285 tracks found at the book's accompanying Web site that will enable the reader to focus on exactly the sound under discussion, whether a vocal effect, an obscure percussion instrument, a scale pattern, a harmonic relationship, or a particular rhythmic device. (Bracketed callouts labeled "Web photo" refer to photographs at the same site.) Whereas licensing issues prevent the quotation of significant portions of the lyrics of the songs under analysis, it is hoped that (1) the range of titles suggested as exemplifying any given technique will permit the reader to recognize at least one familiar song for every given case and that (2) if necessary, the convenient, legal, and inexpensive downloading of the examples referred to here will circumvent any need to purchase a greater number of recordings than desired in order to get full value from this text. In many cases, a lo-fi recording accessed without cost on YouTube (http://www.youtube.com) would serve the intended illustrative purpose.

Some compromises in presentation were necessary in keeping to one volume a text aimed at the novice that delves into its topics in great depth. Clear communication is this writer's goal, and hopefully it has been achieved by streamlining vocabulary and providing all the references that might be deemed helpful, without the use of cumbersome footnotes. Nevertheless, the book's ideas are tightly packed and the reader should not hope to absorb them quickly or in large doses. In fact, the abundance of materials in this book are offered in order that, carefully examined and considered, they may continue to reward quite a deliberate study if desired. The book's contributions will be found most enriching when the text, Web audio examples and photographs, and the cited recordings from 1955–1969 are consulted together, fully compared back and forth. It is hoped that the reader's patience and the investment of time required by some of the more involved discussions will be well repaid. And whereas I have labored for years now to refine this book, errors have undoubtedly escaped my notice, and I would be grateful to readers who might inform me of necessary corrections.

The book is organized so as to cover all fundamental aspects of rock music and its popular cousins in a sequence that will best help the reader grow in knowledge and confidence. We begin with five chapters focusing mostly on uses of instrumentation and voice, as most of these sounds—guitars, bass, drums, keyboards, and vocals—are familiar to most listeners. But our study will probe the depths of the tonal colors, the performance techniques, and the functional values of these forces, establishing as we go some basic systems by which we'll treat matters of melody, harmony, and rhythm throughout the book. Chapter 6 covers the formal sections of the popular song, so that all subsequent discussions may refer to the intro, verse, bridge, chorus, break, or motto in the knowledge that the reader understands what part of a given song is up for discussion. Then, we enter the highly detailed world of pitch, the parameter that most sets music apart from all other arts. One chapter on the principles of melodic construction will be followed by four chapters on various topics dealing with harmony—chords and their connections—in every usage known in the repertoire. Chapter 12 isolates rhythm, and here we cover all matters of tempo, rhythm, and meter. In Chapter 13, the recording techniques of the 1950s and '60s are detailed, so that a listener can learn to become aware of all types of electronic effects brought to bear in a recording, many of them relating closely to the expressive purpose of the song at hand. In Chapter 14, aspects of lyric writing are covered to enable a listener to form his or her own interpretation of their poetic meanings on their own and as tied to the accompanying musical ideas through various critical stances. At the end of the process, a listener should be able to identify the sources of any and all sounds in a recording, understand the purely musical relationships through which they interact, and interpret the meanings suggested by lyrics and music together—not only for any record of the 1950s or '60s but practically for any popular song of the past century or more. Those with stronger musical inclinations should find themselves able as never before to compose, arrange, and produce excellent recordings in most any style popular in this period. As Ringo once directed before a guitar break, "Rock on, anybody!"

Acknowledgments

This book was written with the support of a fellowship from the National Endowment for the Humanities and the Horace H. Rackham Faculty Fellowship Enhancement Award, which provided for a year of time released from teaching responsibilities. Any views, findings, conclusions, or recommendations expressed in this publication do not necessarily reflect those of the National Endowment of the Humanities. I am grateful to the brilliant musicians who graciously gave of their time and expertise in reading and commenting on early chapter drafts: Christopher Doll, Andy Flory, Dai Griffiths, Virgil Moorefield, William Moylan, Shaugn O'Donnell, George Shirley, Mark Spicer, Gordon Thompson, and an anonymous reader contacted by Oxford University Press all prevented some of my unhelpful errors from making it to the final pages.

Music Editor Suzanne Ryan and Associate Editor Norm Hirschy have been generous with their support, brimming over with great ideas, and unusually helpful in realizing the potential of my own point of view and desires in ways I could not envision myself. From start to finish, it has been an absolute pleasure and a terrifically rewarding experience working with Suzanne and Norm.

The recording of the book's accompanying audio examples required the coordination of many people and facilities at the University of Michigan School of Music, Theatre & Dance. Under the auspices and arrangements of Deans Christopher Kendall and Mary Simoni and with the cheerful support and assistance of audio resources coordinator Dave Greenspan, engineers Jason Corey and Kristin Fosdick, Stearns Collection of Musical Instruments Director Chris Dempsey, percussion facilitator Neeraj Mehta, piano technicians Robert Grijalva and Norman Vesprini, and staff and faculty members David Aderente, Lynne Aspnes, Fritz Kaenzig, Ken Kiesler, Marilyn Mason, Edward Parmentier, Stephen Rush, Ramon Satyendra, Michael Udow, and Brent Wagner, I was able to secure the world-class facilities of the Duderstadt Center Audio Studio, the use of many fine instruments, and the services of many Michigan student performers all of whom are credited in the online audio captions. Thanks also to Greg Laman for tutelage and trouble-shooting advice in Logic Pro and to Neile Rissmiller and Elizabeth Burr for desktop and wireless tech support. Recordings were made possible by grants from the School of Music, Theatre & Dance of the University of Michigan that were administered by Julie Smigielski, and from the Society for Music Theory. Scheduling was coordinated by Kimberley Osburn. I am fortunate beyond measure to have such wonderful, generous, and highly professional colleagues.

Notes on the Web Site

A full appreciation of the contents of this text will depend upon a rich interaction with its companion Web site, found at http://www.oup.com/us/thefoundationsofrock. This site is replete with hundreds of audio examples and photographs created precisely to illustrate this book's points as clearly as possible. When the aural examples are studied alongside the text, the reader's experience will be more richly alive and comprehension will be fuller, allowing for an easy, active transfer from the knowledge gained here to the experience of real-world listening. In fact, the ready availability of the book's Web site also means the ready availability of digital versions of all recordings cited in the text, nearly all of which are licensed at the major online repositories (iTunes, Amazon, Wal-Mart, etc.) and presented on YouTube.

Each Web audio example has its own caption, adding cues to help the listener focus on the point at hand and crediting performers. Web photo captions also add information for further clarification. It is recommended that listeners use headphones. Even small earbuds will produce a far better response than do the tiny drivers in laptops, which often cannot convey any bass at all. Most desktop machines include built-in speakers of moderate quality, but the listener may experience severe distortion and clipping from these at louder volume levels. Standalone external monitors are better still as long as the listener can control a good stereo balance.

Contents

The Foundations of Rock

CHAPTER I

Drums, Other Percussion, and a Bit about Rhythm

Trained musicians who are so inclined love to talk about melody, harmony, and intricate rhythmic and formal patterns. In some cases where I've discussed such matters with general audiences that are not so trained, I'm told that it's the basic "sound," more than these more advanced properties, that makes rock music meaningful to them. Their point is well taken. The sound of the sound, its color—the characteristics that enable us to tell one instrument from another or one singer from another or one guitar effect from another—are a very sensible place to begin to point the ear in order to focus on the aural experience. In our first five chapters, we'll cover every single device used to produce the sounds that create the pop music of the 1950s and '60s. First, in chapters 1 through 3, we'll examine the instruments of the rock band from its foundation, drums and bass, through its different kinds of guitars and keyboards. This will be followed in chapter 4 by a look at how every single orchestral, wind-band, and other instrument originally created for preceding styles has been borrowed in our pop-rock repertoire. In chapter 5, we'll consider the ins and outs of vocal sonorities. For each instrument and voice type, we'll discuss pertinent concepts of tone production, the ways in which those sounds function on their own, and the ways in which they combine with other sonic forces to create full textures. Along the way, we'll introduce some important concepts of rhythm and pitch that will prepare us for later chapters on rhythm, melody, and harmony. Our survey begins with the keeping of the beat...

Drums and drumming

The most universal complaint of adults in the 1950s and '60s: "rock 'n' roll is NOISE." There were many reasons for this reaction: rock singers, when they belted out their songs, placed little or no value on any ideal beauty of tone that had been prized for many generations; featured instruments such as guitars and piano often had more of a rhythmic function than one of providing melodic lines that would complement the vocalist's melody; the amplification of electrified instruments and the colorings provided—or subtracted—by the engineers who produced the recordings often seemed to remove subtleties of quiet nuance from the picture and to encourage a shrinking of the overall dynamic range. The recordings, now supplanting live performances as the main source of musical experience, were sometimes played via mistreated vinyl on poor equipment that added heavy distortion to the signal when cranked up to the desired volume. But probably the most important reason for the noise complaint was rock's new emphasis on the drummer. In classical music, only the most massive orchestral music of the previous hundred years would require more than one percussionist, and solo, choral, and chamber music usually employed none at all. A single drummer in a swing band, even though heavily outnumbered and outsounded by melodious brass and saxes, did not have to play loudly to be the group's timepiece. In a jazz trio, where one of three played a trap set, the drummer often used soft-sounding brushes so as to stay out of the pianist's or wind player's way. In rock, the drummer could play as loudly as possible, even when he was one of only four or five group members, even before amplifiers became much more powerful in the late '60s. Drums are the main reason adults relegated rehearsing rock groups to the garage.

The rock drummer maintains the pulse that holds the group together and connects directly with listeners' physiology, driving them to dance, igniting the exuberance that would deafen the young to all requests to turn it down. The drummer is largely concerned with keeping the ensemble together (consider expert session players like Hal Blaine, as heard in records by Frank Sinatra, Elvis Presley, Phil Spector, and the Beach Boys), keeping the energy level at a high roar (think Keith Moon of The Who), taking the group from one section of a song to another through connective and often propulsive fills (Ringo Starr of the Beatles), shaping the groove that controls the performance's flow (Benny Benjamin of Motown), and occasionally taking center stage with imaginative solos (Ginger Baker of Cream). Drummers have a wide range of techniques, styles, and degrees of control or wildness. We'll examine a number of such characteristics by reviewing a few of a drummer's roles, establishing a few basic concepts pertaining to rhythm, and looking at the drum kit itself.

Exceedingly rare is the rock song with no drumming at all. Among them are Elvis's first singles for Sun, including "That's All Right," "Milkcow Blues Boogie," and "Baby Let's Play House," released in 1954–55 before anyone knew drums would be "required." Similarly, only two songs among Bob Dylan's first four LPs, "Don't Think Twice, It's All Right" and "Corrina, Corrina," include drums, but these were cut before anyone—the artist included—knew he was a rocker at heart. Like Dylan's early work, Simon and Garfunkel's "Sounds of Silence" was recorded without drums (and first released that way in 1964 with only two vocals and a lightly picked acoustic guitar), but producer Tom Wilson beefed it up without the duo's knowledge with overdubbed electric guitar, electric bass, and drums for its hit-bound release as a 1966 single. These examples aside, only a few rare top-twenty songs like Chuck Berry's "Havana Moon," Frankie Laine's "Love is a Golden Ring," and Elvis Presley's "Crying in the Chapel" omit drums entirely, and this is always done for a particular effect. Much more often, drums are omitted for just one section of a song as a foil, as in the intros to the Crests' "Sixteen Candles" and Roy Orbison's "In Dreams," and the first verse of James Taylor's "Fire and Rain," allowing the delayed drum entry to provide renewed strength to succeeding passages.

Some rock drumming is virtuosic. Some cases, such as that spotlighted in B. B. King's album, *Live & Well,* suggest origins in the jazz tradition via blues bands. Blues is in fact the basis for some of rock's greatest improvisation, which yields the best extended soloing on drums, as heard in Cream's "Toad" (more or less weakly imitated by Blue Cheer's "Second Time Around," Iron Butterfly's "In-A-Gadda-Da-Vida," the Rascals' "Boom," Grand Funk Railroad's "T.N.U.C.," and Led Zeppelin's "Moby Dick"). The studio version of "Toad" (on *Fresh Cream*) opens with Baker's four toms (entering successively high to low), stating the range to be occupied by a brilliant 3'26" solo featuring two bass drums at 2:45–3:08. The released live version (edited for *Wheels of Fire* but reconstructed for *Those Were the Days*) is nothing but drums from 3:46 to 16:54, with great demonstrations of all kit components brought together by what is hard to believe is one performer. Blues aside, modern jazz inspired such extended solos as heard in Soft Machine's "So Boot If at All" and the Mothers of Invention's "King Kong." Jazz aside, the concerto principle pitting soloist versus orchestra gave rise to the long drum solo in the third movement of Deep Purple's

Concerto for Group and Orchestra. Otherwise, rock's most flamboyant drumming appears in brief bursts, as in the six-second solo in the Ventures' "Perfida," the several solos of Sandy Nelson's "Let There Be Drums," the celebrated patterns of the Surfaris' "Wipe Out," and the manifold sorts of fleeting drum breaks that lead from one section of a song to another in most of the repertoire.

Drums are out front for a variety of reasons, sometimes arbitrary, and it's certainly an unquestioned norm. With the Dave Clark Five, one gets the impression that the drums are mixed to the fore in tracks like "Glad All Over" because (1) not much else is going on and (2) the procedure features the group's leader, a drummer who set up on stage in front of the guitars, as a marketing ploy. Only the first of these two reasons could explain the same characteristic in tracks such as Bob Seger's "Ramblin' Gamblin' Man." In Steam's "Na Na Hey Hey (Kiss Him Goodbye)," the solo drumming beginning at 1:44 seems the result of a post-production decision to mute everything else in the mix momentarily, and the drum solo (plus tambourine) in the Beatles' "Birthday" seems like a stretch intended for band overdubs that never materialized. Clem Cattini goes wild on the skins in Donovan's "Hurdy Gurdy Man" not because the song's poetics demand it, but because he's trying to keep up with hard-rocking bandmates John Paul Jones (bass) and Alan Parker (electric guitar). The dual drummers of the Grateful Dead sometimes blend together in an extended flurry; at other times they have separate agendas (they're quite distinct in "New Potato Caboose," *Anthem of the Sun,* CD remix, 5:53 to the end, with Mickey Hart on the left and Bill Kreutzman on the right). "Listen Here," by Brian Auger and the Trinity, features four jazz drummers pursuing quite different simultaneous ideas. Much more interesting is the work of a single musician, working in counterpoint with his fellow instrumentalists, as with Ringo Starr's playing in the Beatles' "Rain" and "A Day in the Life," Ginger Baker's in Cream's "Crossroads" and "Spoonful" (*Wheels of Fire* performances), or even Gene Chrisman's understated snare in Merrilee Rush's "Angel of the Morning." The contrapuntal potential of the drummer was realized in a new way in the late '60s by multiple miking of the set, allowing different parts of the kit to appear in different parts of the stereo image, as in Blood, Sweat and Tears' "And When I Die."

Usually, the drums are a seat of power, and the unleashing of their fury can suggest life-changing ecstasy in Little Richard's "Tutti–Frutti," psychological volatility in the Jimi Hendrix Experience's "Manic Depression" and Led Zeppelin's "Dazed and Confused," apocalyptic pronouncement in The Doors' "The End," antiauthoritarian bravado in The Who's "Anyway, Anyhow, Anywhere," blistering anger in The Who's "I Can See For Miles," or the threatening total loss of control in The Who's "My Generation." Yes, The Who's Keith Moon was a wild man, and his eventual replacement, Kenney Jones, can be heard first establishing his own Moonish credentials in the Small Faces' "Song of a Baker."

Rudiments, or the snare techniques practiced to perfection by military and orchestral drummers (and the basis of Dead drummer Mickey Hart's mother's award-winning skills), are generally of remote interest here. Occasionally a rock listener hears a flam, where a dynamically accented snare hit is immediately preceded by another for added emphasis, and you've got those short paradiddle drills after the refrain of Neil Sedaka's "Calendar Girl," the upbeats of the Everly Brothers' "Cathy's Clown," and those funny little bits in Dylan's "Most Likely You Go Your Way (And I'll Go Mine)," but the roll is the only other rudimentary "trick" known to rock, and it isn't very common. (Listen to Web audio examples 1.01 and 1.02.) The longest roll of this era may be that by Nick Mason in Pink Floyd's "The Grand Vizier's Garden Party" (directly after the opening flute duet); Ringo plays them only in "All You Need Is Love," "Nowhere Man," and "Being for the Benefit of Mr. Kite," and that's pretty much it for drum rolls in British rock. Americans are much more prone to feature them, as in Perry Como's "Hot Diggity (Dog Ziggity Boom)," James Darren's "Goodbye Cruel World" and "Her Royal Majesty," the Miracles' "Tracks of My Tears," Bobby Hebb's "Sunny," The Mamas and the Papas' "Words of Love," the Outsiders' "Time Won't Let Me," the Mothers of Invention's "Plastic People," The Grateful Dead's "Easy Wind," Sly and the Family Stone's "Stand!," and The Association's "Requiem for the Masses." Seven of these eleven are played by session drummers rather than group members, who are less often trained.

Despite the general disinterest in rudiments, two-stick snare marches make for the most common drum-based symbol in pop, bringing militaristic and patriotic themes into about three dozen hits of the era. Witness inspiring marches in Mitch Miller's "March from the River Kwai," Johnny Desmond's "The Yellow Rose of Texas," Johnny Horton's "The Battle of New Orleans," and Jimmy Dean's "P. T. 109," raw jingoism in Senator Dirksen's "Gallant Men," Ssgt Barry Sadler's "The Ballad of the Green Berets," and Victor Lundberg's "An Open Letter to My Teenage Son," cartoonish battle scenes in the Royal Guardsmen's "Snoopy vs. the Red Baron" and The Fifth Estate's "Ding Dong! The Witch Is Dead," a simple army chant in Art Mooney's "Honey-Babe," a psychedelic bolero in the Jefferson Airplane's "White Rabbit," pitchless poetry in Van Morrison's "Madame George," and dedication in an antiwar pair, the Butterfield Blues Band's "Love March" and Original Caste's "One Tin Soldier."

Rhythm: Beats, meter, and groove

To get any deeper into drumming technique, we'll have to cover a few technical points about how rhythm works. One can't have rhythm without meter. Meter is the imaginary background grid of regularly recurring pulses against which performed rhythmic patterns are heard and interpreted. Meter provides a constant flow of inaudible beats, some of which (or some parts of which) are manifested in the actual rhythms of a song, and some of which pass silently by. In many songs, the drums simply beat out the meter, marking every beat uniformly on the snare for a hard-driving effect; this is true in the Rolling Stones' "(I Can't Get No) Satisfaction," Bob Dylan's "Rainy Day Women #12 & 35," and many early Motown productions with Benny Benjamin on drums (the Four Tops' "It's the Same Old Song," "Shake Me, Wake Me," and "Bernadette," and the Supremes' "Nothing But Heartaches," for example). (Listen to Web audio example 1.03.) Sometimes, only a portion of a song will be drummed this way; note the driving intro to the Box Tops' "The Letter," or the choruses of the Zombies' "She's Not There" and the Union Gap's "Young Girl."

> **Meter:** a grid of regular, inaudible pulses
>
> **Rhythm:** the articulation of time as measured against the underlying meter

Meter, however, is more complex than is realized in these basic examples. In its full glory, it is organized into different levels by regular alternations of strong and weak beats, strong and weak *parts* of beats, and strong and weak parts of the parts. (It even has higher levels that recognize strong and weak *groups* of beats.) Rhythms, in contrast to meter, can provide any combination of strong and weak accents in either regular or irregular patterns. Rhythms often align with meter, or they can syncopate against it by emphasizing normally weak beats (or their parts), thus creating the great off-balance, propulsive tension typical of rock music. Drummers typically will set up regularly recurring rhythmic patterns that may or may not agree with the underlying meter, and then embellish the patterns with new levels of accents on ever smaller parts of beats, and then may change them completely. When a rhythmic pattern recurs throughout a song or a section of a song, it is referred to as the groove—especially when the bass, rhythm guitar, or keyboardist participate—and is often a defining characteristic of a song.

Let's demonstrate these ideas further and at the same time add a bit of detail to the basics, just enough to support our current investigation. (We'll cover aspects of meter much more thoroughly later in our "Rhythm" chapter.) Meters will most often involve recurring groupings of either four beats or three, with the first beat of each group accented in relation to the others. So when one counts a recurring series of regularly spaced beats ("ONE—two—Three—four—ONE—two—Three—four—ONE—two...," with each upper-case word indicating a loud accent and each capitalized initial letter applied to a beat of lesser accent), meter is established. This example, "ONE—two—Three—four—ONE—two—Three—four...," represents quadruple meter (four beats per bar), whereas "ONE—two—three—ONE—two—three—ONE—two—three..." is the basis of triple meter (three beats per bar). (Listen to Web audio examples 1.04 and 1.05.) Think of the first verse of the Turtles' "Happy Together" ("imagine me and you, I do," beginning at 0:08), where the drummer simply articulates every beat on the left channel; can you hear/feel that these beats are grouped into patterns of four beats each? ONE—two—Three—four—ONE—two—Three—four.... The drum rhythm perfectly matches the underlying meter. (Note that the pitch of the recurring vocal pattern, and each underlying chord, drops by step every two bars, or every eight beats. While drummers often set the meter, the chord changes and such vocal patterns as these typically reinforce it.) Other examples of quadruple meter include Elvis Presley's "Hound Dog," Bobby Darin's "Mack the Knife," the Beatles' "Hey Jude," and Marvin Gaye's "I Heard It Through the Grapevine." Despite the fact that these songs all move at different tempos (rates of speed), they all have four beats per bar.

Triple meter occurs much less often than does quadruple, but it's still very popular. The best-known triple-meter songs of our era include Kay Starr's "Rock and Roll Waltz" and Patti Page's "The Tennessee Waltz" (maybe an obvious pair), but they also include examples as different as Elvis Presley's "Are You Lonesome To-night?," Sonny and Cher's "I Got You Babe," the Jimi Hendrix Experience's "Manic Depression," the Beatles' "Dig a Pony," and James Taylor's "Sweet Baby James."

The drummer leads the rhythm section, which also includes the bass and other accompanimental instruments such as rhythm guitar and keyboards. The rhythm section sets the groove, the steady repetitive accompaniment against which the singer(s) and any soloists may have much more varied rhythms. The drummer pretty much controls the pocket, the repetitive pattern basic to the groove. (In its earliest usage, the word "pocket" referred to a flexible space in which the articulation of the backbeat could be delayed; more on this later.) The pocket's pattern is based on how various beats are accented within the meter. Beats have different sorts of functions (and are therefore given different labels) depending on where they fall in the metric pattern: In quadruple meter, odd-numbered beats are strong and the alternating even-numbered beats are weak. In triple meter, the one strong beat, the first of every pattern, is followed by two weak beats. Beat "ONE" is always the downbeat, metrically the strongest beat of each bar, and all others are backbeats. The last beat of the bar, the weakest, is the upbeat. Count a few bars of quadruple meter (ONE—two—Three—four—ONE—two—Three—four...) and try to feel a strong downbeat on every "ONE," a less strong

"Three," and "four" feeling the weakest of all; this is a normal metric accent pattern.

Backbeat drumming, in which beats two and four are accented much more strongly than the metrically strong beats, is a common form of syncopation—a word for a rhythm's accent pattern working against the regular underlying strong-weak pattern of the natural metric accent. We can portray a backbeat rhythm against the quadruple meter by notating the beats articulated by the rhythm spelled out and the silent metric beats shown by parenthesized numerals: (1)—two—(3)—four—(1)—two—(3)—four. (Say the spelled-out numbers out loud, but feel and think the parenthesized numerals silently as thwarted metric accents, all numbers continuing at the same pace; you are now performing both a quadruple meter and a syncopated backbeat rhythm against it.) The drummer is accenting snare backbeats in Web audio example 1.04. To appreciate how common backbeat drumming is in rock music, consider that it is basic to examples as diverse as the Everly Brothers' "When Will I Be Loved," the Supremes' "I Hear a Symphony," Judy Collins's "Both Sides Now," the Mothers of Invention's "Orange County Lumber Truck," and everywhere else that beats two and four are played (particularly by the drummer) louder than the naturally accented beats one and three.

The backbeat rhythm, depending on how it interacts with other instruments, can be energetic, as with the piston-powered "Maybelline," or it can be determined and angry, as in Crosby, Stills, Nash and Young's protest, "Ohio." Parts of beats that fall between the timepoints marked by beat numbers are considered offbeats; these generally divide the beats in half (ONE—and—two—and—Three—and—four—and...) but are actually infinite in number due to the continual subdivision of metric layers. Beats are somewhat plastic as well; in backbeat drumming, the snare may be delayed slightly behind beats two and four. Note Charlie Watts's playing deep in the pocket, holding back the Rolling Stones in "Honest I Do." Rock historian and drummer Gordon Thompson likens this plastic quality of the beat to pitch intonation in a useful way—he finds that many drummers work to delay or "flat" the beat because most musicians tend to rush, "sharping" the beat.

In the first verse of the Turtles' "Happy Together," referred to earlier, every beat is played on both the bass drum and snare; later, in the first refrain, the bass drum calls attention to itself and throws the listener off balance by the kicks heard slightly after the strong beats at 0:22 and 0:23; these forcefully counterbalance the swinging offbeats lazily placed just *before* the beats by the singer in the prior verse. (If you have access to this recording, or a particularly vivid musical memory, think: How are the beats ornamented in "imagine me and you..." or, in the second verse, "if I should call you

10" TOM   12" TOM
16" CRASH
20" RIDE
14" HI-HAT
14" TOM
SNARE
22" BASS DRUM

Photo 1.01. The Pearl Vision trap drum set as seen from the drummer's throne. This is a fusion set, with toms scaled 2" smaller than those in the standard set. Measurements refer to the diameters of the drum shells; this dimension determines the drums' fundamentals. (Photo: Annie Eastman)

> The drum set: bass drum, floor and rack tom-toms, snare, ride and crash cymbals, hi-hat. Following descriptions of the pieces, their typical usages are detailed.

up…"?) One common way to embellish the backbeat is to also play the "and" of two, which appears exactly halfway between two and three: (1)—two—and—(3)—four. This was particularly a hallmark of hits appearing in the years from 1960 to 1962, and can be heard as basic to the groove in the Shirelles' "Will You Love Me Tomorrow" and "Baby It's You," the Mar-Keys' "Last Night," the Beach Boys' "Surfin' Safari," and the Contours' "Do You Love Me," all from that period. (Listen to Web audio example 1.06.)

The trap set

Let's be sure we understand the drummer's equipment so that we'll be able to see how different sounds are created and used for different rhythmic functions. The drum set, or traps, or the kit, consists of a number of drums and suspended cymbals arranged for the convenience of a single seated player. (See Web photos 1.01–1.06.) The larger the multilayered hardwood shell and corresponding drum skin ("head"), the deeper the sound, and so the large bass drum (the one facing the audience, its outer skin a handy location for the band's logo), typically struck on strong beats, provides the group's rhythmic foundation. Drum heads were regularly made from calfskin until the introduction of one- and two-ply Mylar, which could produce a sharper attack, circa 1958.

The bass drum is also called the kick drum because it is struck by a beater hinged to a metal plate depressed by the right foot. One might notice that Dixieland bands once used a very large-diameter bass drum (though still smaller than the slow-responding orchestral bass drum of 32 to 36 inches), and that there is a good range of bass-drum sizes (16 to 26 inches) today; jazz drummers tend to continue to prefer more boom from the bass drum than do rock drummers. Rarely, a rock drummer of the '60s will have two kick drums producing different tones (as with Ginger Baker's pair) or allowing rapid serial two-foot attacks (Keith Moon's); paired bass drums are much more common today, especially in hard rock, and many drummers have a modern double-pedal for a single drum. Other drums become higher in pitch and faster in the bark of the attack as the diameter grows smaller from perhaps eighteen to about nine inches, and consist of any number of tom-toms (the rack toms are mounted atop the bass drum, whereas the large floor tom-tom rests on its own legs) and the narrow 14"-across snare, which has a dozen or so loosely coiled metal wires stretched across its thin lower resonant head, adding a character-istic snap when the upper beater head is struck. (See Web photos 1.07 and 1.08.) All toms and snare are played by the sticks or, fairly commonly in the 1950s and '60s, by wire brushes swept across the heads. Drummers often color the vibrations of their drums by covering them with towels, damping them with cigarette packs, or applying masking or duct tape to the heads, usually so as to subdue any unsatisfying ringing. (Listen to Web audio example 1.07.)

Cymbals of a brass-tin alloy are suspended from their centers on stands that allow them to ring when struck until they fade away or are damped by hand. Different diameters, thicknesses, and other more subtle qualities determine the loudness and reverberation time of various cymbals, and so the rock drummer would typically have at least two for contrasting colors, and perhaps a good number more. Cymbals also produce different sounds depending upon where they are struck. When tapped near the center, on the bell, a purer brass sound with little ringing results, as heard in the intros to the Animals' "We Gotta Get Out Of This Place" (from the third tap; the first two strike more closely to the edge) and Sam and Dave's "Soul Man," or in signaling the verse's return in the Dead's "Easy Wind" (3:33–3:50). When struck toward the rim, a richer, louder crash results; note every downbeat of the intro to Steppenwolf's "Born to Be Wild." (Listen to Web audio exam-ple 1.08.) Struck forcefully at the rim, a cymbal can achieve great sustain; see Paul McCartney's "Singalong Junk." Typically, continuous ride patterns (often articulating both halves of every beat, as one—and—two—and—three—and...) are played through sections of a song on thicker, larger, cym-bals, whereas occasional crashes and splashes from the rims of thinner, smaller cymbals mark musical climaxes or formal turning points, perhaps once every eight or sixteen bars. (Listen to Web audio example 1.09.) Some drummers prefer cymbals pierced by loose rivets for a sizzling ring (see Blind Faith's "Can't Find My Way Home," 0:58).

Completing the basic kit is the hi-hat, which mounts two matched cymbals above and below each other on a stand and brings them together (not too unlike the clashing of two hand-held cymbals in a military band or orchestra) by a pedal controlled by the left foot. (Listen to Web audio example 1.10.) Typical footwork strikes the bass drum on strong beats and the hi-hat on weak beats. (Listen to Web audio example 1.11.) Occasionally, the hi-hat may emphasize a very weak metric position, as in Arthur Alexander's "Anna," where only the second half of Three is struck—musically defining the weakness of the stricken singer—but here the hi-hat is given a stick stroke, not pedaled. The hi-hat can be sticked when the pair is partially open or closed, or the pair may be struck when completely open and then pedaled closed. (Listen to Web audio example 1.12.) All these techniques yield characteristic effects.

Just as cymbals can be pierced by rivets, they can also support a tambourine-like jangle-box; one is heard atop the hi-hat in the Grateful Dead's "Casey Jones" (1:22–1:56). Some trap sets of the '60s would also include cowbell and woodblock, perhaps a pair of bongos, and some players (notably the Grateful Dead's Mickey Hart and Bill Kreutzman) customized their live-performance percussion collections to orchestral proportions, often adding exotic

Photo 1.02. Mike Gabelman on his silver-sparkle Yamaha drum kit. (Photo: Annie Eastman)

non-Western instruments to their arsenals. In recordings, nearly all drumming would be enhanced by tambourines, maracas, and/or other percussion instruments, typically added in overdub sessions; these will be described below after we cover a bit more of the role of the kit, piece by piece.

So the band's foundation is typically laid by strong beats on bass drum and weak beats on hi-hat. This is often ornamented, as when the bass drum adds anticipatory kicks, in a ONE—(2)—and—Three—(4)—and—ONE—(2)—and—Three—(4)—and pattern, in conjunction with the weak-beat hi-hat (pedaled closed on two and four) (compare Web audio example 1.12), as in Roy Orbison's "Blue Bayou," Marvin Gaye's "I Heard It Through the Grapevine," and the chorus of Smokey Robinson and the Miracles' "The Tears of a Clown." In the Orbison recording, note how the bass guitar is locked to the bass drum's rhythm, both setting the groove. A slightly more complex version of this pattern opens the Supremes' "My World Is Empty Without You," again with the bass guitar locked to the bass drum. Sometimes a pattern is created progressively. In Sandy Nelson's "Teen Beat," the bass drum opens with two toms; the snare enters after five seconds of this, and at 0:29 the ride cymbal arrives; it's all traps until guitar and piano enter at 0:34. Sometimes the drummer will drop the bomb (a reference to an unprepared and isolated kick of the bass drum as in the Crew Cuts' "Sh-Boom," at 1:22) or give the bass drum its little solo; note Ringo's unconventional bass-drum march in the Beatles' "Yellow Submarine" (0:10–0:17). The bass drum is all alone in articulating every beat for three bars (1:21+) in Herb Alpert and the Tijuana Brass's "A Taste of Honey," until a sustained trombone alarm warns of the impending verse. This use of the bass drum is repeated in Tommy James and the Shondells' "Hanky Panky" and Nancy Sinatra's "Lightning's Girl," and done with offbeats marked as well (ONE—and—two—and—Three—and—four—and...) in Freddie Cannon's "Way Down Yonder in New Orleans" and Neil Sedaka's "Breaking Up Is Hard to Do." The bass drum affects a door slam in Betty Johnson's "The Little Blue Man" and a door knock in the Stones' "Tell Me (You're Coming Back)." (Conversely, Ray Charles's drummer "knocks" repeatedly on the snare in "Hallelujah! I Love Her So," as does Eddie Floyd's in "Knock on Wood.")

The snare is generally struck by the stick, but the use of brushes continues from earlier jazz practice. In fact, some jazz numbers continue to bring a brushed snare into the top twenty in the 1950s and '60s: Crazy Otto's "Glad Rag Doll" (a honky-tonk number), Eddie Heywood's "Soft Summer Breeze" (piano trio), Nina Simone's "I Loves You, Porgy" (vocal), Rosemary Clooney's "Memories of You" (featuring Benny Goodman's clarinet), and Kenny Ball's "Midnight in Moscow" (a minor-mode Dixieland septet), to mention a few. Otherwise, brushes would be called for most often in soft ballads (Pat Boone's "I'll Be Home," Ray Charles's "Georgia On My Mind," and James Taylor's

"Sweet Baby James"). Phil Ochs uses the brushed snare along with a tack piano and whimsical cowbell to ironic effect in the upbeat narration of the broad-daylight killing of Kitty Genovese in "Outside of a Small Circle of Friends." A more hackneyed result is heard in Teresa Brewer's "A Sweet Old Fashioned Girl," wherein the Jekyll-and-Hyde singer affects an old-fashioned innocence in major-mode sections with smooth strings and brushed snare, but becomes a "crazy rock 'n' rollin' little Goldilocks" in contrasting sections with loud sticked backbeat snare, gritty saxes, and brash trumpet stabs. Although the dance-band rimshot (one stick held against both the batter head and rim, the second stick striking the first sharply) is not part of the 1950s–'60s experience, the snare would frequently be tapped rhythmically on its rim; varied examples include Lonnie Donegan's vaudeville revival, "Does Your Chewing Gum Lose Its Flavor on the Bedpost Overnight," the Johnny Burnette Trio's "Lonesome Tears In My Eyes," Bob Dylan's "Sad-Eyed Lady of the Lowlands," R. B. Greaves's "Take a Letter Maria," Nilsson's "I Guess the Lord Must Be in New York City," and the second verse of "Try a Little Tenderness" as recorded by both Otis Redding and Three Dog Night.

Buddy Holly's drummer, Jerry Allison, added strong toms to "Words of Love," "Not Fade Away," and "Peggy Sue," and that's Allison on the large toms on the Everly Brothers' "('Til) I Kissed You." His style of continuous tom battering was adopted in Tommy Roe's "Sheila" (no surprise there, as Roe sought to fill Holly's shoes in many ways), but also in Barrett Strong's "Money (That's What I Want)." The toms are often heard in cascades highlighting their different pitches (recall Web audio example 1.07), as in the break in the Outsiders' "Time Won't Let Me" (1:43–1:45), the bridge of the Everlys' "When Will I Be Loved," and the intro of the Buckinghams' "Mercy, Mercy, Mercy." Sometimes one or two toms will carry a distinctive repeated tattoo rhythm, as in the Ronettes' "Be My Baby" (one tom doing ONE—(2)—and—Three, answered by another tom and handclaps on four), the Four Seasons' "Big Girls Don't Cry" (one tom hitting (1)—and—a—two—and—(3)—and—a—four—and, with a second tom hitting on Three only), and the American Breed's "Bend Me, Shape Me" (simply one tom's ONE—and—a—two—and—a—Three—and—a—four—and—a).

In that culturally insensitive age, toms were still Native American totems, as in the 1910 Fruitgum Co.'s "Indian Giver" and the Electric Indian's "Keem-O-Sabe." It happens rarely, but toms and snare may be combined in patterns, as in the opening of the Four Seasons' "Walk Like a Man," where the snare is struck four times in the first beat (ONE—ee—and—a), a tom four times in the second (two—ee—and—a), the snare four times again in the third (Three—ee—and—a), and then the bass drum marks the fourth (four!). Long rolls on the tom are rare but can be heard at the beginnings of the Marvelettes' "When You're Young and in Love" and Jimi Hendrix's "May

This Be Love," and in the majestic ending of the Moody Blues' "Peak Hour." In the Beach Boys' "That's Not Me," drummer Hal Blaine breaks out of the groove at 0:17 with lots of confident tone-painting toms as Brian Wilson sings, "I could try to be big in the eyes of the world."

The ride cymbal (or the closed hi-hat) is typically used for a regular repeated pattern, as with the opening of Henry Mancini's "Peter Gunn," the Champs' "Tequila," and The Doors' "The Crystal Ship." Often, this is combined with a backbeat snare pattern, as in the Ventures' "Walk—Don't Run." Sometimes, the ride cymbal provides a change of color for contrasting sections, as in the mood-shifting prechorus of the Zombies' "She's Not There" (at "but it's too late to say you're sorry...") and the tension-ratcheting bridge of Jefferson Airplane's "White Rabbit" ("when men on the chessboard..."). Regular ride patterns seem to be required in slow compound meters (where each beat is divided into three, not the usual two, equal offbeats), as in the Beach Boys' "Surfer Girl" and Percy Sledge's "When a Man Loves a Woman," both of which also feature strong snare backbeats (the ride and snare combining for a "ONE—trip—let—two—trip—let—Three—trip—let—four—trip—let" groove). The ride cymbal illustrates a few suggestive effects, as with the bell portrayed in Trini Lopez's "If I Had a Hammer," the rainfall suggested in the opening half-minute of Jimi Hendrix's "One Rainy Wish," and a meta-phorical accusatory finger wagging in the intro to Gladys Knight and the Pips' "I Heard It Through the Grapevine." Jazz drummer Michael Giles of King Crimson alternates between the bells of two ride cymbals (mixed at the extreme left and right of the stereo image) in "Moonchild."

Ride patterns may be played on a crash cymbal for a raucous tone, as heard in the Rebels' "Wild Weekend"; the crash carries an unusual backbeat pattern in The Mamas and the Papas' "Words of Love." A great variety of color is sought with the crash cymbal, sometimes blending beautifully with other instruments. It is played with a soft yarn or felt mallet for great long-sustaining pink-noise atmosphere in Spirit's pre-Aquarius "Taurus," and pairs of these mallets produce a wonderful soft and shimmering roll on the crash cymbal in the Four Seasons' "I've Got You Under My Skin" (blending with the brass at 0:12+), the intro of the Lovin' Spoonful's "Rain on the Roof," the ending of the Beatles' "Penny Lane" (blending with the harmonium), The Who's "Underture" (there shading the acoustic twelve-string guitar), Fleetwood Mac's "Albatross" (inspiration for the Beatles' "Sun King"), King Crimson's "Epitaph" (merging with the Mellotron's reverb), and the intro to Billy Preston's "That's the Way God Planned It" (for colorful interplay with the organ). (Listen to Web audio example 1.13.) Even without a roll, the sticked crash cymbal is often made to blend with other sounds: with the high partials of a muted guitar in the Beatles' "Girl" (2:00+), and arising out of a shaken tambourine in The Who's "Sparks" (2:13–2:22).

Effects of the crash cymbal alone are quite suggestive and are sometimes central to psychedelia; it can suggest a gong in Buddy Knox's "Ling Ting Tong," the surf in Jan and Dean's "Honolulu Lulu" and "Sidewalk Surfin'" and in Cream's "Tales of Brave Ulysses," and bright sunshine in the Beatles' "Good Day Sunshine." Effects are a bit more metaphorical in the syncopated attention-demanding backbeat crashes in the Hollies' "Stop Stop Stop" and in the clashing "fussing and fighting" cross-rhythms in the Beatles' "We Can Work It Out." But probably most often, the crash cymbal is used to mark off one section from another; note how it's struck every two downbeats only in the bridge of Sam the Sham and the Pharaohs' "Lil' Red Riding Hood"—it's just as important a tool of formal demarcation as Sam's verse-punctuating wolf howl.

As noted earlier, pedaled backbeats and sticked ride patterns are commonly played on the hi-hat. The relentless hi-hat backbeat gives the First Edition's "Ruby, Don't Take Your Love to Town" a constant, palpable tension that musically embodies the singer's inner cursing of his impotence. Often, as in the Coasters' "Three Cool Cats," the hi-hat will mark every beat while the snare smacks the backbeat; this device can be ornamented, as in the intro to John Fred and His Playboy Band's "Judy in Disguise (With Glasses)," where the bass drum adds a compelling kick on the "and" of beat one. See regular sticked hi-hat patterns in the Four Seasons' "Walk Like a Man" and Creedence Clearwater Revival's "Down on the Corner," and a syncopated one in Ringo's mesmerizing hi-hat/toms intro to the Beatles' "Come Together." The last-named recording evokes a suspenseful quality strongly associated with the hi-hat, an association also invoked when it is struck when open and subsequently closed, as in Elmer Bernstein's Theme from "The Man With the Golden Arm" or the oddly derivative "(Theme From) The Monkees." The open-shut technique can also be ultrafunky, as when the backbeat drums in Wilson Pickett's "Mustang Sally" are complemented by the offbeat strike on the open hi-hat just before it is closed on fourth beats. Many rhythmic hi-hat patterns are possible: listen to a variety of them in the intros to Donovan's "Mellow Yellow" and the Beatles' "While My Guitar Gently Weeps," the second verse of Tiny Tim's "Tip-toe Thru' the Tulips With Me," Crosby, Stills, Nash and Young's "Our House," and the verse of Smith's "Baby It's You." The hi-hat contributes great tension to the nervous preparation for the bridge in the Beatles' "This Boy," where Ringo taps the closed hi-hat at 0:58–1:02 but opens it strategically for a touch of ringing at 1:00, 1:01, and 1:02. Another imaginative transitional use comes from Dino Danelli in the Rascals' "It's Wonderful" (0:37), where the open-and-shut hi-hat seems to signal an abrupt end to the proceedings, granting the ensuing verse a fresh start. The Mothers of Invention focus on a complex rhythm in their satirical "America Drinks," wherein the hi-hat is struck closed, struck open and then pedaled closed, at oblivious rhythmic odds with everything else in an intentionally piss-poor ensemble of vocal, bass, piano, flute, and cymbals.

One final topic remains in our introduction to trap-set drumming—the transitional fill, which is a brief ornamented passage used to propel a song from one section into another. The transitional fill also helps mark placement during a recording session in which non-vocal backing tracks may be performed with limited variety, so that a drummer can lead bandmates into and out of sections without their having to rely on each individual's counting of repeated bars. When the fill occurs in returning from a contrasting passage back to the main section (usually a verse), we'll refer to it as a retransitional fill. Ringo Starr, especially in his early work with the Beatles, is the master of the form-defining fill. Listen to how, in "I Saw Her Standing There," he sets up new material, as with the small flam at 0:19 that brings us to the refrain, a more substantial fill moving to the bridge at 0:43, and still wilder retransitions from bridges at 1:09–1:10 and 1:57–1:59. Similar techniques helped put the Beatles on the world map with "She Loves You" and "I Want to Hold Your Hand." Ringo was not alone, of course; a dynamic full-bar snare fill leads from the bridge back to a verse at 1:24 in the Chiffons' "He's So Fine." One widely practiced way to make a transition to verse or chorus sound distinctive was to divide each beat into three—not two—equal parts, so a drummer would work twelve accents (4 × 3) into the time of eight (4 × 2) in a suddenly dramatic bar of quadruple meter. Hear these triplets in Herman's Hermits' "Can't You Hear My Heartbeat" (0:39–0:40), the Dave Clark Five's "Catch Us If You Can," Wilson Pickett's "634–5789" (1:40–1:42), Donovan's "Mellow Yellow" (0:40–0:44, filling two bars), and the Turtles' "Happy Together" (0:38–0:39). (Listen to Web audio example 1.14.) An even more disruptive technique would involve simple but strong syncopation not heard elsewhere; this approach brings an exhilarating anarchy to Cream's "SWLABR" (1:15–1:17) and Steppenwolf's "Born to Be Wild" (2:06). In the large scale, a long interior jam often calls for a wild drum climax to call the song's structure back into being, thus the frenetic retransitional solo by Mitch Mitchell in Hendrix's "Voodoo Chile." It is the balance of regular and surprisingly irregular contributions that makes the good rock drummer much more than a timekeeper.

Secondary percussion: Latin hand percussion and larger items

Even with a strong drummer at the wheel, extra percussion is heard in all but the sparest rock music. Whether to strengthen the backbeat, double a ride pattern with a contrasting color, or provide an unusual accent, members of a battery of more than fifty different available instruments make their appearances one place or another in these songs. Some instruments, like the vibraphone, are available in all studios and heard seemingly everywhere; others, like the vibraslap, seem to be a rare and passing fad. At times, as with the Mothers' "Help, I'm a Rock" and "Lumpy Gravy" theme, a wide range of percussion played at once betrays modernist orchestral ambitions. Whether played by a free pair of hands during the basic recording or overdubbed later (usually while the vocal parts are taped), whether assigned to whomever happens to be free in the studio or requiring the booking of a mallet specialist from the local philharmonic orchestra, it's always fun to try to guess which of the dozens of possible add-ons has been trotted out for a particular effect. With a bit of experience, one quickly learns the favorite percussion sounds of particular producers, the specialties of given studios, and the not-really-so-intangible qualities that nail a particular style.

In our opening chapters, we'll divide the percussion instruments into two groups. We'll cover the nonpitched instruments here, as a natural follow-up to our introduction to the drum kit. Other, pitched, percussion pieces (especially bells and xylophone-type mallet instruments) chiefly used for their melodic and harmonic potential will be covered in Chapter 4, along with other orchestral sweeteners, the strings and winds.

Nonpitched percussion: handclaps...

Frequently, percussion requires no instruments at all. Sometimes it takes no more than an ensemble of handclaps, as in the Marvelettes' (1)—two—and—(3)—four introductory pattern in "Please Mr. Postman," to get listeners dancing. Backbeat handclaps are extremely popular right from Wynonie Harris's "Good Rockin' Tonight" (1948) to the slightly varied patterns of the 1960s girl groups (though the Supremes often preferred to clap on all beats in their 1964 hits) and the let's-all-join-in party atmosphere of the Tijuana Brass's ritual-dance "Zorba the Greek," Mitch Ryder and the Detroit Wheels' "Little Latin Lupe Lu," the Plastic Ono Band's "Give Peace a Chance," and the funky shuffle of the Grateful Dead's "New Speedway Boogie." Even the Boston Pops Orchestra, in a failed attempt to find the beat in the intro to their cover of "I Want to Hold Your Hand," resorted to group handclaps, probably earning its members double scale. Fingers and palms would tap elsewhere, too; perhaps on laps in Buddy Holly's "Everyday" and perhaps on a box in Paul McCartney's "The Lovely Linda." Little Willie John's, and later Peggy Lee's, "Fever" may be the best-known vehicle for finger-snaps, but it's far from alone; the sound is heard in at least thirty hits of the period, helping suggest

...Shaken items: maracas, cabasa, sleigh bells, tambourine, castanets, slapstick, vibraslap, wobbleboard...

settings ranging from the sparse means of a carefree Roger Miller in "King of the Road" to the abundant riches of the princely Temptations in "My Girl." Even foot taps (in Janis Joplin's informal "Mercedez Benz" and Simon and Garfunkel's elegantly scored "The Boxer," 0:31+) and stomps (yes, the Four Seasons' "Walk Like a Man") have their place.

Most nondrummed percussion heard in rock music is from shaken items. Maracas are pairs of shot-filled gourds with handles, once primarily shaken to provide a rumba beat in a Cuban or Puerto Rican band. (Listen to Web audio example 1.15 and see Web photo 1.09.) While they provide a Mariachi flavor in the many hits of the Tijuana Brass and a Brazilian touch to the Critters' "Mr. Diengly Sad," maracas are a staple in all 1960s styles, from Lawrence Welk's "Calcutta" to Elvis Presley's "(Marie's the Name) His Latest Flame," Bob Dylan's "Obviously 5 Believers," Ike and Tina Turner's "River Deep, Mountain High" (2:18–2:46), the Beach Boys' "Good Vibrations" (2:14–2:56), The Who's "Sparks" (softening the overall sound at 3:25+), and the intro of the Classic IV's "Traces." Interestingly, the maracas don't seem to appear in top-twenty hits of the 1950s other than the Bell Notes' "I've Had It" and, more influentially, Bo Diddley's "Say Man" (both of 1959); note the classic Bo Diddley rhythm (ONE—(2)—and—Three—four—(1)—and—two—Three—(4)) reappearing in the maracas, snare, and bass in Elvis Presley's "His Latest Flame." A very close relative of the maracas is the cabasa, a metal shaker around which are strung metal beads; this appears to be the instrument played in Walter Wanderley's "Summer Samba (So Nice)," David Ruffin's "My Whole World Ended," and Chicago Transit Authority's "I'm a Man." (Listen to Web audio example 1.16 and see Web photo 1.10.) More jangly are a strap or stick of sleigh bells, which add a seasonal touch in Barry Gordon's "Nuttin' for Christmas," the Beach Boys' "Little Saint Nick," and Booker T. and the M.G.s' "Jingle Bells"; but that also add spice and color to many other Beach Boys tracks including "God Only Knows" (0:09+) and "Pet Sounds," Marvin Gaye's "Pretty Little Baby," the Ronettes' "Baby I Love You," and the Beatles' "Don't Pass Me By." (Listen to Web audio example 1.17 and see Web photo 1.11.)

The tambourine is the most commonly heard piece of added percussion. It's really versatile—its small drum head may be struck with the palm, tapped with the fingertips or rubbed with friction to produce a thumb roll, it may be struck on the rim or shaken so its jangles cut through any texture, and any of these techniques may be combined in a variety of rhythms for a busy undercurrent. The headless tambourine is shaken and hit against the fist or wrist. (Listen to Web audio examples 1.18 and 1.19, and see Web photos 1.12 and 1.13.) On occasion, the tambourine makes a lingering ethnic characterization, as in Donovan's "The Enchanted Gypsy," "You've Got to Pick a Pocket or Two" (from *Oliver!*), and perhaps also in "I Feel Pretty" (*West Side Story*). But more typically, it has no such programmatic quality. Because its sharp attack and sudden decay can be powerful, it's sometimes mixed much louder than normally featured forces, drowning out the piano in Barrett Strong's "Money (That's What I Want)" and threatening to cover even the voices in Sam and Dave's "You Don't Know Like I Know."

A glance at Figure 1.01 shows a sharp rise in the use of the tambourine in top-twenty songs beginning in 1964–65, peaking with its appearance in 41 of 198 hits of 1966. Interestingly, ten of the twelve tambourine-marked 1964 hits entered the Hot 100 in the June–December period. The Beatles' "Love Me Do," featuring Ringo on the instrument, was a number-one song in the United States that May; could the wide use of the tambourine in pop music of the late 1960s and beyond be one of the great hidden influences of the early Beatles? As for its use, the tambourine is simply struck on the backbeat in more cases, well over a hundred hits, than all other patterns, shaken or struck, combined. For typical backbeat examples, consider the Miracles' "The Tracks of My Tears," the Jefferson Airplane's "Today," or most work by the Wrecking Crew of Gold Star Studios for the 5th Dimension. For the heavily delayed backbeat, listen to the Rolling Stones' most appropriately named "Time Is On My Side." When struck on every beat, the tambourine can suggest compulsive behavior, as in Napoleon XIV's "They're Coming to Take Me Away, Ha-Haaa!" (note the support from bass drum, handclaps, and snare), the bridge of Frankie Valli's "Can't Take My Eyes Off You," or the chorus of the Grass Roots' "Temptation Eyes." When shaken, the tambourine has an ominous quality, suggestive of a rattlesnake's suspenseful warning in Norman Whitfield's productions of "I Heard It Through the Grapevine" for both Gladys Knight and Marvin Gaye or of a simmering frustration in the Beatles' "Day Tripper" and Glen Campbell's "The Universal Soldier." The shake can come to a snappy stop (the Monkees' "Last Train to Clarksville") or be combined with strikes of various rhythms (a backbeat in Bob Lind's "Elusive Butterfly") or with other percussion (backbeat snare and hi-hat in Jr. Walker and the All-Stars' "What Does It Take"). Note how the tambourine is overlapped and answered by a cymbal tapped at the bell for a color transition in the Beatles' "In My Life" (0:28–0:46). Frequently, the tambourine can enter late or stop or be played with a different pattern to demarcate a song's sections; note the various such techniques in the retransition of Dobie Gray's "The 'In' Crowd," the accompaniment to Larry Knechtel's tack piano solo in The Mamas and the Papas' "Dedicated to the One I Love," the coda of the Association's "Windy," the appearance of a second tambourine in the chorus of Diana Ross and the Supremes' "Reflections" (the first one shaken and a second one struck), and the chorus/verse transition in the Union Gap's "Lady Willpower." In fact, the tambourine can so clearly mark section boundaries, its three-second-late entry (0:43) cries out for a retake in Lesley Gore's "California Nights."

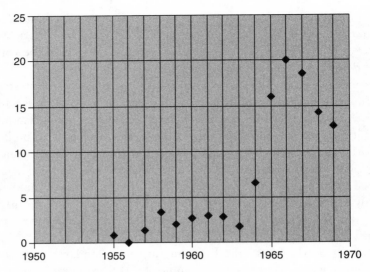

Figure 1.01. Annual percentage of *Billboard's* weekly top-twenty songs with tambourine, 1955–69.

An instrument with a strong Spanish heritage is the castanets, once a pair of hollowed-out pieces of wood clicked in the hand but now usually mounted for easier play. (Listen to Web audio example 1.20 and see Web photo 1.14.) The Spanish theme runs through Major Lance's "The Matador," the Baja Marimba Band's "Ghost Riders in the Sky" (which opens with a mandolin tremolo) and the Young Rascals' "Sueño," but the castanets were also taken over without any cultural context by the Diamonds ("Little Darlin'"), Phil Spector (the Crystals' "Uptown" and "Then He Kissed Me," Darlene Love's "A Fine Fine Boy," and the Ronettes' "Be My Baby"), and the Beach Boys ("Dance, Dance, Dance," 0:23–0:26). The variously sized slapstick, which brings together two hinged slats of wood for a loud slap, is heard in Tennessee Ernie Ford's "Sixteen Tons" and the Beach Boys' "That's Not Me." (Listen to Web audio examples 1.21 and 1.22, and see Web photos 1.15 and 1.16.) The vibraslap, which causes a wood resonator to rattle when a ball attached to it by a steel spring is slapped, is known to me only through three rock songs recorded in Los Angeles within a few months of each other: the Jefferson Airplane's "Two Heads" (2:24–2:25), Spanky and Our Gang's "Give a Damn" (0:50), and the Grateful Dead's "Alligator" (CD remix, 3:21, 3:23, etc.). (Listen to Web audio example 1.23 and see Web photo 1.17.) Another vibrating piece of wood, a panel of masonite about two feet by three that is shaken rhythmically and called of all things the wobbleboard, is the Australian instrument sounding throughout Rolf Harris's "Tie Me Kangaroo

Down, Sport," but which can also be heard in a few British discs including the Yardbirds' "Hot House of Omagarashid" and The Who's "A Quick One While He's Away" (in the cowboy boogie section, "We'll Soon Be Home"). (Listen to Web audio example 1.24 and see Web photo 1.18.)

...**Drums**: bongos, conga, tabla, timbales, orchestral bass drum, timpani...

A number of drums are played in addition to those in the trap set. Three common types are played by the hands: the Latin bongos and conga, and the Indian tabla. Bongos, two small joined drums of different sizes, were popular in Americanizing the 1950s calypso style, as in Terry Gilkyson's and the Hilltoppers' recordings of "Marianne." (Listen to Web audio example 1.25 and see Web photo 1.19.) In the 1960s, they were adopted by a number of Motown artists (appearing in Mary Wells's "The One Who Really Loves You," Marvin Gaye's "Too Busy Thinking About My Baby," Stevie Wonder's "My Cherie Amour"—note the rapid bongo trill in 0:13–0:15, and the Temptations' "Cloud Nine" among many others), were paired with a nylon-string guitar to add a Latin color to the Beatles' "And I Love Her," and added a wild touch to the Yardbirds' "For Your Love."

The much larger and deeper Cuban conga would typically be slapped by both hands; this gives an airy, gentle quality to both Dionne Warwick's "Message to Michael" and the Young Rascals' "Groovin'," brings to life the beating hearts of Tommy James and the Shondells' "I Think We're Alone Now," and itself is paired with a nylon-string guitar in José Feliciano's "Light My Fire." (Listen to Web audio examples 1.26–1.28, and see Web photos 1.20 and 1.21.) The Indian tabla, also a small pair of drums, were not imported into rock music until the Beatles recorded "Love You To," "Getting Better" and others, but were then quickly adopted by Donovan (in three *Sunshine Superman* songs that also feature sitar), the Rascals (in "Sattva" and "Stop and Think," both making use of tamboura as well as sitar and tabla), the Moody Blues ("The Best Way to Travel"), the Association (accompanying the harpsichord-backed bridge in "Windy"), and Led Zeppelin ("Black Mountain Side"). (Listen to Web audio example 1.29, and see Web photo 1.22.) Sticked drums include the brass or steel single-headed timbales (heard panning left—right—left in the opening of Santana's "Evil Ways") and the orchestral bass drum (hit with a soft beater, as in Johnny Horton's "Sink the Bismarck" and Bobby Vee's "Run to Him," the former dropping bombs in the intro and the latter ending with a bass drum trill). (Listen to Web audio examples 1.30 and 1.31, and see Web photos 1.23 and 1.24.)

Much more rock music employs the timpani, tuned drums whose pitch can be adjusted by a pedal. Made of large copper bowls and also known as kettledrums, they are typically used in pairs or groups, each tuned to a different bass pitch and played with soft beaters. (Listen to Web audio example 1.32 and see Web photos 1.25 and 1.26.) High drama, in Ben E. King's "I (Who Have Nothing)," Little Anthony and the Imperials' "Hurt So Bad," and Tom Jones's "Daughter of Darkness," is signaled by the timpani's dark sounds, which may be made even more ominous in an opening roll, as in the Crests' "Gee (But I'd Give the World)," Connie Francis's "Follow the Boys," and Ronnie Dove's "I'll Make All Your Dreams Come True." (A song also may end with a dramatic timpani roll, as happens in Peaches and Herb's "Close Your Eyes.") Timps double for drama and gunshots in Gene Pitney's "(The Man Who Shot) Liberty Valance." A more mysterious atmosphere is created by the free-form timpani rolls, cymbal crashes, and the gradual settling of backing vocalists of uncertain intonation into a recognizable minor key in the opening minute of People's "I Love You." An excellent demonstration of the timpani's dynamic range is heard in Little Peggy March's "I Wish I Were a Princess" (0:15–0:16). A favorite technique of Brian Wilson's was to shroud only the timpani in reverb (compare the timps' sound envelope to that of other instruments in the Beach Boys' "Wouldn't It Be Nice," "You Still Believe in Me," and "Don't Talk (Put Your Head on My Shoulder)." (Lots of reverb had previously been applied to the timpani and other percussion that opens the Four Seasons' "Ronnie.") Owing to its definite pitch, the timpani will often double the bass line (see the Cheers' "Black Denim Trousers" and the Piltdown Men's "Brontosaurus Stomp"), or, rarely, take over that role on its own (as in the "looked good...looked fine" echoes in Manfred Mann's "Do Wah Diddy Diddy"). Moreso than other drums, the timpani can have a huge change of pitch while sustaining a single note, when the pedal is depressed before damping a sounding tone; this produces a trombone-like rising or falling glissando effect, put to good use in Neil Sedaka's "Stairway to Heaven," Johnny Crawford's "Cindy's Birthday," and Chuck Jackson's "I Need You." While other drums cannot produce such a large glissando, a similar effect is sometimes suggested by pressure from the hand tightening a drum head, and thus raising its pitch after it is struck; this technique colors the Moody Blues' "The Sun Set."

...Struck items, louder effects, metal and wood instruments.

The hollow woodblock is struck by the stick, perhaps constantly as in Kathy Linden's "Billy," or in a ricky-tick vaudeville rhythm, as in The Mamas and the Papas' "Words of Love," or in supplying the backbeat, as in the intro and bridge of the Troggs' "Love Is All Around." (Listen to Web audio examples 1.33 and 1.34, and see Web photos 1.27 and 1.28.) The two tuned woodblocks simulating a clock in the Safaris' "Image of a Girl" are actually part of a set of temple blocks (sometimes called Chinese blocks), usually sounding up to five different approximate pitches when struck by a hard rubber mallet. (Listen to Web audio example 1.35 and see Web photo 1.29.) Temple blocks produce a humorous horseclop effect in the Coasters' "Along Came Jones," and suggest a mule in Johnny Horton's "North to Alaska" and a camel in Ray Stevens's "Ahab the Arab." Their use to accompany a mention of coffee in Oliver's "Sunday Mornin'" is a reference to a stylized percolator in an old Maxwell House ad, and they are used for their sound alone, without references to clocks, coffee or camels, in Bobby Vee's "Come Back When You Grow Up" and the Beach Boys "I Just Wasn't Made for These Times."

The cowbell, naturally, opens Hugh Masekela's bucolic "Grazing in the Grass," but it seldom calls forth such an agrarian quality elsewhere, as when it adds accent to Perry Como's "Papa Loves Mambo," Marvin Gaye's "Stubborn Kind of Fellow," the Beatles' "You Can't Do That" and "Taxman," the Chambers Brothers' "Time Has Come Today" (note the heavy reverb on the cowbell), and the Stones' "Honky Tonk Women." (Listen to Web audio example 1.36 and see Web photo 1.30.) The anvil makes a number of appearances in rock music—often in work songs such as Sam Cooke's "Chain Gang," Jimmy Dean's "Big Bad John," and Lee Dorsey's "Working in the Coal Mine," in "work" songs such as the 5th Dimension's "Workin' On a Groovy Thing," in a clever simulation of a railroad-crossing bell in the Cheers' "Black Denim Trousers," and as a psychopath's weapon in the Beatles' "Maxwell's Silver Hammer." (Listen to Web audio example 1.37 and see Web photo 1.31.) Louder effects can be made by a wind machine (see Simon Dupree and the Big Sound's "Kites"), gunshot (heard on second beats of the chorus of Simon and Garfunkel's "The Boxer"), the lion's roar (its player pulls a rope through a hole in a suspended metal tub, or pulls his or her hand along the length of a rope attached to the bottom head of a large drum; it appears in the center of the mix of the Mothers of Invention's "The Return of the Son of Monster Magnet"), and the orchestral siren (opening the Overture to *Fiorello!* and Janis Ian's "Younger Generation Blues"). (Listen to Web audio examples 1.38 and 1.39, and see Web photos 1.32 and 1.33.)

A few metal percussion instruments remain to be covered. The long-resonating Chinese gong or tam tam is the final sound heard on the Moody Blues' LP, *Days of Future Passed,* is heard in a number of Dead tracks (it's struck in "New Potato Caboose" and rolled in "What's Become of the Baby"), Pink Floyd's "Sysyphus," and The Who's "Underture" (9:58+) and "Overture" (9:58+) both. (Listen to Web audio example 1.40 and see Web photo 1.34.) It has a subtle touch at the end of Donovan's "To Susan on the West Coast Waiting." At the opposite extreme are finger cymbals (pairs of tiny cymbals struck together) and crotales (thick brass discs that provide a high definite pitch when struck). (Listen to Web audio examples 1.41 and 1.42, and see Web photos 1.35 and 1.36.) Finger cymbals suggest the Nile valley in Roy Orbison's "Shahdaroba" and places beyond (?) in the Ran-Dells' "The Martian Hop"; crotales are heard in the Beatles' crossfade from "You Never Give Me Your Money" to "Sun King," and in several pitches in the intro to Oliver's "Good Morning Starshine." The bell tree, which nestles between fourteen and twenty-six brass bells along a short rod, are scraped by a metal striker in the openings of Sammy Davis Jr.'s "The Shelter of Your Arms" and Petula Clark's "Kiss Me Goodbye." (Listen to Web audio example 1.43 and see Web photo 1.37.) The Beach Boys' "The Warmth of the Sun" is given a shimmering glow by a bell tree at 0:42. Both finger cymbals and the bell tree sparkle brilliantly in Gary Lewis and the Playboys' "This Diamond Ring" (the former on second beats and the latter on fourth beats, 0:02–0:07). A related but more fragile sound from wind chimes is heard in the opening of the chorus in Simon and Garfunkel's "At the Zoo," the Monkees' "Words," and in the Grateful Dead's "That's It for the Other One" (5:26–5:32 in the CD remix of *Anthem of the Sun*). (Listen to Web audio example 1.44 and see Web photo 1.38.) Wind chimes are usually numerous metal rods of different lengths suspended within a frame, stroked by a metal striker and damped by the bottom edge of the frame.

The simple triangle has wide use, as heard on every other beat two of the instrumental break of the Righteous Brothers' "(You're My) Soul and Inspiration" (1:26–1:57), throughout Lesley Gore's "It's My Party," and in a trill-like tremolo over violin harmonics and flute/alto flute duet in the opening of the 5th Dimension's "Aquarius / Let the Sunshine In (The Flesh Failures)." (Listen to Web audio example 1.45 and see Web photo 1.39.) The ratchety sound of the bicycle bell was first intended to evoke a childhood quality in the Beach Boys' "You Still Believe In Me" (1:27–1:33), but Brian Wilson's initial conception of the lyrics changed after the instrument was recorded with the rest of the band so it now offers a more ambiguous meaning. The bicycle bell

Photo 1.03. Recording the large guiro. Fish guiro and congas are seen to the right. At lower left, the percussionist's silo holds a wide range of sticks and mallets. (Photo: Annie Eastman)

is also heard in a pre–"White" Album between-the-tracks passage of gibberish in the Rascals' "Dave and Eddie." (Listen to Web audio example 1.46 and see Web photo 1.40.) The bicycle horn, also part of "You Still Believe in Me" (2:16, 2:21), marks the Playmates' "Beep Beep" and the Tijuana Brass's "Tijuana Taxi" for rather obvious reasons. (Listen to Web audio example 1.47 and see Web photo 1.41.)

Speaking of ratchets, a well-used orchestral instrument that sets a thin tongue of resonant wood vibrating loudly in rapid repetition at the turn of a crank is called just that, a ratchet; it is notable in several song openings: Dion and the Belmonts' "Kissin' Game" (along with the triangle), the Four Seasons' "Ronnie" and the Ventures' "Hawaii Five-O" (each with drums and timpani), and the Hollies' "Carrie-Anne." (Listen to Web audio examples 1.48 and 1.49, and see Web photos 1.42 and 1.43.) A small ratchet is paired with crotales in the Lemon Pipers' "Green Tambourine," which also pairs toms with the title instrument. The ratchet marks the second beats of Tommy James and the Shondells' "Mirage" and "Crimson and Clover" both. Similar to the sound of the ratchet is that of the Latin guiro, originally a multiply notched hollow gourd against which a wooden stick is scraped but nowadays usually formed of plastic. The Cuban guiro is fairly large, whereas the Mexican version is smaller and often painted to resemble a fish. (Listen to Web audio examples 1.50 and 1.51, and see Web photos 1.44 and 1.45.) The guiro is yet another marker of second beats in Dusty Springfield's "The Look of Love." It plays a two-beat pattern that remains constant through the second verse of the Grateful Dead's "Uncle John's Band," even when the meter changes from four beats per bar to three. The Drifters' "Under the Boardwalk" opens with a syncopated pattern featuring the bass on ONE, the guiro on two, and the triangle on four. The guiro accents the Four Seasons' "Candy Girl" but is heard throughout the Byrds' "So You Want to Be a Rock and Roll Star." A similarly ribbed instrument is the washboard scraped with thimbles or a metal beater, reserved for such jug-band numbers as Country Joe and the Fish's "I-Feel-Like-I'm-Fixin'-to-Die Rag," the Incredible String Band's "Big Ted," and Creedence Clearwater Revival's "Poorboy Shuffle." (Listen to Web audio example 1.52 and see Web photo 1.46.)

Three more instruments come in pairs. Sandpaper-covered sandblocks are brushed together in Tommy Dorsey's "Tea for Two Cha-Cha," Martin Denny's "Quiet Village" (along with woodblock), Ben E. King's "Stand By Me" (every second beat, along with triangle, in the opening), Simon and Garfunkel's "At the Zoo" (fading in and out, 0:48–0:55), and The Doors' "I Can't See Your Face in My Mind" (entering with marimbas, 0:31–0:50). (Listen to Web audio example 1.53 and see Web photo 1.47.) Sandblocks come in different sizes, and the pairs of blocks are often covered with mismatched concentrations of grit for a richer texture. The claves are sticks made of hard wood (usually rosewood or teak) and clicked together, often in a syncopated Latin pattern, as in Elvis Presley's "It's Now or Never" and the Beatles' "And I Love Her," but sometimes in a straight backbeat, as in the Drifters' "On Broadway." (Listen to Web audio example 1.54 and see Web photo 1.48.) They and a ratchet are used throughout the Strawberry Alarm Clock's "Barefoot in Baltimore." Other sorts of rhythm sticks of various tone colors are heard in Annette's "Tall Paul," Benny Spellman's "Fortune Teller" (along with maracas), and The Who's "Magic Bus." Bringing us full circle in our paragraphs on added percussion is Petula Clark's "Round Every Corner," in which two pairs of rhythm sticks simulate group fingersnaps. (Listen to Web audio example 1.55.)

By becoming familiar with representative examples among those cited above, the reader should now be able to recognize all unpitched percussion instruments that appear in popular music of the 1950s and '60s. Even so, it still takes great care sometimes to pick out these sources when used in combination, and when they are used to help accent the simultaneous attacks of guitar chords and other forces. Rhythm instruments articulate the music's foundation, providing the metric framework against which all pitched instruments and vocals find their place even as they create rhythmic matrices of their own. Put in a perhaps more mystical way, rhythm instruments bring the transcendental nature of harmony into our worldly awareness through music's only dimension, that of time.

CHAPTER 2

Guitars, the Bass, and an Introduction to Harmony

It's time to add pitch instruments, the carriers of melody and harmony, to the rhythmic foundation we've built in chapter 1. In chapter 2, we'll concentrate on guitars of all types, their amplification, and the wide variety of guitar effects produced by electronic circuits and performance techniques. Although the guitar is no doubt the most familiar of all rock instruments, and the most played by amateur and pro alike, we'll begin our investigation with the bass. As do the drums with rhythm, the bass defines a song's underlying harmonic structure. So we'll cover the basic aspects of harmony as we examine both the acoustic upright string bass and the electric bass guitar.

The bass

If the bass drum is the foundation of the band's rhythm, the string bass or bass guitar is the band's pitch foundation. (See Web photos 2.01—2.03.) The pitch is so low that it is felt just as much as heard, and so the bass also plays a rhythmic function, often doubling or slightly ornamenting the bass drum's pattern. (The bass/bass-drum doubling in a regular pattern is so common, any deviation seems either bizarre, as in the odd third beats of the first verse of the Jeff Beck Group's "Rock My Plimsoul," where the two have competing patterns, or quite artistic, as when McCartney's bass doubles Ringo's entire kit in an amazingly irregular ten-second duet in the Beatles' "Rain," 2:24+.) Because of the nature of acoustics, other pitch instruments—guitars, upper keyboard parts, strings, and so on—can blend with the upper tones produced by the supportive bass. (This is true when the bass line is played by tuba or bassoon, as well as by a stringed instrument.) Some producers prefer to have the bass blend fully into the ensemble, whereas others will have it stand out from the rest of the mix. Occasionally, the bass will play a melodic or otherwise independent role, thereby demanding a louder voice. The string bass or its electrified counterpart might even have a solo—in an introduction (a string bass opening Roy Orbison's "Dream Baby (How Long Must I Dream)," the electric in Cliff Richard's "Living Doll"), in a transitional bar or two (string bass at 2:27–2:34 in the Beach Boys' "I Know There's an Answer," electric at 0:52–0:57 in the Righteous Brothers' "You've Lost That Lovin' Feeling"), in a verse (string bass in Roger Miller's "King of the Road," electric in J. Frank Wilson and the Cavaliers' "Last Kiss"), or in an extended improvisation (as in Blind Faith's "Do What You Like," Blood, Sweat and Tears' "Somethin' Goin' On," and Led Zeppelin's "Good Times Bad Times"). In Blue Cheer's version of "Summertime Blues," the bass plays the role of the boss's authoritative voice that is given words in most all other performances of the song. We'll first investigate the quality of the bass's sound, and then describe its function.

> **The bass instrument: the string bass, the electric bass, the keyboard bass, and the washtub bass.**

The stand-up string bass (also called the bass viol) has been for the most part replaced by the much smaller electric bass. The electric's more focused tone is in most cases easier to record and to balance in live performances than that of the acoustic forebear, but the noisy-up-close string bass is often preferred for its richer sound at a normal listening distance. (Occasionally, as with some Beatles and Motown productions, the electric bass would be cabled directly to the soundboard, bypassing the colorations and distortions of amplifier and microphone, in an attempt to capture the string vibration at its most essential.) The electric bass's ease of play for a beginner, in that all pitches are fixed by frets on most models and strings are much easier to depress than on the acoustic, combines with its convenient size and ease of sonic control to make it so popular.

It should be mentioned that whereas the function of the bass is present in most recordings, this role is sometimes performed by a keyboard, rather than a stringed, instrument. Particularly when four-piece bands would feature a lead singer who did not play an instrument, a keyboardist would often provide the bass line. Thus, Felix Cavaliere of the Young Rascals furnished the bass line on the pedalboard of his Hammond B-3, and when that could not produce the desired effect in the studio (the organ bass lacked the snappy attack of strings), guitarist Gene Cornish would overdub an electric bass part. Similarly, Ray Manzarek of The Doors would typically perch a Fender Rhodes Piano Bass atop his Vox Continental organ. On this, his left hand would supply a bass line on the two-and-a-half-octave Rhodes keyboard while his right hand would comp or play solo lines on the Vox. Led Zeppelin boasted John Paul Jones, a career studio keyboardist who was also competent on the electric bass guitar. In concert, when Jones played electronic keys, he still managed to cover the bass line with his left hand.

Generally, only a few pioneering pop and rock recordings were made with an electric bass before 1959; Jackie Brenston's very early "Rocket '88'" (1951) is followed by electric-bass hits by Johnny Cash, Little Richard, the Coasters, and Fats Domino. The acoustic and electric instruments, however, enjoyed roughly equal footing in the 1959–63 period. Since 1963, only a handful of holdouts have clung to the string bass in particular styles, and it has enjoyed a new life for occasional sonic effects: it appears in a buzzy imitation of a barber's "trim" in a few seconds of the Beatles' "Penny Lane" (2:04–2:09) and is played by an amateur Bill Wyman of the Rolling Stones—the bow sounds rosinless—in "Ruby Tuesday." It should be noted that two jug bands mentioned in chapter 1 for their use of the washboard, Country Joe and the Fish and Creedence Clearwater Revival, also use in these numbers the washtub bass. This is an overturned metal tub against the bottom of which the player stands a broomstick; a waxed string connecting a rim of the resonant tub with the top of the stick is adjusted for tautness—and thus for rising and descending pitch—by pulling and releasing the stick, and is plucked with the free hand. Folk styles often retained the acoustic bass—Bobbie Gentry's "Ode to Billie Joe," the Stone Poneys' "Different Drum," and Arlo Guthrie's "Alice's Rock & Roll Restaurant" feature the string bass in contrasting acoustic environments. But style does not firmly dictate which type of bass is used; the electric is used in some orchestral backings (Bert Kaempfert's "Red Roses for a Blue Lady," Paul Mauriat's "Love Is Blue"), in eighteenth-century styled chamber arrangements (the Cyrkle's "Please Don't Ever Leave Me"), and in some styles suggestive of jazz (Friend and Lover's "Reach Out of the Darkness" and Van Morrison's "Moondance").

The Beatles and Stones examples mentioned earlier, "Penny Lane" and "Ruby Tuesday," both feature the string bass played with a bow, even though its strings are nearly always plucked by fingers in popular styles. (Listen to Web audio example 2.01.) Other bowed examples include the intro to the Kingston Trio's "M. T. A.," Chuck Jackson's "Tell Him I'm Not Home," the Four Tops' "(It's the Way) Nature Planned It," Judy Collins's "Winter Sky," and James

Taylor's "Fire and Rain." The Beach Boys' "Good Vibrations," in fact, includes both the string bass and the cello bowed in tremolo (back and forth rapidly on the same note) (0:25–0:50 and 3:10–3:13), an exceedingly rare pop-music effect. The strings of the electric bass are also typically set in motion by the fingers, but some players prefer the immediate response from a plastic pick, whose loud attack is evident in Carol Kaye's playing on the Beach Boys' "Sloop John B," Ray Pohlman's on their "Here Today," and John Entwistle's on The Who's "Sparks." (Listen to Web audio examples 2.02 and 2.03.)

One effect possible on the upright bass but not very easily achieved on fretted electrics is the production of quarter tones, which divide in half the smallest usual pitch interval, the half step, also referred to as a minor second. This effect has its most notable appearance in the smug bass descent in Nancy Sinatra's "These Boots Are Made For Walkin'," the opening of which features a line of sixteen bass notes that squeeze into the pitch-space normally occupied by nine. That being said, the glissando, or smooth slide between two notes that may lie far apart, can be very effective on the electric bass—witness the gliss covering half a string length in Dee Clark's "You're Looking Good" and that of a third of a string length that opens The Who's "I Can't Explain." Another very unusual pitch-related effect is created when strings are detuned, usually in order to reach a lower pitch than the lowest string would normally provide. (This and many other abnormal string tunings are far more common on the guitar than on the bass. Today, in fact, bass players can opt for a five- or seven-string model that lowers the bass range considerably beyond that of the traditional four-string instrument.) A detuned bass is the likely reason we hear a low E-flat in the second instrumental break (right after the guitar solo) in the First Edition's "Just Dropped In (To See What Condition My Condition Was In)." Probably because bass strings can become ineffectively flabby (and buzz uncontrollably against frets) when loosened too much for detuning, a regular electric guitar is tuned down two half-steps to cover the bass line in Marcie Blane's "Bobby's Girl." At the opposite extreme, the bass is sometimes heard in very high registers, as in Ronnie Dove's "Kiss Away" (where a bowed string bass almost sounds like a cello), the Beatles' "Rain" (where McCartney drives his Rickenbacker into high terrain), and the Beach Boys' "God Only Knows" (see 0:21–0:24, where Ray Pohlman picks at the top of his six-string Danelectro).

When the bass string is plucked, it will ring until stopped. Depending upon the speed of the bass line, this will usually happen in the normal course of moving from one note to another, but the sustain may be clipped immediately by any of several hand-muting techniques. (In Web audio examples 2.02 and 2.03, note how the bass line is played unmuted first, and then muted.) Note the difference between damped and booming bass notes in the Tymes' "Wonderful! Wonderful!" Paul McCartney mutes the sharp attacks of the Fender Jazz bass in the Beatles' "Glass Onion," and George Harrison clips the authoritative bass notes of their "Maxwell's Silver Hammer" on his Fender Bass VI (a six-string instrument that sounds an octave lower than a regular guitar, a good fit for the guitarist who needs to play bass only occasionally and can thereby maintain familiar fingerings). The damped bass in The Doors' "People Are Strange" seems to take on an oom-pah tuba quality in response to the tack piano and the Brechtian tonal and lyric atmosphere. In the 5th Dimension's "Stoned Soul Picnic," bassist Joe Osborn plays a great variety of note lengths before the really long-sustaining ones appear in 0:31–0:36. This effect can be subtle, but it's just the thing that makes Steve Winwood's bass line so funky in Traffic's "Empty Pages."

Occasionally, the string bass seems to be mixed too loud in relation to other forces (it competes with the vocals in the Everly Brothers' "Ebony Eyes"), but this occurs much more often with the electric, as might be said of Marvin Gaye's "Too Busy Thinking About My Baby," most of Bob Dylan's album *John Wesley Harding* and the Rolling Stones' *Beggar's Banquet*. Sometimes but not often, the electric bass pushes the amplification's gain hard enough to cause distortion at any loudness level; this ranges from the slight over-drive in Bob Moore's solo in Elvis Presley's "(You're the) Devil in Disguise" through James Jamerson's busy parts in the Miracles' "Going to a Go-Go," the Supremes' "Love Is Like an Itching in My Heart," and Martha Reeves and the Vandellas' "Nowhere to Run" and "My Baby Loves Me," to the Stones' "2120 South Michigan Avenue," an ode to the R and B studios of Chess Records where it was cut. As soon as there was a device that could create a fuzz tone at normal amplifier settings, first heard in the Beatles' "Think For Yourself" (the "fuzz" bass doubling a regular bass), its use became familiar, as in the Stones' "Under My Thumb" and "Mother's Little Helper," Music Machine's "Talk Talk," The Who's "Fiddle About" and "Tommy's Holiday Camp," and Deep Purple's "Fault Line/The Painter." Although the low pitch range occupied by the bass is typically too murky to survive much signal pro-cessing, there are just a few examples of heavy echo applied to the bass line including the Rebels' "Wild Weekend," the Beach Boys' "God Only Knows," and the Zombies' "I Want Her, She Wants Me."

Harmony, as supported by the bassist

To understand the bassist's job of laying the pitch foundation, one must understand the basics of harmony. There are seven different degrees in a major scale. They are sometimes called do, re, mi, fa, sol, la, and ti, but we will refer to them numerically, as the first, second, third, . . . and seventh scale degrees. They cycle continuously, so that the scale degree higher than 7 is called either 8 or 1, where the scale begins again an octave higher than the previous first

Harmony and the bass line: the seven degrees of the major scale; chordal roots, thirds, fifths, and sevenths; arpeggiation, harmonic relationships by fifth-related roots, and chordal inversions.

scale degree. (See fig. 2.01.) If you're having trouble placing the sound of the major scale, here are a few examples: in the Beatles' "Hello Goodbye," the line played by the lead guitar at 0:21+ and sung at 0:59+ is the major scale from 1 up an octave to 1. (Listen to Web audio example 2.04.) In the Rolling Stones' "Dandelion," the verse opens with a vocal descent down a one-octave major scale, but from 5 to 5 rather than from 8 to 1. (Listen to Web audio example 2.05.) The opening verse of the Beach Boys' "Heroes and Villains" starts with two scalar descents, both larger than an octave and both replete with repeated pitches: the first, 0:00–0:07, descends 4—3—2—1—7—6—5—4—3—2 and the second, 0:11–0:18, descends in answer, 4—3—2—1—7—6—5—4—3—2—1. Major scales in the bass can be heard at the opening of the Beatles' "All My Loving," moving 2—1—7—6—5—4—3—2—1, and in the verses of Procol Harum's "A Whiter Shade of Pale" (0:26–0:36), descending every two beats, 8—7—6—5—4—3—2—1. (Listen to Web audio examples 2.06 and 2.07.)

Any of these seven scale degrees can serve as the root for a chord built above it. In acting as a chord's foundation, the root is most often played by the bass, especially in metrically strong places—listen to how often chords generally change on first beats. The chord is named by its root (E major and E minor chords have E as their root); when we refer to a scale degree num-

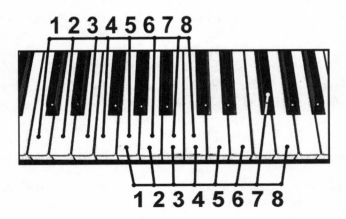

Figure 2.01. Two different major scales as played on a piano keyboard, indicating their scale-degree numbers. Note that there are no keys, black or white, in between degrees 3 and 4 or between 7 and 8, but that there is one pitch that lies between all other adjacent scale members.

ber as the root of a chord with a written symbol, we apply Roman numerals: I is the chord whose root is the first scale degree, IV is the chord whose root is the fourth scale degree, and so on. (Some chords, such as V, are labeled with uppercase Roman numerals; others, like vi, with lowercase. The significance of this difference, based on the quality of the chord—whether it is built from a major, minor, or diminished chord—is a topic covered in chapter 6.) A chord can have any number of members above the root, but there are nearly always at least two additional scale degrees different from the root. The most common kind of chord is the triad, containing three chord members that alternate steps in the scale. (See fig. 2.02.) We speak of the members of a triad as the root, third, and fifth, because each triad contains the third and fifth scale steps counted above its root. The I chord contains scale degrees 1 (root), 3 (third), and 5 (fifth). The IV chord contains scale degrees 4 (root), 6 (third), and 1 (fifth). The V chord contains scale degrees 5 (root), 7 (third), and 2 (fifth). (Listen to Web audio examples 2.08—2.10.)

The bass frequently spells out each chord, one member at a time, in a pattern called arpeggiation. Take, for instance, Elvis's "Hound Dog," in which bassist Scotty Moore plays scale degrees 1—3—5 for the I chord (0:00–0:07), 4—6—1 for the IV chord (0:07–0:09), back to 1—3—5 for I (0:10–0:12), to 5—7—2 for V (0:07–0:13), and to 4—6—1 for IV (0:14–0:15), remaining silent during the final assumed I. (Listen to Web audio example 2.11.) Compare this with the electric bass line in Big Bopper's "Chantilly Lace," which sequences the same chords differently. More complex chord relationships certainly exist, and the chord changes can come faster, but the bassist often maintains the same root-third-fifth arpeggiation pattern, as in the

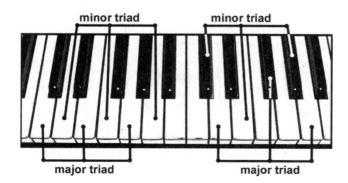

Figure 2.02. Major and minor triads on the piano keyboard, a sample of two each. Note that the major triads are made of the first, third, and fifth degrees of their own major scales. In the minor triads, the thirds are one key lower than would be the thirds of those major triads.

fast-moving bridge of the Box Tops' "The Letter" (0:33–0:45). Sometimes the triad is abbreviated, so the bassist arpeggiates only among the roots and fifths of each chord; this is typical of the early Beatles style. Listen, in "She Loves You," to how McCartney plays only scale degrees 6 and 3 on the vi chord (0:01–0:03), 2 and 6 on ii (0:04–0:06), 4 and 1 on IV (0:07–0:08), and 1 and 5 on I (0:10–0:13); in the following verse (0:14+), he plays mostly roots alone. Listen to Willie Dixon's string bass playing on Chuck Berry's "Maybelline" or Buddy Wheeler's on Duane Eddy's "Shazam!" to see where McCartney learned the idea. The simple alternation of triadic root and fifth can also create a powerful effect in such song openings as Otis Redding's "Dock of the Bay," as played by Donald "Duck" Dunn.

Many chords in popular music contain notes beyond just those three in the triad; most common is the four-member seventh chord. The V^{m7} chord contains its seventh, scale degree four, in addition to the members of the V triad, and so would be arpeggiated 5—7—2—4. The I^{M7} chord is spelled 1—3—5—7. (Appearing more commonly than I^{M7}, I^{m7} is spelled 1—3—5—♭7, where the flat seventh lies between the major scale's sixth and seventh degrees. (See fig. 2.03.) The significance of the various chord labels is discussed in chapter 8. Appendix A lists the spellings of the 120 most commonly heard chordal sonorities in our repertoire, including all of those referred to in this book. The boogie-woogie bass pattern arpeggiates through all four seventh-chord members, sometimes with the sixth above each root as a passing tone between the fifth and the seventh of each chord: 1—3—5—6—♭7—6—5—3 (–1) for I, 4—6—1—2—♭3—2—1—6 for IV, 5—7—2—3—4—3—2—7 for V, and so on. (Listen to Web audio example 2.12.) This is the string-bass pattern in Wynonie Harris's "Good Rockin' Tonight."

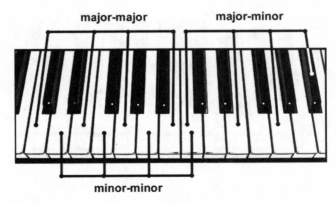

Figure 2.03. Three different types of seventh chords, with different spacings between their roots, thirds, fifths, and sevenths. The types are discussed in chapter 8.

Can you tell which of these scale degrees are omitted in Paul McCartney's electric bass line in the Beatles' "Birthday"? (In the I chord, the "missing" tones are the sixth on the way up and the third in descent.) The thirteenth chord may contain all six different scale degrees above its root: 5—7—2—4—6—1—3, for example. Suspended chords and other anomalies will be discussed in chapter 8.

Now that we know the basics of how chords are constructed, we can cover a bit of how they relate to one another. The lowest notes of the chords typically belong to the bass line, and have a special function in that, for acoustical reasons, they support all tones sounding above in other instruments and vocals. Upper tones in higher-sounding instruments tend to move from one to another for *melodic* purposes; this melodic function may also be adopted by the bass part, but the bass line is also the best place to relate the lowest tone of one chord to the lowest tone of another with *harmonic* value. The basic harmonic relationship is the falling fifth between roots, and the goal of harmony is to arrive on the I chord. In other words, when two chords relate to each other so that the root of the first drops a fifth along the scale to the root of the next, we have the falling fifth and thus the most fundamental harmonic function. The chords V—I exemplify this relationship, because the root of the V chord lies a fifth above that of the I, and we have arrived at a satisfying conclusion in the I chord. (Listen to Web audio example 2.13.) (Note, in the chorus of Perry Como's "Hot Diggity (Dog Ziggity Boom)," how the string bass alternates between roots of the I and the V chords. Same for the electric bass in 1910 Fruitgum Co.'s "Simon Says.") What chord lies a fifth above ii? (The vi chord.) What lies a fifth above V? (Remember that the scale replicates, 8 = 1, so that measuring a fifth above the fifth scale degree takes us to the second scale degree.) A falling-fifths progression may begin with a chord whose root lies anywhere along the scale and then progress to the final I chord though the most basic harmonic function. Beginning on iii, for instance, yields iii—vi—ii—V—I via falling fifths. (Listen to Web audio examples 2.14 and 2.15.)

In most styles of popular music, roots are nearly always played in the bass. But certain chords can be "inverted," with the third, fifth, seventh, or other member occurring in the bass instead. Sometimes, inversions can make for a smoother bass line, as in the phrase, "So how could I dance with another" in "I Saw Her Standing There," where Paul McCartney moves from the root of I (0:20+) to the third of the same chord (0:22), so he can step instead of jump to the root of IV (0:23). At other times, using a chord member other than the root in the bass can cause great instability, as in James Jamerson's sitting on the chordal thirds or fifths in the bass in the Four Tops' "Reach Out, I'll Be There" (as at 0:37, 0:49, 0:57, etc.). The Beach Boys album *Pet*

Photo 2.01. Erik Santos on fretless electric bass. (Photo: Kristin Fosdick)

Sounds has a high concentration of chords with the bass playing nonroots. To create a melodic bass line, rather than one fulfilling a purely harmonic function, the bassist will employ a variety of inversions and connect the more structural bass tones with nonchordal embellishing tones that pass between and lie next to them (note the melodic usage of all sorts of nonroot tones in the bass in many of the audio examples already cited). Often, when the bass arpeggiates through the triad once every bar, or when a large number of embellishing tones may appear, the strongest metric accent—almost always the downbeat—is considered to carry the one true bass note for each chord (although this too may be the location of a rather disruptive substitution). So chordal construction above the root, relationships among chordal roots, the property of chordal inversion, the interrelationship between harmony and melody, and the relationship between pitch and meter are the bassist's concerns when creating a bass line. All of these topics will be explored further in the chapters on harmony and rhythm.

More on bass technique

Even when working apart from the drummer, and even though charged with creating a song's harmonic foundation, the bassist may bring great rhythmic life to a performance. The simple sense of knowing when to repeat notes is a strong rhythmic skill—note its suggestion of halting power in the chorus of the Supremes' "Stop! In the Name of Love" and the increase of adrenaline on the root of V at the end of the bridge of the Beatles' "This Boy" (1:21), where the bass suddenly plays three repetitions per beat and just as suddenly drops an octave then stops playing altogether before the tension-clearing return of I. In a related way, the constant repeated notes opening Tommy James and the Shondells' "I

> **Bass technique:** repeated notes and pedals; arpeggiations and the ostinato; doubling of the bass line.

Think We're Alone Now" makes the sparse later "heartbeat" on the conga all the more effective. The bassist can also create tension between different simultaneously existing levels, when the root of a structural harmony sustains, with an effect called a pedal, below embellishing chords that change in other instruments. This commonly occurs beneath a I chord moving back-and-forth to and from its lower-neighbor chord, as when the bass sustains the first scale degree through chord changes in the verse of Martha and the Vandellas' "Dancing in the Street" or through the entirety of the Beatles' "Tomorrow Never Knows." Much more subtle appearances of the pedal, however, lend grace to the Beach Boys' "Let's Go Away for Awhile" (where two bass pedals support changes in the vibes, acoustic guitars and piano, 0:00–0:17), the intro to Frankie Valli's "Can't Take My Eyes Off You" (the bass holding beneath moving trumpets and horn), and the verse of Dionne Warwick's "(Theme From) Valley of the Dolls" (listen to how long that unchanging first scale degree sustains beneath the large variety of embellishing chords, each unstable relationship between chord and bass tone underlining an unanswered question from the singer).

Rhythm is also an important element of the bassist's arpeggiation patterns. You may note that the several types of arpeggiations listed above feature a rhythmic pattern, as well as a pitch pattern, that is repeated from bar to bar and maintained through the chord changes. This melodic device incorporating repeated pitch and rhythmic elements—and usually embodying an embellished arpeggio—is called an ostinato, and is fundamental to rock music, exemplified in the opening of the Animals' "We Gotta Get Out of This Place," the intro and part of the verse of the Beatles' "Day Tripper" (0:01–0:31), and the contrasting verse (0:08–0:25) and chorus (0:41–0:55) of the Monkees' "Words." But no matter how active or busy the bass may be (witness the Beatles' "Nowhere Man," the Grass Roots' "Midnight Confessions," and Dion's "Abraham, Martin and John"), it is rarely a lead melodic instrument. It just about rises to this occasion by default in the Shangri-Las' barren "Remember (Walkin' In the Sand)" and the unresolving din of the Mothers' "Are You Hung Up?" One can probably speak of the bass as a leading melodic force in the Beatles' "Something," wherein Paul McCartney provides simply elegant, rightly emphasized counterpoint to Harrison's Telecaster guitar.

The bass line is frequently strengthened by doubling. One curious technique is the "tic-tac" bass, created by the simultaneous plucking of the same line on upright and electric basses for a particularly percussive attack. Perhaps appearing first in Fats Domino's "Valley of Tears" and Jill Corey's "Love Me to Pieces" (both from 1957), the sound became closely identified with Nashville's A-Team of session players, particularly Harold Bradley, who added electric to Bob Moore's acoustic in Patsy Cline's "Crazy" and "I Fall to Pieces," Elvis Presley's "Follow That Dream," and in a slew of top hits by Brenda Lee and Bobby Vinton (her "I'm Sorry" and "I Want to Be Wanted (Per Tutta La Vita)," his "Blue Velvet" and "There! I've Said It Again"). It wasn't heard much at all after two hits from early 1967, Frank Sinatra's "That's Life" and Engelbert Humperdinck's "Release Me." Brian Wilson would at times double two electric basses ("God Only Knows," 1:04–2:00; "I Just Wasn't Made for These Times," 0:21–0:30), and George Harrison overdubbed a melodic second bass part over McCartney's line in the Beatles' "I Want to Hold Your Hand" (0:10–0:12) for a very unusual effect. Much more commonly, the bass line is doubled by one guitar (as by Grady Martin's lead guitar in Roy Orbison's "Oh Pretty Woman") or by two (in "Day Tripper"), and sometimes, for overbearing potency, with the same line heard in three different octaves (the Beatles' "Dig a Pony," Led Zeppelin's "Dazed and Confused"). We will later note that this often happens in the minor-pentatonic, as opposed to the major, scale, creating a real uproar in such numbers as Edwin Starr's "War." (The minor-pentatonic world, built of scale degrees 1, $\flat$3, 4, 5, and $\flat$7, will also be seen to be the domain of the bass's great role in creating funk.)

The lowest line from a keyboard or mallet instrument may double the bass, as with piano (Ray Charles's "Hit the Road Jack," the Beach Boys' "Help Me Rhonda"), organ (Elvis Presley's "Bossa Nova Baby," the Supremes' "My World Is Empty Without You"), harpsichord (plus fuzz guitar in the Association's "Along Comes Mary," Donovan's "Sunshine Superman"), clavichord (the Beatles' "For No One"), vibraphone (the Isley Brothers' "This Old Heart of Mine," the First Edition's "Just Dropped In (To See What Condition My Condition Was In)"), or xylophone (the Four Tops' "It's the Same Old

Song"). Tuba (Peter and Gordon's "Lady Godiva"), bass trombone (Edwin Starr's "Twenty-Five Miles"), tenor trombone (Fontella Bass's "Rescue Me"), bass clarinet (the Beatles' "When I'm Sixty-Four," 1:04–1:07), and baritone saxophone (Martha and the Vandellas' "I'm Ready for Love") also commonly double the bass line, as a pop-music analogue to the orchestral roles for tuba, bassoon, and string basses. Some high-register doublings sound unconvincing, as when a trumpet doubles the bass's root-fifth alternation in the intro to Terry Stafford's "Suspicion" or when the lead vocal maintains its bass-doubling roots in the face of moving backing-vocal parts (the chorus of the Cookies' "Don't Say Nothin' Bad (About My Baby)"), or when the bass loses its crucial independence by just playing along with the lead vocal (as in Herman's Hermits' "Dandy," 0:13–0:21, or Crazy Elephant's "Gimme Gimme" Good Lovin'," beginning of chorus).

Stranger still are doublings at pitch levels not matching that of the bass line. Because the deep register can sound muddy, it is rare for the bassist to play two strings at once, but this makes an effective marker of texture change, as in the opening of Joanie Sommers's "Johnny Get Angry," the bridge of

Photo 2.02. The Ovation acoustic guitar. This model, made in 1981, has a rounded fiberglass back. (Photo: Annie Eastman)

the Beatles' "I Want to Hold Your Hand" (0:51–1:02), the first two verses only of the Ventures' "Hawaii Five-O," a transition in the Grateful Dead's "St. Stephen" (2:15–2:17 on the CD's 1971 mix of *Aoxomoxoa*), and a funky variation in Cream's "Sweet Wine" (8:45–9:03 in the *Live Cream* performance). These lines are all in parallel fifths and fourths (outlining the roots and fifths of triads), but the interval size lying halfway between the fifth and fourth, known as the tritone (and known in earlier ages as "the devil in music" for its harsh dissonance), is the distance between bass and guitar in the opening of the Jimi Hendrix Experience's "Purple Haze"; the same tritone is expressed melodically by bass and trombone in the intro and ending to Blood, Sweat and Tears' "Symphony for the Devil" / "Sympathy for the Devil," to appropriate effect. (Listen to Web audio example 2.16.) Much more commonly, a single bass line runs beneath a large protective buffer zone, whereas any combination of high-register voices and instruments can combine together in very close proximity to good effect.

Acoustic guitars

Elvis Presley, Chuck Berry, Buddy Holly, Bob Dylan, Pete Townsend, B. B. King, Eric Clapton, Jimi Hendrix, Joni Mitchell, Johnny Rotten, Bruce Springsteen, . . . : it seems easy to conjure a list of superstar rockers for whom the guitar is an iconic image. The guitar seems to lie at the core of rock music. Yet, among the top ten artists of 1955–2001 as found by Joel Whitburn's tabulation of lifetime performances on *Billboard*'s album charts, only four acts—Elvis Presley, the Beatles, the Rolling Stones, and Bob Dylan—are associated with the guitar, and none of them are usually praised for any particular technical expertise. In Whitburn's review of all-time *singles* charts, guitarists fare even worse, with only Presley, the Beatles, and the Stones among the top ten. Whitburn also publishes analyses by decade; among the top *thirty* album artists of 1955–59, the only guitarists to make the cut are Presley and the Kingston Trio; singles artists in that period include only six guitarists among the top twenty-five: Presley, Ricky Nelson, Bill Haley, the Everly Brothers, Jimmie Rodgers, and Chuck Berry, only the last-named possessing notable technique. Even in the 1960s, with the youth market for albums beginning to grow quickly, guitarists among the top thirty album artists of the 1960s include only the Beatles, Presley, the Ventures, the Kingston Trio, the Beach Boys, and the Rolling Stones. The top twenty-five singles artists of this period include the Beatles, Presley, the Beach Boys, the Stones, Roy Orbison, Nelson, and a lot of non-guitar-playing keyboardists and vocalists. But whereas the era's headliners were not

> The acoustic guitar: contruction; varieties of guitar- and lute-like instruments.

primarily known for their work on the instrument, and whereas those who were revered for its mastery were not among the time's most popular artists, the guitar was simply ubiquitous; it was there in every style and on nearly every recording, even if played by faceless rhythm-keepers. Little Richard did not feature the instrument, and it's not heard on piano-based songs such as Big Bopper's "Chantilly Lace," the Marathons' "Peanut Butter," the Angels' " 'Til," or Buddy Holly's cover of "Valley of Tears." But how many other discs from this fifteen-year period do not have at least a rhythm guitar somewhere in the background? Such recordings are pretty tough to find.

Both acoustic and electric guitars come in an array of types and models; in all, strings are stopped along the fretted fingerboard (on the neck) by the fingers of the left hand (reverse for most lefties) to shorten their vibrating lengths and raise the pitch, or are played open (unstopped by fingers). Finger-picking, plucking with a pick, and strumming is done by the right hand at various distances from the bridge. The bridge marks the constant end of string length and transfers vibration from string to the amplifying box. We'll cover in this section the basic sound properties of the instruments and their closest cousins in the lute and harp families, and their amplification and effects used in the 1950s and '60s, along with enough about performance and arranging techniques to widen and deepen the listening experience considerably.

Acoustic guitars are either of the Spanish classical tradition with nylon strings or of the modern folk tradition, larger with steel strings. (See Web photo 2.04.) Whereas the nylon-string guitar is famous in Mexican and other Latin settings (Grady Martin's playing in Marty Robbins' "El Paso" and in Roy Orbison's "Yo te Amo Maria," Charlie Byrd's playing in "Desafinado"), it is also heard in songs as different as Chubby Checker's "Limbo Rock," Bob Dylan's "Desolation Row" and "Just Like a Woman," Frank and Nancy Sinatra's "Somethin' Stupid," and Mason Williams's "Classical Gas." The steel-string acoustic is strummed by Bob Dylan in "Chimes of Freedom," fingerpicked by Paul McCartney in the Beatles' "Blackbird," and given the lead melodic role by Peter Albin in Big Brother and the Holding Co.'s "Turtle Blues." Guitars have six strings, or, with the twelve-string model, six pairs of strings, the two strings of each pair of the latter tuned either at the same pitch (the unison) or in octaves. The acoustic twelve-string is strummed (the Brooklyn Bridge's "Worst That Could Happen"), fingerpicked (Marianne Faithfull's "As Tears Go By"), or played for a single-line melody (the Seekers' "I'll Never Find Another You"). The acoustic guitar has a top of soft wood, usually sitka spruce, to absorb and color as much vibration from the strings as possible; this sound reverberates in the box and is reflected off the hardwood back, often of mahogany. The tonal color of a particular acoustic is determined largely by the composition of the woods and strings, the tautness of construction, and the dimensions of the box. Generally, a larger instrument produces a deeper sound and has better overall intonation; there is also a small tenor guitar, which can be heard along with string bass, a second acoustic guitar, and banjo on most Kingston Trio hits including "Tom Dooley." In the 1920s, a pre-electric attempt to amplify the guitar resulted in the dobro, a guitar whose bridge lies atop a ten-inch metal resonating cone that opens into the box. Nancy Sinatra's "How Does That Grab You, Darlin'?" opens with a bent note on dobro for a tom-cat effect, and bent dobro strings are heard throughout Jeannie C. Riley's "Harper Valley P.T.A.," but the dobro's strings are more often stopped with a bottleneck slide than by bare fingers, as in the Stone Poneys' "Up to My Neck in High Muddy Water," the Rolling Stones' "You Got the Silver," and Creedence Clearwater Revival's "Green River" and "Lookin' Out My Back Door." The dobro is given a full workout on John Lennon's *Imagine* album.

Related to the dobro is the four- or five-stringed metal-bodied banjo, which features however a head of tight skin on which the bridge sits, adding a snap to the tinny metallic tone. Busy fingerpicking is the norm here, as in the Statler Brothers' "Flowers on the Wall"; other characteristic sounds are the rapid strumming of a single note (strummed tremolo, as in the second verse of the Village Stompers' "Washington Square," 0:23+) and the rapid strumming of a rising chord sequence with the left-hand chord position held in parallel as it climbs the neck, as in the opening of Louis Armstrong's "Hello, Dolly!" Glen Campbell's banjo enters a bar early in the Beach Boys' "I Know There's an Answer" (1:43), contributing to his decision to forego session work for a solo career. Long a banjoist before he picked up the guitar, Jerry Garcia has a fine banjo solo in It's a Beautiful Day's "Hoedown." Much less often heard is the long and narrow, and thus delicate, airy dulcimer, played by Brian Jones in the Rolling Stones' "I Am Waiting" and by Richard Fariña in Judy Collins's "Carry It On." The gourd-shaped lute is also used by the Stones, in "Factory Girl," and elsewhere accompanies the nightingale—lark duet in the "Farewell Love Scene" from the *Romeo and Juliet* soundtrack. The mandolin is like the lute, but much more resonant with its four pairs of strings; its sound is usually given artificial sustaining power by strummed tremolo, as in Dean Martin's "Return to Me," Ray Conniff's "Somewhere My Love," Petula Clark's "This Is My Song," the Nitty Gritty Dirt Band's "Mr. Bojangles," and the introspective suspension of time in the Beach Boys' "Wouldn't It Be Nice" (1:43–1:58). A Greek sort of mandolin, the bouzouki, is heard in Don Costa's "Never On Sunday" and the Stone Poneys' "Sweet Summer Blue and Gold." Another four-string box is the intimate ukulele, often associated with Hawaii (see Tony Bennett's "In the Middle Of an Island") and with vaudeville (Tiny Tim's "Tip-toe Thru' the Tulips With Me"). It also has a poignant role in B. J. Thomas's "Raindrops Keep Fallin' On My Head," which opens with the uke as solo accompaniment, as if the singer is sitting alone with his thoughts on a park bench.

Smaller members of the harp family are often strummed or picked in this music. The autoharp is a table model equipped with buttons that depress preset combinations of closely spaced strings to produce certain chords, so when used it is invariably strummed as a rhythm instrument, as by John Sebastian in the Lovin' Spoonful's "Do You Believe in Magic" and his own "How Have You Been," and in Every Mothers' Son's "I Believe in You." The Irish harp is also played by Sebastian in the Spoonful's "Rain on the Roof." The smaller zither is typically played melodically, most famously by Anton Karas in "Third Man Theme," but also by Donovan in "Atlantis" (entering at 1:18). George Harrison plucks an Indian harplike instrument, the svaramandal, melodically in the transitions of the Beatles' "Strawberry Fields Forever" (panning right to left, first in 1:18–1:20).

The Beatles also introduced to the rock realm three other Indian string instruments: the bowed violin-like dilruba (in "Within You Without You," heard right, imitated by sitar in 2:28–2:42, center, then joined by Western strings, center), the droning plucked tamboura (used traditionally by them in "Love You To" and in a rock context in "Tomorrow Never Knows," and taken over by the Rolling Stones for "Street Fighting Man," Donovan for "Hurdy Gurdy Man," and the Turtles for "Sound Asleep"), and the sitar. (Listen to Web audio example 1.29 and see Web photos 2.05—2.07.) The gourd-based sitar has a small number of stopped-and-plucked strings but gets its characteristically complex metallic ring of high frequencies from the buzz emanating from a flat bridge and from a larger number of differently tuned sympathetic strings, which

Photo 2.03. Erik Santos, right, plays bass; Reg LeCrisp, with Stratocaster, is at left. A hollow-body Epiphone Casino awaits in the background, and a Pod XT digital simulator sits on the piano bench. (Photo: Kristin Fosdick)

are not played but which vibrate harmoniously along with the plucked pitches and their buzzing overtones. Used first by the Beatles as an exotic-sounding guitar in "Norwegian Wood (This Bird Has Flown)," the sitar was quickly adopted by a dozen pop acts or producers of the late '60s, including the Rolling Stones (in "Paint It, Black"), Petula Clark (doubling a guitar in "Color My World"), Donovan, the Moody Blues, the Rascals, and Traffic.

The electric guitar

Leo Fender and Les Paul began developing the electric guitar in the late 1940s. (See Web photo 2.08.) Pioneer performers include Ike Turner, Barney Kessel, Rusty Draper, Boyd Bennett, Danny Cedrone, Scotty Moore, Carl Perkins, Chuck Berry, Paul Burlison, and James Burton. In the new design, an electromagnetic coil placed beneath each string converts metal-string vibrations (which disturb the coils' magnetic fields) into electric voltage changes, which are transduced into sound waves by an amplifier and speaker cabinet. Because of the way strings vibrate in multiple simultaneous divisions along their length, coil pickups will detect differing combinations of string harmonics, and therefore different resulting tone colors, depending on how far away they are placed from the bridge and from various nodes along the strings. Electric guitars sometimes have just a single pickup, but usually have several; one placed close to the bridge will be excited by very fast partials and will conduct a very bright and complex trebly tone, whereas one placed where the neck ends will capture fewer harmonics and produce a mellower, simpler tone. The guitarist can switch between pickups or, on most models, combine the tones from a pair. (Listen to Web audio example 2.17 and see Web photos 2.09—2.11.) Typically, rhythm guitarists will play at the neck pickup (as does Lennon, even when taking lead in the Beatles' "I Feel Fine") whereas lead guitarists, more interested in cutting through the texture, will use the bridge pickup. Wayne Fontana and the Mindbenders' "Game of Love" and Jimi Hendrix's "Belly Button Window" are fine examples of normal rhythm and lead pickup selections by each pair of guitarists. But the bridge pickup is used for many solos, providing for example a clarinet-like color to harmonize with the Beatles' dance-band arrangement for "Honey Pie" (1:32–1:39). The lead guitarist changes from neck to bridge pickup at 1:17 in the Beach Boys' "Pet Sounds"; can you hear the multiple such changes in Crosby, Stills and Nash's "Wooden Ships"? Can you hear where the guitarist changes pickups in Web audio example 2.09? Simultaneously mixed pickups simulate an effect of one line played in octaves in Dee Clark's "Raindrops" (0:37–0:49).

> The electric guitar: construction and varieties.

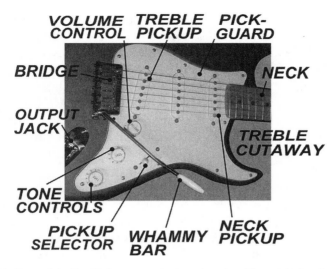

VOLUME TREBLE PICK-
CONTROL PICKUP GUARD

BRIDGE

NECK

OUTPUT
JACK

TREBLE
CUTAWAY

TONE
CONTROLS

PICKUP WHAMMY NECK
SELECTOR BAR PICKUP

Photo 2.04. Parts of the Fender Stratocaster, oriented as played by a right-hander, with the thicker bass strings lying above the thinner treble strings. (Photo: Annie Eastman)

The construction of the guitar's body can also vary considerably. A very solid guitar like a maple/mahogany Les Paul or an ash Fender will absorb little of the string's vibration, channeling most of the string color directly into the electronics (note the trebly Strat sound of the solos for the Beatles' "Nowhere Man" and The Band's "Jemima Surrender"), whereas a semisolid or hollow-body guitar will shape the tone according to its acoustic qualities (note the mellow, jazzy tone of Barney Kessel's work on Julie London's "Cry Me a River" and in the Casinos' "Then You Can Tell Me Goodbye"). (Listen to Web audio example 2.18.) A hollow body will also be more prone to feedback, both because the amplified signal will exert control over the box's acoustics and therefore over the magnetic vibration, and because all strings are more prone to vibrate sympathetically than they would on a solid instrument. Played at the verge of feedback, a hollow Gibson 335 (in Chuck Berry's "Maybelline" or B. B. King's "Sweet Little Angel"), Gretsch Country Gentleman (George Harrison's in the Beatles' "She Loves You") or an Epiphone Casino (McCartney's retransition in the Beatles' "Ticket to Ride," 1:24–1:29) can sound white-hot. Listen to feedback threatening, but never doing more than encroaching, in the Amboy Dukes' "Journey to the Center of the Mind," Cream's "White Room," and Big Brother and the Holding Co.'s "Piece of My Heart," to name just three examples from 1968. Equalization controls on both the guitar and the preamp allow the guitarist to filter treble and bass frequencies to a desired bandwidth; note the very trebly sound of James Burton's Strat in Rick Nelson's "It's Late," the intro to the Grass Roots'

"Let's Live for Today," and in John Fogerty's playing on Creedence Clearwater Revival's "Suzie Q." (Listen to Web audio example 2.19 and see Web photo 2.12.) The odd hornlike sound in the Lovin' Spoonful's "Rain on the Roof" at 1:00–1:08 shows what happens when Zal Yanovsky turns the treble off of his hollow Guild Thunderbird and cranks the amplifier's treble and gain high enough to distort and just begin to feed back. The Vox AC30 amp featured a "Top Boost" circuit that gave Beatle guitars a silver sheen, as with George Harrison's playing of a hollow-body Gretsch on "Words of Love."

Whereas the Hawaiian lap steel guitar began life as an acoustic instrument, it was an early convert to electrification. Played across the lap, the strings are stopped by a sliding steel bar rather than by left-hand fingers; raised by a higher-than-normal bridge, the strings do not touch the fretboard, and thus project a long sustain. The resulting sound is a near-constant set of glissandi between parallel chords, as heard in the Fontane Sisters' "Daddy-O" and the Beatles' "For You Blue" (John Lennon playing). (Listen to Web audio example 2.20.) Because the slide could replicate only parallel versions of the open tuning, a new instrument was developed to enable retunings of the strings during play; this is the pedal-steel guitar, which makes use of various numbers of pedals and knee levers to alter the tuning of the six-to-ten open strings, thus allowing constant changes of intervals and chord members from string to string even though the same straight steel bar is used by the left hand. A number of tuning systems have been developed for this instrument, the sound of which is characterized by a shifting, fluid quality because some or all sounding pitches may change after the strings are set into motion. A volume pedal also allows the player to adjust volume up or down on an already-sounding string for a second dimension of fluidity. Celebrated results of the pedal-steel are heard in Santo and Johnny's "Sleep Walk" (Santo Farina on the Fender steel), Bob Dylan's "Lay Lady Lay" (played by the best, Pete Drake), the Dead's "High Time" and "Dire Wolf" (played by Garcia, who also graces the Airplane's "The Farm" and Crosby, Stills, Nash and Young's "Teach Your Children"), and James Taylor's "Anywhere Like Heaven."

The twelve-string guitar as electrified by Rickenbacker was introduced by George Harrison in the Beatles' film *A Hard Day's Night* and instantly adopted by many of the top British groups (the Animals, the Hollies, Gerry and the Pacemakers, Herman's Hermits, the Searchers, the Rolling Stones, the Zombies, and The Who all used it in 1964–67) as well as the American Beach Boys, Jefferson Airplane, and the Byrds, whose member David Crosby continued to use it in Crosby, Stills and Nash. (Listen to Web audio example 2.21 and see Web photo 2.13.) It was also used for occasional effect by Eric Clapton with Cream ("Dance the Night Away") and by Jimmy Page with Led Zeppelin ("Thank You"). Page often played a cumbersome double-neck Gibson SG in concert, allowing him to alternate immediately between six- and twelve-string necks. One company, Danelectro, even came up with an electric sitar for its Coral line. This guitar had an unusually thick bridge that caused the six plucked strings to buzz. In addition, the lower parts of the strings were enclosed in a plastic chamber that also contained the lower ends of thirteen thin and normally unplayed strings; the chamber would concentrate resonances so that the extra strings would vibrate sympathetically. The buzz combined with the wild resonances closely simulated the very complex sound of the sitar. (Listen to Web audio example 2.22 and see Web photo 2.14.) Heard on more than a dozen hits from the years 1966–70 (including the Cyrkle's "Turn-Down Day," the Animals' "Monterey," the Lemon Pipers' "Green Tambourine," the Box Tops' "Cry Like a Baby," B. J. Thomas's "Hooked on a Feeling," Joe South's "Games People Play," and Stevie Wonder's "Signed, Sealed, Delivered I'm Yours"), the guitar's designer Vinnie Bell (in New York) and Reggie Young (Nashville) got most of the session gigs with this once trendy instrument.

Signal amplification and modification

Beyond factors of the instrument's construction, the signal from any sort of guitar can be further altered by amp circuits that generate tremolo, reverb, and distortion. Tremolo, which rapidly alternates two different volume levels for a wavering effect, can be controlled for depth of distance between the two volumes and for speed of wavering. (Listen to Web audio example 2.23 and see Web photo 2.15.) Of the hundreds of 1950s–'60s songs featuring tremolo on guitar, the Dominoes' "Do Something For Me" and Buffalo Springfield's "For What It's Worth (Stop, Hey What's That Sound)" are among the slowest and Rosie and the Originals' "Angel Baby" and the Animals' "Don't Bring Me Down" are among the fastest. Slow and intense amp tremolo added to the lead guitar in many Everly Brothers' hits ("All I Have to Do Is Dream," "Let It Be Me," "Devoted to You") sometimes seems to suggest tenderness, and at other times ("So Sad (To Watch Good Love Go Bad)") tremulous sobs. The very slow and deep tremolo in Don French's "Lonely Saturday Night" is just pathetic! Heavy moderate-speed tremolo helps Tommy Tedesco's lead guitar cut through the orchestral arrangements for Al Caiola's "The Magnificent Seven" and "Bonanza" themes. Joe South's fast tremolo on the opening of Aretha Franklin's "Chain of Fools" is memorable enough to survive a bad splice to the song proper. The moderate-speed tremolo in the Association's "Never My Love" just swoons, as does the final Telecaster chord in their "Cherish." Fast tremolo adds mystery to the guitar in verses of the Monkees theme, in which we've already noted hi-hat suspense.

> **Amplification and effects:** tremolo, reverb, distortion and sustain, echo, compression, the Leslie, volume/tone-control pedal, talkbox, wah-wah, the Octavia, and phasing.

Reverb, created by bouncing a signal between metal plates, builds an acoustical space around a sound; a guitarist can play dry, or wet with reverb. The Fender amp is fairly universally credited for having the most satisfying reverb effect. (Listen to Web audio example 2.24 and see Web photo 2.16.) Buddy Holly blends his two-part, dual-string Strat playing with a touch of reverb in "Words of Love." Billy Strange soaks his guitar for "The James Bond Theme." Note the additional space opened up when Lennon's reverb-drenched Casino enters to double George Martin's electric harpsichord in the Beatles' "Because" (at 0:12). When Robby Krieger opens The Doors' "End of the Night," his seasick bottleneck slides are awash in murky, dreamy reverb.

Guitar distortion is a large topic, and would theoretically include any alteration to the guitar's sound that jeopardizes its purity or regularity of waveshape. (Web audio example 2.16 features extreme guitar distortion.) The concept could include the breakup caused by a poor connection as when guitar cables or plugs begin to fail, as heard in Chuck Berry's "Come On" or the Beatles' "Chains." It is accepted to call distortion the appropriately fuzzy sound Paul Burlison gets from a loose tube in his amp for the Johnny Burnette Trio's "The Train Kept a Rollin'" and which Grady Martin gets from a blown preamp tube in Marty Robbins's "Don't Worry." But distortion is much more commonly the result of (1) raising the preamplifier's gain in one or more stages past the point where the greatly boosted signal begins to overdrive the amplifier circuits, or (2) adding a "fuzz box" like the Maestro Fuzz-Tone used by the Stones in "(I Can't Get No) Satisfaction" and elsewhere to achieve the same thing, either way clipping the sound and introducing "unwanted" wave-shapes characteristic of the nonlinear electronics but allowing the amplifier to still control the volume of the output level. Examples of songs containing distorted leads that bear such adjectives as raucous, raunchy, sizzling, wild, and blistering include the Kinks' "You Really Got Me" (by Dave Davies), Bob Dylan's "Leopard-Skin-Pill-Box Hat" (Dylan himself), Buffalo Springfield's "Leave" (Neil Young), Traffic's "Dear Mr. Fantasy" (Dave Mason), The Doors' "Hello, I Love You" (Robby Krieger), the Amboy Dukes' "Journey to the Center of the Mind" (Ted Nugent), the Beatles' "Revolution" (both John Lennon and George Harrison), and Creedence Clearwater Revival's "Up Around the Bend" (John Fogerty). Extreme pain runs through the very dirty lead and rhythm guitars of the Plastic Ono Band's "Cold Turkey."

Through the high gain level, distortion compresses the signal, boosting the volume of quieter parts of the waveshape, which thereby also allows the guitar string to sustain its voice much longer than it could without such intervention. This factor is beautifully manipulated by Eric Clapton for rich and climactic solos in Cream's "Sunshine of Your Love" (2:00–2:50) and "SWLABR" (1:17–1:32), and in a more pedestrian way by Randy Bachman in the Guess Who's "American Woman." The Fuzzface distortion pedal was such a constantly used piece of Hendrix's gear, that "Hey Joe" and "Dolly Dagger" are rare in featuring clean Hendrix leads. Distorted lines often combine with others colored differently: the Association's "Along Comes Mary" and the Monkees' "Valleri" double the bass with a distorted guitar; the Electric Prunes' "I Had Too Much to Dream Last Night" runs one guitar's fuzz tone through a fast tremolo and that of a second is heavily colored by the whammy bar and overdubbed backward. In Crosby, Stills and Nash's "Long Time Gone," the dirty guitar grates against the pure flutelike organ the same way that David Crosby's tense vocal grates against Graham Nash's and Steve Stills's cool backing vocal harmonies. By contrast, two fuzz guitars harmonize for duets in Hendrix's "Little Miss Strange," Led Zeppelin's "Ramble On," and Spirit's "Uncle Jack." By the late 1960s, Fender amps had a reputation for a sweet clean tone with excellent reverb, whereas Marshalls had the best range of distortion colors that would fully saturate all ranges of the sound spectrum. But no matter how dirty, grungy, and noisy guitarists could make their tone in 1969, it is nothing compared to the crunch of metal heard decades later. Those interested in learning more about the best-known amps of the 1950s and '60s, all based on tubes rather than solid-state technology, are encouraged to visit the various walk-through demonstrations on YouTube of such models as the Gibson GA-40 (Les Paul); the Fender Tweed, Twin Reverb, and Bassman; the Vox AC15 and AC30; and the Marshall JTM45 (Bluesbreaker) and Plexis.

The guitarist can add electronic boxes to the signal path to generate a growing range of effects. A very early effect is the echo box, which uses a tape-delay system to slap repeated but ever-softer echoes through the signal; it is heard in Eddie Cochran's "Sittin' in the Balcony," the Chantay's' [sic] "Pipeline," Leapy Lee's "Little Arrows" (very effective in suggesting Cupid's darts hitting their mark!), and Jimi Hendrix's "May This Be Love." (Listen to Web audio example 2.25.)

One of the most widely used yet seldom discussed of the guitar effects is the compressor. As suggested in the discussion of distortion, compression is a squeezing of the dynamic range so as to unify the loudness of notes or chords, rounding off peaks at initial articulation and beefing up decay, adding to the tone's sustain. (Listen to Web audio example 2.26 and see Web photo 2.17.) At an extreme level, a compressed guitar can emulate the sound of an organ; many, in fact, think they hear an organ in the Beatles' "I Want to Hold Your Hand," but this sound is just the extreme compression given to Lennon's rhythm chording. The highly compressed signal from James Taylor's neck pickup in "Steamroller" sounds like an electric piano.

Another favorite Beatle method of confusing the sounds of the guitar and the organ was to run the guitar signal into the revolving Leslie speaker normally applied to the signal from a Hammond B-3 organ, adding a Doppler-colored sort of tremolo. This leads to Harrison's Fender Stratocaster effect in the chorus of "Lucy in the Sky With Diamonds," where the swirly guitar doubles the bass (0:50–1:06, right channel), and to his chiming Fender Telecaster arpeggiations in the "magic feeling" section (1:31–1:37) of "You Never Give Me Your Money." (Listen to Web audio example 2.27.) The Leslie was adopted by many, applied to the lead guitar in the Beach Boys' "Pet Sounds," the Zombies' "Beechwood Park," The Who's "Tattoo," Cream's "Badge," the Airplane's "Share a Little Joke," Joe Cocker's "Bird On the Wire," Big Brother and the Holding Co.'s "Summertime," and Led Zeppelin's "Good Times Bad Times" (and applied to an amplified acoustic guitar in Simon and Garfunkel's "America," the Hassles' "Night After Day," and The Band's "Tears of Rage.") But I'm guessing that this wasn't a Beatle invention, as is widely thought; isn't that the Leslie coloring the guitar tone in Jewel Akens's "The Birds and the Bees," recorded more than a year before *Revolver?*

The Beatles are also sometimes credited with the first use of the volume/tone-control pedal in three February 1965 recordings: "Ticket to Ride," "Yes It Is," and "I Need You." This device masks the initial attack and decay of a guitar's tone, controlling all volume changes with an organlike swell pedal (which makes it much easier to control the quicksilvery effect than as attempted in "Baby's in Black," where Lennon continuously turned the volume knob up and down, up and down, on Harrison's guitar as the latter picked the solo). (Listen to Web audio example 2.28.) The Beatles themselves credited the effect to Italian guitarist/engineer Marino Marini, who used it on "The Honeymoon Song (Bound By Love)." It's also heard on the Everly Brothers' "That's Just Too Much," the Lovin' Spoonful's "Daydream," The Mamas and the Papas' "I Call Your Name" (1:19–1:38), the Critters' "Younger Girl," Jimmy Page's addition to Donovan's "Sunshine Superman," and Simon and Garfunkel's "The Boxer" (1:44–2:10).

One of the more humorous guitar effects is Pete Drake's talkbox. Inspired by Alvino Ray's talking steel guitar recordings of the 1940s, Drake fed his barely amplified guitar signal through a plastic tube modulated by a singer's silent mouth shapes, picked up by the vocal microphone, in songs like "Forever." Robbie Robertson used this on The Band's "This Wheel's On Fire" before Peter Frampton made it a household sound in the late 1970s.

Certainly the most celebrated guitar effect of the 1960s is the wah-wah pedal, which uses a very strong filter to control the range of harmonics present in a guitar's tone. (Listen to Web audio example 2.29 and see Web photo 2.18.) (A touch of physics here: when a string is set in motion, it vibrates as a whole, producing the fundamental pitch, but at the same time also vibrates in halves—producing a much quieter overtone, a harmonic, an octave higher—and in thirds, fourths, and ever-smaller units, each producing a much higher pitch in varying ratios of loudness depending upon properties of the vibrating body; this is the principle behind guitar pickups detecting different tones at different places along the string. Every note is a complex of many simultaneous harmonics, and it's actually the ratios of the loudnesses of the various harmonics to the fundamental that gives every sound-producing body, every instrument, its own color.) The wah can change the tone of a sustaining guitar note or chord from relative purity, lacking all overtones, to a very rich one, with a gradual sweep of added harmonics, controlled by rocking a pedal up and down. The pedal gets its name from the sound made when a person changes vowels mid-syllable; if one were to sing a long sustained syllable like uuuuuu uuoooooooooaaaaaaaaiiiiiiiiieeeeeeee on one unchanging pitch, a perceptive ear would hear the added overtones, kicking in one by one, that make one vowel sound different from another. The wah pedal was rarely used before 1968; just how is that effect achieved in Brenda Lee's 1964 record, "Is It True" (0:38–0:42)? Surely the Rolling Stones pioneered this novelty with a Vox pedal two years later in "Have You Seen Your Mother, Baby, Standing in the Shadows?" before Clapton made it a must-have in 1967 in "World of Pain" and "Tales of Brave Ulysses." The pedal became a favorite device of Hendrix in *Axis: Bold as Love* and *Electric Ladyland,* of the Norman Whitfield-produced Temptations in "Cloud Nine" and "Run Away Child, Running Wild," and of Frank Zappa from *We're Only in It For the Money* onward, and was taken up by the Beatles, the Airplane, Pink Floyd, The Band, Jeff Beck, Steve Stills, Blue Cheer, Iron Butterfly, the Small Faces, Soft Machine, and Status Quo before the charting year of 1968 was over. Chicago, Deep Purple, the Supremes, Isaac Hayes, Sly and the Family Stone, and Led Zeppelin soon jumped on the bandwagon to drive the wah into the following decade.

A more specific sort of filtering device powered the Octavia, a box used chiefly by Jimi Hendrix to overemphasize the first overtone of every note. (Listen to Web audio example 2.30.) This enabled him to virtually play along with himself in octaves; note its use in the intro to "Straight Ahead" and in the overdubbed solo (after "help me! help me!") in "Purple Haze." Along with the wah and the Leslie, a primary psychedelic effect was phasing. Often applied in postproduction by the engineer, this would match a replica or an inverted replica of the guitar's signal against the original but slightly sped up and slowed down so that parts of the sound that were exactly out-of-phase (amplitudes of certain frequencies just as far in the positive range for one wavelength as in the negative range for the other) would be cancelled out, so that the resulting sound sort of got wrapped up inside of itself in ever-changing convolutions. (Listen to Web audio example 2.31.) Although applied most recognizably to vocal parts (as in the Small Faces' "Itchycoo Park," the Grateful Dead's "That's It for the Other One," Hendrix's "Little Wing" and in many other places), the guitar is phased along with vocals in the Status Quo's "Pictures of Matchstick Men." A pedal called the Univibe achieved a live phasing effect by using a low-frequency wave to drive a signal and its simultaneous inversion past each other; along with the Fuzzface, the Univibe assists Hendrix in recreating the rockets' red glare in his *Woodstock* performance of "The Star Spangled Banner." The Univibe, incidentally, was to become the basic effect of Robin Trower's 1974 album, *Bridge of Sighs,* which takes its name from the opening lyric of the heavily phased "Itchycoo Park."

Guitar technique

Of course, a player's actions can have the most profound impact on the instrument's resulting sound, and that's what we aim to cover in the remainder of this section on the guitar. Temporary manipulation of the instrument's sound characteristics, playing techniques for both the left and right hands, idiomatic performance practices of both rhythm and lead playing, and a few indications of how different guitars are combined are easily appreciable by the focused ear.

> **Guitar techniques:** alternate tunings, the capo and string length, slide, string bending, hammer-ons and pull-offs, muting and muffling, whammy-bar and wrist-vibrato, strummed tremolo, noise effects, and the harmonic.

First, the player may detune the instrument, either to achieve lower pitches from the low E string, or to arrange for different chord patterns in the left hand or for the use of a slide. Glen Campbell's "Wichita Lineman" and "Galveston" both have a deep "slack" tuning to allow for very low notes in their solos; other examples include the Tijuana Brass's "The Lonely Bull." Ike and Tina Turner's "It's Gonna Work Out Fine," Dick Dale and the Del-Tones' "Let's Go Trippin,'" the Rolling Stones' "Little Red Rooster," Dylan's "Highway 61 Revisited" and "It's Alright, Ma (I'm Only Bleeding)," Cream's "As You Said," Led Zeppelin's "Black Mountain Side," and Richie Havens' "Freedom" all feature detuned instruments for the easy achievement of parallel triads. (Listen to Web audio example 2.32.) (Havens, for example, nearly always tunes to an open D-major or D-minor triad and simply stops all strings with his thumb straight across the fingerboard.) Lower-than-standard pitches are heard in Paul McCartney's playing on the Beatles' "Yesterday," all strings on the acoustic Epiphone tuned down a major second, probably done to find a lower key to better accommodate the top limits of his vocal range.

The opposite approach to detuning is to clamp the neck with a capo to artificially shorten all of the strings. This might be done just a fret or two to improve the vocal ranges, as with the Beatles' "Norwegian Wood (This Bird Has Flown)," or by a considerable amount, to create the sound of a soprano guitar, as in the Hollies' "Look Through Any Window." Capos are placed as high as on the seventh fret, removing a third of the string length, for George

Harrison's exceedingly bright electric twelve-string solo on the Beatles' "If I Needed Someone" and on acoustics for "Here Comes the Sun," and on Steve Winwood's acoustic in Traffic's "John Barleycorn Must Die." (Listen to Web audio example 2.33 and see Web photos 2.19 and 2.20.) Guitarists can also manipulate string length by picking at certain places to emphasize certain overtones; the brightest sound is achieved by picking right near the bridge, where only the fastest vibrations are located; this is where the final chord of John Fred and His Playboy Band's "Judy in Disguise (With Glasses)" is played, as is the lead riff in the Rolling Stones' "Mother's Little Helper" (with the left hand working high on the G string). (Listen to Web audio example 2.34.) Of course, when the strings are plucked *behind* the bridge, only very high pitches of uncertain intonation will be found; this is the effect that ends the Beatles' "Oh! Darling" and that adds novelty half-way through Quicksilver Messenger Service's "Who Do You Love." (Listen to Web audio example 2.35.)

The bottleneck slide (a steel tube is probably used more often than a glass one, but there are all sorts) can easily suggest a rural blues; in the 1930s, Robert Johnson had made the wind howl with his slide in "Come On in My Kitchen" and Huddie Ledbetter had sent shivers up the spine in "Gallis Pole." (Listen again to Web audio example 2.32; see also Web photos 2.21 and 2.22.) Mike Bloomfield calls on this tradition in the postchorus breaks (as at 0:55–0:58) of Bob Dylan's "Tombstone Blues," and Roy Acuff simply plays the rube in "Wabash Cannon Ball." Brian Jones added the slide to many Stones tunes, Duane Allman did the same in supremely liquid fashion to Aretha Franklin's "The Weight," Harrison plays a slide Strat line that doubles Lennon's voice in the prechoruses of "Lucy in the Sky With Diamonds" (0:32–0:49, to contrast with his Leslie'd guitar doubling the bass line in choruses), Steve Cropper colors the chorus's signature lick of Sam and Dave's "Soul Man" (0:40–0:42) with slide, and The Doors and the Dead use it selectively. An odd effect (suggesting a garden's growth?) is heard in the intro and coda of the Four Seasons' "Watch the Flowers Grow," where bottleneck slides along pairs of strings have an atonal relationship with the rest of the pitchwork. A player often achieves a glissando with finger sliding along the neck after a note's articulation. (Listen to Web audio example 2.36.) The effect imitates whistling in the Royal Teens' "Short Shorts" and sounds like water drops in the Chordettes' "Never on Sunday," but the noise of intervening frets only contributes to the Strat's growl in Perry Como's "Kewpie Doll," and the staggering back and forth along the string in the Marvelettes' "My Baby Must Be a Magician" gives the spell-casting ring of a crash cymbal (was Motown too cheap for a gong?) a truly occult power. Large, fast glissi colored with an Echoplex also suggest mystery in the opening of Jimi Hendrix's "May This Be Love." It's usually difficult to sustain a glissed chord, but Bo Diddley does just that in "Road Runner."

Small distances between pitches may be met by bending the string—either after the string is plucked, in which case the pitch will rise (as in Duane Eddy's "Rebel-'Rouser"), or before the string is plucked, allowing a pitch to drop when the string is struck then relaxed (think of the bridge of Elvis's "Can't Help Falling in Love" or the prebent first note in the Troggs' "Wild Thing"). (Listen to Web audio example 2.37 and see Web photo 2.23.) Guitarists can also produce changing pitches with a single pluck by hammering a finger above the one that had stopped the string initially (see Dylan's "Masters of War" and "Oxford Town," or the final chord of James Taylor's "Sweet Baby James") or by pulling off the stopping finger (as Eddie Cochran does in his "Twenty Flight Rock" solo). In Web audio example 2.12, every chordal seventh is accented by a hammer-on. (Listen to Web audio example 2.38.) Either of these techniques, the hammer-on or the pull-off, can be repeated rapidly to effect a trill. Less often, the guitarist can turn a tuning peg to change pitch after a note is struck; recall the opening of the Animals' "When I Was Young." For characteristic uses of these left-hand phrasing techniques, listen to the solos of Buck Owens' "I've Got a Tiger By the Tail" and Don Gibson's "Oh Lonesome Me," and to that by Jimmy Page for Herman's Hermits' "I'm Into Something Good."

Guitarists can also color a note's ability to fully ring, and can produce a muffled percussive attack without definite pitch by muting with either the right or left hand. The right-hand mute is achieved by lightly resting the picking hand's palm on the strings near the bridge, thus controlling the strings' resonance. (Listen to Web audio example 2.39 and see Web photo 2.24.) The effect is classic when pitches just percolate, as in Johnny Cash's "Big Wheels," Jackie Wilson's "Lonely Teardrops," Billy Vaughn's "Wheels," Nancy Sinatra's "Sugar Town," the second lead guitar in the Guess Who's "Shakin' All Over" (with the descending arpeggios), and Johnny Nash's "Hold Me Tight," or when chords become more percussive than pitched, as in the opening of Crosby, Stills and Nash's "Wooden Ships" and Jethro Tull's "Hymn 43" (0:23–0:26). Although not technically muting, a related effect can be achieved when the left hand reduces pressure after the note or chord is struck, but still touches the strings; I suppose it might be called muffling, because that's how the chords sound in Steppenwolf's "Magic Carpet Ride," but it can also produce a staccato line, as in Horst Jankowski's "A Walk in the Black Forest." (Listen to Web audio example 2.40.)

A note about vibrato and tremolo, two terms that are often confused. Vibrato is the decoration of a pitch by rapid alternation with pitches just below, or those just above and below. Many guitar bridges are fitted with a whammy bar that, when pulled, pushed or shaken, will tighten or loosen the strings slightly for a vibrato effect. (Listen to Web audio example 2.41 and see Web photo 2.25.) This effect is perhaps best known in any version of the widely covered "Shakin' All Over," but also portrays the zing of the bow in Connie Francis's "Stupid Cupid," the flowing of the cape in Bob Dylan's "Visions of Johanna" (at 6:27), John Lennon's nod to Jimi Hendrix in the ferocious opening to the Beatles' "It's All Too Much," the incessant sobbing in Eric Clapton's solo for the Beatles' "While My Guitar Gently Weeps," bombs bursting in air in Hendrix's Woodstock performance of "The Star Spangled Banner," and many subtler illustrations. Particularly effective with smaller instruments and best of all with nylon strings, the guitarist can shake the left wrist or forearm to produce vibrato without moving the fingertip pad from the string. In Cream's March 10, 1968, Winterland performance of "Spoon-ful" (*Wheels of Fire*), Clapton displays heavy wrist vibrato in the first seven seconds and again at 0:17, where he plants his left thumb. The opening of "Purple Haze" (following the guitar/bass tritones) shows a range of guitar expression: with his line colored by the Fuzzface distortion pedal, Hendrix slides up to and down from notes, bends notes from a quarter tone to a whole tone, and applies lots of light wrist vibrato. In "Summertime Blues," Leigh Stephens of Blue Cheer shows lots of wrist vibrato during sustained notes and takes full-fingerboard glisses for end-of-note slides.

As opposed to vibrato, tremolo (as we have described a propos the ampli-fier effect) is the decoration of a sound by a rapid alternation of two differ-ent loudnesses. But the term can also be applied to a strumming or picking technique where the same note, note pair, or chord is rapidly repeated with up-and-down right-hand motions. Such a strummed tremolo is heard in Carl Perkins's "Sure to Fall (In Love With You)," as if in imitation of a hillbilly's mandolin; certainly the sound of a Venetian lute is sought by Hank Garland's tremolo in Elvis's "It's Now or Never." The effect adds a touch of drama to the slow intros to the Crystals' "Uptown," the Contours' "Do You Love Me," and the Four Seasons' "Let's Hang On." And rage seems to be behind the tremolo in Townsend's solo in The Who's "I Can See For Miles" (2:11–2:30). Although Dick Dale is probably known chiefly for his descending gliss, extremely fast tremolo picking and pull-offs are important weapons in his "Surfing Drums" and "Mag Wheels."

Perhaps we should pause just to consider a single performance using a number of these techniques. I would suggest Eric Clapton's playing in Cream's *Wheels of Fire* performance of "Sitting on Top of the World," for it is a remarkable example of musical growth to climax in thoroughly exemplify-ing the song's theme, a slavery-rooted complaint about backbreaking work. Supported by fine bass and drums, loaded with reverb and distortion, the intro begins in one of the slowest tempos of the rock era restricted to simple guitar commentary including many repeated tones (0:27–0:33), and steps back to say less with shorter responses to vocal lines in the first verse (note the quick finger gliss in 0:58–1:00 ending with a strong wrist vibrato on the last note, and a few other short glisses in 1:18–1:21). Clapton speaks up a bit more in the second verse, as with the double-stops (two strings played at a time) and the ear-catching octave leap (1:44–1:49). His solo begins low on the third string at 2:25, uses a touch of whammy bar at 2:49–2:51, but then cuts loose at 3:13 for a second solo chorus, with lots of syncopation, playing in the highest register—in fact, playing at the top fret of the first string at 3:26 to descend to more hammer-ons, pull-offs, and faster syncopation continuing through the third verse (4:02+), pushing through the vocals with insistent hard work that can't quit when the singer returns. And all of it—the choices of pitches, the rhythms, the articulations and phrasing—is just so imaginative and compelling. Another great Clapton solo: in "Sleepy Time Time" (*Live Cream*), a bewilderingly large number of different tonal, rhythmic, articulative, and dynamic techniques carry three improvised twelve-bar choruses (2:37–5:16).

A few more effects remain to be covered. Pete Townsend may have invented the pickup-switch toggle, the alternation of pickups during the sustain of a note or chord. (Listen to Web audio example 2.42.) Obviously this entails a change of color, but may also be marked by some percussive electronic switching noise. In his solo for The Who's "Anyway, Anyhow, Anywhere," the toggling can be heard on a single note at 1:11–1:25 and on a chord at 2:34–2:39. Townsend repeats this in a more rhythmic fashion in "I Don't Even Know Myself" (1:28–1:30), as performed at the August 1970 Isle of Wight Festival. At the end of "Manic Depression," Jimi Hendrix achieves feedback on his lead pickup and then switches back and forth between clean and back-feeding pickups. The opening chord of Blue Cheer's "Gypsy Ball" is also thus modulated. Then there is the pick scrape, which can excite all sorts of wild noise as the pick is dragged along a wound string and highly amplified. This sound is perfect in the free-form days of Pink Floyd's "Interstellar Overdrive," suggests the dragging of a phonograph needle across a record in the Balloon Farm's "A Question of Temperature" (0:03–0:07), and is repeated for a Jimmy Page experiment in the chorus of Led Zeppelin's "Whole Lotta Love." Page would also run his guitar fingerboard back and forth across a microphone stand for related effects. (Listen to Web audio example 2.43.) Guitarists are also known to tap on the face or back of their acoustic guitars, usually to keep rhythm, as Lennon helps Harrison through his unusual preverse riffs in the Beatles' "Help!," or as the third guitar so aids the ensemble in Part III ("chestnut brown canary...") of Crosby, Stills and Nash's "Suite: Judy Blue Eyes." But this of course can also be a source of word painting, as in the "rat tat tat tat tat" hammering portrayed by the pick on the guitar face in the Serendipity Singers' "Don't Let the Rain Come Down (Crooked Little Man)."

Much more subtle and musically inspiring is the harmonic. Produced by lightly touching the string at its halfway point (on the twelfth fret), at one-third of its length (seventh fret), or at the quarter mark (fifth fret) for just the moment it is plucked, the resulting pure, high tones are the unadorned overtones located at these nodes along the entire string. Those high-pitched tones in slow tremolo in "For What It's Worth" are Neil Young's alternation of seventh- and twelfth-fret harmonics on his first string, the same harmonics played once by Jimmie Rodgers in "Two-Ten, Six-Eighteen (Doesn't Anybody Know My Name)." Enlightenment is suggested with irony by the silvery fifth-fret, first-string harmonic at the end of the Beatles' "Nowhere Man" solo. Jefferson Airplane's "Triad" includes twelfth-fret harmonic chords. (Listen to Web audio example 2.44.) One harmonic is heard per string over drones of roots and fifths in dobro tremolos before the shuffle begins in Canned Heat's "On the Road Again." Bell-like, they signal the beginning of Part II ("Friday evening...") in Crosby, Stills and Nash's "Suite: Judy Blue Eyes." There are other such natural harmonics, and also artificial harmonics much used in modernist classical music, but they are of little importance in our repertoire.

There were earlier examples of a very hot guitar sound (in Presley's "That's All Right (Mama)," Chuck Berry's "Oh Baby Doll," the Kingsmen's "Money," and Rufus Thomas's "The Dog"), but if the opening of the Beatles' "I Feel Fine" was not the first example of guitar feedback on record, it was certainly its first calculated use for musical value. (Listen to Web audio example 2.45.) In that instance, it was the sound of a note from McCartney's bass amp that began a sympathetic vibration in the fifth string of Lennon's Gibson electric-acoustic, eventually causing the guitar to back-feed through its own guitar-pickup-amplifier circuit. Sometimes used for brief effect just barely under control (Cream's "Toad," *Those Were the Days* remix, 0:57–1:26, and in many Hendrix tracks), variously manipulated feedback would at other times feature in extended jams (as in many Dead tracks including "Feedback"—just that for 8'52" on LP, 7'49" on CD; Chicago Transit Authority's "Free Form Guitar"; and John Lennon and Yoko Ono's "Cambridge 1969"). Perhaps because of its limited capacity for being controllable while it could be highly surprising and individualistic, feedback became synonymous with the great do-your-own-thing experimentation of the 1960s.

Rhythm and lead

Rock bands often have two or three guitar players, one relegated to rhythm and the other one or two, to lead. Assignments don't remain so neat and tidy, because roles often reverse depending on whether a songwriter is playing, because the idea of choosing a preexisting song might have occurred to one member or another, because of singing roles or keyboard assignment, or simply because one or another player invented just the perfect riff to accompany

Rhythm and lead parts: strumming and fingerpicking, the boogie and the shuffle, double-stops, the lead guitar interacting with other parts.

the number. But typically, rhythm players will strum harmonically supportive chords in somewhat repetitive rhythm patterns, whereas lead players pick single-line melodic parts that interact with the lead vocal and then may take their own solo. Rhythm parts can be played on acoustic or electric—or often on an amplified acoustic, as pickups can be fitted to any acoustic instrument—whereas lead players nearly always use an electric. And in many recordings, a single player does it all through overdubbing—in Cream's "Strange Brew," how many guitars does Clapton play? (It's a snappy Gibson SG rhythm guitar on the left and an overdubbed, overdriven Les Paul lead in the center.)

The strummed acoustic is the typical rhythm instrument from folk and country sources; there may be no electric at all in many recordings by Lonnie Donegan, the Kingston Trio, Bob Dylan, Donovan, Judy Collins, the Everly Brothers, Roy Acuff, and The Band. The acoustic may be strummed on backbeats (Buddy Holly's "True Love Ways") or be fingerpicked (Joan Baez's "Silver Dagger," Bob Dylan's "Don't Think Twice, It's All Right," the Beatles' "Julia," Led Zeppelin's "Babe I'm Gonna Leave You"). The main accompaniment to Simon and Garfunkel's "The Boxer" is two fingerpicked guitars. An acoustic twelve-string, once Leadbelly's favorite, may be used for rhythm, as in the Kinks' "Sunny Afternoon," The Who's "Mary Anne with the Shaky Hand," and the Moody Blues' "Send Me No Wine." The New Christy Minstrels have three acoustic rhythm boxes in "Saturday Night": a twelve-string on the left, a simple acoustic in the center, and a banjo on the right. Electrics have been widely used for rhythm right from the jump blues of the early 1950s; note the slow arpeggiations accompanying the whistled tune in the opening of Dick Hyman's or Richard Hayman's recordings of "Moritat," the Theme from the Three-Penny Opera. (Web audio example 11.10 supports a violin melody with arpeggiated electric guitar chords.) Note the tremolo on the electric rhythm chords in the Vogues' "You're the One," the Wrecking Crew's rhythm guitar in the Beach Boys' "Don't Worry Baby," and the rhythmic perfection in Mark Farner's rhythm pattern in Grand Funk Railroad's "Are You Ready." Electric rhythm guitars chime the chord changes once each in the Islanders' "The Enchanted Sea," the bridge of the Beatles' "I Should Have Known Better," the Association's "Cherish," Lulu's "To Sir With Love," and Blood, Sweat and Tears' "You've Made Me So Very Happy." And the staccato "chick" guitar is almost exclusively a backbeat electric rhythm; it's heard in Sam Cooke's "Chain Gang," the Supremes' "Come See About Me," James Brown's "Papa's Got a Brand New Bag," Aretha Franklin's "Baby I Love You," the Temptations' "My Girl," the Mar-Keys' "Philly Dog," and Sonny and Cher's "Baby Don't Go." The chick guitar is played *on* the beat in Fontella

Bass's "Rescue Me" and Cream's "Badge." Its ska role is presented in Desmond Dekker and the Aces' "Israelites."

Two other important rhythm techniques are the boogie and what I call the blues boogie. In the boogie, the guitarist plays the root and fifth of the chord and alternates the fifth with its upper neighbor in the scale, so that the intervals heard are the stable fifth and the more fluid and melodious sixth as the root is sustained below; they are nearly always performed in pairs: fifth—fifth—sixth—sixth—fifth—fifth—sixth—sixth.... You can hear this in a straight rhythm in Chuck Berry's "Oh Baby Doll" and "Sweet Little Sixteen" and in the chorus of Creedence Clearwater Revival's "Travelin' Band," but it's more often played in a swinging shuffle, with the first interval of each pair held about twice as long as the second, dividing each beat into thirds, as in Willie Dixon's bass part to Berry's "School Days," in two electric guitars in the Everly Brothers' "So How Come (No One Loves Me)," and in Johnny and the Hurricanes' "Red River Rock." In the blues boogie, the sixth above the bass does not return directly to the fifth but passes on up to a flat seventh above the root: fifth—fifth—sixth—sixth—flat seventh—flat seventh—sixth—sixth—fifth—fifth—sixth—sixth—flat seventh—flat seventh—sixth—sixth.... This also may appear in either a straight or a shuffle pattern; listen to the Jefferson Airplane's "3/5 of a Mile in 10 Seconds," the Hollies' "Long Cool Woman (In a Black Dress)," James Taylor's "Steamroller," or even the vocal melody of the Beach Boys' "Do It Again." (Listen to Web audio example 2.46.) In addition to the boogie and blues-boogie decorating an empty fifth, the entire triad is often embellished with the neighboring boogie (with the third of the chord moving to its upper neighbor in tandem with the fifth, so that the "boogie" chord constitutes a sixth and a fourth above the stable root) or the passing blues boogie (with the sixth/fourth chord passing up to two notes that are a flat seventh and a fifth above the bass, both members of the I^{m7} chord). Note, in Robert Johnson's "When You Got a Good Friend" (1936), that the blues-boogie shuffle is heard over the I chord and is then transposed so it is heard, with the appropriate moving scale tones, over the IV chord. This is fundamental to rock guitar, and is heard all over, in Tommy Tucker's "Hi-Heeled Sneakers," in Big Brother and the Holding Co.'s "Turtle Blues," and in the chorus's backing vocals in the Ad Libs' "The Boy From New York City" (ooh-aah, ooh-aah, cool cool Kitty, tell us about the boy from New York City... ").

There are as many lead guitar roles and techniques as there are players. An acoustic usually takes the job when it's one of several (Glen Campbell's "Gentle on My Mind," Simon and Garfunkel's "Mrs. Robinson," Paul McCartney's "Junk" and "Every Night"), and an acoustic twelve-string makes occasional lead appearances (Al Martino's "Mary in the Morning," the Beatles' "I've Just Seen a Face," Peter and Gordon's "I Don't Want to See You Again,"

The Mamas and the Papas' "California Dreaming"). Electric twelve-string leads are more common, as in the Beatles' "A Hard Day's Night," the Jefferson Airplane's "Let's Get Together," the Beach Boys' "Help Me Rhonda," the Byrds' "Mr. Tambourine Man," The Who's "I Can't Explain," and the Animals' "San Franciscan Nights." One way that lead players cut through the texture is to play double stops. George Harrison was highly unusual in playing his early Beatles leads in octaves, as in "Please Please Me," "From Me to You," and in the coda of "This Boy," but Jimi Hendrix followed him in the opening of "Fire" and in "Third Stone From the Sun." Much more typical is to hear double-stopped lines in other relationships, as in Chuck Berry's solo in "Memphis," Paul Burlison's solo in Johnny Burnette's "Lonesome Tears in My Eyes" (copped by John Lennon for the coda of the Beatles' "The Ballad of John and Yoko"), and Van Morrison's intro to "Brown Eyed Girl." It's the double stop by which Chuck Berry nails the car horn in "Maybelline" and the train whistle in "Let It Rock," and Willie Woods bends one of the two picked strings for a characteristic effect in Jr. Walker and the All Stars' "Shotgun." Buddy Holly just goes ahead and riffs through full chords in the "Peggy Sue" solo.

Simple speed is key in Arthur Smith's "Guitar Boogie," Jeff Beck's "Jeff's Boogie" with the Yardbirds and his own group's "Blues DeLuxe," Eric Clapton's "I'm So Glad" with Cream, and Alvin Lee's "I'm Going Home" for Ten Years After; add a touch of the frenetic for Roger McGuinn's lead playing in the Byrds' "Eight Miles High." Some lead playing is just really bad; Ritchie Valens can probably be forgiven his three-note solo in "La Bamba" (if it's harder to understand his late vocal entrance immediately following), but I don't know how the ineffective playing on Tommy James and the Shondells' "Crystal Blue Persuasion" (every note picked with the same articulation, notes repeated arbitrarily) got past a producer, label execs, critics, and consumers. Another flaw to watch out for is a guitarist's not knowing when NOT to play; Mike Bloomfield, for instance, doesn't seem to know the value of a rest or of sustained tones in "Albert's Shuffle" (*Super Session*).

The lead guitar doubles the voice or just about any instrument. It will very often double the bass or another guitar; the bass riff in the Animals' "It's My Life" thus gains strength; a fuzz guitar doubles a clean one in the Chambers Brothers' "Time Has Come Today"; the intro of the Temptations' "Cloud Nine" has a wah guitar doubled by one without; the introductory bass is doubled by a muted guitar in Tommy James and the Shondells' "I Think We're Alone Now"; the bass ostinato in the Mothers' "Directly From My Heart to You" is doubled by a majestic guitar; in Big Brother and the Holding Co.'s "I Need a Man to Love," James Gurley's guitar doubles the bass ostinato while Sam Andrews's lead is wild. (Listen to Web audio example 2.47.) Keyboards are often involved in guitar doubling: the Four Seasons' "Tell It to the Rain" opens with a new color when a guitar doubles a tack piano at the octave, the opening piano riff in the Beatles' "Hey Bulldog" is doubled first by Harrison's distorted SG and then by McCartney's bass; guitar and bass are joined at 0:07 by harpsichord in the Association's "Windy," and guitar and organ double for the main riffs in Music Explosion's "Little Bit O' Soul" and The Band's "Chest Fever." (Listen to Web audio example 2.48.) String doublings are rare, but a violin section doubles the lead guitar solo in the Vogues' "You're the One." Other pairings include guitar with blues harp (three titles on *Fresh Cream*), flute (Donovan's "There Is a Mountain" and Frank Zappa's "Peaches en Regalia"), sax (Rusty Draper's "Are You Satisfied?"), horn (Frankie Valli's "Can't Take My Eyes Off You"), orchestra bells (the T-Bones' "No Matter What Shape (Your Stomach's In)" and the Grateful Dead's "St. Stephen"), and xylophone (Perry Como's "Hot Diggity"). The whole band can join in (Los Bravos's "Black is Black," the Mothers of Invention's "You're Probably Wondering Why I'm Here," Blues Magoos' "(We Ain't Got) Nothin' Yet," and The Doors' "Wild Child"), but a simple guitar/vocal doubling can be riveting (the Beatles' "Happiness is a Warm Gun" [0:45–1:34], Jimi Hendrix's "If 6 Was 9," Led Zeppelin's "You Shook Me"). Sometimes the guitar is doubled at an interval other than octave or unison, as in Gary Lewis and the Playboys' "Save Your Heart for Me," which doubles the guitar in thirds with a whistler, and Spirit's "Fresh Garbage," where the melody is doubled in fifths by vocal, bass, electric piano, and guitar. (Listen to Web audio example 2.49.)

It is also important to recognize how guitars interact with each other—they may have a congenial duet or a duel to the death. (Listen to Web audio example 2.50.) Jerry Cole and Barney Kessel collaborate for the dreamy sound that opens the Beach Boys' "Wouldn't It Be Nice." John Lennon and George Harrison sound as one in the celebrated harmonized dual-Strat "solo" of the Beatles' "And Your Bird Can Sing." "Our Guessing Game" showcases one of many Moody Blues duets. The Beatles' "Michelle" blends Paul's large Epiphone "Texan" acoustic, John's nylon-string guitar, and George's acoustic twelve-string, all capoed at the fifth fret. The two leads in Crosby, Stills and Nash's "Marrakesh Express" are divided by extreme stereo placement. Contrast is the order of the day in the Beau Brummels' "Just a Little" (note the nylon-string, the electric with fast tremolo, and the acoustic in the break). Two lead guitars play Q&A in The Doors' "Maggie McGill." Stephen Stills and Neil Young fight it out in Crosby, Stills, Nash and Young's "Almost Cut My Hair," as do Eric Clapton and Dave Mason in Delaney and Bonnie and Friends' "Only You Know and I Know." The Beatles trade solos in "The End," with Paul's sustaining Fender Esquire, George's sublime Telecaster, and John's belligerent Casino each taking the spotlight three times in turn, an effect mimicked by an overdubbed Steve Howe alone in Yes's "All Good People." The working tape of the Beatles' "Let It Be" has simultaneous (but separately recorded) solos by Lennon and Harrison; in the mixing process, one was chosen for the single and the other appeared on the album. The two oddly simultaneous guitar solos in Fabian's "Tiger" seem like the result of a mixing error, where one should have been entirely muted, rather than leaving intact a nonfunctional dialogue between two instruments.

Other than a greater emphasis on thick distortion, a few digital developments in guitar synthesis and amplifier emulation, and the addition of a scant few new virtuosic techniques by the likes of Eddie Van Halen, very little has changed in guitars and guitar playing in the decades following 1970. Hopefully, the fan of this more recent pop-rock music would be able to learn the materials outlined in this chapter and be able to hear them at work in any of their favorite recordings. And pop-rock performing and songwriting readers should now be able to form their own band and begin quickly working their way through old, new, and original songs alike. Just a few more points on instrumental and vocal resources in the two following chapters....

CHAPTER 3

Keyboards and a Summary of Early-Rock Instrumentation

If the best-known guitarists of the 1950s and '60s were not the most popular artists of that era, pianists and organists received even less recognition. True, rock 'n' roll began to make noise under the fingers of Little Richard, Fats Domino, and Jerry Lee Lewis at a time when other pianists like Nat King Cole, Ray Charles, Dave Brubeck, Roger Williams, and Henry Mancini were top-drawer attractions. But how many keyboardists rose to a similar stature before Elton John, Carole King, Stevie Wonder, Rick Wakeman, Keith Emerson, and Billy Joel did in the 1970s? Most toiled in obscurity through the 1960s—Ian Stewart was a full member of the Rolling Stones in all but publicity; session players such as Floyd Cramer, Nicky Hopkins, Larry Knechtel, Al Kooper, Leon Russell, and John Paul Jones were only sometimes credited on the records on which they contributed key parts. It is little known that Aretha Franklin played many of her own keyboard parts, and the group keyboardists who were most indelibly linked to their instruments, principally among them Felix Cavaliere of the Rascals and Rod Argent of the Zombies, were never household names. Keyboardists rarely enjoyed front-line status on stage; their instruments often kept them behind the guitar players or off to the side. For the most part, keyboardists of the 1960s were either faceless session players or jack-of-all-tradesmen in their groups, switching back and forth among bass, guitar, and keys.

But just as with the guitar, keyboards—grand and upright piano, tack piano, electric piano, electric organ, harpsichord, celesta, Moog, Mellotron, and others—are heard everywhere. Even the pipe organ, too gargantuan, expensive, and difficult to maintain to be at home in a recording studio, finds its way into a few rock tracks. There is even more variety in style and method with keyboard than with the guitar; players' roots may lie in gospel, jazz, or other traditions; some players were classically trained for a number of years, whereas others could only pick at the instrument finger by finger. All usages have their own rewards. Keys may be central to a recording, used simply for coloration effects, used to augment the bass line, or may play a rhythmic role. This chapter will focus on the contrasting tones of the various instruments and some basic performance techniques that yield characteristic keyboard sounds, and then we'll summon ideas from throughout the first three chapters in a survey of the uses of all rock instrumentation in a sampling of twenty-five rock recordings from the period 1955–69.

Photo 3.01. Christopher Street at the Steinway grand piano. Two microphones are placed at different positions along the bridge, near where the hammers strike the strings. The strings' vibrations are molded and amplified by a soundboard (unseen) of Sitka spruce and reflect off of the raised lid. (Photo: Kristin Fosdick)

Pianos—acoustic and electric

The piano is most useful when taken advantage for its full texture, as any number of its eighty-eight keys can sound simultaneously. When depressed, the key allows a hammer to strike a string (or up to three strings tuned to the same pitch) with a strength and resulting loudness controlled by the

> **The piano:** construction, gospel and classical styles, as a rhythm instrument, solo techniques, coloristic effects, the electric piano.

player's pressure. The strings sound for as long as the keys are depressed; when the fingers are removed, the strings are instantly silenced. Players may circumvent this muting with the damper pedal, which holds the dampers away from the strings, allowing the sound to sustain through any changes of notes or chords, as long as the pedal is depressed. This is demonstrated most self-consciously in The Who's "Welcome," at 4:04–4:11 and 4:21–4:33. With a grand piano, the sound carries from the spruce soundboard to the reflective hardwood lid, which is usually open for recording, with microphones placed inside. (Listen to Web audio example 3.01 and see Web photo 3.01.) Upright pianos are also frequently used in studios; their tone is generally less rich, mostly because the string length is considerably shorter than that of a concert grand, but also because their pedals are far less effective. (Listen to Web audio example 3.02 and see Web photos 3.02 and 3.03.) The grand is heard in the Beatles' "The Long and Winding Road," Pink Floyd's "Sysyphus," and The Band's "Sleeping," whereas the upright is played in Crazy Otto's "Glad Rag Doll," Sly and the Family Stone's "Hot Fun in the Summertime," and The Band's "The Night They Drove Old Dixie Down."

Gospel playing, involving a generally chordal style across the entire range of the keyboard, maintains fairly pure major or minor-pentatonic scales with little alteration. (The minor-pentatonic scale, spelled 1, ♭3, 4, 5, ♭7, is to be discussed in detail in chapters 7 and 10.) This style is strongly evidenced in tracks such as Ketty Lester's "Love Letters" (a clear predecessor of Larry Knechtel's playing on Simon and Garfunkel's "Bridge Over Troubled Water" and Billy Preston's on John Lennon's "God"), the Temptations' "I Wish It Would Rain," Aretha Franklin's own playing on "A Natural Woman (You Make Me Feel Like)," and Bob Dylan's on "Day of the Locusts." Jazz styles erupt in Louis Prima's "Jump, Jive, an' Wail," and in Blood, Sweat and Tears' "Smiling Phases" and "Sometimes in Winter." Spirit's "Caught" revives the parallel dissonant chords of the great bop pianists. Classical backgrounds are evidenced in long quotations of Bach's C-major Prelude from Book I of the Well-Tempered Clavier in both Procol Harum's "Repent Walpurgis" and Phil Ochs's "I've Had Her." Tchaikovsky is a stylistic source of some of the playing in Roger Williams's "Autumn Leaves" and even more of that in Ferrante and Teicher's "Theme from 'The Apartment.'" More interesting is the air from a Schoenbergian planet that wafts through Ian Underwood's spliced-in contribution to the Mothers' "The Little House I Used to Live In." The piano plays a leading role in Arthur Alexander's "Where Have You Been (All My Life)" (with its one-finger solo, 1:45–1:58), Gerry and the Pacemakers' "How Do You Do It?" (its break played by producer George Martin), the Moody Blues' "Go Now!" (featuring a bluesy solo by Mike Pinder), Blood, Sweat and Tears' "Spinning Wheel" (with its extensive jazz choruses), Chicago's "Colour My World" (instantly recognizable by its lugubrious arpeggiations), Isaac Hayes's "Hyperbolicsyllabicsesquedalymistic" (featuring six minutes of piano improvisation, all on one chord), and the New Colony Six's "Things I'd Like to Say" (which ends with a brief piano coda unrelated to the song's tune).

The piano, along with bass and drums, is often considered part of the rhythm section. With good reason—frequently, its primary job is to put rhythm to harmonies. And the mostly untrained performers often exhibit flat fingers and stiff wrists that make it difficult to achieve the independence of fingers and flexibility of motion required for much more. The pianist may simply bang out repeated chords, as with Jerry Lee Lewis and Little Richard, or may repeat chords more softly, as in the Young Rascals' "Groovin'." (Listen to Web audio example 3.03.) The piano may push the backbeat (the Four Seasons' "Big Girls Don't Cry") or the offbeat (note the piano's right-hand chords off the third and fourth beats in the verse of the 5th Dimension's "Stoned Soul Picnic"). (Listen to Web audio example 3.04.) Very often, when the beat is uniformly divided into triplets, three parts instead of two, it is the piano that clarifies the twelve-parts-per-bar meter, as in Paul Anka's "Put Your Head on My Shoulder," James Brown's "Please, Please, Please," and Sly and the Family Stone's "Hot Fun in the Summertime." (Listen to Web audio example 3.05.) Somehow, the pianist fouls up this rhythm at 1:55–1:56 in Rosie and the Originals' "Angel Baby," just drowning the feel.

Boogie, blues boogie, and boogie-woogie parts are a big part of the piano's rhythm arsenal, brought to bear in Danny and the Juniors' "Rock and Roll Is Here to Stay," Steve Lawrence's "Go Away Little Girl," and the Mothers of Invention's "Cheap Thrills." (Listen to Web audio example 3.06.) The pianist alone has an idiomatic rhythmic technique, whereby the right hand rocks between the thumb's single note (often a root, but perhaps another chord member) and other notes in the fingers, usually hitting the thumb every weak half of the beat. (Listen to Web audio example 3.07.) By referring back to figure 2.02, the reader might visualize how the right hand's thumb on the root of a major triad can alternate with the chord's third and fifth as played by the same hand's middle and pinky fingers, with a rocking motion back and forth between them. This rocking right-hand accompaniment is heard with different rhythms in the Stones' "Ruby Tuesday," the Young Rascals' "A Girl Like You," the Monkees' "Daydream Believer," and the Beatles' "Hey Jude." (One wonders whether Paul McCartney might have known that the rocking left-hand octaves on which he bases the Beatles' vaguely eighteenth-century-styled "Martha My Dear" is a standard Mozartean accompanimental pattern.) A related playing of neighbor chords, sort of like a chord-based boogie pattern in a free rhythm, accompanies the Rascals' "I've Been Lonely Too Long" and Sly and the Family Stone's "Everyday People."

For coloristic effect, the pianist may tinkle in the high register; note the nonchalance given Elvis Presley's "Heartbreak Hotel" by Floyd Cramer's piano. The high-pitched single line in the piano is so forcefully played at 0:26–0:42 in Gene Pitney's "I'm Gonna Be Strong," it sounds at first like a guitar. The pianist may boom out a part in the bass register, for a similarly contrasting color, as in Buddy Holly's solo for "Think It Over" (0:51–1:13) or Soft Machine's "Box 25/4 Lid." The right hand may carry a melody in octaves, as heard in the opening of the Chiffons' "One Fine Day" and as characteristic of Roger Williams's "Born Free," Ferrante and Teicher's "Tonight," and other adult-contemporary favorites. Rolled chords may be the order of the day, as in Henry Mancini's solo in "Love Theme From Romeo and Juliet." A right-hand tremolo, where the thumb alternates very rapidly with an upper finger (usually spaced a sixth above the thumb), brings more or less of a barrelhouse color to Dylan's "Temporary Like Achilles" and the Beatles' "Good Day Sunshine" (more) and Roger Williams's "Near You" (less). The same barrelhouse might also be suggested by the energetic knuckle gliss, where the thumb, a knuckle, or a fingernail is rapidly scraped down—or less often, up—either the white or black keys, as in Jerry Lee Lewis's "Great Balls of Fire" (0:58, 1:00), Freddie Cannon's "Action" (that's Leon Russell on piano), Tommy James and the Shondells' "Hanky Panky," and Archie Bell and the Drells' "I Can't Stop Dancing." (Listen to Web audio example 3.08.)

Floyd Cramer is typically identified with Nashville's "slip-style" playing, where a *very* short note leads immediately to an accented one a step above, as if in emulation of a bent string (it actually has precedent in an eighteenth-century Italian keyboard style). (Listen to Web audio example 3.09.) This effect is similar to the grace note, which is a very fast initial ornament usually sounded by a different finger than the one playing the following accented pitch. In true slip style, however, the *same* finger hits an ornamental black key and then slides upwards to fall on the adjacent white key. Again, referring back to figure 2.02 may help the reader visualize how some major triads (like the one identified on the bottom left of the figure) have black keys just below the triad thirds, often the recipient of the slipping finger. The awkwardness of the technique leads to interesting rhythms, as the accented resolution is often a mite delayed. This effect colors tracks such as Andy Williams's "Hopeless," many of Patsy Cline's and Brenda Lee's hits, Cramer's own "Last Date," Bobby Vinton's "Roses are Red (My Love)," Tom Jones's "I'll Never Fall in Love Again," Young-Holt Unlimited's "Soulful Strut," and Nicky Hopkins's contribution to Jefferson Airplane's "A Song for All Seasons."

Sometimes a piano's intense dissonance will have a coloristic effect (in Joanie Sommers's "Johnny Get Angry"), as will an out-of-tune instrument (Richard Hayman and Jan August's "A Theme From 'The Three Penny Opera' (Moritat)," Ernie K. Doe's "Mother-In-Law," and Etta James's "Something's Got a Hold On Me"). Most adventurous is when a player works not with the keyboard, but with the harp inside: The Mothers' "The Return of the Son of Monster Magnet" and "The Chrome Plated Megaphone of Destiny" feature lots of plucking of the piano's strings; the latter ends with indefinite sustain, mocking the piano chord held for forty-five seconds at the end of the Beatles' "A Day in the Life." In "Song of the Naturalist's Wife," Donovan vocalizes into the strings with the dampers raised (0:15–0:39), leading to a rush of Aeolian harp-like sympathetic vibrations. The strings are scraped in the Grateful Dead's "That's It for The Other One" and plucked to accompany the beasts of the wild surf emblematic of Jim Morrison's torment in The Doors' "Horse Latitudes." (Listen to Web audio example 3.10.) The piano that opens the Beach Boys' "You Still Believe in Me" has an eerie steely sound because of the bobby pins clipped to the piano's strings and the unrelieved holding down of the damper pedal for extra sustain. A final color effect also takes a bit of preparation; the honky-tonk style is best recreated on a tack piano. For this, tacks are inserted into the felts on each hammer of an upright instrument. It's also quite effective if some of the multiple strings per note are not in tune with each other; see the simulated honky-tonk effect created in Web audio example 9.04. Johnny Maddox's "The Crazy Otto" sounds like it comes directly from a nickelodeon, and the sound is also central to Jim Lowe's "Green Door" and the Dixiebelles' "(Down at) Papa Joe's." The tack piano is heard in Bob Dylan's "Ballad of a Thin Man," the bridge (1:42–2:43) of the Beach Boys' "Good Vibrations," The Doors' "Love Her Madly," and the Beatles' "For You Blue."

The electric piano, although bereft of many tonal qualities of its acoustic forebear, had portability and control on its side, especially in touring situations. It came in several makes, each having its own characteristic sound produced by a thin steel reed or a heavier tone bar set in vibration with a gust of wind or a piano's felt hammer, the resulting vibration picked up by electromagnets as with a guitar then amplified. The electric piano would be fitted with a sustain pedal and perhaps a tremolo switch. The best-known early model is the five-octave Wurlitzer, famed for its appearance in Ray Charles's "What'd I Say" and also heard in Joe Zawinul's playing on Cannonball Adderly's "Mercy, Mercy, Mercy" and in Spooner Oldham's on Aretha Franklin's "I Never Loved a Man." (Listen to Web audio example 3.11 and see Web photo 3.04.) The Wurli is characterized by a "bark" produced when keys are sharply attacked. The Hohner Pianet (introduced in 1962) was the Beatles' favorite; it's played through the *Help!* album and in "I Am the

Walrus," and given heavy distortion by Nicky Hopkins in "Revolution." Paul McCartney's Pianet solo at 2:03–2:14 in "Come Together" makes for excellent chamber music with his own bass line. The Pianet also appears in the Zombies' "She's Not There," the Association's "Never My Love" (on the left, along with tremolo guitar; do not confuse it with the electronic organ that enters, right, at 0:34), Three Dog Night's "Mama Told Me (Not to Come)," and The Who's "The Acid Queen."

Steel bars gave the Fender Rhodes (introduced in 1965) its own watery sound; the Rhodes is played by Billy Preston in the Beatles' "Don't Let Me Down" Before it gained widespread use in the 1970s. (Listen to Web audio example 3.12.) The ultrafunky Hohner Clavinet Model C (introduced in 1968) had two magnets per pickup, like a guitar's humbucker arrangement. Before Stevie Wonder made this sound famous in "Shoo-Be-Doo-Be-Doo-Da-Day," it was played on Sam and Dave's "I Thank You"; a bit later, it was altered with a wah pedal on The Band's "This Wheel's on Fire" and "Up on Cripple Creek." (Listen to Web audio example 3.13.) The Beatles would also distort the natural sound of the acoustic piano by running it through an overdriven guitar amplifier, as done in "Ob-La-Di, Ob-La-Da," or through an organ's Leslie cabinet, as in "Birthday" and "Don't Pass Me By," but the Hollies seem to have anticipated this trick by a year in "Pay You Back With Interest."

Organs—wind-powered and electric

Pipe organs, built in majestically different styles over more than six centuries, traditionally use wire trackers to enable a number of keyboards and pedalboards to allow air compressed by bellows to enter tin or wood pipes, all chosen by a set of player-engaged knobs called "stops" and designed to produce a range of colors emulating flutes, trumpets, and other wind effects. A "chiffy" sound, for instance, is most characteristic of some attacks, produced by a particular nick in the corresponding pipes. The general middle register is covered with eight-foot stops, but sixteen-foot stops are used for the bass pedals, and four-foot and smaller lengths create higher pitches. (Listen to Web audio examples 3.14 and 3.15, and see Web photos 3.05–3.08.) Because these massive instruments are permanently installed in churches, cathedrals, and large theatres, they are typically heard only in live concert recordings, as in a few by Frank Zappa (on *Uncle Meat*) and Deep Purple (*Concerto for Group and Orchestra*)—both recorded at the Royal Albert Hall in London. It's a Beautiful Day went remote to work with a theatre organ in "Soapstone

The organ: pipe organs; electronic organs; harmonium, accordion, and calliope.

Mountain." In the 1970s, large-scale prog rockers such as Rick Wakeman of Yes would bring them to more frequent prominence.

Electric organs were among the most commonly used instruments of the era, featuring in more than four hundred recordings from my listening sample. They were produced in large vacuum tube-based consoles, as with the multimanual five-octave Hammond and Lowrey (each of which was manufactured in numerous models), and in more portable solid-state varieties, notably the extremely popular four-octave Vox Continental and Farfisa Compact. As with the pipe organ, there is little to distinguish in the sound's envelope (the progression of attack, sustain, and decay of any given note or chord) produced by any of these keyboards; each key is primarily either "on" or "off," although a swell pedal can control the overall volume. The Hammond B-3 is known for both its "percussive" effect, which does impart a sharp attack, and the loudness of its key click. An obvious use of the swell pedal on a Hammond is heard in Ruby and the Romantics' "My Summer Love," 1:47–1:56. It's treated more subtly in the Turtles' "Happy Together," where the organ at first has only little touches (0:27–0:28), but a sustained octave creeps in at 1:04, moving with a crescendo to the chorus at 1:11. The volume of each hand, melodic line, or keyboard manual is not separable, and there is no sharp attack or gradual decay. Organists could, of course, play long sustained tones, as in Percy Sledge's "When a Man Loves a Woman" or Smith's "Baby It's You," or very short staccato tones as in all of the Bill Black Combo's hits or Walter Wanderley's "Summer Samba (So Nice)." Occasionally, the organist will play in two-part counterpoint, as in the opening of the Cyrkle's "Red Rubber Ball" and the Young Rascals' Renaissance-like intro to their cover of "A Place in the Sun." Brian Auger and the Trinity provide conspicuously classical organ arrangements in their settings of Fauré's "Pavane" and Albinoni's "Adagio Per Archi e Organo." Some of the many interesting doublings of an organ line occur with the electric guitar in the Animals' "Don't Let Me Be Misunderstood," the nylon-string guitar in the Seekers' "Georgy Girl," and the celesta in the Cascades' "Rhythm of the Rain."

The console organs feature mixture stops, adding overtones of complex ratios to the fundamental, as well as the octave harmonics that come with simple 2:1, 4:1, 8:1,... ratios. With this mixture feature, the organist can generate a complex, piercing texture of lines added in parallel thirds or fifths above a single melody, as in Bobby Bland's "I'll Take Good Care of You," the Beach Boys' "Be True to Your School," Ruby and the Romantics' "Our Day Will Come" (1:33–1:54), the Casinos' "Then You Can Tell Me Goodbye," and the Zombies' "Time of the Season" (1:22–1:52). (A simple octave doubling is heard in the Shirelles' "Big John.") Multiple manuals are registered with different stops and therefore yield contrasting colors when played in alternation; a good example of manual changes on a Hammond B-3 is heard in the Young Rascals' "Since I Fell For You." The deep-bass pedalboard undergirds the chorale played by Rick Wright in Pink Floyd's studio version of "A Saucerful of Secrets" (8:39+).

The Hammond's sound is created by metal tone wheels whose strobing parts (their speed determined by key selection) would be read by electro-magnets; a large variety of tone colors is available from presets, drawbars, and stops that would introduce overtones in different concentrations. The attached Leslie cabinet includes a two-speed rotating horn for a wide tremu-lant effect. (Listen to Web audio examples 3.16–3.19.) A Hammond M-3 is heard in Booker T. and the M. G.'s "Green Onions," and a Hammond M-102 is the chief instrument of Procol Harum's "A Whiter Shade of Pale." The B-3, however, is the most-used Hammond, and is heard in Don Rondo's "White Silver Sands" (note the big swell), Ray Charles's "One Mint Julep" (in a jazzy Quincy Jones arrangement), Dave "Baby" Cortez's "Happy Organ," Robert Maxwell's "Shangri-La" (full tremulant here!), Bob Dylan's "Like a Rolling Stone" (Al Kooper playing), the Beatles' "I Want You (She's So Heavy)" (with Billy Preston), most of the Rascals' great hits (note the large vibrato in "Good Lovin'" and the growth of the opening V^{m7} chord in B-3 and guitar at 0:00–0:04 in "I Ain't Gonna Eat Out My Heart Anymore"), Billy Joel's early work with the Hassles and Attila, and perhaps at its most intense in "Fire" by the Crazy World of Arthur Brown. The Leslie is easily identified in Blood, Sweat and Tears' "You've Made Me So Very Happy" and Eddie Floyd's "Bring It On Home to Me," but it is also interesting to trace in the Beach Boys' "Good Vibrations," where Larry Knechtel plays with Leslie in the verses but without for choruses. (It's a different organ, played by Dennis Wilson, that has the heavy echo for the retransition at 2:14–2:56.)

Lowrey models tended toward theatre organs, and featured more garish effects. A combination of harpsichord, vibraphone, music box, and guitar stops is said to be the registration on a Lowrey Heritage Deluxe DSO respon-sible for the opening keyboard arpeggiations in the Beatles' "Lucy in the Sky With Diamonds," and a Lowrey is central to The Band's "Stage Fright." A variation on the Lowrey follows a thematic statement in Charles Randolph Grean Sounde's otherworldly "Quentin's Theme," and the wah effect in The Who's "Baba O'Riley" and "Won't Get Fooled Again" is not from a synthe-sizer but from a Lowrey Berkshire Deluxe.

The transistorized and therefore ultraportable Vox Continental (intro-duced in 1962) and Farfisa were fully electronic; tone would be generated by a sine or sawtooth wave (in the case of the Continental), or by a sawtooth or square wave (in the edgier-sounding Farfisa), each of which waves would be modulated by a given frequency to create each pitch of the range. Compared to the consoles, minimal tonal variety was available with the few overtone drawbars on these simple instruments, which would have a tremolo switch and sometimes vibrato and reverb controls. (Listen to Web audio examples 3.20 and 3.21, and see Web photo 3.09.) Note the funky reverb on the Vox Continental backbeat chords in the Turtles' "You Showed Me." The Vox is certainly the workhorse of all the pop-group's organ combo needs, showing up in recordings by the Animals (with Alan Price's solo in "The House of the Rising Sun"), the Beatles, the Box Tops, the Castaways, the Dave Clark Five, Manfred Mann, the first three Monkees albums, Music Explosion, Strawberry Alarm Clock, the 1910 Fruitgum Co., Paul Revere and the Raiders (note the disturbing tremolo in "Hungry," 1:56–2:10), the Rivieras, the Royal Guardsmen, the Status Quo, and many others. It receives John Lennon's elbow gliss in the Beatles' "I'm Down," is the garage-band's friend in the Castaways' "Liar, Liar," ? (Question Mark) and the Mysterians' "96 Tears" and Music Explosion's "Little Bit O' Soul," and is the spectacular hard-rock core vehicle of The Doors' "Light My Fire" and Iron Butterfly's "In-A-Gadda-Da-Vida." The harsher Farfisa is known from Sam the Sham and the Pharaohs' "Wooly Bully" and "Lil' Red Riding Hood," the Swingin' Medallions' "Double Shot (Of My Baby's Love)," Tommy James and the Shondells' "I Think We're Alone Now" and "Mirage," and Pink Floyd's "See Emily Play," "The Scarecrow," and "Set the Controls for the Heart of the Sun" (featuring Rick Wright's highly active swell pedal, 3:58–4:04). Two other late-'60s electronic keyboards were the Gibson G101 (adopted by Ray Manzarek for The Doors' *Waiting for the Sun*) and the cylindrical Tubon, which sounds like a set of bagpipes in the Lovin' Spoonful's "Lovin' You."

All of these organ models are polyphonic, allowing the playing of multiple keys at once. Another group of electric organs based on a single oscillator were monophonic, capable only of a single note at a time, and therefore used only for the playing of melodies. These include the Univox, the Ondioline, the Musitron, and Selmer's Clavioline. As with the polyphonic models, they're also widely used, as in Kai Winding's "More" (Ondioline), Del Shannon's "Runaway" and "Hats Off to Larry," Diane Renay's "Navy Blue," Terry Stafford's "I'll Touch a Star," Tommy Roe's "Sweet Pea," and Brenton Wood's "Gimme Little Sign" (Musitron), and the Tornadoes' "Telstar" and the Beatles' "Baby You're a Rich Man" (Clavioline).

A few acoustic wind-governed keyboards belong in this category. The bellows-powered harmonium, its tone generated by harmonica-like reeds, is the wheezy pump-organ sound heard in the Hollies' "Dear Eloise" and the Beatles' "We Can Work It Out." (Listen to Web audio example 3.22 and see Web photo 3.10.) A hand-held version of this, the accordion, opens and closes the bellows with arm motions rather than foot pedals. (Listen to Web audio example 3.23 and see Web photo 3.11.) Capable of melodic and multivoiced play over chords chosen by button, the accordion captures the street sounds of Paris in both Dinah Shore's "Chantez-Chantez" and the Young

Rascals' "How Can I Be Sure," suggests a lederhosen band in Elvis Presley's "Wooden Heart," rouses the wedding dancers in Will Glahé's "Liechtensteiner Polka," and makes no particular references in Cathy Carr's "Ivory Tower" or the Beach Boys' "God Only Knows" (intro) and "Wouldn't It Be Nice" (note the short notes on piano, organ and two accordions, 0:24–0:35, as against sustained notes from three saxes). The steam organ, the calliope, is played for carnivalesque irony in Country Joe and the Fish's "I-Feel-Like-I'm-Fixin'-To-Die Rag," and recordings of this sound are shredded into second-long fragments by George Martin's tape operators and the Beatles in the tape mélange that conveys the whirlwind din of the circus in "Being for the Benefit of Mr. Kite." The calliope is only weakly suggested by an electric organ in Freddie Cannon's "Palisades Park." And the keyboard heard in Whistling Jack Smith's "I Was Kaiser Bill's Batman" and Blood, Sweat and Tears' "Meagan's Gypsy Eyes" sounds more like the Emenee chord organ, a toy, than anything else.

The organ's close association with the church was exploited in 1950s recordings such as the Cowboy Church Sunday School's "Open Up Your Heart," Patti Page's "Go On With the Wedding," and Don Cornell's "The Bible Tells Me So," and would appear in more generally secular later settings, as with the chapel reference in Big Bopper's "Big Bopper's Wedding" and the quotation of Mendelssohn's *Wedding March* in the Brooklyn Bridge's "Worst That Could Happen," the gospel/liturgical break in Dion's "Abraham, Martin and John," and the suggestion of a funeral parlor in the Grateful Dead's "Black Peter" (1:31–1:54). A more metaphorical reference might be gleaned in the Beatles' evangelical "The Word," where the bright mix of partials from the blending crash cymbal and harmonium might symbolize a spiritual sort of enlightenment. But the organ can have other connotations as well; the sudden, unprepared entrance at the very end of Janis Ian's "Society's Child (Baby I've Been Thinking)" of a Hammond with an ugly minor tonic chord with its lowered third, despite the song's unresolved but attempted orientation towards the heroic, attests to a horrible pessimism. A carbon-copy tragic ending seems to be the hopeless conclusion of the Raiders' "Indian Reservation (The Lament of the Cherokee Reservation Indians)."

Other acoustic keyboards

One keyboard used with surprising frequency in the pop world of the late 1960s is the harpsichord. Much more delicate than the piano's, the | **The harpsichord, clavichord, and celesta**

harpsichord's sound was produced by keys that would force quills to pluck taut steel strings. Long considered to have been replaced in Mozart's day by the fortepiano and then the modern piano, the harpsichord was given new life close to two hundred years later in an effort to create historically accurate performances of Bach and then for its own sake in modernist compositions. (Listen to Web audio example 3.24 and see Web photos 3.12 and 3.13.) It appeared in only fifteen top-twenty hits in the ten years from 1955 through 1964. At this time, it was often played like a jazzy sort of light piano with a chord-rolling full sound augmented by a second set of strings so everything would sound in overripe octaves, as in Lawrence Welk's "Tonight You Belong to Me," Rosemary Clooney's "Mambo Italiano," Billy Vaughn's "The Theme from The Three Penny Opera (Moritat)," and the Ames Brothers' "Melodie d'Amour."

Two late-1964 usages of the harpsichord, in the Beach Boys' "When I Grow Up (To Be a Man)" and the Righteous Brothers' "You've Lost That Lovin' Feelin'," seem to have kindled a new rage for the sound, as it would then be used in fifty top-twenty hits over the next five years, and in fifty important minor hits and album cuts of the same brief period, often as part of the explosion of psychedelia. The most recognizable appearances in the late '60s include the Supremes' "Love Is Here And Now You're Gone," the Beatles' "Piggies" (united with elegant eighteenth-century strings to contrast with rude hog grunts for an Orwellian social statement), the Rolling Stones' "Lady Jane" (an Elizabethan ballad also cast with nylon-string guitar and dulcimer), Ed Ames's "My Cup Runneth Over" (nicely blending the harpsichord on the left with the glockenspiel on the right), the Moody Blues' "House of Four Doors" (a musical history lesson in which a lute passage with two flutes suggests the Renaissance, two harpsichords and cello stand in for the eighteenth century, a piano takes off on the Tchaikovsky B-flat Minor Concerto, and a rock band brings us to the twentieth century), the Left Banke's "Walk Away Renee," Judy Collins's "Both Sides Now," The Doors' "The Soft Parade" (note the switch at 1:06 from a darker to a brighter manual), the Dead's "Mountains of the Moon" (two harpsichords, left and center, plus two acoustic guitars), Paul Mauriat's "Love Is Blue" (harpsichord the solo instrument, plus orchestra), the Bee Gees' "Turn of the Century" (with a more classical arrangement than many), and the Stone Poneys' "Different Drum."

Of course, there was also an electric harpsichord, best known as the opening instrument in the Beatles' "Because" but also heard in Jimi Hendrix's "Burning of the Midnight Lamp," the Monkees' "Hold On Girl," Jefferson Airplane's "Two Heads," Neon Philharmonic's "Morning Girl," and a small handful of others. Before the electric harpsichord had been invented, George Martin wished the sound into existence with his "wind-up piano," by which he would overdub a piano part an octave too low onto a tape track running at half speed so that when the tape played at full speed, the keyboard part sounded in the desired octave and with the clipped articulation and rapid decay more characteristic of the harpsichord than of the piano it was played on. This recording trick was behind the two-part Bach-like solo on the Beatles' "In My Life" as well as other tracks for the Beatles and other members of Martin's artist stable.

Another early keyboard used in some rock tracks is the clavichord, the mechanics of which may be thought of as a cross between the piano and the guitar. Like the former, keys in a range of about four octaves cause a hammer to strike and set into motion one or more strings. Instead of a felt hammer, however, the key controls a brass blade called a tangent, which stops the string(s) as does the left hand of a guitarist; pitch is controlled by how far away each key (and tangent) is from the bridge. Its mechanics are loud and the desired tones soft, but of course in the rock world, it may be recorded at any desired volume. (Listen to Web audio example 3.25 and see Web photos 3.14 and 3.15.) Paul McCartney first played the keyboard part for the Beatles' "For No One" on piano and then doubled it on clavichord (the quieter keyboard best heard at 0:00–0:24), finally also reinforcing the low part on his bass guitar. The clavichord is also heard in the Rolling Stones' "In Another Land" (at 1:06–1:40), and an electric clavichord is credited in John Sebastian's "Fa-Fana-Fa."

One more older keyboard is often heard: the nineteenth-century celesta, a four-octave instrument controlling felt hammers that play a set of bell-like steel bars, which ring over a set of wooden resonator boxes until damped by pedal. A common member of the orchestra, the celesta is best known from Tchaikovsky's "Dance of the Sugarplum Fairies," perhaps the reason that Nelson Riddle's orchestra features the instrument in the opening line, "Fairy tales can come true, it can happen to you," in Frank Sinatra's "Young at Heart." (Listen to Web audio example 3.26 and see Web photos 3.16 and 3.17.) It accompanies a lullaby in Elvis's "Big Boots," suggests a heavenly abode in Bobby Goldsboro's "Honey," paints mortal dreaming in the Chordettes' "Mr. Sandman," and even plinks as a rainshower in both the Cascades' "Rhythm of the Rain" and the Ronettes' "Walking in the Rain." It's the main instrument in the Tymes' "Wonderful! Wonderful!" as well as Buddy Holly's "Everyday" and two derivative usages—the Rascals' "Of Course" and the Moody Blues' "Emily's Song." It's quite effective alone above the string bass in Marvin Gaye and Tammi Terrell's "Ain't No Mountain High Enough" before the string players pick up their bows at 0:16. The celesta strengthens George Harrison's guitar solo in the Beatles' "Baby It's You," and is abused for a maudlin sentimentality in Mike Douglas's "The Men in My Little Girl's Life" and O. C. Smith's "Little Green Apples." The only sound more like a music box is just that: The Mamas and the Papas' "John's Music Box" features quite a resonant example, and a music box and celesta are actually paired in the opening of Blood, Sweat and Tears' "40,000 Headmen."

Electronic keyboards

The mid-twentieth century also saw the creation of four new instruments that use keyboards: the Ondes-Martenot, the Electro-Theremin, the Moog synthesizer, and the Mellotron. The first three are approaches to the joining of oscillators, filters, and amplifiers to create and control new electronic colors, and the fourth is virtually a tape library of samples at the control of a keyboardist who would typically simulate the sound of flutes or strings. We'll review these from a historical standpoint and discuss their use in pop-rock recordings.

> Electronic music: the oscillator, Theremin, Moog, tape music, and the Mellotron.

Electronic music begins with the oscillator, originally a vacuum tube generating a radio frequency far above the human hearing range of about 20–20,000 cycles per second. It was discovered in the second decade of the twentieth century that if the frequency of one oscillator (vibrating at, for example, 170,000 cycles per second [cps]) were combined with that of another (at 168,000 cps), they would produce an audible frequency (2,000 cps) based on the difference between the two competing frequencies. (This difference is based on the principle of beats, which has another practical value in allowing a player to adjust the tuning of two strings that are almost at the desired pitch relationship.) This discovery led to the production of the Theremin, an instrument built of three oscillator coils, two of which had large brass antennae that protruded about a foot each out of the cabinet. (Listen to Web audio example 3.27 and see Web photos 3.18 and 3.19.) The antennae were used to capture the electrical capacitance in a player's hand held in proximity, which would control the frequency of the oscillator. One such oscillator, controlling the gain of an amplifier tube, would dictate the loudness of the instrument; the closer the player's left hand came to that antenna (within a range of three to eighteen inches or so), the softer the resulting sound would get. The other two oscillators included both a fixed one, of 170,000 cps, and a variable one controlled by the right hand that, when combined with the fixed 170,000 cps wave, would produce a difference tone ranging from zero to 2,000 cps (the closer the right hand would get to the antenna, the larger would be the difference tone and therefore the higher the pitch), altogether making for an audible range of five-to-six octaves in pitch. With the two hands waving about the antennae, the Theremin player could get an excellent wobbling vibrato and tremolo, and superb glissandi, all with a tone that resembled that of a cello. RCA made several hundred Theremins in the 1920s and '30s; the instrument is heard in the soundtrack from the film *Spellbound* (1945) and during the rock era was played by Lothar and the Hand People.

Pitch was very hard to control in the Theremin, and so in 1928 the Ondes-Martenot was introduced, allowing a keyboard played by the right hand to modulate the variable oscillator for pitch while the left hand could switch among filters that would color the waveshape. Like the Theremin, the monophonic range was about six octaves. The player also had the option of sliding a finger along a ribbon for a glissando effect. The Ondes-Martenot was used by many European orchestral composers in midcentury, but can also be heard along with full orchestra in the Beatles' "Good Night," as well as in the Four Preps' "26 Miles (Santa Catalina)." The player of the Electro-Theremin, invented by Paul Tanner, would guide a device along a keyboard diagram to control the pitch of an oscillator's sine wave (totally lacking in harmonics for a relatively pure tone). Glissandi were natural, but the device included switches that could control articulation to a degree. The left hand turned a volume knob. Tanner plays his instrument on the Beach Boys' "Good Vibrations" and "I Just Wasn't Made For These Times," and it also colors Steve Lawrence's "Go Away Little Girl" (doubling a violin line), Diana Ross and the Supremes' "Reflections" (note the changing filterings) and "Forever Came Today," and many television ("My Favorite Martian") and film produc- tions of the 1960s. Other monophonic oscillator-based parts are heard in the Ran-Dells' "Martian Hop," the Rolling Stones' "Please Go Home," "She's a Rainbow," and "2,000 Light Years From Home," the Mothers' "The Return of the Son of Monster Magnet" and "Brown Shoes Don't Make It," the Zombies' "Butcher's Tune," the Cowsills' "Indian Lake," and the Temptations' "Run Away Child, Running Wild" and "Psychedelic Shack."

In the 1960s, the oscillator was transistorized, and pitch would be pro- duced in various devices by applying a variable voltage to the oscillator, a technique that became the heart of the modular synthesizer. As produced by Moog circa 1966, the synthesizer used oscillators to produce four or five basic waveshapes: the sine wave; the sawtooth and triangle waves, which include all harmonics in different ratios; the square wave, which includes only the

Photo 3.02. The first commercially produced Moog modular synthesizer, sold in 1964. (Photo courtesy of the Stearns Collection of Musical Instruments, The University of Michigan)

fundamental and every odd-numbered harmonic; and the pulse wave, which could function as a switch. (Listen to Web audio example 3.28 and see Web photo 3.20.) The Moog would be programmed through a patch bay whereby cables would create a signal path among oscillators, filters, mixers, and amplifiers so that various modules would control each other affecting the tone color and envelope of every resulting sound. The Moog had a keyboard as an optional component, and a ribbon controller for glissandi. Its first pop uses were programmed by Paul Beaver for the Monkees' "Daily Nightly" and "Star Collector" and for Jackie Lomax, and by Mike Vickers in four tracks for the Beatles' *Abbey Road* (featuring the Moog's noise generator in "I Want You (She's So Heavy)"). The triangle wave seems to be behind Spirit's "It's All the Same," we hear a square wave in the second verse of the Turtles' "You Showed Me," and a sawtooth-based sound is heard in John Sebastian's "What She Thinks About." In *Uncle Meat*, Frank Zappa experiments with several early synthesizer modules made by Maestro that do not involve keyboards. The Moog and mass-produced hardwired models Minimoog and the single-oscillator Micromoog were followed by important other analog synthesizers such as the Buchla and the ARP 2600 in the early 1970s, before digital synthesis was commercially developed by mid-decade.

Another early component of electronic music dating from the 1950s and early '60s involved the manipulation of recording tape. Works such as Karlheinz Stockhausen's *Gesange der Jünglinge* and Steve Reich's "Come Out" made the magnetic tape recorder an instrument and made tape editing a part of the compositional process. Interest in this work consumed John Lennon, who produced musique concrète works "Tomorrow Never Knows" and "Revolution 9" with the Beatles and *Unfinished Music No. 1: Two Virgins* and *Unfinished Music No. 2: Life With the Lions* with Yoko Ono. The electroacoustic music of Edgard Varèse influenced both Frank Zappa and James William Guercio (particularly in the latter's production of several 1967 works by the Buckinghams). Very closely related interests were also registered by Grateful Dead members Tom Constanten and Phil Lesh (students for a brief time of Luciano Berio), particularly in *Anthem of the Sun* and, judging by "Chushingura," also by Jefferson Airplane.

But the most important way magnetic tape played a role in rock instrumentation was in the Mellotron. In this keyboard instrument, each key on the player's manual pulled a different length of magnetic tape across a tape head. Each bank of tapes (one length, about seven seconds' worth, for each key) contained three channels, each of which was devoted to a vocal part or an orchestral instrument; a tape might have on its three channels flute, trumpet, and violin. Each key would start and stop a recording of that instrument playing that particular pitch. But only the sustaining sound was recorded, and the starting and stopping of the Mellotron tapes was abrupt, with nothing of the noises, spikes, tonal changes, or decays of the instruments' normal envelopes. The drive mechanism was also equipped with a pitch-bend knob. So its products sounded backward, or otherwise unusual. (Listen to Web audio example 3.29 and see Web photos 3.21–3.23). Introduced by the Beatles in "Tomorrow Never Knows" and more famously as the three flutes opening "Strawberry Fields Forever," the Mellotron became the darling of the first progressive rock groups such as the Moody Blues (beginning with a Fall 1966 single, "Love and Beauty," but more famously in "Nights in White Satin" and beyond, as when drummer Graeme Edge would intone his spacey poetry over multiple Mellotrons drenched in reverb and pitch bends) and King Crimson (in three tracks on *In The Court of the Crimson King*). It's also heard throughout the Zombies' *Odessey and Oracle* and the Stones' *Their Satanic Majesties Request* (played by John Paul Jones, who would later contribute Mellotron parts to Led Zeppelin), and in many late-1960s tracks by the Bee Gees, Pink Floyd, and Traffic.

Putting It All Together

It would be useful to focus on a wide range of individual recordings at this point, reinforcing the reader's newly acquired skills in identifying rock sounds, and examining how instrumental colors and functions are combined to create the ensemble for each record. We'll cover here a representative sample of twenty-five rock records from the 1950s and '60s in the chronological order of their popularity, looking only at their instrumental textures, and see if any trends of historical interest begin to emerge.

25 Great Hits I: Both here and at the end of chapter 11, we look at the same selection of twenty-five rock recordings. At this point, we focus on the various approaches to rock instrumentation in these songs.

Bill Haley and His Comets' "(We're Gonna) Rock Around the Clock" (first charting in May 1955) is typical of early rock instrumentation, with drums, upright string bass, lead guitar, and alto saxophone (saxophones will be covered in chapter 4). The song is announced by snare alone; each phrase of the introductory map of the clock is presented in stop time, where the singer works alone with occasional punctuations from the rhythm section. As the verse begins (0:13) ("Put your glad rags on..."), the string bass enters with plucked boogie arpeggiations of each chord: I (0:13–0:17)—IV (0:17–0:19)—I (0:20–0:22), and so on. Here, the drummer has two featured parts: a ticky-tack stickwork on the rim of the snare drum, plus percussive flams on toms to mark phrase endings (as at 0:14 and 0:17). Danny Cedrone's lead guitar, a hollow-body switched to neck pickup throughout, plays jazzy chords off the beat through verses then takes a solo at 0:44–1:00,

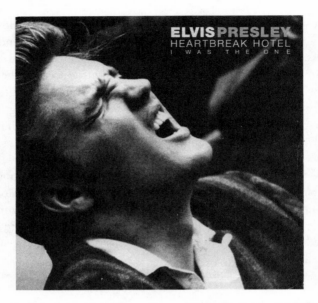

Photo 3.03. Sleeve from the 1996 45-rpm reissue of "Heartbreak Hotel" / "I Was the One," which included a previously unreleased alternate take as well as the original hit of each side of Elvis's first charting record.

featuring a very rapid tremolo (0:44–0:49, again at 0:55–0:56), returning for a concluding gesture (2:01–2:10) before the wacky drums have the last word. In the fourth verse (1:16–1:31) ("When it's eight, nine, ten, eleven too..."), note that the drummer smacks a tambourine instead of his toms. Through the verses, the sax repeats the first scale degree under both I and IV chords, moves to its upper neighbor, 2, for the V chord, and then returns to 1 over I. The same 1—2—1 "tune" of repeated notes is given the spotlight at 1:32–1:47. For the most part, rhythmic rather than color events provide textural contrasts.

Compare Elvis Presley's "Heartbreak Hotel" (March 1956). This opens with the same stop-time arrangement, Elvis singing alone with his phrases punctuated by the rhythm section of drums, piano, and electric guitar. Bill Black's upright string bass joins as solo accompaniment to the voice (0:08–0:21), with as much stepwise connection as arpeggiation in its supportive melody. D. J. Fontana's drums enter (0:28) in the second verse, Scotty Moore's lead guitar following soon thereafter (0:31), both understated here, but Scotty has a very hot solo at 1:21–1:30, featuring double stops (including a double-stopped unison repeated note). In the third verse, Floyd Cramer's piano moves to the high register to balance the bass. The piano supports the guitar solo with mid-register shuffle chords but when Scotty drops out, the piano returns nonchalantly to the tinkly high pitches, the funky bass continuing below. Both Haley's and Presley's records get their tension from the interaction between the vocal and instruments, and the sharp dissonances in the solos, but the arrangement for Presley has more subtlety.

Buddy Holly's "That'll Be the Day" (August 1957) opens boldly with the headliner's bright Stratocaster solo riff, which then quietly moves to a boogie figure underneath the choruses. The guitar solo features double stops (0:49–0:57 and again at 1:05–1:12), but also falls back on the boogie (0:57–1:01). The chorus (0:04–0:19) is propelled by strong backbeat snare ((1)—two—(3)—four), with the ride cymbal added for verses (0:19–0:34) ("Well you gave me all your lovin' and your turtledovin'..."), providing a climax with triplets on the snare at 0:31–0:34. The recording ends with a brief snare roll. Completing the rhythm section, a string bass alternates roots and fifths, playing only on the strong beats, ONE and Three.

The Everly Brothers' "Wake Up Little Susie" (September 1957) opens with a pair of acoustic guitars, one repeating chords as the other adds a bluesy progression (compare the texture of Simon and Garfunkel's arrangement a decade later of "Mrs. Robinson"). Chet Atkins enters at 0:29 with his open-body electric lead guitar, chiefly filling in the corners after vocal phrases, especially after "what're we gonna tell your mama?," a textural technique later adopted by George Harrison with the early Beatles. Drums and string bass enter together at 0:05. The bass alternates roots and fifths, playing just on first and third beats—just as in the Holly track. The drums carry a strong backbeat, and throw out some fills (as at 0:17–0:21) as if attempting to arouse Susie, in perhaps more than one sense of the word.

An electric guitar riff, this time a double-stopped idea from a hollow Gibson 335, opens Chuck Berry's "Sweet Little Sixteen" (February 1958), which from the first chorus through the end reduces his role to a boogie rhythm. Drums provide a simple backbeat pattern, with the first tom fills at 0:45–0:46 leading to slightly more flamboyant playing as the track moves on. In the first chorus, Willie Dixon confines his electric bass to an alternation of roots and fifths on strong beats, but he becomes more animated with full arpeggios in the stop-time verses (beginning at 0:23+) and in later choruses. Lafayette Leake improvises at the piano with his right hand in the high register, beginning quietly and simply, but adding a knuckle gliss (at 0:48–0:49)—a figure that dominates the first half of his solo (1:30+), before wildly dividing serial beats into hammered triplets. Thus, all performers but Berry himself drive the track to ever-rising tension.

In the Marvelettes' early Motown effort, "Please Mr. Postman" (September 1961), piano, electric bass, and drums make up the rhythm section. The drummer has a busy backbeat from 0:08 onward, playing (1)—two—and—(3)—four on his snare while he taps every half beat on the ride cymbal.

He adds fills to take the song from one section to the next, as after the first chorus (0:23–0:24). The bass has a few patterns, opening with a pedal on scale-degree 1 (0:00–0:04), repeated with a ONE—and—two—and—(3—4) rhythm for two bars then sitting out for a bit. Mostly, though, the bass alternates roots and fifths of chords on strong beats ONE and Three, as done by string bass in the Holly and Everlys' tracks, but occasionally these notes are repeated eight to the bar for stronger rhythm. An electric rhythm guitar hides deep in the background, but can occasionally be heard (perhaps most clearly at 0:29–0:30) arpeggiating chords. Handclaps round out the nonvocal texture in the intro and at 1:44+.

Handclaps mark the opening of the Four Seasons' "Sherry" (August 1962), which also begins with congas, a backbeat tambourine, and electric bass. An electric guitar switches from a lead to a rhythm pattern at 0:09 when the voice and piano chording begin. Toms are evident only at climaxes, such as 1:03–1:05 and 1:57–1:59.

The Crystals' "He's a Rebel" (September 1962) features studio greats Hal Blaine on drums and Larry Knechtel on piano. Blaine opens with a snare backbeat and tom fills, as a string bass largely alternates roots and fifths, one note per beat. It's easier to hear the bass line when it is doubled by a baritone sax, which enters in the second verse (0:25) ("When he holds my hand I'm so proud..."). The piano is initially a color instrument, endlessly repeating a figure in the high register for the intro and verses, but moves to rhythmic chords in the mid-register for choruses (as at 0:42+). The sax has a peppy solo (1:11–1:27) deep in the baritone register, augmented by a busy backbeat in Sonny Bono's handclaps, (1)—two—and—(3)—four.

More subtlety appears in the arrangement of the Beatles' "I Want to Hold Your Hand" (January 1964). For clarity's sake, we'll refer here specifically to the stereo mix that appears on the *Past Masters, Vol. 1* compact disc. Let's examine the instrumental texture channel by channel, moving from the left side of the stereo image, through the center, to the right. On the left is the basic rhythm track, with Ringo Starr's drums, Paul McCartney's bass, and John Lennon's rhythm guitar. The drums feature several highly energetic loud crash cymbal strikes in the intro, and then move to a backbeat pattern in the verse (0:08+) ("Oh, yeah, I'll tell you somethin'..."), with a loud ride accompaniment and notable fills (as at 0:20–0:22). McCartney's Höfner bass moves from rapidly repeated notes in the intro to a pattern of mostly roots in the verse/refrain, in what's called (because of its notation) a dotted rhythm: ONE—(2)—and—Three—four—ONE—(2)—and—Three—(4)—and. Lennon, whose three-quarter-length Rickenbacker is run through a compression circuit so heavy it sounds like an organ, plays a boogie pattern in the intro and rhythmic chords in the verse. Overdubs appear in the center, where handclaps add a very busy backbeat, (1)—two—and—(3)—and—four, to the verse and Harrison adds a short bass line at 0:10–0:11 and 0:17–0:18 to mark an unexpected chord change. The right channel is devoted to Harrison's lead guitar track, played on a hollow-body Gretsch Country Gentleman. Many different techniques are demonstrated here, including crying slides of single notes (0:11), rising slides of full chords (0:27, 0:49), and slow arpeggiations of chords in the bridge (0:51+). Also in the bridge, drums drop the ride cymbal and move to the hi-hat for hits repeated every half beat, eight to the bar. Uncharacteristically, McCartney's bass thickens the low texture with double stops (0:58–1:03). An edit tacks onto the right channel a final I chord from a Gibson acoustic-electric guitar. Instruments are mined for power even as the lyrics attempt to coax with grace.

The electric guitar is right out front of the Animals' "House of the Rising Sun" (August 1964), thanks to Hilton Valentine's clean arpeggiation of every chord in his lead playing. Bassist Chas Chandler plays roots on every downbeat. John Steel's drums enter with the singer, Eric Burdon, at 0:11, mostly with a ride-cymbal rhythm and hi-hat pedaled closed on backbeats. At 0:35, just before the second verse ("My mother was a tailor…"), Alan Price adds sustained chords on the Vox Continental; soon, he has more rhythmic contributions, sometimes doubling the guitar, and he takes a solo at 1:54, which climbs to a high register then (at 2:11) descends back to his work area in the middle of the keyboard. Drums become more active circa 2:56 for the fifth and sixth verses ("Well, I got one foot on the platform…"), for a rousing finish with organ out front and guitar strumming away, with the original cymbal patterns reappearing for the close. This song does not contain contrasting verses, choruses, and a bridge, but rather repeats the same strophic section for six hearings, and thus takes advantage of changes in instrumental patterns to build intensity through the repeating stanzaic structures.

A guitar riff doubled for color and strength is the core hallmark of Roy Orbison's "Oh, Pretty Woman" (August 1964). The song's intro begins with drums alone: the bass drum is hit on every beat—four on the floor—and the snare doubles this rhythm as the closed hi-hat is struck on every upbeat. After one bar (0:02), specialist Grady Martin enters with his arpeggiated riff, 5—5—7—2—4, on an acoustic twelve-string guitar. After two looped playings of this (at 0:07), the guitar line is doubled by both electric bass and electric lead guitar. After two more hearings (0:11), the line is doubled by a second electric guitar and punctuated by a baritone saxophone. This texture leads to the first chorus (0:15+), where high-register chords enter on the piano and where the bass adopts a post-McCartney dotted rhythm, the snare still struck on every beat. In the bridge (1:05+), the first lead guitar chimes the changes (a technique made famous by Harrison) with heavy amp tremolo, and the piano becomes more tinkly. The drums change here to a busy backbeat, (1)—two—and—(3)—four on the snare, with tom fills (as at

1:19–1:21) for, overall, a very Beatle-y arrangement. Many elements of this instrumental arrangement are highly memorable.

The Beatles themselves up the ante with contrasting guitar colors in "Ticket to Ride" (April 1965). This track opens with Harrison's electric twelve-string Rickenbacker tattoo (on the right of the digital mix for the *Help!* CD), and then the band is signaled by Ringo's brief snare roll. In the verse, his pattern (heard left) becomes an unusual chamber music for drums, with the bass drum establishing strong beats, ONE—(2)—and—Three—(4), one tom hit on (1)—two—(3–4)—and, and the snare sounded only on (1—2—3)—and—(4). Completing the percussion, a tambourine is struck on every backbeat. (At the bridge, 1:08+, the tambourine is shaken and the backbeat is marked by snare and handclaps. Ringo changes the snare/tom pattern for the third verse, at 1:27+.) McCartney's Höfner bass opens (left) with a repeated pitch doubling the bass drum rhythm, and Lennon's repeated open strings on his new Stratocaster (center) double McCartney's bass. Harrison enters with his own Strat part, with wavering chords articulated by the volume-tone control pedal at the refrain's stop-time passage (0:28–0:30). Lennon's Strat drops out for the bridge, but McCartney adds a blistering hot hollow-body Epiphone Casino lead for a solo retransition (1:24–1:28), blending with the continuing twelve-string and with Lennon's open-string return (at 1:27). The Casino returns at 2:47 for a solo through the coda. Despite the song's many varieties of color, not the least of them the celebrated contrast of the electric twelve-string riff and the Casino solo, the infectious rhythm of Ringo's drums may have as much to do with the resulting charm as do any of its other instrumental effects.

We have seen wholesale changes in texture from one section to another become a common technique, and this is no more characteristic than in Lou Christie's "Lightin' Strikes" (December 1965). Drums, bass, piano, and electric guitar form the rhythm section: the piano is stratified, with low-register octaves in a dotted rhythm (doubled by the bass) supporting high-register chords; a tom fill announces the drums as they enter with electric guitar at 0:02, the drums moving to a snare backbeat and guitar chords heard in a dramatic two-bar pattern: ONE—(2—3—4—1—2)—Three—four. Doubling the bass, dotted-rhythm octaves are added by bari and tenor saxes at 0:04. This additive texture continues through the verse, and then at 0:22 ("Every boy wants a girl...."), the bass alone has the low-register dotted rhythm, with the piano introducing a right-hand fingers/thumb rocking pattern in the high register. The drums adopt a light ride texture here but mark FOUR on the snare. The guitar chimes chord changes on every downbeat. At 0:30, both sustained saxophone lines and orchestral chimes are added. A change marks the opening of the prechorus (at 0:36) ("When I see lips..."), where all beats are struck on the drums. For the chorus (0:44+), the bass walks, the saxes move, the piano reenters, and the guitar has a new unobtrusive chick on backbeats. The electric guitar solo (1:47–2:01) by a new instrument is likely overdubbed. All changes of texture support the song's dramatic demeanor.

Aside from introducing the sitar in a major hit, the Rolling Stones' "Paint It, Black" (May 1966) makes do with largely rudimentary forces. Brian Jones plays his sitar melody as an introduction and throughout most of the song, but the opening also features Keith Richards with repeated notes on the electric guitar; this guitar simply chords through verses. Charlie Watts's drums enter at 0:08, ushering in the chorus, where Bill Wyman begins playing roots on his bass and Watts hammers every beat on the snare. In the verse (0:26+), announced by a crash cymbal, the drums move to a snare backbeat pattern. A tambourine is also used in verses (best heard when shaken at 1:27–1:39), and a strummed acoustic guitar is revealed at 1:30–1:37. The acoustic and tambourine share a triplet-laden bolero rhythm (ONE—two—trip—let—Three—four—trip—let—ONE—two—trip—let—Three—trip—let—four—trip—let) in the coda (2:22–2:35). This is one of the unusual Stones rockers in which Keith Richards's rhythm guitar does not speak with central authority.

Color doublings open the Lovin' Spoonful's "Summer in the City" (July 1966) as a repeated two-note descending melodic figure, ^{b}6—5, covers the first three beats of each introductory bar. This simple motive is performed in octaves by Zal Yanovsky's lead guitar (left), the bass (right), and a Hohner Pianet attributed to co-composer and non–group member Mark Sebastian (also right). This blend is answered every fourth beat by a smash on the snare and bass drum, until a slide on the electric bass introduces the first verse (0:07+) ("Hot town!..."), wherein a snare backbeat, guitar chords, and the electric piano carry the rhythm. Energy picks up at 0:18–0:21 ("hotter than a matchhead"), with Pianet and snare marking ONE—and—two—and, suddenly switching to a tom and Pianet for Three—and—four—and. The chorus (0:21+) ("But at night it's a different world...") introduces John Sebastian's autoharp, which along with the electric guitar chimes every chord change on strong beats (two per bar). At 0:26, an acoustic rhythm guitar and a hi-hat pedaled closed on backbeats are added for thicker texture. This additive trend breaks at 1:09–1:20, where a doubling of Pianet and lead guitar, supported at 1:18+ by a Vox organ pedal on a first scale degree octave, takes center stage over a field recording of car horns and jackhammer. The crash cymbal contributes in a subtle way to increasing tension, by reserving itself for every two downbeats in the verse, then being articulated every downbeat in the second half of the chorus, progressively heating up as does the summer city day. Although the song presents a great deal of color contrast that illustrates its many facets, this is another track in which all elements are shaped by key rhythms.

Photo 3.04. The first compact disc release of Bob Dylan's *Blonde on Blonde*, which edited the program of the double-album so as to fit onto a single disc.

Bob Dylan opens "Visions of Johanna" (*Blonde on Blonde*, July 1966) simply with his acoustic six-string and harmonica, but a snare rudiment announces the first verse (0:13+) ("Ain't it just like the night..."), which adds a very dry electric chick rhythm guitar, a busy bass, and Al Kooper's Hammond organ. An instrumental interlude (1:26+) is assigned just to the harmonica and crash cymbal, with light acoustic guitar from the composer. In the second verse (1:36+) ("In the empty lot..."), Robbie Robertson adds acidic Stratocaster commentaries through his bridge pickup, including many bent notes (as at 1:42–1:43) and bent double stops (4:27–4:52), with a withering whammy exposing "her cape of the stage [that] once had flowed" (6:27–6:28).

Brian Wilson is rightly praised for his complex and inventive arrangement for the Beach Boys of "Good Vibrations" (October 1966). Here, every section of the song has its own texture, partly because each was recorded separately and then edited together into a seamless whole. The sparse first verse has Larry Knechtel repeating chords every beat on a Hammond with rotating Leslie. Underneath, a two-bar Fender bass melody, on (1)—and—two— Three—(4)—and—ONE—two—(3—4), is sequenced successively lower. This is repeated at 0:13 ("I, I looked in her eyes"), with the addition of two piccolos sustaining over a falling flute line. In every odd bar (the first and third of four), bongos double the bass rhythm; every fourth beat is struck by either a tambourine or bass-drum-and-snare combination, in alternation.

In the chorus (0:25+) ("I'm pickin' up good vibrations..."), backbeat toms and tambourine, with the bass melody now steady at one note per beat, and a new cello repeating a single note in a bowed-tremolo triplet, provide a newly regular backdrop for Paul Tanner's unusual Electro-Theremin. In the bridge (1:41+) ("...–tations; I don't know where..."), a tack piano, jew's harp, and bass relegated to strong beats only repeat a whole new sound, to which is added at 1:55 a new electronic organ, bass harmonica, and sleigh bells shaken on every beat. A splice at 2:13 brings in the transition, where Dennis Wilson sustains chords on an electronic organ, maracas are shaken on every beat, and at 2:35 the bass begins playing one note per beat and a second electronic organ adds a high-register idea to balance the bass. (Note that the Dylan, Lovin' Spoonful, and now Beach Boys songs all employ contrasting interludes with suddenly pared-back forces.) This section leads to chorus and coda, which revert back to the previous chorus's instrumentation. As opposed to our previously chosen examples, in which other musical elements might claim a lion's share of the song's success, the unusually impressionistic colors of "Good Vibrations" seem to be of central interest in creating this song's experimental quality of evanescence.

The Doors' instrumentation in "Light My Fire" (June 1967) is very simple in contrast. John Densmore opens with a backbeat snare pattern that is maintained for the whole song. This supports Ray Manzarek's baroque

Photo 3.05. The first release of Jimi Hendrix's "Little Wing" was on *Axis: Bold as Love.*

Vox Continental tattoo, aided by a busy bass line overdubbed by Manzarek himself. At 0:09, the verse ("You know that it would be untrue...") opens, relegating the bass to one note per beat (the second of which is highlighted by a leap to a high register, always initiating a descending arpeggiation from there) and the organ to simple syncopated chords roughly doubled by those on composer Robbie Krieger's slower-to-attack distorted Gibson SG. Little in the song changes, except when singer Jim Morrison drops out for the guitar/organ solos, which imitate each other briefly with a turn figure at 4:44–5:00.

"Little Wing" (*Axis: Bold as Love,* February 1968) is representative of the Jimi Hendrix Experience. This track opens with a multipart guitar solo on the rhythm pickup, featuring expressive hammer-ons, with Hendrix adding a glockenspiel at 0:04 to double occasional key pitches. Heavy phasing is added to the guitar at 0:23. Mitch Mitchell's drum fill at 0:31+ prepares the first verse ("Well, she's walkin'..."), where Noel Redding's bass is added to the drums. This remains the song's whole texture but for an overdubbed guitar solo (1:40+), announced by a sustained whammy chord (1:36+) on the first guitar. The solo is run through a Leslie speaker in addition to being phased and highly distorted, for a characteristically other-worldly Hendrix performance.

Cream arranges some texture changes in "White Room" (*Wheels of Fire,* July 1968), which is introduced by an unusual five-bar tattoo that reappears here and there to announce structural points. The tattoo blends Eric Clapton's long-sustaining double-stopped electric guitar with similar long notes from Felix Pappalardi's double-stopped viola, while Jack Bruce intones roots on his bass on every downbeat, which rhythmic event is also marked every bar by Ginger Baker's crash cymbal. A timpanist is also busy with an unusually willful rhythm repeated in every bar: ONE—two—trip—let—Three—four—and—five. At 0:23, the tattoo gives way to the first verse ("In my white room..."), from which point onward Clapton's distorted guitar is unleashed, Bruce articulates every beat on his bass, and Baker plays a busy backbeat on closed hi-hat (right) and other pieces (left). A drum fill at 0:58–0:59 leads to the chorus, where Clapton's wah guitar, all silver horses and yellow tigers, is added and is to sustain through the second verse (1:20+).

Pink Floyd create a similarly sparse yet unusual sound world in "Remember a Day" (*A Saucerful of Secrets,* August 1968 in the United Kingdom). Composer Rick Wright carries the texture on piano, aided by Roger Waters's bass, Syd Barrett's acoustic guitar, and a wildly atonal bottleneck-slide guitar part from Barrett, as well. Drums, heavy on the toms, are added at 0:17 by producer Norman Smith when drummer Nick Mason is too dumbfounded to produce a part. The verse ("Remember a day before today") begins at 0:25, with the piano establishing three different registers through its rising chords, acoustic chords strummed on every second beat, and the bass playing roots only (repeating scale degrees 1, ♭7, and 4). A single break in the otherwise hypnotic texture is afforded by a soft mallet roll on a crash cymbal at 1:37, in approaching the unconventional song's bridge.

Instrumentation helps tell the story in Marvin Gaye's "I Heard It Through the Grapevine" (November 1968). A terraced opening reflects the singer's growing suspicion: a single fourth beat articulated by snare and tambourine brings in the Wurlitzer's introduction (marking ONE—(2)—and—Three—four...), which is meshed with an open fifth repeated every beat on an electronic organ. At 0:04, a bass drum adds a and—ONE—(2)—and—Three—(4) rhythm as the hi-hat is pedaled closed on every two and four. At 0:09, the tambourine starts to shake ominously, and energy picks up further at 0:13 with the organ's new boogie pattern and an entry of two electric guitars—one with a chick backbeat on two and four, the other doubling the organ boogie. Suddenly, at 0:17–0:21, a French horn rises an octave—sudden enlightenment! Only the bass and regular drum pattern still need to begin, which they do at 0:20, so as to prepare the vocal entry. Bongos and violins are added beneath the verse. At 1:03–1:10, the violins have repeated bowed-tremolo notes that drop down an octave, inverting the horn's opening motive. How do we know this octave is so indicative of sudden enlightenment? At 2:57, Marvin sings, "I know that you're lettin' me go" on the same rising-octave figure.

All of The Who's grandiose rock opera *Tommy* (June 1969) has a remarkably thin arrangement, because the band aimed to perform the work on tour with as few extra performers as possible. But as are its other musical aspects, its instrumentation is a marvel of detail. The "Overture" (the purpose of which is to set the stage for the coming opera by citing its prominent tunes) begins with Pete Townshend's electric guitar chords on the left, John Entwistle's bass and Keith Moon's cymbal crashes on strong beats center, and Townshend's overdubbed piano doubling the guitar on the right. At 0:16 (with the first of several foreshadowings of the "See me, feel me" tune from "Go to the Mirror"), the bass articulates downbeats with electric piano and guitar as Townshend's added acoustic guitar (right) is strummed in rapid tremolo. Drums join only at 0:32, with everyone attacking every beat. The drums loosen up at 0:36, at which point Entwistle's French horn doubles both guitars. At 1:11, the horn breaks into broad melody, quoting the tune, "He seems to be completely unreceptive." Townshend's overdubbed sustained Hammond chords appear at center for a climactic hearing of the "listening to you, I get the music..." melody. For an exotic touch, Moon adds timpani (3:05–3:06) and a gong (3:28–3:48), striking the latter every two bars (heard center). As a transition to the introduction of Captain Walker, the lowest string of Townshend's acoustic is tuned down a major second, and the horn announces "It's a boy!," recapturing the ear-catching role of the brass instrument in "Grapevine." The gravity of the repeated remark, "A son!," is emphasized by crash cymbals and ching-a-ring tremolos on acoustic guitar, piano, and timpani.

"Come Together" (October 1969) will represent the Beatles once more. Its complexities are subtle. In the intro, we hear Harrison's distorted Les Paul and McCartney's bass (descending with a great slide on every fourth beat) on the left, handclaps (and John's Lennon calling "shoot me!") with very heavy echo on every downbeat in the center, and Ringo's drums on the right. The drums present an elaborate rhythm: bass drum and crash cymbal sound on ONE—and, a closed hi-hat is sticked with a triplet on a half beat: two—trip—let—and, and then a tom carries the triplet: Three—trip—let—and—trip—let—four—trip—let—and. The verse calls forth a new drum pattern, with eight snare hits per bar, and then ends (0:30–0:35) with a portentous dotted-rhythm bass-drum solo in stop time through a sustained electric bass note. Lennon adds his distorted Casino at 1:10–1:15 and again in the break (2:02–2:24), where he is joined by McCartney's overdubbed Pianet part. Harrison overdubs a two-part Les Paul idea at 2:14–2:27, this color supported by a shaken maraca (which reappears in the coda, 3:35+). The retransition (2:25–2:31) to the verse is a beautiful rhythmic confusion of bass, Harrison's first Les Paul (left), and McCartney's Pianet (moving to center). As a final touch, Harrison adds a sustained two-voice Les Paul at 3:01–3:11 that is colored by a volume-tone control pedal. Here, color could not be more closely married to pitch and rhythm.

Our final example is Creedence Clearwater Revival's "Down on the Corner" (October 1969), a throwback to a traditional rock instrumentation. Like "Grapevine," this song exhibits a terraced introduction: Doug Clifford's hi-hat struck every beat is doubled at 0:02 by a cowbell and shaken maraca, is joined at 0:05 by a riff on Stu Cook's bass and John Fogerty's lead electric guitar, and then at 0:13 a drum fill ushers in two electric rhythm guitars played by John and Tom Fogerty. A crash cymbal at 0:32 announces the verse, whereupon the drums feature backbeat snare. The lead guitar solo (1:16–1:33) carries a double-stopped idea throughout.

Although trends and stylistic variety have been suggested in the preceding survey, it should be noted that all of the instrumental techniques appearing in these very different songs have been previously covered in these first three chapters. It's now up to the reader to see how the elements discussed here apply in other, and later, examples. Even though I have sought to concentrate thus far on uses of drums, guitars, and keyboards, we have not been able to avoid recognition of the saxophone in early examples and, in later ones, many other instruments including piccolo, flute, French horn, glockenspiel, jew's harp, violin, viola, and cello. It is now time to turn to all these colors and more, in chapter 4.

CHAPTER 4

Sweetening with Band, Orchestral, and Other Instruments

The instruments covered thus far are basic to all rock and most pop music. But every instrument common to the wind band and the orchestra, and many from folk usage are heard in the pop-rock literature as well. At times, an orchestra or band of any size appears as a whole and on its own; at others, a record producer will book expert performers—session musicians—to add soloists, small groupings, or large sections of instruments to a rock group for just the right touch of sweetening. We'll discuss and provide examples of each member of the woodwind, brass, percussion, and string sections, so you'll be able to recognize all of their colors and understand a bit about how they're used. Along the way, we'll take note of several other less formal instruments that don't have orchestral roles but have found their way into our repertoire nevertheless.

Woodwinds

Woodwinds are no longer all made of wood (the flute family is made of platinum, gold, or silver alloys and the saxophones are of brass), but they all involve applying vibration to a column of wind. The clarinets and saxes feature a single vibrating reed, whereas oboes and bassoons have a bound pair of reeds that vibrate together. In each, the player plays higher and higher pitches by successively shortening the length of the vibrating pipe, which is done by removing fingers from pads, keys, or holes, beginning at the end furthest from the mouth. The flute and much smaller piccolo have relatively pure tones because their pipes are cylindrical in shape, and the air is set in motion directly without a reed. The clarinet is also cylindrical and its sound resembles that of a square wave. The oboe, English horn, bassoon, and saxophones have conical shapes and a more piercing sound. In each, the player controls articulation, phrasing, vibrato, dynamics, and intonation by mouth control.

> **Winds:** the flute, piccolo, oboe, clarinet, bassoon, saxophone, mouth music, and recorder.

The solo flute, strongest in the upper register, is often used to present a melody (as the featured instrument in Moe Koffman's "Swingin' Shepherd Blues" and Lalo Schifrin's "Mission Impossible"), take a solo (as in Marvin Gaye's "Hitch Hike" and with severe note bends in The Mamas and the Papas' "California Dreaming"), or double a vocal melody (as Clement Barone's piccolo does in the bridge of the Four Tops' "Bernadette"). It may also play a countermelody—a tune different than, but played simultaneously with, the main melody (as in the second verse, 0:38–1:00, of the Ventures' "Hawaii Five-O"). The flute may answer phrases (Dee Clark's "Just Keep It Up" and the Vogues' "Turn Around, Look At Me"), or appear in between sections (as in the interludes of the Moody Blues' "How Is It (We Are Here)"). Characteristic effects are high trills (in the Four Aces' "Mister Sandman," and for "a fleeting glance" in Johnny Mathis's "A Certain Smile," 0:44–0:46), tremolo (hear Harold McNair's work in the Rascals' "It's Love" and Donovan's "Lalena"), and chirping (the Moody Blues' "Legend of a Mind") and fluttering effects (often achieved by rolling the tongue, as in Gene Pitney's "Mecca" and Linda Scott's "Bermuda"). (Listen to Web audio examples 4.01 and 4.02, and see Web photos 4.01 and 4.02.)

Two flutes often work together, as when playing lines a third apart (the opening of Patti Page's "(How Much Is) That Doggie in the Window," the ending of Gale Garnett's "We'll Sing in the Sunshine"), in octaves (as at the end of the Beatles' "You've Got to Hide Your Love Away," in a stylized adaptation of Dylan's closing harmonica codas), or in unison (Billy Vaughn's "A Swingin' Safari," the opening of the Beach Boys' "Sloop John B"). Occasionally, the flute choir articulates repeated chords as would a rhythm instrument (as in the intro to Percy Faith's "Theme From a Summer Place"). An excellent duet of flute and alto flute opens the 5th Dimension's "Aquarius," Ray Thomas double-tracks a flute/alto flute duet himself in the Moody Blues' "Dear

Diary" and "Eyes of a Child," and Blood, Sweat and Tears open with a flute trio in "Variations on a Theme by Eric Satie." At the top of the Beach Boys' "Good Vibrations," the flute and piccolo sustain against a moving bass flute, whereas flute and piccolo play in octaves in the opening of Stevie Wonder's "My Cherie Amour." Flute and Vox Continental double for a solo in Manfred Mann's "Pretty Flamingo," and the flute is paired with trumpet in the opening duets of the Buckinghams' "I'll Be Back" and "Foreign Policy." Flutes also sound good with reverb, as shown in Glen Campbell's "By the Time I Get to Phoenix," the Beach Boys' "God Only Knows," and the Left Banke's "Walk Away Renee." The piccolo may suggest whistling, as in the Four Lads' "Standing on the Corner," a military fife, as in Jimmy Dean's "P.T. 109" and the Fifth Estate's "Ding Dong! The Witch Is Dead," and a bird's song, as in Bobby Day's "Rockin' Robin," or simply be used to balance the low end, as when contrasting with the bass in Stevie Wonder's "For Once in My Life" or the bassoon in Smokey Robinson's "The Tears of a Clown."

The piercing quality of the oboe gives it a plaintive and melancholy sound, and it often accompanies texts portraying loneliness (as in Gerry and the Pacemakers' "Don't Let the Sun Catch You Crying," Ray Charles's cover of "Eleanor Rigby," the "lost" intro to the Happenings' "I Got Rhythm," the Classics IV's "Traces," and Gary Puckett and the Union Gap's "Over You") or wistfulness (as in Glen Campbell's now horrendously un-PC "Dreams of the Everyday Housewife"). At another extreme, the oboe can also sound playful when given a jaunty rhythm, as are the pair opening Donovan's "Jennifer Juniper." (Listen to Web audio examples 4.03 and 4.04, and see Web photos 4.03 and 4.04.) Given its double-reed likeness to the eastern shawm, it frequently paints an Arabic landscape, as in Ray Stevens' "Ahab the Arab" or the Monkees' ersatz-psychedelic "Take a Giant Step." It's very effective when given the main tune, as in Paul Mauriat's "Love Is Blue," Johnny Mathis's "Misty," or the Flying Machine's "Smile a Little Smile For Me" (oddly here, the closing tune played by the oboe had first appeared in the introductory trumpet). Two oboes in thirds take the break in Peter and Gordon's "I Don't Want to See You Again." The oboe enjoys countermelodies in The Mamas and the Papas' "Words of Love" (1:03+), Jefferson Airplane's "rejoyce" (2:08–2:28), and David Ruffin's "My Whole World Ended." The deeper English horn (a large oboe with a bulbous bell) is heard in the Four Seasons' "Big Man in Town," Marianne Faithfull's "As Tears Go By," The Doors' "Wishful Sinful," and Lesley Gore's "California Nights."

The clarinet is front and center in Dixieland arrangements such as Louis Armstrong's "Hello, Dolly!" and the Village Stompers' "Washington Square." (Listen to Web audio example 4.05 and see Web photo 4.05.) It has a few lead roles, as in Mr. Acker Bilk's tremolo-heavy "Strangers on the Shore" (which probes its introspective lowest notes at 0:09 and elsewhere) and Chris

Barber's "Petite Fleur." The clarinet leads both the Mothers of Inventions's "Dwarf Nebula Processional March & Dwarf Nebula" and the "March for No Reason" in King Crimson's "Epitaph." The latter also features bass clarinet, which is often paired with its more common cousin; both are heard together in Jaye P. Morgan's "If You Don't Want My Love," Tennessee Ernie Ford's "Sixteen Tons" (in octaves), the Beach Boys' "I Just Wasn't Made for These Times" (in dissonant parallel fourths, with the Electro-Theremin doubling an octave above the bass clarinet), the Beatles' "When I'm Sixty-Four," and Spirit's "Ice." Frank Zappa scores the highly unusual contrabass clarinet along with piano, trumpet, and string quartet in an atonal peek inside the corrupted mind of City Hall Fred in the Mothers' "Brown Shoes Don't Make It."

Rounding out the traditional orchestral woodwinds is the bassoon. (Listen to Web audio example 4.06 and see Web photo 4.06.) It has only a very small role as the bass instrument in a rock ensemble, such as when it chugs out the roots on the downbeats of intros and choruses of Sonny and Cher's "I Got You Babe." Instead, it has rare but easily noticed solo roles, as when it plays the clown in the intro to Smokey Robinson and the Miracles' "The Tears of a Clown" and when it doubles the whistled tune in the first bridge of the New Vaudeville Band's "Winchester Catherdral." More often, the bassoon participates in a woodwind chamber ensemble, as when two flutes, clarinet,

Photo 4.01. Ross Leavitt, soprano saxophone; Joe Girard, baritone saxophone. (Photo: Annie Eastman)

oboe, and bassoon collaborate in Harpers Bizarre's "The 59th Street Bridge Song (Feelin' Groovy)," when two oboes, flute, French horn, and bassoon play in Donovan's "Jennifer Juniper," or when the flute is joined by oboe (at 0:10) and then bassoon (0:19) in an imitative texture in The Mamas and the Papas' "Dancing Bear." The traditional woodwind quintet (flute, oboe, clarinet, French horn, and bassoon) is occasionally called for, as in Phil Ochs's "I've Had Her."

The wind instrument logging most rock appearances is, of course, the band-oriented saxophone, which at one time was more ubiquitous than the guitar itself. Built in four common ranges (soprano, alto, tenor, and baritone), the two inner sizes are heard most often; there is also a rarely played bass saxophone. The use of the saxophone as both a melodic and an accompanimental instrument declined significantly in 1964, a year in which we have witnessed other radical changes in instrumentation. Table 4.01 attempts to track the usage of the five different-sized saxophones through our listening sample in recordings that feature only a single one, noting the instances in which the sax has a leading role (as in an entirely instrumental record) or takes a solo. (Listen to Web audio example 4.07 and see Web photos 4.07 and 4.08.) The soprano saxophone seems to make six appearances, including three as soloist (Bobby Vee's "Charms," the Rascals' "It's Wonderful," and the Mothers' "Call Any Vegetable"). The alto sax is heard in thirty-four solos from the years 1955–63 (3.8 per year, leading Billy Vaughn's "Melody of Love" and the hits of Bill Black's Combo, and including King Curtis's solo for the Coasters' "Yakety Yak"), whereas it is heard in only three solos from the period 1964–68 (0.6 per year, including Gladys Knight's "I Heard It Through the Grapevine"). The robust tenor, used much more overall, declines from eighty-eight solos in 1955–63 (9.8 per year, leading Mitch Miller's "Theme Song from 'Song for a Summer Night,'" contributing to Little Richard's hits and including Boots Randolph's playing in Johnny Tillotson's "Poetry in Motion") to twenty solos in 1964–68 (four per year, including the hits of the Classics IV and The Doors' "Touch Me"). The baritone sax, by contrast, seems to enjoy some new interest in the mid-1960s, climbing from three solos in 1960–63 to six in 1964–66, nearly all in Motown productions but also featuring in Lesley Gore's "Maybe I Know" and the Toys' "Attack" (with great registral contrast against the three ultrahigh vocals). The only bass sax appearances of which I am aware are in a 1965 solo in the Four Seasons' "Little Boy (In Grown Up Clothes)" and another from 1968, The Bonzo Dog Band's "My Pink Half of the Drainpipe."

The saxophone is difficult to play with truly satisfying intonation (it's wild in the Hilltoppers' "The Kentuckian Song," redolent of decadence in the Mothers' "Overture to a Holiday in Berlin," and both alto and bari are inexplicably sharp in Ron Holden's "Love You So"). But it has an occasionally useful gravelly

Table 4.01 Frequency of appearances of saxophones in *Billboard*'s weekly top-twenty songs, 1955–69. Shown for each size saxophone in each year are instances of solo or leading role/total appearances in recordings that feature a single saxophone.

Year	Soprano	Alto	Tenor	Baritone	Bass
1955		7/9	12/18	0/1	
1956		4/6	12/13		
1957		3/4	8/15	0/3	
1958		5/8	14/16	0/3	
1959		4/12	5/11	0/4	
1960		6/13	8/11	1/2	
1961	0/1	2/6	10/13	1/3	
1962		1/5	11/14	0/2	
1963	1/1	2/3	8/12	1/4	
1964		1/2	3/8	2/6	
1965		0/2	5/7	3/7	
1966			5/7	1/7	
1967	0/1	1/1	4/4	0/5	
1968	1/2	1/5	3/2	0/2	
1969	1/1	5/7	4/5	0/1	

sound, created when the player excites nonharmonic multiphonics from the horn. Note how the alto's first chorus in the Champs' "Tequila" is played clean and the second, dirty. This color creates great effect in Little Richard's "Can't Believe You Wanna Leave" (the tenor matching the vocal texture), at the end of the tenor solo in Brenda Lee's "Sweet Nothin's" (1:36–1:39, immediately imitated by Lee in some bluesy shouts), and with the dirty tenor buzzing for obvious reasons through Chubby Checker's "The Fly." By contrast, the amateurish alto honking by Mike Love in the Beach Boys' "Shut Down" allows much too strong a first overtone, producing a strong buzzing octave that's just out of control in 0:55–1:04 and not particularly expressive of anything. The saxophone can also have a very breathy sound, and this noise, if desired, can be captured with a close miking technique, as done with Stan Getz's "Desafinado" and Dusty Springfield's "The Look of Love." Chris Wood runs his sax through a wah pedal on Traffic's "Glad," Frank Zappa uses a ring modulator to create two lines in octaves from a single alto performance in "King Kong," and an alto sax is sent through a phaser in Blood, Sweat and Tears' "Variations on a Theme by Eric Satie." One sax is often paired with another (two tenors ply the waves in Frankie Ford's "Sea Cruise," alto and tenor play in unison on Van Morrison's "Domino," and tenor and bari play in octaves in the Supremes' "Baby Love") or with a trumpet (alto and trumpet move from unison to harmony in Hugh Masekela's "Grazing in the Grass"), or grouped in small reed sections (as in the Beatles' "Lady Madonna" and the Stones' "Honky Tonk Women").

Many other wind instruments are too informal for the band or orchestra, but are right at home in pop-music recordings. Several involve reeds, as do the harmonica (often played as a blues harp), and the Melodica. There are several different harmonicas; most allow both the inhaling and the expulsion of air, and some include a sliding switch to obtain pitches outside the major scale. Some, like the bass harmonica, are much larger than others. (Listen to Web audio example 4.08 and see Web photo 4.09.) The blues harp, by which players generally restrict their playing to scale degrees 1, ♭3, 4, 5, and ♭7, is heard in such numbers as Bob Dylan's "Pledging My Time," Little Stevie Wonder's "Fingertips," the Rolling Stones' "Not Fade Away," Millie Small's "My Boy Lollipop," and Count Five's "Psychotic Reaction," as well as many Cream performances. Major-mode playing is heard on Roy Orbison's "Blue Bayou," Dylan's "Just Allow Me One More Chance" and many others, and Frank Ifield's "I Remember You." The chromatic harmonica is played on Billy Vaughn's "When the White Lilacs Bloom Again," Patti Page's "Allegheny Moon," and Stevie Wonder's "For Once In My Life," and the bass harmonica chugs away on the Beach Boys' "I Know There's an Answer," the Beatles' "Being for the Benefit of Mr. Kite," and Simon and Garfunkel's "The Boxer." The harmonica's sound can be varied with a tremolo produced by the rapid wavering of hands cupped around it and by pitch bends. Like the harmonicas, the Melodica also works with reeds vibrated by breath, but the breath is directed by a short keyboard, so its sound is something like that of a harmonium. This may be the leading instrument on Henry Mancini's "Moon River" and may be heard on the Marvelettes' "The Hunter Gets Captured by the Game."

The kazoo is a short metal or plastic tube with a thin cellophane or fiber diaphragm that amplifies whatever pitch is voiced by the singing—not humming!—player's vocal cords. (Listen to Web audio example 4.09 and see Web photo 4.09.) It's often used in a jug band setting (Country Joe and the Fish's "I-Feel-Like-I'm-Fixin'-To-Die Rag," which also includes a jew's harp and someone's blowing on tuned wine bottles, and Arlo Guthrie's "Ring-Around-a-Rosy Rag") or music-hall satire (David Gilmour's playing in Pink Floyd's "Corporal Clegg"), and it can sound populist, sneering, and silly (the Mothers' "God Bless America," Ginny Arnell's "Dumb Head"), but it can also be used as a legitimate wind instrument, as with the countermelody in Dion and the Belmonts' "Little Diane." In their apparent quest to use everything imaginable, the Beatles get a similar sound from comb and tissue paper, with lots of reverb, in "Lovely Rita."

The jew's harp, whereby the vibration of a thin metal reedlike spring set into motion by finger-plucked trigger is conducted through a metal frame held against the teeth, allowing the vibration to be amplified and colored by the size and shape of the oral cavity, is heard in the opening of the Spokesmen's tongue-in-cheek "The Dawn of Correction" and the bridge of the Beach Boys' "Good Vibrations" (1:42–2:43). (Listen to Web audio example 4.10 and see Web photo 4.09.) The ocarina or sweet potato, an enclosed clay bowl with fingerholes, was much more popular in the 1940s (Bing Crosby's "Sweet Potato Piper" runs four ocarinas up against an orchestra), but it has a solo in the Lovin' Spoonful's carefree "Henry Thomas" (0:36–0:44, heard along with slide whistle, 0:00+, and jew's harp, 0:08+) and Senator Bobby's farcical "Wild Thing" (played along with kazoo), and it seems dead serious as the main melodic instrument in Hugo Montenegro's "The Good, the Bad and the Ugly." A group of simple party horns is heard at the end of most mixes of the Rascals' "It's Wonderful," a slide whistle appears in Mitch Ryder and the Detroit Wheels' "Sock It to Me—Baby!" and Procol Harum's "Mabel," a tin Irish whistle is played in the Incredible String Band's "Lordly Nightshade" and the Irish Rovers' "The Unicorn," and a siren-type whistle is heard in Jaye P. Morgan's "Pepper-Hot Baby," Bob Dylan's "Highway 61 Revisited," and Ray Stevens' "The Streak." A drum major blows a police whistle in the Overture to *The Music Man,* and the same effect is used as a metaphorical wakeup call back to reality in the Mothers of Invention's "Status Back Baby" and then as a sign of a referee in the opening to Mel and Tim's "Backfield in Motion."

The centuries-old recorder had some use in folk settings; made in many different sizes, a quartet of different recorders can be heard in Led Zeppelin's "Stairway to Heaven." The soprano recorder is played by Terry Kirkman in the Association's "Along Comes Mary" and the lower-pitched alto recorder is heard in both Brian Jones's countermelody to the Stones' "Ruby Tuesday" (which might be heard as an answer to the ocarina in the Troggs' "Wild Thing") and Grace Slick's sensitive playing in Jefferson Airplane's "Comin' Back to Me." (Listen to Web audio example 4.11 and see Web photo 4.10.) The Beatles responded to this trend with a plastic recorder, heard along with the flutes and bass harmonica in "Fool on the Hill," and Cream used two plastic recorders in "Pressed Rat and Warthog." Paul McCartney was taught how to play the recorder by Margaret Asher, who had previously taught the oboe to Beatles producer George Martin, at the Guildhall School of Music and Drama in London. Finally, non-Western wind instruments sometimes make their way into rock releases as with the Beatles' "The Inner Light," which features the Indian sahnai, an oboelike double-reed instrument.

Wind-band arrangements have been very effective in the pop-rock world. One of Randy Newman's first major successes was his 1969 wind arrangement for Peggy Lee's "Is That All There Is?," perfectly capturing the lurid side of the carnival. George Martin brought back the 1930s English sweet band for the Beatles' "Honey Pie." Frank Zappa lends the wind band a new life with speed-adjusted tape and solid-state electronic alteration in many tracks for *Uncle Meat* and *Weasels Ripped My Flesh*. Deep Purple's "April" pits woodwinds against strings in between sections for church organ and rock band for a unique twelve-minute track.

Brass

Also wind-powered but classified separately from the instruments we've just covered are the brass family. The French horn (simply, the "horn"), the trumpet, cornet, flügelhorn, trombone, bass

> **Brass:** The French horn, trumpet, flügelhorn, trombone, and tuba.

trombone, and tuba are the brass instruments of choice for rock musicians, their producers, and arrangers. In all of these, a cup- or funnel-shaped mouthpiece enables the player to buzz the lips to set vibrating the air contained in a brass tube, which ends in a flared bell for amplification. By adjusting lip tension and air speed, the player can determine whether the tube's fundamental or one of its harmonics will sound. (The column of air vibrates in several simultaneous divisions, just as does a string. The woodwind player must also be able to overblow to activate different harmonics, but for not nearly as many as must a brass player.) For each harmonic, the player can choose as many as seven different pitches, controlled by either a combination of spring-back piston or rotary valves opened by the fingers, or in the case of the trombones, the position of the slide which is let out by the right hand to different lengths, all of which adjustments—valve or slide—control the total length of the tube. Breath control is responsible for most of the resulting tonal qualities, but the brass player also has a collection of mutes (most common are the straight mute, the cup mute, the wah-wah mute, and the plunger). Sometimes, the performer is asked to aim into the stand or play from offstage (offmike) to reduce the instrument's force and brilliance. In addition, the French hornist must constantly fine-tune the pitch by working the free hand in the bell, which can also mute the sound when blocking enough of the opening. Although the trombonist can produce a real glissando simply by pulling or pushing the slide, all brass—particularly the horn with its wide range—are capable of the lip gliss, where the player skips up from one pitch to others through a series of harmonics.

The French horn sometimes presents an opening melody in an instrumental piece, as with Ferrante and Teicher's "Exodus" or Henry Mancini's "Days of Wine and Roses," or is reserved for a later, contrasting section, as in Percy Faith's "Theme From a Summer Place" or Al Caiola's "Bonanza," but is used much more often to underscore a song with a countermelody, as in Sam Cooke's "Cupid," Peter and Gordon's "True Love Ways," the Four Tops' "Bernadette," and the Bee Gees' "Words." (Listen to Web audio example

Photo 4.02. Eric Brummitt on French horn. (Photo: Annie Eastman)

4.12 and see Web photos 4.11 and 4.12.) An opening horn duet is heard in both Mary Wells's "My Guy" and Engelbert Humperdinck's "Release Me (and Let Me Love Again)." The horn can have a wistful, nostalgic quality, put to advantage in Bobby Vinton's "Mr. Lonely," Aretha Franklin's "A Natural Woman (You Make Me Feel Like)" (1:08–1:30), the Beatles' "For No One," and the Young Rascals' "I've Been Lonely Too Long" ("as I look back…"). Used more forcefully, it can seem to sound a warning, as in the Cheers' "Black Denim Trousers" and Marvin Gaye's "I Heard It Through the Grapevine" (with its octave gliss at 0:17–0:21). Other glisses appear in Little Anthony and the Imperials' "Goin' Out of My Head" and The Who's "Pictures of Lily" (apparently symbolizing John Entwistle's solution at 1:28–1:36 to the delicately phrased "childhood problem"). The solo horn from 2:30 to the end in Elvis Presley's "Don't Cry Daddy" seems a subtle rewrite of the flügelhorn solo from the Beatles' "Mother Nature's Son."

Members of the trumpet family (including the shrill piccolo trumpet, and the mellower cornet and flügelhorn) are heard in 120 top-twenty songs of 1955–69, far more than any other brass instruments, and more than double the number of appearances for the most widely scored woodwind type, the flute. The piccolo trumpet makes its sole appearance in the Beatles' "Penny Lane" (1:09–1:26 and 2:20–2:49, left); classical player David Mason had been contracted for the session after McCartney had heard him play the Bach F-major Brandenburg Concerto on television. The cornet is standard in the Dixieland band, and so is heard in Louis Armstrong's "Mack the Knife" and "Hello, Dolly!," Kenny Ball's "Midnight in Moscow," and the Village Stompers' "Washington Square," but is also played by Nat Adderly in duet with "Cannonball" Adderly's alto sax in "Mercy, Mercy, Mercy" and "Why? (Am I Treated So Bad)." The deeper flügelhorn is featured in Randy Brecker's solo in Blood, Sweat and Tears' "Without Her" and in octaves with trumpet in their "And When I Die"; it becomes a much more familiar sound in the 1970s, particularly in the hands of Chuck Mangione.

Special trumpet effects are somewhat rare: the fingered trill is demonstrated in the low register in the intro to Blood, Sweat and Tears' "You've Made Me So Very Happy" and a tremolo between two pitches is heard in the Bar-Kays' "Soul Finger"; glissandos are lipped in "Soul Finger" as well, in the extreme in Perez Prado's "Cherry Pink and Apple Blossom White" and Louis Prima's "Wonderland By Night," and also in some sassy rolling notes in Priscilla Wright's "The Man in the Raincoat." Double- and triple-tonguing allows rapid articulation in Hugh Masekela's "Grazing in the Grass" and the Mothers of Invention's "You Didn't Try to Call Me." (Listen to Web audio example 4.13 and see Web photo 4.13.) Mutes are used widely, as in the solo in Patti Page's "The Tennessee Waltz" (1:33–1:50, recorded far from the microphone), in the New Vaudeville Band's "Winchester Cathedral" (straight mute), and in Ray Davies's cool cup-mute closing improvisation of Petula Clark's "Downtown." Wild wah-wah trumpets are given a low-register repeat of their introductory figure as if attempting to calm down in preparation for Shirley Bassey's vocal in "Goldfinger," and are used by a whole trumpet section in Bobby Darin's "Beyond the Sea." Another effect is created with Miles Davis's heavy tape echo in the introduction to Bitches Brew. Intonation is generally not an issue with fine studio players (often imported from the local orchestra)—it can be just stunning in its perfection, as in the Grass Roots' "Midnight Confessions" (note the trumpets in the bridge, 0:52–1:01, and the trombones in the following verse, 1:09–1:19). But then again there's the case of the Buckinghams' "Kind of a Drag." Here, trumpets accompanied the organ solo playing so sharp that they were wisely mixed out of the original monophonic single. The stereo mix (used in lip-synched television appearances in 1967 and thus audible on YouTube), however, retains them in all of their ugly exuberance.

The trumpet is generally too loud to be assigned a countermelody part outside of a full brass section (note how the trumpet is brought into the chorus of Mark Lindsay's "Arizona" for contrast with the quiet verses), but one is attempted underneath the second verse of the Bee Gees' "How Can You Mend a Broken Heart." It's much more often in the forefront with a solo, as in Brenda Lee's "Losing You," Herb Alpert and the Tijuana Brass's "The Lonely Bull," Barbara George's "I Know (You Don't Love Me No More)," and the Drifters' "On Broadway." One might compare trumpet parts in Ben E. King's "Spanish Harlem" and Bruce Springsteen's much later "With Every Wish." In the Young Rascals' "How Can I Be Sure," a solo trumpet (1:22–1:30) builds great tension in a high-register countermelody, culminating in a big full-brass break (1:48–2:04). The trumpet is often given room to improvise, as in Bert Kaempfert's "Red Roses for a Blue Lady," Al Hirt's "Java," the Byrds' "So You Want to Be a Rock 'N' Roll Star," and in a swirl of trumpets and trombones that suggest insanity in Elvis Presley's odd flip-side, "Edge of Reality."

The trumpet has a few ready-made associations, as with patriotism (sounding martial in Ray Charles's "America the Beautiful"), all things regal (the Hollies' "King Midas in Reverse"), Latin drama (Procol Harum's "Conquistador" and the intro to Zager and Evans's "In the Year 2525") and, in pairs, the Mexican mariachi band (Bob Moore's "Mexico" and Jay and the Americans' "Come a Little Bit Closer"). Trumpets can sustain for a subdued organlike quality (as in Percy Sledge's "When a Man Loves a Woman" or the Turtles' "Happy Together"), solo with clipped articulation for a jaunty nonchalance (Herb Alpert's "A Taste of Honey," Dionne Warwick's "Walk On By"), or stab with brash punctuation (Sammy Davis Jr.'s "Something's Gotta Give," Len Barry's "1–2–3," or portraying a "nagging irritation" on (4)—and—ONE stabs in the Supremes' "Love Is Like an Itching in My Heart"). They can screech in the stratosphere (the American Breed's "Step Out of Your Mind," Tommy James and the Shondells' "Sweet Cherry Wine," and just before the alto solo in Blood, Sweat and Tears' "God Bless the Child") or, in three anomalous 1968 hits (Hugo Montenegro's "The Good, The Bad and the Ugly," Gary Puckett and the Union Gap's "Lady Willpower," and O. C. Smith's "Little Green Apples"), send a symbolic signal that a modulation is about to occur. One trumpet is often paired with another (in unison and then in thirds in Bob Crewe's "Music to Watch Girls By," to refer to a cigarette jingle in Arthur Conley's "Sweet Soul Music," and somehow to suggest cunning seduction in Tom Jones's "Delilah" and "Love Me Tonight"), with a trombone (in the Toys' "A Lover's Concerto" and before the last bridge in Jay & the Americans' "This Magic Moment"), with a saxophone (tenor and muted cornet sustain in octaves for the break in Bobby Lewis's "Tossin' and Turnin'" and "One Track Mind"; tenor and trumpet pair off in the Four Seasons' "Let's Hang On"), or with a vocalist (as when the trumpet's tune is joined by Dionne Warwick's vocalized upper harmony in "I Say a Little Prayer").

Although chiefly a bass-register instrument, the trombone plays well in its upper range, with solo melodies in the Four Freshmen's "Charmaine," the Fleetwoods' "Mr. Blue," and Ronnie Dove's "Cry," and a countermelody under the second verse of Billy Vera and Judy Clay's "Storybook Children." (Listen to Web audio example 4.14 and see Web photos 4.14–4.16.) Unison trombones carry the tune in its more traditional range in Ray Anthony's "Peter Gunn." It suggests a standard bass line (supporting I—IV—V—IV with a bass line of roots only) in the opening of Merrilee Rush's "Angel of the Morning," and sustains a bass pedal in the Four Seasons' "Working My Way Back to You" (0:27–0:32), Herb Alpert and the Tijuana Brass's "A Taste of Honey" (1:23+), and the Temptations' "Ain't Too Proud to Beg" (0:33+). The pedal is particularly effective on the bass trombone, as in Ray Anthony's "Peter Gunn" (on the right) and the Beach Boys' "Here Today" (which also provides a very low glissando at 0:08–0:15). The trombone is closely associated with the march, and thus provides the contrasting section of Mitch Miller's "March from the River Kwai/Colonel Bogey" and is of course a traditional member of the Dixieland band, joining with cornet, clarinet, and others in numbers mentioned in this context previously. In block harmony with horns, it announces a modulation and a new section in Mason Williams's "Classical Gas."

The glissando is naturally the trombone's most conspicuous effect, and it suggests a lascivious phallic thrust in David Rose's "The Stripper" and Peter and Gordon's "Lady Godiva," a raucous rakishness in Dylan's "Rainy Day Women #12 & 35," and perhaps more innocent associations in Ray Stevens's "Harry the Hairy Ape" and the 5th Dimension's "Sweet Blindness." But the trombonist can wobble the slide for a wide vibrato, providing a very weak-kneed lack of support for Gene McDaniels' "Tower of Strength." A trombonist sets the tone for Major Lance's "The Monkey Time" and "Hey Little Girl" with loud first-beat blats that would be considered to be in very poor taste in other genres. Because of the muddy low register, trombones do not often pair up in separate parts, but they do so quite effectively in Benny Spellman's "Lipstick Traces (On a Cigarette)." A different ensemble decision, to have the trombone double the singer in the bridge of the Buckinghams' "Don't You Care," works out rather disastrously, to my ear. Naturally, the trombone can double an electric bass quite well, as does a bass trombone in Edwin Starr's "Twenty-Five Miles," doubling trumpets as well in a minor-pentatonic line in the verse.

The tuba plays in its high register for a solo in Jackie DeShannon's "What the World Needs Now Is Love" but is otherwise relegated to the bass line. Here, it will appear either on its own (in James Ray's "If You Gotta Make a Fool of Somebody," Simon and Garfunkel's "The Boxer" (4:20+), The Band's "Rag Mama Rag") or doubling the electric bass (as in Peter and Gordon's "Lady Godiva" and Mary Hopkin's "Those Were the Days," 3:13+). (Listen to Web audio example 4.15 and see Web photo 4.17.)

Groups of brass nearly always include saxophones as well, either in a big-band arrangement as in Richard Maltby's "Theme From 'Man With the

Photo 4.03. Neil Sisauyhoat on glockenspiel. Behind him, left to right, we see the marimba, xylophone, guitar amplifier, tubular bells, and mallet silo on floor. (Photo: Annie Eastman)

Golden Arm,'" James Brown's Famous Flames (two trumpets, trombone, and three mixed saxes as in "I'll Go Crazy" and "Papa's Got a Brand New Bag"), or a Muscle Shoals section like the single cornet with two tenors and baritone in Aretha Franklin's "I Never Loved a Man (The Way I Love You)." Similar groups were heard in the studios of Motown (for Stevie Wonder's "Uptight (Everything's Alright)") and Stax (for Wilson Pickett's "In the Midnight Hour"). Brass players always have the last word in arrangements that build up from nothing to a big finish, ranging from Ssgt Barry Sadler's "The Ballad of the Green Berets" to the Beatles' "Hey Jude."

Mallet instruments and other pitched percussion

We turn next to the percussion section, chiefly to the pitched instruments that were not covered earlier alongside the drums and hand percussion in chapter 1. Four instruments, the xylophone, marimba, vibraphone (vibes), and orchestra bells (glockenspiel), are mallet instruments, each laid out with dozens of long bars arranged like a keyboard.

> **Pitched percussion:** the xylophone, marimba, vibraphone, glockenspiel, tubular bells, hand bells, steel drums, and water glasses.

Generally, the xylophone's range extends a bit higher than that of the others, and the marimba's (and certainly the bass marimba's) extends lower. (Listen to Web audio examples 4.16 and 4.17, and see Web photos 4.18 and 4.19.) But composition of the bars is the chief determinant of sound color: the xylophone has very hard wooden bars that sound brittle, brilliant, and have little or no sustain, although modern instruments are fitted with resonator tubes beneath each bar to improve that a bit. The xylophone can be heard in the Beach Boys' "All Summer Long," Lesley Gore's "You Don't Own Me" (with lots of tape echo through the introduction), and in a virtuosic display by Ruth Underwood, in the Mothers' "Wowie Zowie." Paul McCartney seems to be playing a toy xylophone in the second verse of "Junk." The marimba has larger rosewood bars and cylindrical resonators for a richer but more of a hollow tone, particularly in the deeper registers. To get the effect of a long note on either a xylophone or a marimba, the player must roll two mallets for a single-pitch tremolo; this is done on the xylophone (on, perhaps, wrong notes?) in the solo of Betty Everett's "The Shoop Shoop Song (It's In His Kiss)," and on the marimba in Sam Cooke's "It's All Right" and Herb Alpert and the Tijuana Brass's "Tijuana Taxi" (soloing at 1:02–1:24). The marimba opens Kyu Sakamoto's "Sukiyaki" and Herb Alpert's "A Taste of Honey," and is the featured instrument of Ben E. King's "Spanish Harlem" and Billy Joe and the Checkmates' "Percolator (Twist)." A bass marimba supports Zal Yanovsky's vocal imitation of Howlin' Wolf in the Lovin' Spoonful's "Voodoo in My Basement."

The much more often heard vibraphone has bell-like metal bars, resonator tubes, and a damper pedal that can allow quite a bit of sustain when engaged. In addition, a small speed-adjustable single-blade electric fan is placed at the top of each tube to produce a discontinuous flow of vibrating air into the resonators and therefore a strong tremolo. (Listen to Web audio example 4.18 and see Web photos 4.20 and 4.21.) The sustain pedal is demonstrated in the Arthur Lyman Group's "Love for Sale," in the intro to Shelley Fabares' "Johnny Angel," and in Herman's Hermits' "I Can Take Or Leave Your Loving" (which opens unpedaled for six seconds, followed by the pedaled remainder). The fans are turned off in Mary Wells and Marvin Gaye's "Once Upon a Time" and are given an excellent audition in the opening of the Supremes' "I Hear a Symphony." They rotate slowly in the Beach Boys' "Let's Go Away for Awhile" and Pink Floyd's "Set the Controls for the Heart of the Sun," and very quickly in the Temptations' "It's Growing." Vibes provide soft backing with strings after the first chorus in the Guess Who's "These Eyes" and have a subtle role in the Turtles' "She's My Girl." Frank Zappa recoups the vibraphone's jazz history when it interrupts the flow of *Lumpy Gravy* with several appearances of the "Oh No" theme. The vibes are often used to double the bass, as in transitional licks between verses of the First Edition's "Just Dropped In (To See What Condition My Condition Was In)." They retain a featured role when played by Buzzy Linhart in John Sebastian's "Magical Connection" but have a secondary yet familiar rhythmic role in the Supremes' work of 1964 through 1966. Steam's "Na Na Hey Hey Kiss Him Goodbye" features two vibes parts. In terraced recordings, where the sound grows and grows with the continual addition of instruments, the vibraphone often begins the process softly, as in the bridge (1:50+) of the Righteous Brothers' "You've Lost That Lovin' Feelin'" (where vibes and bass alone support Bill Medley's vocal), Bobby Hebb's "Sunny" (where vibes and bass alone accompany the first verse), and Simon and Garfunkel's "Bridge Over Troubled Water" (vibes are added to the already featured piano for Artie's second verse at 1:45). Notably, Phil Spector's Wrecking Crew performed in both the Righteous Brothers and the Simon and Garfunkel productions. Arthur Lyman's "Yellow Bird" offers a good comparison of vibraphone (beginning with the melody on the right) and marimba (entering 0:04 to accompany on the left); at 1:02–1:36, the marimba takes over the melody in tremolo while the vibes provide harmony.

Usually played with a brass mallet, the very high-pitched glockenspiel is heard quite often, and indeed can be difficult to discern from the highest register of a vibraphone with its fan turned off. (Listen to Web audio example 4.19 and see Web photo 4.22.) The glock often doubles the lead melody to help it cut through the full ensemble, as in the Shades of Blue's "Oh How Happy," Don Costa's "Never On Sunday," and the Grateful Dead's "St. Stephen" (1:38–1:29). It also may have its own glittering independent line cutting through, as in Neil Sedaka's "Calendar Girl," James and Bobby Purify's "I'm Your Puppet," Simon and Garfunkel's "Scarborough Fair/Canticle," and Cream's "Passing the Time."

Two instruments based on tuned bells are tubular bells (orchestral chimes) and Swiss hand bells. Tubular bells, rising to fame in 1974 by way of Mike Oldfield's recording named after the lead instrument, had already received quite a bit of work in the '50s and '60s. This tall rack of eighteen to twenty hanging cylinders of tubular brass would be struck by a wooden or rawhide hammer and left to ring or be damped by pedal. (Listen to Web audio example 4.20 and see Web photo 4.23.) Chimes may have their own tune, as in the opening of the Sand Pebbles' "Love Power," or may mark important harmonic pitches, as in the Association's "Cherish" (alternating fifth and first scale degrees on each chord at 0:18+ in the verse), but they have trouble escaping association with the chimes of the village square (as in Les Baxter's "Wake the Town and Tell the People," the Royal Guardsmen's "Snoopy's Christmas," and Glen Campbell's "The Universal Soldier") and more particularly of the church (for the "chapel in the pines" in Lou Christie's "Lightnin' Strikes," for "bells will ring" in the Dixie Cups' "Chapel of Love," and for related places in Donnie Brooks's "Mission Bells," Brenda Lee's "Rusty Bells," Herman's Hermits' "East West," and the Righteous Brothers' "He"). In the Diamonds' "The Church Bells May Ring," they do so with a swinging, rocking solo (0:42–0:51). Handbells are shaken by a wooden handle by choir members, each of whom is responsible for two or more. A single handbell is rung at the mention of a fireman in the Beatles' "Penny Lane," but several are at work, along with tubular bells, in the intro to the Rascals' "A Beautiful Morning" and in Cream's "Those Were the Days" (at 0:26+).

Photo 4.04. The string quartet. From left front we see Fabián López, first violin; Megan Fergusson, viola; Nicholas Finch, cello; and Jeanine Markley, second violin. (Photo: Annie Eastman)

Finally, we take note of the steel drums and water glasses. The former is traditionally a Trinidadian and Jamaican adaptation of differently sized oil drums whose tops are banged into facets that, when struck, provide approximate pitches. They provide a Caribbean flavor for the Hollies' "Carrie-Anne" and also, a bit incongruously, for the Happenings' Sanskrit-tongued "Where Do I Go/Be-In/Hare Krishna." Water glasses, perhaps crystal goblets, produce mesmerizing tones when their edges are rubbed by wet fingers; this is the technique behind Paul McCartney's "Glasses" (1:29, followed by the snippet of the piano-based "Suicide"). When filled with different amounts of water, the rubbed glasses can be tuned to a scale and take on a richly harmonic tone (like that of Benjamin Franklin's glass harmonica), but such usage is unknown in our repertoire.

Stringed instruments

The string section completes our instrumentation palette. The modern orchestral strings consist of the violin, viola, cello, and string bass. These four are alike in construction except for their increasing size, and in playing technique except for decreasing agility of response as the strings get thicker and longer. With spruce tops and maple backs and sides, the basic acoustical properties of these instruments—string vibration transferred to a resonating, amplifying box through a bridge—are similar to those of the acoustic guitar, but there is much more attention given to the carving of the top in addition to the accurate placement of a bass bar along the inside of the top and a sound post that transfers the bridge vibration directly to the resonant back, to help achieve the desired rich overtone patterns across the pitch and loudness spectrums. These instruments are generally bowed, giving the player constant control over very expressive changes in articulation, phrasing, vibrato, and dynamics. There are many different bowing techniques: many successive notes can be played on a single bow for a smooth phrase, or the bow may change direction for each note for more of a detached sound; the notes will have a very short staccato sound if the bow is bounced off of the string. Alternatively, the strings may also be plucked. One player can appear alone as a soloist, a chamber group can be formed with one player per part in just about any combination, or small sections can grow intro a chamber orchestra with multiple players per part (although, because of phasing problems, it generally sounds best when there are not two per part; one weak pair is heard in the Joe Jeffrey Group's "My Pledge of Love"). As the string bass has already been covered in chapter 2 as provider of the bass line, this role will not be reviewed here. (Listen to Web audio examples 4.21–4.23, and see Web photos 4.24–4.28.)

Strings: The violin, viola, cello, concert harp, and cimbalon; the full orchestra.

Strings may be integral to a recording, as in Dinah Washington's "What a Diff'rence a Day Makes," or constitute a post-production add-on of little consequence, as in the imitation of the singer in Brenda Lee's "I'm Sorry," the filler punctuation added by Snuff Garrett to Bobby Vee's "Stayin' In," and the many Buddy Holly demos such as "Raining in My Heart" and "It Doesn't Matter Anymore" given posthumous strings by Dick Jacobs. A very common role for strings is as background sweetener, through organ-like sustained chords, as in the Everly Brothers' tender "Let It Be Me," the Beach Boys' "Don't Talk (Put Your Head on My Shoulder)" (1:01+) and "God Only Knows" (second verse and thereafter), or the Box Tops' "The Letter." Some string parts can work in the background and still help tie everything together; as an example, follow the two violin sections in Lulu's "To Sir With Love," and you'll hear that the dissonance created by the fifth and fourth over the bass to which the opening fifth and third move at 0:05 never resolves until the very final chord of the recording. Strings may play a rhythmic role, as in Chuck Jackson's "I Don't Want to Cry," Aretha Franklin's "A Natural Woman (You Make Me Feel Like)," and Shadow Morton's strident pre-"Love Child" arrangement in the Shangri-Las' "I Can Never Go Home Anymore" (at the shouts of "Mama!," 2:06+). At the opposite extreme, rhythm can be totally lacking, as in the high pedals of the last verse, 1:37–1:49, of the Beatles' "Yesterday" or the high violin section in Nilsson's "Everybody's Talkin'," which tries to ascend from its two-verse-long pedal on fifth scale degree up to the first, rising up 5—6—7 only to fall back to 5. Or, both rhythmic and static aims can be combined, as in the violins' pedal with Morse-code-like repeated articulations in Glen Campbell's "Wichita Lineman." Extremely high violin melodies are rare, but are heard in the Four Seasons' "Will You Love Me Tomorrow" (2:28–2:35) and the Supremes' "In and Out of Love" (1:53–1:57).

Les Baxter's "The Poor People of Paris" makes for an excellent illustration of contrasting bowing techniques, with a violin section articulating each of the first four phrases differently. The first phrase is played very much off the string, violin notes bouncing over harp arpeggiations; the answering second phrase is played in long sustained bows. In the second verse, the opening phrase is played with all notes plucked, and is answered by a final fourth phrase in bowed tremolo. Similar contrasts can be heard in the Stone Poneys' "Different Drum"; note how the solo passage (harpsichord and plucked string bass) is followed by a bridge of two phrases. The first phrase and a half ("oh, don't get me wrong…") has a solo cello arpeggiating very much off the string, and the bridge's last few bars ("all I'm sayin's I'm not ready…") end with long sustained bows in the strings. Elsewhere, off-the-string staccato bows are heard in Cilla Black's "You're My World," the chorus of Mary Hopkin's "Those Were the Days," and in the second chorus of James Taylor's "Carolina in My Mind." Trills, the rapid alternations of two pitches a step apart, are not heard much in this literature, but they do simulate sobbing in Roy Orbison's "Only the Lonely (Know How I Feel)." Fingered tremolo, for a rapid alternation of two pitches more than a step apart, can be heard in the violins' introduction to Donnie Brooks' "Doll House," but bowed tremolo, where the same pitch is bowed in rapid repetition, is much more common. This technique brings the tension of high drama to the intros of Paul Anka's "Destiny" and Gary Puckett and the Union Gap's "Young Girl," and a tingling excitement to the opening of the Delfonics' "La-La Means I Love You." Bowed tremolo reminds the listener what a "symphony"—of course, a metaphor for the same tingling excitement noted in the Delfonics—might be like at 0:26–0:27 in the Supremes' "I Hear a Symphony," and provides the material for a wavelike undulation of dynamics in the intro to Gerry and the Pacemakers' "Don't Let the Sun Catch You Crying."

String glissandi are very common; note how the opening descending cello gliss in Johnny Mathis's "Wonderful! Wonderful!" balances those rising whistled glisses. The orchestral glissandi in the Beatles' "A Day in the Life" are its album's (or any album's) most imitated moment, coming back in John Fred and His Playboy Band's "Judy in Disguise (With Glasses)," Johnny Rivers' "Summer Rain," the Arbors' "The Letter," and Moby Grape's "The Place in Time." Glisses sound maudlin when done with bowed tremolo in Bobbie Gentry's "Ode to Billie Joe" and sickly in the intro to Elvis's "Don't Cry Daddy." Plucked violin strings provide text-painting in Carole King's

"It Might as Well Rain Until September" and Tony Bennett's "Firefly," show just an expert sense of ensemble in Andy Williams's "Can't Get Used to Losing You," provide a tentative intro to set up a big climax in Marvin Gaye and Tammi Terrell's "Ain't No Mountain High Enough," and swing with anticipation in Arif Mardin's arrangement for the Young Rascals' "A Girl Like You." Sustained violin-section harmonics provide a superhigh glassy coloring to the opening of Bobby Vinton's "Mr. Lonely," the Temptations' "(Loneliness Made Me Realize) It's You That I Need" (1:17–1:28), Robert Knight's "Everlasting Love," and Nancy Sinatra and Lee Hazelwood's "Lady Bird" (1:38–2:03) and "Some Velvet Morning." In the 5th Dimension's expertly scored "Aquarius/Let the Sunshine In," the opening flute/alto flute duet joins with a tremolo-struck triangle over atmospheric violin harmonics before the electric bass and drums fade in.

The solo violin can suggest many styles. Helmut Zacharias is clearly a classically trained violinist in his solo work for the pop tune, "When the White Lilacs Bloom Again," and the anonymous violinist who provides the obbligato line in Carla Thomas's "Gee Whiz (Look at His Eyes)" clearly has similar chops. The violin carries a tune above electric guitar arpeggiations in Web audio example 11.23. At the opposite end of the style spectrum, the Appalachian fiddle appears in Hank Williams Sr.'s Cajun-style "Jambalaya (On the Bayou)" and the Beatles' more Texas swing-based "Don't Pass Me By." Probably the best rock fiddling is David LaFlamme's, as in It's a Beautiful Day's "Don and Dewey," but this sound is a country staple, from the double stops of Dale and Grace's "I'm Leaving It Up to You" to the doubling of the pedal-steel in Charley Pride's "Is Anybody Goin' to San Antone." The electric violin (initially an orchestral violin with a transducer attached to the bridge) is introduced by Sugar Cane Harris in a number of Frank Zappa tracks on *Hot Rats, Burnt Weeny Sandwich,* and *Weasels Ripped My Flesh.* John Cale, the best-known solo violist in rock, often played with amplification as well, as in the Velvet Underground and Nico, where he could hide behind Lou Reed's vocal reverb and a celesta ("Sunday Morning") or generate an awful feedback-inducing screech ("Heroin").

Outside of roles in larger groupings, the viola is pretty rare, but it is heard in beautiful counterpoint with a violin in the Hassles' "Every Step I Take (Every Move I Make)" and two violas play unassuming rhythm parts in the Beatles' "Hello Goodbye." The more distinctive solo cello gets much more work, from Peter and Gordon's "Knight in Rusty Armour" to Judy Collins's "Lord Gregory" (where it provides her sole accompaniment). The solo cello in its various registers has a wonderful interaction with acoustic guitar in Moby Grape's "He" and with a nylon-string guitar in Phil Ochs's "Pleasures of the Harbor." Two celli are played in unison by Jack Bruce in Cream's "As You Said" and "Passing the Time," and in harmony by John Lodge in the Moody Blues'

"Emily's Song." An interesting effect is created in the Bee Gees' "New York Mining Disaster 1941 (Have You Seen My Wife Mr. Jones)," where backing vocals in the chorus sound like a pair of cellos, only to be replaced by the real thing in the second verse. Pairs of violins are used fairly often, as in the duets of Ray Charles's "Crying Time" and Brook Benton's "So Many Ways."

I've listed a few solo appearances of string instruments, but these examples are few and far between, as string players are usually bought in bulk. Rock recording is unusual work for a lot of these people, who spend lifetimes improving their own interpretations of particular works for performances in front of audiences who themselves may have heard the repertoire many times over. Conversely, in the rock world, any number of string players will show up, typically for an overdub session, never before having seen their part, which they must sight-read while the conductor alone hears through headphones the previously recorded band and vocal parts. It was common in the '60s for concert performers to add their parts to a rock group's recording, collect their flat fee, and never know to which kids' record they had contributed. You will hear snide references from this crowd to "footballs," the empty notation of slow-moving bar-long white oval whole notes, perhaps twenty in a song, as opposed to the much more complex "black" pages filled with many hundreds of rapid-fire small-part-of-a-beat notes that can make classical string playing so demanding. But regardless of how the parts are written, string instruments sound good in various groupings, and we'll look at some of these here.

First is the string quartet: two violins, viola, and cello. (Listen to Web audio example 4.24 and see Web photos 4.29 and 4.30.) Introduced to the rock world via the Beatles' "Yesterday," where string parts were taken with only a few adjustments directly from McCartney's guitar playing, the quartet is heard alone in Simon and Garfunkel's "Old Friends" and Blood, Sweat and Tears' "The Modern Adventures of Plato, Diogenes and Freud," along with acoustic guitar in the Young Rascals' "No Love to Give," the Turtles' "Lady-O," and the Monkees' "I Wanna Be Free," and with one or two other classical instruments in the Left Banke's "Pretty Ballerina," Phil Ochs's "Flower Lady," and Donovan's "Lalena." The Temptations' "I Could Never Love Another (After Loving You)" is a good example of the basic range of each instrument: the recording opens with the solo cello, doubled an octave higher by the viola at 0:06, and joined by the two violins at 0:11, with the same line in three registers altogether. The Beatles' "Eleanor Rigby" places two players on each part for added strength, for an octet that plays a different four-line arrangement in each verse. For the Beatles' "She's Leaving Home," Mike Leander scored a sensitive nonet of harp and strings that vividly characterizes a lonely girl and her selfish parents. Many other chamber combinations involving strings populate the rock canon.

Like instruments also gather into sections small or large, everyone playing the same part. Groups of violins alone take the melody in the breaks of Lesley Gore's "You Don't Own Me," Dusty Springfield's "I Only Want to Be With You," and the New Colony Six's "Things I'd Like to Say," and provide the countermelodies to the second verses of Marianne Faithfull's "As Tears Go By" and Oliver's "Jean." Two violin sections a third apart take the instrumental break in the Drifters' "Under the Boardwalk," and two sections also play in the Classics IV's "Traces" (in both second verse and bridge). A viola section has a rare appearance on its own in the intro and break of Jaye P. Morgan's "The Longest Walk," in the break in Don Cornell's "Hold My Hand," and as a countermelody in the verse of Carla Thomas's "Gee Whiz (Look At His Eyes)"; violin and viola sections play the break in counterpoint in the Shirelles' "Will You Love Me Tomorrow" (1:59–2:13). Cello sections are not heard on their own, but in counterpoint with violas (the Troggs' "Love Is All Around") or violins (breaks in Bob Lind's "Elusive Butterfly" and The Mamas and the Papas' "I Saw Her Again"). Sections have staggered entries in Chad and Jeremy's "A Summer Song" (note the way the vocal duet is answered in the last two verses by violins, then violas, and then celli) and Petula Clark's "Don't Give Up" (listen as the celli enter in 1:53, violas in 1:55, first violins in 1:57, and second violins in 1:59). Paul Mauriat's "Love Is Blue" has an arrangement of increasing depth, whereby violins provide a countermelody to the oboe's opening tune, the bridge (0:55–1:13) features violins with the tune and violas providing counterpoint, and the third verse (1:18–1:38) assigns the melody to the cello section. Size of section may reflect historical style; the eighteenth century is best suggested with small independent sections, as in the Beatles' "Piggies" and one portion (2:00–2:18) of The Doors' "Touch Me," and a large, lush group will reflect more of a Romantic nineteenth-century style, as in Nelson Riddle's arrangements for Nat King Cole and Frank Sinatra, Paul Riser's for the Temptations (particularly the exciting work for "You're My Everything"), or Jimmie Haskell's big finish for Simon and Garfunkel's "Bridge Over Troubled Water." But there may be no such characteristic relation, as when a large string orchestra plays variations of Pachelbel's seventeenth-century Canon in Los Pop Tops' "Oh Lord, Why Lord."

One last member of the orchestral string section is the concert harp, which can play every note within a six-octave range. (Listen to Web audio example 4.25 and see Web photos 4.31 and 4.32.) It's almost always used with strings as part of a larger chamber or orchestral ensemble; it has a rare solo appearance in the Miracles' "I'll Try Something New" (solo, 1:11–1:24). It gives its name to the arpeggio, which may be extended over several octaves and played quite rapidly; see the Four Aces' "Mister Sandman" and the Grass Roots' "Bella Linda" (1:29–1:51). The glissando is also quite characteristic of the harp, used in Teresa Brewer's "A Tear Fell" and Emilio Pericoli's

"Al Di Lá." Harmonics are quite effective, as in Donovan's "Lalena" (1:00+) and the opening of Mary Hopkin's "Y Blodyn Gwyn." The harp evokes angels (Jimmy Clanton's "Venus In Blue Jeans"), the hereafter (Dion's "Abraham, Martin and John," between verses), hallucinations (Tommy James and the Shondells' "Mirage"), and transfigurative ecstasy (the Young Rascals' "A Girl Like You," 2:04–2:08). It signals a retransition, sometimes with cinematic pretensions, in both the Cowsills' "The Rain, the Park & Other Things" and the Bee Gees' "I Started a Joke."

An unusual string instrument, not a usual member of the symphony orchestra although it may appear with one, is the Hungarian cimbalon, sort of a large zither. (Listen to Web audio example 4.26 and see Web photo 4.33.) The cimbalon is a table-mounted, trapezoid-shaped harp played with sticks or mallets. Strings are arranged in courses (multiple strings tuned to the same pitch) in two groups. The group closest to the player constitutes a chromatic scale running a bit more than an octave, whereas the group further away from the player is tuned to allow for easily formed harmonic relations. Oddly, there are two bridges, each of a different height, running along each side of the harp; every odd string runs from the high bridge on the left to the low one on the right and every even string runs from the low bridge on the left to the high one on the right. This alternation of diagonal orientations allows the right hand and left hand each to have easy access to one of the two interlocked whole-tone scales (1—2—3—#4—#5—#6 and ♭2—♭3—4—5—6—7)! The cimbalon opens the Hollies' "Stop Stop Stop" and Mary Hopkin's "Those Were the Days," providing each with an east-European flavor, and it can also be heard in The Doors' "Alabama Song (Whisky Bar)" and the Association's "Pandora's Golden Heebie Jeebies." On each of the mallet instruments, metal, hard-rubber and soft-yarn mallets produce different tones.

The full orchestra has a significant role in some popular-music styles of the 1950s and '60s, but quite a limited one in rock. The booking of a large studio for so many performers, even for small flat fees, would drive up recording expenses to such a degree that label executives habitually approved of such arrangements only for fully composed music, where the sessions would require minimal rehearsal time, and in styles for which audiences loyal to that style were guaranteed. By the late '60s, this approach was still viable in producer/arranger-dominated pop music, but became impractical for the rock band's slow-to-germinate conception of their work. Whereas twenty-nine of the top-twenty hits of 1955 (as by Perry Como, Doris Day, and the Four Lads) and eleven of them in 1956 (Sammy Davis Jr., Jerry Vale, and Andy Williams) involved full orchestra, an average of only 3.7 top-twenty recordings annually over the following thirteen years used an orchestra, and these were by and large adult-oriented recordings by the likes of the Mormon Tabernacle Choir, Robert Goulet, Barbra Steisand, Petula Clark, and Tom Jones. Tellingly, neither of the two 1960s rock albums most notable for their use of orchestra, the Beatles' *Sgt. Pepper's Lonely Hearts Club Band* and the Moody Blues' *Days of Future Passed,* yielded a top-twenty hit. The rock orchestra was, and was to remain, an experimentalist's palette, surfacing in such one-off collaborations as the Beatles' worldwide satellite broadcast of their partly live June 25, 1967, performance with orchestra of "All You Need Is Love," the Rascals' unrecorded concert with the American Symphony Orchestra, Joseph Eger conducting, at the Garden State Arts Center (Holmdel, New Jersey), on July 11, 1968, and Deep Purple's *Concerto for Group and Orchestra* recorded with Malcolm Arnold and the Royal Philharmonic Orchestra on September 24, 1969, at the Royal Albert Hall.

Because the choice of instrumentation has an impact upon the way a song's vocals are supported, the manner in which a song's formal structure is articulated, the coloring of expressive qualities inherent in melodies and harmonies, and the physical embodiment of rhythm, the listener will do well to listen carefully to all manner of sound and technique of performance in order to gain an even more subtle understanding of instrumental roles than we have been able to relate in these pages. In our next chapter, we'll see how vocal colors and technique can range almost as widely as can the instrumental, and then we'll move on to those matters of form, melody, harmony, and rhythm on their own terms.

CHAPTER 5

Vocal Color, Technique, and Arrangement

The sound of the sound is often centered on a force not yet reckoned with—that of the human voice. Each singer has such a distinctive tonal quality, range, and method of articulation, and his and her work is so usually at the core of a recording's means of expression, that they are identified far more easily by even the most casual listener than are most of the instruments—let alone instrumentalists—that accompany them. Each singer should be thought of as an instrument—the primary source of vibration is a column of air, and one that is not at all regular in shape, creating an individual set of ratios of harmonic overtones for any singer. But the resonating body includes more than just the column of air, because all of the bones and tissues in that column's proximity—particularly the relationships of the tongue and soft palate—affect the tone color. The singer can support their breath with a taut diaphragm muscle squeezing the lungs uniformly for a larger-than-life tone (try singing along with the well-supported "hey!...hup!" backing vocals in the introductory backbeats in the Vogues' "Five O'Clock World"), or can vocalize with more of a natural speaking mechanism, yielding much more variety of less-controlled breathing patterns (and often a resulting lack of control over precision in pitch, dynamics, and other tonal factors).

Tautness or relaxation of the facial, neck, and chest muscles will determine how open or closed parts of the air column are, how much resonance the neighboring tissues with their varying densities will provide, and how natural the vibrato may be. In addition, the singer can control groups of muscles to focus the tone at different resonating points—the singer may move between a chest tone, a head tone, a falsetto or a nasal tone, depending upon where the vibration is shaped most strongly. If you can successfully imitate the tone qualities of a favorite singer, you are (most likely unconsciously!) manipulating many or all of these parameters. We'll cover here some of the most characteristic effects that make voices sound different, some of the varied ways the vocal instrument can be used, and some aspects of arranging for lead and backing vocals.

Vocal range and color

The lowest male voice range is that of the bass. (Listen to Web audio example 5.01.) Some of the absolutely lowest singing can be heard in Ray Walter's opening to Elvis Presley's "(Now and Then There's) A Fool Such As I," John Entwistle's "Boris the Spider" for The Who, and the beginning of every verse of Moby Grape's "Murder in My Heart for the Judge." The infrequent exposure of the low bass often seems to be reserved for contrast against an ultra-high voice, as against the falsetto in the Diamonds' "She Say (Oom Dooby Doom)" and with Nick Massi's brief solo lines against the reigning Frankie Valli in the Four Seasons' first hits, "Sherry" (Nick: "why don't you..."), "Big Girls Don't Cry" ("silly boy"), and "Walk Like a Man" ("he said...," "I'm gonna..."). Bass vocalists range from Joe Williams's jazzy sonorities through a reverent Ed Ames's deep resonance ("My Cup Runneth Over") and an insincere Frank Zappa's breathy sound focused in the mouth ("Fountain of Love") to a shunned Johnny Cash's toneless yet powerful cadences in "Rock Island Line" and "Folsom Prison Blues." The bass solo may be comic, as in the many interjections by Will Jones for the Coasters (in "Charlie Brown": "why is everybody always pickin' on me?"), Benny Spellman's line, "sent from down below," clarifying the abysmal origin of the title character in Ernie K. Doe's "Mother-In-Law," and all of the "Popeye" interruptions in the Orlons' "South Street," "Don't Hang Up," and "Not Me." The bass voice is the seat of authority, at least from a mocking point of view, in "Summertime Blues" as done with interjecting stop-time lines by both Eddie Cochran and The Who. Perhaps there's also something reassuringly sincere about the bass register; it was often used for spoken, "from-the-heart" inner verses as by Hoppy Jones of the Ink Spots, and it would be the

> **Vocal ranges:** bass, baritone, tenor, alto, and soprano.

natural site of support for Senator Everett McKinley Dirksen's jingoistic "Gallant Men" and Victor Lundberg's over-the-edge "An Open Letter to My Teenage Son" ("your mother will love you no matter what because she's a woman, [but] if you decide to burn your draft card then burn your birth certificate at the same time; from that moment on, I have no son!"). In many vocal groups, the bass blends into the other parts without much recognition on its own; Melvin Franklin of the Temptations, for instance, scarcely gets more than a solo moment over the course of five years' worth of hits before "Run Away Child, Running Wild" (1:50–1:54), in which all five partners trade lead lines. Perhaps Franklin's greatest-ever moment in the spotlight is in intoning the mesmerizing introduction, "You are under my power—it is the power of love!" in a guest role for the Marvelettes' "My Baby Must Be a Magician."

The high bass range is considered that of a baritone, home to a wide range of characterizations. (Listen to Web audio example 5.02 and see Web photo 5.01.) From the early-electrical recording tradition of Crosby and Sinatra in the 1930s, some soft baritone crooning continues two decades later (Alan Dale's "Sweet and Gentle," Pat Boone's "Friendly Persuasion"), but interest in that sound soon passes. Brook Benton normally sings in the higher tenor range, but can surprise with strong bass-baritone cadences, as in "Thank You Pretty Baby." Nat King Cole's velvety tone with fast vibrato is that of a light baritone. Dean Martin has an annoying scooplike glissando that with his mumbling conveys just too much nonchalance to be taken seriously. (His fan base, however, was so steady that Barry Young could make a small career by imitating Dino's chesty timbre, register, inflections, and freedom of rhythm.) Elvis Presley shows both a deep baritone and a light, supple, airy tenor range in numbers such as "Follow That Dream" and "Such a Night." Tone colors range from the almost-yawning breathiness of Bill Medley in the Righteous Brothers' "(You're My) Soul and Inspiration" through the dark sound focused in the back of the throat of Chuck Jackson, as in "I Don't Want to Cry," to the sustained pinched nasal tones of Adam Wade in "Ruby." Note how Denny Doherty's fairly pure but colorless baritone lines, though carrying the lead melody in The Mamas and the Papas' "Monday Monday," are often overshadowed by Cass and Michelle's harmony parts, so vibrant are their vocal instruments.

The tenor voice is the highest male range in the rock world, and by far the most prevalent. (Listen to Web audio example 5.03.) The voice can be clear and focused in the chest, as with Clyde McPhatter in "Treasure of Love," crystal clear with a head tone, as with Eddie Kendricks in the Temptations' "The Way You Do the Things You Do" and "My Girl," or can be rougher around the edges and concentrated in the sinus cavities (opened by a collapsed palate) for more of a nasal sound, as in Ray Charles's "Hit the Road Jack." It can be noisy with breath, as in Andy Williams's "I Like Your Kind of

Photo 5.01. Alex Brumel recording a tenor part. His headphones carry a mix of his line and the piano's, as well as talkback from the engineers, mixed at his own preference. (Photo: Kristin Fosdick)

Love"; Jackie Wilson has a dramatic vibrato and full diaphragm support, but not a trace of breathiness in "Doggin' Around." Smokey Robinson's is a similarly bright tenor with strong vibrato when not expressed in its usual falsetto, as demonstrated in "Bad Girl." Little Willie John sings "Leave My Kitten Alone" with lots of vibrato, and that of B. B. King is also strong whether he's singing sweetly or shouting angrily. Van Morrison sings expressively, with a well-supported head tone and large dynamic range. James Taylor's well-supported head tone is just a bit more nasal. Chris Montez is striking in "The More I See You" for his complete lack of vibrato. Johnny Mathis has a relaxed voice, with a constant wide tremolo and some long-sustained tones, as in "It's Not for Me to Say." His tone is deeply affected by the fluttery beats caused by an excess of loose breath not compressed by the diaphragm and meeting minimal resistance in the vocal path. Mathis is just about imitated by Dee Clark, who focuses at the palate but blends in some sinus resonance in "Raindrops" for a bit more nasality. Mark Farner of Grand Funk Railroad judiciously modulates his light strong tenor with a sometimes wide vibrato; he seems to be the vocal model for Brad Delp's work with Boston. Three tenors in particular have very strong tremolos: Aaron Neville, in "Tell It Like It Is" (although the original 1967 master is not nearly as mannered as is the remake that replaced it in the late 1990s), Phil Ochs, in "Flower Lady," and Robin Gibb, in the choruses of the Bee Gees' "I've Gotta Get a Message to You" and certain words in "How Can You Mend a Broken Heart" ("and," 0:42, "rain," 0:52, "down," 0:54–0:55). Vocal tremolo can also be simulated electronically, as done for Donovan in "Lalena" and "Hurdy Gurdy Man."

Roy Orbison's tenor is obviously untrained but very expressive; his voice is basically focused in the chest but without diaphragm support, and can move to the mouth where his vibrato is fast and shallow, all demonstrated in "Only the Lonely (Know How I Feel)." A very weak but sympathetic tenor leads the Left Banke through "Walk Away Renee." Mike Love squeals out the lead vocals of "Surfin'" and "Surfin' Safari" with no support at all, but with an earnestness that brings us along. Over the years, many have pointed to Bob Dylan's indefinite pitch and gravelly tone as non-musical, but to those with any rock ears, he is very expressive in these domains and particularly in the way he modulates dynamics (see particularly "You're No Good"); his voice should simply be prized for its humanity and range. In comparison, Art Garfunkel produces perfect intonation and a choirboy's tone, but the voice is tiny next to Dylan's. Less flattering sonority comes from tenors Rick Nelson (an empty voice with no vibrato, no support); Ringo Starr, who sings nasally, tonelessly and sharp, but is charming in the Beatles' "Yellow Submarine" ("in the TOWN," 0:00–0:02!); Jim Morrison, whose weak, clipped vocals don't seem to distract from the star's authoritative persona in The Doors' "Hello, I Love You" and "Touch Me"; the Standells (muffling their sound production in the back of the throat for "Dirty Water"); Fabian (weak intonation, no sustain at all in "Turn Me Loose"); and Sonny Bono (what a really nasal tenor!). Jerry Garcia brings in a hung jury—his light and sweet voice is extremely vulnerable, but at times is quite expressive. Note, for instance, his nicely modulated vocal dynamics (0:23–0:30, 0:44–0:55) that perfectly complement his masterpiece of pedal steel articulation in "Dire Wolf."

The lowest women's voices in rock can be grouped together in the alto category. (Listen to Web audio example 5.04 and see Web photo 5.02.) Nina Simone (what perfectly centered pitch!), Rosemary Clooney (what a relaxed, open, and heavy vibrato in "Hey There" despite an eight-month pregnancy!), Gisele MacKenzie, and the breathy June Christy were major stars in the '50s. But this range simply wasn't popular in the '60s. One might classify Shelley Fabares as an alto because she lacked a soprano's upper reaches (in fact, note how the backing singers in "Johnny Angel" take over her higher notes at "I'm in heaven," 0:47–0:48, and "other fellas," 0:57–0:58), but she can't reach her low notes either (she's sharp at "exist," 0:26–0:27). A great though not exactly chart-topping breathy alto with large dynamic range and no vibrato is Nico, singer in the Velvet Underground's "Femme Fatale." Classified in between the alto and the soprano would be the mezzo-soprano, of whom there are a few. Among these, Jo Stafford demonstrated elegant enunciation and vowel qualities, Jaye P. Morgan displayed a large chest voice, Peggy Lee had a fine head tone, Brenda Lee had a very wide range, and in "Just a Little Bit of Rain," "2:10 Train" and "Different Drum," Linda Ronstadt showed perfectly centered intonation and a fast regular vibrato, demonstrating great flexibility as she would constantly nail her low notes with plenty of subtle grace.

In parallel with the men, most successful female rock singers possess a very high range, as sopranos. (Listen to Web audio example 5.05.) An operatic coloratura soprano, Nelcy Walker, actually has a go in the Mothers of Invention's "Dog Breath, in the Year of the Plague." Patti Page exercised a very large range, perfectly centered pitch without inflection and an unchanging clear tone; as with most old-school singers, her expression lay mostly in control of the dynamic range. Dionne Warwick is a trained soprano with regular vibrato, and strong sustain. Nancy Wilson wins the prize for clearest enunciation of consonants. Joan Baez colors her head tone with a fast, deep vibrato and belts out long-sustained vowels. Diana Ross's head tone is sometimes very nasal, as in "Baby Love." Judy Collins projects a perfectly clear head tone with a strong fast vibrato. In "Those Were the Days," Mary Hopkin shows a young but big and strong breathy tone with fast and shallow vibrato. Julie London is breathy as a saxophone—one can trace the noise right along with the pitch when she's close-miked, as in "Cry Me a River." In "The Girl From Ipanema," Astrud Gilberto's just as breathy, but her lack of vibrato makes for a very volatile and vulnerable pitch. In contrast, Lani Hall's soprano in Sergio Mendes and Brasil '66's "Mas Que Nada" has a crystal pure intonation and a light touch that can still call on dynamic strength. Mama Cass Elliot shows off her great flexibility in an effortless octave leap at 1:10 in The Mamas and the Papas' "I Call Your Name." The female counterpart of Bob Dylan is Janis Joplin, whose amazing voice with its strong diaphragm and fast vibrato is astoundingly underappreciated for its dynamically expressive compass. One aspect is exemplified in Big Brother and the Holding Co.'s "I Need a Man to Love": Janis can shred her voice into multiple parts, singing with a silvery delivery that has a noisy shadow (as at 1:06–1:11), or integrate the parts into a shouting whole (1:11+); all complement beautifully the dirt coming from Sam Andrews's Gibson SG. A second aspect: note how, in "Summertime," Janis can use her vibrato throughout sustained tones ("eaSY," 0:50–0:53), or just at their end ("RICH," 1:13–1:17).

There probably aren't as many hard-to-listen-to women as there are men in rock, but Sue Thompson ("James (Hold the Ladder Steady)") has an annoyingly nasal voice. The most horrific soprano voice is that of Mrs. Miller, apparently marketed out of cruelty. Her "Downtown" showcases a hideous vibrato and a loss of rhythmic control that she seems to stretch and pull inadvertently as if she's forgotten the words, or forgotten to breathe, for the lamest possible rise to anticlimax in 2:14–2:21. The sustained, high-pitched vocalizations of Yoko Ono, as in *Two Virgins* and "Cambridge 1969," are vilified probably because they lack lyrics as much as for their perceived drawbacks in tonal quality or melodic invention. The Chantels is an unusual vocal group that might be mentioned at this point in that all five are sopranos with similar ranges; lead soprano Arlene Smith tries to stand out by singing on the top of the pitch—not quite sharp, but above her partners—for some jarring "unisons" in "Look In My Eyes" (0:40, 1:31). This singing on top of the pitch is practiced by many, both men and women: compare the Imperials in "Tears on My Pillow," lead singer Shirley Owens Alston in the Shirelles' "Dedicated to the One I Love," the Dovells' "Bristol Stomp," Barbara Mason in "Yes, I'm Ready," Carol Jackson in the Sapphires' "Who Do You Love," and the Intruders in "Cowboys to Girls." Even though at times grating, it's a far superior sensation to the incongruously dubious pitch of Hayley Mills' "Let's Get Together," Sunny and the Sunglows' "Talk To Me" and Sandie Shaw's "(There's) Always Something There to Remind Me."

Vocal technique

Many rock vocalists reach out to their audience largely through the physicality of their singing, the degree to which the sounds of their voice suggest in the listener, at least unconsciously, just what their oral cavity is experiencing—it

> Vocal technique: enunciation, tone, falsetto and other effects, dynamics, and ornamentation.

can be quite a sensual communion. Elvis Presley was a singer who, in his early years, used every bit of his oral physicality in creating and modulating his vocal tone, to the point where he would insert made-up syllables just to keep up the activity. Listen to the wide dynamic range, the Dean Martin–like scoops and casual enunciation, the movement between a nasal quality and focus at the back of the mouth, a concentration at the palate, and the emotive air inserted between syllables in "That's When Your Heartaches Begin." Listen to the word slurring in "Mean Woman Blues" and the rearticulation of syllables, "Ho-ho-hold me close" in the opening line, "I-I-I love you" in the refrain, and "lo-hoving yehou etern nally" in the retransition of "I Want You, I Need You, I Love You." Other tracks that demonstrate great physical manipulation of many parts of the vocal instrument include Ray Charles's "Georgia On My Mind," Buddy Holly's "Reminiscing," Mark Lindsay's lead singing in Paul Revere and the Raiders' "Good Thing" (compare the lead line with Terry Melcher's very clean backing vocal), Mick Jagger's vocal in the Stones' "Paint It, Black," Van Morrison's in "Brown Eyed Girl," John Fogerty's in Creedence Clearwater Revival's "Proud Mary," and Joe Cocker's in "With a Little Help From My Friends."

A number of these recordings might strike some listeners as evidence of great inconsistency of tonal quality. Classical singers traditionally strive for constant beauty of tone, but this is rarely of interest to rock vocalists, who wish to be expressive in as many domains as possible, and who reject the dogma of there being one "right" way to do anything. One of the common results of this aesthetic is singing in multiphonics, as we've noted with Janis Joplin, whereby the voice is split into various strands that will produce separate waveshapes. They are typical of the shout, but may be produced at any volume level. An inability or unwillingness to draw forth multiphonics is the chief reason that no matter how many blue notes he may sing and how many syncopations he might try to work into his mostly square melody, Pat Boone never sounds the least bit like Little Richard. It's what combines with a heavy dose of ornamentation and what bridges a large dynamic range in Johnnie Ray's "Cry." It's what adds the rare but the most personal touch to Patsy Cline's "Sweet Dreams (Of You)," it makes for a sultry, fragile sound in the words "the easy way" (0:25–0:27) in Brenda Lee's "Break It to Me Gently" and puts a TNT-degree of grit into "love me right" (1:35) in her "Dynamite," conveys an indecisive thinking-out-loud roughness to the beginning of every verse of Maxine Brown's "All in My Mind," helps John Lennon mold his loose imitation of Dylan in the Beatles' "You've Got to Hide Your Love Away" ("small, 0:17–0:18, "clowns," 1:23–1:24), unleashes all anger when Marvin Gaye "FOUND OUT yesterday" (0:42–0:43) in "I Heard It Through the Grapevine," brings out the desperation in David Ruffin's leads for the Temptations in "Ain't Too Proud to Beg" and "I Wish It Would Rain," and entails much of the character in James Brown's, Etta James's, and Wilson Pickett's vocal personae. And sometimes the all-out multiphonic-laden shout just erupts, as when James Brown shouts "ow!" (7:24+) like a preacher exhorting his crowd to respond in "Prisoner of Love," when Paul McCartney breaks down and cries through the choruses of the Beatles' "Oh! Darling," and when John Kay explodes into space with heavy-metal thunder throughout Steppenwolf's "Born to Be Wild." Listen to the tonal contrast in Sly and the Family Stone's "Dance to the Music," where Cynthia yells (0:01–0:11, 1:44–1:46), Freddie the tenor ornaments his lines with falsetto (0:38–0:45), Larry the bass sounds as hollow as possible (1:08–1:14), and Sly responds with rabble-rousing multiphonics (1:23–1:30).

Falsetto itself represents another manner of tonal inconsistency, as it strips away the lower tones from a vocal product, leaving only the highest remnants. Somewhat like a flute because it's almost a pure tone with few harmonics—and never attaining that head-tone ring produced by the perfectly focused lock of overtones sought by the operatic singer—the very high and exceedingly light falsetto voice is created by the complete relaxation of one of the two main sets of voice-related muscles. It's close to the head tone; note in "La-La Means I Love You" how the Delfonics' lead tenor begins in a very high head tone but then switches into falsetto. Falsetto had forerunners in Robert

Johnson, Howlin' Wolf, and Bill Kenny of the Ink Spots; it was a mainstay of doo-wop, known from such titles as the Diamonds' "Why Do Fools Fall in Love" (what a sustained tone in 0:50–1:01!—is there one any longer?). Falsetto first scale degrees were part of Little Richard's signature and the technique as a whole was a larger part of Frankie Valli's; little else remained of Tiny Tim's. The effect allowed a superhigh climax ("but that's the chance you've gotta take," 2:05–2:13) in Roy Orbison's "Only the Lonely (Know How I Feel)"; it was Curtis Mayfield's "normal" sound in the Impressions' "We're a Winner." Not entirely the province of males, Wanda Jackson provides evidence in "Let's Have a Party," and the Supremes use it ("hooo," 0:16–0:17) as both a symbol of ringing telephones and a reference to an early Beatles hallmark in "Back in My Arms Again," although some would interpret these as examples of pure head tones rather than falsetto. Emphasizing the break, one can move directly from full voice to falsetto and back again; this is the yodel, and it too is very characteristic of rock singing, perhaps coming from Hank Williams Sr.'s "Love Sick Blues," "Long Gone Lonesome Blues," and the like. Buddy Holly's hiccup ("Peggy Sue" is loaded with them) is closely related, and this led to many such hits by Buddy Knox, Bobby Vee, and Tommy Roe. But then again, the ultimate in hiccupping may be heard in the Fendermen's "Mule Skinner Blues," and the model for this goes back to the early 1930s. Frank Ifield recontextualized the yodel by excising its hillbilly roots in "I Remember You." Nino Tempo and April Stevens made an interesting yodeling brother-and-sister duet in their "Whispering." Late-1960s yodels include parody in the "rutabaga" song of the Mothers' "Call Any Vegetable" and two-part full-voice reminiscences of back-to-the-hills calls in The Band's "Up on Cripple Creek" (3:01–3:13).

Photo 5.02. Nina Sturtz pauses between vocal takes in the tracking room. The glass doors to the left lead to the studio's isolation booth; the window behind allows a view to and from the control room. (Photo: Kristin Fosdick)

All techniques discussed thus far are worked into the regular sung line, but a number of other effects stand out strongly. Unvoiced artifacts (not involving the vocal cords) mark dozens of songs from our sample, both in whistling (performed as a solo in Don Robertson's "The Happy Whistler," in parts in Roger Miller's "England Swings" and Whistling Jack Smith's "I Was Kaiser Bill's Batman," and in chorus in Mitch Miller's "March from the River Kwai") and whispering (the backing vocalists admonishing Ronnie Bennett, "Remember!," as if through her superego, in the Shangri-Las' "Remember (Walkin' In the Sand)," Ringo's benediction to the "White" Album in "Good Night," Nancy Sinatra and Lee Hazelwood imitating a train by whispering the title of "Jackson" every beat, and Graeme Edge whispering along with the sung lines of the Moody Blues' "Don't You Feel Small"). There's a bit of humming, in the Chordettes' "Born to Be With You" and in Thurston Harris's and Bobby Day's versions of "Little Bitty Pretty One," and a big yawn is captured for the Beatles' "I'm Only Sleeping." There's loud weeping (Clyde McPhatter in the Dominoes' "The Bells"), hysterical laughing ("the Surfaris' "Wipe Out"), painful groaning and shrieking (Plastic Ono Band's "Cold Turkey"), brash yet innocent stuttering in the Beatles' "Why Don't We Do It In the Road," lisping (Barry Gordon's "Nuttin' for Christmas"), tongue-rolling (Billy Stewart's intro to "Summertime"), lip-buzzing (Larry Williams's "Slow Down"), tongue clicks (Jimi Hendrix's "Purple Haze"), vocal wah effects (Big Brother and the Holding Co.'s "Light Is Faster Than Sound"), cartoon voices (Betty Johnson's "The Little Blue Man"), and imitations of animal howls (Rufus Thomas's "The Dog"), car noises (the Medallions' "Speedin'"), and arrows flying (Sam Cooke's "Cupid"), among the more interesting.

Expressive singing combines these techniques and more, with special care to mix loud and soft dynamics with improvised embellishments. A sudden outburst of sustained climactic ornamentation, as unleashed in Tony Williams's second bridge retransition (1:52–1:54) for the Platters' "The Great Pretender," reveals plainly what his "heart can't conceal." Strong accents and sudden reversions to extreme quiet in Elvis Presley's "I Forgot to Remember to Forget" ("NEver MISS her") exaggerate aspects of a wide dynamic range otherwise held back by a flippant delivery. Elsewhere, as in the ardent "Heartbreak Hotel" and the angry "If I Can Dream," Elvis's expressive character is largely determined by his energy level. In "I Got the Feelin'," James Brown phrases "baby, baby, baby" (0:48–0:55) with a ghost articulation that plays with the inaudible. Marvin Gaye's "Pride and Joy" features lots of dynamic shadings over a wide register. Dynamic growth can be obvious, as when in Johnny Rivers's "Baby I Need Your Lovin'" the dynamics come way down for the second half of the third verse and the celesta enters to support the female backing vocalists' line, "I need you and I want you," repeated endlessly with ever-rising intensity. Expression can be subtle, especially as when John Lennon sings with sensitive articulation in "had to LAUGH" (0:33–0:34) and "I saw the photoGRAPH" (0:39–0:41) early in the Beatles' "A Day In the Life," a five-minute epic that must be paced with soft contrasts in the beginning in order to create an effective loud extreme in due course. Anger wells up gradually over the full course of Janis Ian's "Society's Child (Baby I've Been Thinking)," well expressed through measured dynamic growth. Country singing, as in Tammy Wynette's "D—I—V—O—R—C—E," is laden with trademark one-note ornaments and dynamic emphasis. A more detailed and methodical study of vocal ornamentation will be undertaken in our chapter on melody.

Vocal ensemble

Two or more singers can work together in many different ways. If they are singing the same text in the same rhythm, they may have the same pitches (and be singing in unison), or they may have different pitches (and be singing in harmony, homophonically, as in Sam

> **Vocal ensemble:** balance and texture in settings for two, three, or more voices; choral arrangement; voices and instruments.

Cooke's and Lou Rawls's singing in "Bring It On Home to Me," Sam above Lou; or in Sam and Dave's "You Don't Know Like I Know," Dave Prater above Sam Moore). If the two are singing in different rhythms, their melodies most likely have different pitches as well, and they are singing polyphonically, as in the verses of the Chiffons' "Sweet Talkin' Guy." In the case of a duet, where two are singing in harmony, one melody leads by virtue of its leading toward well-defined structural pitch goals, as in moving to a second scale degree over the V that resolves to the first scale degree with the ensuing I. Often, the lead vocal is above, and a harmony vocal is sung below; this is the case in the verses of Smokey Robinson and the Miracles' "You've Really Got a Hold On Me," the Everly Brothers' "Devoted to You," and Simon and Garfunkel's "Scarborough Fair." Just as often or more, however, the lead vocal is below, and a descant part is sung above; this is heard in Bing Crosby and Grace Kelly's "True Love," Carl and Jay Perkins in "Sure to Fall (In Love With You)," Rick Nelson's "Hello Mary Lou," The Who's "Substitute," the Fortunes' "You've Got Your Troubles," Frank and Nancy Sinatra's "Somethin' Stupid," Ray Charles's "Here We Go Again," Simon and Garfunkel's "Homeward Bound" and "Mrs. Robinson," and Paul McCartney's singing above John Lennon in many early Beatles hits.

The two parts in a duet may move together in parallel motion, with both melodies a constant interval apart, as in sweet parallel thirds or sixths (see the Everly Brothers' "Take a Message to Mary" and the bridge of their "All I Have to Do Is Dream," the Fleetwoods' "Come Softly to Me," Neil Sedaka's

"Calendar Girl," and Don and Juan's "What's Your Name"), a single line doubled in octaves (as in the Sunnysiders' "Hey, Mr. Banjo," Dick and Dee Dee's "Young and In Love," the Rolling Stones' "I'm Free," and in the blues section of the Beatles' "Happiness Is a Warm Gun," 0:45–1:34), lines locked in empty parallel fifths (much of the Electric Prunes' *Mass in F Minor,* Spirit's "Fresh Garbage," the bridge of James Taylor's "Blossom," and much of the bridge of Crosby, Stills and Nash's "Lady of the Island," which finally settles into a sixth), or, least often, lines a fourth apart (as in the bridge of John Fred and His Playboy Band's "Judy in Disguise (With Glasses)," 1:06–1:16: "Come to me tonight..."). The two may relate to each other in oblique motion, with one voice moving as the other holds (as in the Coasters' "Yakety Yak," the Everly Brothers' "Cathy's Clown," the opening of the Beatles' "Please Please Me," Patience and Prudence's "Tonight You Belong to Me," and much of Simon and Garfunkel's "Sounds of Silence," where Paul sustains many repeated harmony pitches below Artie's leading lines), or, least often, contrary motion, where the two melodies move generally in opposite directions (as in the DeJohn Sisters' "(My Baby Don't Love Me) No More"). Largely because siblings have such similar physiology, it's easy for the Everly Brothers or the DeCastro Sisters, or especially the Kalin Twins, to blend perfectly. Even more to the point, a solo singer will very often double-track his or her vocal by overdubbing a second, and sometimes even a third, vocal on top of the first, either in unison (as in the verses of Andy Williams's "Can't Get Used to Losing You") or in harmony (as in many hits by Patti Page and Neil Sedaka; even Elvis tries this once in "I'm Yours").

Vocalists often strive for an independent texture. In many songs, two singers trade lines or verses (Louis Prima and Keely Smith, "That Old Black Magic"), often to come together later on in harmony (Brook Benton and Dinah Washington's "Baby (You've Got What It Takes)," Marvin Gaye and Tammi Terrell's "Ain't No Mountain High Enough," Sonny and Cher's "I Got You Babe"). Elsewhere, voices may oppose each other as if representing different parts of a singer's persona, as when the bass, who normally adds complementary counterpoint to the upper parts in the Dell-Vikings' "Come Go With Me," has a dramatic moment in the solo spotlight when he begs, you "never give me a chance!" answered by a high tenor's anguished "aah!" as if we've heard a desperate plea from the nether regions seconded by the leaping heart. Other independent lines come to mind: Mike Love's bass part in the chorus of the Beach Boys' "Help Me Rhonda," the soaring of soprano Millie Kirkham over Elvis Presley's lead in "My Wish Came True," the quite unroyal female descant vocalized with no words above Johnny Cash's "Ballad of a Teen Aged Queen," or the independent parts of the Everly Brothers' duet, "Love Hurts," and Jack Bruce's self-duet, "Boston Ball Game." Vocal parts can imitate each other, either in short bursts (note how a lead singer is echoed

Photo 5.03. Nina Sturtz routining a number. The black disc suspended in front of the microphone is a spit guard that also reduces explosive vocal sound. (Photo: Kristin Fosdick)

twice in the American Breed's "Bend Me, Shape Me": "madly (madly), madly (madly)") or in a full canonic round (Perry Como's "Catch a Falling Star" and "Round and Round," Donovan's "Happiness Runs"). Such adherence to rule, though, is rare in rock music. More common is the quodlibet, where two or more independent tunes (one of them sometimes well known) are joined together in harmony, as in the appearances of "Auld Lang Syne" in the G-Clefs' "I Understand" and of "Frère Jacques" in the Beatles' "Paperback Writer," or Simon and Garfunkel's pairing of "Scarborough Fair" and "Canticle"; newly composed melodies are performed separately and then in counterpoint in many Broadway shows (as in "The Bum Won" in *Fiorello!*), in the Beatles' "I've Got a Feeling," and the Moody Blues' "Lazy Day" and "Melancholy Man."

Arrangements in three or more vocal parts seldom involve fully independent polyphony (but hear Bruce Johnston above Carl Wilson above Brian Wilson in the coda of the Beach Boys' "God Only Knows," The Mamas and the Papas' "Safe in My Garden," or the Association in "Requiem for the Masses"), except when there is a soloist-vs.-chorus situation, which will be discussed later in this chapter. Otherwise, three-part settings are generally homophonic, with the same rhythm and lyrics in all parts, and differ as to whether the lead melody is on top (as when Judith Durham has the one female part in the Seekers' "I'll Never Find Another You," or in the McGuire Sisters' "It May Sound Silly," the Beach Boys' "Surfer Girl," and the first and last sections of Crosby, Stills and Nash's "Suite: Judy Blue Eyes") or smack in the middle, with both descant and lower harmony parts (as in the Fontane Sisters' "Eddie

My Love," the McGuire Sisters' "Sugartime," Jerry Garcia's buried lead in the Dead's "Uncle John's Band" and Colin Blunstone's in the Zombies' "Time of the Season"). Occasionally, as with the Cookies' "Chains" and the Beatles' "This Boy," the lowest of three homophonic parts is the leader. In less frequent four-part block harmony, the top part is sometimes the lead vocal, as in the Guess Who's "Share the Land," but more common is the barbershop arrangement, where the second highest part leads, as in the Four Freshmen's "Charmaine" and the Chordettes' version of "Eddie My Love."

Because of the difficulties involved in keeping parts from duplicating each other, a five-part vocal setting is much less common in rock, and would typically not involve homophonic parts, although the Zombies' unusual track, "Changes," is just that—an intricate five-part vocal block arrangement. In "In the Still of the Nite," a lead singer and fairly independent bass leave three others in the Five Satins to work out homophonic trios; this is characteristic of many doo-wop groups. The 5th Dimension range from the essentially unison writing for "Up-Up and Away" to a balanced variety of unison singing against vocal duets, trios, and quintets through the various phrases of "Stoned Soul Picnic." Even four-part settings often subdivide into groupings, as when the Harry Simeone Chorale made a hit with the two-part harmony above the two-part droning fifths in "The Little Drummer Boy."

One interesting texture occurs at various levels when singers enter one at a time, all sustaining until a full chord is heard, as in the four voices that open Danny and the Juniors' "At the Hop," the three voices that enter individually through the verses of the Beach Boys' "In My Room," or over the course of an entire song like the Beatles' "You Won't See Me," where McCartney sings the first verse double-tracked at the unison, the second verse adds Lennon and Harrison in two descant falsetto parts, and the third verse adds a high first-scale-degree pedal on top of everything else. This serial addition of vocalists seems to be a favorite way to invoke tolling bells, as in the Diamonds' "The Church Bells May Ring." Or it may make for an orgasmic retransition, as in the Beatles' "Twist and Shout" (Lennon begins sustaining members of V^{m7} with 5 at 1:25, Paul adds 7 at 1:27, George chimes in with 2 at 1:29, Lennon reaches over to complete the seventh chord with 4 at 1:30, and then John and George just scream in multiphonics while Paul adds the falsetto gliss at 1:33–1:36). Or, the falsetto may be association-free, as in the bridge of Betty Everett's "The Shoop Shoop Song (It's In His Kiss)," in The Band's "The Weight" ("and you put the load right on me") and in Eric Burdon and the Animals' "Sky Pilot" (arpeggiating ii with "you'll never, never, never reach the sky").

Choirs can take on a specific character; they can range from the divine to the mundane, for example, from a chapel choir (the Rolling Stones' "You Can't Always Get What You Want") through a spiritual anthem (Ed Ames's "Who

Will Answer"), a motto for everyman (Ray Stevens's "Everything is Beautiful"), a treble boys choir (Mary Hopkin's "Those Were the Days," 2:27+), a group of kids (Frank Sinatra's "High Hopes"), a group of infantile girls (Paul Evans's "(Seven Little Girls) Sitting in the Back Seat" and Brian Hyland's "Itsy Bitsy Teenie Weenie Yellow Polka Dot Bikini"), to female felines (meowing through Little Willie John's "Leave My Kitten Alone").

Of great interest are the myriad ways in which a lead singer can interact with a group of backing vocalists. A responsorial chorus will echo the leader in some way, often to repeat the idea that will become the song's title (as in Chuck Berry's "Thirty Days," Ray Charles's "What'd I Say," Marvin Gaye's "Hitch Hike," the Drifters' "Under the Boardwalk," and the Beach Boys' "Don't Worry Baby"), to repeat other of the lead singer's phrases (the Beatles' "Twist and Shout") or perhaps even complete the lead singer's lines (the Supremes' "Come See About Me"). (See the backing vocalists' completion of the lead singer's thought in Web audio example 4.12.) The manic backing singers of the Friends of Distinction complete a declarative conjugation of the lead singer's question, "can you dig it?" in "Grazing in the Grass": "I can dig it, he can dig it, she can dig it, we can dig it, they can dig it…" Often, the chorus provides sustained syllables ("aah" in The Who's "We're Not Gonna Take It!") or repetitive scatting ("ba da, ba da da da" in The Mamas and the Papas' "Monday Monday") behind the lead singer, supplying harmony and perhaps some rhythm. The chorus can take the reins away from the lead singer, by taking the first line of a section (as in the questioning verses of Betty Everett's "The Shoop Shoop Song (It's In His Kiss)," the bridge of Bobby Helms's "My Special Angel," or the last verse of Jo Stafford's "It's Almost Tomorrow") or by emphatically repeating a word or phrase, leaving the leader to respond (the Marvelettes' "Please Mr. Postman": "WAIT!," the Ronettes' "Be My Baby," the Beatles' "Help!," Bobby Darin's "Things,") or seem to intervene on his behalf (as the Jordannaires plead, "let him be your teddy bear" at the end of Elvis Presley's "(Let Me Be Your) Teddy Bear").

It is often provocative to consider just what persona is portrayed in the solo/chorus relationship: are they split parts of the same psyche? (Lou Christie's superego seems to try to "STOP!" himself in the prechorus of "Lightnin' Strikes.") Do they support each other (consider the odd result of the Supremes' "Back in My Arms Again," where Flo and Mary sing as a supportive part of Diana, even though Ross relates their stories that had gone contrary to her own experience) or are they embattled (as in Ray Charles's "Hit the Road Jack")? As with the chorus of Greek drama, do the backing singers seem to express a more universal truth, or one more palatable to the masses than the individual is able to convey? Such seems to be the effect of the "whitebread" choruses that underline the thoughts of the idiosyncratic lead singer in Elvis Presley's "Love Me," Ray Charles's "I Can't Stop Loving You,"

Walter Brennan's "Old Rivers," Dean Martin's "Everybody Loves Somebody," and Joe Cocker's "Feeling Alright."

Finally, one must observe how the vocal and instrumental parts work together. Much of this topic will be fodder for the coming chapters, but we should just mention here the role of a cappella singing in rock textures. Rarely in rock will an entire composition be for vocals only, but the Grateful Dead experiment with eight minutes and fourteen seconds of this in "What's Become of Baby," as Jerry Garcia's voice is filtered and split by a tape manipulation into three separate strands, all heard over only a soft-mallet gong roll. Otherwise, the Dead often performed the three-part "And We Bid You Goodnight," Phil descant, Jerry lead, Bob bass, without accompaniment, and there is an a cappella verse at 4:01+ in their "Uncle John's Band." More often, an opening vocal will appear without accompaniment and then the rhythm section will enter belatedly, either mid-verse (after four bars in the Regents' "Barbara-Ann") or after a full verse (the Four Freshmen's "Charmaine"). Text-painting seems to be behind this technique in the Young Rascals' cover of "A Place in the Sun," where Eddie Brigati sings the opening line slowly, all on his own, but the band enters, appropriately picking up the tempo, at the words, "movin' on." Occasionally, as in the Monotones' "Book of Love," the bridge will be reserved for an ear-catching a cappella display.

A final note on texture

Assuming that the reader can now aurally distinguish one instrument and voice type from another, and is sensitive to the many performance techniques discussed in our five opening chapters, it should be suggested that any attention devoted to a recording's full texture would be amply repaid. The listener should ask questions such as, how does the bass line relate to upper parts? How do doublings, pairings, or other groupings of sonorities create unified new timbres and contrasts between them? Do contrasting timbres work more at carrying the harmony, developing melodies, or asserting rhythms? How does texture change through the course of a song: Is it constant? Is brass added to the chorus to punch it up? Are vocal forces changed in the bridge? Does an extended introduction present vocal or instrumental parts one by one (The Mamas and the Papas' "Monday Monday," John Fred's "Judy in Disguise")? Is the rhythm section's entry delayed (B. J. Thomas's "Raindrops Keep Fallin' On My Head")? Or does the texture build up over an entire song through gradual additions of forces from a very sparse opening melody to a full-blown ending (Roy Orbison's "Running Scared," the Beatles' "Hey Jude," Simon and Garfunkel's "Bridge Over Troubled Water")?

The creation of texture, typically a group endeavor but also the specialty of the arranger (think of Paul Riser's strings for Motown or Richard Hewson's different colors for each verse of Mary Hopkin's "Those Were the Days") and the producer (for what, after all, is Phil Spector best known?), is also the great separator between the songwriter (Bob Dylan) and the composer (Brian Wilson). Because most popular musicians are usually familiar with just a handful of instruments at most, and sing with unconscious abandon, the reader thus far will probably know more about the overall realm of instrumentation and vocal production than all but the most inquisitive and experienced professional performers.

CHAPTER 6

Forms: Phrases and Sections

What provides the shape of musical matter? What are the fundamental ways of establishing repetition and contrast? What gives us the sense that some musical ideas lead logically to others? What creates a sense of balance and what puts it in peril? These are some of the questions that lead us to consider music's formal structure—how phrases are constructed, how they are grouped together to form sections, and how sections relate to each other to form complete songs. Our earlier coverage of the fundamentals of rhythm and harmony, along with our detailed understanding of texture and color, will be quite useful as we approach these issues.

Phrases in combination

A musical phrase is a lot like a verbal phrase—it expresses something of a complete idea and comes to something of an ending. It may be analogous to a complete sentence, especially in that it may act like either a question or a statement, depending on the harmony to which it leads. It often consists of a four- or eight-bar segment, but phrase lengths can vary widely, and their trajectories and endings will typically match the grammatical shape and purpose of the accompanying lyrics. Later chapters on melodic construction and rhythm will investigate aspects of the interior of phrases in more detail, but for right now we really only need to recognize the goal of the phrase, its ending, the cadence, in order to understand how phrases work together.

> **Phrases:** cadences, the simple and double period, open phrase groups, bar form, adaptations of the twelve-bar blues pattern, the SRDC form.

There are basically three types of cadence: the full cadence, which ends with the V chord moving to I (rhetorically suggesting a strong declaration), the half cadence, which ends on V (rhetorically posing a question), and (occurring much less often) the deceptive cadence, which moves from V to something other than the expected I (its rhetorical analogue perfectly captured by its name). (Listen to Web audio examples 6.01–6.03. To hear phrases in context: See also Web audio example 4.06, at 0:17–0:20, for a phrase ending in a full cadence; Web audio example 4.06, at 0:09–1:10, for a phrase ending in a half cadence; and Web audio example 4.01, at 0:19–0:23, for a phrase ending in a deceptive cadence.) Other phrase endings appear—there may be a softer motion to I than from the harmonically demanding V, as from IV or from ii. A reminder as to the scale-degree membership of the I, ii, IV, and V triads is provided in figure 6.01. (See Web audio example 4.17 for phrases ending IV—I.) Alternatively, a phrase may end much more ambiguously on some chord other than I or V; the phrases, for example, in the Beatles' "A Day in the Life" lead the listener through a maze of cadences so weak (as on ii^{m9} at 0:22–0:24 and on IV at 1:05–1:11) they would be considered as phrase endings only because of the succeeding encroachment of recognized recurring phrase beginnings. Sometimes, harmonic arrival does not synchronize with

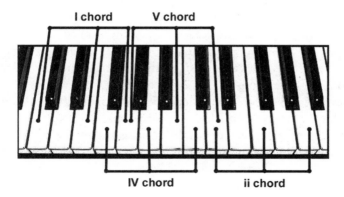

Figure 6.01. Four important triads in one given key: the I chord (made up of scale degrees 1, 3, and 5), V (5, 7, and 2), IV (4, 6, and 1), and ii (2, 4, and 6).

text endings, rhythmic groupings may be asymmetrical, or phrases may seem to overlap in some way. At such times, it may not seem desirable to declare a clear-cut cadence, because doing so would contradict what the song seems to be trying to express. The aware listener is constantly comparing the example at hand to norms but must be flexible enough to recognize the strong event that seems to transcend the usual constraints. At bottom, an understanding of the norms permits the appreciation of the revolutionary statement.

Let's look at some examples and see how phrases might be identified and how they relate. Louis Armstrong's ballad, "What a Wonderful World," provides some good things to talk about. Consider how the verse begins, progressing to the line "I think to myself, 'what a wonderful world.'" The next lyric also leads eventually to the same line of text, and we recognize a refrain—a recurring element of text that is conveniently chosen as the song title. This recurrence strongly suggests two phrases, each ending with the refrain, begging us to compare the harmonies at the two parallel points. The first phrase seems to end on I, the chord heard at the first instance of the word "world," but six beats (1.5 bars) of I fall into two beats (a half-bar) of V for a half cadence before the second phrase begins. The second phrase ends unequivocally with V (supporting the word, "wonderful") moving to eight beats (four full bars) of a decorated I ("world"). Thus the second phrase ends with a full cadence that seems to answer the half cadence of the first phrase and bring the verse to a satisfying close. Also note how the I at the end of the second phrase is stronger than that near the end of the first, by virtue of the singer's melodic goals: the I near the end of the first phrase supports a melodic 3, while the full cadence supports a melody that has reached its goal, coming to rest 7—1—2 ("wonderful")—1 ("world"). (Web audio example 3.26 answers a half cadence at 0:18–0:19 with a full cadence, the melody reaching a final 1, at 0:38.)

Consider the chorus of Peter, Paul and Mary's "Puff (The Magic Dragon)." Note how it moves to V for a half cadence ending its first eight bars, at "the land called Honalee" (0:25). This phrase is followed by a repetition of the opening melody and text, leading in another eight bars to V—I, a full cadence where "Honalee" is repeated (0:38). Again, melodic goals lead us to hear closure, as the half cadence supports 2 whereas the full cadence finds completion in the line, 6—1—7—2—1, bringing 2 down to its goal. In both the Armstrong and PP&M songs, repetition is used at different points in the phrases, but still helps us mark structural points. We recognize a satisfying unit made up of such pairs of parallel phrases, where a half cadence in an opening phrase is answered by a full cadence ending a second phrase. Such a complete pair is called a period, and is a very common pattern for a unit such as a verse or a chorus, particularly in songs derived from the Tin-Pan Alley tradition. One more such example, from the verse of the Turtles' "She'd Rather Be With Me." Here, the first line, about "some girls," finds cadence with the words, "handle everything they see," with a melodic 2 and 5 over a harmonic V, for a half cadence at the end of four bars. The second line, now about "my girl," contrasts the ending of the first phrase with the title sung to a 3—2—1 descent over a full cadence, again completing a parallel four bars. The Turtles use the period structure to compare the roving, unfulfilled quality of most girls (V) to the homing, satisfied nature of the singer's girl (V—I). Other songs among many that feature periods include the verses of Eddie Fisher's "On the Street Where You Live," Sammy Davis Jr.'s "I've Gotta Be Me," Buddy Holly's "True Love Ways," Neil Sedaka's "Breaking Up Is Hard to Do," Gene Pitney's "Town Without Pity," Bob Dylan's "Love Minus Zero / No Limit," and the Classics IV's "Traces." Whereas the period is heard more often in verses than choruses, Rick Nelson's "Hello Mary Lou" and Petula Clark's "My Love" demonstrate that a chorus can be so constructed. Note how each of these sections, whatever their formal function, features a full cadence answering a half cadence, thus constituting a two-phrase period. (Can you hear the period relationship in Web audio example 4.02?)

Some periods, like that of the Classics IV's "Traces," are large enough (this song's verse having a sixteen-bar antecedent phrase answered by an eighteen-bar consequent phrase), and their phrases easily enough separable into two halves, that they constitute what is called a double period. In "Traces," consider how the first eight bars (up to "bits and pieces") seem to be a phrase ending away from tonic, followed by another eight bars ending (after "traces of love") on a strong V. These sixteen bars are followed by an exact musical repetition of the opening eight bars, and this is then followed by a line very similar to the second eight bars, but extended a bit longer so as to end with a full cadence ("traces of love with me tonight"). As with the simple period relationship, there are two phrases, each with the same musical opening. The half cadence is answered by the full cadence, but each seems to contain two divisible gestures. The same double-period structure makes for verses in Henry Mancini's "Moon River" and Bob Dylan's "Blowin' in the Wind."

Some sections of songs consist of groups of phrases that conclude with half cadences. These, which lack the closed finality of periods, are simply called open phrase groups. Because they often lead with a great deal of anticipation to the following section (which should, hopefully, answer the open phrase group with a full period), these incomplete groupings are often found to be the basis of bridge passages, which have the dual jobs of providing contrast to prior verses and choruses, and preparing the return of a succeeding verse. Note the tension created by the half cadences at the ends of the bridges of the Everly Brothers' "All I Have to Do Is Dream" (ending at 1:02–1:06 with the text, "I'm dreaming my life away"), Bob Dylan's "Just Like a Woman" ("ain't it clear…" at 2:37–2:43), the Beatles' "I Want to Hold Your Hand" ("I can't hide, I can't hide, I can't hide!," 1:03–1:11) and "Nowhere Man" ("the world is at your command," 0:42–0:47), and the Association's "Cherish" ("...that you are driving me out of my mind," 1:46–1:52). (Hear retransitional half cadences in Web audio examples 4.23, at 0:50–0:59, and 5.05, at 0:45–0:50.) But a verse can also constitute an open phrase group, as half cadences are found at the ends of verses in the Stones' "As Tears Go By" (0:38–0:41), the Turtles' "Happy Together" (0:20–0:23), and The Band's "Up on Cripple Creek" (0:30–0:33). Some songs, in fact, are open phrase groups in succession, never achieving full-cadence closure but having to fade away while still incomplete, as occurs in the Lovin' Spoonful's "Daydream." Their "Rain on the Roof" has the audacity to simply end on a V^{m7} chord. The Mamas and the Papas' "California Dreaming" might have ended the same way, as every phrase ends with a half cadence, but a i chord is tacked onto the end to simulate a full cadence.

Another very common grouping, this of three phrases, produces what is called bar form. Here, a first and second repeating or mostly repeating phrase, both ending with half or otherwise nontonic cadences, are followed by a contrasting third phrase ending in full cadence. Consider the Brooklyn Bridge's "Worst That Could Happen." The first phrase ends after four bars with scale-degree 5 in the bass but IV sustaining above for an ambiguous harmony overall and a weak cadence, ironically supporting the text, "this time you're really sure." We are then led through a mostly repeating phrase to a V four bars later, ending "so safe, so sane, and so secure" with a strong half cadence. These two phrases might be heard together as a two-part open phrase group, except that they are followed by a lone climactic phrase with an extended length of eight bars, culminating in the resigned title and ending with a full cadence, a refrain that demands grouping with the prior two phrases for a bar form, four-plus-four-plus-eight. The Cuff Links' "Tracy" features the same four-plus-four-plus-eight grouping of three phrases in bar form. (Web audio example 5.04 features an irregular 8+4+7 bar form with eight bars leading to V at 0:21–0:22, followed by a four-bar phrase also ending on V, at 0:30, and concluding with a seven-bar phrase with a full cadence.)

A far more common 4+4+4 bar form is heard in the twelve-bar blues. In a standard blues, bar form is suggested by the lyrics, whereby the first line is repeated and the third line is different (each of the three lines containing four bars). But in twelve-bar rock blues, this lyric convention is usually unobserved. Also in blues, the cadences are somewhat softened: the first four bars may have no harmonic motion at all, simply prolonging I for that entire phrase. The second four bars typically move from two bars of IV to two of I, making for the weak plagal decoration of tonic. The third phrase of four bars typically moves from V to a concluding two bars of I, often through an intervening, softening bar of IV that eases the full cadence. So bar form is represented by a first tonic-prolonging phrase containing a very weak, or possibly no, cadence, varied repetition of that phrase with a weak plagal (IV—I) cadence, and a contrasting third phrase with a stronger (although sometimes softened) full cadence. This is of course the format for Bob Dylan's "Outlaw Blues" and Johnny Cash's "Folsom Prison Blues," but also for the verses of Chuck Willis's "C. C. Rider," the Beatles' "Can't Buy Me Love," Gary U.S. Bonds' "New Orleans," Donovan's "Sunshine Superman," and the Temptations' "I Wish It Would Rain"; the choruses of most of Little Richard's and Chubby Checkers's hits, Chuck Berry's "Roll Over Beethoven," Roy Orbison's "Ooby Dooby," Ray Charles's "What'd I Say," Buddy Holly's "Peggy Sue," James Brown's "I Got You (I Feel Good)," the Beach Boys' "Little Deuce Coupe"; and the instrumental breaks of the Beatles' "A Hard Day's Night," Jimi Hendrix's "Come On (Part I)," and the Surfaris' "Wipe Out." The twelve-bar structure becomes a primary one for hard rock through the Yardbirds ("Jeff's Boogie"), Cream ("Strange Brew," "Sleepy Time Time"), The Doors ("Summer's Almost Gone," "Maggie McGill"), Jeff Beck ("Let Me Love You," "The Hangman's Knee"), and Led Zeppelin ("How Many More Times," all on one chord; "The Lemon Song"). (Can you hear the twelve-bar structures in Web audio example 3.11?)

Whereas the twelve-bar blues pattern remains intact through much of rock music, whether in the covering of old songs by Robert Johnson, Willie Dixon, or Big Mama Thornton or in new compositions, it is actually a source for many more flexible forms adapted by stretching in lots of pop music. In the Beatles' "Day Tripper," note how the verse ("Got a good reason...") contains two four-bar phrases that mimic the blues form, right down to the repeated lyric in the second phrase. The third phrase, however, does not follow the blues' simple V—IV—I—I pattern. Instead, the highly chromatic response wanders widely as it takes the singer "so long to find out" that he has been led down the garden path in an extended eight-bar third phrase unrelated to the blues or to any other prior model. (A related, though much simpler, deviation had occurred in the chorus of Jan and Dean's "Surf City.") A sixteen-bar blues is quite common with a division other than that heard in "Day Tripper." In most cases, the opening phrase is often an eight-bar verse, all on tonic, leading to a chorus that occupies the normal second and third four-bar phrases of a blues. Gene Vincent's "Be-Bop-A-Lula," Dion's "Ruby Baby," Robert Parker's "Barefootin,'" and Little Willie John's "All Around the World" all work this way, although the last also has an extended third line. Another common extension occurs in the third phrase, where V—IV—I—I (one bar each) is given an inner repetition, thus extended to V—IV—V—IV—I—I, making a fourteen-bar blues overall. Such is the case with Jackie Wilson's "Baby Workout" and the Beach Boys' "Surfin'"; Mongo Santamaria extend this to sixteen bars with one more extra V—IV in the third phrase of "Watermelon Man," the Jaynettes get sixteen bars in "Sally Go Round the Roses" by tacking two extra bars of I instead onto the Jackie Wilson structure, and Brook Benton and Dinah Washington extend the pattern differently in "Baby (You've Got What It Takes)," the last line of which moves V—IV—V—IV—IV—V—I—I, for sixteen bars. In the Rolling Stones' "19th Nervous Breakdown," the third line is much more direct harmonically, but it morphs into a chorus that extends the form to seventeen (4 + 4 + 9) bars with an extra IV—I tag. One fun example is the Fendermen's "Mule Skinner Blues," whose first phrase consists of five bars of I, second phrase follows three bars of IV with three and a half of I, and third phrase leads three bars of V through two of IV to four of I, for a mule-stubborn 20.5-bar (5 + 6.5 + 9 bars) structure. Some blues are extended simply through a really slow tempo; Wilson Pickett's "Mustang Sally" preserves all the normal blues chord ratios in a twenty-four-bar pattern with lots of slow grinding. See if you can determine how each of the following adjusts the twelve-bar blues structure with expansions and, in rare cases, contractions: B. B. King's "Let's Get Down to Business" (a very irregular 14 bars), The Doors' "Love Me Two Times" (15), Ray Charles' "I Got a Woman" (16), It's a Beautiful Day's "Don and Dewey" (16), Bob Dylan's "Obviously 5 Believers" (20) and "Highway 61 Revisited" (22), the Temptations' "The Way You Do the Things You Do" (23), Cream's "Sunshine of Your Love" (24), the Capitols' "Cool Jerk" (26), the Grateful Dead's "Easy Wind" (27), and James Brown's "Cold Sweat" (30). In some of these cases, the chord relationships get much more advanced than the simple model we've presented, but this shouldn't make it too difficult to follow the underlying three-phrase structure.

One other phrase combination occurs quite often, enough so to give it a name and compare examples. This is a four-phrase pattern that we'll refer to as SRDC, as its components always perform the functions of Statement—Restatement—Departure—Conclusion. The Restatement phrase may cadence the same as did the first Statement (Bobby Darin's "Dream Lover") or differently, and in fact the first two phrases may form a periodic subgrouping (as in the Highwaymen's "Cotton Fields") or an open phrase group (as in the Rooftop Singers' "Walk Right In" and Marvin Gaye's "I Heard It Through the Grapevine"). The fourth phrase may recap the opening material, for an *aaba* pattern (the Turtles' "You Baby"), or may present new melodic ideas, *aabc* (the Bee Gees' "(The Lights Went Out In) Massachusetts"). Often, an SRDC is the basis of a verse with refrain. This is the case in the Stones' "As Tears Go By," which overall forms a four-part open phrase group. Jimmy Gilmer's "Sugar Shack," by contrast, is an SRDC-shaped verse-refrain section ending with a full cadence. This pattern seems to be common, for some reason, with female vocalists and girl groups, as it is characteristic of Mary Wells's "My Guy," Little Eva's "The Loco-Motion," and the Crystals' "Then He Kissed Me," but it's also a Beatles favorite ("Please Please Me," "Eight

Days a Week"). Smokey Robinson and the Miracles repeat the last phrase of the verse-chorus pairing in "I Second That Emotion" for an unusual SRDCC form. The SRDC appears in the work of even the least conventional artists, as with the Velvet Underground ("I'm Waiting for the Man") and the Mothers of Invention (the "Smother My Daughter with Chocolate Syrup" section of "Brown Shoes Don't Make It," which is very closely related to the form of the recurring tune in Arlo Guthrie's "Alice's Restaurant Massacree").

SRDC (heretofore invoked in comparing phrases within a section) is of course also the pattern established through larger-scale groupings, as when a pair of verses leads through a bridge to a third verse that seems to tie together all four sections. This hearing is particularly pertinent when the third verse seems to be the consequent of an action in the bridge (Pat Boone's "Love Letters in the Sand"), or when it is extended with ending material not present in the first two verses, typical of a Broadway finish ("A Wonderful Guy" from *South Pacific,* Steve Lawrence's "Portrait of My Love," the Seekers' "Georgy Girl"). The bridge of the Association's "Cherish" leads to a verse (2:18+) with a radically new harmonization and a somewhat elevated function as if the listener has been scaling a monumental peak ever since the song's intro. Sometimes the large SRDC is marked only by an abbreviated last verse, suggesting that only one of its two phrases is necessary, as in Johnny Mathis's "Misty" or Bobby Helms's "My Special Angel," or when the last verse ends with a full cadence instead of the half cadences of previous verses, as in Scott McKenzie's "San Francisco (Be Sure to Wear Flowers in Your Hair)" or B. J. Thomas's "Raindrops Keep Fallin' On My Head." Any of these large SRDC structures may then lead to a further bridge and a repeat of the DC sections, or perhaps more likely, an instrumental break that wipes the slate clean.

Functions of song sections

Most songs group related phrases into sections that function as verse, chorus, or bridge, and then combine a number of these different sections to

The one-part formal contrasting textures.

create contrast in a balanced presentation. A surprisingly large number of songs, however, violate this norm by containing only a single form of a section that is repeated for the song's duration without contrasting material. Clearly, folk songs are the historical basis for this stanzaic procedure, as in Fats Domino's "Bo Weevil" and Joan Baez's "All My Trials," and in folk-derived and -styled story-songs (the Kingston Trio's "Where Have All the Flowers Gone," Bobby Gentry's "Ode to Billie Joe," and forty-five Dylan recordings officially released through 1969). But this one-part form occurs in many styles, ranging among Les Paul and Mary Ford's "Hummingbird," Brook

Benton's "Thank You Pretty Baby," Mickey and Sylvia's "Love Is Strange," the Supremes' "Baby Love" and "Come See About Me," the Four Seasons' "Opus 17 (Don't You Worry 'Bout Me)," Nancy Sinatra's "These Boots Are Made for Walkin'," Them's "Gloria," the Rolling Stones' "Midnight Rambler" and "Gimme Shelter," Jimi Hendrix's "Purple Haze" and "Manic Depression," and the Mothers of Invention's "Trouble Every Day." Sometimes, this is a result of the chorus taking on the same tune or harmonic structure as heard in the verse, as in the Diamonds' "Silhouettes," Perry Como's "Ko Ko Mo (I Love You So)," the Highwaymen's "Michael," Ben E. King's "Stand By Me," the Marvelettes' "Please Mr. Postman," or the Kingsmen's "Louie Louie." The unabating repetition can be a major flaw despite strong material, as in the Supremes' "Where Did Our Love Go," and when the material is weak, as in Gene Simmons's "Haunted House," one wonders how the recording could have been produced and released at all.

Sometimes, given a compelling lyric, even the most economical musical material can be repeated without contrast, as in Buffalo Springfield's intensely concentrated "For What It's Worth (Stop, Hey What's That Sound)." Usually, as with The Mamas and the Papas' "California Dreaming" or Classics IV's "Spooky," there is enough interest within the section that it can stand alone. Sometimes, each repeated section is given enough variation to counter the overall repetition, as in Simon and Garfunkel's "Overs," but the escalating instrumentation of Ssgt. Barry Sadler's "The Ballad of the Green Berets" is not enough to begin to save it. Sometimes, the tension that would come from hypothetical contrasting sections is just not desired, as in the Young Rascals' ultrarelaxed "Groovin.'" Sometimes, the goal-free nature of the repetition underlines the hopelessness of the text, as in Bob Dylan's eleven-minute "Desolation Row," whereas at others, the pattern refuses to budge despite ever-changing images in the lyrics, as in his "I Shall Be Free." Rarely, the form of a verse is so dramatically tensile, as is the case with Roy Orbison's "Only the Lonely (Know How I Feel)," that two verses without a contrasting section is all that is necessary.

Much more common is the song with multiple sections arranged to take advantage of both repetition and contrast. Arrangers and members of good bands will emphasize the contrast of a new section by introducing new accompanimental materials: note how the violins begin to climb in the bridge of the Drifters' "Up On the Roof" and how Grady Martin drops his lead-guitar ostinato to ring out chiming chord changes in syrupy amp tremolo in the chorus of Roy Orbison's "Oh Pretty Woman." Occasionally, songs contain sections that are so different in rhythm, texture, tempo, and tonal materials that they hardly belong together. Such is the case in Cher's divorce-broken "You Better Sit Down Kids," but the Moody Blues' "Question" survives its abrupt changes by virtue of a bigger-than-any-one-of-us scope. Pete

Townshend can be called the father of prog rock for his early experimentation with suite-like tableaux that sometimes avoided recapitulation of previously heard sections, as in The Who's "A Quick One While He's Away," or the "Overture" to *Tommy,* itself a great instrumental number of symphonic import that contains changes of texture, tonal center, meter, and instrumentation with much more memorable materials and powerful construction than "A Quick One." A very common large-scale scheme is a holdover from Tin Pan Alley: the AABA structure, a specific form of the large SRDC. Here, one section (usually a short verse or verse/refrain) is repeated before giving way to a contrasting section, which then leads to a rehearing of the original structure. It is a highly satisfying form, in that the listener gets to enjoy the first part a second time through before it is withheld, and yet contrast makes the return all the sweeter. The AABA structure is usually extended to AABABA, with the contrasting chorus or bridge itself appearing twice. We must stress that the use of the terms "verse," "chorus," and others for sections in pop music of

Photo 6.01. Rock 'n' roll, the quintessential American invention of the 1950s. Collected are album covers by Elvis Presley, Duane Eddy, Bo Diddley, Lloyd Price, Fats Domino, the Crickets, and the Isley Brothers. (Photo: Annie Eastman)

the 1950s and beyond often differs from earlier usage, as regarding the music of Irving Berlin, Cole Porter, George Gershwin, Richard Rodgers, and their contemporaries.

This chapter will continue with a detailed look at each type of section that appears in a rock song, but first let's get an overview of how the arrangement of a set of contrasting sections can contribute to a song's character. Listen to the Beatles' "I Want to Hold Your Hand." Here, a brief instrumental introduction climaxes on a V^{m7} (0:04–0:07), and the first verse enters with powerful anticipation ("Oh yeah, . . .) before that V^{m7} can even let go. The verse consists of three phrases, the first two of which do not cadence strongly, ending both times on a weak iii chord, the first time after four bars ("understand," at 0:13–0:14) and then after another four ("hold your hand," 0:20–0:22). Despite a weak harmony, the cadence of the second phrase defeats the vocal descents that have characterized the song thus far with a daring, desperate vocal leap of an octave, marked by the first divergence of Paul and John from the same melody, prompting a feverish fill from Ringo. The third phrase (0:22–0:29) is likewise four bars in length, but is powered by its chords changing twice as fast (two per bar rather than the previous one per bar), the new harmonic tempo underlining the joy realized by John and Paul's breaking into vocal harmony with their parallel thirds at 0:23–0:25, by the repetition of the lyric that constitutes a refrain, and also by the strength of the full cadence (V—I, 0:27–0:29) that provides a powerful end to the verse, heard altogether as an asymmetrical three-phrase period in bar form. As the song exemplifies AABA form, a second verse follows (0:29–0:51), essentially a repeat of the first except for its pleading lyric being different until the refrain appears. The song moves to the contrasting bridge at 0:51. Despite the limited instrumentation, the guitar texture changes by virtue of McCartney's double stops in the bass (actually introduced in the second refrain, providing a touch of continuity over the interrupted divide between sections), the abandonment of Lennon's driving boogie rhythm part heard throughout the verses, and the introduction of Harrison's delicate lead-pickup arpeggiations, one per bar (reflecting the reduced rate of chord changes).

The relaxation of instrumentation in "I Want to Hold Your Hand" is accompanied by a similar gesture in the tonal materials, as the seventh scale degree is lowered a minor second throughout this section, the lowered note appearing primarily in George's guitar. After a four-bar phrase (through the introspective "happy inside," 0:51–0:58) that ends with a weak cadence, the bridge shifts up a few gears into a rousing retransition (0:58–1:11) made all the more powerful in comparison by the bridge's relaxed opening, with Lennon re-starting his guitar boogie, the new phrase held for a full off-balance seven bars ending on a V^{m7} that makes the bridge an open phrase group based on the same demanding material that was first heard as the song's introduction, there minus the vocal "I can't hide" declarations. A third verse (1:11–1:33) repeats the first, and a second bridge (1:33–53) introduces for variety's sake a new descant vocal part added by McCartney above Lennon's lead vocal. For added ear-catching power at the V^{m7} retransition, Lennon overdubs a falsetto "ooh" (1:52–1:53; this is where the young women in the audience would shiver and shake with greatest abandon) that brings everything to a boil for the fourth verse (1:54–2:24), once again a repeat of the first.... Until, that is, it goes unexpectedly astray with a change of chord for a deceptive cadence at 2:14–2:15, requiring a coda that pulls sharply back on the reins with two bars of cross-beat chords (2:18–2:19) before the final I arrives (2:20) for a crisp ending. Dynamic formal ingenuity, honed to a razor's edge in this, their fifth British single, is one of the strongest factors in the Beatles' explosive introduction to America.

Pop and rock songs nearly always have both a verse and a chorus. The primary difference between the two is that when the music of the verse returns, it is almost always given a new set of lyrics, whereas the chorus usually retains the same set of lyrics every time its music appears. If there is a chorus, the title will typically appear there and then there will be no need for a refrain within the verse structure, but both may be present. When a verse contains a refrain, it is typically the final line (as in Johnny Rivers's "Mountain of Love" and Creedence Clearwater Revival's "Proud Mary": "rollin' on the river"), but the refrain may instead open the verse (Lesley Gore's "You Don't Own Me," Frank Sinatra's "That's Life," Herman's Hermits' "No Milk Today"). Whether or not the refrain or chorus contains the title of the song (Dylan, for example, frequently will not contain his titles in their lyrics at all, an approach to be adopted by many alternative-rock acts in the 1990s), these passages of repeated text will sum up the song's main theme ("it cannot be a part of me for now it's part of you" is the refrain of the Monkees' "Tapioca Tundra"), which theme is illustrated in the changing texts of the verses as through different chapters of a story, or different instances of an idea played out in the singer's experience.

> **Sections:** the verse, the chorus, the refrain, the prechorus, the bridge, the instrumental break and solo, the motto and tattoo, the introduction and coda, editing and form.

In addition to the lyric function, the larger-than-life chorus often has a thicker texture, and perhaps more dramatic harmonies, melodic shape, or rhythms than are characteristic of the verse, which often settles down to its individualistic, sometimes intimate nature. The relatively stable chorus usually ends on a satisfied I harmony, but it can lead to V and a retransition to the verse, as in Dusty Springfield's "You Don't Have to Say You Love Me." As mentioned earlier, the chorus may share the same melody used in the verse (see Peter, Paul and Mary's "Puff," Chuck Berry's "Sweet Little Sixteen," or

Bob Dylan's "I Want You"), but this is unusual. Sometimes the chorus ends with the same melodic idea that had ended the verse, enabling a preordained effect in the Beatles' "Let It Be," but this is also somewhat unusual. More often, verse and chorus will have the same chord progression but different melodies, as in Lou Christie's "Two Faces Have I," Jerry Butler's "He Will Break Your Heart," and the Grass Roots' "I'd Wait a Million Years."

Various techniques might join the verse to the chorus, usually functioning to raise the value of the latter, as if it requires its own introduction, or in some dramatic instances, as if it's been achieved after a difficult search. The Beatles' "She Loves You" is an interesting experiment in that the refrain of its verse ("because she loves you, and you know that can't be bad...") is stretched to two phrases, becoming an independent section of its own, perhaps vying for the label of chorus itself before it is usurped after two hearings by a much stronger candidate for that role ("she loves you, yeah, yeah, yeah..."). In Brian Hyland's "Itsy Bitsy Teenie Weenie Yellow Polkadot Bikini," after the verse ends squarely on I, the chorus is introduced by a stand-alone line, "one, two, three, four, tell the people what she wore!" and the clank of a cowbell to suggest the stunning nature of the revelation to follow. O. C. Smith's "Little Green Apples," as different as is the song, takes the same cue, completing its verse and then musing, "and if that's not lovin' me, then all I've got to say..." before moving into the chorus. James Taylor's "Sweet Baby James" also finds a way to move from his Berkshires-based verse to his cowboy-waltz chorus ("Good night, you moonlight ladies...") via the transitional passage, "there's a song that they sing...."

A very common way of joining separate verse and chorus is through the prechorus, a form seemingly invented in 1964 and remaining extremely popular through the remainder of the decade. Often, a two-phrase verse containing basic chords is followed by a passage, often harmonically probing, that leads to the full chorus. As a model example, let's examine Merrilee Rush's "Angel of the Morning." Its verse contains two phrases, each covering the basic I—IV—V—IV expansion of tonic twice. The trombone then leads to a darker color for the four-bar prechorus that introduces a new tone in the lyric ("I see no need to take me home..."), as the singer realizes that her sense of self is stronger than any dependence upon an unstained reputation. Her confidence rises to full glory in the two-phrase title-based chorus that repeats the verse's progression three times before poignantly turning away for a soft ending. A comparison of this self-assured large-form statement with the more tentative SRDC setting of the Shirelles' "Will You Love Me Tomorrow," an earlier setting of a poetic theme similar to that heard in "Angel," suggests a great shift of societal mores in the meantime. The SRDC scheme and verse—prechorus—chorus pattern are in fact closely related; in songs that do not contain a chorus, among them James and Bobby Purify's "I'm Your Puppet" and the Delfonics' "La-La Means I Love You," the Departure-gesture that precedes each refrain (at "I'm yours to have and to hold" in the former and "Now, I don't wear a diamond ring" in the latter) has the same formal function as a prechorus, but clearly the stage is smaller.

The prechorus is useful when verse and chorus are extremely different in some aspect, as in the contrast between present-set verses and past-memory choruses in the Shangri-Las' "Remember (Walkin' In the Sand)," whose prechorus interrupts, "oh no, oh no..." The prechorus can occur whether the verse itself is an open phrase group (as with the Ronettes' "Walking in the Rain," the Zombies' "She's Not There," the Cyrkle's "Red Rubber Ball," Bob Dylan's "One of Us Must Know (Sooner or Later)," Tommy James and the Shondells' "I Think We're Alone Now," the Small Faces' "Itchycoo Park," and the Flying Machine's "Smile a Little Smile For Me") or a period (Gary Lewis and the Playboys' "She's Just My Style," the Temptations' "Get Ready," Lulu's "To Sir With Love," and the Soul Survivors' "Expressway to Your Heart"). The Cowsills' "The Rain, the Park & Other Things" moves to a prechorus ("but I knew...she could make me happy...") after a verse of only a single phrase, albeit one of eight bars with a slow harmonic tempo; the chorus ("I love the flower girl...") does not yield the catch-all title of this unusually constructed song. Blood, Sweat and Tears' "You've Made Me So Very Happy" has unusual ratios, with a six-bar single-phrase verse leading through a rhythmically and harmonically intensified four-bar prechorus ("I chose you for the one...") to a six-bar chorus. Steppenwolf's "Born to Be Wild" has an extended verse (eight bars of I)-refrain ("Yeah, Darlin,' go make it happen...") pattern repeated before the first appearance of the prechorus ("like a true nature's child..."). Sometimes, as in the Foundations' "Baby, Now That I Found You" and Big Brother and the Holding Co.'s "Piece of My Heart," the final cadence of the verse takes a dark turn before the prechorus appears, adding yet a further gradation in the process of achieving continuity.

Most pop songs also have a bridge, a section that provides greatest contrast to the verse. If the chord changes are simple in the verse, they may become complex in the bridge, and similar contrasts may hold true for other musical qualities: texture may thin out, melody may move to a different register, the key may change, the lyrics may become deeply introspective or begin to reach out more desperately. Sometimes the bridge reflects a singer's consideration of an alternative view to that expressed in the song's main thrust. The bridge nearly always builds to an anticipatory V or V^{m7} in a retransitional motion ending an open phrase group with a call for the return of I in a verse or chorus, sometimes with an exciting vocal spilling-over, as in Johnnie Ray's "You Don't Owe Me a Thing," Elvis Presley's "Tryin' to Get to You," Jackie Wilson's "Lonely Teardrops," and the Platters' "The Great Pretender." But the bridge may be followed instead by an instrumental passage, which is usually a verse without lyrics, the melody taken by or varied by an instrumental solo. Rarely, the retransitional function of a bridge will be performed in some other section; the Moody Blues' "Go Now!" has such an unusual form in that its chorus seems to meander its way to a pause on a half-cadence as if concluding a bridge, then continues with a very short verse.

Of the songs of our sample that contain a bridge, more than 250 of them end on a strategic V. These include Eddie Fisher's "Heart," Jimmy Jones's "Handy Man," the Association's "Cherish," and the Troggs' "Love Is All Around." In many of these 250, the V is intensified by a preparatory alteration of the major scale, the raising of the fourth scale degree, that gives new power to the V harmony as its root, 5, is loudly called forth by that alteration of the scale degree below it. One can hear this intensified V in Andy Williams's "Butterfly," the Fleetwoods' "Mr. Blue," Bobby Lewis's "Tossin' and Turnin,'" the Marcels' "Blue Moon," the Crystals' "Then He Kissed Me," Bob Dylan's "If Not For You," Betty Everett's "The Shoop Shoop Song (It's In His Kiss)," and the Mothers' "Go Cry On Somebody Else's Shoulder." In a similarly large number of songs, a further step along these lines is taken: This retransitional alteration of scale is balanced at the beginning of the bridge by an alteration in the opposite direction, the lowering of the seventh scale degree, which strengthens the IV harmony as the new pitch leads down convincingly to 6, the third of the IV chord. Thus, the dual alterations allow the bridge to take a relaxed initial step back from the major scale, falling flat to emphasize IV, as if to recoil for a farther jump through a raised scale degree to move up two fifths (IV to I, then I to V) to the sharp side, emphasizing V. Such drama is created by calculated changes of scale degree in Elvis Presley's "Love Me," Shelley Fabares' "Johnny Angel," the New Vaudeville Band's "Winchester Cathedral," and the Beatles' "Back in the U.S.S.R." and "Hey Jude."

If the verse begins on a chord other than I, the bridge will often lead to whatever triad lies a fifth above that, colored to sound like the V of that returning chord; this is true of Los Bravos's "Black Is Black" and the Grass Roots' "Midnight Confessions," the bridges of which both end on VI, leading to verses that begin on ii. And non-V endings can be very effective; Crosby, Stills and Nash's bridge to "Marrakesh Express" (beginning, "I've been saving all my money...") melts easily into the returning verse through a retransitional IV. Dusty Springfield's "Wishin' and Hopin'" has a bridge that culminates on a deceptive cadence, moving from its V to six bars of vi. And other chords can substitute for the retransitional V, as does the ♭VII of the Monkees' "She," as will be covered in the chapter on modal harmony. A bridge may sound particularly weak if it ends on I; such seems to be the case with Tommy Roe's "Sheila" and the Shades of Blue's "Oh How Happy." Because it ends on I, the bridge of? (Question Mark) and the Mysterians' "96 Tears" leads to an unusual ambiguity, sounding as if a new verse might already be underway (??). The Monkees are clever in ending the bridge of "Pleasant Valley Sunday" on I, as it writes large the suburban garage band's incompetence as they try to learn their signature guitar riff. The bridge of The Doors' "Touch Me," also ending on I, seems like a grand baroque parody with its lyric, "Now, I'm gonna love you 'til the heavens stop the rain," ridiculing a half-forgotten promise by misquoting a harmonic cliché. A little variety would help the bridges of the Sweet Inspirations' "Sweet Inspiration" and the Joe Jeffrey Group's "My Pledge of Love," both of which contain sixteen bars of the same non-V chord. Gerry and the Pacemakers end the bridge of "I Like It" with a valid ii—V motion, but then repeat it, undercutting its strength with a narcissistic second look.

Occasionally, the bridge will have a "hidden" relationship to earlier material; that of the Supremes' "You Can't Hurry Love" is based on the harmonies iii—vi—ii—V from the last half of the chorus, but played twice as slowly and given a new melody. The chord progression, I—IV—V—I, from the verse of Music Explosion's "Little Bit O' Soul," is given a new melody and is transposed to a different key so that its bridge ends on the desired V of the original key. Such procedures add unexpected unity. The two most common problems with bridges: appearing too early, as after only a single verse in the Dave Clark Five's "Because," and not appearing at all, as in Little Peggy March's "I Will Follow Him," which relentlessly alternates four choruses with the same number of verses—an effective portrayal of destiny, but one not particularly interesting to follow.

As far as these major sections go, some songs defy convention. Bobby Vinton's "There! I've Said It Again" has choruses and bridges but no verses. The Hollies' "Look Through Any Window" has three different sections (beginning with the ostensible chorus, "Look through any window…," continuing with what ought to be a verse, "Where do they go (Movin' on their way)…," and following with what might be a bridge, "You can see the little children…"), but then all three sections are repeated without any changes of text for an overall recurring three-part form lacking the sense of balance that comes from new verse lyrics or from ending with a chorus. The Human Beinz's "Nobody But Me" is a driven, compelling song, despite its verse containing only a single repeated word ("no"), the same word each verse, its litany of dances (shing-a-ling! skate! boogaloo! filly!) leading to a twelve-bar blues as strong as a chorus yet never reappearing, and its apparent chorus featuring only a single word ("nobody"); the group's energy need bow to no norms. Strangely, the bridge leads directly to the song's ending in Sam and Dave's "Soul Man" and also in both Aretha Franklin's "I Never Loved a Man (The Way I Love You)" and her "Think." Like "Groovin'," the 5th Dimension's "Stoned Soul Picnic" avoids tension-based form, but not by lacking for contrast. It has an unusually mercurial structure, fluid but not goal-directed, whereby its first prechorus ("there'll be lots of time and wine," 0:31+) is followed not by the chorus but by an abbreviated verse (0:36+); the chorus, once it finally appears (0:49–0:59, following a prechorus with a new text, "red-yellow honey, sassafras, and moonshine"), is structured on the materials of the verse; and an extended chorus (1:28–1:49) leads to a bridge that begins deceptively just like another verse ("there'll be trains of blossoms"), takes some unexpected harmonic turns before the prechorus (now "can you surrey?," 2:13+), and returns us to the verse...instead of to the chorus. The form flows as freely as do the libations. But such eccentricities don't always work well: in the case of Gene Pitney's "That Girl Belongs to Yesterday," the young composers (it's a November 1963 Jagger–Richard original), seem to miss the import of their own signal, as two verses teasingly demand a chorus with a big V, dramatic vocal tremolos, and unison instrumental cross-rhythms (1:23–1:27), but instead continue with just another verse.

Perhaps the strongest contrast can be brought to the verses, choruses, and bridges of a song by an instrumental passage. It may be referred to as a solo if dominated by a single saxophone, guitar, or other individual, or simply as a break if scored for an ensemble. It may closely follow the structure of a previous section; one interesting example is the guitar solo in Big Brother and the Holding Co.'s "Piece of My Heart," which is a jam based on the song's introduction, repeating the chords of the opening two bars for four hearings before moving through the next four bars, leading to a climactic retransitional V. (This significant passage is not present in the song's model recording by Erma Franklin.) Less often, the break may be something entirely new, as in the twelve-bar "solo" scored for piano doubling twelve-string guitar in the Beatles' "A Hard Day's Night." The solo's melody may be exactly as heard previously with words (the Beatles' "I Should Have Known Better"), with new ornamentation (Wes Montgomery's "Windy"), or the break may involve a great degree of free improvisation (the Beatles' "Day Tripper," Cream's "SWLABR"), perhaps extending for a long period of numerous choruses swapped from player to player as in traditional jazz (The Doors' "Light My Fire," Cream's "Spoonful"). The instrumental section of the Mothers of Invention's "America Drinks" is a barely recognizable instrumental version of the just-past "the other night we painted posters" passage, leading to a number of Stravinsky quotes over a big forty-second jam on a retransitional V^{m7} for a traditional rock structure with some unusual twists; it even ends with a ringmaster's piano ching-a-ring later used to prepare the third verse of the Beatles' "Being for the Benefit of Mr. Kite." Of course, when the Grateful Dead begin to jam ("Dark Star" being the primal example), they enter a new space that leaves the song's structure far behind, and their return to four dimensions could just as easily occur during a completely different song from the one out of which they had vanished. Pink Floyd's "Careful With That

Axe, Eugene" lacks structure entirely, being in its *Ummagumma* incarnation a nearly nine-minute one-chord jam with minimal textural shaping; in "A Saucerful of Secrets," the thirteen-minute jam is more a suite of three-minute sections traded by four band members.

Another formal unit can be referred to as a motto when sung, or as a tattoo when played instrumentally. This is a short, one-phrase unit that may reappear as if to bring the song back into focus, perhaps to call extra attention to the following verse or, if the phrase had functioned as the song's introduction, to make it seem as if we are off to a fresh start. A simple example of a tattoo would be the solo repeated tom figure that reappears at times throughout the American Breed's "Bend Me, Shape Me." Another example is the syncopated descending series of parallel triads set for two trumpets, tenor and bari saxes, and electric bass that reappears through Wilson Pickett's "In the Midnight Hour." A classic introductory tattoo is played by trombones sustaining 5 and 1 while trumpets above move repeatedly from I to a lower neighboring triad, ♭VII, in Stevie Wonder's "Uptight (Everything's Alright)." The Animals' "It's My Life" opens with a tattoo doubled in guitar and bass. Another tattoo appears later in their "We Gotta Get Out of This Place," with the syncopated parallel fifths scored for organ, bass, and guitar; the figure is heard several times including the ending. George Harrison opens the Beatles' "Something" with an exquisite guitar tattoo that signals the return of each verse. Cream introduce some verses in "White Room" with a guitar-ensemble tattoo that runs for nine bars, five beats in each bar.

Vocal mottoes are much less common than their instrumental cousins, but they do exist in roles independent from verses and choruses. The Four Seasons employed mottoes in both "Dawn (Go Away)" and "Walk Like a Man," the latter featuring simply a falsetto setting of the title that announces each verse. In "Paperback Writer," the Beatles experiment with a rich six-part polyphonic vocal rendering of the title in a motto that remains separate from the title's appearances elsewhere in the refrain. The motto is a featured part of another song with very unconventional form, Friend and Lover's "Reach Out of the Darkness." Here, a brief percussive intro with drums, bass, and congas leads to the song's opening motto ("I think it's so groovy now...," 0:09+), sung four times by Cathy Post, joined midway at the unison by husband Jim. Cathy and Jim then sing the title-based chorus in harmony with backbeat tambourine (0:26+), Jim sings the song's single verse with harpsichord ("I knew a man," 0:45+), leading to the chorus (1:12+) and another hearing of the motto (1:30+). This prepares Jim's lead vocal and Cathy's descant in the single bridge that leads to a retransitional V (1:47+), followed by another chorus and an ending with the repeated motto—a hodgepodge of varied sections in a song celebrating the bringing together of disparate souls.

Our coverage of formal functions is left with two of the most important sections of a song from a marketing standpoint, but least important from a structural view: the introduction and the coda, the first and last parts of the recording, respectively. An old-fashioned number, and indeed the cover of a much older number, will have an introductory stanza (called the "verse" in the golden era of Tin-Pan Alley) that leads to a dramatic sustained V, followed by the song proper with altogether new material; this is the case in Lenny Welch's "Since I Fell For You" and the Happenings' "I Got Rhythm." This pattern is modeled by John Lennon in the Beatles' "If I Fell." Similarly old-fashioned is the slow intro, perhaps lacking a tempo altogether, as heard in Rosemary Clooney's "Hey There," Elvis Presley's "True Love," and the Crests' "Gee (But I'd Give the World)"; the effect is regained late in the '60s by the molasses-slow Vanilla Fudge to introduce their version of "Eleanor Rigby." (A slow intro leading to a dramatic half cadence is heard in Web audio example 4.13.) In live performances beginning in 1964, the Beatles got right down to business by simply arpeggiating the introductory V^{m7} in their concert arrangement of "Twist and Shout." The intro can consist of a tattoo also unrelated to the body of the song, as appears in The Doors' "Light My Fire" in a red-hot Vox organ sequence that leads to a beckoning V. The material of the intro may be based on a later section from within the song; for example, the intros of the Beatles' "Can't Buy Me Love" and "Help!" are rearrangements of later choruses. The Supremes' "I Hear a Symphony" has a harmonically complex yet texturally subdued instrumental intro for bass, vibes, and crash cymbal that comes from a later tag ending minus the vocal part ("I'm lost in a world..."), for a very innovative piece of construction. Every once in a while, particularly in a live performance, the artist will provide a false intro, leading the audience to expect one work and suddenly entering another, as when on his *Live in Concert* album, Ray Charles offers for a disguise the opening bars of Beethoven's "Für Elise," only to turn to "I Got a Woman." The half-minute introduction to the Beatles' "Love You To," played by George Harrison and Indian musicians, follows a North-Indian form involving two rapidly descending sitar arpeggiations, a freely improvisatory sitar melody introducing first all the tones of the scale over tamboura drones and then a melodic idea from the song to follow in a rhapsodic rush, until the tabla enter to set the song's pulse.

Coda techniques are just as varied. Some songs end cold, as happens in Fats Domino's "It's You I Love," The Who's "Pictures of Lily," and "Gloria" as performed by both Them and the Shadows of Knight. But far more often, the final idea is repeated, usually coming to rest only in the imagination as the engineer fades out the sound prior to the conclusion of the recording. In such cases, the song may have its structural ending ornamented by later phrases that add no essential new info, but ease the listener out of the experience, as in Buddy Holly's "Reminiscing" or the Shirelles' "Will You Love Me Tomorrow." The ornamentation may take the form of extensive improvisation, as in Smokey Robinson's sublime falsetto ending to the Miracles' "The Tracks of My Tears," an anonymous oboist's awkward additions to the Monkees' "Daydream Believer," or Eric Clapton's taking us out of Cream's "White Room." "His Holy Modal Majesty," on the Mike Bloomfield—Al Kooper—Stephen Stills *Super Session* album, concludes with a five-minute free-for-all for bass, drums, organ, and electric guitar, most of which fades out to leave the guitar on its own for a final minute without rhythm section. Songs that fade out on record were usually given a cold ending for concert or televised performances—see such examples as the Four Seasons' "Let's Hang On" and the Supremes' "My World Is Empty Without You" in DVDs of the Ed Sullivan shows and other televised performances often heavily abbreviated to conform to tight programming requirements.

There are many ways that repetition can bring a song to its close. Sometimes, the last vocal line is repeated instrumentally, as in Peter and Gordon's

Photo 6.02. The most soulful music of the '50s and '60s appeared on these labels, all independent except for the major label, Mercury. Seen are records created by Philly Groove (The Delfonics), Motown (The Supremes), Tamla (Smokey Robinson and the Miracles; Stevie Wonder), Stax (Sam and Dave), ABC Paramount (Ray Charles), Volt (Otis Redding), Atco (Arthur Conley), Phil-L.A. of Soul (The Fantastic Johnny "C"), Philles (The Ronettes), Atlantic (Aretha Franklin), Chess (Billy Stewart; Chuck Berry), King (James Brown), Soul (Jr. Walker and the All Stars), Tamla-Motown, as licensed for the U.K. (The Four Tops), Mercury (Brook Benton), Gordy (The Temptations), Red Bird (The Shangri-Las), Imperial (Fats Domino), Gamble (The Intruders), and Scepter (The Shirelles). (Photo: Annie Eastman)

"A World Without Love" and the Beatles' "Yesterday." Sometimes, a refrain, motto, or tattoo is given varied reharmonization; this is suggested by the Beatles' "She Loves You" and carried out in The Mamas and the Papas' "Dedicated to the One I Love" and the Cyrkle's "Red Rubber Ball." Or the last line can be heard in a new texture, as in the overlapping vocal phrases of the Turtles' "You Showed Me." In a number of cases, the final cadence is evaded harmonically, requiring one or two rehearings in what might be termed the one-more-time coda, finally set right at the end of the Beatles' "I Want to Hold Your Hand" and "I Will," Billy J. Kramer and the Dakotas' "Bad to Me" (written by Lennon), and Bob Dylan's "I Threw It All Away." Sometimes repetition can be so continuous as to function as a be-here-now mantra that savors the moment to promote a transcendent anthemic experience, perhaps the goal of the Beatles' "Hey Jude" (one spiritual step beyond their frenzied repetitions in "Long Tall Sally"), Donovan's "Atlantis," or Tommy James and the Shondells' "Crimson and Clover."

Codas work in other ways, too; one is the false ending. The band can stop, perhaps leading some unsuspecting listener into early applause, and then pick up again as if no ending had been suggested. Such occurs in Bobby Freeman's "Do You Want to Dance," Don Gardner and Dee Dee Ford's "I Need Your Loving," Little Stevie Wonder's "Fingertips," the Gentrys' "Keep on Dancing," Sonny and Cher's "I Got You Babe," and Cream's "I'm So Glad." Sometimes the pause is followed by unrelated material, as with Jimi Hendrix's "Bold As Love" or Spanky and Our Gang's "Like to Get to Know You." The Beatles pioneered both the fade-out—fade-in coda, heard in "Rain," "Strawberry Fields Forever," and "Helter Skelter," and also used by Led Zeppelin in "Thank You"; and the cold ending followed by an unrelated coda, as with the Maori finale to "Hello Goodbye." In response to the Beatles, the Rolling Stones experimented with an unusual format with their single, "Dandelion" / "We Love You," so that each song fades out only to be answered by a faded in-and-out fragment taken from the other side. The unrelated coda also appeared in the form of a tempo change in the Beatles' "Ticket to Ride" (compare Wayne Fontana and the Mindbenders' "Game of Love"), new parts for strings, choruses, and radio in the Beatles' "I Am the Walrus," a context-free piano solo added to the New Colony Six's "Things I'd Like to Say," and a change of meter at the end of Blood, Sweat and Tears' "Spinning Wheel."

An earlier paragraph covered a few unconventional approaches to form. Even further removed are a number of compositional approaches that appear, for one reason or another, arbitrary. One early sort of mishap was caused by the restrictive allowable length of a 45-rpm single; often, a very long recording had to be divided into two parts, one for each side, even though only the A-side, which would usually fade out, would be marketed. One of the most arbitrary dividing points is heard in Billy Vaughn's version of "The Shifting Whispering Sands," where a long narration comes to a very premature cadence. There are many ways in which harmonic relationships, chord progressions, and asymmetrical phrase lengths can seem arbitrary, but the artist who experimented most with the formal ramifications of such arbitrary factors was surely James Brown. Originally, his concert performances, such as of "Prisoner of Love," would have seemingly unrelated stretches of music, but this approach to odd phrasing infiltrated his studio work as well in 1969. Improvisation over a basic riff in "Give It Up or Turnit a Loose" follows 31 bars of I^{m7} with 14 of IV, 17 of I^{m7}, and 10 of IV, before returning to I at 2:39. Form is similarly arbitrary in his "Mother Popcorn (You Got to Have a Mother For Me)" and "Get Up I Feel Like Being a Sex Machine," the latter capturing a discussion between Brown and his partner Bobby Byrd, as to whether it's time (after more than two minutes of an uninterrupted I^{m7} chord) to "take 'em to the bridge." (This is surely what Robert Plant is referring to when his auto-conversation concludes, "where's that confounded bridge," at the end of Led Zeppelin's similarly arbitrary and funk-based "The Crunge.") Bob Dylan, probably improvising as he recorded, would routinely add a seemingly flexible number of lines to his verses; in "Only a Pawn in Their Game," the weakly uneven number of lines that appear one after another seem to be pushed around simply to fulfill instantly decided-on functions, just as are the lyrics' sadly manipulated souls in this ballad of Medger Evers's death. This works just fine on solo guitar, but Dylan gets intro trouble when he's part of an ensemble, as his bass players err at 6:29 in "Visions of Johanna" and at 1:21 and 2:01 in "If Not For You" because of formal confusion that follows his apparently un- or under-rehearsed extra repetitions of lines at those points. Another artist who veered into the arbitrary was Brian Wilson, who in 1966–67 experimented with the splicing together of separately recorded "feels"; what was monumental in "Good Vibrations" turned somewhat unintelligible in "Heroes and Villains." Such a postmodern pastiche worked better in the hands of Frank Zappa, whose Mothers' "Plastic People"—a mélange of satiric quotes from "Louie Louie" through "Havana Moon," "Baby Love," and Stravinsky's *Rite of Spring* and *Firebird,* each phrase sporting its own instrumentation, tempo, meter, and texture, with sections often spliced together just as Wilson was attempting to do for the Beach Boys—was a masterful capturing of the stratified phraseology of Stravinsky's own later work so as to comment on the artificially layered nature of contemporaneous American society and its fragmented constituent psyches. In the Mothers' very different "Cruising for Burgers," every two lines have a different meter, tempo, instrumentation, texture, and tonal language. One wonders if the Mothers' art was also behind such conflations of seemingly unrelated sections as those heard in The Doors' "The Soft Parade."

Many rock aficionados with a little knowledge of sonata form—considered by many to be the apex of thematic/formal organization in Western musical history—claim to find it lurking in countless places in the popular repertoire. I, by contrast, can point to only one pop-rock example from our period for which a comparison to sonata form might have some relevance: Frank Zappa's "Peaches en Regalia." A brief introduction ending on V (heard four times), leads to what might be called the first theme, a phrase ending in a weak cadence, repeated for a period. This is followed by a sequence that modulates to the key of V. A second theme, a wah-guitar solo in the key of V, leads to a regal closing theme a half step above V, and a brief developmental passage that regains V in a retransition that recapitulates the introduction and first theme in the original key. All of this is unusually consistent with the outer conventions of sonata form, which would then continue with recapitulatory second and closing themes—this time without modulation away from I—but instead, Zappa rests after the return of the first theme.

The reader is encouraged to discover for him- or herself some of the many ways that formal arrangement can add to the power or the expressiveness of a song; a few more examples that would repay study are the Beatles' "Happiness Is a Warm Gun" and "You Never Give Me Your Money," and the Mothers of Invention's complete album, *Absolutely Free,* each side of which is an oratorio composed of six or seven numbers. In the last, see if you can hear, for example, the variation of returning material in "Brown Shoes Don't Make It" (the expository sketch at 0:20–0:46 growing into the grandiose climax at 6:06–6:45). Such large works of the Beatles and Zappa also invoke the occasional appearance of a reprise, the return of a previous idea after a great deal of intervening material, as heard in the return of the introductory "Sgt. Pepper" theme near the end of that album, the "You Never Give Me Your Money" tune later on in "Carry That Weight" (for the Beatles), the recurring theme, "What's the Ugliest Part of Your Body?" through various tracks on *We're Only in It for the Money,* and, at a more abstract level, the notion of opening and closing the otherwise instrumental album, *Burnt Weeny Sandwich,* with throwback vocal numbers "WPLJ" and "Valarie" (the Mothers of Invention). These early attempts at super-large forms came to be repeated more sure-handedly in the songs and albums of the 1970s, just beyond our defined repertoire.

CHAPTER 7

Melody: Materials and Patterns

Melody, that setting of pitch to rhythm that is hummable, sung to words, playable on a flute, or the basis of a transfigurative guitar solo, is the essence of music. For many, the tune is synonymous with the song. It works integrally with the chords that accompany it, because it evolves out of the play of harmony and voice leading. Its structure, its points of cadence, are key in determining phrase lengths and formal relations. The colorings of the scales and modes that provide it with substance, sometimes including exotic alterations of scale degrees, along with the large variety of repeating, sequencing, and contrasting patterns that mold those raw materials into its various contours, go a long way in determining a song's atmosphere and providing a singer with means of expression. This chapter will cover the pitch relations basic to melody, and will set the stage in many ways for the following four chapters on harmony's many colors and purposes.

Pitch collections

Pitch collections, modes, scales, and tonal center are ways of thinking about the pitch materials present in a given song, and some basic ways in which

they can relate to each other. We have already investigated the major scale, composed of scale degrees 1, 2,
3, 4, 5, 6, and 7. (Recall that 8 = 1.) The reader may
wish to refer back to figure 2.01 throughout the fol-

> **Pitch collections:**
> major, minor, and
> chromatic scales.

lowing coverage of scales and intervals. The scale is an ordered collection of
pitches, but they rarely appear in that sequence in a real song. Something
like what the alphabet does with the letters occurring on this page, the scale
is merely a convenient, largely abstract, way of collapsing all of a song's regularly occurring pitches into a simple, useful array. We say that a song is in
the major mode if it is fairly consistent in preferring the seven degrees of the
major scale; it's not that other pitches can't occur—we've already seen, for
instance, how the lowered seventh and the raised fourth scale degrees can
be quite useful—but the song will sound major when the seven unchanged
tones of that scale are the naturally occurring pitches of the song's collection.
The scale contains the most important ingredients of a song, but some notes
outside the scale will invariably spice it up some, too. Before we proceed to
examining the relationships of scales to the vocal and instrumental melodies
of particular songs, we shall explore in greater detail the construction of
scales and the nature of the intervals between scale degrees. And even though
our focus will be melody, we will need to regularly contextualize this discussion with harmonic groundings, relating tunes to their supporting triads and
larger tonal context.

There are many different kinds of scales, and they sound different from
each other because each has its own ordering of differently sized steps. In the
major scale, for instance, the minor seconds from 3 to 4 and from 7 up to 1 (or
8) are half the size of all the other steps, 1 to 2, 2 to 3, 4 to 5, 5 to 6 and 6 to
7, which are major seconds. The adjacent pitches of the major scale represent
seconds of different sizes because the larger ones have additional "chromatic"
tones between them that do not belong to the scale. (All members of the scale
are considered "diatonic," as opposed to the chromatic in-betweeners.) The
complete chromatic scale includes such outlying pitches between diatonic
scale degrees 1 and 2, 2 and 3, 4 and 5, 5 and 6, and 6 and 7, but not between
3 and 4 or between 7 and 1. Whereas the relative placement of diatonic and
chromatic tones is not readily apparent on any other instrument, keyboards
(and keyboard-like percussion instruments) are arranged so that when played
in the key of C major, all of the white keys represent members of the diatonic
scale and all of the black keys are chromatic. (The C-major scale is indicated
above the keyboard in fig. 2.01, whereas the G-major scale, which requires
one black key to make the correct pattern of major and minor seconds, is
indicated below the same keyboard.) Any pitches, diatonic or chromatic, may
be heard in a song, but only one version of a scale degree (such as 6) will

always be heard as more natural than another (such as the chromatic lowered sixth or the raised sixth).

Because of this asymmetrical division of the scale, intervals of the same general size can still be different. For instance, the third from 1 to 3 sounds different from the third between 2 and 4 because they each span different numbers of chromatic notes. Intervals formed by combining scale degrees 1 and 3, 4 and 6, or 5 and 7 are large thirds, called major thirds, because they each span across two chromatic tones, or a total of four chromatic and diatonic tones, above the given bottom note. The thirds combining scale degrees 2 and 4, or 3 and 5, or 6 and 1 are smaller than major thirds by one chromatic tone, and are called minor thirds. We noted earlier that major seconds are found between scale degrees 1 and 2, 2 and 3, 4 and 5, 5 and 6, and 6 and 7, but the smaller minor seconds are measured between scale degrees 3 and 4, and between 7 and 1.

Intervals can be measured between chromatic scale degrees or among mixed chromatic and diatonic scale degrees as well. The chromatic tone that lies between 1 and 2 may be considered ♯1 (a raised first scale degree) or ♭2 (a lowered second), and this chromatic pitch lies what sounds like a minor second away from either 1 or 2. We shall use the sharp sign (♯) and the flat sign (♭) only to indicate deviations by chromatic step from the major scale. (Thus, a scale spelled 1—2—3—4—5—6—♭7—8 is just like the major scale except that its seventh degree is lowered chromatically.) The interval from 3 to ♯5 is a major third, and that from 1 to ♭3 is a minor third. The span from 4 up to 2 is a major sixth, whereas one from ♯4 up to 2, or one from 4 up to ♭2, is a minor sixth. Unisons (two tones usually performed by different forces that match the same pitch), fifths, fourths, and octaves do not have major and minor varieties, but are considered perfect intervals when they measure diatonic notes above the first scale degree. The interval from scale degree 1 up to 4 is a perfect fourth, ♭6 up to ♭3 is a perfect fifth, and 5 up to the next 5 is a perfect octave. All interval sizes, some to be discussed only later, are listed in table 7.01 and illustrated in figure 7.01.

The chromatic scale is the ordered collection of all twelve pitches available to practically all rock systems, with every note in the scale a minor second away from its neighbor. (All of the frets on a guitar fingerboard are a minor second apart; the guitarist can play a major scale only when he or she recognizes when to stop strings on adjacent frets for minor seconds and when to skip frets for major seconds.) So the twelve pitches of the chromatic scale, which may be thought of as the seven-pitch major scale plus the five chromatic pitches completing the minor seconds that do not occur naturally, could be spelled 1—♯1—2—♯2—3—4—♯4—5—♯5—6—♯6—7 in ascent and would normally be spelled 7—♭7—6—♭6—5—♭5—4—3—♭3—2—

Table 7.01 Common interval sizes

Interval names	(most common scale degree pairs forming them, lower pitch given first)
minor second	(2-♭3, ♯2-3, 3-4, 4-♯4, ♯4-5, 5-♯5, ♯5-6, 6-♭7, 7-1)
major second	(1-2, 2-3, ♭3-4, 4-5, 5-6, ♭6-♭7, 6-7, ♭7-1)
augmented second	(1-♯2, ♭6-7)
minor third	(1-♭3, 2-4, 3-5, 4-♭6, ♯4-6, 5-♭7, 6-1, 7-2)
major third	(1-3, ♭2-4, 2-♯4, ♭3-5, 3-♯5, 4-6, 5-7, 6-♯1, ♭7-2, 7-♯2)
perfect fourth	(1-4, 2-5, ♭3-♭6, 3-6, 4-♭7, ♯4-7, 5-1, 6-2, ♭7-♭3, 7-3)
augmented fourth	(1-♯4, 4-7)
diminished fifth	(7-4)
perfect fifth	(1-5, ♭2-♭6, 2-6, ♭3-♭7, 3-7, 4-1, 5-2, ♭6-♭3, 6-3, ♭7-4, 7-♯4)
augmented fifth	(1-♯5, 5-♯2)
minor sixth	(1-♭6, 2-♭7, 3-1, 4-♭2, ♯4-2, 5-♭3, ♯5-3, 6-4, 7-5)
major sixth	(1-6, ♭2-♭7, 2-7, ♭3-1, 4-2, 5-3, ♭6-4, 6-♯4, ♭7-5, 7-♭6)
augmented sixth	(♭6-♯4)
diminished seventh	(♯4-♭3, 7-♭6)
minor seventh	(1-♭7, ♭2-♭1, 2-1, ♭3-♭2, 3-2, 4-♭3, 5-4, ♭6-♭5, 6-5, ♭7-♭6, 7-6)
major seventh	(1-7, ♭2-1, ♭3-2, 3-♯2, 4-3, ♭6-5, ♭7-6)
perfect octave	(1-1, ♯1-♯1, 2-2, ♭3-♭3, 3-3, 4-4, ♯4-♯4, 5-5, ♯5-♯5, 6-6, ♭7-♭7, 7-7)

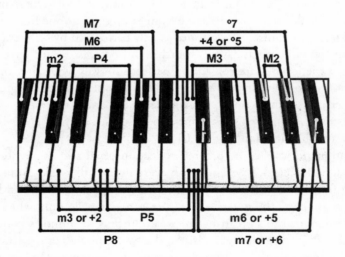

Figure 7.01. Examples of the common intervals a perfect octave and smaller. M = major, m = minor, ° = diminished, + = augmented.

♭2—1 in descent. Except for fine distinctions made by singers and some instrumentalists in some styles, we think of ♯1 as sounding the same as does ♭2, and ♯5 sounding the same as ♭6 (these pairs of like-sounding scale degrees are certainly played at the same guitar fret or on the same keyboard key). Microtones do exist between pitches a minor second apart, and can be used expressively by singers, guitarists, and others, but in tonal music they are considered to be ornaments of intervals based on larger steps. We do not normally speak of a chromatic mode in rock music, because all twelve different pitches almost never have equal value in these styles; the natural version of scale-degree 2, for instance, nearly always has precedence over ♭2 or ♯2. Some "classical" styles, by contrast, can be thought of as sounding in the chromatic mode, when all twelve pitches have equal value. Note that in such a case, no pitch can act as tonal center, as 1 does in the major mode, because no structural hierarchy of relationships, and therefore no point of reference, exists in the chromatic mode. These styles are often called "atonal" and are exceedingly rare in rock music, although Pink Floyd, Frank Zappa, and others occasionally have produced passages that would qualify.

The huge majority—by thousands—of top-twenty songs from the 1955–69 period are squarely in the major mode. These include such disparate recordings as Chuck Berry's "Thirty Days," the Diamonds' "Why Do Fools Fall in Love," Fats Domino's "Valley of Tears," Perry Como's "Catch a Falling Star," Andy Williams's "Lonely Street," Chubby Checker's "The Twist," the Chordettes' "Never on Sunday," Elvis Presley's "Good Luck Charm," Ray Charles's "Busted," Mary Wells's "My Guy," Billy Joe Royal's "Down in the Boondocks," Lou Rawls's "Love is a Hurtin' Thing," Van Morrison's "Brown Eyed Girl," Sammy Davis Jr.'s "I've Gotta Be Me," and Aretha Franklin's "Share Your Love," to cite one hit from each year. Even if a song seems to emphasize minor triads (containing minor thirds above roots, as in 2—4—6 or 6—1—3), it may eventually find its way to the tonal center of a major key. This is the case in the opening of the chorus of Bobby Vee's "The Night Has a Thousand Eyes": " 'cause the [vi] night has a thousand eyes, and a thousand [ii] eyes [V] can't help but [I] see...." The tonal center, and thus the mode, are determined much more by the cadential goals of a song than they are by the openings of phrases, which may start anywhere.

The cliché that the major mode projects happy feelings whereas sad songs must be in the minor mode is often borne out, but then there is a song like Guy Mitchell's "Heartaches By the Number," which seems to intend no irony whatsoever in making a thoroughly happy-go-lucky major-mode tune of his heartaches and troubles. Lloyd Price's "Stagger Lee," a tale of a sickly wife and gunshots, is likewise incongruously upbeat and in the major mode. Bob Dylan's "Don't Think Twice, It's All Right," by contrast, sets the blithe tone of the words in the bright major-mode spirit, barely covering the dark tone kept just under the surface; see also his "Boots of Spanish Leather." Many major-mode blues exist, from Ivory Joe Hunter's "Since I Met You Baby" to Wilbert Harrison's "Kansas City" and Hank Ballard and the Midnighters' "Let's Go, Let's Go, Let's Go." But when the tale is just too sweet, as in Paul Evans's "Happy-Go-Lucky Me" or Gerry and the Pacemakers' "I Like It," the major-mode setting can make for a sickening, cutesy washout. For some reason, 1967 was a year that the hard-rocking Who and Rolling Stones briefly abandoned darker modes to revel in the major-mode atmospheres of "Happy Jack," "Pictures of Lily," "Dandelion," and "She's a Rainbow." Most rhythm-and-blues is also more at home in other modes, but with such songs as "Cyprus Avenue" and "Madame George," Belfast-born Van Morrison wins the title of major-mode soul singer.

Whereas the ordered major scale is not typically represented in melodic writing, there are a handful of melodies that follow it at some length. Here are a few of the more interesting examples: In the bridge of Georgie Fame and the Blue Flames' "Yeh Yeh," the vocal melody constitutes a pair of rising major scales, altered so that the first scale includes some lowered notes (1—2—3—4—5—$\flat$6—$\flat$7—7—8 starting at 0:49) and the second one includes one raised one (1—2—3—4—5—6—7—$\sharp$1—2, starting at 1:04), exemplifying our previously stated precept that for added power, a bridge may move from the flat side to the sharp side. Note how much more unpredictable, and therefore more interesting, such lines are than the straight and pure octave-long major scales, both ascending and then descending, in the verses of Paul Anka's "(All of a Sudden) My Heart Sings." In the verse of Ike and Tina Turner's "River Deep, Mountain High," Tina rises from the first scale degree up to $\flat$7 and no higher; from here, she can only drop, $\flat$7—6—5—4 over a IV chord. An unaltered major scale governs the melody of the Beach Boys' "Heroes and Villains"; its verse is a classic period, opening with a descending scale from 4 down more than an octave to 2 on a half cadence at 0:07, answered by a second phrase beginning on the same 4 but descending all the way to 1 on the full cadence at 0:18. The major scale is also featured in Smokey Robinson and the Miracles' "I Second That Emotion" (another verse period, the first phrase descending from 6 to 1, then rising to 3, the second dropping from 6 to 1 and remaining there for a stronger close) and Bob Dylan's "Sad-Eyed Lady of the Lowlands" (which moves in 1:42–1:51 through a dramatic major-scale descent to a half cadence: "[5—6—7] my [8] ware- [7] -house [6] has [5] my [4] Ara- [3] -bian [2] drums"). See if you can follow the various five-note fragments of a major scale, 1—2—3—4—5, 4—3—2—1—7, and 2—3—4—5—6, in the verse melody of the Mindbenders' "A Groovy Kind of Love."

Although not as strongly highlighted as vocal melodies, instrumental lines may feature passages from the major scale, never of more structural value than when in the bass line. Note Paul McCartney's major scale from 2 down more than an octave to 1 in the bass at 0:01–0:04 of the Beatles' "All My Loving"; in the bridge of "Lady Madonna," his bass traverses a full twelfth. A similar depth is reached but much more slowly, step by step, in Procol Harum's "A Whiter Shade of Pale." Much more typical is the briefer bass descent in the verse of Skeeter Davis's "The End of the World," which descends 1—7—6—5—4 through a sequence of dropping chords, well suited to portray the singer's depression. (Listen to Web audio example 7.01.) Melodic instruments other than the bass may perform scales, usually to add a colorful filler in between phrases, as with the organ's two-octave descent in Merrilee Rush's "Angel of the Morning," the twelve-string guitar's scales in Peter and Gordon's "Nobody I Know," or the celesta's descent in the coda of the Dixie Cups' "Chapel of Love." Such scales may also provide a deeper background structure that disappears unnoticed behind stronger voices, as in the volume-pedal colored second guitar's rise of a full twelfth on the second beat of every bar behind the guitar solo of the Beatles' "Day Tripper."

Although it appears far less often than the major, the minor mode is used quite a bit, appearing about 75 times in our top twenty. It is characterized by the substitution of ♭3 for scale-degree 3, a preference in most cases for ♭6 over 6, and in some contexts, for ♭7 over 7. Note that the triad built on the first degree of a minor scale is spelled 1—♭3—5; think of these scale degrees in the opening three notes of the melody of the Four Lads' "Istanbul (Not Constantinople)," or the opening notes to the words, "there's a man who..." in Johnny Rivers's "Secret Agent Man." This arpeggiation sounds different from the I triad in a major mode, 1—3—5. We say that the I chord of a major mode, and any triad with a major third and perfect fifth, such as 4—6—1 or 5—7—2, are major triads. We will use lowercase roman numerals to indicate minor triads built on those indicated scale degrees, so we understand that the i chord in a minor mode, spelled 1—♭3—5 and characterized by the minor third between 1 and ♭3, is itself a minor triad. The minor triad is also heard on scale degrees 4—♭6—1 in the minor mode (forming the iv chord in a minor key), but can also be heard in the ii, iii, and vi triads of the major mode, because they all share the same-sized thirds and fifths: 2—4—6, 3—5—7, and 6—1—3, respectively. Three major triads normally appear in the minor mode: ♭III (spelled ♭3—5—♭7; note the major third from ♭3 to 5), ♭VI (♭6—1—♭3), and ♭VII (♭7—2—4). These, in fact, are the contexts that allow the melodic lowered seventh scale degree in the minor mode. Songs in the minor mode frequently use both ♭7 and 7, as when James Brown's "It's a Man's, Man's, Man's, Man's World" features the minor v chord (5—♭7—2) within verses (as at 0:15 and 0:19), but requires the more structural major V chord (5—7—2) at cadences (as at 0:25–0:29). In Simon and Garfunkel's "A Hazy Shade of Winter," ♭7 rises to Paul Simon's lead vocal part when the ♭III chord appears (0:16), and then the appearance of raised 7 is reserved for the climactic cadence (0:28): "[5/i] Time, time, time, see what's [♭3] be- [4/♭VII] -come of [4—5] me [4] while [5] I [♭6/iv] looked around for my [5] pos- [4] -si- [♭7/♭IIIᴹ⁷] -bilities. [5] I [♭6] was [5] so [4/♭VII] hard [♭3] to [2] please but look a- [♭3/i—1] -round, [5] leaves [♭3] are [4/♭VII] brown and the [♭6/♭VI] sky is a [7/V] ha- [5] -zy [7] shade of [♭3/i] win- [1] -ter." (In this slash notation, where the Arabic number appears to the left of the Roman Numeral, the vocal pitch is indicated over the supporting harmony. Referring to the example just presented, the words "Time, time, time" are all recited on 5 while accompanied by i; the word "become" is sung with ♭3 on the first syllable, and 4 sung on the next, right as the chord changes to ♭VII.)

People speak of a minor scale (in fact, most classical musicians are taught three different minor scales), but—this collection being more abstract than most—the concept is generally not too helpful in understanding the mode's pitch usage. The sixth and seventh scale degrees, as we have hinted, are problematical, but it is enough to remember that in minor, the sixth degree is lowered (appearing as ♭6) unless it is part of a melody moving up to the regular seventh scale degree, and that the seventh scale degree is the same as heard in the major mode unless a noncadential context favors the ♭III or ♭VII chord (thereby allowing ♭7 to appear instead of 7) or unless ♭7 appears melodically on the way down to ♭6. (Figure 7.02 will aid the reader in visualizing these scale degrees.) We normally wish to avoid steps larger than the major second between any versions of the otherwise flexible sixth and seventh scale degrees, which in melodies will normally lie a major second apart, so where ♭6 appears, the surrounding tune will take the seventh degree down with it to ♭7. One exception to this rule is the Armenian-inspired instrumental number, Ralph Marterie's "Shish-Kebab," which routinely spells its melodic scale degrees 5—♭6—7—1—7—♭6—5 for a non-Western melodic effect. (Listen to Web audio example 7.02.) (Keith's "Tell Me to My Face" features a similarly large augmented second between ♭3 and ♯4 in another exotic scale that seems like a Moroccan reference.) Although there is no single minor scale, stepwise melodic material in the minor mode perhaps reaches its greatest lengths in the Kinks' "Sunny Afternoon" and the Moody Blues' "Melancholy Man."

The lowered melodic inflections of the minor mode (♭3, ♭6, and ♭7) are normally chosen to illustrate the tragic (Ben E. King's "I (Who Have Nothing)," Diana Ross and the Supremes' "Love Child," Don Fardon's "(The Lament of the Cherokee) Indian Reservation"), the grim (the Animals' "The House of the Rising Sun," the Turtles' "Grim Reaper of Love," the Rolling Stones' "Paint It, Black," Cher's "Bang Bang," Zager and Evans's "In the Year 2525 (Exordium and Terminus)"), the melancholic (The Mamas and the Papas' "California Dreaming," Janis Ian's "Insanity Comes Quietly to the Structured Mind," Mary Hopkin's "Those Were the Days"), the lonely

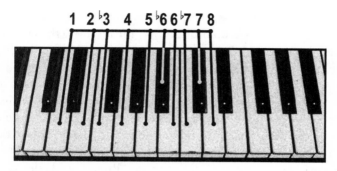

Figure 7.02. Elements of the minor mode.

(Jackie Wilson's "My Empty Arms," Herman's Hermits' "No Milk Today"), the cruel (Ray Charles's "Hit the Road Jack," the Four Seasons' "Beggin'" and "C'mon Marianne"), and sometimes the mysterious (the Chordettes' "Zorro," the Searchers' "Love Potion Number Nine," The Doors' "People Are Strange," the First Edition's "Just Dropped In (To See What Condition My Condition Was In)"). This can go way too far in bathetic drama, as in Paul Anka's "(All of a Sudden) My Heart Sings." There are a few minor-mode blues, as by Ray Charles ("I Don't Need No Doctor," "Unchain My Heart," "Don't Set Me Free"), and with B. B. King's "The Thrill Is Gone." Just as we saw with the major mode, the minor can sometimes appear for incongruous reasons, not seeming to fit the positive moods in Jimmie Rodgers's "Kisses Sweeter Than Wine," Simon and Garfunkel's "We've Got a Groovey Thing Goin'," or, from the soundtrack of *The Sound of Music*, "My Favorite Things." A prevailing genre of the period was the minor-mode instrumental hit, examples including the Ventures' "Walk—Don't Run," Ferrante and Teicher's "Exodus," Kenny Ball's "Midnight in Moscow," the Village Stompers' "Washington Square," the Chantay's' "Pipeline," the Marketts' "Out of Limits," the Bob Crewe Generation's "Music to Watch Girls By," and Paul Mauriat's "Love Is Blue." Two rock albums chock full of minor-mode music are the Moody Blues' *Days of Future Passed* and the Beatles' *Abbey Road*.

It can be very effective to contrast major-mode and minor-mode passages within the same song, especially as the major mode will typically sound bright against the darker quality of the minor mode. When this involves the alteration of a scale's tones, we call this mode mixture, and it can be as brief as a few chords—not even lasting a full phrase—or may involve the pitting of a song's sections in different modes against one another. One highly abbreviated form of mode mixture occurs when a major I chord unexpectedly appears at the end of a minor-mode song, instantly brightening and in some contexts redeeming the proceedings with a raised third scale degree before all would be lost in the minor-mode doldrums. (See, for instance, the ending of Web audio example 4.05.) This happens occasionally in rock, as in the final chords of Brian Hyland's "Sealed With a Kiss" and Jefferson Airplane's "Today." Most brief examples of mode mixture will be covered in a later chapter on modal harmony, but we may list here a number of ways that major/minor mode mixture may heighten the contrast between songs' sections: a minor introduction may precede a major-mode song (Brenda Lee's "Rusty Bells," the Beatles' "Do You Want to Know a Secret"), minor-mode verses will often give way to major-mode choruses (Del Shannon's "Runaway," Lesley Gore's "You Don't Own Me," Dusty Springfield's "You Don't Have to Say You Love Me," Paul Revere and the Raiders' "Kicks," the Beatles' "Girl") or minor-mode verses will lead to a major-mode bridge (Paul Mauriat's "Love Is Blue"). The contrast of the minor and the major mode's different sixth scale degrees is the point of the melody of "Do You Want to Know a Secret," the introduction of which opens with $\flat 6$ decorating the reciting tone, 5, leading to a verse that proceeds to ornament that 5 with its natural-6 upper neighbor: "[5/i] You'll never know how much I [$\flat 6$/iv] really [5/i] love you; [5/$\flat$III] you'll never know how much I [4/$\flat$II] really [5/V^{add6}] care. [6/I] List- [5] en, [iii—$\flat$iii—ii] [2] do [3] you [4] want [5/V^{m7}] to [6] know [7] a [6/I] sec- [5] -ret."

Rarely, verses in major will be followed by a minor-mode chorus (Marvin Gaye's "Pretty Little Baby," the Beatles' "Fool on the Hill"), the bridge may be the only section in minor (as in Ivo Robić's "Morgen" or the Beatles' "Here, There and Everywhere"), or perhaps the instrumental break of a major-mode song will appear in minor (the Four Seasons' "Tell It to the Rain"). Occasionally, a major-mode song will end in minor for a tragic effect, as in the tongue-in-cheek final verse of Georgie Fame's "The Ballad of Bonnie and Clyde" or the thoroughly pessimistic organ tag to Janis Ian's "Society's Child (Baby I've Been Thinking)." One particularly expressive use of large-scale mixture is in the Crystals' "Uptown," where the singer's heartthrob is just one member of an unruly mob through the minor-mode verses but rises to royal stature in the major-mode choruses.

Many who have had classical training might think of the minor mode as the opposite of the major, because most composers of the period roughly occupying the years 1725 to 1900 would indicate that this or that piece is in A major or in F minor. But such an opposition makes no sense in rock music, because although the minor mode does appear regularly, other nonmajor modes occur with comparable frequency. The scale that, next to the major, has most import in rock music is that of the minor-pentatonic, which is the sole melodic resource for some 130 of our top-twenty songs. This label, the minor-pentatonic, simply refers to a five-note scale that

The major- and minor-pentatonic scales.

has a minor third above tonic. There is also a major-pentatonic, and we shall cover that momentarily. The minor-pentatonic scale, closely linked to the blues, is spelled 1—♭3—4—5—♭7. (See fig. 7.03 and listen to Web audio example 7.03.) None of the steps are minor seconds (and other sharply dissonant intervals heard among members of the major collection are also lacking here), giving the collection a mellower tone than that typical of the major or minor modes. Note that within this limited scale, the only triads with roots, thirds, and fifths available are 1—♭3—5 and ♭3—5—♭7, so harmonic support must draw chord members from outside the scale except in rare cases such as Edwin Starr's "War," which supports a minor-pentatonic vocal simply with octaves on alternating first and lowered third scale degrees. (Usually, when the accompaniment supplies a lowered third, as for the i chord in Aretha Franklin's "Chain of Fools," the end result sounds minor, rather than a bluesy minor-pentatonic.)

It ought to be noted, too, that minor sevenths as well as roots are available within the scale for I^{m7}, IV^{m7}, and V^{m7} chords, even though their thirds and/or fifths might not be present, allowing for a much greater flexibility in adding sevenths to these basic chords. (In the major-minor system, sevenths are heard as dissonances that tend strongly to resolve to consonant intervals; conversely, they behave with absolute freedom in the minor-pentatonic system.) This propensity for added chordal sevenths can be heard in such songs as Bob Dylan's "In My Time of Dying," Wilson Pickett's "Funky Broadway," or the Isley Brothers' "It's Your Thing," where singing is done over an unchanging I^{m7} chord, or Edwin Starr's "Twenty-Five Miles," where the vocal is supported by major I^{m7} and IV^{m7} chords.

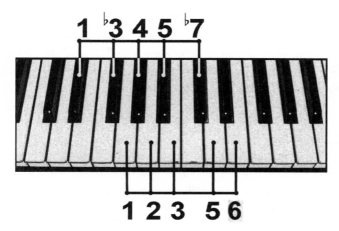

Figure 7.03. Examples of the minor-pentatonic (above) and major-pentatonic (below) scales.

Note that in all these cases, the I triad is major, drawing its third from outside the pentatonic scale. Usually, in fact, use of the minor-pentatonic will involve melodic material sung or played by soloing instrumentalists restricted to that scale while the harmonic accompaniment will draw freely from the major scale, and all will together actually sound as if the major mode is predominant but subject to heavily bluesy melodic inflections. (Listen to Web audio example 7.04.) Singers working completely in the minor-pentatonic world while their accompanying instrumental parts followed the major were typical in blues ancestry through figures such as Robert Johnson and Ledbetter, and carried the technique into early rock performances. One such example has Clyde McPhatter riff on the line, "[5] something like [5—4—5] teas- [4] -ing [♭3—1] me," at 1:16–1:20 in the first bridge of the Dominoes' "Do Something For Me. In the second bridge (compare 2:15–2:18 to the foregoing passage), McPhatter sits out while the line is presented by the backing chorus in the pure major mode. The minor-pentatonic—over—major system governs such disparate songs as Chuck Berry's "Maybelline," James Brown's "Please, Please, Please," Patsy Cline's "Walkin' After Midnight," the Dave Clark Five's "Can't You See That She's Mine," Marvin Gaye's "Ain't That Peculiar," and the Supremes' "Love Is Like an Itching in My Heart," which was Diana Ross's first foray into the minor-pentatonic. Despite the large supportive role of the major mode in these songs, one must realize how important are the minor-pentatonic tones of the vocalist; when Donovan sings from the major scale with a few chromatic ornaments in "Sunshine Superman," the tune is hardly recognizable as a blues! And the total freedom of all members of the minor-pentatonic scale to behave in any way they wish, without communicating any built-in desires to resolve or reach for goals, can be easily demonstrated by having a five-year-old novice play whatever their hands want to do on the pentatonically related black keys of the upper half of a piano keyboard while someone a bit more accomplished accompanies them on the lower half with a blues in E-flat major. The results will sound amazingly good, because the child is playing from the scale that, pitchwise, just cannot yield a bad melody!! In the minor-pentatonic system, tension is created by the use of tones drawn from outside the scale, and by a strong reliance on syncopation and other accentual clashes. These techniques bring life to the 8—8—♭7—8—5—♭5!—4—1—♭3—1 ostinato in Cream's "Sunshine of Your Love." Much heavy metal of later years would preserve such minor-pentatonic riffs but abandon the major-mode harmonic underpinnings so important in rock's formative decades.

The minor-pentatonic scale can also be a source of ornamental devices. Otherwise major-mode melodies can be given minor-pentatonic ornaments basic to blues singing, as with Little Esther Phillips's "Release Me," Nancy Wilson's "(You Don't Know) How Glad I Am," Lesley Gore's "It's My Party" (note the inflection of "but he's supPOSED to be MINE"), Linda Ronstadt's vocal in the Stone Poneys' "Different Drum," or Jerry Garcia's work in the Dead's "Black Peter" (as in his graceful roulades in "laying," 0:27, and "who," 1:20–1:22). Frequently, songs in other modes will contain minor-pentatonic references in little guitar interjections (as in George Harrison's Gretsch additions to the verses of the Beatles' "She Loves You") or in full-blown solos, as in Buck Owens's "I've Got a Tiger By the Tail," Jimmy Page's addition to Herman's Hermits' "I'm Into Something Good," Vic Flick's solo on Peter and Gordon's "A World Without Love," or Frank Zappa's extended jam following a quote of Gustav Holst's "Jupiter" theme in the Mothers' "Invocation and Ritual Dance of the Young Pumpkin." In fact, Sugar Cane Harris's electric violin seems to be calibrated to play only tones from the minor-pentatonic as he solos in Zappa's "Willie the Pimp," "The Gumbo Variations," and "Directly From My Heart to You." The rock guitar solo appears to blister most readily in the minor-pentatonic, as in Bill Justis's "Raunchy," Mitch Ryder and the Detroit Wheels' "Devil With a Blue Dress On," Buffalo Springfield's "Leave," The Doors' "Soul Kitchen," and Jimi Hendrix's "May This Be Love." Hendrix has an idiosyncratic twist, often playing tones of the minor-pentatonic scale plus their double-stopped parallel fourths above, as in the introductory and final gestures of "Castles Made of Sand."

An important nontriadic structural group of minor-pentatonic scale degrees is what can be called the blues trichord. A look at the scale will indicate that four different groupings of three adjacent pitches (1—♭3—4, 4—5—♭7, 5—♭7—1, and ♭7—1—♭3) all contain the same combination of three intervals: major second, minor third, and perfect fourth. These patterns combine countless times as three-note groupings in blues melodies. (Listen to Web audio example 7.05.) In other words, although the minor-pentatonic is a five-note scale, often hearing only a blues trichord from that scale allows one to infer the blues context. This leads to Peggy Lee's chant, "I'll say it again" on 5—♭7—5—♭7—8 at every chorus cadence in "I'm a Woman." And the "hey, hey, hey, hey, yeah!" chant on 8—♭7—5—♭7—8 in Gary U.S. Bonds's "New Orleans," and the "I can't get no!" protest in the Stones' "(I Can't Get No) Satisfaction," and the entire vocal material of Canned Heat's "On the Road Again" and Led Zeppelin's "Living Loving Maid."

Longer scale passages occur frequently in descending minor-pentatonic cascades, as in the central section of the Beatles' "Happiness Is a Warm Gun," where Lennon sings in octaves, a distorted guitar doubling along: "[5/I^m7] I [♭7] need [5] a [♭3] fix [1] 'cause [♭3] I'm [5] goin' [4—♭3—1] down, [5] down [♭7] to [5] the [♭3] bits [1] that [♭3] I [5] left [♭7] up [5—♭7] town." Also see the refrains of Little Richard's "Miss Ann," Elvis Presley's "So Glad You're Mine," the Beatles' "I Saw Her Standing There," Jack Bruce's repeated a cappella cries of "all right" in Cream's "Cat's Squirrel," and the instrumental introductions or tattoos of Roy Orbison's "Candy Man," Marvin Gaye's "I'll Be Doggone," Bob Dylan's "Obviously 5 Believers," and Johnny Rivers's "Memphis."

Just as with the previously discussed major-minor mixture, it is very common to juxtapose minor-pentatonic and major phrases or sections within songs. In "(We're Gonna) Rock Around the Clock," Bill Haley and His Comets linger in the suggestive minor-pentatonic world when promising what rocking the night will bring but behave in the innocent major mode in references to broad daylight. (See also Haley's "Dim, Dim the Lights" for the same metaphoric contrast of these two scales.) Chuck Berry mimics this in the major-mode verses of "Rock and Roll Music" as contrasted against its $\flat$7-heavy choruses. In Buddy Holly's "That'll Be the Day," it's primarily $\flat$3 that brings the chorus from the major world of the verses into the minor-pentatonic. The Beatles' "Can't Buy Me Love" features the reverse: a minor-pentatonic twelve-bar verse-refrain, with a major-mode chorus, whereas their "She's a Woman" contrasts a minor-pent verse with a major-mode bridge.

The major-pentatonic scale, far less common than the minor-pentatonic, may be spelled 1—2—3—5—6, and thus sounds like a major scale with its minor seconds removed. (Listen to Web audio example 7.06; please refer back to fig. 7.03.) It carries even less tension than does the relatively tranquil minor-pentatonic, because of the more peaceful major I triad at its core; this is well demonstrated in the verses of Johnny Mathis's wavelike song, "Wonderful! Wonderful!": "[6/I] Some- [5] -times [3] we [2] walk [3] hand [5] in [6] hand [5] by [3] the [2] sea [3] and [5] we [6] breathe [5] in [3] the [2] cool [3] sal- [5] -ty [6] air; [2/IV] you [1] turn [6] to [5] me [6] with [1] a [2] kiss [1] in [6] your [5] eyes...." Note how all four scale members that appear in the first phrase (2, 3, 5, and 6) move a fourth higher in the second (to 5, 6, 1, and 2), when the I chord is replaced by IV. The "missing" fourth and seventh scale degrees will have harmonic value as members of various accompanimental chords, not least the all-important V, and these tones might even appear fleetingly in the melody, but will not be considered regular scale degrees. The scale is common in many folk settings, including non-Western tunes; it is in fact perfectly represented in the vocal melody of Kyu Sakamoto's hit, sung in Japanese, "Sukiyaki." Tony Perkins gets a Hawaiian sound by singing few notes outside of the major-pentatonic scale in "Moonlight Swim." The southern Appalachian tune "Silver Dagger" is one of many major-pentatonic melodies (including "Wildwood Flower," "Ranger's Command," "Colours," and "Satisfied Mind") sung by Joan Baez. Donovan's "There is a Mountain" is a joyous airing of the scale, as are the verses of Jimi Hendrix's "May This Be Love" and "One Rainy Wish." Van Morrison adds a Scotch-Irish entry with the seven-minute major-pentatonic melody to "Astral Weeks." Instrumental ostinati often lie in the major-pentatonic realm; note the guitar tattoos of the Temptations' "My Girl," 1—2—3—5—6—8, which is then immediately transplanted via the IV chord to tones (4—5—6—1—2—4) outside the scale, just as did Mathis's melody. For other major-pentatonic instrumental riffs, see the Rivieras' "California Sun," Gary Lewis and the Playboys' "She's Just My Style," John Fred and His Playboy Band's "Judy In Disguise (With Glasses)," and the unison alto/tenor sax doubling of the tattoo in Van Morrison's "Domino." Some tunes (such as Sam Cooke's "Chain Gang") add the seventh scale degree as an ornament to the major pentatonic, whereas others (the Young Rascals' "Groovin'") occasionally add the fourth.

Five other scales normally associated with the music of much earlier eras

Other diatonic materials: the aeolian, dorian, mixolydian, lydian, and phrygian modes; the blues scale.

were given new life in rock music. Referred to as the medieval modes, these are the aeolian, dorian, mixolydian, lydian, and phrygian scales. Each is a seven-note scale with two minor seconds, and so these are cousins of the major scale (which, centuries ago, was known as ionian). They are spelled as follows, in order of popularity, and examples are illustrated in figure 7.04:

Dorian: 1—2—♭3—4—5—6—♭7   (minor seconds: 2—♭3, 6—♭7)

Aeolian: 1—2—♭3—4—5—♭6—♭7   (minor seconds: 2—♭3, 5—♭6)

Mixolydian: 1—2—3—4—5—6—♭7   (minor seconds: 3—4, 6—♭7)

Lydian: 1—2—3—♯4—5—6—7   (minor seconds: ♯4—5, 7—1)

Phrygian: 1—♭2—♭3—4—5—♭6—♭7   (minor seconds: 1—♭2, 5—♭6)

The dorian mode is similar to the minor, but its always-natural sixth scale degree colors the major IV chord that is not typical of the minor key; the alternation of a minor i chord and a major IV chord is therefore the readiest identifying feature of the dorian mode. (Web audio example 5.01 is introduced with a i—IV alternation.) This chord pair is heard in the intro of Jorgen Ingmann's "Apache," the verses of the Turtles' "You Showed Me," the chorus of the Electric Prunes' "I Had Too Much to Dream (Last Night)," the bridge of Brian Hyland's "Sealed With a Kiss," the tag ending of Del Shannon's "Keep Searchin' (We'll Follow the Sun)," and just about all of Santana's "Evil Ways." (Listen to Web audio example 7.07.) Of these examples, the Hyland passage makes most pronounced melodic use of the characteristic

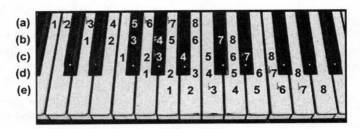

Figure 7.04. Examples of the (a) phrygian, (b) lydian, (c) dorian, (d) mixolydian, and (e) aeolian scales. Remember that the sharps and flats do not necessarily indicate black keys but, rather, deviations from membership in the major scale.

dorian sixth scale degree: "I'll [6/IV] see you [5] in [4] the [5/i] sunlight, [1] I'll [6/IV] hear your voice [5] ev- [4] -ery- [5/i] where." The Renaissance-era dorian tune, "Greensleeves," was recorded by the Jeff Beck Group; this also features the dorian sixth degree in the melody: 1—♭3—4—5—6—5—4—2—♭7.... In both of these, and also in Simon and Garfunkel's "Scarborough Fair/Canticle," 6 is used as an upper neighbor to 5. About twenty-five top-twenty songs from our era are entirely or largely in the dorian mode; these and others include the Animals' "Monterey," the Moody Blues' "The Sun Set," the Association's "Along Comes Mary," Simon and Garfunkel's "Sounds of Silence," The Doors' "Soul Kitchen," Strawberry Alarm Clock's "Incense and Peppermints," and Hugo Montenegro's "The Good, the Bad and the Ugly."

The aeolian mode can be heard as a version of the minor, but its harmonic accompaniment will not include a major V chord because its seventh degree is always lowered, whether featured in the tune or not. (Listen to Web audio example 7.08.) Note how the descent through ♭7 to 5 is featured in tunes such as the Animals' "Don't Let Me Be Misunderstood," "[1/i] Baby, do you [2] un- [♭3] -der- [2/♭VII] -stand me [2—1—♭7] now, [♭6/♭VI] sometimes I feel a little [5/V] mad." At other times, ♭7 approaches 8 directly, as in the Rolling Stones' "Play With Fire," which opens with a pentatonic-like tune that is filled in as aeolian: "[♭7/i] Well, [8] you've [♭3] got [1] your [♭7] dia- [8] -mond, and [5] you've [♭7] got [8] your [♭3] pret- [1] -ty [♭7—8] clothes...[1] but don't [♭3] play [4] with [5] me, 'cause you're [♭6] playin' with [5] fire." Note here also how ♭6 is used as a neighbor to 5, as opposed to the 6—5 idea in our dorian examples. The aeolian scale is heard in a few more than twenty top-twenty songs of the era and in many others not as popular, most notably in Johnny and the Hurricanes' "Crossfire," Dave Brubeck's "Take Five," Booker T. and the M. G.s' "Green Onions," the verses of the Hollies' "Bus Stop," Bob Dylan's "All Along the Watchtower" and "As I Went Out One Morning," the Ventures' "Hawaii Five-O," Big Brother and the

Holding Co.'s "Ball and Chain," and Henry Mancini's "Love Theme From Romeo and Juliet."

The mixolydian scale is just like the major mode but for its lowered seventh scale degree, making a diatonic major V chord impossible. The major ♭VII chord, all of which tones (♭7—2—4) are neighbors to members of the I chord, often substitutes in cadential situations for the unavailable V. (Listen to Web audio example 7.09.) Only a handful of mixolydian melodies are found in the era's top hits, and these nearly always involve some mixture from the major mode. The first phrase of the instrumental, Herb Alpert and the Tijuana Brass's "The Lonely Bull" (3—4—5—4—3—2—♭7—♭7—1—2—1—5—5—1—5—♭7), for instance, is fully mixolydian, but the verse concludes as a period with the major-mode's full cadence, V—I. The verse of Jay and the Americans' "She Cried" is strongly mixolydian, but the bridge contains changes of scale degree. Likewise, the chorus of Lesley Gore's "She's a Fool" is the only mixolydian section in that song. The Kingsmen's "Louie Louie," with its thirdless I and IV chords but its repulsive minor v, has a mixolydian vocal. The Kinks' "Tired of Waiting for You" ("[1] So [2] tired, [1] tired [2] of [3] waiting, tired [4] of [5] waiting [6] for [♭7—6—5] you") and the Stones' "Lady Jane" have beautiful mixolydian melodies, the latter introduced on dulcimer, harpsichord, and nylon-string guitar. Jimi Hendrix's expansive octave-doubled guitar tune in "Third Stone From the Sun" is in a placid mixolydian.

The lydian and phrygian scales are quite rare. (Listen to Web audio examples 7.10 and 7.11.) The former is represented by Donovan's "Peregrine," suggesting a north-Indian influence by way of Scotland: "[1] Oh [2] your [3] boats [2] up- [1] -on [7] the [6] sea [5] are [6] ve- [7] -ry [8] beau- [7] ti- [6] -ful [5] to [♯4] view [3] by [♯4—5—6] me, [5] by [6—5—♯4] me, [3] by [♯4—5—6] me, [5] by [6—5—♯4] me, [3] I [♯4] hope [5] by [6—1—3] you." The lydian is also heard in much of the Beatles' "Blue Jay Way," and by strong yet deft melodic touches of ♯4 in the Left Banke's otherwise major "Pretty Ballerina." The phrygian mode, characterized by the minor second above 1, is heard in the unusual alteration of ♭II and i, as in Bob and Earl's "Harlem Shuffle" : "You [♭7—♭6/i] move [♭7] it [♭6] to [1] the [5] left, [♭3] yeah, then you [5] go for [♭3] yourself.... [4/♭II ᵐ⁷] Now [♭7] take [♭6] it kind- [4] -a [♭7—♭6] slow with [4] a [♭7] whole [♭6] lot- [4] -ta [♭7—♭6] soul; [♭2] don't [♭7/i] move [♭6] it [♭6—♭3] too [5] fast...." The same i—♭II—i alternations occur in the Great Society's (less so the later Jefferson Airplane's) "White Rabbit," the Chantay's' "Pipeline," Crosby, Stills and Nash's "Wooden Ships," and Quicksilver Messenger Service's "Calvary."

Another scale with historical connections is the whole-tone scale, so called because its six scale degrees, 1—2—3—♯4—♯5—♯6, are all a whole-step (a major second, as opposed to the half-step minor second) apart. (Listen to

Web audio example 7.12.) This collection was heard quite often in music composed in the late nineteenth and early twentieth centuries, but is rare in rock; its use is probably imported from jazz (as from Oscar Peterson or Bill Evans) as opposed to the impressionists such as Debussy who made it famous. Because of its totally symmetrical structure, no relational syntax—and therefore no sense of a tonal center—is built into the system. Because of this issue, the whole-tone scale does not exist on its own in rock, but functions only as a momentary ornament of the major scale. Fleeting examples are heard near the end of Dionne Warwick's "Alfie" (2:01–2:06), where time stops so that the vibes may continue to move in whole steps following a vocal major second, and in Stevie Wonder's "My Cherie Amour," where a hidden whole-tone chord at 0:44–0:46 plants the seed for the great whole-tone scales (doubled in major thirds) later to be unleashed over the introductory V in his "You Are the Sunshine of My Life."

A traditional use of ♭5 instead of the natural fifth scale degree occurs in the so-called blues scale. But it is exceedingly rare to throw 5 over for ♭5 in rock music; the latter is normally a momentary ornament to a scale featuring a natural 5 that lies more at its core. Two songs that do threaten to elevate a horrific ♭5, however, are Nancy Sinatra's "These Boots Are Made for Walkin'" ("[♭7] one of these days these [8] boots [♭5] are gonna walk [4] all [♭3] o- [2] -ver [1] you") and the Plastic Ono Band's "Cold Turkey," which duplicates the Beatles' "Glass Onion" in having ♭5 sung over the minor i triad.

Most of the other top-twenty hits not accounted for in this chapter are songs whose melodies mix and match phrases from several scales, or are grounded in one particular mode but are ornamented by momentary alterations of scale degree so frequently as to render allegiance to a single underlying scale questionable. And then there are the rare non-hits like Pink Floyd's "Let There Be More Light" and "Astronomy Domine," which feature fully indeterminate scales.

Unpitched song

It must be mentioned here that a great deal of the pop-rock repertoire involves melody that is either entirely unpitched, as with the spoken word, or

Unpitched song: the spoken word.

where pitch is used more like a speech inflection than in representation of some particular tonal pitch collection. These approaches are adopted for a surprising variety of purposes. The spoken-word genre of course contains a few comedy and novelty records, such as Jack Ross's "Cinderella," Jose Jimenez's "The Astronaut," Napoleon XIV's "They're Coming to Take Me Away, Ha-Haaa!," Bill Cosby's unclassifiable "Little Ole Man (Uptight—Everything's

Alright)," the Hollywood Argyles' "Alley Oop," and such imitations as of Yogi Bear in Boyd Bennett and His Rockets' "Boogie Bear" and the Ivy Three's "Yogi." Mel Blanc himself interjects cartoon voices in Pat Boone's "Speedy Gonzales." Very often, a spoken recording is simply one of a narrator telling a sappy or a humorous story, as in Billy Vaughn's "The Shifting, Whispering Sands," Bill Parsons' "The All-American Boy," Wink Martindale's "Deck of Cards," Rolf Harris's "Tie Me Kangaroo Down, Sport," the Barbarians' "Moulty," Mike Douglas's "The Men in My Little Girl's Life," Peggy Lee's "Is That All There Is?," and Johnny Cash's "A Boy Named Sue." In both Tennessee Ernie Ford's "Ballad of Davy Crockett" and Jan and Dean's "Dead Man's Curve," only the last verse is spoken to heighten the immediacy of the story's final chapter. And that's why the last verse of the Irish Rovers' "The Unicorn" breaks the fourth wall by ending with the spoken line, "and that's why you've never seen a unicorn to this very day."

Occasionally, poetry is not set to song but intoned as read, in the Moody Blues' *Days of Future Passed* album, a slew of Graeme Edge's later spacey contributions to that group, The Doors' "Horse Latitudes," the Soft Machine's "Why Are We Sleeping?," Cream's "Pressed Rat and Warthog," and a number of discs by Rod McKuen. Correspondence has more impact when read aloud than when set to music, and so that is done with Pat Boone's "I'll Be Home" and Victor Lundberg's "An Open Letter to My Teenage Son." In a few cases, such as Lolita's "Sailor" and the Sandpipers' "Guantanamera," tunes first sung in a foreign tongue are later given a spoken voice-over translation that also breaks the presentational fourth wall as a direct aside to the listener. Tributes and odes are often spoken, as in Tommy Dee's "Three Stars," Senator Everett McKinley Dirksen's "Gallant Men," and It's a Beautiful Day's "Galileo." Parody records may be spoken too, as with the Detergents' "Leader of the Laundromat." Phil McLean's "Small Sad Sam" remains faithful to the tone of Jimmy Dean's delivery of "Big Bad John," as do the final-verse references in Dean's own "P.T. 109."

The spoken word may be that of the auctioneer (Leroy Van Dyke's "Auctioneer"), the announcer (as with the reverberating opening airport announcement in Rose Garden's "Next Plane to London" or in the Rolling Stones' "On With the Show"), the dance caller (Ray Bryant's Combo's "The Madison Time," Chubby Checker's single line, "how low can you go?," inserted at a few points in "Limbo Rock," or Archie Bell and the Drells' "Tighten Up"), the record producer (coaxing Senator Bobby through "Wild Thing"), the entertainment director (Shirley Ellis's "The Name Game"), the bailiff (Shorty Long's "Here Comes the Judge," the Unifics' "Court of Love"), the drill sergeant (the Monitors' "Greetings (This Is Uncle Sam)"), or a chanting crowd (the Routers' "Let's Go (Pony)"). Jim Morrison provides a three-minute incantation in The Doors' "The End" and shouts the anti-invocation, "You cannot petition the Lord in prayer!" in "The Soft Parade," Robert Plant intones a story in Led

Zeppelin's "How Many More Times," and a Scotsman's diatribe ends Pink Floyd's "Several Species of Small Furry Animals Gathered Together in a Cave and Grooving with a Pict." The Marvelettes' "My Baby Must Be a Magician" opens with Melvin Franklin of the Temptations intoning a deep-bass inducement to hypnotic trance. The singer may quote a poem through the spoken word, as does Donovan in "Goo Goo Barabajagal (Love Is Hot)," or may quote a tale, as he does in "Riki Tiki Tavi." Authority figures, especially fathers, are imitated with spoken lines in Eddie Cochran's "Summertime Blues" and the Lovin' Spoonful's "Did You Ever Have to Make Up Your Mind?" John F. Kennedy's American University speech of June 10, 1963, on Peace is sampled in the Buckinghams' bold tape piece, "Foreign Policy."

The fourth wall may be represented by a spoken introductory frame that could simply be the unedited count-in, as with the Beatles' "I Saw Her Standing There" or Sam the Sham and the Pharaohs' "Wooly Bully," a proclamation of the song's title, as with the Champs' "Tequila," Alvin Cash and the Crawlers' "Twine Time," or Cozy Cole's "Topsy II," or an introductory aside to the listener, as with Frankie Laine's "Moonlight Gambler," the Kingston Trio's "Tom Dooley," Bob Dylan's "Baby, Let Me Follow You Down," Sonny Bono's "Laugh at Me," the Mothers' "Call Any Vegetable," or Jimmy Ruffin's "I've Passed This Way Before." Sometimes, a final frame appears at the end of the recording, as when a comment appending Blood, Sweat and Tears' "Spinning Wheel"—"that wasn't too good" and its attendant laughter—is not trimmed away. Sometimes, the frame is observed mid-song with a transitional aside, as in the explanation offered by Lou Monte in "Lazy Mary (Luna Mezzo Mare)" or when Stevie Wonder reaches out beyond the singer's persona to voice the entertainer's entreaty, "you know, when times are bad, I want you to always remember...," just before the last chorus of "A Place in the Sun." Sometimes, a girl group's spoken introductory line is not addressed to the listener but still eases the recording into the world of song, as when the Angels suggest the warning to come in "My Boyfriend's Back," when the Shirelles open "Foolish Little Girl" by scolding, "you broke his heart and made him cry...," or in the Shangri-Las' gradual shift from recitative to aria in "Leader of the Pack."

A technique heard frequently since Hoppy Jones of the Ink Spots made it effective in the 1930s, is for a singer to drop the vocalizing and shift to the spoken word for an introspective later verse or bridge, as if speaking from the heart, reaching the audience with inner thoughts in a more direct way than an "artificial" melody is able to do. This is an expressive effect that does not cross the frame; examples include the Diamonds' "Little Darlin'" ("Little Darlin', I NEED you...") and Elvis Presley's paraphrase of Shakespeare in "Are You Lonesome To-night?" The effect becomes far more artificial than would be a tune when the words are stretched out in a slow rhythm like "please accept my a—pol—o—gy" by Brenda Lee in "I'm Sorry." In "Hey There," Rosemary Clooney's sung vocal is put into the background with augmented reverb to allow her dry spoken verse to assume center stage.

The spoken word also allows conversations between duo singers, as with Mickey and Sylvia in "Love Is Strange" or Dinah Washington and Brook Benton in "Baby (You've Got What It Takes)." It may suggest such things as the division of the psyche as when the singer's better half interrupts James Darren's "Conscience," aliens communicating on a radio as in Jimi Hendrix's "Third Stone From the Sun," or trading disses as with Johnny O'Neal's "Ugly Woman," Bo Diddley's "Say Man," Ike and Tina Turner's "It's Gonna Work Out Fine," Jimmy Soul's "If You Wanna Be Happy," and Otis and Carla's "Tramp." Speaking can rise to emotional heights with extramelodic pleading (Joe Tex's "I Gotcha," the Mothers' "Go Cry On Somebody Else's Shoulder") and can descend to inner depths ("and there ain't nothin' I can do about it" in the Supremes' "Love Is Here and Now You're Gone"). A number of examples employ speech-song, where pitch, even definite pitch, is used as an expressive speech device, but no tonal melody is intended; Bob Dylan's "Stuck Inside of Mobile With the Memphis Blues Again," the Syndicate of Sound's "Little Girl," the Troggs' "Wild Thing," the Kinks' "Dedicated Follower of Fashion," the Chambers Brothers' "Time Has Come Today," Three Dog Night's "Mama Told Me (Not to Come)," and John Lennon's responses (1:49–2:01) to Ringo's verses in the Beatles' "Yellow Submarine" are good examples, but Johnny Tillotson's "True True Happiness" shows where it can go wrong. A few proto-rap examples of highly rhythmic spoken text with exhaustive rhyming existed before 1970, including Pigmeat Markham's "Here Comes the Judge." Broadway offers a great example of polyphonic spoken word in the show-opening "Rock Island" from *The Music Man,* the Mothers of Invention present a barbershop rendition of four-part spoken word ("it can't happen here...") in Part III of "Help, I'm a Rock," and a number of songs have patter as an objective ("Ya Got Trouble," *The Music Man,* Joe Tex's "Skinny Legs and All"). Perhaps the most unusual spoken-word record of all time, though, is a continuous rant seemingly improvised by Albert King in the Stax Studio, released as "Cold Feet." Here, over a twelve-bar blues, the singer complains continuously, "[ya] keep raisin' sin about playin' this chord, ya ain't hittin' the B♭ right; [I've] been hangin' around this studio for three days in a row now, there ain't nobody can get a hit out of here but Sam & Dave..."

This coverage of scales and other pitch collections has given us aural command over all of the raw materials available to rock composers and performers. We now turn to the ways in which these elements were given life and meaning in phrases through different contours, patterns, and directionality.

Melodic Contour and Ornamentation

One way of characterizing melodic construction is to examine a melody's range. Some tunes have a very narrow range, perhaps existing mostly in strings of repeated pitches. The verses of Chuck Berry's "Maybelline" motor right along, their cylinders always firing on ♭3; Bob Dylan mimics this approach by reciting on 5 for "On the Road Again," "Bob Dylan's 115th Dream," and "Tombstone Blues." Little Richard, Larry Williams, and Jerry Lee Lewis favor repeated tones for emphasis of their lyric content, and Creedence Clearwa-

> **Melodic contour:** range, syllabic and melismatic tunes, steps and skips, repetition, compound melodies, sequences, direction toward a goal.

ter Revival revive the same fixation in their verses of "Travelin' Band." In the repeated-note bridge (1:01–1:08) of "So Long, Frank Lloyd Wright," Simon and Garfunkel suggest the run-of-the-mill quality of other architects, and perhaps even Wright's flat, prairie-inspired horizontal cantilevered lines as well, through the long-repeated 1.

In the verses of Beatles' "Strawberry Fields Forever" (as at "living is easy with eyes closed"), John Lennon obliquely contrasts his repeated vocal pitch against the descending inner-part Mellotron line for an introspective look, and in contrast, Paul McCartney belts out repeated notes once he finds a pitch he likes in order to shout out a frustrated point ("silly people standing there who disagree...") in the Beatles' "Fixing a Hole." I suppose Ed Ames's "Who Will Answer," largely intoned on an unchanging first scale degree, perhaps to underline its focused seriousness, is the ultimate in non-moving melody. Note how Sonny and Cher change at 0:11 from a repeated-note idea to a moving one to balance the phrases of the verses of "I Got You Babe." The Association provide a strict-as-a-dictionary repeated-note intoned definition for "Cherish" but also express what it's like to be "out to lunch" in the constrained repeated-note verses sung before meeting a liberating force in "Along Comes Mary." The repeated note can be expressive instrumentally, too; note the cross-accent and the pairs of bent and straight notes in the guitar introduction to the mono mix of the Rolling Stones' "Time Is On My Side."

In other songs, the main tune will alternate between two pitches; so McCartney decorates the first scale degree with its ♭7 lower neighbor as he sings the verses of the Beatles' "Sgt. Pepper's Lonely Hearts Club Band," and so Eric Clapton gets across the psychedelic images of Cream's "Tales of Brave Ulysses." Many mysterious lines in the Beatles' "A Day in the Life" ("nobody was really sure if he was from...," "tu-u-u-urn you-ou-ou-ou o-o-o-o-o-o-o-n...") depend on the repeated alternation of two pitches a second apart for their effect, and a similarly mystical line, "we have all been here before" illustrates a sense of "Déjà vu" when sung in alternating steps by Crosby,

Stills, Nash and Young in muted, off-mike vocals. Chuck Berry typically alternates tones a minor third apart, as in "Havana Moon" (1 and 6) and "Too Much Monkey Business" (1 and ♭3), and so the latter pattern is recreated by Steppenwolf as an homage in "Berry Rides Again."

Still other tunes are characterized by a very wide range. In "True Love Ways," Buddy Holly demonstrates a very large range as he pours out his heart. Roy Orbison, in particular, climaxes in "Only the Lonely (Know How I Feel)" with a multioctave outburst. In "Pride and Joy," Marvin Gaye begins with a low Nat King Cole–like texture and opens up to achieve a much higher Smokey Robinson–like silky quality. Beginning with the bridge of the Righteous Brothers' "You've Lost That Lovin' Feelin'," Bill Medley and Bobby Hatfield trade lines, harmonize in thirds (2:15–2:30), then trade tortured two-bar segments in ever higher registers, Hatfield in falsetto, building the tension up to the arrival of the last chorus (2:56+). Their "Ebb Tide" is a similar rise-to-climax song, where the rise of vocal register works along with the additive wall of sound and growing strength of harmonic motions, but it's not clear why growth is so clearly indicated—doesn't an ebb tide progress from peak to trough? Note how Chuck Berry uses different vocal ranges and textures to illustrate a change of narrative perspectives in "Little Queenie," where most verses are sung in a high tessitura at definite pitch, but the verses preceded by the transitional adverb, "meanwhile" (as at 0:38–0:55), move to a low range for inner thoughts that are expressed in a contrasting speech-song introduced long before Bob Dylan led imitators into this arena.

We can also divide melodic tendencies into the rat-a-tat syllabic approach, where nearly every syllable is sung on its own pitch (more prevalent in hard-rocking styles), and the flowing melismatic style, where two, several, or many notes are sung on a single syllable (more prevalent in pop styles). (Listen to Web audio example 7.13.) Tunes built of repeated notes (discussed above) are by definition syllabic, but this group can also include melodies that move by step or skip in any combination. Melismas can be acrobatic, reaching over the break into the falsetto, as when Johnny Moore sings "lots of pretty girls with figures they don't try to *hide*" in more than a two-octave range, a great contrast from his earthy low notes for "huggin' with your baby, last row in the balcony" in the Drifters' "Saturday Night at the Movies." Little Richard has a beautiful "gal" that Pat Boone strains to describe with a similar melisma (0:24) in "Tutti-Frutti."

Melismas may often be gospel-motivated, as in Aretha Franklin's "Baby I Love You" (note how her "oh!" reaches up to a high 1 in 1:21–1:22) and "I Never Loved a Man (The Way I Love You)" (see how "why" at 0:17 with its ghost yodel is followed by a descending pentatonic melisma and "whoa" has a melisma at 0:31–0:33 that begins soft and ends on a high-register yelp). Jackie Wilson opens "Please Tell Me Why" with an extensive ten-second gospel melisma on the word "I." The very slow last line of Billy Stewart's "Summertime" evolves into the very rare pop vocal cadenza on "do——————n't you br . . . . cry," with melismas among the featured ornaments.

Melismas are perhaps most expressive when reserved for the final retransitional V of the bridge, as in Johnnie Ray's "You Don't Owe Me a Thing" (which emphasizes the homonyms of "a loan" and "a-lo-ho-hone"), Guy Mitchell's "Singing the Blues" ("cry-hy-hy-hy over you"), Jackie Wilson's "Lonely Teardrops," the Penguins' "Earth Angel," the Platters' "The Great Pretender," the Five Satins' "In the Still of the Nite," Carl Perkins' "Lend Me Your Comb," and Elvis Presley's "Tryin' to Get to You," for some of the sometimes virtuosic hallmark rockabilly and doo-wop examples of improvisatory lead-ins to the returning verses that follow. Simple but seductive are the melismas sung in parallel thirds by Eric Clapton and Jack Bruce on the final word of each title-bearing refrain in Cream's "Sunshine of Your Love."

Some melodies move in entirely stepwise motion, some largely by skip, and others mix the two approaches effectively, perhaps reserving a wide leap for sudden emphasis. Among the melodies that skip, the outlines of arpeggios are frequent melodic shapes. Consider Ray Charles's "Busted," most of the melody of which simply arpeggiates descending triads: the opening 5—3—1 arpeggiates the I chord, then 8—6—4 represents IV, followed by 9—7—5 for V. Members of the I chord, 1—3—5, open the tunes of Bill Haley's "Rock Around the Clock," Chubby Checker's "Limbo Rock" and Simon and Garfunkel's "The Big Bright Green Pleasure Machine" (arpeggiating in full 1—3—5—8—3), and do so in a different order in Buddy Holly's "Oh, Boy!," Herman's Hermits' "Dandy," and Creedence Clearwater Revival's "Down on the Corner." The verse of Harry Belafonte's "Banana Boat (Day-O)" simply arpeggiates the I chord: 3—5—3—5—3—5—8, and these are the only tones of Bob Dylan's "Oxford Town," as if the situation of that song is so foundationally clear and true that it needs no interpretive non-I tones for fancy decor. In the chorus of "Things," Bobby Darin alternates arpeggiations, all in the same rhythm, of V^{m7} (5—7—2—4), I (5—1—3—5), and V^{m7} (5—7—2—4) once again. Phrases ending 5—3, hovering over an unvoiced foundational 1, can have a wistful quality, as they do in Don Gibson's "Oh Lonesome Me." The phrases of the Righteous Brothers' "You've Lost That Lovin' Feelin'" combine to create a large dramatic arch based on the slightly decorated arpeggiation of a I chord: Bill Medley's vocal begins low on 5, goes through 1 to a decorated 4–3 figure resolving at "close" (0:01), continues up to 8 at "no" (0:11) and rises again to 3 on "Baby" (0:27). The minor i triad is also a source of melody, as in the opening 5—1—♭3—5 of the Beatles' "Your Mother Should Know," the bridge of which works its way to a retransitional arpeggiation of V^{m7} on "[5] sing [7] it [2] a- [4] -gain." For an instrumental arpeggiation of a minor i triad, one can't beat the Vox organ's introduction to Iron Butterfly's "In-A-Gadda-Da-Vida."

Ostinato figures, which usually involve rhythmically repeated arpeggiations, are not typical of vocal lines. Ostinati more commonly form melodies for guitar, bass, piano, and saxophone. Note, however, how many twelve-bar blues numbers repeat the first line, supported by I, note-for-note in their second phrase, even though IV supports it there. This is another example of the harmonic flexibility of the minor-pentatonic scale, the source for the melodies of such songs behaving this way as the Cadillacs' "Speedo," Little Richard's "Ooh! My Soul," Little Willie John's "Leave My Kitten Alone," Gene Vincent's "Be-Bop-a-Lula," Elvis Presley's "Too Much," Freddie Cannon's "Tallahassee Lassie," and Wilbert Harrison's "Kansas City." But it's also the principle behind the highly repetitious ♭3—2—1 tune in the refrain of Buffalo Springfield's "For What It's Worth (Stop, Hey What's That Sound)."

Sometimes, melodic skips seem to connect portions of two different parts of the range, leading to compound melodies that one singer performs by moving back and forth between them. Andy Williams's "(Where Do I Begin) Love Story" is a good example: "[♭3/i] Where [5] do I [♭3] begin [5] to tell [♭3] the sto- [5] -ry [♭6] of [5] how [4/V^{m7}/7] great a love [2] can be, [4] the sweet [2] love sto- [4] -ry [5] that [4] is [♭3/i] older than [8] the [8/i/♭7] sea, [i/♭6] [♭3] the sim- [8] -ple truth [♭3] a- [4] -bout [♭3] the [2/V^{m7}] love she brings [7] to me; [8] where [2] do [♭6] I [5/i] start?" (In this slash notation, the Arabic number *following* a Roman Numeral indicates that the bass carries a tone other than the root, as it moves to 7 under the V chord at "great.") Note how the tune seems to be composed of large skips: two bars of ♭3 skipping down to 5 and back, two of 4 leaping up to 2 and back, then two bars of a lower ♭3 jumping up to 8 and back, leading then through another two bars, now with 2 leaping up to 7, finally ending on 5. Note also how each two-bar pair contains the same rhythm but on a different chord, each chord containing the pair of skipping melodic tones: i (♭3—5)—V^{m7} (4—2)—i (♭3—8)—V^{m7} (2—7), ending on i (5). But another way to hear this tune is as a combination of two different stepwise lines moving together in parallel sixths: ♭3 stepping down to 2 to 8 to 7, all over the simultaneous lower line, which steps down 5—4—♭3—2; the effect is one of desperate searching for an answer, the vocalist looking first to one line and then to the other, constantly alternating up and down between the two virtual voices.

The two compounded "Love Story" lines move in parallel sixths, but other intervallic structures exist for such polyphonic melodies, as with the oblique lines in Buddy Holly's "Raining in My Heart," which alternates each rising scale degree in the line, 5—♯5—6—♭7, with the 3 above, the lower line suggesting perhaps an inner location for the heart, the repeated upper tones, perhaps, raindrops. It's often useful to hear melodies as divided into different register-bound ideas. Rick Nelson's "It's Up to You" features a wonderfully surprising melody when the repeated line, 3—5—7—6, is followed by a third phrase treating this idea as divided into two halves ("make up your mind!") and sequencing just the upper half, 3—5—9—8. The division of each line into two two-note fragments seems to portray two alternatives that must yield to a decision, and the eventual sequence at heightened pitch seems to bring out the singer's demanding impatience. A more involved compound line composed by Nilsson is the basis of Blood, Sweat and Tears' recording of "Without Her."

Sequencing, the repetition of a melodic pattern in the same rhythm but a step or more away, is a fairly widespread way to build pop tunes, but—probably because of its dependence on harmony in agreement with a seven-note scale—is fairly rare in hard rock. Consider Frank Sinatra's "Strangers in the Night." The opening phrase consists of three gestures, each based on the same melodic idea that first begins on 1, is repeated a step down beginning on 7, and then is sequenced down to begin on 6, cadencing weakly on IV. The second phrase is also made of three gestures, again the same pattern sequencing down by step, but this time beginning a step higher on 2 to end with a V^{m7}—I full cadence for a period built of two different sequences. Recall the bridge of Roy Orbison's "Oh Pretty Woman." Although it is sung in two vocals a third apart, one can hear in each of them a sequence of an idea repeated a step lower then a step lower, 4—3—2, 3—2—1, 2—1—7, these gestures in the lead vocal corresponding with chord changes and lyric structure: "[4/ii] Pretty [4—3] wo- [3] -man, [3/V^{m7}] stop [2] a while; [3/I] pretty [3—2] wo- [2] -man, [2/vi] talk [1] a while; [2/ii] pretty [2—1] wo- [1—7] -man, [1/V^{m7}] give [7] your [7—6] smile [7] to [7—8/I] me." The entire sequence is then repeated before moving into the retransitional phrase. One example in a minor key is Bobby Rydell's "Sway," the verse of which moves ♭6—5—4 over iv, to 5—4—♭3 over i, to 4—♭3—2 over V^{m7}, to ♭3—2—1 over i.

All of these sequences involve brief ideas composed of steps, but a melodic fragment built of skips may also be sequenced, as is the chorus of Terry Gilkyson and the Easy Riders' calypso number, "Marianne," where 3—5—1—3—2—4 drops to 2—4—7—2—2—1, adjusting at the end for the period's full cadence. Brenda Lee's "All Alone Am I" opens with 8—6—4 sequenced to 7—5—3. A tune with more daring skips of sevenths, in fact one more in an instrumental style than a vocal one, occurs in the verse of the Rolling Stones' seventeenth-century-like mixolydian tune "Lady Jane," where the line, "your time has come, my love," is set to 8—2—8 (supported by II^{m7})—♭7—2 (over v); this is sequenced down to ♭7—1—♭7 (over I^{m7})—6—1 (IV).

All of the sequences cited thus far descend, but rising ones are just as plentiful. Note the simple glockenspiel idea, 3—2—1, 3—2—1, that is then sequenced a step higher (4—3—2, 4—3—2) in the Four Seasons' "Rag Doll"

(0:21+). Floyd Cramer's "Last Date" includes the line, 1—2—3 over I, followed by 2—3—4 over V, 3—4—5 over I^{m7}, and then 4—5—6 over IV (0:26–0:33). This rising sequential line later becomes the basis of the "and I try, and I try…" sequence of mounting frustration in the Rolling Stones' "(I Can't Get No) Satisfaction." Cream's "Dreaming" includes a classical-sounding sequence in the break (1:00–1:08), where Bruce's bass imitates Clapton's guitar sequence in octaves. Another wonderful guitar sequence ends the break of Creedence Clearwater Revival's "Proud Mary" (1:43–1:51). Can you hear the rising melodic sequence in the chorus of the Dixie Cups' "Chapel of Love"? Leaping sevenths are tempered by descending scales in the Beach Boys' "Don't Worry Baby" (0:34–0:41): 6 leaping up for a descent, 5—4—3—2, sequenced to 7 up to 6—5—4—3—a melody that many years later found its way into John Lennon's "(Just Like) Starting Over" (0:53–1:02).

Phil Spector uses sequence to pose and then answer a question in Ike and Tina Turner's "River Deep, Mountain High," in which "Do I love you, my oh my?" is set on a ♭VII chord, repeating a rising arpeggio 2—4—♭7, and the immediate answer, "River deep, mountain high!," comes in the same rhythm a step higher on the repeated affirming I triad, 3—5—8. Sometimes, a sequence can all represent a single harmony, even though some tones might not belong to the chord. In the bridge's retransition in the Chiffons' "One Fine Day," the entire phrase, "[7] you'll [5] come [7] to [8] me [6] when [8] you [9] want [7] to [9] set- [9] -tle [4] down, [5] hey!," is supported by the retransitional V^{m7}, but note the 8 and 6 that are not part of that 5—7—2—4 chord; they exist as compound-melody passing tones (7—8—9 over 5—6—7) within the sequence, and function to prolong the drama of the V^{m7}.

Occasionally, a sequence is deliberately broken but still recognizable. In the verse of the Turtles' "Happy Together," the vocal first moves among pitches ♭3—2—1—2—♭3, then among 2—1—♭7—1—2, then among 1—♭7—♭6—♭7—1. Next, one should expect the seventh scale degree to come down through the sixth to 5, but because of the minor-mode inflections, the singer does not wish to move from ♭6 up to the 7 that is required for the cadential V harmony, so he instead moves, in a contrasting rhythm, to chord tone 2 and passes *down* through 1 to 7, then leaps *up* to 5 rather than passing down to it. The 7—5 of the sequence is preserved, but partly hidden by the new rhythm, the presence of other tones and an inversion of the direction of the structural 7—5 interval. Can you hear the melodic sequences in the Teddy Bears' "To Know Him Is to Love Him"? Herb Alpert and the Tijuana Brass's "Tijuana Taxi" and "Spanish Flea"? Spanky and Our Gang's "Sunday Will Never Be the Same"?

It is possible to sequence ideas by skips instead of by steps, but this is much less common. It tends to happen in thirds, sometimes aligning all in a single harmonic identity without the need for passing tones, as exhibited in the Chiffons example. The chorus of Petula Clark's "Kiss Me Goodbye" also exemplifies, as it descends 1—2—3—2 through 6—7—8—7 to 4—5—6—5. The structure of the bridge of the Bee Gees' "I Started a Joke" is very classy, composed of two phrases: the first (1:02–1:12) a sequence that descends by step, the second (1:15–1:26) a sequence that drops by thirds as the singer falls out of bed: the first phrase descends with 8—6—7—8 (over vi) stepping down to 7—5—6—7 (over iii), to 6—4—5—6 (over IV), and to 5 (over I, for a weak plagal cadence), then the second continues the descent, only faster: 5—3—4—5 (over iii) skipping down to 3—1—2—3 (over vi) and to 1—6—7—8 (over IV), to 5 (over V). Note how, even though different chord colors (iii, vi, and IV) appear, the first notes of each term in the skipping sequence, 5 then 3 then 1 then 6-to-5, define a descending I chord, making the second phrase a highly ornamented version of I (embellished through the sequence) moving to V (for the retransitional half cadence).

Melodies may begin on any scale degree and progress in many potential ways, but sooner or later, one can define a phrase as either goal-directed or not. Depending upon the harmony represented in the phrase's cadence, the ultimate goal of 1 may be approached (usually, by step from 2 or from 7) but not quite reached, may be reached but not given full harmonic support, may be fully realized, or may be ignored altogether. Note how disciplined and normal is the 5—4—3—2—1 chorus-ending line, "if you wanna dance with me," in Chuck Berry's "Rock and Roll Music." The same conclusion brings a resolute attitude to every verse of Bob Dylan's "With God on Our Side." Paul Anka's "Lonely Boy" is so simple and repetitive, it's dull, but it does exemplify a slightly ornamented line descending from 3 to 1; some deviation through an ascending skip away from one or two of its notes would have helped it immensely. Sam Cooke's "Wonderful World," on the other hand, has a nicely varied line that constantly approaches 1, but alternates appearances of this plan with motions to 3 and to 4 before finally settling on 1 at the end of the highly satisfied refrain.

A common ornamentation of the 3—2—1 line is to first ascend from 3 to 5; the lead vocal in the Beach Boys' "Sloop John B" ornaments the opening 3 with its upper neighbor, 3—4—3, twice before moving up to 5 in order to descend to 2 for the end of the first phrase on a half cadence (the same structure is taken for the verse of Glen Campbell's "Rhinestone Cowboy"). The second phrase of "Sloop" then eventually descends through the ornamented line 4—3—2—1, both recalling elements of the opening 3—4—3 gesture and sequencing the 5—4—3—2 descent of the first phrase a step lower to land on a full cadence. Bob Dylan's "One More Night" is a nicely ornamented descent from 5 after an opening I arpeggiation, a very common late-eighteenth-century tune structure. The line opens on 1 (0:11), drops to 5 but then arpeggiates up through 3 (0:14) to 5 (0:17), and then

Photo 7.01. Folk turns into rock. Covers of albums by Joan Baez; Simon and Garfunkel; Bob Dylan; the Kingston Trio; the Cyrkle; Odetta; Peter, Paul and Mary; and Pete Seeger. (Photo: Annie Eastman)

descends through 4 (0:25), 3 (0:28), and 2 (0:29) to 1 (0:30); note how each of these tones is ornamented, and also how the phrase's chord changes support each descending melodic tone, one of the many ways that harmony and melody are structurally related. Similarly, a melody might use sequence to build an arch-shaped structure, as in the Drifters' "Save the Last Dance for Me." Here, the verse opens with a 1—2—3—2 gesture (0:02–0:03) that is sequenced up to 2—3—4—3 (0:12–0:13) at a full cadence; the following phrase moves up more quickly as the singer gets more anxious ("but don't forget who's taking you home and in whose arms you're gonna be..."), as 3—4—5 now rises by step all the way to 8 and then falls; the refrain falls stepwise from 5 to 1 completing an octave-sized arch while stating the hoped-for goal.

The path of the Beatles' "The Long and Winding Road" is divided into several conflicting motions, but it does find its way home through a cadential rise from 5 through 6 and 7 to 8. Can you hear through the ornamentation in Dionne Warwick's "(Theme From) Valley of the Dolls" to the deeper-level 3—2 melodic structure of the opening phrase (0:15–0:42), leading to a period-concluding second phrase (0:42–1:07) that is based on a large-scale 3—2—1 melody? Although the Beatles claim that their "Nowhere Man" "knows not where he's going to," can you hear how the tune's structure is ironically very goal-directed through a stepwise descent from 5, most tones of which are ornamented by little sequencing subphrases?: "[5/I] He's a [8] real [7/V] no- [6] -where [5] man, [4/IV] living [6] in his [5] no- [4] -where [3/I] land, [2/ii] making [4] all his [3] no- [2/iv] -where [1] plans [2] for [1/I—2] no- [1] -body." What happens to the melodic shape of Frankie Valli's "Can't Take My Eyes Off You" once "at long last love has arrived"? Where does the 5 heard many times in James Taylor's "Sweet Baby James" finally reach the first scale degree? All of these directed lines have been drawn from examples in the prevailing major mode, but ♭3—2—1 descents are common in dorian songs, too, as in The Doors' "Light My Fire," "Soul Kitchen," and "Hello, I Love You."

Such descent to 1 signifies a satisfied closure, but this effect is not always desired in a pop song. Sammy Davis Jr.'s "I've Gotta Be Me" ends dramatically on 5 for a searching effect. Bob Dylan adds a tender, vulnerable quality to many of his phrases by ending on 4 over a I chord with which it does not agree; this is the ending of many verses of "Visions of Johanna" and is so frequently heard elsewhere that it might be referred to as the Dylan cadence. Glen Campbell's "The Universal Soldier" ends with the lyric "this is not the way we put an end to war" on an ambiguous 2 doubled in multiple registers without clear harmony, for an appropriately unresolved setting. Listen to the implications of hanging threats in the unfinished melodic motions in the chorus of the Rolling Stones' "Get Off Of My Cloud." These examples can be heard as avoided closures, because their melodic motions might induce a listener to expect an ending with a full cadence supporting a 1 that does not materialize. But other songs do not lead a listener to expect any motion in particular; we have already noted this quality in minor-pentatonic melodies (by which any stepwise descent to 1 would have to involve a tone from outside the scale). The minor-pentatonic verses of the Monkees' "(I'm Not Your) Steppin' Stone," firmly in the "Gloria"-glorifying proto-punk groove, defy any need to point to particular melodic goals. The improvised major-pentatonic chanting by which Yoko Ono and John Lennon intone various newspaper clippings in "No Bed for Beatle John" illustrates that this scale may avoid goal-direction as well. The verses of Jimi Hendrix's "Bold as Love" have no recognizable cadential gestures, thus phrase rhythm and form are difficult to comprehend, and the vocal melody cannot be said to be directed at all. Is there any obvious pitch direction in the vocal lines of Pink Floyd's "See Emily Play" or Donovan's "Epistle to Dippy"?

Our final topic of melodic phrasing involves a closer look at ornamentation. Some ornamentation occurs at such deep levels it is always considered essential to the tune (such as those passing tones within the expanded retransitional V^{m7} in the Chiffons' "One Fine Day"), whereas other ornamentation exists so much at the surface that it can be created by the performer through improvisation, and thus may be different with every performance. Typically, lighter ornamentation might take place within verses so that they are all of a regular similarity, whereas heavier, freer, ornamentation may take place in the solo. Sometimes, the final hearing of the verse, once repetition has made its content and supportive structure well known, is adapted by the singer to a nearly unrecognizable degree; see, for example, José Feliciano's "Light My Fire." We'll just mention here some of the small-scale ornaments that can be employed, often extemporaneously, by singers.

> Melodic ornamentation: articulation, glissando, neighbors, mordents.

We might begin by looking at a few negative examples. The syllabic style, preferred as we've said in hard rock, is relatively unornamented; think of Jim Morrison's delivery in The Doors' "Hello, I Love You." But the singer can further reduce the artistry of the phrases as syllabically composed by clipping each note as short as possible. When the sustain is removed from every vocal note in the verses of the Outsiders' "Time Won't Let Me," for example, suggesting the breathless impatience of the lyric, the idea of ornamentation (which prolongs, rather than shortens, ideas) is completely foreign to the aesthetic. Such clipped articulation is common, appearing in such passages as the first verse of the Four Aces' "Mister Sandman," the unison staccato delivery of Somethin' Smith and the Redheads' "It's a Sin to Tell a Lie," Elvis's coy baby-boy phrasing in "(Let Me Be Your) Teddy Bear," and the sharply slicing sound of "every glove that laid him down or CUT HIM TILL he cried out" in Simon and Garfunkel's "The Boxer." Compare these examples with even the simplest vocal ornament, perhaps a bent note, which requires that note to be sustained in order to be misshapen. This, a favorite country technique, can be synonymous with the southern drawl that indicates total patience with the world. That's the attitude of Roger Miller in "King of the Road," and the same bent notes are recreated in Jody Miller's parody, "Queen of the House."

Related to the bent note is the glissando, usually referred to as a scoop or a portamento when done vocally. When done slowly or otherwise accented, this effect injects a highly informal quality into the quality of expression. Nat King Cole's "(Get Your Kicks On) Route 66" swings with accented vocal scoops on every note. The scoops get slurpy in Al Alberts's lead vocal for the Four Aces' "Love is a Many-Splendored Thing." Partly because of his mumbling, Dean Martin pushes nonchalance to the edge of incoherence with the many glisses in "Memories Are Made of This," and Troy Shondell sounds just plain drunk with the sloppy scoops to nearly every note in "This Time." Patsy Cline's portamentos, with a touch of growl, are on the other hand quite effective in "Walkin' After Midnight." When James Brown stops time cold in his stretched-out portamentos on "I'll" in "I'll Go Crazy" (0:16–0:17) and "feel" in "I Got You (I Feel Good)" (1:40–1:42), he's reveling in the sensuous. Lou Reed conveys vulnerability as he scoops to find his pitch in the Velvet Underground's "Sunday Morning." Choral or harmonized scoops can be highly infectious, as in the intro to the Bachelors' "Diane," the chorus of the Beatles' "Rain," and portions of Sonny and Cher's "Plastic Man."

Another country technique is to add an accented neighbor (appearing on the strong part of a beat), usually the upper neighbor, to many notes (which subsequently appear at their normal pitch in a metrically weaker place). These are constant in Tammy Wynette's "D-I-V-O-R-C-E," the excessive upward and downward motions to the ornamented pitches make it sound as if her voice is controlled by some outward force pushing and pulling her off her pitch. Upward-resolving neighbors are paired with a nasal vocal and a fiddle in unison with pedal steel for the full country effect in Charley Pride's "Is Anybody Goin' to San Antone." The country inflection was taken up in many other rock styles; note the soulful upper-neighbor decorations to IV (0:18–0:19) and to V (0:22–0:23) in Doris Troy's "Just One Look." Consider the many notes ornamented by those a step away in Fats Domino's "Blueberry Hill," Carl Perkins's "Sure to Fall," and Patsy Cline's "I Fall to Pieces" and "Sweet Dreams." The Everly Brothers give us undiluted Kentucky pronunciations along with the hillbilly neighbors in "I Wonder If I Care as Much," and their drooping a cappella neighbors in thirds truly do "sigh" in the intro to "Sigh, Cry, Almost Die." Neighbor notes are not always accented; in fact, a structural note may move to its neighbor and back, sometimes repeatedly. Listen to Aretha Franklin's repetitious-as-a-set-of-links neighbor-ornamentation of "chayiayiayiayian" over straight backing vocals in the coda (2:19–2:21) of "Chain of Fools." Similarly, Kenny Rogers ornaments a structural tone with its repeated neighbor in "I fo-ound m-y mi-nd in a brown paper bag..." in the First Edition's "Just Dropped In (To See What Condition My Condition Was In)." Such slow trills also mark the Coasters' "Searchin'" and the ends of the choruses of Petula Clark's "Don't Give Up."

Notes graced by rapidly executed neighbors that leave once and return to the structural tone are called mordents. The last notes sung in Web audio example 7.13 consist of a mordent. They are a feature of Jerry Lee Lewis's imitation of Al Jolson in "Rock-A-Bye Your Baby With a Dixie Melody," and are a constant part of John Lennon's singing with the Beatles. Patsy Cline works mordents into her nicely improvised ornamentation in "Crazy," which also includes broken syllables, strong dynamic contrasts in her voice, and the reservation of multiphonics for her retransitional "oh" at 1:32. Ronnie Bennett sings with very light ornaments, as with the mordents in "say you LOVE me" (0:25) in the Ronettes' "Be My Baby." Stevie Wonder's "A Place in the Sun" is highly ornamented; note the mordent at "like a branch on a tree, I keep reachin' TO be free." One of the many trademark formulas used by Gary Puckett and the Union Gap in their repetitive hits, "Woman, Woman," "Young Girl," and "Lady Willpower" was to have the lead singer ornament a chord mixing tones from outside the predominant major scale with a vocal mordent that emphasizes its foreign color; this occurs on iv at "that's really killing ME" in "Woman," on III^{m7} at "get out of HERE" in "Girl," and on iv at "I'll take good care of YOUR love" in "Lady." In "To Sir With Love," Lulu features a variety of graces: multiphonics break up her vulnerable ego at "I" (0:30–0:31 and 0:39), mordents color her "days" (0:12) and "nails" (0:19). She reserves vibrato for phrase endings, as at "gone" (0:22–0:24) and "on" (0:37–0:38), but beautifully mixes mordents and vibrato as she decides to take a stand at "try" (0:54–0:58). Note also her sensitive placement of notes, not always on the beat; she is slightly late, as if in denial, with "the time has come..." (1:22–1:33) and "...for closing books and long last looks must end," for which the composer ought to be congratulated for a conflict of internal rhyme. It's an intriguing vocal melody, beginning unprepared with accented non-chord tones, 6—5—4—3 over I, leading to a transcendent, soaring maturity.

Melody is a combination of both pitch and rhythmic materials, and we have concentrated almost entirely on the former. This is not because rhythm is of less importance but mostly as preparation for the following four chapters on harmony. The next chapter beyond these, on rhythm, meter, and tempo, will contextualize ideas presented in all preceding chapters including the role of rhythm in melody. The listener should also understand that melodies become far more complex than may have been suggested here. Heavy chromaticism, for instance, is not common in rock music, but all of the scales and modes outlined here are subject to some degree, varying from style to style, of chromatic ornamentation. Materials that are discussed here as separate topics find their ways into combinations of contrasting ideas in a single specimen. Whether songs are composed of simple and repetitive, or complex and difficult-to-categorize, melodic patterns, the listener should try to appreciate the stylistic ancestries and expressive values of each tune's components and overall effect.

CHAPTER 8

Chord Construction

It is through harmonic relationships that musical material most effectively points toward goals or digresses from them, follows expected norms or shocks the listener, and expressively supports the melody. Whereas rhythmic propulsion drives the listener's body to dancing synchronization, and the singer's melody and the words it carries reach the listener's consciousness, a song's harmonic relations touch or inspire the heart and soul only in mysterious, unseen ways. And so, the topic of harmony might seem at first a bit more abstract than music's other aspects, with their more direct appeal. But it is this mysterious, intangible allure that makes an understanding of harmony's hidden nature so enticing and rewarding. And the sometimes intricate, sometimes bold nature of harmony is so centrally important, it is usually the only aspect of music that is notated in any way by rock composers and pop singer-songwriters, who often write some references to the chord changes along with their lyrics. But even most pop and rock musicians, particularly those guitarists who begin learning their craft with left-hand chord patterns, don't have a complete conscious understanding of how chords relate to each other, and are not aware of the vast materials available in this area. To the uninitiated, or even to the professional writer about popular music who comes to this book thinking that harmony is a concept confined to the employment of backing singers, this chapter will no doubt present manifold unexpected complexities. But it contains everything necessary to build a comprehensive and fully detailed understanding of its topic, and a careful digestion of its contents—whether or not one plays an instrument, composes, sings, or simply listens—will add immeasurably to the experience of this music.

In the world of pop music, the word "harmony" is normally associated with backing vocals, as these parts usually add different scale degrees to those sung by the lead vocalist. Our use of the term is going to be much broader. For us, any time two or more different tones are sounded together, whether produced by singers, instruments, or both in combination, we are going to speak about the way those tones combine with each other in terms of harmony (which topic covers the makeup of chords and the functional ways in which they relate to each other) and counterpoint (which has to do with the support and combination of different melodic lines based on the intervals between them, but which can also govern many relationships between successive chords). In most classical music and in some forms of popular music, the roles of harmony and counterpoint often compete for supremacy at any given moment, but generally balance each other in the long run. In most rock music, by contrast, harmonic relationships are generally more diverse and of more structural value than are contrapuntal ones. In this and the following three chapters, we aim to introduce the reader to the most common ways, and a good number of less common ones, that chords can relate to one another in pop music.

Consonance and dissonance

Many basic concepts of harmony have already been introduced, particularly in chapters 2 and 7. In previous discussions, we have constructed various scales and noted the melodic intervals they contain, have built triads and seventh chords on different scale degrees, and have seen how the falling fifth motion from

> **Consonance and dissonance:** harmonic intervals, consonant chords (major and minor triads, the power chord, the added-sixth chord).

one root to another is the central harmonic relationship. All of these ideas will be basic to chapters 8 through 11, but we must first examine a concept even more fundamental: that which relates consonance and dissonance.

Table 7.01 and figure 7.01 listed all available melodic intervals composed of one note following another. But these intervals can also relate tones that sound simultaneously, as harmonies. By virtue of the qualities of particular harmonic intervals—which are created when we combine two, three, four, or more notes at a time—triads, seventh, and ninth chords have different degrees of stability and instability. Certain intervals above the bass, including thirds, fifths, sixths, and octaves, are nearly always consonant and stable, whereas other intervals including seconds, fourths, and sevenths are always dissonant and unstable. To be more specific, consonances as measured above the lowest sounding tone include the perfect unison, major and minor thirds, perfect fifths, major and minor sixths, perfect octaves, and larger intervals such as major and minor tenths created by adding octaves to smaller consonances. (An octave plus a third forms a tenth.) All other intervals are dissonant. In traditional counterpoint, dissonant intervals resolve to consonant ones, but in rock music they are often treated more freely, generating tension that never goes away.

Consonant chords

Nearly all triads heard in popular music combine three different note names relating to each other as root, major or minor third, and perfect fifth. These individual intervals are consonant with the root in the bass, and their products are therefore considered consonant chords. (Whereas triads are restricted to three different note names, they may include any number of actual notes, with any of the three appearing doubled as unisons or doubled in multiple octaves.) As we have seen, those triads with a perfect fifth and the major third above their roots are called major triads, and those including instead minor thirds above their roots are minor triads. (Please refer back to fig. 2.02.) Both, being fully consonant, are considered stable, but they sound different because of the different qualities of their respective thirds. Many say that in comparison, the major chord sounds bright and cheerful, the minor chord dark and grim. Major triads include those with scale degrees 1—3—5, or 4—6—1, or 5—7—2, and such chromatic combinations as 2—♯4—6, ♭7—2—4, and others—any combination of a major third (equal to the combined size of two adjacent major seconds such as 1—2 and 2—3 forming 1—3) and perfect fifth (equal to the sum of three major seconds plus a minor second) above the root. Minor triads are made of scale degrees 2—4—6, 3—5—7, 6—1—3, 1—♭3—5, and other similar combinations of minor third and perfect fifth above the root. In the major scale, diatonic triads built on the first, fourth, and fifth scale degrees, referred to as the I, IV, and V chords, respectively, are always major. Diatonic triads built on the second, third, and sixth scale degrees—ii, iii, and vi—are always minor. (Recall that uppercase Roman numerals designate chords that contain major thirds above the root, whereas lowercase Roman numerals indicate chords that contain correspondingly minor thirds.) Through the use of chromatic tones, both major and minor triads can be built on any of the twelve different scale degrees; a lexicon of the most common chords in pop music appears as the Appendix.

After covering all of the different qualities of chords (triads, seventh chords, and others) used in popular music, and their immediate voice-leading contexts, we shall investigate in chapter 9 how these different chords built on all of the diatonic scale degrees relate to each other in a larger context by studying chord progressions, then examine in chapters 10 and 11 how such chord progressions can be modally and chromatically altered and, from an even larger perspective, how different tonal centers can relate to each other.

There are actually four basic types of chords that are fully consonant: the very common major and minor triad, and the much less common power chord and chord of the added sixth. Power chords contain only two distinct tones a perfect fifth apart, and would thus more correctly be termed intervals than chords, except that they are typically used as alternatives to triads (. . . and usually at amplifier levels loud enough to demand recognition as chords). The added sixth chord has four different pitches, one each of all sizes of consonant intervals above the root: major third, perfect fifth and major sixth. At this point, it would be useful to compare the sounds of these four consonant types of chords. The major triad is heard with tones 1—3—5 arpeggiated in the upbeat opening vocal line of Bill Haley and the Comets' "(We're Gonna) Rock Around the Clock." (Listen to Web audio example 8.01.) The same three scale degrees making the I triad are heard together through much of the accompaniment to Donovan's joyful "There Is a Mountain." The Hollywood Argyles' "Alley Oop" moves through four different major triads: first, it sustains the I chord for more than a minute, moves to IV at 1:10, then to II (a chromatic chord including 2, ♯4, and 6) at 1:15, and then to V at 1:19. (Listen to Web audio example 8.02.) The chorus of the Plastic Ono Band's hopeful "Give Peace a Chance" alternates two important major triads: I supports "all we are," then V accompanies "saying is 'Give Peace a,'" before I returns for "'Chance.'" As noted in chapter 7, in the climax of the chorus of Ike and Tina Turner's "River Deep, Mountain High," the ecstatic vocal melody for "Do I love you, my oh my?" arpeggiates the third, fifth and root of the ♭VII chord (2—4—♭7—♭7, 2—4—♭7) before the following line sequences the title to the same arrangement of members of the I chord (again, arpeggiating up from the third, rather than the root, of the chord: "[3] Riv- [5] -er [8] deep, [3] moun- [5] -tain [8] high"). The Beatles produce many major triads involving chromatic scale degrees, as when "And I Love Her" ends on the VI triad (6—♯1—3), and the intro to "Do You Want to Know a Secret" moves through ♭II (♭2—4—♭6), going to great lengths to emphasize the second hearing of the word, "really" in an unusual area at 0:09. (Listen to Web audio example 8.03.) This last chord has a particularly dark color even though it is a major triad, because it is built on the shadowy lowered second scale degree, mixing cues for great rhetorical richness. In contrast, the major triad that ends "And I Love Her" has an unusually bright quality because it contains the raised first scale degree. (Listen to Web audio example 8.04.) Both of these major triads, $^\flat$II and VI, include the same chromatic note ($^\flat 2 = ^\sharp 1$), but the different contexts give them completely different qualities.

Minor triads built on the first scale degree, i, are heard in the lonely openings of Brian Hyland's "Sealed With a Kiss" and the Beatles' "Things We Said Today." Before making its way to the $^\flat$II chord, the "Do You Want to Know a Secret" intro moves first from i to iv (at 0:03, emphasizing the *first* use of "really") and back to i (0:04). (Listen to Web audio example 8.05.) The final chord of "And I Love Her" sounds all the brighter because of the song's previous heavy emphasis of minor triads; the verses all begin with introspective alternations of ii ("I give her") and vi ("all my love") chords, the dead-serious minor pair heard three times before moving on to the more optimistic major chords, IV (0:21), V (0:23), and I (0:25, McCartney's accenting an added sixth on the downbeat). The verses of Dion's "Abraham, Martin and John" have a quietly mournful quality due to their strings of minor triads; the first line moves I—iii—ii—I; the two minor chords are reversed in the next line, I—ii—iii—V. The third line becomes more poignant still by surrounding these two minor chords with yet another pair, the bookending vi chord: " [vi] He freed a lot of [iii] people, but it [ii] seems the good they [vi] die young." (Listen to Web audio example 8.06.)

Defiantly simple power chords, which come to the fore in heavy metal and punk, have quite an old history of forebears, if heard sparingly before the 1970s. Some early folk-based tunes, like the Ames Brothers' "My Bonnie Lassie" and the Harry Simeone Chorale's "The Little Drummer Boy," employ droning vocal fifths as if in simulation of bagpipes. Other early examples, like Chuck Berry's "Havana Moon," might suggest primitive cultures with alternations of empty fifths (Berry's chorus alternates I^5 with $^\flat VII^5$, but the verse is all I^5 and VI^5). (Listen to Web audio example 8.07.) Proto-hard rock examples include the Dave Clark Five's "Catch Us If You Can" (whose guitar power chords alternating I^5—VI^5 in the verse lead to vocal fifths in the chorus, moving II^5—III^5—I^5—VI^5—II^5—III^5—VI^5), Paul Revere and the Raiders' "Just Like Me" (which repeatedly mirrors the I^5(0:07)—$^\flat VII^5$ (0:08) descent with a IV^5(0:09)—V^5 (0:10) ascent, these fifths accounting for every note performed by the bass, guitar, lead vocal, Vox Continental organ, and backing vocals), the Animals' "When I Was Young" (its verse alternating I^5—$^\flat VII^5$ before the two-part guitar riff descends IV^5—III^5—II^5—I^5), the Kinks' "Tired of Waiting for You" (I^5—$^\flat VII^5$ heard ten times in the chorus!), the Troggs' subdued "Love Is All Around" (introduced with I^5—IV^5—V^5—IV^5, repeated), and Cream's "Sunshine of Your Love" (whose forceful "I've been waiting for you" refrain, beginning at 0:50, presents three hearings of V^5—$^\flat VII^5$—IV^5—V^5). The opening of Marvin Gaye's "I Heard It Through the Grapevine" owes its ominous quality partly to the empty fifths on the Wurlitzer, just as the bare I^5 chord in McCartney's guitar provides a haunting atmosphere for the opening of the Beatles' "Yesterday." Rarely will the bass play double-stopped power chords alone, but such is the case through the first two verses of the Ventures' "Hawaii Five-O."

The added-sixth chord, overloaded with blissful consonances, is much more prevalent in the 1950s and '60s than later. (Listen to Web audio example 8.08.) Earlier custom would have phrases end on I with the singer cadencing on 6, as in Eddie Fisher's unabashedly romantic performance of "On the Street Where You Live," and still earlier references—as with Freddie Cannon's cover of the 1922 hit, "Way Down Yonder in New Orleans"—are chock full of such "tender sighs." The major-chord-plus-major-sixth sonority evokes simple satisfaction as the final guitar sound in songs as different as Hank Williams Sr.'s "Hey, Good Lookin'," Chuck Berry's "Rock and Roll Music," and Sam Cooke's "You Send Me." The Beatles defied their producer, who argued ineffectively against their ending "She Loves You" with the gleeful added-sixth chord that they articulated with three sustained vocals: Paul on 8, George on 6, and John on 5. In this case, Harrison's added tone is dramatically necessary because the final sonority says "you know you should be *glad*," shining a bright light on 6, which throughout the song had languished in the shadows as the root of the minor vi chord ("you know that can't be *bad*," 0:29–0:31). The added-sixth chord is rarely built on scale degrees other than 1, but it can be heard with 5 as its root at 0:35 and elsewhere in the 5th Dimension's jazzy "Stoned Soul Picnic."

Dissonant triads

Dissonant sonorities may be categorized as to those based on triads other than major and minor, and those containing dissonant intervals

> **Dissonant triads:** the diminished and augmented.

added to any of the consonant chords or substituting for any of their members. There are two common dissonant triads: the diminished, which would appear diatonically only in scale degrees 7—2—4, and the augmented, which requires at least one chromatic note, as in 5—7—♯2 or 1—3—♯5. Neither contains a perfect fifth but is based instead on a dissonant, non-perfect fifth. Recall that "perfect" intervals—the unison, fourth, fifth, and octave—do not appear in major or minor forms. If a perfect interval is reduced in size by one minor second, we say it is diminished. If a perfect interval is enlarged by one minor second, it is augmented. (Similarly, a minor interval is reduced by a minor second to become diminished, and a major interval grows a minor second to become augmented. The diminished seventh, as from 7 up to ♭6, and the augmented ninth, as from 5 up more than an octave to ♯6, are the specific intervals of this group most frequently encountered in popular music.) Thus, the diatonic fifth measured above scale degree 7 is not perfect, but diminished; a diminished triad such as vii°,

7—2—4, contains a minor third and diminished fifth above the root. An augmented triad such as V⁺, 5—7—♯2, contains a major third and augmented fifth above the root. (Note the degree symbol used in chord symbols to indicate a diminished fifth and the plus sign used to indicate an augmented fifth.)

These two dissonant triads, the diminished and augmented, are highly unstable and their imperfect fifths tend to resolve according to contrapuntal norms: the note functioning as the lowered fifth of the diminished triad usually moves down by minor second when the chord changes, and the raised fifth of the augmented chord resolves up by minor second. In pop music, the diminished triad nearly always appears on the second scale degree, forming a generally maudlin and dejected ii° with its members, 2—4—♭6. In resolving to the following chord, the chordal fifth ♭6 (borrowed from the minor mode) tends to drop the minor second to 5, which might be the root of a V chord (as ii° goes to V in the verse's repeated progression, I—vi^m7—ii°—V^m9/m7 (0:15–0:22), in Santo and Johnny's "Sleep Walk"). The 5 of the resolution from ♭6 might act as the third of a iii chord as ii° goes to iii in Herb Alpert's "This Guy's in Love With You": "[♭VII^M9] When you smile I can [I] tell we [IV^M7] know each other [ii°] very well; how [iii] can I [vi] show you...." Alternatively, ♭6 might resolve to the fifth of a I chord (as ii° goes to I in the verses of Jay and the Americans' "Cara Mia" and the Hollies' "The Air That I Breathe"). (Listen to Web audio example 8.09.)

The augmented triad appears by far most often as an altered V chord. (Listen to Web audio example 8.10.) This V⁺ may have an introductory function, creating strong tension as the unstable opening chord in Chuck Berry's "School Days," Aaron Neville's "Tell It Like It Is," or the Beatles' "Oh! Darling," or acting as the culmination of an intro that may have begun elsewhere, as in Gene Pitney's melodramatic "Town Without Pity," the Beach Boys' colorful "The Warmth of the Sun," or Joe Cocker's frisky "Delta Lady." In a related manner, the V⁺ may appear at the end of a song's bridge, as its tension can make for a very dynamic retransition to the following verse. This occurs in fairly subdued form in Patience and Prudence's "Tonight You Belong to Me" and the Caravelles' "You Don't Have to Be a Baby to Cry," but in a far less restrained manner in the Beatles' "From Me to You," the Dave Clark Five's "Glad All Over," and Martha and the Vandellas' "Dancing in the Street."

Aside from its introductory and bridge-ending roles, the augmented triad has a third usage; this is a chromatically passing function usually appearing over the first scale degree. In this case, the I chord usually appears in its major form and then becomes augmented as its fifth rises from 5 to ♯5; the melodic motion continues by passing intensively up to 6, which is usually harmonized by IV (as in Jay and the Americans' "Some Enchanted Evening," at 0:27–0:29, and Lesley Gore's "It's My Party," at 0:03–0:04) but may instead be supported by vi (as in Herman's Hermits' "There's a Kind of Hush," 0:24–0:26)

Photo 8.01. First pressings of some of the Beatles' first releases. Seen are a German release of "My Bonnie," British (Parlophone) and U.S. (Tollie) releases of "Love Me Do," British (Parlophone) release of "Please Please Me," Canadian (Capitol of Canada) release of "From Me to You," Australian (Parlophone) and American (Swan) releases of "She Loves You," American (Capitol) release of "I Want to Hold Your Hand," and an American E.P. of four songs released by Vee-Jay. (Photo: Annie Eastman)

or by ii (as in Roy Orbison's "Crying," 0:18–0:20). (Listen to Web audio example 8.11.) Note that in several of these cases, the melodic 5—#5—6 motion turns around to pass in descent from 6 through ♭6 back to 5 (ii descending through ii° to I in "Crying" and IV dropping through iv to I in "It's My Party"); "There's a Kind of Hush," to be different, continues on up to ♭7 (supported by I^m7). See if you can trace the similar line in the verses of the Guess Who's "Laughing." Some gaudier songs employ augmented triads in both their chromatically passing and retransitional functions. This is true of both the Dave Clark Five's obsequious "Because" (the verse of which opens I—I⁺—vi—I^m7, like "Kind of Hush," and continues through ii to cadence on V⁺, leading then to the I—I⁺—IV—iv motion of "It's My Party") and the Monkees' camp "Tapioca Tundra" (the verse of which opens I—I⁺—vi, and whose bridge leads to the retransitional V⁺).

Seventh chords based on major and minor triads

The most common dissonant sonorities in rock music, however, are seventh chords, whereby sevenths are added to the root, third, and fifth of any of the chords we have already covered. In some popular styles, particularly when the chordal seventh appears in a melodic line such as that of the lead vocal, that note will move down by step at the next chord change, discharging its energy on reso-

lution. In other uses, however, the sevenths do not resolve but sustain some degree of tension without relief. The degrees of perceived tension and the needs for resolution are different from style to style; based on an understanding of stylistic practices, we sometimes expect the seventh to resolve, we sometimes wish it to resolve and it frustrates us by not doing so, and we sometimes have no expectations. Three different sizes of sevenths can be added to triads: the major seventh (such as 7 above 1), the minor seventh (4 above 5), and the diminished seventh ($\flat$6 above 7). We'll examine the construction of various seventh chords according to the underlying sonorities that are so ornamented, and discuss normal resolutions when counterpoint plays a role.

The major triad can take either a minor or a major seventh. (Please refer back to fig. 2.03, which illustrates examples of three different types of seventh chords on the keyboard.) The major triad with minor seventh undeniably creates the most widely heard seventh chord in all pop-rock music and appears on nearly any scale degree, but is most at home in its diatonic form on the fifth, 5—7—2—4, the pitches sung at "sing it again" (0:24–0:26) in the Beatles' "Your Mother Should Know." (Listen to Web audio example 8.12.) The potential power of this V^{m7} chord is exercised in the culmination of the Beatles' vocal arpeggiation on "ah" in the retransition from the instrumental break to the verse in "Twist and Shout" (1:24–1:36), as John provides the root with 5, George adds 7, Paul sings 2, and then John tops the chord off with 4 before all three break into various shouts. Normally, when contrapuntally active, the major-minor seventh chord (as the major triad with minor seventh is called) resolves with root descending a fifth to the next root, and with the dissonant seventh falling by step to the third of the resulting chord. Thus, the retransitional V^{m7} of "Twist and Shout" leads to the opening I of the ensuing verse; the melodic motion is most clearly articulated in the oft-repeated title, with "Twist and" sung on 4 over V^{m7} (0:10–0:11), "Shout" on its resolution, 3 over I (0:11–0:12).

Chromatic versions of the major-minor seventh chord also normally move down by fifth, as when II^{m7} (2—$\sharp$4—6—1) descends to V, or when VI^{m7} (6—$\sharp$1—3—5) goes to II. (Listen to Web audio example 8.13.) Note how the II^{m7} chord ups the ante in "Don't Think Twice, It's All Right," when the cadence of the repeated first line (I—iii—vi—vi, IV—IV—V^4—V^3, two beats per chord) is altered upon repetition (at 0:22+) to I—iii—vi—vi, II^{m7}—II^{m7}—V^{m7}—V^{m7}. A very commonly occurring bridge construction is that of Betty Everett's "The Shoop Shoop Song (It's in His Kiss)," where roots descending in fifths support alternating chromatic major-minor seventh chords and diatonic chords: III^{m7}—vi—II^{m7}—V^{m7}. The bridges of many songs, the Rolling Stones' "Time

Is On My Side," Wayne Fontana and the Mindbenders' "Game of Love," and the New Vaudeville Band's "Winchester Cathedral" among them, end with II^{m7}—V^{m7}. The VI^{m7} chord is particularly useful as a cadential goal when a first phrase opens on I and the second phrase opens a step higher, on ii. In Dionne Warwick's "Alfie," the first phrase moves from I to a half cadence on VI^{m7} (0:13–0:14), preparing the second phrase (each phrase opening with the same question, "What's it all about?") when the cadential root, 6, drops a fifth to the opening ii of the second phrase. The same harmonic strategy governs the first two phrases of Frank Sinatra's "My Way."

Another contrapuntal resolution, much less common, also exists whereby the root of a major-minor seventh chord slides down by minor second. This happens most often when $^\flat VI^{m7}$ ($^\flat 6$—1—$^\flat 3$—$^\flat 5$) slides down to V^{m7}, one chordal seventh sliding down to another. (Listen to Web audio example 8.14.) This descent often decorates a cadential V, as in the chorus of Johnny Rivers's "Secret Agent Man" or in the verses of the Box Tops' "The Letter," Creedence Clearwater Revival's "Suzie Q," and Three Dog Night's "One," all of which end $^\flat VI^{m7}$—V^{m7}—i^{m7}. The $^\flat VI^{m7}$ chord can likewise intensify the V-culminating bridge retransition, as in the Turtles' "She'd Rather Be With Me" and Sam and Dave's "You Don't Know Like I Know."

Sometimes, counterpoint takes the day off and the dissonance of the major-minor seventh chord is never resolved. Often, the I chord takes a minor seventh (1—3—5—$^\flat 7$ in all) that acts as a full member of the I sonority. In fact, this is the single accompanimental sonority throughout Bob Dylan's "In My Time of Dying," "Masters of War," and "Ballad of Hollis Brown," Sonny and Cher's "The Beat Goes On," a number of Creedence Clearwater Revival songs ("Born on the Bayou" among them) and a raft of late-'60s soul records, those of Wilson Pickett ("Funky Broadway") and James Brown ("Licking Stick," "Say It Loud—I'm Black and I'm Proud") emulated by the Isley Brothers ("It's Your Thing"), Sly and the Family Stone ("I Want to Take You Higher"), and the Temptations ("Don't Let the Joneses Get You Down," "Ball of Confusion"). On occasion, what sounds like a tension-filled introductory V^{m7} (normally demanding a resolution to I) will suddenly deflate when the listener finds out that this major-minor sonority wasn't a V^{m7} at all, but a I^{m7} that continues as such with no resolution; the repeated opening major-minor seventh chords of Sam the Sham and the Pharaohs' "Wooly Bully" that cause momentary confusion when they go nowhere make the point, and Chris Montez's "Let's Dance" creates a similar issue. But as stated earlier, the major-minor sonority can appear on any scale degree without contrapuntal pull toward resolution. Going back to Arthur Crudup's electric guitar chording in "That's All Right," the I, IV, and V scale degrees all may carry added minor sevenths, and this is a hallmark of many blues- and funk-based examples. Note how, in Gladys Knight and the Pips' "The Nitty Gritty," the I^{m7} heard through the verse gives way to IV^{m7} (4—6—1—^{b}3) in the chorus. See also Sam and Dave's "Hold On! I'm Comin'." The Beatles extend the scale-degree basis for such chords, opening up avenues for all rock music, in such passages as the repeated I^{m7}—II^{m7}—IV^{m7}—I^{m7} verse of "Sgt. Pepper's Lonely Heart's Club Band," which requires an alteration of the scale—a raised fourth scale degree—in the II^{m7} chord (0:23–0:24), over and above the alterations of seventh and third degrees in the I^{m7} and IV^{m7} chords, respectively. (Listen to Web audio example 8.15.)

The major-major seventh chord appears twice diatonically, on I^{M7} (1—3—5—7) and on IV^{M7} (4—6—1—3), and—particularly in soft, breezy jazz contexts—on many other scale degrees chromatically. (Listen to Web audio example 8.16.) The I^{M7} chord is perhaps most easily identified as the wistful final-sounding sonority in Patti Page's "Old Cape Cod," Henry Mancini's "Days of Wine and Roses," Lenny Welch's "Since I Fell For You," Little Anthony and the Imperials' "Goin' Out of My Head," the Zombies' "Tell Her No," Petula Clark's "This Is My Song," Peaches and Herb's "Close Your Eyes," the Vogues' "Turn Around, Look at Me," and the Beatles' "I Will." (Can you tell where major sevenths are added to the tonic chords in Web audio example 2.14?) This convention is slightly twisted by the ending of the Association's "Cherish," which settles into a wildly intense yet slow electric-guitar tremolo on ^{b}III^{M7} (^{b}3—5—^{b}7—2). The I^{M7} chord is marked by high-register descending string arpeggiations in Stevie Wonder's "My Cherie Amour" (0:54–0:56), all tones pouring themselves into a retransitional V$^+$, and is sustained by the organ through the verse of Brook Benton's "Rainy Night in Georgia." It is the opening sonority of Johnny Mathis's "Misty" and Dionne Warwick's "(Theme From) Valley of the Dolls."

> **The major-major seventh chord.**

Another common use of I^{M7} repeatedly alternates this chord with a neighboring ii^{m7}; they occur in this ordering in such songs as Barbara Lewis's "Hello Stranger," Smokey Robinson and the Miracles' "Ooh Baby Baby," and Peter, Paul and Mary's "Leaving On a Jet Plane," and are reversed when repeated in the verses of the Righteous Brothers' "(You're My) Soul and Inspiration," Blood, Sweat and Tears' "You've Made Me So Very Happy," and the Guess Who's "These Eyes." (Listen to Web audio example 8.17.) Major-major seventh chords on roots of ^{b}VII and I alternate in the verse of the Buckinghams' "Don't You Care" and the coda of Strawberry Alarm Clock's "Incense and Peppermints." The chord's other diatonic form, IV^{M7}, also appears chiefly in conjunction with I. The IV^{M7}—I pair forms the verse's fragile phrase ending (0:06–0:15) in Paul McCartney's "Junk." Note the alternation of IV^{M7} and I^{M7} in both the pained piano-driven "don't . . . stop" chorus of Dionne Warwick's "Walk On By" and in the nostalgic intro to Simon and Garfunkel's "Old Friends." The sonority occurs on various scale degrees in songs steeped in vulnerable sentimentality, such as the Association's "Never My Love" (particularly at 0:57–1:02 in the bridge, where V^{M7}—I^{M7}—IV^{M7} appears) and the Classics IV's "Traces" (tracing at one point, 0:43–0:49, IV^{M7}—$^{\flat}VI^{M7}$—$^{\flat}II^{M7}$). Another frequent job for I^{M7} is to support 7 within a contrapuntal line descending chromatically from 8 to 6; thus begin Frankie Valli's "Can't Take My Eyes Off You," the Beatles' "Something," and B. J. Thomas's "Raindrops Keep Fallin' On My Head." (Listen to Web audio example 8.18.) In the Supremes' "Stop! In the Name of Love," the vibraphone creates a IV^{M7} by sustaining a stubbornly dissonant 3 against IV, continuing also with this non-triadic tone over V, at 0:27.

The minor-minor seventh chord (minor seventh added to minor triad) appears diatonically on three scale degrees: ii^{m7} (2—4—6—1), iii^{m7} (3—5—7—2),

> **The minor-minor seventh chord.**

and vi^{m7} (6—1—3—5), and chromatic versions exist too. (Listen to Web audio example 8.19.) We've just seen how ii^{m7} often alternates with I^{M7}. The chord also prepares V well, as the root of ii drops the harmonic fifth to the next. Thus, the chorus of the Forum's "The River Is Wide" opens, "...the river gets [ii^{m7}] wide, the river gets [V^{m7}] long now, the water runs [I] deep..." and the refrain of the Happenings' "See You in September" ends, "or [ii^{m7}] lose you [V] to a summer [I] love...." Although it lacks 1, the iii^{m7} chord often acts as a slightly shaded I when it immediately follows the tonic, as in the opening line, "through the [I] corridors of [iii^{m7}] sleep, past [IV^{m7}] shadows dark and [I] deep" in Simon and Garfunkel's "Flowers Never Bend with the Rainfall." As here, iii^{m7} tends to move to IV. (Listen to Web audio example 8.20.) This motion is heard three times in succession in the Association's "Cherish," in a series beginning with "you don't know [iii^{m7}] how many times I wished that I had [IV] told you...." The reverse, IV—iii^{m7}, is heard four times in succession to close the wah-guitar theme in Frank Zappa's "Peaches en Regalia," iii^{m7} clearly substituting there for I^{M7}. Strange is the verse of The Doors' "Light My Fire," which four times (0:09–0:24) alternates v^{m7} (5—$^{\flat}$7—2—4) with iii^{m7} (rectifying the previous chord's $^{\flat}$7 as it moves to 7, the scale degree's diatonic form) before moving to a more predictable IV for the chorus (0:25+).

Often, the iii^{m7}—IV motion is part of a larger ascent from I to IV or one that reaches all the way to V, with chords appearing on every scale degree. Thus, the bridge of the Beatles' "Sexy Sadie" repeats this motion: "[I] one sunny day the [ii^{m7}] world was waiting for a [iii^{m7}] lover, [IV^{M7}]...." Gary Puckett and the Union Gap's "Lady Willpower" repeats I—ii^{m7} in its verse, moving through iii^{m7} (0:41) to IV (0:42) to arrive at the prechorus. Similarly, Brenton Wood's "Gimme Little Sign" turns from its thrice-repeated ii^{m7}—I verse to push stepwise up to V: "and when I'm [ii^{m7}] feelin' blue, and [iii^{m7}] I want you, there's [IV] just one thing that [V] you should do."

Perhaps because it contains all of the tones of the I chord, the vi^{m7} chord is not heard often. When it does appear, it usually drops a fifth to ii, as in the verse of the Monkees' "Daydream Believer" ("the [I] six o'clock al- [vi^{m7}] -arm would never [ii^{m7}] ring [V]") and in the prechorus of the Beatles' "Fool on the Hill" ("they can [I] see that he's just a [vi^{m7}] fool; [ii^{m7}] they don't [V^{m7}] like him..."). But vi^{m7} also makes odd appearances, as when it slides through $\flat VI^{m7}$ to V^{m7} at the end of the bridge, on "waitin'," in Oliver's "Jean." This song is introduced by our final consonant sonority that can also take an added seventh, the added-sixth chord. This chord is fairly rare, and seemingly always a form of V. The guitar's opening chord to "Jean," for instance, arpeggiates 5—7—4—7—3, including the sixth and seventh along with root and third but omitting the fifth. (Listen to Web audio example 8.21.)

To suggest great instability, the chordal seventh may be placed in the bass, beneath the triad itself. One of the most remarkable parts in the bass litera- ture occurs in 1:47—2:02 of the Beach Boys' "Here Today," where rapidly repeated bass notes are all sevenths, 1 appearing beneath ii, in alternation with $\flat 7$ placed below I. Also on this album, *Pet Sounds,* "God Only Knows" has few roots in the bass, as does the passage 2:07–2:18 from "Sloop John B." Instability also occurs, however, when a chordal fifth is placed in the bass; note the unsettling effect achieved thus by James Jamerson in the Four Tops' "Reach Out I'll Be There," at 0:49 and 0:57.

Seventh chords based on dissonant triads

Other third-based chords: the fully- and half-diminished seventh chords; ninth, eleventh, and thirteenth chords.

Sevenths may be added to either augmented or diminished triads, and these are among the most dissonance-filled chords to get regular work in the literature. With the augmented triad, it is always a minor seventh added on top. (Listen to Web audio example 8.22.) In fact, this sound is usually created when the fifth of a structural V^{m7} chord rises chromatically to form 5—7—$\sharp 2$—4 ($V^{m7/+}$); such an event brings the bridge to its culmination in the Reflections' "(Just Like) Romeo and Juliet" and takes the intro to its brink in the Beach Boys' "The Warmth of the Sun."

The diminished triad may take either a diminished seventh (creating alto- gether what is called the fully diminished seventh chord) or a minor seventh (the half-diminished seventh chord). The fully diminished seventh has three different behaviors: it may (1) embellish a chord whose root it shares, it may (2) lead to a chord whose root is a minor second higher than any one of its tones, or it may (3) lead to a chord whose root is a minor second lower than any of its tones. All of these resolutions are plotted in figure 8.01. The first usage is called the common-tone diminished seventh chord, and typically ornaments I. (Listen to Web audio example 8.23.) The progression may begin with the stable chord that is being embellished, so "Bali H'ai" from *South Pacific* and Arthur Lyman's West-Indian "Yellow Bird" both begin on I and move to i°⁷ (1—♭3—♭5—°7, perhaps more easily imagined when spelled 1—♯2—♯4—6, the third, fifth, and seventh all neighbors to members of I), resolving directly back into I. But more often, the °7 chord comes between IV and I, allowing 4 to move to ♯4 while 6 and 1 sustain as common tones in moving from IV to the i°⁷, and then permitting stepwise resolutions to 3 and 5 in resolving i°⁷ to I. This progression is heard in Bing Crosby and Grace Kelly's "True Love" ("I [I] give to [IV] you, and you [i°⁷] give to [I] me"), Neil Sedaka's "Calendar Girl" ("[IV] Yeah! Yeah, my [i°⁷] heart's in a whirl [I] . . ."), the Lovin' Spoonful's "Daydream" ("[IV] And even if [i°⁷] time ain't really [I] on my [VIᵐ⁷] side . . ."), and Arlo Guthrie's "Alice's Restaurant Massacree" ("[IV] just a half a mile from the [i°⁷] railroad tracks [I] you can get . . .").

The second function of the fully diminished seventh is performed by the leading-tone diminished seventh chord. Its root rises by minor second in resolution, usually to I, but any major or minor triad may be so decorated by a prior fully diminished seventh chord when the root of the stable chord is approached by minor second from below. (Listen to Web audio example 8.24.) This °7 chord may be sustained for tense moments of villainous suspense, marking the points of greatest danger in the narratives ("and then he turned on the buzz saw!") of the Coasters' (and Ray Stevens') "Along Came Jones." In a novel twist, the Beatles' "Because" ends on a vii°⁷ chord that resolves only with the beginning of the album's following song, "You

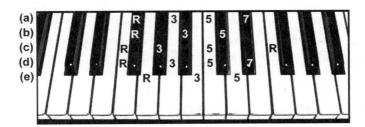

Figure 8.01. Keyboard representation of (a) a dissonant fully diminished-seventh chord and its four common resolutions, where R = chordal root, 3 = chordal third, 5 = chordal fifth, and 7 = chordal seventh. In (b), the dissonance resolves as a common-tone diminished seventh into a major triad; melodically, R holds while 3 and 5 both move to the new 3, and 7 resolves to 5. In (c) and (d), the dissonance resolves as a Broadway diminished seventh to a minor triad and a major-minor seventh chord, respectively; in the latter, only the root of the dissonance need move at all. In (e), the dissonance resolves as a leading-tone fully diminished seventh chord; melodically, the root and third of the dissonance both normally resolve into the new root.

Never Give Me Your Money." More often, vii°⁷ resolves directly to I as a mix-ture-based substitute for V^m7—I, as when the title is sung in *Carousel*'s "If I Loved You," or in the bridge of Sam Cooke's "You Send Me" ("At [ii^m7] first I thought it was [vii°⁷] infatu- [I] -ation ..."), or when the chorus is approached in Diana Ross and the Supremes' "Someday We'll Be Together" ("[IV] and just as sure, my, my baby [vii°⁷] as there are stars above I wanna say ... [I] Someday ..."). The chorus of Frank Sinatra's "Strangers in the Night" con-tains a pair of different leading-tone chords: "[iii] Strangers ..., we were [♯i°⁷] strangers ... when we [ii] said our first hello ... [vii°⁷] little did we know ... [I] love was just a [vi] glance ..."]; ii is also thus embellished in both the verse of the Beatles' "If I Fell" (at 0:22) and the intro to the Casinos' "Then You Can Tell Me Goodbye" (I—♯i°⁷—ii^m7—V^m9/m7). Bobby Helms gives IV its own leading-tone chord in "My Special Angel" ("[IV] sent from [V] up a- [I] -bove [iii°⁷—IV] ...") and the Beatles apply the leading-tone chord to V in "Michelle" ("words that [♯iv°⁷] go together [V] well ...").

To my knowledge, the third type of fully diminished seventh chord, which contains one note that moves down by minor second to the following root, has never been recognized with its own label. I think of it as the Broadway seventh, because it is ubiquitous in show tunes from "I Got Rhythm" to "Hello Dolly" and beyond. It will often ornament ii, as in the bridge of Bobby Vinton's "Blue Velvet" ("[iii] but when she [♭iii°⁷] left, [ii] gone was the [V] glow ...") and the verse of the Monkees' "Tapioca Tundra" (I at 0:34—III⁺ at 0:36—vi at 0:38—♭iii°⁷ at 0:39—ii at 0:40). (Listen to Web audio example 8.25.) At least two songs embellish a surprising major triad on III with its Broadway neighbors: the Buckinghams' "Susan," as the bridge opens ("[ii] No other [iv°⁷] girl could ever take place of [III^m7] you"), and the Classics IV's "Traces," in the verse's second phrase ("[ii] tickets torn in [♭VII] half, [iv°⁷] memories in [III^m7] bits and pieces"). The second and fourth verses of Jimmy Ruffin's "What Becomes of the Broken Hearted" are unusual in that they are harmonized differently than are the first and third. The even-numbered verses contain a Broadway seventh applied to iv^m7 (as ♯iv°⁷, ♯4—6—1—♭3, heard at 1:19, partially slides down to reveal iv^m7, 4—♭6—1—♭3, at 1:22).

Just as the diminished triad seems most comfortable on the second scale degree, so does the half-diminished seventh chord. Originally part of a ii^m7/°—V^m7—I cadence, as in *Damn Yankees*' "Heart" and *Oliver*'s "As Long as He Needs Me," ii^m7/° (2—4—♭6—1) goes to V^m7 through an intervening ♭VI^m7 in Mama Cass's cover of a 1931 hit, "Dream a Little Dream of Me" ("[ii^m7] birds singing in the [ii^m7/°] sycamore tree, [♭VI^m7] dream a little dream of [V^m7] me"). (Listen to Web audio example 8.26.) Otherwise, ii^m7/° will approach I directly, as in the Mothers of Invention's "Brown Shoes Don't Make It" ("She's a [I] teenage baby and she [I^m7] turns me on; I'd like to [IV] make her do a nasty on the [ii^m7/°] White House lawn; I'd [I] smother ...")

and the Buckinghams' "Susan" ("I'm losin' my [vi] mind, losin' my [ii$^{m7/o}$] mind, I'm wastin' my [I] time..."). Another highly dissonant sonority related to the ii$^{m7/o}$ is the II$^{m7/o}$ (2—#4—♭6—1), a sort of a seventh chord that is not based on a recognized triad at all, having a major third and diminished fifth. (Listen to Web audio example 8.27.) This chord directly precedes the V that ends the chorus of Bobbi Martin's "For the Love of Him." The same sonority appears on the fifth scale degree, 5—7—♭2—4 in the Four Lads' "No Not Much!" (ending ii^{m7}—V$^{m7/o}$—I), Blood, Sweat and Tears' "Just One Smile" (ending each chorus with V$^{m7/o}$—I), and the Spiral Starecase's "More Today Than Yesterday" (the chorus of which ends "but [vi] only half as [II^{m7}] much as to- [IV] -mor- [V$^{m7/o}$] -row"). This construction is exceedingly rare.

Ninth, eleventh, and thirteenth chords

Just as sevenths may be added to triads; ninths, elevenths, and thirteenths are used as well, generating ever more complex constructions. One song that demonstrates this added complexity is the Beatles' "She's Leaving Home." The song depicts a young woman's moment of elopement, and her increasing distance from her parents is emblematized by the distance of given sonorities from purer ones. String players have a telling moment to themselves at the same point in every verse: When the daughter is in her bedroom (0:12–0:16), a solo cello plays under an unchanging vi chord in the harp; when "she goes downstairs" (0:35–0:39), an added part for four unison violins ends in dissonant parallel ninths; by the time "she is far away" (2:38–2:42), the cello line—now doubled by string bass—supports all manner of thick seventh and ninth chords from ten string players alienated by a dissonant haze.

Ninth chords come in many varieties. On I, the major ninth with minor seventh (1—3—5—♭7—2) was a favorite of James Brown; his "Please, Please, Please" and "I Got You (I Feel Good)" both end with the sound, and horns in octaves arpeggiate the chord at the end of every refrain in the latter. (Listen to Web audio example 8.28.) It's also the rapid-fire repeated guitar chord of "Papa's Got a Brand New Bag." But Chuck Berry knew the chord too, ending "Roll Over Beethoven" with I$^{M9/m7}$. It's also part of the folk tradition, and is fingerpicked on a nylon-string acoustic by Bobbie Gentry to open "Ode to Billie Joe." The V chord is often so decorated (5—7—2—4—6) when a phrase cadences with a non-resolving 6 in the melody, as in Henry Mancini's "Moon River" (ending the verse's antecedent phrase) and in Jewel Akens's somewhat less formal "The Birds and the Bees," the lead vocal nonchalantly—perhaps suggestively—leading with unresolved ninths at 0:14 ("trees") and 0:16 ("above"). The sound appears on IV in The Band's "The Weight" (where the vocal entries stagger on "*and* you put the load right on me," adding 1, 4, and 5 to overtax the supporting IV chord, 0:47–0:52). The bridge of Bobby Vinton's "Please Love Me Forever" features a rich display of this chord in a root descent in fifths to the retransitional V; the bridge consists entirely of the following: III$^{M9/m7}$—VI$^{M9/m7}$—II$^{M9/m7}$—V$^{M9/m7}$. (Listen to Web audio example 8.29.)

The major ninth-major seventh combination, by contrast, seems only to be used on I, V, and on $^\flat$VII. Paul Riser writes I$^{M9/M7}$ in his lush arrangement for the Temptations' "My Girl" (note the strings at 1:16–1:17 and through the coda), and the Association open "Everything That Touches You" with this chord. (Listen to Web audio example 8.30.) In fact, the intro to their "Cherish" alternates twice between I$^{M9/M7}$ and $^\flat$VII$^{M9/M7}$. The Association's "Windy" also decorates $^\flat$VII this way ("[I] who's trippin' [$^\flat$VII$^{M9/M7}$] down the [IV] streets of the [I] city?"), but hard rockers like the sound, too: The Who's "We're Not Gonna Take It!" has $^\flat$VII$^{M9/M7}$ accompany an attention-get-ting call: "Hey you smokin' Mother Nature?" The major ninth rarely appears over a minor triad, but the final organ chord of the Animals' "The House of the Rising Sun" is an unsatisfied i$^{M9/m7}$, and a fleeting sonority like this is heard on v among a highly jazzy series of chords ending the bridge of the 5th Dimension's "Stoned Soul Picnic" (V^{M7} [2:08]—v$^{M9/m7}$ [2:09]—IV^{M7} [2:10]). Another rarity is the augmented triad with major ninth, but V$^{M9/M7/+}$ graces the long-held end of the antecedent phrase of Dionne Warwick's "Alfie" (0:35–0:37).

The minor ninth works well on the V chord, nowhere else, and nearly always takes the minor seventh. (Listen to Web audio example 8.31.) It is heard throughout the Casinos' "Then You Can Tell Me Goodbye" (as in "[I^{M7}] Kiss me each [vi] morning for a [ii^7] million [V$^{m9/m7}$] years. Organist Billy Preston brings this chord to the Beatles' "I Want You (She's So Heavy)," where it appears first in the intro (at 0:05) and later in harshly repeated organ, guitar, and bass chords (through 0:54—1:03), apparently driving the singer mad.

More rockers were interested in the augmented-ninth chord, originally as a decorated V (5—7—2—4—#6), #6 grating against the chordal third just a minor second above. (Listen to Web audio example 8.32; the chord is also heard at 0:42–0:45 in Web audio example 4.23.) Perhaps first appearing in the Miracles' "Shop Around" (note how Smokey Robinson sings 2—4—5—#6 at "my Mama told ME" [0:26–0:28]), it appeared in songs as diverse as the Beatles' "You Can't Do That" (while insisting "because I told you before!"), the First Edition's "Just Dropped In (To See What Condition My Condition Was In)" ("I [i] found my mind in a brown paper bag but [V$^{+9/m7}$] then. . .") and Cream's "Outside Woman Blues" (emphasizing the wife's drudgery of "cookin' your food, doin' your dirt"). The Beatles had the idea to move this jarring sonority to first-scale-degree function, which they did in "Taxman" (at 0:12–0:13, personifying the vile title character); the chord was instantly adopted by Jimi Hendrix for "Purple Haze" (the verse of which runs three times through the progression $I^{+9/m7}$—$\flat III^5$—IV) and by David Gilmour for Pink Floyd's "Corporal Clegg," and became a hallmark of proto-heavy metal, as in Deep Purple's "Hush" ("They got it early in the morning…"), Steppenwolf's "Born to Be Wild" (eight bars of $I^{+9/m7}$ on rhythm guitar following the eight-bar organ solo), and Led Zeppelin's "Lemon Song" (0:03–0:04). By the late '60s, the augmented-ninth chord might appear anywhere a major-minor seventh chord would be useful: on IV in the Box Tops' "The Letter" (0:09), on VI in Blood, Sweat and Tears' "Spinning Wheel" ($VI^{+9/m7}$—II^{m7}—$V^{+9/m7}$—I heard three times in the second verse), and on $\flat VI$ in Deep Purple's "April" (the work's third section repeats I—$\flat VII$—$\flat VI^{+9/m7}$—V). As yet another variation on the augmented-ninth chord, Joe Hinton signals that his forthcoming song, "Funny," is to be taken ironically when the intro ends with $V^{+9/m7/+}$ at 0:13.

Eleventh chords with perfect fourths (or elevenths) above the bass are usually heard as voice-leading phenomena, particularly as suspension chords when their thirds are omitted (a topic that is discussed later in this chapter). But occasionally, as when Bob Dylan sings 4 over a final I or I^{m7} chord (as in many verses of "Visions of Johanna," "Most Likely You Go Your Way (And I'll Go Mine)," and "Absolutely Sweet Marie"), one might consider them true eleventh chords. Another case in point is the opening sonority of the Beatles' "A Hard Day's Night," where the bass has 5 and the twelve-string electric and piano share $\flat 7$—2—4—8. Some would call this a $v^{11/m7}$, but the $\flat 7$, 4, and 2 form a neighbor triad to I (as evident in the cold ending of all live performances, which concludes $\flat VII$—I, effectively dulling any consideration of $\flat 7$ as the V chord's +9th) while 1 anticipates its role as the first root of the ensuing verse. Occurring over 5, this startling chord is perhaps best thought of as a dissonant sort of V with contrapuntal relationships to I. A few chords contain augmented elevenths. In Sammy Davis Jr.'s "Something's Gotta Give," Sy Oliver's punchy band ends with a dissonant I^{+11} chord, perfectly symbolizing the "immovable force" with which the singer contends. The same sharp dissonance has a softer effect when created by the addition of a descant "ba—ba—pa—ba" vocalization (1:38–1:44) added to the trumpet solo in Dionne Warwick's "I Say a Little Prayer," where she nonchalantly sings the line 7—5—$\sharp 4$—3 over I.

Thirteenth chords are the limit for stacked thirds, as they may contain versions of all seven scale degrees. Country and rockabilly stars of the '50s would end a song with the guitar-friendly $I^{M13/M9/m7}$ chord, as with Mary Ford's "The World is Waiting for the Sunrise," but jazz-oriented recordings would end the same way, especially with the thirteenth on top, as does Bobby Darin's "Mack the Knife." (Listen to Web audio example 8.33.) The Beatles, whom we've seen to like messy introductory V chords, picked this one up from George Harrison's love of Carl Perkins; the slow intro to "Do You Want to Know a Secret" ends on a slowly arpeggiated $V^{M13/M9}$ (5—2—5—6—3 on guitar). Thirteenth and eleventh chords wash over Crosby, Stills and Nash's dreamy "Guinnevere" so as to make one forget the pull of dissonance. In "Fire," on the other hand, The Crazy World of Arthur Brown add a thirteenth to an augmented ninth chord (5—7—2—4—#6—3) to get hellfire, screaming "you're gonna burn!" as they illustrate harmonically.

Other dissonant harmonic forms

Chord-based dissonance can be controlled by several contrapuntal devices such as the pedal, suspension, and anticipation. The pedal might be related to the idea of a polychord, whereby one triad sounds over another. This is rare, out-

> **Other dissonances:** the pedal, suspension, and anticipation; fourth-based chords.

side of when Bob Dylan blows I in his harmonica while playing IV on his guitar (as in the break, 7:10–7:12, of "Ballad in Plain D"), or in the chain of polychords in the piano solo opening the album version (it was excised from the single) of James William Guercio–produced Chicago's "Does Anybody Really Know What Time It Is?" Much more often, triads move above an unchanging pedal of a single note or perfect fifth, usually sounding in the bass, and nearly always acting as the stable tone or interval while upper parts create dissonance against it. Most common is the 1-and-5 fifth pedal that sustains beneath changing I—♭VII—I chords, as in the introductions to Martha and the Vandellas' "Dancing in the Street," Stevie Wonder's "Uptight (Everyting's Alright)" and the Beatles' "Got to Get You Into My Life." (Listen to Web audio example 8.34.) The lead guitar's 1–5 fifth also won't let go, despite pleas from the singers to set them free, as it sustains through the repeated I—♭VII—v^m7—♭VI motion in the Supremes' "You Keep Me Hangin' On." The verse of the Association's "Along Comes Mary" repeats the progression i—ii—i^m7—ii over a sustaining 1/5 pedal. Similarly, the progression I—ii—iv—I is repeated over an unchanging 1 pedal in Robert Knight's "Everlasting Love."

As one might guess from having examined so many possible different chord formations commonly appearing as variations on or substitutions for V, that dynamic scale degree supports more different kinds of dissonant motion above it than do others. Often, 5 appears below what might otherwise seem like the I triad in cadential situations. (In fact, some may hear this as a I chord with its fifth in the bass.) But this is usually an illusion. In this case, the dissonant fourth above the bass (the first scale degree) and the sixth above the bass (3) usually resolve down as a pair to the third and fifth above the bass, respectively, uncovering the normal V triad. (Listen to Web audio example 8.35.) This is heard in countless examples, such as the Beatles' "Ob-La-Di, Ob-La-Da" (the dissonant chord heard at 0:31, for "Desmond and Molly," resolving to V at 0:33 for "Jones"), Dickey Lee's "Laurie (Strange Things Happen)" (0:39–0:41), and Billy J. Kramer and the Dakotas' "I'll Keep You Satisfied" (as the verse ends, "I'll keep you" at 0:16 resolving the dissonances to V for "satisfied" at 0:17). In "It's Wonderful," the Rascals alter the third scale degree so that $\flat$3 and 1 resolve to 2 and 7 respectively over 5, interrupting the key word "deceiving" as the change marked by minor-mode mixture takes place at 0:12–0:13. The same tension, "I" over 5, remains unresolved to portray the singer's suddenly ungrounded world in the Brooklyn Bridge's "Worst That Could Happen." The verse of this song opens with I moving to ii^{m7} and back to I, all over 5; at song's end, the hyperclimactic 5 arrives in the bass at 2:13, sustains through the singer's frightening hallucination of Mendelssohn's *Wedding March* in trumpets and organ (0:27–0:38), and continues through the coda for a never-resolved rehearing of the opening pedal progression. (This instance seems based on the verse of the Association's "Cherish," which repeated the motion from I^{M9} [0:09] to ii^{m7} [0:11], both over 5, to $\flat$VII^{M9} [0:13] on its own and back to ii^{m7} over 5 [0:16].)

Also quite common, though, is a different use of 5 as a pedal appearing in more than twenty-five hits of the 1960s, and that is as support for the notes of a IV triad. (Listen to Web audio example 8.36.) We shall use slash-chord notation to indicate a chord that appears above a non-root scale degree in the bass, as in the case of IV/5, where the IV chord appears above the bassist's 5. This in particular is the piano chord that Paul McCartney sounds repeatedly after singing the title in the chorus of the Beatles' "The Long and Winding Road" (0:04–0:06), and it's also the culmination of the intro to the Hollies' "He Ain't Heavy, He's My Brother" (0:10–0:12), the end of the verse of the Beach Boys' "Don't Worry Baby," and the end of the bridge of Barbara Acklin's "Love Makes A Woman." In all of these examples, the IV/5 chord moves to I, but it can also resolve to a normal V, as in the end of the intro to the Buckinghams' "Susan" (I—ii—iii—IV/5—V) and the climax of the verse in B. J. Thomas's "Raindrops Keep Fallin' on My Head" (through "I'm never gonna stop the rain by complainin'" in the last verse). Oddly, IV/5 moves instead through iii/5 to ii/5 and *then* to V^{m7} to close the bridge of Aaron Neville's "Tell It Like It Is." A very different situation is at work when 5 is part of a moving bass line beneath an unchanging chord above. (Listen to Web audio example 8.37.) This occurs in the Classics IV's "Traces," when vi ("Traces of") moves through vi/5 ("love long a-") to $\sharp$iv$^{m7/o}$ ("-go that") and then to IV^{M7} ("didn't work out right...."). Clearly, 5 is here a passing tone from 6 down to 4 and even though it sounds in the normally supportive bass line, it itself is a dissonance against the three sustaining consonant upper notes.

Sometimes unchanging tones can sustain in high registers while chords change below. These are called inverted pedals, and they're heard in the top backing vocal in the third verse of the Beatles' "You Won't See Me," in a high-register balalaika-like guitar tone through the last verse of their "Back in the U.S.S.R.," and in the high violins on 5 through two verses of Nilsson's "Everybody's Talkin'."

The 4–3 suspension occurs where the arrival of a chordal third is delayed by the presence of a dissonant fourth above the bass. The fourth is struck right along with the root and fifth, and then descends by step to the third, finally making the triad fully consonant. The V chord, perhaps unsurprisingly, is the one most often decorated with a suspension. (Listen to Web audio example 8.38.) Examples include the final chord of the bridge in the Beach Boys' "In My Room" ("[IV] laugh at yester- [V^4 at 0:28] -day [V^3 at 0:30]"), the verse-ending pedal-controlled guitar chord in Beatles' "Wait" (0:55–0:56), the sustaining harmonium in the bridge of their "We Can Work It Out" ("and there's no [$^\flat$VI] ti- [V^4] -ime for [V^3] fussing and [i] fighting..."), and on every structural V of Bobby Hebb's "Sunny." The suspension can be decorated, as in the accompanimental $V^{4\text{-}3\text{-}2\text{-}3}$ resolution of Bob Dylan's "Sad-Eyed Lady of the Lowlands," ending the line, "who among them do they think could bury you?," with such a decoration so as to emphasize the stronger cadence here than those carrying simple $V^{4\text{-}3}$ resolutions at "missionary times" and "prayers like rhymes." Much more often, the fourth is left unresolved, demanding attention that is never paid. (Listen to Web audio example 8.39.) The verse of Dylan's own "One of Us Must Know (Sooner or Later)" is just this impudent ("[IV] you shouldn't [I] take it so [V^4] personal"), and this became a Mamas and the Papas fingerprint, as in "California Dreaming" (where both six-string and the twelve-string guitars end the intro on the hanging $V^{m7/sus4}$ chord, and vocalists adopt this for the song's chorus endings as well, as at 0:39; better behaved are the $V^{4\text{-}3}$ suspensions at "grey," 0:15–0:16, and "day," 0:22–0:24). The same idea colors "Dedicated to the One I Love," the unresolved V^4 both played in the opening chord, $V^{m7/sus4}$, and sung at the end of the bridge, "something that everybody needs." The same bold $V^{m7/sus4}$ sustains through most of the chorus of Blood, Sweat and Tears' "You've Made Me So Very Happy" before falling (at 0:48) to a meek I^{M7}.

The 4-3 suspension will occur above scale degrees other than 5 in the bass. The consequent phrases of Paul Mauriat and His Orchestra's "Love Is Blue" end $i^{4\text{-}3}$ (as at 0:31). With the Stones, Keith Richards plays normally resolving suspensions in "Honky Tonk Women" with $IV^{4\text{-}3}$ (after "Memphis" and then again after "shoulder") and then with a parallel $V^{4\text{-}3}$ (after "a ride"). Sometimes, for greater tension, the root will not be in the bass; in the Beach Boys'

"Darlin'," for instance, a suspension on the intro's IV chord sounds with scale degrees ♭7 on top and 4 also above the bass 1, as if fourths rather than thirds were being stacked. In "Darlin'," the ♭7 moves to 6 (back and forth, in fact), and only when the chord as a whole shifts to the intro's V (0:16) does it become clear in retrospect that the bass tone has been 1, the fifth of IV. In rare cases, the suspension is particularly effective because it delays the arrival of a third of unexpected color. Paul McCartney exploits this trick in the opening of the chorus of his "Junk," where a presumed IV chord is completed in an unexpectedly minor form, as iv, in "[iv$^{m7/sus4}$] 'Buy! [iv^{m7}—I] Buy!' says the [V] sign...." In the Zombies' "Maybe After She's Gone," the 4-3 suspension at 0:26–0:27 resolves to reveal a chromatically altered major II chord, which settles into a IV that leads to a sequenced 4-3 suspension over I (0:30–0:31).

An imaginative arrangement can give the metaphorical effect of a long-held suspension, too. In Lulu's "To Sir With Love," two violin sections open the intro with sustained 5 and 3 over I, moving to 5 and 4 over V^{m7} at 0:05. This dissonant 4 is a chordal seventh that does not immediately resolve. But much later, after the coda's final cadence, the violins return with a high-register, long-sustaining 5/3 that seems to finally answer the opening as the long-unsatisfied 4 finally resolves to 3. Rock's greatest suspensions, however, are anything but metaphorical, occurring rather in a powerful Townsend-driven descending series of 4–3 resolutions that forms the basis of each verse of The Who's "Pinball Wizard," as in "Ever [I^{sus4-}] since I was a young boy, I [I^3] played the silver ball; from [♭VII^{sus4-}] Soho... [♭VII^3] must have played... [♭VI^{sus4-}] ain't seen nothin'... [♭VI^3] any amusement hall... [V] deaf, dumb and blind kid." Consider the even more remarkable long-range sequence of suspensions in "Cousin Kevin" (0:00–0:49), also from *Tommy*.

The opposite of a suspension is an anticipation. Here, the one note that does not belong to the chord with which it appears arrives *too early,* belonging instead to the following chord. Perhaps the most apt use of this technique occurs in James Jamerson's bass playing in the Supremes' "You Can't Hurry Love." This song, all about the dangers of giving in to anticipation, portrays the error in its chorus, where the impatient bass jumps from 4 to 1 (at 0:20) before everyone else can move ("you [IV] just have to [I] wait!"), and leaps from 3 to 6 (0:23) before iii moves to vi. Otherwise, most nonchord tones will tend to be neighbors, as a chordal third may move to a fourth and back, or a fifth may move to a sixth and back. Instrumentally, these often appear as guitar hammer-ons, perhaps in a boogie, but not necessarily—see Bob Dylan's "Oxford Town" for lots of free hammer-on neighbors.

Some chords are not built of stacked thirds, and then invariably involve some sort of dissonance. The final sound in the Grateful Dead's "Uncle John's Band," for instance, simply has a fifth on top of a fifth, 5—2—6 at that—not close to the expected I chord. Streams of parallel fourths are often used

Photo 8.02. The Stones as marketed in the United States. Seen are American albums *Flowers, Let It Bleed, Beggar's Banquet, Get Yer Ya-Ya's Out, December's Children (and everybody's)*, and *Between the Buttons*, and 45 sleeves for "Jumpin' Jack Flash" and "She's a Rainbow" (with its homage to the *Pepper* cover). (Photo: Annie Eastman)

for exotic appeal (as in Booker T. and the M.G.s' "Chinese Checkers" or Bobby Goldsboro's "Me Japanese Boy, I Love You") or to suggest alienation (as with the clarinet in fourths above the bass clarinet, the latter also doubled an octave higher by electro-theremin) in the Beach Boys' "I Just Wasn't Made for These Times" and the piano-guitar opening of Spirit's "Cold Wind." The parallel fourths sung in a descant line above the melody in the chorus of Keith's "98.6" suggest that the singer's fever lingers yet. The counterpoint-driven augmented fourth, 8 over ♭5 (at 0:09), in Ray Ceroni's guitar intro to the Bell Notes' "I've Had It" is resolved rockabilly fashion to a perfect fifth (8 over 4), but this same dissonant interval is hammered continuously with no thought of resolution in Jimi Hendrix's guitar above Noel Redding's bass for the opening of "Purple Haze" and is doubled by trombone and bass in the opening and coda of Blood, Sweat and Tears' "Symphony for the Devil."

A singular example of contrapuntal dissonance is achieved in James Brown's "Ain't It Funky Now," where every instrument has its own collection of scale degrees: bass in the center on 1, right-channel rhythm guitar on 1 and 2, left-channel rhythm guitar on ♭3, 4 and 6, trumpet on 1, 3, 5, 6, and ♭7, and the late-entering organ on 1, 2, 3, ♯4, 5, 6, and 7. Nothing is arranged into triads. "Wrong" notes seem to be intended with the dissonances of the soprano sax/sped-up electric guitar/vocals-and-drums waltz, "No one will know if you don't want to let them know" section of the Mothers of Invention's "Call

Any Vegetable," and totally free dissonance reigns in extensive instrumental passages of King Crimson's "Moonchild" as well as many electronic concrète or saxophone-oriented Mothers numbers, including "Are You Hung Up?," "King Kong," "Didja Get Any Onya," "Prelude to the Afternoon of a Sexually Aroused Gas Mask," and "Toads of the Short Forest." A conscious effort to emulate the complex dissonances of Edgard Varèse is made by producer James William Guercio in orchestral overdubs for moments in the Buckingham's "Remember," "Foreign Policy," and "Susan." These passages lie a small step from full atonality. In the coming discussions of how chords relate to one another in larger contexts, we will for the most part revert to far more rudimentary sonorities, principally triads and seventh chords.

This chapter has presented a superficial view of chords examined in isolation and in how they are connected to their immediate surroundings through both harmonic and melodic tendencies. But the study of harmony truly belongs to a higher level of organization and purpose, at which individual chords work together to express larger and more abstract ideas through phrase-based voice-leading connections and harmonic progressions. These are the topics of the following three chapters, beginning with functional relationships in progressions that remain within the major scale, and then moving to the more exotically colored harmonic relationships based on all manner of chromaticism.

CHAPTER 9

Diatonic Harmonic Function

One speaks of chord progressions, and these typically involve strongly harmonic relationships between the roots of the chords involved. But sometimes different chords appear in succession that have little or nothing to do with *harmonic* root relationships—sometimes, *melodic* concerns predominate, as when chords are fixed against a given melody, or when chords are chosen because some buried line can be heard moving through one chord tone into another as chords change, without regard to how any roots relate or even how the main melody moves. Sometimes this moving line occurs in the bass, and sometimes it is confined to inner parts, as in tones within chords on the guitar, piano, or backing vocals. (Listen to Web audio example 9.01.) These moving inner parts can be supported by what are called passing or neighboring chords, which connect more stable surrounding chords that may themselves have progressive root function whereas the chords between them have only a contrapuntal essence, existing only to provide a sonorous textural context for moving melodic lines. In our continuing investigation of harmony, we will take up in this chapter the issue of functional root motions, the progress of one chord to or through another, and the sorts of contrapuntal melodic relationships that can exist between and among chords. In chapters 10 and 11, we shall focus on the implications that nonmajor contexts may have for these basic relationships, and how mode mixture and chromatic harmony can color them further. Just as the more innocent and perhaps naïve quality of the major mode gradually became somewhat supplanted by modal systems in the rock music of the later '60s, our discussion will turn in due time from the harmonic implications of diatonic, major-mode functions to those of more revolutionary alternatives.

Fifths falling toward the tonic

The reader may recall from previous discussions that all tonal music gravitates toward the I chord, the tonic. This, the triad whose root is the first scale degree, is home base. We've seen how a rock

> **Harmonic progression:**
> falling fifths
> (iii—vi—ii—V—i).

artist might do nothing but ride on the I or I^{m7} chord through a verse (as in Chuck Berry's "Maybelline" or Sonny and Cher's "Baby Don't Go"), a chorus (Donovan's "The Trip" or Sam and Dave's "You Don't Know Like I Know"), a jam (beneath Clapton's solo in Cream's "Spoonful" or Hendrix's in "Machine Gun"), or an entire structured song (Henry Mancini's "Peter Gunn" or Aretha Franklin's "Chain of Fools"). But this unyielding approach is quite unusual; far more common is the music that presents harmonic variety and one way or another finds its way to I for closure. A song will usually open on a I chord, but that is not always the case; verses of both the Chiffons' "He's So Fine" and the Beach Boys' "Darlin'" begin with a repeated ii—V motion, and both James Ray's "If You Gotta Make a Fool of Somebody" and the Beau Brummels' "Laugh, Laugh" start on a repeated iii—vi motion. (Listen to Web audio example 9.02.) Bob Dylan's "Mr. Tambourine Man" begins on IV, and the Beatles' "She Loves You" and the Supremes' "My World is Empty Without You" begin on vi. These songs all find their tonics eventually, with a rush of familiarity that often seems like the dissipation of clouds, particularly when a major-chord tonic displaces the apparent centricity of a minor-chord opening—"She Loves You" wouldn't present such a joyful effect were it not for the "displaced" vi chord that constantly shadows the I.

Much rarer than the nontonic opening is the song that ends on a chord other than I, but this event can suggest a great sense of lasting uncertainty, as when the unresolved narrative of the Bee Gees' "New York Mining Disaster 1941 (Have You Seen My Wife Mr. Jones)" ends on a doubtful ii. Typically, this ending will conclude a song of dubious mode, as when The Doors' "Light My Fire" ends on what had first worked as an introductory V, or when the Jefferson Airplane's "Somebody to Love," with its strong dorian flavor, ends on IV. Tonic is hard to identify for quite a while in the Beatles' "And

I Love Her" until it becomes apparent at the end of the refrain that the verse had begun with an alternation of ii and vi; the song's final chord, then, is a refreshing and surprisingly stable VI. Even "She Loves You," in which the joyful I chord defeats the glum vi, ends with the added-sixth chord, George Harrison singing the root of vi right along with tonic harmony to encapsulate the song's main conflict in one single, final sonority.

Note that both introductory motions mentioned above, ii—V (in the Chiffons and Beach Boys examples) and iii—vi (in James Ray and the Beau Brummels), constitute falling fifths from root to root: 2 down to 5 and, in the second type, 3 down to 6. Both are instances of what has been called the basic harmonic progression, falling in fifths, in which the root of one chord becomes the fifth of the one that follows. The closure that comes with V—I, therefore, represents the strongest harmonic motion of our repertoire.

Many who disparage rock music as containing "only two chords" are, when they are accurate, likely basing their criticism on songs that contain nothing but V and I. These songs often contain what might be called the "Tom Dooley" pattern, after the Kingston Trio's folk song that follows three bars of I with a single bar of V, and then answers with an opposing phrase: three bars of V leading to a final bar of I. Consider other instances that appear in the verses of the Beatles' "When I'm Sixty-Four" and Janis Joplin's "Me & Bobby McGee." This pattern, or a rhythmic variation of it (such as two bars of each chord: I—V, V—I, as in the Hilltoppers' "Marianne" or the opening lines of Frank and Nancy Sinatra's "Somethin' Stupid") characterizes dozens of well-known songs. (Listen to Web audio example 9.03.) (Many older-generation listeners who would complain that rock music is barren in being confined to two chords should likewise have to account for Eddie Fisher's "Cindy, Oh Cindy," or Nat "King" Cole's "That's All There Is to That," or the Mills Brothers' "Cab Driver," or Al Martino's "Spanish Eyes," presumably examples of an acceptable style of two-chord music!) I and V are the only chords one hears in the opening of the verse in John Fred and His Playboy Band's "Judy in Disguise (With Glasses)," the entirety of the verses of the Dixiebelles' "(Down at) Papa Joe's" and the New Vaudeville Band's "Winchester Cathedral," and the chorus of the Rolling Stones' "Honky Tonk Women." It's a simple, basic relationship great for crowd singalongs, which is why the Plastic Ono Band's "Give Peace a Chance" is so effective and direct in getting its message across without distraction.

The strength of the V—I connection also helps us understand the great tension created by the song introduction that ends on V. Buddy Holly's guitar intro to "That'll Be the Day," which ends on V, is a modified form of the classic guitar intro gracing many of Robert Johnson's recordings, "Crossroads Blues" and "Kindhearted Woman Blues" among them, but Holly may have learned it from Fats Domino, whose "Blue Monday" opens with the same gesture. (Listen to Web audio example 9.04.) This is also heard in the turnaround between verses of Bob Dylan's "Leopard-Skin-Pill-Box Hat." Sometimes a fast song is introduced by a slow passage that works its way to a V where time stops still—such is the case with Bobby Vee's "Take Good Care of My Baby" and the Beatles' "Do You Want to Know a Secret." Sometimes the intro is just a simple statement of V, as in the vibes arpeggiation that opens Shep and the Limelites' "Daddy's Home," or the growling organ's and guitar's V^{m7} introducing the Young Rascals' "I Ain't Gonna Eat Out My Heart Anymore." In other cases, the route to the introductory V is fraught with harmonic complexity, as in John Lennon's highly tentative groping that finally finds a ii—V gesture (0:14–0:18) in the beginning of the Beatles' "If I Fell."

The V—I fifth-progression is extrapolated by a second fifth when ii moves to V, which then usually follows straight to I: the ii—V—I progression. The bridge of Johnny Ray's "You Don't Owe Me a Thing," beginning with one bar of ii^{m7} (at 0:48), going through a bar of V^{m7} (0:50) and leading to two of I (0:52), is the model for many similar bridge openings, as in the Tymes' "So Much in Love." The bridge in Gerry and the Pacemakers' "Ferry Cross the Mersey" opens with the same proportions but in halved values, so that the full pattern takes place in two bars instead of four. One of the musical contributors to the overly sappy quality of Bobby Goldsboro's "Honey" is the squareness of the two-bars-per-chord approach to I—ii—V—I in its verses (a pattern halved in the similarly hypersentimental choruses of the Bee Gees' "I've Gotta Get a Message to You" and the Irish Rovers' "The Unicorn"). (Listen to Web audio example 9.05.) The same device seems more appropriate in Cher's "You Better Sit Down Kids," where the easy-to-follow quality of the progression brings the difficult discussion down to a level the kids can understand. More typically, asymmetry will make things interesting, as when the Beatles' "Penny Lane" opens with a full bar of I leading to a bar divided into two beats of ii^{m7} (0:03) and two of V (0:05), before the harmony turns elsewhere. Or, interest can be created by added sevenths and ninths; the verses of the Delfonics' "La-La Means I Love You" begin with a repeated pattern of two bars of I^{M7} leading to one of ii and one of V$^{M9/m7}$ before turning elsewhere for the prechorus. The strength of direction and the ubiquity of the I—ii—V—I progression forces the ear to hear the repeated I—ii—I—V in the chorus of Paul McCartney's "Every Night" (0:51+) as containing a second "I" that isn't a tonic in its own right as much as an ornament to the stronger V, to which it resolves. In a very strong way, the I chord really exists in this case only as support for the first scale degree as part of a more regular hypothetical V with 4–3 suspension. (Listen to Web audio example 9.06.)

Extrapolating by one more fifth motion, we often hear the I—vi—ii—V—I progression leading back to I through three successive descending fifths between roots. This progression is basic to doo-wop music, which leads to half cadences in repeated phrases, one bar each on I—vi—ii—V before I is finally regained in the verse's fourth phrase. (Listen to Web audio example

9.07.) Examples abound: the Chordettes' "Eddie My Love," the Diamonds' "Silhouettes," and the Crew Cuts' "Sh-boom" created the style, fully formed at the outset and stultified in such records as the Poni-Tails' "Born Too Late" and Mark Dinning's "Teen Angel." An imaginative, unpredictable vocal melody helps disguise the regularity of the underlying progression in the verse of Little Anthony and the Imperials' "Tears on My Pillow" and some added dissonance makes it a bit more bearable in Percy Faith's "Theme From a Summer Place" and the Beatles' "This Boy."

Adding yet another fifth motion to the opening of this progression gives us iii—vi—ii—V—I, a long string that begins at quite a remove from I. This distance along the chain of fifths is a large part of what makes iii (3—5—7) a mysterious chord in its own right—it contains two elements (scale degrees 3 and 5) of the I chord, and also two elements (5 and 7) of V, giving it a conflicted identity that, so distant by fifths from I, is held by a weaker gravitational force than the stronger closer-to-tonic chords previously discussed. For these reasons, iii often appears when a special sort of sensitivity is desired. And for whatever reason, the long iii—vi—ii—V—I chain rarely appears unaltered in the major mode. The iii often does lead to vi, but usually in a melodic/contrapuntal role, where iii is heard with its fifth (scale degree 7) in the bass as part of a descending 8—7—6 bass melody, supporting a passing I—iii/7—vi progression. (Listen to Web audio example 9.08.) (Recall that slash notation, such as for iii/7, indicates a triad appearing over a particular scale degree in the bass.) This sound is well known from the chorus of Percy Sledge's "When a Man Loves a Woman," and the verses of Procol Harum's "A Whiter Shade of Pale" and Jack Bruce's "Theme for an Imaginary Western."

Because vii° is a diminished triad, it rarely if ever appears in an extension of the falling-fifths series adhering to a major scale, preparing iii. But an entire circle of fifths, containing roots on every scale degree, does appear in the minor mode, where chords progress i—iv—♭VII—♭III—♭VI—ii°—V—i. (Listen to Web audio example 9.09.) Note that here, the melodic fifth between the roots of ♭VI and ii is diminished, bringing extra tension to the end of the progression. The full minor-mode circle is heard in songs as diverse as Joe Harnell's "Fly Me to the Moon" (chorus), Dusty Springfield's "You Don't Have to Say You Love Me" (verse), the Beatles' "You Never Give Me Your Money" (intro and first two verses), and the Hare Krishna chant in *Hair*.

Root motion by third

Just as the descending fifth can represent the arpeggiation of the two bounding members of a triad (its fifth and root), progression between roots a third apart—often suggesting triadic arpeggiation—is harmonically valuable. Sometimes the

Harmonic progression: descending thirds (I— vi—IV—ii—vii°—V).

descending fifth is in fact divided into thirds; the I—vi—IV string, for instance, appears just as commonly as does I—vi—ii. In fact, because ii and IV share two tones (scale degrees 4 and 6), these two chords are functionally interchangeable though they have different colors (IV being major, ii, minor) and different roots. (Listen to Web audio example 9.10.) Thus, the I—vi—IV—V progression is interchangeable with doo-wop's I—vi—ii—V, and is heard in such songs as the Penguins' "Earth Angel," the Five Satins' "In the Still of the Nite," the Diamonds' "The Church Bells May Ring," and the Quin-Tones' "Down the Aisle of Love." The equivalent I—vi—ii—V and I—vi—IV—V progressions are perhaps the single most constant element in early sixties pop music, appearing in countless examples of proto-soul music (Ben E. King's "Stand By Me" and the Ronettes' "Be My Baby"), garage-band hits (Gary U.S. Bonds's "Quarter to Three" and the Swingin' Medallions' "Double Shot (Of My Baby's Love)"), and numbers by vocal soloists (Neil Sedaka's "Breaking Up is Hard to Do," Dion and the Belmonts' "Runaround Sue," and Johnny Tillotson's "Poetry in Motion"). The climactic third phrase of Frank Sinatra's "Strangers in the Night" moves from a colorful progression, "[iii] Strangers in the night, two lonely people, we were [#i°7] strangers in the night, up to the moment when we [ii] said our first hello; [vii°7] little did we know," to a more controlled, clichéd retransition with "[I] love was just a [vi] glance away, a [IV] warm, embracing [V] dance away, and . . . ." Figure 9.01 indicates the large decline in popularity of these two sister doo-wop progressions following their 1962 peak.

A related version of the I—vi—IV—V progression might be referred to as the "offset doo-wop" pattern. Here, the I—vi—IV—V motion is divided into two pairs of chords that are rotated, resulting in a IV—V—I—vi progression, now ending in a weak cadence. (Listen to Web audio example 9.11.) Examples are found in the refrain of Bob Dylan's "Blowin' in the Wind" ("the [IV] answer, my [V] friend, is [I] blowin' in the [vi] wind..."), the bridge of the Beach Boys' "Surfer Girl" ("[IV] we could [V] ride the [I] surf to- [vi] -gether"), and the D-gesture (of the SRDC form) of the Rolling Stones' "As Tears Go By" ("[IV] Smiling faces [V] I can see, [I] but not for [vi] me..."). Perhaps rock music's longest chain of descending thirds follows the opening fifth motion ("Close your [ii^m7] eyes and I'll [V] kiss you, to-") in the Beatles' "All My Loving," which then moves "[I] -morrow I'll [vi] miss you, re- [IV] -member I'll [ii] always be [♭VII] true [V^m7] and then...") in its first line, an all-third descent to the half cadence in six chords. For other examples of the offset doo-wop, see the bridges of both the Isley Brothers' "This Old Heart of Mine (Is Weak for You)" (0:30–0:36) and the Beatles' "I Want to Hold Your Hand" (0:51–0:57), and the chorus of the Forum's "The River Is Wide."

Third-related chords, however, serve a contrapuntal role as much as they do a harmonic one. Just as iii shares two members each with I and with V, vi

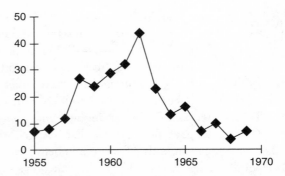

Figure 9.01. Numbers of *Billboard*'s weekly top-twenty songs including the unadorned I—vi—ii—V or I—vi—IV—V progression, 1955–69.

does the same with I (each containing scale degrees 1 and 3) and with IV (having 6 and 1 in common). So vi can alternate with I as an ornament to tonic, its root acting as a melodic, contrapuntal neighbor to the fifth of I while 1 and 3 sustain in both chords. Recall in Web audio example 8.13 how I alternates with vi; in the second alternation, supporting the words "neighbored by a six chord," the singer is alternating the fifth scale degree with its melodic upper neighbor, 6. Only one harmonic function is expressed, but its quality changes, when I—vi—I—vi is heard in scores of songs, such as Buddy Holly's "Maybe Baby" ("[I] Maybe baby, [vi] I'll have you..."), Elvis Presley's "(Marie's the Name) His Latest Flame" ("a very old [I] friend [vi] came by to- [I] -day, [vi] 'cause he was [I] tellin' every- [vi] -one in town a- [I] -bout the love that [vi] he had found..."), Little Eva's "The Loco-Motion" ("[I] everybody's doin' a [vi] brand new dance now..."), Bob Dylan's "Stuck Inside of Mobile With the Memphis Blues Again"("Oh, the [I] ragman draws [vi] circles [I] up and down the [vi] block..."), and the Small Faces' "Itchycoo Park" ("[I] It's all so [vi] beautiful, [I] it's all so [vi] beautiful..."). Dusty Springfield's "I Only Want to Be With You" uses well-placed and rhythmically varied repetitions of chords to greatly expand an underlying I—vi—IV—V—I structure: we hear one bar (four beats) each of I—vi—I—vi, then two beats each of IV—V—IV—V, one bar each of I—vi—IV—V, two beats each of IV—V and finally one bar of I. The chorus of Simon and Garfunkel's "Mrs. Robinson" is built on a similar, but simpler expansion of I—vi (repeated)—IV—V.

Pop music is full of other third-related pairs of chords that together express a single harmony but present a neighbor motion in one voice that alters the quality of the overarching sonority from major to minor or vice-versa. One good example of how one chord can embellish another whose root lies a third away is provided in Scott McKenzie's "San Francisco (Be Sure to Wear Some

Flowers In Your Hair)." Note how the third verse adds new embellishing chords to a harmonic structure that had been presented without them in the first two verses: the first verse (0:05+) progresses with four beats (one bar) per chord, "[vi] if you're [IV] going to [I] San Fran- [V] -cisco,..."], a pattern that is repeated for the second line. In the third verse (1:50+), one bar of vi, "[vi] For those who," is followed by two beats per chord, of "[ii—IV] come to [I] San [iii] Fran-," then a full bar of V ["-cisco"]. Here, one clearly hears ii—IV substitute for the underlying IV, and I—iii for the prior I. Underlying harmonies are thus given changing qualities on the surface. Similarly, the descending-third progression I—vi—IV—ii can fill in a falling fifth within the I—vi—ii—V progression, as in Shelley Fabares' "Johnny Angel," which also expands ii by repeating the IV—ii pair: "Johnny [I] Angel, how I [vi] love him, he's got [IV] something that I can't re- [ii] -sist, but he [IV] doesn't even know that [ii] I-I- [V] -I ex- [I] -ist."

Such third-related chord pairs do not necessarily provide the forward direction that would be expressed by a fifth descent, but they do convey a sense of complexity and sensitivity, as if a single overarching harmony can be appreciated as multifaceted in some way. The second half of the Troggs' "Love Is All Around," for instance, proclaims, "There's [IV⁵] no beginning, there'll [II⁵] be no end," and even though triadic thirds are not articulated in these open-fifth power chords, the listener contrasts the implied natural major sound of IV with the minor sound of ii, given the major-mode context that associates the "happy" major sound with an optimistic "beginning" and the darker minor quality with "end." In another example, consider how the richness of Judy Collins's "Both Sides Now" is enhanced by the quirky metric rhythm with which its chords change, sometimes on the first beat of a bar, sometimes on the third. Its opening line describes clouds as "[I] Bows and [IV/1] flows of angel [I] hair and ice cream [iii] castles [IV] in the [I] air...," moving from the light imagery of angel hair and confection to the weighty stone of a castle at the turn from a major triad, I, to a minor one a third above. The same basic harmony is represented by both I and iii, but its color and density change suddenly. Even where specific word-painted images are not readily apparent, it is the sensitivity of the color change that is of central value, which is why tender ballads such as McKenzie's, the Troggs,' and Collins's tend to feature this relationship. One last example makes this point as well: Merrilee Rush and the Turnabouts' "Angel of the Morning," which supports an optimism despite such emotionally difficult lines in its prechoruses as "and if we're victims of the night" and "I won't be blinded by the light" with repeated tangled *rising* changes from ii to IV.

Occasionally, a single harmony might be represented by three chords working together. For instance, I may move to iii through vi. (Listen to Web audio example 9.12.) Both vi and iii are third-related to I, the basic underlying major-chord root function that is colored by the related minor triads that appear with gentle neighbor-note shifts. In 0:13—0:16 of the Beatles' "She Loves You," this expansion of the I—iii relationship helps portray the shadowy idea that we have seen to pervade this song: "you [I] think you've lost your [vi^{m7}] love, well I [iii] saw her...." In the Beatles' "Across the Universe," John Lennon uses the same chord connection to help us picture drifting waves: "[I] pools of sorrow, [vi] waves of joy are [iii] drifting through my open mind." (Note the vibrantly ironic major quality of "sorrow" and the minor mode of "joy," seemingly refracted in a mingled blend of imaginary waves.) The three-chord connection also appears in Petula Clark's "Downtown," where it provides contrast to an otherwise bustling exuberance with a deeply introspective moment: "[I] someone who is just like you and [vi] needs a gentle hand to [iii] guide them along." You'll find the same connection in lines like "I'm alone in the dark" (Chicago's "Make Me Smile") and "I close my eyes..." (Classics IV's "Traces"). So third-related root motions might sometimes indicate progress, as when dividing fifth motions to new harmonies, and at other times—as when arpeggiating from I to iii as a substitute for I/3—suggest different tonal facets of the same harmony.

The three harmonic functions

We tend to speak of three core harmonic functions: those of the tonic (I), the dominant (V), and the intermediate harmony that leads to V. This last, which we will call the pre-dominant, may be ii (which falls a fifth to V, giving it a harmonic preparation) or it may be IV or vi, the roots of each of which can move to V by step, and therefore contrapuntally. In this sense, IV is a lower neighbor to V and vi is the upper neighbor to V. From either direction, the preparatory chord is subservient in importance to the strongly functional V, but it serves a purpose in hinting that V is coming, building a sense of expectation. All chords can be classified according to these three functions as either exemplifying them, as for example does I, or by embellishing or substituting for them. Thus, in the doo-wop progression, I—vi—IV—V, the functions of I and V are understood by their respective names, IV acts as the pre-V, and vi embellishes the motion from I to the pre-V. This sort of understanding helps the listener distinguish between structural, goal-related chords, and others that are more superficial and ornamental, providing color and transition. Often, position in the song's form, melodic direction, and rhythmic placement of changing chords help to contribute to the sense of which chords are structurally crucial and which are of lesser structural importance. Sometimes, though, such sorts of accents

> **Harmonic functions:** the tonic, the dominant, and the pre-dominant.

bring unnatural emphasis to embellishing materials; the listener often walks a fine line in judging such relationships. A structurally less significant event may be stretched all out of proportion, sometimes in order to create tension by "throwing away" a deeper value through lack of emphasis. As another way of considering this, the reader should be cautioned not to equate structural value with artistic importance; often, a listener's favorite sounds are the ephemeral, transient ones that ornament a steady underlying structure that provides integrity and direction. It is the combination of harmonic functions and various sorts of contrapuntal relationships that, in addition to textural, formal, and rhythmic accents, allows the domain of harmony to exhibit mind-boggling complexity and sometimes confusion, yet also be governed in meaningful ways at any level of structure or detail.

The complaint is indeed a truism that there is a great body of pop music from our period featuring only three chords. When this is the case, the three in question are more often than not I, IV, and V, each chord performing one of the three basic harmonic functions. Many blues numbers contain these chords (sometimes ornamented) and no others. Many dozens of such songs, related to the blues or to any number of other styles, can be represented by the following cross-section, one song from each year of our period that contains no chords but the basic harmonies I, IV, and V:

Joni James, "You Are My Love" (first charting October 1955)

Nervous Norvous, "Transfusion" (June 1956)

Ernie Freeman, "Raunchy" (November 1957)

Buddy Holly, "Rave On" (May 1958)

Bo Diddley, "Crackin' Up" (July 1959)

Johnny Horton, "Sink the Bismarck" (March 1960)

Chris Kenner, "I Like It Like That" (May 1961)

Chubby Checker, "Limbo Rock" (September 1962)

The Crystals, "Do Doo Ron Ron (When He Walked Me Home)" (April 1963)

Jay and the Americans, "Come a Little Bit Closer" (September 1964)

Bob Dylan, "Desolation Row" (*Highway 61 Revisited,* October 1965)

The Beach Boys, "Sloop John B" (April 1966)

The Who, "Happy Jack" (April 1967)

Manfred Mann, "The Mighty Quinn (Quinn the Eskimo)" (March 1968)

Joe South, "Games People Play" (January 1969)

Many passages, such as the riff underlying the intro and entire verse of the Music Explosion's "Little Bit O' Soul," present a simple I—IV—V—I progression with equal durational values on each chord. (Listen to Web audio example 9.13.) Much more rhythmic variety is heard in Janis Joplin's "My Baby," which repeats the I—IV—V pattern in the verse, but the I chord is heard as two bars of three beats each, the IV is heard in one such bar, and then V is expanded to a bar of four beats. Occasionally, as with Bob Dylan's "Mr. Tambourine Man," the progression is thrown a bit off balance by dispensing with the opening tonic, and jumping right in with IV—V—I. In a number of cases, vocal texture breaks the pattern in half: the verse/chorus arrangement of the Beatles' "Twist and Shout" has John sing lead over I, answered by Paul and George on the other chords ("[IV] shake it up, [V] baby!"). This is done twice as slowly in the Angels' "My Boyfriend's Back," in which Peggy sings "my [I] boyfriend's back and you're gonna be in trouble," to which Phyllis and Lana respond, "[IV] hey la, hey [V] la!...," and the directness of the progression, without fancy embellishment, shows that they mean business.

The other important pre-V chord is vi, although it certainly appears far less often than does IV in this role. Tommy James and the Shondells' "I Think We're Alone Now" is a good example. Its verse moves from I to the V-preparatory vi through iii (the underlying I—vi—V being a variant on the I—vi—iii pattern discussed earlier) and then leads to the half cadence from above: "[I] 'Children be- [iii] -have!,' [vi] that's what they [V] say when we're together." This is then repeated before the prechorus reemphasizes by further repetition the iii ("runnin' just as fast as we")—I ("can") third-relation for tension-releasing minor-major contrast. The verse of the Grass Roots' "Midnight Confessions" has a similar approach to the half cadence, but the chords change twice as slowly and so the phrase is not repeated: "[ii] the sound of your footsteps [I] telling me that you're near, [iii] your soft gentle motion, baby, [vi] brings out the need in me that [V] no one can hear."

This I—iii—vi—V idea is actually a substitute for a much more common approach to V from below. In I—iii—IV—V, the bass, carrying roots, moves up directly from 1 to 3 before stepping to 4 and then continuing by step to 5. (Listen to Web audio example 9.14.) This makes for a single coherent, goal-directed gesture. The bass line to this progression is often counterpointed by a commonly heard line in the melody, 8—7—6—7—think of the "oh—oh, oh—oh" backing vocals in the between-the-verse vamps of Peter, Paul and Mary's "If I Had a Hammer." At other times, the upper voice descends straight down, 8—7—6—5, moving from the root of I to the root of V in both outer voices, both in nearly completely stepwise motion, but in contrary directions (8—7—6—5 sung over the bass's 1—3—4—5). This latter model is the basis of Donovan's "Hurdy

Gurdy Man": "[I] Thrown like a star in [iii] my vast sleep, I [IV] open my eyes to [V] take a peep" (progression repeated); note that the individual tones of the 8—7—6—5 descending vocal line are simply repeated, and even repeated as suspensions over each chord change, making for a particularly sharp dissonance that truly opens the eyes with a vocal 7 suspended over the bass 4, for a vertical augmented fourth. These melodies may be sung, or may simply get buried among the rhythm instruments, as when the I—iii—IV—V succession appears four times straight in Herman's Hermits' "Mrs. Brown You've Got a Lovely Daughter." The progression is well known in the verse of the Beach Boys' "I Can Hear Music" and the chorus of Jay and the Americans' "Walkin' in the Rain." The half-cadential V is given a 4–3 suspension when it ends its I—iii—IV—V phrase twice in a row in both Bob Dylan's searching "Sad-Eyed Lady of the Lowlands" and in the coda of the Seekers' fancy-free "Georgy Girl." On occasion, ii^{m7} will substitute for IV; note the I—iii—ii^{m7}—V progression in the bridge of the Beatles' "I Feel Fine" ("[I] I'm so [iii] glad that [ii^{m7}] she's my little [V] girl..."). A more involved version of this expands I with its upper iii before beginning a descending chain of thirds, as in Mary Hopkin's "Goodbye": "[I] Please don't wake me until [iii] late, to- [vi—IV] -morrow comes, and [ii^{m7}] I will not be [V] late...."

Sometimes IV^{M7} will appear in the I—iii—IV—V progression, extending the third scale degree from the iii chord, making for a slight, almost damaged pre-V sound in Peter and Gordon's "I Go to Pieces": "[I] When I see her comin' [iii] down the street, [IV^{M7}] I get so shaky and I [V] feel so weak...." In other cases, the IV^{M7} proves too fragile to rise at all: see Gary Puckett and the Union Gap's "Woman, Woman." Here, the verse progresses normally, beginning with an antecedent phrase ending on a half cadence: "[I] Something's wrong be- [iii] -tween us that your [IV] laughter cannot [V] hide." But the singer cracks in the soon-to-appear minor iv chord ("you're not satis*fied*"), only to remain devastated through the chorus, trying to rise to V but continually falling back, as if sobbing relentlessly, unable to push through the third scale degree that sustains through IV, before finally regaining composure at the end of the refrain: "[I] Wo- [iii] -man, Wo-o [IV^{M7}] -o-o-o- [iii] -man, [IV^{M7}] have you got [iii] cheating on your [ii] mi-hi-hi- [V] -ind...." Despite several attempts, the weak IV^{M7} will never work here as a pre-V; Puckett's V can only be reached through a stronger harmonic preparation, the falling fifth from ii. The cuckold must gird his loins through ii in the accusatory "mi-hi-hi-ind" moment. Interestingly, a similar weakness is overcome in the bridge of the Beatles' "Nowhere Man" when ii replaces IV as a pre-V coming from iii: "Nowhere [iii] man, please [IV] listen, you don't [iii] know what you're [IV] missing, nowhere [iii] man, the [ii^{m7}] world is at your command [V^{m7}]...." See also the vulnerability playing in the iii—IV alternation in the bridge ("tonight with words unspoken...") of the Shirelles' "Will You Love Me Tomorrow" and the wistful quality of the same idea in the bridge of Harold Dorman's "Mountain of Love."

Neighboring chords

We turn now to chords that have no harmonic value at all, but function purely as contrapuntal ornaments, supporting melodic ideas in upper or inner parts or existing only to create melodic motion in the bass. Usually, these chords involve neighbor notes (notes adjacent to more struc-

> **Contrapuntal chords:** chords with neighbors in upper voices, chords with roots as neighbors, the deceptive cadence.

tural tones, to which they typically resolve) or passing notes (moving in a stepwise manner from one structural tone to a different one). Aside from its role as a pre-V, the IV chord may act as a neighbor to I. This comes about both because its root lies a step above the tonic's chordal third, and because the third of the IV chord, scale degree 6, lies a step above the fifth of I. Thus, the succession I—IV—I can support one melodic motion from scale degree 3 to its upper neighbor and back down, and another melodic motion from 5 to its upper neighbor and back down. (Listen to Web audio example 9.15.) This actually constitutes the "boogie" formation, which may occur over a bass that moves 1—4—1 or sustains the 1 pedal as 1—1—1. See how this is done in the piano intro to the Young Rascals' "I've Been Lonely Too Long," which is probably derived from the constant I—IV—I—IV alternation in the verse of Wilson Pickett's "In the Midnight Hour," a song the Rascals had covered. The piano similarly introduces neighboring IV chords over 1 in the bass in Sly and the Family Stone's "Everyday People." In this succession, it is impor- tant to remember that the IV chord, whether 4 or 1 lies in the bass, is simply an embellishment to I, to which it returns rather than moving on to V. Both tonic-neighboring and dominant-preparing roles of IV may be juxtaposed; note the common bridge design, IV—I, IV—V, as in the Monotones' "Book of Love": "[IV] Chapter One says to love her, you [I] love her with all your heart; [IV] Chapter Two says you tell her you're [V] never, never, never, never, never gonna part, and...."

Tonic is often sustained through a repeating, neighboring I—IV vamp; this appears six times in succession in the chorus of the Vogues' "Five O'Clock World," and sixteen times in the mechanical verse of the Five Americans' "Western Union." One would easily lose count of the I—IV alternations in the guitar intro to the Temptations' "The Way You Do the Things You Do," the verse of their "My Girl," the chorus of their "Ain't Too Proud to Beg," and the gospel piano-and-bass intro to their "I Wish It Would Rain." Both

I and IV chords are typically given minor sevenths in soul records originating further downtown from the uptown Tempts; note the I^{m7}—IV^{m7} alternation throughout the Fantastic Johnny C's "Boogaloo Down Broadway" and, for that matter, Traffic's "Feelin' Alright?" (Listen to Web audio example 9.16.) But the seventh on IV alone makes the repeated I—IV^{m7} alternation ultra-funky in ? (Question Mark) and the Mysterians' "96 Tears," where the organ's eight-times-repeated third of I drops a minor second to ♭3 over IV, also pumped eight times, before being regained with the returning tonic. In 1968–69, major sevenths appear on both I and IV chords in alternation in three songs, unknown elsewhere: Archie Bell and the Drells' "Tighten Up," Blood, Sweat and Tears' "Variations on a Theme by Eric Satie," and Chicago Transit Authority's "Does Anybody Really Know What Time It Is?"

The IV—I motion is known as the plagal "Amen" cadence, and it has that comforting, reassuring quality in such endings as to the verse of Johnny Rivers's "Summer Rain": "[IV] sitting here by [I] me, yeah, [IV] she's here by [I] me." (The "Amen" is heard in Web audio examples 4.17, 5.04, and 9.07.) Perhaps the pious "Amen" association lies behind the decision to have an angelic choir singing the Rolling Stones' repeated line, "You [I] Can't Always Get What You [IV] Want." And perhaps it can be considered a divine rapture that hovers over much of Lou Reed's "Heroin," which simply alternates I with its neighboring IV. Rapture is replaced by a smug self-assuredness when the I—IV—I "Amen" cadence is punctuated by a syncopated rhythm, with I articulated on ONE—(+)—two, the IV punched out on the Three (+)— a— (4), and the final I held back until (4)—and. This syncopation ends the choruses of Lesley Gore's "It's My Party" (as at 0:12–0:16) and other top-ten hits of 1961–63 such as the Cookies' "Don't Say Nothin' Bad (About My Baby)" and Barbara George's "I Know (You Don't Love Me No More)."

The contrapuntal I—IV—I idea can be expanded just as we have seen with I—IV—V. Thus, several chords in succession may serve only contrapuntally to colorize the tonic, delaying any motion to V or to a pre-V. In this manner, I—vi—IV—I is repeated for the verse of Eddie Fisher's "Cindy, Oh Cindy," constitutes the expansive first four chords of Henry Mancini's "Moon River," and provides both an opening line for the verse and an instrumental coda for the final tonic of the Cyrkle's "Red Rubber Ball." The chordal structure of the verse of The Band's "The Weight" is simply this succession heard four times. The opening tonic of Peter, Paul and Mary's "Puff (The Magic Dragon)" contains bass/vocal counterpoint that may have been the model for "Hurdy Gurdy Man," quoted above: Mary ornaments her lead vocal 8—7—6—5 descent with two arpeggiations (7—5 and 6—8): "[8/I] Puff, the magic [7/iii] dra- [5] -gon [6/IV] lived [8] by the [5/I] sea," filling in the gap from root down to the fifth of tonic harmony vocally. Follow the same counterpoint underlying the opening phrase of Bobby Vinton's "Please Love Me Forever."

A controversy of sorts has arisen in the academic community over the fact that the powerful tonic-searching V harmony does not properly lead to IV, normally a pre-V chord. In fact, this does not occur in the tonal music of centuries past, but seems to happen with regularity in our repertoire. It is most common in the final, third, line of the blues, where a bar of V moves to a bar of IV before landing on two bars of I. Actually, what is happening here is a combination of two normal tonal behaviors: V leads to I, but that I is at the same time ornamented by its prior neighboring IV chord. V doesn't lead *to* IV as much as it goes to I *through* IV. (Listen to Web audio example 9.17.) I refer to this as the softened blues cadence, because the IV chord cushions the fall from V to I. The Trashmen's "Surfin' Bird" (sixteen bars of I, two of V, two of IV, then eight of I) is a typical appearance of this structure in an adaptation of the blues form. The softened cadence can have an introductory function, as in the horns in Smokey Robinson and the Miracles' "I Second That Emotion," or can even mitigate the usually intense retransitional V at the end of a bridge, as in the Beatles' "I Saw Her Standing There." Elsewhere, in the chorus of "I've Just Seen a Face," the Beatles use this descending counterpoint to illustrate falling: "[V] falling, yes I am [IV] falling, and she keeps [I] calling..." The inevitable nature of the descent inspires the verse and the chorus of Crosby, Stills, Nash and Young's "Helpless." The softened cadence seems like an expression of comfort when Herman's Hermits sing, "[V] somethin' tells me [IV] I'm into something [I] good." Blues-toned pop takes advantage of the effect in many contexts, as heard three times in succession in the relaxing verse of Jimi Hendrix's "The Wind Cries Mary," four times straight in Van Morrison's "And It Stoned Me," and in strategic chorus cadences of Creedence Clearwater Revival's resigned "Bad Moon Rising" ("[V] there's a [IV] bad moon on the [I] rise"), "Lodi," and "Fortunate Son."

An oft-repeated alternation of V and IV before the latter finally falls to I seems a favorite pattern of Memphis and Detroit soul, as when the third line of an expanded blues appears thus in a famous Temptations refrain: "you could have [V] been anything that you [IV] wanted to, and I can [V] tell [IV] The Way You Do The Things You [I] Do." Similar alternating expansions reflect stasis in Otis Redding's "(Sittin' On) The Dock of the Bay": "[V] look like [IV] nothin's gonna change, [V] everything [IV] still remains the same ...." One hears the pattern in the verse of Aretha Franklin's "Respect" and, suggestive minor sevenths everywhere, in the D-gesture of Wilson Pickett's "In the Midnight Hour": "I'm gonna [V^{m7}] take you girl and [IV^{m7}] hold you, [V^{m7}] do everything I [IV^{m7}] told you in the midnight [I] hour." Sometimes, instead of falling to I, the final IV in the repeated pattern moves to a structural V, as in the Rolling Stones' performance of "Time Is On My Side": "[V] you'll come [IV] runnin' back, [V] you'll come [IV] runnin' back, [V] you'll come [IV] runnin' back to [V] me!" Similarly, the I—V—IV—V, as if providing extra accent to the V, is a repeated riff in such songs as the Four Seasons' "Big Girls Don't Cry," the Tremeloes' "Here Comes My Baby," and Tommy James and the Shondells' "Crimson and Clover."

The softened blues cadence is also key to the first real cliché of rock (which virtually replaced the pop cliché, I—vi—ii—V, in terms of popularity): the repeated riff, I—IV—V—IV. (Listen to Web audio example 9.18.) Although heard in such varied styles as the chorus of Jay and the Americans' "Let's Lock the Door," the bridge of the Righteous Brothers' "You've Lost That Lovin' Feelin'" ("[I] baby, [IV] baby, I'd [V] get down on my [IV] knees for [I] you [IV—V—IV]..."), and the verses of Wayne Fontana and the Mind-benders' "Game of Love" and Janis Joplin's "Piece of My Heart," it is as the core of many a mid-sixties garage-band classic that the progression is best remembered. Compare the Kingsmen's "Louie Louie" (I^5—IV^5—v—IV^5),

Photo 9.01. American pop in the '60s. Pictured are albums by the 5th Dimension, the Turtles, the Association, the Young Rascals, Creedence Clearwater Revival, the Strawberry Alarm Clock, the Beach Boys, and Sonny and Cher. (Photo: Annie Eastman)

the McCoys' "Hang On Sloopy," the verse of the Stones' "Get Off Of My Cloud," the Young Rascals' "Good Lovin'," and the Troggs' "Wild Thing." (In "Louie," the IV chord is sometimes expressed as an open fifth, sometimes as a complete major triad.) But this combination of the dynamic full cadence with the soft "Amen" ending is not singular to rock music, and may not always be related to blues—especially noted when we hear Frank Sinatra sing "[V] I did it [IV] My [I] Way."

A very different but similarly unexpected substitution for the direct V—I close is afforded by the deceptive cadence, whereby vi substitutes for I in following the cadential V. In this event, vi sounds like a "damaged" I, or perhaps the effect suggests that V escapes its duty to drop to I by slipping slyly to its upper neighbor instead. (Listen to Web audio example 9.19.) A painful ending is suggested at the refrains of the Everly Brothers' "Crying in the Rain," but no such trouble accompanies the closure-evading "just one more time" cadence of Maurice Williams and the Zodiacs' "Stay." The V—vi motion is the product of momentum in the second half of the verse of the Young Rascals' "I've Been Lonely Too Long," which rises to V for a deceptive cadence (0:46), only to rise again in faster note values (actually much more than "cut in half") for a successful second attempt at regaining tonic: "[I] Now I find that [iii] I can choose, I'm [IV] free, [V] oh, yeah! [vi] so funny I [ii] just have to laugh, [vi] all my troubles been [ii] cut [iii] in [IV] half, I've [V] been [I] lonely...." In the "(Theme From) The Monkees," a chorus ends with a deceptive cadence, "[IV] we're too [V] busy [I] singin' to [IV] put any- [V] -body [vi] down," in order to prepare the next verse, which begins on vi.

Sometimes, vi acts as a complete neighbor to V, in a V—vi—V decoration of dominant function. In the chorus of Janis Joplin's "Get It While You Can," a deceptive vi returns right back to V for a half cadence: "[V] don't you turn your back on [vi] love, no [V] no!" The chorus of Lesley Gore's "Maybe I Know" expands on this idea, beginning with descending thirds that expand the pre-V ("[vi] maybe I know that [IV] he's been a-cheating, [ii] maybe I know that..."), followed by the deceptive cadence ("...[V] he's been un-[vi] -true..."), circling back to the pre-V and full cadence ("...[IV] but [V] what can I [I] do?"). And sometimes V does not go *to* vi, but *through* vi to I, as a variant on the softened blues cadence: Creedence Clearwater Revival performs this both in "Proud Mary" ("[V] big wheels, keep on turnin',' [vi] Proud Mary keep on burnin, [I] rollin'...") and in "Who'll Stop the Rain" ("[IV] and I wonder, [V] still I wonder, [vi] who'll stop the [I] rain"). Occasionally, the texture will lead the ear against hearing V—vi as a deceptive motion; when Jan and Dean have all parts suddenly moving in parallel motion at "[V] won't come [♭VI] back from [IV] Dead Man's [V] Curve!," both ♭VI and IV are heard as having equal value, the V embellished by a pair of neighbor chords. The upper neighbor here does not sound at all like a substitute goal but only an ornament to V.

The tonic itself is often expanded by the use of ii as its upper neighbor, usually with the two chords in repeated alternation. Either can be accented: most songs start on tonic and then waver from there, such as the Young Rascals' relaxed "Groovin'," with a moderate full bar per chord ("[I] Groovin' [ii^{m7}] on a Sunday after- [I] -noon; [ii^{m7}—I] really [ii^{m7}] couldn't get away too [I] soon"). Others start on ii, emphasizing the minor quality, and drop to I on metrically weaker bars, as with Smokey Robinson and the Miracles' "If You Can Want" and the Beatles' "Don't Let Me Down." (Listen to Web audio example 9.20.) The succession may be rapid, alternating chords every two beats, as in Marvin Gaye's "Too Busy Thinking About My Baby," or it may be slow, as in the four bars per chord in the chorus of Sonny and Cher's "Baby Don't Go." Sometimes the minor ii is accented, and its potential pre-V energy is stored in I before it turns and steps upward, eventually gaining its V, as in the Righteous Brothers' "You've Lost That Lovin' Feelin' " ("You never [ii^{m7}] close your eyes anymore when I kiss your [I] lips, and there's no [ii^{m7}] tenderness like before in your finger- [I] -tips; you're trying [ii^{m7}] hard not to show it [iii] (baby) but [IV^{M7}] baby, [V] baby, I know it. . . .") Brenton Wood takes exactly the same approach in the chorus of "Gimme Little Sign." Rarely, the neighbor ii will take an upper neighbor itself, but iii acts as the neighbor to a neighbor in the repeating I—ii—iii—ii chorus, two beats per chord, of James and Bobby Purify's "I'm Your Puppet."

With the alternation of I and ii, the tonic often takes the major seventh, softening its effect somewhat in a vague fog, as in Peter, Paul and Mary's "Leaving On a Jet Plane": "all my [I^{M7}] bags are packed, I'm [ii^{m7}] ready to go, I'm [I^{M7}] standin' here out- [ii^{m7}] -side your door . . . ." This sonority also colors Barbara Lewis's tonic-accented "Hello Stranger," as it does passages that begin on ii^{m7}, such as the verses of Blood, Sweat and Tears' "You've Made Me So Very Happy" and the Guess Who's "These Eyes." The ii often takes more than its seventh; it is not uncommon for this chord to carry the fifth scale degree over from I as a suspended fourth, adding considerably to the haze; the verse of Thunderclap Newman's "Something in the Air" alternates I with a neighboring ii$^{m7/sus4}$ twice, and that of Mercy's "Love (Can Make You Happy)" alternates I^{M7} with ii$^{m7/sus4}$ eight times. In some cases, the fifth scale degree is added not among the upper voices, but in the bass itself, making this chord function as a V chord even though the seventh scale degree is not present (the seventh of ii^{m7}, the first scale degree, acts as a suspended fourth, displacing the 7); the rhythm section plays a ii^{m7} chord, but the bass player makes it function as V$^{M9/sus4}$ by playing 5 as a root. The verse of Madeline Bell's "I'm Gonna Make You Love Me" exemplifies this: "[I^{M7}] I'm gonna do all the things for you a [V$^{M9/sus4}$] man wants a girl to do, oh [I^{M7}] baby (oh)

[V$^{M9/sus4}$] (baby)…." The hazy V$^{M9/sus4}$ is also heard as the retransitional V of "Windy," as she flies "above the clouds." In rare cases, ii over its own root is understood to serve as a substitute for V by supporting a half-cadential scale-degree 2 in the melody, as a half-cadential V often does. The first phrase of the Mindbenders' "A Groovy Kind of Love" concludes this way, "When I'm feeling [I] blue, all I have to [V] do is take a look at [I] you, then I'm not so [ii] blue." Both the Departure-gesture of Mary Wells' "My Guy" and the chorus of the Mothers of Invention's "Hungry Freaks, Daddy" conclude an alternation of ii with iii as a tonic substitute, ending on ii as a V substitute! Bob Dylan has a root-position ii triad fill in for V in a full cadence ending the chorus of "Sad-Eyed Lady of the Lowlands": "My [I] ware- [iii] -house [IV] has [I] my A- [IV] -rab- [I] -ian [V] drums, [ii] should I leave them by your [V$^{4-3-2-3}$] gate? Or, [ii] Sad-eyed lady, should I [I] wait?" More quizzical yet is the Hollies' "Look Through Any Window," which simply ends cold on ii.

Passing chords

Stepwise motion between root-position neighbor chords can often have a primitive or primal sim-plicity when all parts move in parallel motion, as in the stark refrain of "Dead Man's Curve" illustrated earlier. This may be even more true of root-position

> **Contrapuntal chords:** passing chords with ascending and descending roots.

passing chords, often articulated with fifths and even octaves moving in paral-lel above the roots between one structural chord and another a third or more away. Chords moving in block formation in this manner seem to destroy the notion of counterpoint altogether—one simply hears the entire texture moving in one joined-together force. This lockstep propensity can be offset somewhat by a melody that skips between chord members or even moves in contrary motion against the bass. But regardless of style and contrapun-tal roles, passing functions that either expand a single harmonic function or move from one to another occur very often in our repertoire.

First, let's look at passing functions that expand the I, the pre-V, and then the V. We know that direct motion from I to iii helps expand the single tonic harmony with a neighbor motion, as scale degree 1 moves to 7 while both 3 and 5 sustain as common tones to both chords. But ii may often appear as a passing chord between I and iii. In the opening of the verse of the Beatles' "If I Fell" ("if I [I] give [ii] my [iii] heart…"), note that there are two vocal lines against the bass, which rises through chord roots 1—2—3: Paul sings 1—2 (moving in parallel octaves with the bass) and then drops to 7 (moving in contrary motion to the fifth of iii), while at the same time John sings below him 3—4—5 (all three notes moving in parallel tenths above the bass). This song is a fine study in contrasting different sorts of vocal motions against contrapuntal and harmonic chord connections: it contains examples of parallel, similar but not parallel, contrary, and oblique motions in John's and Paul's vocal parts. (Oblique motion is defined as one voice moving while another sustains.) See also the I—ii—iii passing motion in the verse of the Turtles' "It Ain't Me Babe."

Tonic can be expanded with nested passing and neighboring motions in the repeated I—ii—iii—IV succession, where the resulting IV falls as a neighbor chord into the following I. A few more Beatles examples are in order here: In the verse of "Here, There and Everywhere," note how McCartney's lead vocal leaps against stepwise block vocal harmonies in the line, "[I] Here, [ii—iii] making each [IV] day of the [I] year [ii—iii] changing my [IV] life with a . . . ." The lead vocal begins in parallel motion and then goes against the bass in the chorus of "Getting Better": "you've [I] got to admit it's getting [ii] better, a little [iii] better all the [IV] time." In the refrain of "I Shall Be Released," The Band works in completely contrary motion against a rising bass: "[I] any day now [ii] any day now [iii] I [IV] shall be re- [I] -leased." There's no repetition of this refrain; the simple "Amen" cadence renders that unnecessary.

Photo 9.02. An album of historical interest. Seen, at bottom, are the original U.S. stereo and British mono covers of *Sgt. Pepper's Lonely Hearts Club Band*. At upper left is the inner sleeve for the first U.S. pressing. At upper right is a U.S. picture disc manufactured by Capitol in 1978. Also included are 45 sleeves for the title track as issued in 1978 in the United Kingdom and the United States. At center is the gatefold photo as packaged for the album's compact disc release. (Photo: Annie Eastman)

The pre-V function is typically expanded with passing motion in either ascending or descending motions involving ii and IV, or a descending motion from vi to IV. This is emphasized by repetition in the set-up for the refrain in the Supremes' "Come See About Me": "it keeps me [ii] cryin', [iii] baby, for [IV] you, keeps me [ii] sighin', [iii] baby, for [IV] you, so won't you hurry …." The bridge of Los Bravos's "Black Is Black" opens with this rising expansion: "[ii] I can't choose, I got [iii] too much to lose, my [IV] love's too strong"; note the emphatic quality afforded by the singer's doubling the bass line in octaves. The Cowsills' "The Rain, the Park and Other Things" opens intriguingly off-tonic, with this same expansion, two bars per chord; the resulting IV resolves to I as a neighbor chord: "[ii] I saw her sitting in the rain, [iii] raindrops falling on her, she [IV] didn't seem to care, she sat there and smiled at [I] me."

The IV—iii—ii descent occurs about as often as does this ascent; it has a full pre-V function in the Supremes' "Baby Love": "[ii] tell me, what did [I] I do wrong to [IV] make you [iii] stay a- [ii] -way so [V] long, oh …." The same progression, one chord per bar, is given a very different melody in the Mindbenders' "A Groovy Kind of Love," where the tune matches the bass in parallel tenths on the downbeats, finally has a suspension, but then descends the scale on third and fourth beats: "when you're close to [IV] me, I can feel your [iii] heart beat, I can hear you [ii] breathing near my [V] ear, wouldn't you a- [I] -gree …." The vi—V—IV passing motion is much less common than these other types, due to the harmonic domination normally held by V, but V is thus beaten down as a passing chord in the Rolling Stones' "Under My Thumb," part of the pounding coming from the authoritative parallel fifths between lead vocal and bass: "Under my [vi] thumb, the [V] girl who [IV] once had me down, under my [vi] thumb, the [V] girl who [IV] once pushed me around." Jagger couldn't have chosen a better harmonic-contrapuntal device to portray a once-strong girl (V?) as powerless under his forces. The bridge of Clarence Carter's "Slip Away" also works this way, turning first from vi—V—IV to I and then to a retransitional V.

Because the vii° triad is rarely used in rock music, when V is expanded with passing chords, the gap filled is typically not that which comes from rising from 5 to 7 in the bass, but that between the root and the lower fifth of the harmony, passing from V down through IV and iii to ii. This is found mostly in turnarounds, where a song's section ends on V, and the texture passes down V—IV—iii—ii on the way to I beginning the following passage. Bob Dylan does this instrumentally in "If Not For You" to link the bridge's retransitional V (after the line, "without your love I'd be nowhere at all, I'd be lost if not for you") to the beginning of the following verse. In "Sweet Caroline," Neil Diamond links the end of his chorus to the following verse this way: "[I] I've been inclined to believe it never [V] would [IV] and [iii] now [ii] I…." A 5 pedal in the bass helps make it clear that V is being expanded through surface chord changes at the end of the bridge of Aaron Neville's "Tell It Like It Is," when ii is not quite reached by the passing descent: "[iii] but if you want me to [IV] love you, then baby I [V] will, [IV/5] girl you know that I [iii/5] will; [V^{m7}] Tell it like it...."

Finally, stepwise passing chords can fill the gap between two structural harmonies, such as I and V, or between ii and V, whose roots lie some distance apart. The instrumental intro to the Buckinghams' "Susan" is a good basic example, where we hear one bar each of I—ii—iii and then an accelerated motion, half a bar each of IV/5 and the goal, V. The bridge of both the Buckinghams' "Hey Baby (They're Playing Our Song)" and the Turtles' "You Baby" follows a neighboring I—IV—I succession with the stepwise rise from I to the retransitional V. Bob Dylan, who frequently uses root-position passing chords, builds the verses of "Like a Rolling Stone" thus: "[I] Once upon a time you [ii] dressed so fine, you [iii] threw the bums a dime [IV] in your prime, [V] didn't you?," naturally ending the first of the song's many interrogatives ("how does it feel?") on the questioning V. See also the chorus of Johnny Tillotson's "Poetry in Motion."

The gap between ii and V is similarly filled with stepwise root motion in many songs. Note the change in texture in both instruments and vocals at the entry of this repeated idea in the Four Seasons' "Dawn (Go Away)": "[ii] Think! [iii] what a [IV] big man he'll [V] be, [ii] Think! [iii] of the [IV] places you'll [V] see," the lead vocal repeatedly descending stepwise 8—7—6—5—4—3—2 against the bass rise, 2—3—4—5, for expert contrary motion. No such finesse is considered in Martha and the Vandellas' feverish "(Love Is Like a) Heat Wave": "[ii] Could it be the [iii] devil in me, or is [IV] this the way love's sup- [V] -posed to be?" Here, Martha sings pretty much like mercury in the thermometer, rising in strict parallel octaves with the bass. This song is the likely model behind the bridge for the Outsiders' "Time Won't Let Me," parallel octaves and all.

The falling fifth from iii to vi is also treated to intervening passing chords in many songs. Even though this bass line passes through 7, the vii° chord is typically avoided here; instead, an altered iii, with major third and added minor seventh (III^{m7}), typically appears in its place above 7. Thus, the first line in Louis Armstrong's "What a Wonderful World" follows an expansion of I with this descent: "I see [I] traces of [iii] green, [IV] red roses [iii] too, [ii] I see them [I] bloom [III^{m7}/7] for me and [vi] you." The bridge of Dee Clark's "Raindrops" works the same way: "There [IV] must be a cloud in my [iii] head, [ii] rain keeps falling from my [I] eye-eyes. [III^{m7}/7] Oh no, they can't be [vi] teardrops, for a [II] man ain't supposed to [V] cry."

The chords and the relationships among them covered thus far account for all of the harmonic materials in a vast amount of pop music. For nearly all other more elaborate examples, these diatonic progressions and connections are of structural value. In such cases, the underlying diatonic substrate may be altered or ornamented in ways that have yet to be discussed, or several passages with different tonal centers may be combined in ways we have yet to acknowledge. Chapters 10 and 11 will explore these more adventurous, experimental enrichments and will conclude with a summary of the formal arrangements of interactions of all sorts of harmonic procedures that support melodic constructions found in contrasting thematic sections in the same twenty-five songs sampled for their use of rock instrumentation at the end of chapter 3, in an attempt to tie together many of the techniques addressed throughout the book.

CHAPTER 10

Harmony in Minor and Other Nonmajor Modes

Nearly every harmonic and contrapuntal relationship discussed thus far in our examination of harmony has been illustrated with examples in the major mode. This is because the major mode is the fundamental backdrop for, and the normal context of, popular music of the 1950s and '60s. Throughout the era, however, as seen in chapter 7, the minor mode also appeared with some regularity, and later in this period rock music developed a dependency upon the minor-pentatonic mode. In addition, five other scales that had been described as early as the ninth century, the medieval modes, have varied degrees of relevance for the songs we're studying. All of these collections have been treated already in our chapter on melodic organization, but they also have important implications for the nature of harmonic relationships in pop and rock music. In particular, as degrees change in relation to each other among the various scales, chords take on differing characteristic sets of qualities in the different modes. All of these collections but the minor-pentatonic are considered diatonic modes, each comprising seven different scale degrees within the octave, all degrees a second apart from each of their neighbors.

To make matters more interesting, the especially nuanced expression of musical ideas takes frequent advantage of the mixture of modal scale degrees.

So whereas a song may fundamentally conform to the regular elements of one given mode, it may have its scale degrees altered through the borrowing of—or may make reference to—foreign scale degrees taken from any contrasting mode. Often, for example, borrowing iv from the minor mode into major works well because the altered third, ♭6, pulls down strongly by minor second to the root of the following V. A more radical borrowing might occur when a song in the major mode contains passing elements of the dorian mode, perhaps in order to contrast the two different emotional qualities suggested by the major and dorian scales. (Listen to Web audio example 10.01.) A few very gnarly songs, as we shall see, seem to exist largely for the purpose of making the "home" scale fully ambiguous through a thoroughly confusing mixture of contradictory degrees. In all modal settings, both the simple and the complex, everything we have already learned about harmonic and contrapuntal function will be seen to operate largely as it does in the major mode, but every scale has its characteristic harmonic pleasures and pains. We shall first examine qualities of the minor mode, turn next to the medieval modes, look then at the minor-pentatonic, and finally illustrate more or less indeterminate modes. Matters involving chromatic alterations of scale degrees, those not borrowed from diatonic modal scales but altered for other purposes, will be covered in chapter 11.

Harmonic implications of the minor scale

First, a reminder as to the nature of this scale. In comparison to the major scale, 1—2—3—4—5—6—7—1, the minor mode replaces 3 with the note one minor second below, ♭3, but usually keeps other scale degrees from 1 through 5 constant. Otherwise, melodic context for degrees 6 and 7 determines scale membership. (Please refer back to fig. 7.02.) When the melody ascends, 5 moves through 6 and 7 just as in the major scale; when the tune descends, on the other hand, 1 drops through ♭7 and ♭6 to 5. (Listen to Web audio example 10.02.) This dependence on context is heard to a degree in the makeup of certain minor-mode chords. Characteristically, the minor mode presents the tonic as a minor chord (i)

> **Harmonic support in the minor mode:** the minor scale and its resulting chords and characteristic progressions; cycles of falling fifths (i—iv—♭VII—♭III—♭VI—ii°—V—i); borrowing of minor into major; the i—♭III—V arpeggiation; passing chords descending from i to V; V and ♭VI; iv in minor; ii° borrowed into major; the minor v; mixture of major scale degrees into minor; modal substitution.

and, at least in cadential situations, presents the V chord as major, with its third, 7, rising to 1 when V resolves to i. In our repertoire, ♭7 tends to appear as the third of a minor v chord only as contrast to the more prevalent major V. But the major chord, ♭VII, does play a role, most often in supporting ♭7 when that pitch descends melodically. The ascending succession, ♭VII—i, is more characteristic of some medieval modes, but can occur in early or middle portions of minor-mode phrases. Occasionally, in noncadential passages, V^{m7} may be replaced by $vii°^7$, which chord contains all the contrapuntal values of V^{m7} (scale degrees 7, 2 and 4, plus an additional ♭6, all of which tend to move stepwise in their resolutions to members of i.) But in resolving to i, $vii°^7$ lacks the harmonic pull of the falling fifth of V—i. The major triad, ♭III (incorporating ♭7 as its fifth), is the only chord normally built on a minor mode's third scale degree, with the natural 7 rarely acting as its fifth. The unaltered rising melodic 6 rarely serves as root or fifth, but can appear as third; ♭VI, iv, and ii° chords are considered normal forms, as opposed to vi, IV, or ii, respectively. But each of these alternates does appear if melody so demands.

All of these attributes make the minor mode by far the most complex, and the most fraught with minor-second and diminished-chord tension, of all of rock's tonal systems. To summarize, unless mode mixture is at work, triads (and corresponding seventh chords) nearly always take the following roots and qualities in the minor mode: $i^{(m7)}$, $ii°^{(m7)}$, $♭III^{(M7)}$, $iv^{(m7)}$, $V^{(m7)}$, $♭VI^{(M7)}$, and a descending $♭VII^{(m7)}$; but IV, v, and $vii°^7$ appear often enough to give this environment rich expressive variety. We shall continue with examples of characteristic minor-mode harmony by examining chord progressions and characteristic minor-mode colors, making some reference to borrowings of this material into the major mode and of major-mode material into the minor.

In discussing the harmonic value of the diminished triad, it has already been mentioned that the minor mode often hosts full cycles of falling fifths. (Listen to Web audio example 10.03.) The beginning of the Beatles' "You Never Give Me Your Money," is a case in point, where the full cycle of fifths is heard in the introduction and in each of the two opening verses, the first of which is "[i^{m7}] You never give me your [iv^{m7}] money, [$♭VII^{m7}$] you only give me your [$♭III$] funny paper [$♭VI^{M7}$] and in the middle of ne- [$ii°^7$] -goti- [V^{m7}] -ations, you [i] break down." Note how easily the harmony slips from the highly dissonant $ii°^7$ to the driving V^{m7} twice as quickly as the previous chords had moved, changing after two beats instead of adhering to the previous durations of four, pushing with increased drive to the cadential resolution. The tension is relieved after the second verse (and, in the same manner, in going from verse to chorus in Dusty Springfield's "You Don't Have to Say You Love Me") by switching to a new section ("Out of college, money spent...") completely in the more carefree major mode.

Usually, falling fifths do not work their way through the whole cycle from tonic to tonic this way, but are restricted to narrower terrain, as in the repeated phrases moving to half cadences in the Four Seasons' "Beggin'" (their hit single flanked by two other minor-mode examples, "Tell It to the Rain" and "C'mon Marianne"): "[i] Beggin' [♭VI] beggin' you, [ii$^{m7/°}$] put your lovin' [V^{m7}] hand out, baby." Tension exists not only in the diminished triad but also in the diminished fifth, ♭6—2, traversed by the bass to achieve it. The ii$^{m7/°}$ chord may be borrowed into major, as in the verse of the Buckinghams' "Susan," where its ♭6 contrasts with the less intense 6 heard twice before and once afterward in the diatonic neighboring ii chord: "[I] Susan, [ii^{m7}] looks like I am [I] losin','[ii^{m7}] I'm losin' my [vi] mind, (losin' my mind) [ii$^{m7/°}$] I'm wastin' my [I] time [ii^{m7}—V^{m7}]..." The mysterious quality of the Beatles' "Because" is by and large a product of its minor-mode structure that trails off in every verse, and indeed at the end of the entire song, by ending on a revolving-door diminished seventh chord. This highly unstable chord makes several appearances in the song, and is always left unresolved except when followed by the brief major-mode bridge: "ah—[ii$^{°7}$] love is old, love is [IV] new; love is all, love is [V^{m7}] you."

A frequent device in the minor mode is to move from i to the cadential V through ♭III, which gains some mid-point stability by virtue of its major-triad color. (Listen to Web audio example 10.04.) Herman's Hermits' "No Milk Today" illustrates: "[i] No milk today, my [♭III] love has gone away, the [V^{m7}] bottle stands for- [i] -lorn, a [V^{m7}] symbol of the [i] dawn." The Crystals' "Uptown" is built on the same motion. Often, this i—♭III—V progression, a bass arpeggiation of the tonic triad, has a deeper structural role, as in Tom Jones's "Delilah." Here, the verse ("[i] I saw the light on the night that I passed by her [V] window...") expands the minor tonic, and then the chorus begins on the strong major-mode ♭III ("My, my, my Delilah..."), and moves through various chord changes expanding ♭III, only to drive to a retransitional V (between "no man could free" and the next verse's "At break of dawn"). This structure, moving from verse through chorus and retransition, also undergirds the Beatles' "Your Mother Should Know": "[i] Let's all get up... [—♭III]...your mother should know. [—V^{m7}] sing it again." It is further embellished in Mary Hopkin's "Those Were the Days," establishing i in the verse and moving through ♭III ("forever and a day") and V—i in the chorus. In rare cases, this structure so emblematic of the 1—♭3—5 minor triad is imported into the major mode, where it may have the same structural role; see Madeline Bell's "I'm Gonna Make You Love Me," which moves from the major I embellished through the verse ("I'm gonna do all the things for you...") to ♭III, with which the chorus begins ("and I'm gonna make you love me..."), and then to V^{m7} at the retransitional end of the chorus (the repeated "Yes I will"). With the verse-ending words, "Look out, it's comin' in your direction," the singer tries to signal the chorus's surprising impending arrival of the impossible to predict ♭III, foreign to the major mode but seeming to signify here a transcendent love.

The stepwise descent in the bass to V is of great significance in the minor mode. It is intensified by the heavy minor second between ♭6 and 5, so we will first examine these degrees as roots of ♭VI—V (looking also at V—♭VI), and then consider these chords as part of a larger descending pattern. Immediately following a blistering Hammond organ line by Billy Preston, the Beatles' "I Want You (She's So Heavy)" piles up on the emerging intensity by following the ♭VI^{m7} chord with an augmented half-cadential V$^{m7/+}$ at 2:04–2:08: "She's So [i—i/♭3—II$^{m9/m7}$—♭VI^{m7}] heavy [V$^{m7/+}$—i] heavy, heavy, [i/♭3] heavy [II$^{m9/m7}$—♭VI^{m7}—V$^{m7/+}$]." This is, in fact the progression that recycles forever instrumentally as the song's coda, and ♭VI^{m7}—V$^{m7/+}$ are the last two chords heard before the tape was cut at Lennon's direction. The verse section of Paul Mauriat's "Love Is Blue" contains an antecedent phrase that moves from i to ♭III (0:22), and a consequent phrase that repeats that and ends i [0:28]— ♭VI [0:29]—V^{m7} [0:30]—i$^{4-3}$ [0:31], ornamenting the full cadence with the "heavy" ♭VI preparation and a weighty 4–3 suspension. The cadential V^{m7} is similarly approached by ♭VI^{m7} in B. B. King's "The Thrill Is Gone," and the opening (*non*cadential) part of the phrase uses this intense neighbor relationship in the bridge of the Hollies' "Bus Stop": "[♭VI] Every morning I [V^{m7}] would see her [i] waiting at the [♭VI] stop, sometimes she'd [ii°] stop and she would [V^{m7}] show me what she [i] bought."

The direction of the ♭6—5 minor second is reversed in the minor-mode deceptive cadence, where V moves to ♭VI instead of to i. This is particularly surprising in the coda of a major-mode song, where a final major-chord I is expected, just as it had always followed V through the rest of the song. Examples of this surprise are found in the Four Lads' "No, Not Much!," which moves from the bridge to the coda with ii^{m7}—V—♭VI^{m7}—V^{m7}, adding a final ii^{m7}—V$^{m7/o5}$—I, and in the Beatles' "I Will." Here, a three-times repeated "one more time!" ending shifts surprisingly to a ♭VI, a "misstep" long sustained as if the music is momentarily lost before righting itself with the "corrected" I chord: [two beats each chord: I] For the [IV] things you [V^{m7}] do en- [one beat each chord: vi] -dear you [IV] to [I] me, [♯i^{o7}] oh, [two beats: ii] you know [two beats: V^{m7}] I [eight beats!: ♭VI] will, I [eight beats: I] will." This deceptive motion is of course especially effective when the vocal line ends on its final 1, as McCartney does here, rising from 7 to 8 at the ♭VI misstep.

But the ♭VI—V motion of the minor mode is probably best known through the longer stepwise descent, i—♭VII—♭VI—V. (Listen to Web audio example 10.05.) The Beach Boys' "Good Vibrations" is an evocative example: "[i] I love the colorful [♭VII] clothes she wears, and the [♭VI] way the sunlight plays upon her [V] hair." (Note that the song's chorus, "I'm diggin' up…," begins on the major-mode ♭III, and completes the arpeggiation to V to prepare the following verse.) The verses of Del Shannon's

"Runaway," Zager and Evans's "In the Year 2525," the Turtles' "Happy Together," and the flute solo of the Moody Blues' "Nights in White Satin" are just a few of the many celebrated examples of this descending passing-chord progression.

The rising approach to V in minor, through iv, probably occurs less often than does the descent from ♭VI, but it is not uncommon. The verse of Lesley Gore's "You Don't Own Me" repeats this idea within the phrase, "[i] You don't [iv] own me, [V] I'm not just [iv] one of your [V] many [i] toys....," before the entire phrase itself is repeated. An effective combination of both minor-mode stepwise approaches to 5 is particularly appropriate for depicting the painful memory that inspires the Beatles' otherwise major-mode "If I Fell"; it appears at 0:38–0:39, in the half-cadential turnaround between the first and second verses, with a 4–5 rise in McCartney's bass supporting the contrary ♭6–5 descent way above in George Harrison's overdubbed twelve-string Rickenbacker: "that [ii^{m7}] you...would [V^{m7}] love me more than [I] her; [iv—V^{m7}]."

In the minor mode, probably more often than it is heard as a preparation for V, iv functions as a neighbor to i, where its third, ♭6, drops by step to the fifth of i as its root, 4, steps down to the tonic's lowered third. The i—iv—i expansion of tonic is a typical opening environment-setting gesture, sort of a warm-up before any real motion takes place. (Listen to Web audio example 10.06.) It is heard as the first three chords of both the Beatles' "Do You Want to Know a Secret" ("[i] You'll never know how much I [iv] really [i] love you") and Mary Hopkin's "Those Were the Days" ("[i] Once upon a [iv] time there was a [i] tavern"). It may be the minor-mode device imported most often into the major mode, as in the Beatles' dramatic conclusion to "Happiness Is a Warm Gun," where the many-times repeated I—vi—IV—V ("bang bang, shoot shoot") doo-wop progression is countered by the climactic iv in a suddenly free rhythm: "[iv] Happiness is a warm, yes it is, [I] gun," whereupon the greasy doo-wop resumes. The strongest cadence of the Monkees' "Tapioca Tundra" contrasts the overriding major mode with borrowings of ♭VI as well as iv: "it [ii] cannot be a [♭VI] part of me, for [iv] now it's part of [I] you."

Nearly as often, the similarly functioning minor mode's ii° chord may appear as a neighbor to I in the major mode. When heard immediately after the diatonically clean IV-I motion, this mode mixture brings taut emotion to the verse of Jay and the American's "Cara Mia": "[I] Cara mia, [iii] why [IV] must we say good- [I] -bye? [ii°] Each time we [I] part, my [IV] heart wants to [V] die." A multiplicy of chord substitutions is heard when ii° resolves not to I, but to the fragile, sometimes plaintive minor iii chord that we know often plays the tonic-substitute role. As with John Lennon's "Happiness is a Warm Gun," this mixture is wiped away by a clichéd doo-wop reference in Herb Alpert's "This Guy's in Love With You": "[♭VII^{M9}] when you smile, I can [I]

Photo 10.01. London's hot guitarists. Records by Ten Years After, Cream, the Jimi Hendrix Experience, Led Zeppelin, and the Yardbirds. (Photo: Annie Eastman)

tell we [IV^M7] know each other [ii°] very well; how [iii] can I [vi] show you I'm [IV] glad I [V] got to know you. . . ."

The pathos of the minor v is central to the tragedy underlying the Shangri-Las' three-minute saga, "I Can Never Go Home Anymore." The lead singer rebels against her mother, voicing plans to run away with a bass descent to the minor v until a friend-advisor curtly interrupts her with a cautionary "Don't!" placed firmly on the time-suspending major V: "[i] I'm gonna hide [♭VII] if she don't leave me alone, [♭VI] I'm gonna run a- [v] -way [V] (Don't! 'Cause you can [i] never [♭VII] go home any- [♭VI] -more. [v] Listen! [V] Does this sound familiar?)." The minor v goes uncorrected in the prechorus of the Zombies' modally complex "She's Not There": "but it's too [IV] late to [iv] say you're [i] sorry; how would I [v] know, why should I [i] care?"

Much more often, as in the Shangri-Las example but rarely to such a stark degree, a chord employing ♭7 (most often ♭VII) leads to a corrective chord employing the raised 7, either in the V^m7 or in a vii° chord. The bridge-ending refrain of the Kinks' "Set Me Free" is the normative example, the raised 7 breaking out of a slew of minor-mode scale degrees: "so if I [♭VI] can't have you to my- [♭III] -self, [i] set [♭VII] me [V] free! [i] Set [♭VII] me [V^sus4] free!" The effect is a bit more maudlin in Cher's kiddie spaghetti western, "Bang Bang": "[i] I was five and he was six; we rode horses made of sticks. [♭VII] he wore black and I wore white, [V^{m7}] he would always win the fight..." In Paul McCartney's "Maybe I'm Amazed," ♭VII is the product of a descending sequence of chords in dropping neighboring fourths (V dropping to II, the pair repeated a step lower as IV falls to I, and then a full major second lower again as ♭III falls to ♭VII), the sequence broken when ♭VII finds the cadential V: "[IV] Maybe I'm a- [I] -mazed at the way you [V] pulled me out of [II] time, [IV] hung me on a [I] line, and [♭III] maybe I'm amazed at the [♭VII] way I really [V] need you." Rarely, the corrective raised 7 will be supported by vii°, but this must pass immediately to i as it's a highly weak and dependent diminished triad. The midpoint of the verse of the Bee Gees' "Lonely Days" regains tonic this way, after ♭VII had previously settled on ♭III, with a vii° chord that lasts for only a single passing beat: "[i] Good morning, [♭VI] Mr. Sunshine, [♭VII] you brighten [♭III] up my day; [♭VI] come sit be- [iv] side me in your [♭VII] way. [vii°—i] I see you [♭VI] every morning...." The vii°⁷ chord can appear in the major mode, but not as a rectification of ♭VII. In this context, it is a minor-mode substitution for V; see the bridge of Sam Cooke's "You Send Me" ("at [ii^{m7}] first, it was [vii°⁷] infatu- [I] -ation") and, allowing the chord a longer sustain, the verse of Diana Ross and the Supremes' "Someday We'll Be Together" ("[I] You're far away from me, my love, [IV] and just as sure, my, my baby, [vii°⁷] as there are stars above I wanna say, I wanna say, I wanna [I] say, (Some [V] day we'll be to- [IV] -ge- [I] -ther)").

Just as useful as minor-mode scale degrees are in major keys, major-scale degrees can be mixed into minor for characteristic effects. None affects the mode more strongly than the altered third scale degree, and so the ending of a minor-mode song is often supercharged with a final major tonic; the one-more-time coda of Brian Hyland's "Sealed With a Kiss" performs this twist, as does the oft-repeated ending of the Turtles' "Happy Together." But the effect need not be reserved for the very end of the song. In many records, the major I brings mode change from one section to another. In the verse of "Knight in Rusty Armour," Peter and Gordon repeat an antecedent phrase that had decorated an underlying I—♭III—V arpeggiation to the half cadence, completing the consequent phrase with an altered full cadence that prepares for the major-mode chorus: "[i] Long ago in [V] days of old there [i] lived a knight who [♭VI] wasn't quite as [♭III] bold as a knight should [V] be; he [i] rode an old grey [V] mare called Bess, [i] searching for a [♭VI] damsel in dis- [♭III] -tress just to see if [V] he could set her [I] free." Note how freedom is expressed with the liberated third scale degree, not unlike the effect gained by the ♭7—7 rectification just discussed in the Kinks' hit of six months earlier, "Set Me Free." The major I also ushers in major-mode sections in Lesley Gore's "You Don't Own Me." The Zombies' "She's Not There" and "Time of the Season," on the other hand, find the major I at the ends of refrains, but these chords are always followed by a direct return to the contrary minor mode. Both songs contain the same progression, where major I takes its modal cue from a borrowed major IV chord: in the former, "[♭VI] her eyes were [i] clear and bright [IV] but she's not [I] there"; in the latter: "it's the [♭VI] time of the [i] season for [IV^m7] lo- [I] -vin'." The appearance of the major I in the minor key is greatly expanded by the change of mode from minor to major with competing song sections, as in the Exciters' "Tell Him," the Turtles' "Elenore," and the Beatles' "Things We Said Today."

The raised sixth scale degree in the major IV chord usually has a different role in minor-mode songs. It is typically part of a descending chromatic line, in which 6, supported by the major IV chord, drops through ♭6 to 5 over either V or I. Note how IV moves to ♭VI, supporting an inner-voice change from 6 to ♭6 on the way to 5 in the Animals' "The House of the Rising Sun": "There [i] is a [♭III] house in [IV] New Orleans [♭VI] they [i] call the [♭III] Rising [V] Sun." Here, the first arpeggiation that rises from i seems to deflate in New Orleans whereas the second is strong and direct. In the Beach Boys' major-mode "Surfer Girl," Brian's heart is undone by the similar deflation of IV to iv within a 7—♭7—6—♭6—5 descent: "[I] Little [vi] surfer, [IV] little [V] one, [I^M7] made my [I^m7] heart come [IV] all un- [iv] -done." The descending chromatic line, 8—♭7—6—♭6—5, is quite obvious in the highest part in the introduction to Chicago's "25 or 6 to 4": a progression heard four times with a full bar each of i—♭VII—IV^m7 followed by a half-bar each of ♭VI^M7—V^m7. The same repeated line is buried in the same rhythm within the acoustic guitar in Led Zeppelin's "Babe I'm Gonna Leave You," although the chords are different: i—i^m7—vi^m7/°/1—♭VI—V. The change from IV to iv is a climactic event in all of Gary Puckett and the Union Gap's first four records; perhaps sensing a certain staleness, their next and last top-ten disc, "This Girl is a Woman Now" harmonizes the 6—♭6 descent differently, all over a tonic pedal: I—II/1—iv/1—I. The major IV chord can also have a neighboring function expanding the opening tonic; the i—IV—i succession actually represents a reference to the dorian mode borrowed into minor-mode contexts in songs such as the First Edition's "Just Dropped In (To See What Condition My Condition Was In)" (" I [i] woke up this mornin' with the [IV] sun down, shinin' [i] in") and, with some elaboration, the Box Tops' "The Letter" ("[i] Gimme a ticket for an [♭VI] aeroplane, [♭VII^m7] ain't got time to take a [IV] fast train, [i] lonely days are gone...").

The borrowing of the major mode's third scale degree into minor is reversed in some major-mode songs that borrow ♭3, often with ♭III—i forming a united pair of chords (both supporting ♭3) that seems to provide a segue to the newly minor tonic. This mixture results in a surprising opening to the bridge in the Beatles' "Here, There and Everywhere," which opens with ♭III—i, leading to a repeated phrase that first settles into the minor i ("I want her [♭III] everywhere, [i] and if [iv] she's beside me, [V^m7] I know I need [i] never care"), and then with the repeat returns to I for the following verse ("[iv] but to love her [V^m7] is to need her [I] every- [ii] -where..."). Rather than bringing out a deflatory effect, Brian Wilson finds a way to suggest growth in the expansion of modal materials in the Beach Boys' "The Warmth of the Sun": "What [I] good is the [vi] dawn [♭III] that [i] grows into [ii] day [V—V^+]?" A more extensive string of minor-mode chords imported into the Supremes' major-mode song, "I Hear a Symphony," opens the door momentarily to a flat-side fantasy: "[iv] I'm lost in a world [♭III] made for you and [i] me [V^m7]." The contrast of major and minor sections of songs occurs in the less natural order, beginning in major but containing parts in the minor, in rare examples such as the Beatles' "Fool on the Hill."

A few minor-mode songs have chord successions whose functions seem quite different from those discussed thus far. Despite a lack of strong and direct harmonic drive, they can usually be understood as containing substitutions for the more regular relationships with which we're familiar. A case in point is Lesley Gore's "California Nights." Its chorus contains major triads that are not at home in either major or minor modes: "I [i] love California [♭II, that's ♭2—4—♭6] nights, when I'm walkin' with [VII, that's 7—♯2—♯4] you, hand in hand by the [V] shore, [iv] yes, [V] I [i] love...." Here, ♭II—VII—V seems to form a warped descending arpeggiation of the V triad, substituting for the much more common ii°—♭VII—V^m7 succession. In fact, ♭II—because it contains both 4 and a version of the second scale degree—substitutes for the minor mode's V^m7 with some regularity; see, for example, the ♭II turnaround in the Beatles' "Things We Said Today" (1:13–1:14). In the Moody Blues' "Nights in White Satin," ♭II assumes its common role as a substitute for the cadential V^m7 brought about by an ornamented i—♭III—V arpeggiation: "[i] Nights in white [♭VII] satin, [i] never reaching the [♭VII] end, [♭VI] letters I've [♭III] written, [♭II] never meaning to [i] send." Actually, all of these chords would represent diatonic triads in the phrygian scale, but the song soon turns to IV ("'cause I love you..."), and finds the major-mode V in the flute solo for two chords that are foreign to the phrygian mode. Because of the strong V, this song might be considered to be a minor-mode song with heavy reliance upon phrygian and then other (major? dorian?) elements. The Rolling Stones' "Paint It, Black" may have been a model; this song has strong modal qualities (once cadencing "[♭III] girls go [♭VII] by, dressed [i] in their summer clothes") despite the opening's minor-mode i ["I see a red door and I"]—V "want it painted black"] alternation. The chorus moves through a string of major chords, culminating in the strong retransitional IV—V: "[i] I [♭VII] have to [♭III] turn my [♭VII] head un- [IV] -til my darkness [V] goes." Such combinations of mode mixture and functional substitution can make the already complex minor mode quite rich.

Characteristics of the medieval modal systems

The medieval modes are chiefly ingredients for melodic material, but in our repertoire these tunes are nearly always always given harmonic support. The members of the harmonies that result may conform to all of the scale degrees in the given mode, but much more likely, the accompaniment of the song in question will fall into either the major or minor mode, with more or less mixture coming from one or more of the variegated medieval modes. Each mode has its own characteristic combination of relationships among scale degrees, and thus its own set of member chords. (Please refer back to fig. 7.04.) Table 10.01 lists the five medieval modes that exist in the pop-rock music of our period, indicates the constituent scale degrees (which forms should be familiar from chapter 7), and then lists the natural forms of triads (and seventh chords) made from the diatonic scale degrees of each mode. Note that not every scale degree is represented as a root in every mode; the "missing" chords, such as those built on the 6th degree of the dorian scale, the 5th and 7th of the phrygian, the 3rd of the mixolydian, and the 4th and 7th of the lydian, do not normally exist in native forms. The phrygian and lydian are the modes that appear most seldom, largely because of the lack of functioning V and IV chords, respectively. A number of the more colorful chords, such as the minor v and phrygian major ♭II, make for such ungainly progressions at times that modal impurity is frequently demanded.

The five modes are listed in order of increasing differences from underlying minor or major scales, with loyalty to either of these two types determined by the quality of the respective third scale degrees. The aeolian mode shares all seven scale degrees of the descending minor scale; the common dorian is the same as this but raises the 6th scale degree, while the rare phrygian adjusts the aeolian structure only through ♭2. The mixolydian and lydian differ from the major scale by one degree each, but the mixolydian allows for

Table 10.01 Scale degrees and triadic (and seventh chord) forms present in the medieval modes

Mode	Scale degrees	Diatonic chord forms
The "minor" types:		
Aeolian	1 - 2 - ♭3 - 4 - 5 - ♭6 - ♭7	i$^{(m7)}$, ii$^{o(m7)}$, ♭III$^{(M7)}$, iv$^{(m7)}$, v$^{(m7)}$, ♭VI$^{(M7)}$, ♭VII$^{(m7)}$
Dorian	1 - 2 - ♭3 - 4 - 5 - 6 - ♭7	i$^{(m7)}$, ii$^{(m7)}$, ♭III$^{(M7)}$, IV$^{(m7)}$, v$^{(m7)}$, ♭VII$^{(M7)}$
Phrygian	1 - ♭2 - ♭3 - 4 - 5 - ♭6 - ♭7	i$^{(m7)}$, ♭II$^{(M7)}$, ♭III$^{(M7)}$, iv$^{(m7)}$, ♭VI$^{(M7)}$
The "major" types:		
Mixolydian	1 - 2 - 3 - 4 - 5 - 6 - ♭7	I$^{(m7)}$, ii$^{(m7)}$, IV$^{(M7)}$, v$^{(m7)}$, vi$^{(m7)}$, ♭VII$^{(M7)}$
Lydian	1 - 2 - 3 - ♯4 - 5 - 6 - 7	I$^{(M7)}$, II$^{(m7)}$, iii$^{(m7)}$, V$^{(M7)}$, vi$^{(m7)}$

the crucial IV function, so it is prioritized above the very rare lydian, which does not. In terms of harmonic constituents, note that only the lydian has a naturally occurring major V chord; that harmony, however, would take the major seventh—not often heard in conjunction with V. Additionally, the diminished triad is really only at home in the aeolian mode, where it shares the ii° function that is also heard in minor. In fact, any song that seems for the most part to be in the minor mode but makes cadential use of the minor v may be considered to be aeolian. Both the dorian and mixolydian take minor ii and major IV, but their tonic chords are of differing qualities. The lydian scale is the only one that produces a naturally major triad on II.

These are the basic differences between the various modes, the sonic hallmarks of which can be learned through heavy exposure to rock music, whether the mode is pure or a product of the mixture of two or more scales. Generally, one must listen to both the melodic and the harmonic elements of a modal song to determine the relative strengths of the possibly competing modes at work in one or both domains. Here, we shall examine the characteristic harmonic sounds of each mode, and then look at the most common modal chord successions that lead to ambiguity by being shared by more than one source mode. Then, following a discussion of harmonic support for the unrelated minor-pentatonic mode, we shall finally look at a few examples that confound the ear with very heavy mode mixture, trademark signs of particular artists.

The aeolian mode is the source of a fair amount of folk-based popular music. Simon and Garfunkel's "Sounds of Silence," with its moody i, ♭VII and then more optimistic ♭VI and ♭III chords ("[i] Hello, Darkness, my old [♭VII] friend, I've come to talk with you a- [i] -gain, because a vision softly- [♭VI] -y creep- [♭III] -ing..."), is entirely aeolian. Although the Peruvian Quechua melody of their "El Condor Pasa (If I Could)" features the minor-mode's raised 7 as a minor-second ornamental neighbor to 8 in the verses sung by Paul ("[5] I'd [8] ra- [7] -ther [8] be [2] a [♭3] spar- [2] -row [♭3] than [4] a [5] snail"), this song's *chords* use ♭7 exclusively ("... [♭III] snail, [♭VII] yes I [♭III] would, [♭VII] if I [♭III] could I [♭VII] surely [i] would"), going on to introduce ♭VI to clinch the aeolian mode in Artie's bridge ("A- [♭VI] -way, I'd rather sail away like a [♭III] swan..."). Perhaps a subset of this folk category is the aeolian twelve-bar blues, including such examples as Johnny and the Hurricanes' "Crossfire" and Booker T. and the M.G.s' "Green Onions"; the aeolian mode is the only home of the i, iv, and v^{m7} chords heard in these songs and others, such as Fleetwood Mac's "Black Magic Woman." The stubborn, determined ♭7 that refuses to be ameliorated as 7 is perfect for the relentless outrage behind Crosby, Stills, Nash and Young's aeolian "Ohio": "[i] Tin soldiers

> **Harmonic support in the aeolian mode:** ♭VII, ♭III, and v for ♭7; ♭VI and iv for 6.

and [♭III] Nixon [♭VII] coming," with ♭6 reserved for the bridge: "[iv^m7] Gotta get down to it, [♭III] soldiers are cutting us down." The Rolling Stones' early "Play With Fire" incorporates only i, ♭III, and ♭VII chords in its verse/refrains. The rudimentary song lacks a contrasting bridge, but the lowered ♭6 scale degree appears in Jagger's vocal above a supporting ♭VI in the refrain to distinguish this pitch collection from that of the dorian mode : "[♭7/i] but don't [♭3/♭III] play [4/♭VII] with [5/♭III] me 'cause you're [♭6/♭VI] playin' with [5/i] fire." The lack of firm direction posed in Neil Diamond's first single, "Solitary Man," by the ambivalent ♭VII as modal substitute for V, coupled with phrases that trail off indecisively on iv (or, ending the second verse, the dissonant hammer-ons of iv^M9), underline the singer's lack of goals: "[i] Belinda was [iv^M9] mine till the [♭III] time that I [i] found her [♭III] holdin' [iv] Jim, [♭III] lovin' [iv] him." The sung second scale degree keeps these chords from suggesting the phrygian mode, but the chords make the aeolian mode absolutely clear only in the chorus: "[♭III] Don't know that I [♭VI] will, but un- [♭III] -til I can [♭VII] find me a girl who'll [♭VI] stay...." Note how typical it is for aeolian songs to support verses with i and ♭III, and to save chordal appearances of either the telltale ♭6 (accompanied by ♭VI or iv) or 2 (♭VII) for a contrasting section, only late in the game nullifying the possibility of a dorian or phrygian interpretation.

In contrast, the dorian mode—the most frequently occurring medieval mode in rock—is usually announced immediately through a rather brash relationship. Most particularly, the strongly pungent augmented fourth between scale degrees ♭3 (the third of i) and 6 (usually the third of IV or the fifth of ii) is typically at work in either a featured part or behind the scenes in alternations of i with a neighboring chord, such as i—IV—i or i—ii—i. (Listen to Web audio example 10.07.) Either one of these common expansions of tonic is enough to iden-

> **Harmonic support in the dorian mode:** i, ♭III and IV^M7 for ♭3; IV and ii for 6; ♭VII for ♭7 or 4; the dorian–aeolian shift.

tify the dorian context. Sometimes a dorian folk tune is given a full harmonic setting, as in Simon and Garfunkel's "Scarborough Fair/Canticle," or Traffic's "John Barleycorn." In the latter, we hear "There [IV] were three [i] men, came [♭III] out [♭VII] of the [i^susM9] west, their [IV] fortunes [♭III] for [♭VII] to [i^susM9] try." Even if the accompaniment is modally noncommittal, as with the i—♭VII—i neighbor alternations behind The Doors' "Break On Through (To the Other Side)" and the Moody Blues' poetically related "The Sun Set," the vocal line is typically clear in featuring the raised 6; in The Doors, "[5] you know [4] the [5] day destroys [4] the [5] night, [♭7] night divides [6] the [5] day" and in the Moodies, "[♭3] when the sun [2] goes [1] down, and the [2] clouds all [1—6] frown, [5] night has [6] be- [1] -gun [2] for [♭3] the [♭3—4—♭3] sun- [2] -set." Sometimes, harmonies will provide dorian support for a minor-pentatonic tune, as with the Blues Magoos' "(We Ain't Got) Nothin' Yet": "[1/i] One [♭3] day [1] you're [♭7/♭VII] up [5] and [♭7] the [1/i] next [♭3] day [1] you're [4/IV—♭3] down." This vertical mode mixture can be heard in other songs such as Booker T. and the M. G.s' "Hang 'Em High," Stevie Wonder's "Fingertips," Marvin Gaye's "I Heard It Through the Grapevine," and Sergio Mendes and Brasil '66's "Mas Que Nada"; all feature the minor i chord and major IV.

One of the most important chord successions in all of early hard rock can be traced to the modally adventurous Zombies. The dorian idea behind the intro to their "She's Not There" (charting first in the United Kingdom in August 1964) appeared next in the Byrds' Britain-inspired "Eight Miles High" (April 1966) and then in a slew of records immediately thereafter. In the Zombies' prototype, i alternates with the ii, below a syncopated Hohner electric piano melody that passes from 5 through 6 (over ii) to ♭7 and then back through 6 to 5 beneath the lyric, "[i] Well no one [ii] told me a-[i^{m7}] -bout [ii] her [i—ii—i] (the) [ii] (way she lied) [i^{m7}—ii—i—ii]." This syncopated dorian alternation is the basis of the vamp following the second verse of "Eight Miles High" (i—ii^{m7}—i^{m7}—ii^{m7}), also the bed of the song's guitar solo, intro, and coda. Rock jams and pop songs both took up this often-syncopated structure with a vengeance, as we find it in the Association's "Along Comes Mary" (moving over a tonic pedal and through a sustaining vocal 5: "[5/i] Everytime I think that I'm the [ii/1] only one who's lonely someone [i^{m7}] calls on [4/ii/1—♭3] me"). It's also the basis of the extended solos on Vox Continental and Gibson SG in The Doors' "Light My Fire," the solos in the Mothers of Invention's "Call Any Vegetable" from Frank Zappa's guitar and Bunk Gardner's soprano sax (both of which prepare the "a lot of people don't bother about their friends in the vegetable kingdom" coda), the verse of the Classics IV's "Spooky" ("In the [i^{m7}] cool of the evenin' when [ii^{m7}] everything is gettin' kinda [i^{m7}] groovy [ii^{m7}]..."), the Hammond organ solo of Santana's "Evil Ways," the jazzy verse to Van Morrison's "Moondance" ("Well it's a [i] marvelous [ii$^{m7/sus4}$] night for a [i^{m7}] moondance [ii$^{m7/sus4}$] with the [i] stars up a- [ii$^{m7/sus4}$] -bove in your [i^{m7}] eyes"), and many more. Closely related—practically the same thing—is the dorian alternation of i and IV, heard in the Door's "Soul Kitchen" and in the long instrumental jams of The Doors' "When the Music's Over" and Frank Zappa's "Son of Mr. Green Genes." An alternation of i^{m7}—IV^{m7} is given great tension, expressive of the singer's pain, through the conspicuous vocal addition of ♭5 over the tonic chord in the Plastic Ono Band's "Cold Turkey," "[i^{m7}] temp'ature's risin' [IV^{m7}/1—i^{m7}], fever is high [IV^{m7}/1—i^{m7}]...," before the ♭3/6 augmented fourth is exposed most harshly in a chord pair in the chorus, "Cold [♭III] turkey has [IV] got me [♭VII] on the [i^{m7}] run."

A number of pop songs contrast one section in dorian against another in a different mode. Brian Hyland's "Sealed With a Kiss," for instance, has a minor-mode verse/refrain, but as seen in chapter 7, its bridge lies in a pure dorian. That is, until it finds the retransitional major V to return to the minor-mode verse: "I'll [IV] see you in the [i] sunlight, I'll [IV] hear your voice every- [i] where. I'll [IV] run to tenderly [i] hold you, but [II] darlin', you won't be [V] there." Del Shannon's "Keep Searchin' (We'll Follow the Sun)" has a minor-mode verse, a major-mode chorus, and a repetitive dorian i—IV cadence that forms the song's coda. In Paul Mauriat's "Love Is Blue," the major-mode bridge and minor-mode verse are joined by a repeated dorian i—IV vamp (1:13–1:17) also used for the intro and coda. Some songs are more complex, blending modes by beginning in a clearly dorian scale but shifting to aeolian as 6 is replaced by ♭6, all within the same section. This flatting clouds over "Eight Miles High," dropping to ♭VI just as the singer's airplane—and apparently his state of consciousness—first touches down, rebounds, and then cadences there firmly: "[i] Eight [ii] miles [♭III] high, [♭VII] and when you touch [♭VI] down, [♭III] you'll find that it's [♭VII] stranger than [♭VI^M9] known." Much of this pattern—the dorian-to-aeolian change and the colorful ♭VI^M9 cadence—is repeated in the Turtles' "You Showed Me," if the details differ: "[i] You [IV^m7] showed me how to [i] do ex- [IV^m7] -actly what you [i] do, how I [♭VI] fell in [♭VII] love with [i] you; [♭VI] oh [♭VII] it's [i] true, [♭VI] oh, [♭VII] I love [♭VI^M7] you." The dorian-to-aeolian shift is telescoped in the Strawberry Alarm Clock's "Incense and Peppermints": "[i] Good sense, [IV] innocence, [i^m7] cripplin' mankind [♭VI^M9]," which then moves to a strange chorus of minor triads descending by minor second, "[i] who [vii] cares what [♭vii] games we [IV] choose," an apparently hamfisted reharmonization of the classic chromatic melodic descent from 8 to a dorian 6 in such songs as "A Taste of Honey" ("I [i] dream of [i^M7] your first [i^m7] kiss and [IV] then"). See also both the verse and bridge sections of Hugo Montenegro's "The Good, the Bad and the Ugly," each of which moves from dorian to minor. In very rare cases, the dorian mode will only emerge after extended play in the aeolian. The Crazy World of Arthur Brown's "Fire" illustrates: a minor-pentatonic tune is supported by tonic expansion, and then moves through a passing dorian ii to a cadential mixture-colored I chord: "[i] Fire, [♭VII/1] I'll take you to [i] burn. [♭VII/1—i] Fire, [♭VII/1] I'll take you to [i] learn. [♭VII/1—i] I'll [ii] see you [♭III] burn, [ii—I]."

The mixolydian mode is represented chiefly by contrasting through repeated alternation, a major tonic chord with its major ♭VII lower neighbor. (Recall the introduction to Web audio example 4.19.) The mixolydian is a some-what uncommon pop-rock phenomenon. Some folk tunes, such as Judy Collins's "Lord Gregory," and folk-inspired tunes, such as Donovan's "The Fat Angel," are completely mixolydian, but nearly all songs with mixolydian sections have modal

Harmonic support in the mixolydian mode: i—♭VII—i; mixture of mixolydian into major.

contrast with other passages. This is true of the mode's earliest rock appearances, from 1958 and 1959: the Champs' "Tequila" alternates I and ♭VII until 0:42, where IV^{m7} appears en route to a major V. The Four Preps' "Big Man" is militantly major, but the folk-guitar turnaround at 0:46 touches on the mixolydian, with this half cadence: I—IV—I—♭VII—I—V. Little Anthony and the Imperials seem to add a racist touch to "Shimmy Shimmy Ko-Ko-Bop," wherein the "uncivilized" mixolydian lowered seventh portrays the primitive "native girl" with its I—♭VII—I opening. Although not a folk song, the Vogues' "Five O'Clock World," with its mechanistic alternation of I with ♭VII^{add6}, uses the goal-less mixolydian framework to suggest repetitive drudgework, before everything lightens up with the five o-clock whistle. Significantly, the ♭VII^{add6} possesses all of the tones of the minor v^{m7}, but it is hard to hear such a function in an otherwise major-mode context. This is true even when 5 appears in the bass, as in Donovan's "The Fat Angel." The ♭VII-in-the-major-mode effect portrays hopelessness in both the verse/refrain of Jay and the Americans' "She Cried" and the chorus of Lesley Gore's "She's a Fool."

The mixolydian is suggested in a few garage-band numbers from the mid-'60s, such as the Kingsmen's "Louie Louie" (with its modally ambiguous, bare-bones riff I^5—IV^5—v—IV^5) and the Seeds' "Pushin' Too Hard" (repeating the I—♭VII alternation underneath a minor-pentatonic vocal line). Providing tonal contrast against the major-mode verses and bridge, the chorus of the Kinks' "Tired of Waiting for You" alternates I^5 and ♭VII^5 underneath a mixolydian vocal so exhausted it drops further and further behind the beat, fighting inertia just as much as does the lowered seventh scale degree. The rare ♭VII^{M7} chord, emphasized with a guitar's pedal-controlled volume fluctuations, provides a bitter mixolydian touch to the chorus of the Beatles' "Ticket to Ride," which is in a straightforward major mode otherwise: "[vi] She's got a ticket to [IV^{m7}] ride, [vi] she's got a ticket to [♭VII^{M7}] ri-hi-hide, [vi] she's got a ticket to [V] ride, but she don't [I] care." This is typical of the mixolydian—just furnishing an off-color touch to a predominantly major-mode song. Our last example also employs the striking ♭VII^{M7} chord: Herb Alpert's "This Guy's in Love With You": "[I] You see this [IV^{M7}] guy, this guy's in love with [♭VII^{M7}] you."

The phrygian and lydian modes are both rare in the pop-rock literature. All that is required to refer to the phrygian scale is the use of minor i and major ♭II chords. Our three best phrygian examples, curiously, all have California roots. While the Chantay's dark "Pipeline" (first a local hit with the Los Angeles surf crowd) must be considered to be in the minor mode because of its functional Vs, it has strongly phrygian characteristics, including its cadence, iv—♭III—♭II—i. In the San Francisco–based Jefferson Airplane's

Harmonic support in the phrygian mode: ♭II—i; phrygian inflections of other modes; ♭II and tonicization.

Photo 10.02. Acid rock as recorded in Los Angeles. Pictured are album covers from the Grateful Dead, Jefferson Airplane, The Doors, Spirit, and Big Brother and the Holding Co. (Photo: Annie Eastman)

premetal chorus of "Crown of Creation," the second scale degree sounds both as 2 in v and as ♭2 in ♭II, but the latter sounds diatonic, the former, ornamental: "[i^m7] You [v] are the [♭II] crown of cre- [i^m7] -ation." Crosby, Stills and Nash's haunting "Wooden Ships" (cowritten by Hollywood-born David Crosby and Los Angeles transplant Stephen Stills) has a thoroughly phrygian verse: "If you [i^m7] smile at me, I will [iv^M9/m7] understand [♭II] 'cause that is something [i^m7] everybody everywhere does in the [iv^M9/m7] same [i^m7] language."

From there, appearances of the phrygian mode become very sketchy. Is Vaughn Monroe's "Riders in the Sky (A Cowboy Legend)" in the phrygian mode? Its only chords are i, ♭III, ♭VI, and iv, all of which are diatonic in the phrygian, but the singer articulates 2, making this an aeolian song. Perhaps closer is Bob and Earl's "Harlem Shuffle," which follows a long-held i chord (0:07–0:31) with ♭II^m7 (sustaining from 0:32 to 0:39), returning directly to i (heard from 0:40 through 0:47), all of which constitutes the song's entire, repeated, structure. This tale of a slide-based dance, referring to the limbo, answers the question, "how low can you go," with the sunken ♭II chord. But it's not strictly phrygian, because of the minor seventh added to ♭II, which is the nondiatonic lowered first scale degree. (Bob and Earl were both from Los Angeles, the latter once a member of the Hollywood Flames—further evidence of a local interest in the phrygian sound.) Whereas the Lemon Pipers' "Green Tambourine" is basically in the major mode, mixture gives phrygian scale degrees a strong presence: "[I] drop your silver [V] in my [IV] tambour- [I] -ine...Now [♭III] listen while I [♭II^add6] play-ay-ay-ay-ay my green tambour- [I] -ine." Time stops still on ♭II with a rhythmic breakdown ironic for a song about a percussion instrument, when the chord lingers through a vocal suddenly enhanced by tape echo. Functionally, the ♭II seems to result from a paraphrase of the verse's thrice-heard V—IV softened cadence, as the surprising ♭III continues the descent of major triads a major second apart by dropping to ♭II.

The ♭II chord appears in very few other examples of this era, gaining new life years later with heavy metal. Occasionally, though, it will color an already stated V, as it does on a single beat in the Casinos' "Then You Can Tell Me Goodbye": "[I] Kiss me each [vi] morning for a [ii^{m7}] million [V$^{m9/m7}$] years, [♭II$^{#9/m7}$—I^{M7}] hold me each [vi] evening...." This ♭II chord looks especially complex because of its label, but aside from its root (which slides chromatically between 2 and 1), all of its tones represent either the sustaining of a note from the prior V$^{m9/m7}$, or the anticipation of a note from the following i^{M7}; it functions to blur the motion from V to I. (Listen to Web audio example 10.08.) This chromatic passing motion, 2—♭2—1, underlies the most common nonphrygian use of ♭II, as a color substitute for V^{m7} following a pre-V in the major mode. This is a hallmark of the bossa nova style captured in Simon and Garfunkel's "So Long, Frank Lloyd Wright," the consequent phrase of which cadences I (0:50)—ii (0:52)—♭II^{M7} (0:54)—I (0:57). The Lettermen's arrangement of "The Way You Look Tonight" follows a thoroughly conventional major-mode verse with the odd retransition, I—♭III—II—♭II, to the next verse, which begins on I. This may be thought of as the major-triad version of the "Incense and Peppermints" minor-triad slide. The same idea appears in related forms in Pink Floyd's "The Narrow Way" (I^{m7}—IV—♭III—II^{m7}—♭II^{m7}—I^{m7}) and in a more interesting twist in the Beatles' "Sexy Sadie." Here, the ascending succession of the bridge is followed by a complementary descent: "[I] she came along to [ii^{m7}] turn on every- [iii^{m7}] -one, [IV] Sexy [II^{m7}] Sadie, the [♭II^{M7}] greatest of them [I] all; Sexy [VII^{m7}] Sadie...." Just as the ♭III—♭II motion of "Green Tambourine" continues a preexisting line in an unexpected way, the lascivious minor-second slides in the bass line, 2—♭2—1, of "Sexy Sadie" serve to prepare the opening of the verse, which drops in the bass from 1 to the strange VII^{m7} chord on 7. In all of these examples, ♭2 is understood as a chromatic, not a diatonic, scale degree, and therefore makes only tangential reference to the phrygian mode.

There exists one further category of ♭II chords, but these are all illusory. In such songs as Jefferson Airplane's "White Rabbit," the Monkees' "Words," and the Rolling Stones' "Mother's Little Helper," ♭II appears early in the game, but is soon reinterpreted as having a more common function in relation to another chord that itself is reinterpreted as tonic. In each of these songs and others, the meaning of ♭II changes when it acts in some way other than ♭II (becoming ♭VII in the Airplane and Stones examples, and reheard as ♭VI in the Monkees). This technique of reinterpretation, known by the awkward word tonicization, is a form of chromaticism and will be covered in the following chapter. It might be mentioned here, however, that the "White Rabbit" example is far from straightforward. In the Airplane's recording, what is first heard as the alternation of an empty fifth and the major triad a minor second above, may sound at first like I⁵ alternating with its ♭II, but these chords are subsequently understood to truly be vi–♭VII in a minor-pentatonic system: "...and the [VI⁵] ones that mother gives you don't do [♭VII] anything at all, go ask [I] Alice [♭III] when she's [IV] ten feet [I] tall." When this song had been performed by lead singer Grace Slick's former group, The Great Society (as in the live 1965 performance at the Matrix in San Francisco appearing on the LP, *Conspicuous Only In Its Absence*), the opening alternation repeats for a long-extended jam, creating a strong Californian phrygian effect.

The lydian mode is the only one sharper than the major mode, as its only difference from that norm is its raised 4th scale degree. For all practical purposes, the ♯4 works only as the third of the major II chord, because the other scale-based chords that would include ♯4, the diminished ♯iv° and minor vii triads, as well as the V^{M7} seventh chord, are of extremely limited value. The II triad, by contrast, is the one chord most commonly altered through the chromatic process, as will be discussed in chapter 11, and so nearly none of its appearances can be decisively linked to lydian modal tendencies. In nearly all music, the natural 4th scale degree is diatonic, and only in the rare case where ♯4 is treated as *the* normal form of the fourth scale degree can one speak convincingly about the lydian mode. One strong candidate is the Beatles' "Blue Jay Way." This song was composed by George Harrison, who constantly explored unusual scales, beginning with his earlier song, the dorian "Don't Bother Me." This, in fact, may be a musical inclination behind his influential study of Indian ragas, which brought new non-major scales to many rock domains in the years after his first such experimentation in 1965. In "Blue Jay Way," ♯4 is the only note lying between scale degrees 3 and 5 that is sung or played by an instrument. Perhaps contesting the source as the lydian scale is the frequent use of ♯2, which appears, always in the featured lead vocal ("(1) there's [♯2] a [♯4] fog [♯2] u- [1] -pon [♯2] L. [3] A."), far more often than the diatonic 2 (which appears at only one place in the chorus, in the backing vocals). The strong ♯2 would likely lead a listener to decide that this song is not based on a Western scale at all, but on one spelled as 1—♯2—3—♯4—5—6—7. The song's lack of harmonic motion

> **Harmonic support in the lydian mode:** the difficulty of diatonic support for ♯4; II—I; II—IV; cadencing on II; references to ♯4 in the major mode.

(C is sustained as the song's only chordal root) does not support a Western-mode analysis.

Donovan's "Peregine" is a similar and perhaps more convincing example, in that the melody of its main section (repeated in 0:50 to the end) is completely lydian, but, as with the Beatles, the tune is supported only by an unchanging Eastern open-fifth drone and a doubling of the melody on the sarod and harmonium. Our study of lydian melodies must also address the Left Banke's "Pretty Ballerina," which uses a piercing ♯4 to portray the eye-blinding danger of a disarming beauty. But the tune also depends upon ♭7 until it is rectified by 7 in the verse's final cadence, making the opening phrases sound like a mixolydian-lydian mix. Scale degree ♯4 is also replaced by 4 as the cadence approaches: "[1/I] I [8] had [♭7] a [6–5] date [♯4] with [3] a [♯4] pret- [3] -ty [♯4] bal- [3] -ler- [♯4] -in- [5] -a, [1] her [8] hair [♭7] so [6] bril- [5] -liant [♯4] that [3] it [♯4] hurt [3] my [♯4] eye- [5] -es, . . . [♭7/♭VII] was I sur- [8/IV] -prised, [6–5–4] yeah, [4] was I sur- [5/♭III] -prised, no, [7/V] not at [8/I] all." As with the Beatles and Donovan examples, this song's harmony remains fixed on I through the lydian-tinged passage, but moves to other chords when the mode adjusts. Note that all of the song's triads, I, ♭III, IV, V, and ♭VII, are major and their constituent members do not conform to a single scale. (In fact, this represents an example of major-triadic doublings of roots that lie along a minor-pentatonic scale, 1—♭3—4—5—♭7, unusually taking place in a decidedly major-mode context.) So in none of these examples of tunes featuring ♯4 does the supporting harmony relate to the lydian mode.

The lydian scale is marked by that most dissonant of intervals, the augmented fourth, involving the tonic scale degree in the distance from 1 to ♯4. Therefore, the combination of I and II triads exposes this dissonance as measured from the root of the I chord from wherever ♯4 appears as part of II. So the alternation of I and II chords would be a strong lydian fingerprint. Examples of this actually abound. The affect can be one of a transcendent escape from the major mode. This has been heard on Broadway ever since Leonard Bernstein introduced the idea in the magic of "Tonight," from *West Side Story*, where the augmented fourth is emphasized by the sustaining tonic pedal underneath the II chord: "To- [I] night, to- [II^M9/1] night, won't [I] be just any [II^M9/1] night." (Listen to Web audio example 10.09.) Note that with the added ninth, this II/1 chord fills the augmented fourth with a complete string of major seconds involving scale degrees 1, 2, 3, and ♯4, invoking wonder as much as anything. Although quite at home on Broadway, this I—II alternation appears in some pop songs, as in the verse of the Turtles' "You Know What I Mean": "[I] Shouldn't we two [II] be together, [I] you know what I [II] mean, to [IV] be with you is [ii] something I could

[♭VII] dream (you know what I) [V] (mean)." Note the change from ♯4 to 4 in the latter half of this phrase, although the transcendence of the dream remains intact.

Whereas II moves only once to I without alternation in the bridge of the Amboy Dukes's "Journey to the Center of the Mind," this chord portrays fantasy directly: "For [vi] it's a land un- [IV] -known to man where [II] fantasy is [I] fact." Here, the stark parallel octaves moving 2–1 in both lead vocal and bass make rock-hard the factuality of I as opposed to the unbound, evanescent quality of II. In the chorus of "Temptation Eyes," the Grass Roots emerge from a minor-mode verse to an open transcendence; as with Bernstein, the alternation here occurs over a tonic pedal: "[I] Temptation [II/1] eyes lookin' [I] through my my my [II/1] soul, [I] temptation [II/1] eyes, you've gotta [IV] love me, gotta [V^{add6}] love me to- [i] -night." As the lyric moves from soul to physicality, ♯4 is replaced by 4, and even 3 by ♭3, in order to prepare for the minor-mode verse. Occasionally, I can be replaced by IV (which still contains the key 1, forming the augmented fourth with ♯4) in the alternation with II, as in the daydream of Otis Redding's "(Sittin' On) The Dock of the Bay": "[I] Sittin' in the mornin' [II] sun, I'll be [IV] sittin' when the evenin' [II] come. . . ."

This last example illustrates how a phrase can end on II, creating a sort of hyper-half-cadence, useful in many rock songs when a more normal V simply doesn't go far enough. This ending often signals fantastic change, just as we saw above in the I—II—I—II succession. Examples begin chronologically with the Vogues' 1965 hit, "Five O'Clock World." We have already seen how this song's verse displays workday drudgery through the mixolydian mode; the verse ends with a whistle that signals the end of the workday, and the expectant chorus ushers in the brighter major mode, only to end with a fully transcendent II as the singer imagines the coming freedom: "and there's a [I] five o'clock [IV] me in- [I] -side my [IV] clothes [I] thinkin' that the world looks [II$^{M9/m7}$] fine, yeah." The singer then actually trails off with a gleeful, anticipatory yodel while the mixolydian workday setting, not yet over with in reality, returns underneath as if from a flashback with diaphragm-strengthened work grunts from the backing vocals, preparing the way for the coming verse. This turn to II to suggest fantasy is composed out more freely following the bridge of Blood, Sweat and Tears' "Sometimes in Winter," where the cadence, "It's a [I] cold [vi] room and the [IV^{M7}] walls ask where you've [II] gone," leads to flute and flügelhorn fantasias on the lingering II. This effect had actually been achieved two years earlier with a bit more arousal in The Doors' "Light My Fire," where the chorus ending leads to an improvisatory jam with the line, "[IV] try to set the [I] night on [II] fire!" A more spiritual transcendence is suggested in the refrain of Traffic's

"Heaven Is In Your Mind": "[♭VII] guiding you [IV] visions to [I] heaven, and [♭VII] heaven is [I] in your [II] mind," with a spiritual ascent traced by the vocal line rising from 4 (over ♭VII) to 5 (over I) and then, as if breaking an invisible barrier with hardy parallel fifths, rising still further to 6 (over II). See also the end of the chorus of Joan Baez's "The Night They Drove Old Dixie Down." (With a bit more complexity, Web audio example 4.04 ends on II, as its second half progresses i—ii/1—i—ii/1—iv—V—VI^{m7}—II, combining suggestions of aeolian and lydian practice in a fundamentally dorian atmosphere.)

It was stated earlier that the primary function of II is a chromatic one, and this is nearly always operative when II leads to V, a descending-fifth motion that mimics the major-triad quality of V—I in the chords that lie a fifth above, combined with the highly goal-directed rise from ♯4 (the third of II) to 5 (the root of V). This common chromatic use of II will be covered in chapter 11, but we shall explore one other chromatic appearance of ♯4/II here before we depart the topic of the lydian mode. This pertains to the unexpected chromatic fall from ♯4 to 4, continuing to 3, that occurs when II leads through IV to I. (Listen to the final four chords of Web audio example 4.25.) In Procol Harum's "Homburg," in which the I—II—IV—I chain is heard above a sustaining tonic pedal, this 5—♯4—4—3 descent forms the vocal line, but in most rock songs, the chromatic line is buried among inner parts. The chord succession seems to carry a "tamed" quality, as the brash, expectant II is replaced by the mundane IV, which is already falling on its way to I. (One theorist of popular music, Naphtali Wagner, has referred to this taming effect as the "domestication" of ♯4.) Nowhere is this pair of hopeful and deflated sentiments better contrasted than in the refrain of the Beatles' "Yesterday," where the optimistic quality of the singer's belief is tempered by the fact that the past, seen wistfully, is gone: "oh [I] I be- [II] -lieve in [IV] yest- [I] -erday." Bob Dylan, who heard this progression first in the intro to the Beatles' "She Loves You" (although this appearance was anticipated by two years in Bobby Vee's "More Than I Can Say"), similarly portrays magic with II and something more dismal with its quenching by IV in "She Belongs To Me." The verses of this song depart from the twelve-bar blues model, in that the final third line of each verse replaces the more usual V with a startling II that implies extraordinary powers: "she can take the [II] dark out of the nighttime and [IV] paint the daytime [I] black." Lulu's "To Sir With Love" blends a "Yesterday"-like nostalgia with a soaring maturity as the singer prepares for transition to a new life; each of its verses presents our chord succession twice: "[I] Those schoolgirl days [II] of telling [IV] tales and biting [I] nails are gone, but in my mind [II] I know they [IV] will still live [I] on and on." In "Atlan-tis," Donovan repeats the four-chord succession I—II—IV^{M7}—I, adding to this a half-bar turnaround on V each time like a mantra as he conveys the fanciful legend.

Whereas these cannot strictly be considered examples of the lydian mode because 4 rather than ♯4 is always heard as diatonic, they have been treated here because of the characteristic augmented fourth against the tonic—basic to the lydian mode—that is brought out in each of them. In some cases, even when II does not lead to V but is followed by a non-functional drop to I, this strange and wondrous dissonance is nullified if the melody has ♯4 rise to 5. This contextualizes ♯4 in relation to 5 and not to 1, and therefore defuses the "magic" effect. This is exemplified in Patty Duke's "Don't Just Stand There," where she sings 4 going to 5 via ♯4 as IV moves to I via II: "If [I] something is [vi] wrong, give me just [IV] one little [II] sign, if there's [I] someone else...."

Much more surprising is the Turtles' "She'd Rather Be With Me," which lies somewhere in between the examples above. The Turtles' bridge com-prises the line, "Me, oh [I] my, lucky [I^{m7}] guy is what I [IV] am, tell you [II^{m7}] why, you'll under- [♭VII] -stand, she don't [V^{m7}] fly although she [I] can [♭VI^{m7}—V^{m7}]." Here, the lead singer bases his tune on a rising chromatic line, 3 (over the initial I, at "Me") moving to 4 as an accented neighbor to 3 ("guy," over I^{m7}), rising then to ♯4 ("why," over II^{m7}), culminating in 5 (at "fly," on V^{m7}). What's interesting is the fact that this ♯4—5 progression, normally a dilution of the lydian fourth, is interrupted by a backsliding ♭VII, which pre-vents ♯4 from rising directly to 5 on the surface, therefore calling attention to the augmented fourth arising from the featured ♯4 of II and the fifth of the previous IV chord. So although technically not examples in the rare lydian mode, these songs and many others take the stark ♯4 from that rare domain for illustrative purposes.

Finally, a number of songs carry modal chords and chord successions that could in themselves represent more than one mode but depend upon their surroundings for context. The modal loyalty of each can only be deter-mined, if indeed it may be with any certainty, by the consideration of the melodic and harmonic values of all scale degrees involved. Table 10.02 lists a number of such chords and successions and the modes suggested by rep-resentative examples that feature them. For each type, songs are listed in chronological order of chart appearance. Significantly, all of these examples with the exception of eight precursors are from the heavily modal years, 1965–70.

Table 10.02 Modal chords and chord successions, and the modes they typically suggest

Chord(s)	Examples (and functions)
v	Joan Baez, "All My Trials" (mixolydian, with major-mode cadence: I—v—I—iii—IV—I—vi—ii—V—I)
	Fontella Bass, "Rescue Me" (mixolydian chorus: I—IV—♭VII—v)
	The Hollies, "Bus Stop" (aeolian: i—♭III—♭VII^m7—i—iv—v—i, with minor-mode bridge)
	Simon and Garfunkel, "A Hazy Shade of Winter" (aeolian: i—♭VII—♭VI—v—♭VII, then minor-mode chorus)
	The Grass Roots, "Let's Live for Today" (aeolian chorus: i—v—♭VI—♭VII—i, but major-mode bridge)
	The Moody Blues, "Twilight Time" (aeolian: i—♭VI—v—i)
	Mason Williams, "Classical Gas" (aeolian: i—♭VII—v—i)
	Cream, "White Room" (introductory iv—♭III—i—♭VII—v^m7 tattoo thoroughly aeolian but based on roots of minor-pentatonic; verse and chorus major with major triads on these roots plus ♭VI as well)
	The Ventures, "Hawaii Five-O" (dorian mixture in aeolian context: v—i—♭VII—i—♭III—i—♭VII—♭III—v—i; mixture in final chord: ♭VI—♭VII—I)
	Henry Mancini, "Love Theme From Romeo and Juliet" (aeolian: i—v—♭VI—♭III—iv—i, with appearance of phrygian ♭II in bridge)
i—♭VII—i	Ben E. King, "I (Who Have Nothing)" (aeolian but for one V: i^9-8—♭VII^9-8—i^9-8—♭VII^9-8—♭III—V^m7—♭VII—♭VI—i)
	Bob Dylan, "North Country Blues" (aeolian but only faintest touches of 6th scale degree in melody)
	Nancy Sinatra and Lee Hazelwood, "Lady Bird" (aeolian? no 6th scale degree at all)
	The Doors, "Unhappy Girl" (aeolian: i—♭VII—i—v—iv—i)
	The Rolling Stones, "Jumpin' Jack Flash" (pentatonic-minor verse: I^♯9—♭VII—I^♯9)
	Steppenwolf, "Born To Be Wild" (dorian chorus)
♭VI—♭VII—i	Ferrante and Teicher, "Exodus" (dorian but aeolian ♭VI and minor-mode cadence: i—IV—♭VI—♭VII—i—v—♭III—IV—V)
	Bob Dylan: "All Along the Watchtower" (aeolian)
	The Cowsills, "Hair" (♭VI borrowed into dorian: i—♭III—i—♭III—v—♭III—v—♭VII to ♭VI—♭VII half cadence)
♭VI—♭VII—I	The Beatles, "P. S. I Love You" (major mode with aeolian cadence)
	The Beatles, "With a Little Help From My Friends" (major mode with aeolian fanfare and final cadence)
	The Beatles, "Lady Madonna" (major mode with aeolian cadence)
	The Rolling Stones: "Gimme Shelter" (mixolydian: I^5—♭VII^5/1—♭VI^5/1—♭VII^5/1—I^5)
i—♭III—i	The Grass Roots, "Let's Live for Today" (aeolian verse)
	Hugo Montenegro, "The Good, the Bad and the Ugly" (dorian bridge)
	The Zombies, "Time of the Season" (aeolian prechorus)
I—♭III—IV	The Everly Brothers, "Wake Up Little Susie" (major with mixture from minor-pentatonic)

Carl Perkins, "Lend Me Your Comb" (major with mixture from minor-pentatonic)

The Beatles, "Please Please Me" (major with mixture from minor-pentatonic)

Steppenwolf, "Born To Be Wild" (dorian verse: I♯9—♭III—IV—i)

♭VII—IV Martha and the Vandellas, "Nowhere to Run" (dorian)

The Who, "I Can't Explain" (major-mode with minor-pentatonic inflections)

The Rolling Stones, "The Last Time" (mixolydian)

The Beatles, "You're Going to Lose That Girl" (major with chromaticized final cadence)

The Beach Boys, "California Girls" (chromaticized major with minor-pentatonic inflections; sustained over 1 pedal in intro)

The Hollies, "Look Through Any Window" (mixolydian chorus)

The Beatles, "She Said She Said" (mixolydian)

Paul Revere and the Raiders, "Hungry" (chorus moves from mixolydian to major)

The Rolling Stones, "Lady Jane" (mixolydian with chromaticized D-gesture)

The Association, "Never My Love" (chromaticized major)

Tommy Boyce and Bobby Hart, "I Wonder What She's Doing Tonite" (chromaticized major)

The Chambers Brothers, "Time Has Come Today" (mixolydian but one major-mode V for half cadence)

The Moody Blues, "Peak Hour" (mixolydian I—v^{m7}/♭7—IV—I but later use of II$^{M9/m7}$—I^{m7})

The Status Quo, "Pictures of Matchstick Men" (chromaticized major, even with later ♭VI—♭III—♭VII succession)

The Rolling Stones, "Jumpin' Jack Flash" (minor-pentatonic chorus: ♭III—♭VII—IV—I)

Donovan, "Hurdy Gurdy Man" (chromaticized major)

Bloomfield, Kooper and Stills, "His Holy Modal Majesty" (mixolydian)

The Beatles, "Hey Jude" (major mode with chromaticized coda)

The Flirtations, "Nothing But a Heartache" (aeolian but bridge moves from phrygian to minor)

Cream, "Badge" (bridge is ♭III^{M7}—♭VII—IV in dorian; verse has aeolian touch of ♭VI: i—IV—v—♭VI—i—ii—i$^{M9/m7}$)

The Who, "We're Not Gonna Take It" (chromaticized major)

The Grateful Dead, "St. Stephen" (mixolydian but one major-mode V for half cadence)

Chicago, "Make Me Smile" (chromaticized major)

Traffic, "Empty Pages" (chromaticized major? no melodic 7th scale degree during Pianet solo)

The Moody Blues, "And the Tide Rushes In" (mixolydian)

The Moody Blues, "It's Up to You" (mixolydian)

James Taylor, "Fire and Rain" (major with mixolydian mixture: I—v^{m7}—IV—I$^{9-10}$—V—♭VII)

The minor-pentatonic mode

As stated in chapter 7, the minor-pentatonic scale is spelled 1—♭3—4—5—♭7 (please refer back to fig. 7.03). It is actually a purely melodic collection, responsible for almost all vocal and lead-guitar activity in the blues, and most chords in the system must draw from outside of this group for their members. Typically, the five scale degrees act as roots for major triads all around, and therefore only ♭III among them would contain all members of its triad within the scale. But even so, such

> **Harmonic "support" in the minor-pentatonic mode:** acoustic doublings in unisons, octaves, fifths, and major triads; characteristic progressions I—♭VII—I; I—♭III—IV—I; I—♭VII—♭III—I; I—♭VII—IV—I; I—♭III—IV—V—I; V—IV—I; related scales and mixture involving minor-pentatonic materials.

a chord does not make for a harmonic phenomenon. There can be some sense of counterpoint, in that ♭VII can resolve to I, or IV to ♭III, as neighboring chords, but there is no semblance of harmonic function other than the absolute basic V—I progression. When chords do progress by fifth along the minor-pentatonic roots, such as through I—IV—♭VII—♭III, it is much more likely that they are part of a minor or aeolian system. (Note that all five degrees of the nondescript minor-pentatonic scale are also members of the minor, dorian, aeolian, and phrygian modes!)

Instead of thinking of these chords as harmonic entities, one should regard them as simple acoustic doublings, almost as very thick single notes. Triads built on the minor-pentatonic-scale roots tend to connect with each other in all-parallel motion, like blocks moving up or down as one piece. The following paragraphs will clarify the nature of this acoustical doubling, provide conflicting examples that seem to interject independent parts into the otherwise block-voiced minor-pentatonic system, and finally look at a small handful of highly experimental songs that, although not part of this system, seem to draw inspiration from it.

The doubling of the minor-pentatonic scale begins with unison and octave doublings of a moving line, typically of a chantlike nature. Think of the backing vocalists who respond to the lead singer with a unison "hey—yeah" on the minor-pentatonic pitches, 8—♭7—5—♭7—8 in Gary U. S. Bonds's "New Orleans," or all of the singers chanting "bop ba" and similar scat syllables on the minor-pentatonic line, 8—8, 8—♭7—8—8, 8—♭7—8—8—♭3—8—♭7— 8 in Cream's "Sweet Wine." It is this approach to textural doubling that led the way to octave doubling among bass and guitars in minor-pentatonic lead riffs to such songs as the Yardbirds' cover of "I'm a Man" (1—♭3—4—♭7—1) and, with one chromatic passing tone, Led Zeppelin's "Heartbreaker" (1—♭3—4—♯4—5—♭7). On rare occasion, the major-pentatonic scale or a subset of it (usually spelled 1—2—3—5—6, but there are variants) can be treated this way—consider the bass/piano octave doublings of 8—6—5—6—8 in the introductions to Gary Lewis and the Playboys' "She's Just My Style" or John Fred and His Playboy Band's "Judy in Disguise (With Glasses)."

Often, the minor-pentatonic tune is doubled in pure fifths. (Listen to Web audio example 10.10.) These are just like the fifths that would form the distances between roots and fifths of triads, but the result should be more properly heard as a single line with a "thickened" doubling, as a Hammond melody played with a mixture stop that adds a perfect fifth above every note played. The guitarist's open-fifth power chords operate most effectively in a minor-pentatonic song, as with the I^5—$^\flat\text{VII}^5$—I^5 neighboring motion upon which Link Wray and His Ray Men built "Rumble." Perhaps the first such examples came from large brass arrangements, as with Jimmy Smith and the Big Band's "Walk on the Wild Side," which arranges open-fifth doublings of the succession, I^5—IV^5—V^5—$^\flat\text{VII}^5$—V^5—IV^5—$^\flat\text{III}^5$—I^5, or the Contours' Smokey Robinson-penned hit, "First I Look at the Purse," which contains the intro vamp, I^5—$^\flat\text{III}^5$—IV^5—$^\flat\text{III}^5$—I^5. But early examples also included solo keyboard work: The electric piano's slow I^5—$^\flat\text{III}^5$—IV^5 intro to Ritchie Barrett's "Some Other Guy" gave John Lennon the idea for his piano intro to "Instant Karma" eight years later. The heyday for this technique, whether arranged for band or covered by a single electric guitar, was 1966, in the repetitive riffs of such hits from that year as the Kinks' "Till the End of the Day" (I^5—$^\flat\text{VII}^5$—$^\flat\text{III}^5$—I^5), Sam and Dave's "Hold On! I'm Comin'" (I^5—$^\flat\text{III}^5$—IV^5—I^5), the Young Rascals' "You Better Run" (I^5—$^\flat\text{VII}^5$—I^5—$^\flat\text{III}^5$), and Eddie Floyd's "Knock on Wood" (I^5—$^\flat\text{III}^5$—IV^5—V^5—$^\flat\text{VII}^5$—V^5). It is important to note that whereas these "chords" provide the accompanimental backdrop, the lead singer (or indeed, further instrumental riffs, as with the trumpets and saxes in the Sam and Dave number's 8—$^\flat$7—5—5—$^\flat$7—8 ostinato played over each different fifth) will typically move independently, also staying largely within the confines of the minor-pentatonic resources. All parts may proceed with their own pentatonic melodies, either performed as a solo, or in one or more simultaneous lines doubled in octaves, fifths, or triads. Remember that there is no concept of consonance and dissonance at work with this scale, so any such combinations may appear at any time. The pentatonic line may even appear in parallel fourths, as in the intro to the Jimi Hendrix Experience's "Castles Made of Sand."

But it is as parallel major triads that these doubled lines take their thickest texture. The guitarist will often form a barre chord, moving up and down the fingerboard with an unchanging left-hand position, the entire sonority moving up or down as a block. (Listen to Web audio example 10.11.) One early example is performed on the lone acoustic guitar that opens the Champs' "Tequila," as the tonic alternates with its pentatonic lower neighbor, $^\flat$VII. Curiously, the bass soon enters, supporting $^\flat$VII with the 5th scale degree, insisting that the chord is v, not $^\flat$VII. (It really makes little difference; the

1—5—1 alternation in the bass sounds like an arpeggiation of the root and fifth of the I chord, while the guitar ornaments I with neighbors; it's possible to hear no *harmonic* motion from tonic at all despite the 5—1 in the bass.) This I—♭VII—I motion is the most important of all minor-pentatonic chord pairs, basic to such songs as Little Anthony and the Imperials' ultra-primitive "Shimmy Shimmy Ko-Ko-Bop" and the Seeds' primal "Pushin' Too Hard." Note, though, that the strident I—♭VII, ♭VII—I motions that foment revolution in Jefferson Airplane's "Volunteers" are not played as barre chords, and include some contrary motion between guitar lines as the chords change. Even where all vocal and instrumental parts may not move in block fashion, these passages are still heard as inspired by the minor-pentatonic doubling technique if the context of that scale holds strong against any modal mixture.

A second important succession of major triads in the minor-pentatonic is I—♭III—IV—I. This and all passages that pit I against ♭III or V against ♭VII take advantage of the colorful alteration of scale degree that takes place as one chord is replaced by the other: 3 in the I chord is replaced by ♭3 in the ♭III, and ♭7 in ♭VII is replaced by the 7 in V. Despite the color effect, and the lack of contrapuntal lines for the most part, ♭III is heard as an extension of the I chord, and so I—♭III—IV—I works sort of like an expanded tonic moving to a neighboring IV with a return. (But still, try to listen in melodic, not harmonic, terms, focusing when necessary on sometimes hypothetical parallel motions against the bass.) The Everly Brothers provide a very early example of this succession as an intro to "Wake Up Little Susie," but note that even though they play ♭III and IV as barre chords, I is not in parallel (one can hear 3 as the highest note in the guitar's I chord, but then roots on top of ♭III and IV). Bob Dylan gets fully parallel block motion in his rural guitar playing of I—♭III—IV—♭III—I in "Highway 61 Revisited." In "It's Alright Ma (I'm Only Bleeding)," Dylan tunes the guitar to an open major chord, sounding this succession for his intro riff with parallel ease. Pete Townshend electrifies exactly these same fingerings and rhythms in the intro to The Who's "I Can See For Miles." The parallel I—♭III—IV—I chords appear as contrast to an overriding major mode in tag riffs everywhere, from the Four Seasons' "Sherry" (punctuating the cadences that precede bass Nick Massi's question, "Why don't you come out?") to Aretha Franklin's "Think" (the "Freedom!" section). The Yardbirds play an adaptation of these chords, I—♭III—IV—iv—I, in parallel motion in "For Your Love," but note how a backing vocalist introduces counterpoint by descending 8—♭7—6—♭6—5 against this succession. The chords are also arranged out of parallel voicing in the Supremes' "Love Is Like an Itching in My Heart" and heard over an unchanging 1 pedal in the Temptations' "(I Know) I'm Losing You." Hendrix's famous "Purple Haze" verse is out of parallel by virtue of the ornamented tonic, as it repeats $I^{\sharp 9/m7}$—♭III—IV.

There are two other minor-pentatonic formations involving a trio of triads: I—♭VII—♭III—I, where I moves to its lower neighbor but returns only indirectly when ♭III—I unfolds the tonic chord (as in the Kinks' "All Day and All of the Night," involving the lead vocal in the parallel chords as well), and I—♭VII—IV—I, in which ♭VII falls as a neighbor to IV just as IV does to I. This progression has already been discussed as it appears in modal contexts, and it is in most contexts best understood as a chromaticized major-mode construction. But it can hold sway in predominantly minor-pentatonic songs or sections as well, such as the chorus of The Who's "I Can't Explain" and the Rolling Stones' "Midnight Rambler" (had Jagger and Richard heard this succession in Bob Seger's "Ramblin' Gamblin' Man" of a year earlier?). Because in I—♭VII—IV—I the successive roots are so far apart, chord members are often voiced out of parallel motion, bringing some semblance of voice leading into the proceedings and working against the block-doubling phenomenon. Smoother voice leading is key in Martha and the Vandellas' "Nowhere to Run" and in the I—IV—I, IV—♭VII—IV neighboring motions of Buddy Holly's "Not Fade Away."

There are two core combinations of four minor-pentatonic chords that seem to occur more regularly than others. One omits ♭VII for a strong harmonic element in I—♭III—IV—V—I, and the other omits V for a simple pair of neighboring chords, I—♭III—IV, ♭VII—I. The former grouping tends to appear in all-parallel doublings, as in the introductory riffs to Carl Perkins's "Lend Me Your Comb" (quoted mid-verse in the Beatles' "Please Please Me") and Ike and Tina Turner's "It's Gonna Work Out Fine," and the chorus-ending tags of both the Rip Chords' "Hey Little Cobra" and the Young Rascals' "Love Is a Beautiful Thing." The latter, I—♭III—IV, ♭VII—I, may appear in parallel, as with Cream's "SWLABR," but will just as often inspire some counterpoint, as in the introductory tattoo in the American Breed's "Bend Me, Shape Me," where the trumpet moves in contrary motion against the guitar and bass.

The entire scale often appears doubled in major triads, typically in relation to a falling cascade, as in the I—♭VII—V—IV—♭III—IV—V structure of Benny Spellman's "Fortune Teller" or the straight I—♭VII—V—IV—♭III—I descent introducing Wilson Pickett's "In the Midnight Hour" (which had to be the inspiration for the signature riff of Creedence Clearwater Revival's "Proud Mary," which introduces a few non-parallel voicings that emphasize the ♭7 / 7 and ♭3 / 3 contrasts). Some songs, however, are built on a rise and fall suggestive of harmonic motion; such is heard in Bobby Freeman's "C'mon and Swim": I—♭VII—I—♭III—IV—V—IV—I (compare with Paul Revere and the Raiders' "Hungry"). Both the verse and chorus of Tommy James and the Shondells' "Hanky Panky" ornament a twelve-bar blues I, IV—I, V—IV—I progression by embellishing each structural chord with its own minor-pentatonic lower neighbor until time gets short in the third line, where the lower neighbors are compacted right into the structural chords as minor sevenths: I—♭VII—I, IV—♭III—IV, I—♭VII—I, V^{m7}—IV^{m7}—I. (The final I moves to a lower neighbor as well, but only in the portamento of the whammy bar.)

This technique of parallel major triads on roots taken from a minor-pentatonic scale is adapted in a few songs based on related scales. The Grateful Dead's "That's It For the Other One," for example, has a passage in the "Cowboy Neal at the wheel" section (2:38–2:45, sung to the words "comin' around in a circle," appropriately enough) that has all parts descend a differently formed pentatonic scale: I—♭VII—♭VI—IV—♭III. Similarly, one may think of the Monkees' garage-band classic, "(I'm Not Your) Steppin' Stone," which has bass and Vox organ in parallel motion for I—♭III—IV—♭VI—I (although one backing singer consistently drops, 8—♭7—6—♭6—5, against this rising succession, introducing three successive melodic minor seconds, as well as contrary motion).

A few songs get much further from the simple major-triad doubling of minor-pentatonic roots, but seem related to this minor-pentatonic practice of nonfunctional triadic doublings of scale degrees. All of the (major) triads, I, ♭III, IV, V, and ♭VII, of the Left Banke's "Pretty Ballerina" are built on the degrees of the minor-pentatonic scale, but as we have already seen, the vocal melody moves from mixolydian/lydian to major, and the song's counterpoint (articulated with harpsichord and chamber strings) is quite strong, using lofty stylistic airs to completely mask the simple parallel nature of the chord collection's usual rude behavior. In composing "I Am the Walrus," John Lennon set out to write an intentionally opaque lyric as a joke on those "expert textperts" who would analyze his every word. His accompanying music is identically obscurantist. Although it is basically functional with strong V—I relationships, the chord colors seem all wrong. Eventually, one recognizes that Lennon is working only with major triads (and a few spicy added tones here and there), and that their roots are all members of the aeolian scale. In applying a minor-pentatonic practice to a very different scale, Lennon's entire chord vocabulary is I, II, ♭III, IV, V, ♭VI , and ♭VII. There is little attempt at parallel motion, outside of the "[♭VI] waiting for the [♭VII] van to [I] come" cadence. (Curiously, for added modal confusion, the song's coda pairs a long descending aeolian scale in the low strings against a rising dorian scale in the violins.) A rather perplexing usage produces the occult sound of the Marvelettes' "My Baby Must Be a Magician." Here, many chords appear to be of the "wrong" quality, not following a single parent mode, but they are not all major. All of the roots adhere to the mixolydian scale and the series lacks any harmonic drive in its ordering, but the chords (some moving in parallel, some not) are altered without regard to chromatic norms, and thus the resulting effect is more akin to the nonfunctional substitution triads of modal systems. The song's chords progress, with repetitions stripped away, thus:

I—♭VII^m9—VI—II—IV—I—ii—vi—V—vi—IV—iii—ii—IV—ii—I. As a final example along these lines, Iron Butterfly's "In-a-Gadda-Da-Vida" may prove more influential to the post-'60s future of heavy metal than the more-often-cited Led Zeppelin in the nonfunctional and nondiatonic basis of its chord relationships. Its tonic chord remains minor, but all other sonorities are major. Although the entire scale is not represented by roots (we have rather a sort of a pentatonic scale, as it includes five members), enough information is provided to declare them all members of the dorian scale: i—II^m9—IV— II^m7, V—III^m7—VI—i. (These scale degrees, it is true, are also members of the mixolydian and major scales, but these are ruled out by the minor tonic chord.) The overall effect, quite bombastic in its rhythmic stretching-out via organ and guitar noodling, is one of parallel block major triads very much in a non-major context.

Mode mixture in acid rock

Perhaps initially guided by the modal literature of folk music, a few British groups of the mid-'60s—notably the Beatles, the Rolling Stones, and the Zombies—experimented with mode mixture. This began simply and inno-cently enough, but a transition took place through the music of the Byrds so that by the late '60s any regularity of pitch relations exploded in full-blown acid rock into highly ambiguous and certainly nonconformist approaches to altered scale degrees and syntactical harmonic nonsequiturs, all perfectly emblematizing the altered states of consciousness explored in the music of the Grateful Dead, the Jefferson Airplane, The Doors, Pink Floyd, and Jimi Hendrix. Early experimentation is heard in the Zombies' "She's Not There" (basically dorian, with alterations featuring ♭6 and, at the cadence, the raised 3), the Beatles' "Think For Yourself" (dorian with flashes of a cadential 3 in a minor-pentatonic ♭III^m7—IV^M9—I^m7 cadence) and "Strawberry Fields Forever" (major with scale degrees ♭7 and #1 featured in the I—v^m7—VI^m7—IV— VI^m7—IV—I verse/refrain), and the Stones' "Mother's Little Helper" (aeolian with an ostentatious ♭II chord right off the bat, at 0:20).

Gene Clark's compositions for the Byrds include some tonal relations just as brash as, and more outlandish than, Jim McGuinn's electric twelve-string itself. Representative is "I Knew I'd Want You," which is basically in the aeolian mode but moves through the phrygian to end an antecedent phrase on a dorian IV and then end the consequent on the aeolian half cadence, substituting ♭VII for V: "[i] I'd like to [♭VII] love you [♭VI] with all of my [♭III] heart; [♭III] you had me on [♭II] your trip [i] right from the [IV] start. [♭VI] And when you [i] looked at me [iv] with love in your [i] eyes, I [♭II] knew I'd want [♭VII] you, oh yeah." This is adventurous harmony, but still, the 1965 lyric delivers a conventional love song. The mode play in The Doors' "The Crystal Ship," with its alterations of 3rd, 6th, and 7th scale degrees and its softened precadential harmony, makes for a beautiful painting of the intangible quality of verging off into sleep: "Before you [i] slip into un- [v] -consciousness, I'd [IV^M7] like to have an- [♭VI] -other kiss, an- [I] -other [IV^m7] flashing [V—IV] chance at [V] bliss, an- [♭VII] -other [I] kiss, an- [♭VII] -other [I] kiss.... [♭VI—♭III—♭VII—V^m7]."

Jimi Hendrix's "Drifting" floats through nonharmonic relations until it gently settles home with a soft V—IV—I landing. The intro defies its mixolydian basis with a lydian ♯4 in a shock of Debussian parallel triads, I—♭VII—II—IV—I, leading to a verse that adds 7 to the prior mix of scale degrees: "[I] Drifting on a [vii] sea of forgotten [♭VII] teardrops on a [iii] lifeboat sailing [V—IV] for [vi] your [V—IV—vi] love, [IV] sailing [I] home [♭III^M7—IV—♭III^M7—V]." The texture's odd pitchworld is complemented by aural glimpses of a backward guitar and a highly irregular meter, with chords initially sustaining for one bar (four beats) each until the mode-interrupting V appears; this and the following chords are then measured in half beats, with V receiving three half-beats, IV getting two, vi eleven, V three, IV two, vi eight, and IV three, returning to a full bar per chord once "home" has been reached on the stable tonic. The effect is one of a sailboat meeting a sharp gust of contrary wind and then a momentary lapping of small irregular waves.

Other good examples include Pink Floyd's "See Emily Play" (in which neighbor relations dominate over harmonic ones in the verse, I—V—ii—IV^M7—I, and color-changing chorus, VI—V—II^m7—I), The Great Society's "Didn't Think So" (which moves from the aeolian through the exceedingly rare locrian mode—1—♭2—♭3—4—♭5—♭6—♭7—to settle into the minor-pentatonic), the Jefferson Airplane's "D.C.B.A.-25" (its title rebranding the chemical abbreviation of L.S.D. with the four major triads on D, C, B, and A that furnish the chordal materials), and the Dead's "High Time" (which hides its tonal center through the harmonically ambiguous verse, ♭VII—vi—III—II—IV—I—♭VII—IV—V, mixing different forms of the 4th, 5th, and 7th scale degrees; the 2nd and 6th degrees soon get their comeuppance in the bridge). The bittersweet mixed-mode harmony of acid rock does as much as its fantastic tone colors to distance its listeners from reality.

Hopefully, the reader will by this point be pleasurably immersed in the lofty and expressive harmonic adventures led by the ear and hand of the period's most imaginative rock musicians. There remains only one other core aspect of harmonic relationships, that of chromaticism, which is the use of one or more altered scale members to emphasize others, sometimes to the point where the tones given added significance may even take on the status of tonic themselves. This is the material of chapter 11, following which we shall turn to the topic of rhythm.

CHAPTER 11

Chromatic Harmony

It will be recalled that roots descending in fifths create the most compellingly directed harmonic motion. Normally, as these roots progress through the diatonic degrees of a major key, a variety of major and minor triads results. The progression, ii—V—I, for instance, has a minor triad followed by two major triads. When seventh chords descend by fifths, there is even more variety in the qualities of the chords in relation to one another. However, all of these chord qualities are adjustable through the chromatic alterations of tones that can make any minor triad into a major one by raising the third of the chord by a minor second. Chromatic inflection, which often leads to unusual chords that may substitute for more basic ones, often works to emphasize a diatonic pitch, such as when #4 (perhaps as third of a major II appearing in place of the diatonic ii) lends added weight to 5 (root of the ensuing V chord). (Listen to Web audio example 11.01.) Through chromatic alteration, one might build a progression of all-major triads or all major-minor seventh chords in descending fifths, as with VI^{m7}—II^{m7}—V^{m7}—I. (Listen to Web audio example 11.02.) This might be labeled the "Lazy River" progression, immortalized with two bars per chord in that 1932 classic by Hoagy Carmichael that was covered in the rock era by Bobby Darin. (Darin also resurrected the same progression in the verse from the 1938 hit, "You Must Have Been a Beautiful Baby.") An even older example of the progression is heard in "Shimmy Like Kate" (1923), a song covered by the Olympics. The reader may recall the succession of fifth-related major triads in Web audio example 9.03b, which followed iv with the progression I—VI^{m7}—II—V^{m7}.

> Chromatically altered chords in descending fifths and the artificial V.

This string of major-minor seventh chords also appears in many newly composed pop songs, such as Neil Sedaka's "Happy Birthday, Sweet Sixteen" and "Calendar Girl": "[IV] yeah, yeah, my [i°^{7}] heart's in a whirl, I [I] love, I love, I love my little [VI^{m7}] calendar girl every [II^{m7}] day (every day), every [V^{m7}] day (every day) of the [I] year (every) [IV] (day of the) [I] (year)." It's a characteristic sequence in early R and B, as in the Dominoes' "Sixty Minute Man," jump swing (Boyd Bennett's "Seventeen"), rockabilly (Carl Perkins's "Right String But the Wrong Yo-Yo"), blues (Jesse Fuller's "You're No Good," as covered by Bob Dylan), and vaudeville-based numbers ranging from the Beatles' "When I'm Sixty-Four" and the Mothers of Invention's "Smother My Daughter in Chocolate Syrup" passage from "Brown Shoes Don't Make It" to Country Joe and the Fish's "I-Feel-Like-I'm-Fixin'-To-Die Rag" and Arlo Guthrie's "Alice's Restaurant Massacree." In the ending of a bridge, VI^{m7}—II^{m7} can lead to a retransitional V^{m7}, as in Sam Cooke's "You Send Me": "Now I find myself [VI^{m7}] wanting to [II^{m7}] marry you and take you [V^{m7}] home." In Blood, Sweat and Tears' "Spinning Wheel," the first verse presents the VI^{m7}—II^{m7}—V^{m7}—I progression three times in succession, but in the second verse, each step is intensified by #9 chords.

Chromatically altered major-minor seventh chords can appear on any scale degree, whether or not they are joined in chains. In fact, they most commonly appear one at a time, and nearly always progress in root motion by descending fifth to a simple major or minor triad. In this way, the major-minor chord emulates the quality of V^{m7}, so that one can hear a major-minor chord on any scale degree acting as an artificial dominant when it descends by fifth. We'll cover examples of this function by investigating, in order, the use of artificial dominants applied to V itself, to ii, to vi, to iii, and to IV. The artificial dominant is also the essence of the concept of tonicization—a process that allows a chord other than I to behave as a tonic—and so this concept will be a recurring theme of the chapter.

II^{m7} moving to V is by far the most common of the artificial dominants, appearing in hundreds of songs in our sample. It is perhaps heard most often in retransitions, setting up the final bridge-ending V^{m7} with chromatic emphasis as the #4 of II pulls to the dominant's 5. A listing of one representative example per year will demonstrate the many stylistic contexts enjoyed by this very common function:

Eddie Fisher, "I Need You Now" (first charting September 1954)

The McGuire Sisters, "Something's Gotta Give" (June 1955)

Pat Boone, "I'll Be Home" (February 1956)

Andy Williams, "Butterfly" (February 1957)

Frankie Avalon, "I'll Wait for You" (October 1958)

The Platters, "Enchanted" (March 1959)

The Safaris, "Image of a Girl" (June 1960)

Bobby Lewis, "Tossin' and Turnin'" (April 1961)

Brian Hyland, "Sealed With a Kiss" (June 1962)

The Caravelles, "You Don't Have to Be a Baby to Cry" (November 1963)

The Rolling Stones, "Time Is On My Side" (October 1964)

Gerry and the Pacemakers, "Ferry Cross the Mersey" (February 1965)

Frank Sinatra, "That's Life" (November 1966)

The Happenings, "I Got Rhythm" (April 1967)

Aretha Franklin, "The House That Jack Built" (August 1968)

Bob Dylan, "To Be Alone With You" (*Nashville Skyline,* May 1969)

In contrast to these often spectacular rushes to conclusion and other typically cadential uses of the major II chord, the II–V progression may appear in a brash opening gesture. A verse or chorus may begin with a chromatically altered I—II—V motion, instead of the more placid diatonic I—ii—V, as in dramatic songs such as "Climb Every Mountain" from *The Sound of Music* and the chorus of Sly and the Family Stone's "Stand!"

Often, the diatonic ii chord will be preceded and emphasized by its own artificial dominant, the chromatically altered VI$^{(m7)}$. (Listen to Web audio example 11.03.) In this chord, the first scale degree is raised to $\sharp 1$, usually acting as a chromatic passing tone rising from 1 through $\sharp 1$ to 2. This device helps move a static I up to a higher level in the Edwin Hawkins Singers' "Oh Happy Day": "Oh happy [I] day (oh happy) [IV] (day), oh happy [I] day (oh happy) [VI$^{m7/+}$] (day) when Jesus [ii] washed (when Jesus) [V] (washed), when Jesus [ii] washed...." Note here how the opening alternation of I and IV is freed to move up a step to an alternation of ii and V by virtue of the passing VI^{m7}, which leads through its $\sharp 1$ from I to ii. Notice also the further chromatic alteration that augments the fifth in the artificial V chord resulting in the collection of scale degrees 6—$\sharp 1$—$\sharp 3$ (=4)—5. In most cases, however, VI^{m7} is simply used as a colorful substitute for its diatonic version, in the I—VI^{m7}—ii—V progression, repeated in the verses of the Four Seasons' "Big Girls Don't Cry," the Rooftop Singers' "Walk Right In," Barbara Lewis's "Baby I'm Yours," and the Lovin' Spoonful's "Daydream."

The major III chord works as an artifical V of vi in many songs, including the bridge of the Beatles' "This Boy" ("oh and [IV] this boy would be [III^{m7}] happy just to [vi] love you, but oh [I^{m7}] my...") and the opening of the verse of Peter and Gordon's "A World Without Love" ("[I] Please lock me a- [III^{m7}] -way and [vi] don't allow the day..."). (Listen to Web audio example 11.04.) Pairs of artificial dominants are often sequenced together, most commonly when the falling fifth, III^{m7}—vi, is repeated down a step with II^{m7}—V, often supporting an entire bridge and leading logically to its V retransition, as in Pat Boone's "Love Letters in the Sand," Betty Everett's "The Shoop Shoop Song (It's In His Kiss)," and the Monkees' "Tapioca Tundra."

The major III also has a second important function, as a deceptively resolving artificial dominant when it moves not to the expected vi but to IV instead. (Listen to Web audio example 11.05.) In moving to either IV or to vi, III contains the chromatic ♯5 that rises by minor second to 6. Thus the III can be heard as a colorful expansion of an opening tonic in the progression I—III—IV, heard in dozens of songs including Johnny Burnette's "You're Sixteen" ("You come [I] on like a dream, [III] peaches and cream, [IV] lips like strawberry [I] wine") and Smokey Robinson and the Miracles' "The Tears of a Clown" ("there're some [V] sad things known to [III] man, but ain't [IV] too much sadder [ii$^{m7/o}$] than the tears of a [I] clown"). A surprising enlightenment, an unexpected second thought, is portrayed directly this way in the Young Rascals' "A Girl Like You": "[III^{m7}] It's nothin' like I ever [IV] thought it would be...." Occasionally, III^{m7} participates in a "Lazy River"-like stream of all-major-minor seventh chords leading to V instead of to I; such is the structure of the bridge of the Four Seasons' "Sherry": "(Why don't you) [III^{m7}] (come out) to my twist party, [VI^{m7}] (Come out) where the bright moon shines [II^{m7}] (Come out) we'll dance the night away, [V] I'm gonna make you mi-yi-yine." See also the bridge of Bob Dylan's "Country Pie."

The major triad built on the seventh scale degree, VII, can function as the artificial V of iii with its ♯2 pulling up to 3 in resolving to iii, doing so in the DeCastro Sisters' "Teach Me Tonight" (1:17), the Righteous Brothers' "He" (0:49), Mel Carter's "Hold Me, Thrill Me, Kiss Me" (fifth bar of the bridge), the Sopwith Camel's "Hello Hello" (opening of the bridge), and only a very small number of others. This chord, however, more often ornaments I as a lower-neighbor substitute for V in a I—VII motion (as in Brenda Lee's "I'm Sorry" and Frank Ifield's covers of two decades-old songs "I Remember You" and "I'm Confessin' (That I Love You)"). It may also move to V in a colorful expansion of V analogous to the previously discussed use of III to expand I. (Listen to Web audio example 11.06.) The VII—V expansion is heard in the intro to Dion and the Belmonts' "Sandy" and the chorus of Lesley Gore's "California Nights": "[i] Love California [♭II] nights when I'm walkin' with [VII] you hand in hand by the [V] shore, yes I...."

Because chromaticism would be required to create *either* a major or a minor triad on the seventh scale degree, there is never an artificial V built on ♯IV and applied to that area. (Actually, Carly Simon's 1973 hit, "The Right Thing to Do" may be the first song to descend by perfect fifth to a VII chord, but it is from ♯iv, not from the artificial dominant, ♯IV: "you're [♯iv] with me [VII^{m7}] now and as [iii]· long as you stay…." Here, ♯iv acts as ii of iii.) ♯IV appears rarely, always as either a neighboring chord to V (at the end of the bridge of the Dovells' "Bristol Stomp") or as a chromatic passing chord from IV to V (in the chorus of Mercy's "Love (Can Make You Happy)": "[I^{M7}] love can [ii^{m7/sus4}] make you happy [IV] if you find someone who- [♯IV] -o [V] cares to [I^{M7}] give…").

All of these alterations, most of which produce artificial Vs, involve changing a naturally minor triad into a major one. But one artificial V is altered differently: the V^{m7} that is applied to IV is an unaltered major I triad with a chromatic minor seventh added, I^{m7}. (Listen to Web audio example 11.07.) Sometimes the minor seventh is added to I within the basic I—IV—V progression for a bluesy touch, as when the lead guitar adds that note in the "(Theme From) The Monkees": "Hey, Hey, we're the [I] Monkees [I^{m7}], and [IV] people say we [V] monkey a- [I] -round [I^{m7}]…." Songs in minor keys, of course, do require alteration of the third of the tonic chord to create the I^{m7}; an instance is heard in the verse of Mary Hopkin's "Those Were the Days": "[i] once upon a [iv] time there was a [i] tavern, [I^{m7}] where we used

Photo 11.01. Post-*Pepper* British experimentation. Albums by Soft Machine, King Crimson, the Moody Blues, Yes, and Pink Floyd. (Photo: Annie Eastman)

to raise a glass or [iv] two...." One important value for I^{m7} is in introducing the bridge that begins on IV, a very common procedure; the Beatles' "From Me to You" is a case in point: "I got [v^{m7}] arms that long to [I^{m7}] hold you and [IV] keep you by my side; I got [II^{m7}] lips that long to kiss you and [V] keep you satis- [V$^+$] -fied." Note the I^{m7}—IV motion that is repeated exactly a step higher, II^{m7}—V, another common example of pairs of artificial dominants, one emphasizing IV and the next strengthening V, that are often sequenced together to form the bridge. This same pair forms the basis of the bridges of two late-1966 hits, Frank Sinatra's "That's Life" and the New Vaudeville Band's "Winchester Cathedral." The first chords of the same sequenced pair, I—IV, are stretched out rhythmically as II—V (and in pitches as well, as the chromatic line descends 8—7—♭7 instead of moving directly from 8 to ♭7) in the verse of the Beatles' "Something": "[I] Something in the way she [I^{M7}] moves, [I^{m7}] attracts me like no other [IV] lover, [II^{m7}] something in the way she wo- [V] -oos me." In this song, the quickening pace and the continued surprising chromaticism suggest a leap at what remains on the tip of the tongue, never to be caught.

All of these chromatically altered chords represent artificially colored falling-fifth motions of harmonic value. But just as do diatonic chords, altered chords have many contrapuntal uses as well. One use, which is often referred to as the double-plagal cadence, is in some ways the opposite of the chromatically enhanced falling-fifth progression through artificial dominants. In the double plagal, a chain of descending fourths emerges, with a major IV of IV created by lowering the root of the vii° chord to ♭7, creating the ♭VII—IV—I motion. (See the four-chord intro to Web audio example 4.07.) In this chord succession, ♭VII resolves to IV with a transposed version of the same descending neighbor motions (here 2—1 and ♭7—6) used by IV in resolving to I (6—5 and 4—3). Originally appearing in 1957–60 as an ornamental guitar figure (see the main Bo Diddley riff in Buddy Holly's "Not Fade Away," the intro to Paul Anka's "Lonely Boy," and the cadence of the Everly Brothers' "Love Hurts"), this function emerged in broader rhythms in the soul music of late 1964 (The Four Tops' "Baby I Need Your Loving," intro) and early 1965 (Martha and the Vandellas' "Nowhere to Run," chorus) to become a rock mainstay (The Who's "I Can't Explain," Them's "Gloria," Paul Revere and the Raiders' "Hungry," and the Beatles' "With a Little Help From My Friends" and coda of "Hey Jude").

Other chromatic neighbor tones exist; in the chorus of the Rivieras' "California Sun," a VI chord may at first appearance be expected to act as an artificial V of ii, but instead connects a prior I to a pre-dominant by arpeggiating down in the bass, 8—6—4, to support an unusual inner-voice 1—#1—1

> **Contrapuntal altered chords: the double-plagal cadence and other neighbor functions; support for passing tones.**

Table 11.01 Common chromatic lines given various chordal supports

---

Supported voice: 1—#1 (♭2)—2 (—♭3)
  Lesley Gore, "Judy's Turn to Cry": I—♭II—#IV—V
  Beatles, "Hey Bulldog": iv—♭II—ii° (—iv^m7)

Supported voice: 3—4—#4—5
  Four Lads, "Standing on the Corner": vi—IV^M7—#iv^m7/°—vi^m7
  Foundations, "Build Me Up Buttercup": iii—VI—IV—II—V

Supported voice: 5—#5 (♭6)—6—♭7 (—7)
  Otis Redding, "These Arms of Mine": I—I⁺—IV—I^m7
  Dave Clark Five, "Because": I—I⁺—vi—I^m7
  Beau Brummels: "Just a Little": I—♭VI—IV—♭VII
  Herman's Hermits, "There's a Kind of Hush": I—I⁺—IV—I^m7
  Beatles, "Hey Bulldog": i—♭VI—vi°—i^m7
  Mason Williams, "Classical Gas": ♭III—♭VI—IV—♭VII (—V)

Supported voice: 5—#5 (♭6)—6—♭6—5
  Carla Thomas, "Gee Whiz (Look at His Eyes)": I—I⁺—IV—iv—I
  Elvis Presley, "Surrender": i—♭VI—vi°—♭VI—i
  Dave Clark Five, "Because": I—I⁺—IV—iv—I
  Billy Strange, "The James Bond Theme": i—♭VI—vi°—♭VI—i
  Gary Lewis and the Playboys, "Green Grass": I—III^m7—IV—iv—I
  'Buckinghams, "Don't You Care": I^M7—I^m7/⁺—IV—iv—I

Supported voice: 5—#5—6—♭7—6 (—♭6—5)
  Buckinghams, "Kind of a Drag": I—I⁺—I^add6—I^m7—IV (—iv—I)
  Guess Who, "Laughing": I—I⁺—I^add6—I^m7—IV (—iv—iii—V^sus4)
  Joe Jeffrey Group, "My Pledge of Love": I—III^m7—vi—I^m7—IV (—iv—I)
  Garland Green, "Jealous Kind of Fella": I—I⁺—vi—I^m7—IV

Supported voice: 8—7—♭7—6 (—♭6—5—#4—4—3)
  Murmaids, "Popsicles and Icicles": I—iii—♭VII—IV (—iv—V)
  Mary Poppins soundtrack, "Chim Chim Chiree": i—i^M7—i^m7—IV (—iv—i)
  Bob Dylan, "Ballad of a Thin Man": i—i^M7—i^m7—i^add6 (—i^m6)
  Kinks, "Set Me Free": i—i^M7—i^m7—IV
  Beatles, "Here, There and Everywhere": I—iii—♭III—ii
  Left Banke, "Walk Away Renee": I—V—v—IV (—iv—I—IV—II)
  Mothers of Invention, "How Could I Be Such a Fool": I—iii—♭VII—ii
    (—♭VI—i)
  Frankie Valli, "Can't Take My Eyes Off You": I—I^M7—I^m7—IV
    (—iv—I—II^m7—iv—I)
  Strawberry Alarm Clock, "Incense and Peppermints": I—vii—♭vii—IV
  Johnny Rivers, "Summer Rain": i—i^M7—i^m7—i^add6
  Dionne Warwick, "(Theme From) Valley of the Dolls": I^M7—I^m7—IV^M7 (—iv^M7—I^M9/^M7)
  B. J. Thomas, "Hooked on a Feeling": I—V—I^m7—IV (—iv—I)
  Ray Stevens, "Mr. Businessman": I—I^M7—I^m7—IV (—iv—I—II^m7—V^m7)
  New Colony Six: "Things I'd Like to Say": I—V—♭VII—VI
  Frank Sinatra, "My Way": I—I^M7—I^m7—VI^m7
  Bob Dylan, "Lay Lady Lay": I—iii—♭VII—IV
  B. J. Thomas, "Raindrops Keep Fallin' On My Head": I—I^M7—I^m7—IV

(continued)

Table 11.01 Continued

Supported voice: $\flat 7$—6—$\flat 6$—5(—$\sharp 4$—4—3)

   Patience and Prudence, "Tonight You Belong To Me": I—I^{m7}—IV—iv—I

   Bob Dylan, "It's Alright, Ma (I'm Only Bleeding)": I^{m7}—I^{add6}—I$^+$—I

   Yardbirds, "For Your Love": $\flat$III—IV—iv—i

   Beatles, "Eleanor Rigby": i^{m7}—i^{add6}—i$^+$—i

   Lovin' Spoonful: "Summer in the City": i^{m7}—vi^{o}/^{m7}—$\flat$VI—V

   Monkees, "(I'm Not Your) Steppin' Stone": $\flat$III—IV—$\flat$VI—i

   Donovan, "Hamstead Incident": i^{m7}—IV—$\flat$VI—V

   Beatles, "Lucy in the Sky With Diamonds": I^{m7}—vi^{m7}—iv—I

   Foundations, "Baby, Now That I've Found You": I^{m7}—IV—iv—I

      (—II^{m7}—ii^{m7}—V^{m7}—I)

   Beatles, "Dear Prudence": I^{m7}—I^{add6}—I$^+$—I

   Beatles, "While My Guitar Gently Weeps": i^{m7}—IV—$\flat$VI^{M7}—i

   Led Zeppelin, "Babe I'm Gonna Leave You": i^{m7}—vi^{o}/^{m7}—$\flat$VI—V

   Nilsson, "I Guess the Lord Must Be in New York City": I^{m7}—IV—III—$\flat$III (—II^{m7}—

   V^{m7}—I)

Supported voice: 6—$\sharp 5$ ($\flat 6$)—5 (—$\sharp 4$—4)

   Joni James, "You Are My Love": vi—vi^{M7}—vi^{m7} (—II^{m7})

   Don Cherry, "Band of Gold": vi—$\flat$VI—I

   Domenico Modugno, "Nel Blu Dipinto Di Blu (Volare)": vi—vi^{M7}—vi^{m7} (—vi^{add6})

   Buckinghams, "Susan": vi—ii^{m7}/^{o}—I

Supported voice: 5—$\flat 5$—4 (—3)

   Ral Donner, "Girl of My Best Friend": V—$\flat$V—IV

   Beatles, "Strawberry Fields Forever": V—V^{M7}—V^{m7} (—vi)

Supported voice: 3—$\flat 3$—2 (—$\flat 2$)

   Chimes, "Once In Awhile": iii—$\flat$iii—ii

   Cathy Jean and The Roommates, "Please Love Me Forever": iii—$\flat$iii—ii

   Dick and Dee Dee, "Young and In Love": iii—$\flat$iii—ii

   Beatles, "Do You Want to Know a Secret": iii—$\flat$iii—ii

   Beatles, "If I Fell": iii—i^{o7}—ii

   Brenda and the Tabulations, "Dry Your Eyes": iii^{m7}—$\flat$iii^{m7}—II^{m7}—$\flat$II^{m7}

Supported voice: $\flat 3$—2—$\flat 2$—1

   Castells, "Sacred": $\flat$III—II—$\flat$II—I

Supported voice: 2—$\sharp 1$—1

   Beatles, "And Your Bird Can Sing": iii^{m7}—VI^{m7}—I

---

neighbor motion: "They're [I] out there havin' [VI] fun in the [IV] warm Cali- [V] -fornia [I] Sun." The same I—VI—IV motion adds exotic spice to Crosby, Stills and Nash's "Marrakesh Express": "[iii] I've been savin' all my [I] money just to take you there, [VI] I smell the garden in your [IV] hair...."

In addition to such support of upper-voice neighbor tones, chromatic chords are also useful in supporting contrapuntal passing tones. Occasionally, chromatic tones pass in what seem to be "backward" directions, as when the lydian $\sharp 4$ leads not up to 5 (as would be supported by an artificial V to V) but down from 5 to 4; this is usually set with I—II—IV—I, as in the magical opening of

Lulu's "To Sir With Love," Bob Dylan's "She Belongs to Me," Procol Harum's "Homburg," Marianne Faithfull's "As Tears Go By," and the chorus of the Beatles' "Yesterday." In the bridge of Cream's "SWLABR," this #1—1 motion (with 1 supported both by I and by the chromatic ♭VI chord) passes down a further step to 7 within the retransitional dominant: "[VI] Comin' to me with that soulful look on your [I$^{#9/m7}$] face, [♭VI] Comin' lookin' like ya never ever done one wrong [V] thing." All sorts of chromatic lines in upper and inner voices are set with varying chordal supports, as suggested in table 11.01.

Of course, parallel chords many times invoke heavily doubled passing chromatic motion, as in the chorus of the Kinks' "Tired of Waiting For You," where a repeated alternation of I and V moves through #I to approach the repeated II—VI sequence, sort of a ruder version of the more contrapuntal support for #1 noted earlier in bridging the halves of the same sequence in "Oh Happy Day." In the bridge of "Way Down Yonder In New Orleans," Freddie Cannon's band simply links IV and II by passing through III and ♭III chords along the way, all voices moving in parallel with the bass. Also see Gerry and the Pacemakers' cadence to "How Do You Do It?," which passes ♭VII—VII—I at 0:19–0:20. The motion is also heard in the Jimi Hendrix Experience's "The Wind Cries Mary" and reversed for a more startling effect with seventh chords in the Beatles' lascivious "Sexy Sadie," which moves I—VII^{m7}—♭VII^{m7} at 0:25–0:29. See also the the opening of the chorus of Sly and the Family Stone's "Everybody Is a Star." The Spencer Davis Group's "I'm a Man" boasts a testosterone-charged series of all-chromatic major parallel triads in its chorus, "I'm a [III] man, yes I [♭III] am and I [II] can't help but [i] love you so."

Many other chordal progressions involve chromaticism simply to introduce unexpected chord colors, sometimes implying no particular voice-leading or harmonic values at all. One such case is The Doors' "Touch Me," the chords of which are organized in sequences of chord pairs, each pair comprising two roots in a rising third, altogether requiring quite a long time to find the key center,: "Come on,...come on, now [#IV] touch me, Babe, [#vi] Can't you see that [VII] I am not afraid? [II] What was that [VI] promise that you made? [#i] Why won't you [II] tell me what she said? [IV] What was that [I] promise that you made?" The Everly Brothers' "Poor Jenny" leaves behind its strict sequences of chords in falling thirds when its pratfalling lyric calls for disruptive chromatic chords that struggle to find their way back to tonic: "I [I] took my little Jenny to a [vi] party last night, at [♭VI] one o'clock it ended in a [iv] heck of a fight; when [♭II] someone hit my Jenny she went [I] out like a light, [II] Poor [V] Jenny." Bob Dylan's "Nashville Skyline Rag" has an unexpectedly nonfunctional chromatic sequence in its bridge, which turns from a quite normal II^{m7}—V motion (0:24–0:26) to a bizarre twist a step

> **Chromatic color chords:** unconventional mixture and unorthodox cadences.

higher, III^{m7}—VI^{m7} (0:28–0:30). A seemingly nonfunctional sequence serves
the purpose of providing a transition between different tonal areas in Frank
Zappa's "Peaches en Regalia," whereby pairs of stepwise-descending chromatic chords rise until the dominant key is found: v—IV, $^\flat$vii—$^\flat$VI, $\sharp$i—VII,
VI—V. Note that the second chord of each of the first two pairs sounds like
an artificial V of the first chord of the following pair.

Through the combination of chromaticism and contrapuntal progressions, quite novel combinations of scale degrees can result, as when a
descending-fifths progression is followed by a descending-third progression
with a passing "tonic" thrown in for good measure. Thus the bridge of Gene
and Debbe's "Playboy": "[iii] I never [VI^{m7}] knew that love could [II] hurt
me like this 'til [I] you came along with your [$^\flat$VII] kiss [V^{m7}]." The bridge
of the Turtles' "She'd Rather Be With Me" has a related twist on the I^{m7}—IV,
II^{m7}—V sequence by moving through chromatic thirds from IV *down* to
V: "me, oh [I^{m7}] my, lucky guy is what I [IV] am, tell you [II^{m7}] why you'll
under- [$^\flat$VII] -stand, she don't [V^{m7}] fly although she [I] can [$^\flat$VI^{m7}—V^{m7}]."
The $^\flat$VII—V^{m7} cadence first appeared in 1958–60 with songs including
Link Wray and His Ray Men's blues adaptation, "Rumble," Duane Eddy's
"Because They're Young," and Joan Baez's "Fare Thee Well," and was imme-
diately picked up in Al Caiola's rugged orchestral hits, "The Magnificent
Seven" (0:15–0:17) and "Bonanza" (0:26–0:27) before it became a mainstay
in all rock styles of the '60s.

Another unusual chromatic technique has one triad slide to another, all of
whose members are a minor second from those of the first, but whose roots
are related by thirds. Thus, the Marvelettes' "The Hunter Gets Captured By
the Game" opens with a nonfunctional v—VII progression, whereby 5 (the
root of v) leads to $\sharp$4 (the fifth of VII), $^\flat$7 (third of v) leads to 7 (root of VII),
and 2 (fifth) leads to $\sharp$2 (third). The strangeness continues; here is the entire
first line: "[v] Everyday things [VII] change and the [iv$^{m7/\circ}$] world puts [V^{m7}]
on a new [iv^{m7}] face…" The VII chord prepares two members (7 and $^\flat$3) of
iv$^{m7/\circ}$ as common tones, ultimately serving to introduce scale degree 7 of V^{m7},
which resolves normally to 8 as the chord moves deceptively from V^{m7} to iv^{m7}.
After this song's pungent opening phrase is immediately repeated, it never
again recurs.

One of the more exceptional functions of chromatic chords is to serve as
an unorthodox cadence point. The major II chord functions not as artificial
dominant to V, but as a dead-end color chord in the Departure-gestures of
Barry Mann's "Who Put the Bomp (In the Bomp, Bomp, Bomp)": [I] Who
was that [III] man? I'd [IV^{M7}] like to shake his [II^{m7}/$\sharp$4] hand." Here, the
dead end is made the more stark by the inversion of the II chord, the gesture
ending with $\sharp$4 played by the bass as the culmination of a 3—4—$\sharp$4 rise. See
also the Rolling Stones' "Time Is On My Side" (at 0:26), the Beatles' "Eight

Days a Week" ("[vi] Hold me, [IV^{add6}] love me; [vi] hold me, [II] love me! I [I] ain't got..."), and Bob Dylan's "Don't Think Twice, It's Alright" ("When your [I] rooster crows at the [I^{m7}] break of dawn, [IV] look out your window and [II^{m7}] I'll be gone..."). As mentioned in chapter 10 in relation to the lydian mode, the verses of Otis Redding's "(Sittin' On) The Dock of the Bay" and Joan Baez's "The Night They Drove Old Dixie Down," among several others, end on II. All chromatic major chords that can serve as artificial dominants can also serve as unexpected cadence points; unlike II, however, which is usually followed by a phrase beginning with I, the others seem to be followed with only rare exceptions by their natural goals at the beginnings of the following phrases. For instance, the verse of Gary Lewis and the Playboys' "Sure Gonna Miss Her" ends with VI^{m7}, leading to a refrain that begins a fifth lower, on ii. The same exact relationship is heard in the first two phrases of Dionne Warwick's "Alfie," in moving from the verse to the bridge in the Stones' "Dandelion," in moving from the bridge to the verse in Los Bravos's "Black Is Black," in moving from the instrumental break to the chorus in Neil Diamond's "Girl You'll Be a Woman Soon," and in moving from the bridge to the repeated intro in the Grass Roots' "Midnight Confessions." Although this predictive role is by far the most common one for a phrase-ending VI, in rare occasions, as in the Beatles' "And I Love Her," Chad and Jeremy's "A Summer Song," and The Band's "This Wheel's On Fire," a song will end surprisingly on a fresh and nonresolving VI. When IV—V is followed not by I but by VI, this does not have the effect of a deceptive cadence but one by which VI substitutes for I in a hyper-full cadence, with the normal 1 replaced by ♯1.

When one phrase settles unexpectedly into an ending on III, the next typically begins in one of two places. One is on vi, fulfilling the artificial dominant's destiny, as in the move from the verse to the bridge in the Beatles' "I Should Have Known Better" (0:40), or from the verse to the chorus in Tommy Roe's "Dizzy." The other is on IV, for a deceptive resolution of the III function, as in the coda of the Beatles' "I Want to Hold Your Hand" (2:16). Very rarely will a phrase or section end on III without such a logical follow-up, but it is just this disjunction that creates discontinuity following the Repetition-gesture (ending on III) moving at 0:23 to a Departure-gesture beginning on ii in Mary Wells' "My Guy," following the open-ended prechorus of the American Breed's "Bend Me, Shape Me" ending on III^{m7} with a chorus starting on I, and following the III^{m7}-ending bridge of the Everly Brothers' "Let It Be Me" With a I-opening verse. Cadences on a major VII chord are exceedingly rare, but such stopping points are heard at the end of the chorus of the Flamingos' "I Only Have Eyes For You" (the cover of a 1934 hit), halfway through the bridge in the Dreamlovers' "When We Get Married," and at a strong deadend towards the end of the ever-questioning, never-resolved verse of Dionne Warwick's "Alfie": "...what's it [ii] all about, when you sort it [iii] out, Alfie?

[I^{M7}—IV] Are we meant to take more [VII^{m7}] than we give? Or [IV] are we meant to be kind? [V^{M9}] And, [V$^{M9/+}$] if. . . ."

The discussion ending chapter 10 pertaining to unconventional mode mixture, with descriptions of such songs as Pink Floyd's "See Emily Play," includes examples related to those discussed immediately above, where chromatically created major triads do not observe expected voice-leading or harmonic goals, but instead lead to highly colorful yet nonfunctional harmonies. Perhaps the unconventional Doors reign supreme in concocting unexpected turns of chromaticism in such songs as "Strange Days" (whose instrumental break repeats, without direction, the chord succession I—III—$^\flat$III—$^\flat$VII) and "Yes, The River Knows" (whose verse emblematizes the free, rhapsodic quality of a river's eddies: "[I^{M7}] Please believe me, [$^\flat$VI] the river told me [vii^{m7}] very softly [ii] wants you to hold me, ooh [VI$^{4–3}$]").

Tonicization and modulation

Two central and mutually related topics remain in our coverage of chromatic harmony: tonicization and modulation. Both involve the chromatic redesignation of scale degrees such that an area other than tonic actually takes on all of that function's attributes,

> **Tonicization:** pivot chords; tonicization in major of vi, $^\flat$III, IV, V, and other areas.

with its own pre-dominant and dominant functions supported by any chromatic changes necessary to create the new scale. For instance, if the 5th scale degree is to take on a tonic quality, the 4th scale degree must be changed to $\sharp$4 so that V (the triad spelled 5—7—2 in terms of the original tonic) may have its own dominant (2—$\sharp$4—6) and so that a new major scale emerges, as 5—6—7—1—2—3—$\sharp$4—5 mimics the major scale with 5 as its home base. Both tonicization and modulation involve this set of displaced chromatic and functional properties, but tonicization is a temporary toniclike emphasis of a nontonic area whereas modulation involves a permanent abandonment of one tonal center for another.

Major or minor chords on any scale degrees, diatonic or chromatic, of either major or minor keys may become tonicized, but some areas act as tonic much more often than others. We shall look first at tonicizations of areas in major keys, then of those in minor, proceding in each domain from most to least commonly tonicized area. But before we turn to that, we should make clear one agent at work in most instances of tonicization and modulation: the pivot chord. The pivot chord is transitional in that it has functional value in both the original and the new tonal areas. In tonicizing the V area, for example, the vi chord may be treated as a transitional pivot, because it might first be heard as vi of the original key, but if it moves to a chromatically altered II chord, vi will in retrospect be heard as ii of V, proceeding then to the II, which will be heard as V of V. So in this case, the chord spelled 6—1—3 can express clear functions in both the original and tonicized areas. This pivot function, although not always clearly identifiable or even desirable, is almost as important in tonicization and modulation as the artificial dominant, which helps clinch the establishment of a new tonal area. In the example cited here, the tonicization of V, the pivot chord (vi) prepares the artifical dominant (II) and so both chords play major roles in the tonicization of V.

Many songs move their tonics up a step by having V reinterpreted as IV of the new area. This is true in Creedence Clearwater Revival's "Lodi," in which V is reheard as the new IV at 1:54–2:00, and in Sly and the Family Stone's "Everybody Is a Star," where the V introduced at the end of one chorus at 0:52 is reinterpreted by a chromatic change of scale as the new IV of the following scatted chorus (0:53+). (Listen to Web audio example 11.08.) Note the same relationship in moving from verse to chorus in the Bee Gees' "I've Gotta Get a Message to You": ".... Now for [I] once in your life you're a- [ii] lone, but you [pivot chord: V = new IV] ain't got a dime, there's no [artificial dominant: VI = new V] time for the phone; I've just [prior II = new I] gotta get a message to [prior iii = new ii] you...." Perhaps rock's most esoteric use of the pivot chord is heard in the Cyrkle's cover of the Beatles' "I'm Happy Just to Dance With You." In the original, a chorus in the tonic is answered by a bridge that begins with a tonicized vi, so the song as composed is already tonally rich. In John Simon's arrangement, the Cyrkle add two pivot-chord tonicizations of their own, setting practically each phrase in a new key: first, the original V is reinterpreted as IV (tonicizing II), and then the new I is twisted to become IV (of the original VI); at the beginning of the bridge, the just-tonicized VI changes mode to become the Beatles' vi.

In major keys, the goal of tonicization more often than any other is most likely the vi just witnessed. This is a natural point of gravitation, as the aeolian form of vi shares exactly the same seven scale degrees as the original tonic; one need only change 5 to ♯5 if a major dominant chord is desired for a true minor built on vi. (Listen to Web audio example 11.09.) Examples include the refrain of Del Shannon's "Little Town Flirt," a portion of the verse of the Five Americans' "Western Union," the bridges of the Beatles' "We Can Work It Out" and "When I'm Sixty-Four," and dorian versions of vi in both the verse of the Beach Boys' "Wendy" and the "Status Back Baby" fantasy in the Mothers of Invention's "America Drinks."

Three other areas in major keys are exceedingly common goals of tonicization: ♭III (as in moving to the bridges of both Herman's Hermits' "Mrs. Brown You've Got a Lovely Daughter" and the Beatles' "You're Going to Lose That Girl," and in moving to the choruses of both the Temptations' "Get Ready" and Petula Clark's "Don't Sleep in the Subway"), IV (as in the chorus of the Four Seasons' "Walk Like a Man," in the bridges of the

Beatles' "From Me to You" and "I Want to Hold Your Hand," and the Hollies' "Carrie-Anne"), and V (as in moving to the chorus of Jr. Walker and the All Stars' "(I'm a) Road Runner" and the bridge of the Music Explosion's "Little Bit O' Soul"). (Listen to Web audio examples 11.10– 11.12.) Heard less often are tonicizations of ii (as in Simon and Garfunkel's "Homeward Bound"), VI (Lou Christie's "Lightnin' Strikes"), III (the Beach Boys' "Wouldn't It Be Nice"), iii (Shirley Bassey's "Goldfinger"), II (Jimmy Ruffin's "What Becomes of the Brokenhearted"), and ♭VI (the Brooklyn Bridge's "Worst That Could Happen"). (Listen to Web audio examples 11.13–11.18.) Far less common still are tonicizations of ♭VII (Blood, Sweat and Tears' "Sometimes in Winter"), ♭II (the Turtles' "The Story of Rock and Roll"), and ♯iv (Aretha Franklin's "Respect"). (Listen to Web audio examples 11.19–11.21.)

Strong tonicization is applied to few degrees in the minor mode. In fact, only one area, ♭III, is sustained with any regularity, and this is the minor mode's natural goal for the same reason vi is in a major context: the major

Tonicization in minor of ♭III.

scale for ♭III requires no alterations from the minor tonic's aeolian backdrop. (Listen to Web audio example 11.22.) This i—♭III motion takes place in dozens of aeolian and minor-mode songs, such as moving to the bridge of the Box Tops' "The Letter" and to the choruses of Paul Revere and the Raiders' "Kicks," Neil Diamond's "Solitary Man," the Beach Boys' "Good Vibrations," and Tom Jones' "Delilah." Other rarely heard tonicized areas in minor include ♭II (chorus of the Turtles' "She's My Girl"), II (at 2:08-2:11 in the Chris Barber Jazz Band's "Petite Fleur"), iii (Marion Marlowe's "The Man in the Raincoat"), and III (announced by horns and trombones in Mason Williams's "Classical Gas"). (Listen to Web audio examples 11.23–11.26.)

All of these different tonicizations, despite the occasional far-ranging differences between home and visited scales, represent relationships among tonics that are somewhat organic, or are at least contextualized by the contrasting lyric texts in passing from one phrase or section to another. The difference of tonal center often helps portray a contrast of mood or perspective that is usually made clear in the lyrics. Sometimes, as in Johnny Cash's "I Walk the Line," where each verse is sung in a somehow arbitrarily different key, and in the 5th Dimension's more structurally integrated tonal relations of "Up–Up and Away," migration seems to be exactly the point. The unexpected tonal shifts in Tommy Roe's "Dizzy" are enough to make any sensitive listener's head spin. Lyric-explained tonal careening is characteristic of the wild tonicizations in Jan and Dean's "Drag City" and "The Little Old Lady (From Pasadena)," whereas the tonal excursions of Jimi Hendrix's "Drifting" are supported by a text that carries the listener to unexpected places much more gently. In other cases, however, when an instrumental passage appears in a key other than tonic, particularly if it is not closely related (in other words, if chromatic alterations are required for more than one or two scale degrees), there may be no corresponding lyric and so the instrumental passage takes on the quality of a fantasy, somehow outside of the more tangible scheme represented by the vocal portions of the song. This technique was very popular in orchestrally backed songs of the 1950s (as in Caterina Valente's "The Breeze and I (Andalucia)" and Dick James's "Fascination"), but was also used for sax solos (the Fontane Sisters' "Rock Love," the Four Aces' "Melody of Love").

Modulation may involve the same processes (possibly involving a pivot chord) used in tonicization, but there **Modulation.** is no attempt to regain the original tonic. The most commonly heard technique whereby the original tonic is forsaken for another tonal center is known as the "truck driver's modulation." Here, the tonic is replaced by a new center lying a minor or major second above. These motions may occur in series; one song may include as many as six modulations (as does Sandy Nelson's "Let There Be Drums"), rising by step so that I, #I, II, #II, III, and IV may each work as successive tonics in their own right. In the most common manifestation of a truck driver's modulation, one may hear a song's chorus move to a cadence on V^{m7}, a moment of purchase at which point one can imagine a clutch being depressed; this is followed by the shift to a major chord a minor second higher, acting as the artificial V of the new tonic, which is gained as the clutch is released. The shift has the same transcendent effect of hyper-arrival noted in the chromatic V—VI cadence of The Band's "This Wheel's on Fire." (Listen to Web audio example 11.27.) Whereas the ultimate origins of this technique have not been traced, immediate forebears to the pop-rock literature include the Mills Brothers' "The Glow-Worm" (1952) and Patti Page's "(How Much Is) That Doggie in the Window" (1953). Figure 11.01 indicates the number of shifts per song heard each year in records that reached the weekly top-twenty. The truck driver's modulation is ubiquitous through our period of study; during the 1960s, the modulation rising by major second gains in frequency. It is eventually recognized as an artificial technique common to manufactured hits and Vegas arrangements; one never hears the Rolling Stones, for instance, practice this although The Who experimented with it in live performance. Well-known examples include the McGuire Sisters' "Sugartime," David Seville's "Witch Doctor," Bobby Darin's "Mack the Knife" (sporting five such shifts), Lorne Greene's "Ringo," and the Toys' "A Lover's Concerto." In some cases (Zager and Evans' "In the Year 2525 (Exordium and Terminus)") the shift accompanies a narrative transition, in some (Frank Sinatra's "That's Life") we hear a grand finish, but in others (Bobby Hebb's "Sunny"), the repeated "surprise" seems an overblown attempt to compensate for a weak formal structure.

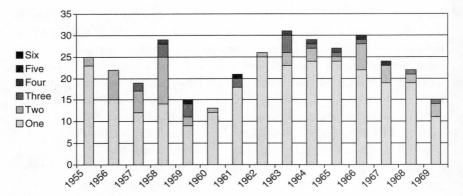

Figure 11.01. Incidence of Truck-Driver's Modulations in all hits to reach the weekly Top Twenty in 1955–69, indicating for each year the numbers of songs containing one TDM, songs containing two TDMs…and songs containing six TDMs.

All of the topics covered in these past four chapters—the balance of counterpoint and harmony, the relationship of consonance and dissonance, the construction of individual sonorities and their functional relationships, modal systems, chromaticism, tonicization and modulation—show the two- and three-minute songs of this literature to contain many of the tonal elements of interest in song literatures of prior centuries and far more as well, because of the infusion of blues-based minor-pentatonic language into the tonal system once common to the swing, the Tin-Pan Alley, the parlour song, the operetta, and the European classical song that came before. More than forms, more than tonal color and rhythm, more than melodic techniques and the composition of lyrics, it is the principles of harmony and counterpoint that would remain relatively stable from their amalgamation in the 1950s and '60s through the rest of the pop-rock era. Not that genres such as heavy metal and hip-hop have not introduced new tonal relationships in the twenty-first century; it's just that they are still working within the same tonal background present in the 1950s and '60s.

Interpreting melodic and harmonic values

So as to tie together many of the ideas covered in the past six chapters, and particularly to show how all aspects of harmony and melody are interdependent, and how these aspects of music have a fundamental bearing on the creation and perception of form, let's review the same twenty-five songs discussed at the end of chapter 3, now from a perspective that will illustrate the wide variety of approaches taken in these more recently covered topics.

Our earliest chosen examples are among the simplest. Bill Haley's "(We're Gonna) Rock Around the Clock" and Elvis Presley's "Heartbreak Hotel" are both in one-part forms, one strophe following the other without chorus or bridge, both songs also using only I, IV, and V chords with their sevenths. Haley's strophe has a twelve-bar structure, the last eight of which form the title-based refrain; even the instrumental break takes this shape. All five of Presley's eight-bar verses, plus the similarly built break, share the same structure; in this case, the "so lonely, baby" refrain occupies just the last four bars of each verse. Arpeggiation of 1—3—5 is a key part of Haley's melody, both in the V-attaining intro and the verse melodies, but, as was mentioned previously, the refrain follows the daytime verse with a shift from the night's suggestive minor-pentatonic mode to the major-scale pitches of broad daylight. Presley's melody does not make use of arpeggiation, but instead mixes a reciting tone on 8 with a largely minor-pentatonic melody, featuring the 5—♭7—8 blues trichord. A surprisingly jazz-flavored tag ending appears with the final chords, ♭II^{M7}—I^{M7}.

> **25 Great Hits II:** The same twenty-five recordings analyzed at the end of chapter 3, now approached from the perspectives of form, melody, and harmony.

Buddy Holly's "That'll Be the Day" sets virtually the same tune for both verses and choruses, which alternate, but the different word rhythms and different rates of chord changes help set them apart: In the verse, chords take one bar each: IV—I—IV—I—IV—I—II—V. The chorus moves more slowly at first but then ends irregularly: two bars of IV are answered by two of I; another three of IV then lead to two beats of V and two of I. Holly uses minor-pentatonic materials in an otherwise major-mode context to vocally emphasize his feelings of betrayal, ornamenting "bye" and "cry" with broken, repeated vowels on a painful ♭3.

The Everly Brothers' "Wake Up Little Susie" is unassumingly complex. Its harmonies are simple; except for the intro, which contrasts an alarming minor-pentatonic trichord, I—♭III—IV—♭III—I, strummed in one guitar against a sustained major-mode tonic chord in the other, the song contains nothing but the same I, II, IV, and V triads used by Holly. The song's form, however, is quite unconventional and somewhat misdirected. The four-bar intro is followed by a motto consisting of the song's title. Not really a chorus (because it is harmonized differently in its several reappearances), the title is repeated here on I for eight bars, and this is followed by what might be called a verse ("We've both been sound asleep...," 0:16) because it reappears once with different lyrics ("The movie wasn't so hot...," 1:17), for eight bars on IV. This leads to a repeated motto (0:26+), this time sung on V, IV, and two bars of V, which prepares the bridge (0:31+, "what're we gonna tell your mama"), oddly tonicizing that V all the way through its eight bars by alternating V with its own artificial V, the major II chord. At 0:42, harmony returns to I for yet another motto, now on I—V—I. Although the large-scale I—V—I basis is not in itself unusual, its usage here has a disorienting, confused effect, because the I—IV motion into the first verse (0:16+) has the same relationship as does the V—I that returns to the motto (0:42+). This leads to a new section ("Well, I told your mama that you'd be in by ten...," 0:47), four of I going to four of IV, interrupted by the V—IV—I motto, which leads to the song's only cadence, "we gotta go home," with Don's leading lower voice going home to tonic, right down the major scale 3—4—3—2—1, while Phil shadows his every move in the descant part a third above. The introductory guitar figure comes in at 1:02, followed by first motto (1:08), second verse (1:17), bridge (1:33, skipping the V—IV—V motto), I—V—I motto (1:43), then a fade-out on the introductory figure without a second hearing of the "new" section and, more significantly, without ending with the descending cadence. The formal disorientation and lack of resolution portray well the couple's harsh return to their post-"sleeping" realities.

Like Haley, Presley, and Holly, Chuck Berry relates all of his strophes very closely in "Sweet Little Sixteen." Here, there are definitely distinguishable verses (three of them) and choruses (four: at the beginning and end, and surrounding the piano break), but only because of the recurring lyrics. All sections have the same sixteen-bar harmonic formula: two of V^{m7}, two of I, these four bars repeated, then two each of IV—I—V—I. This and the accompanying tune were borrowed in Bobby Rydell's "Kissin' Time" (no legal problem there) and

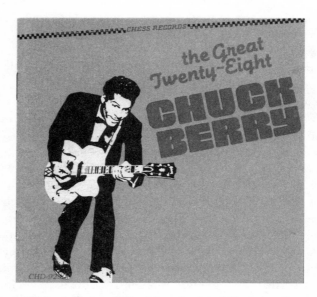

Photo 11.02. A 1984 compilation of Chuck Berry's original Chess recordings.

the Beach Boys' "Surfin' U.S.A." (plagiarism lawsuit!). Although the melody is often altered as it reappears, most lines in the chorus descend ♭7—6—5 except when Berry tells us which of the long litany of American cities is his own home town by pushing up to 8 and dropping to 1 at "all over St. Louis"!

Our next recording, the Marvelettes' "Please Mr. Postman," was also copied by another artist, in this case by Dee Dee Sharp in "Mashed Potato Time." As in several previous examples, both verse and chorus share a harmonic frame for a one-part form; here, it's two bars each of I—vi—IV—V. The form balances three choruses and three verses asymmetrically (Cho—Vs 1—Vs 2—Cho—Vs 3—Cho—Coda, "Wait a minute!," repeated on the chorus structure). The melody is hexatonic—it never takes a blue note and never introduces 7; it thus sounds compliant and restrained, raising only a faux protest to the postman with such ultrasecure major-pentatonic melodic lines as 6—5—3—2—1 and 5—3—1 arpeggiations.

The Four Seasons' "Sherry" features diatonic, modal, and chromatic progressions: the intro presents a half-bar each of the descending-fifth cliché, I—vi—ii—V (repeated), which then underlies both a title motto (0:09+, repeated) and a verse (0:17+, heard four times). The second verse (0:34+) is punctuated with the "Wake Up Little Susie" blues trichord as a tag, I—♭III—IV—I (0:45+). The bridge (0:50+), on the other hand, uses an ultra-chromatic variation on the "Lazy River" fifths-descent, with two bars each of III^{m7}—VI^{m7}—II^{m7}—V^{m7} (most of these supporting an energetic lead-vocal arpeggiation in the highest register), stopping time on this last for the "mi-yi-yine" melisma at 1:02. The effect seems clear; the tame diatonic music supports a polite invitation, even requests for a mother's permission; the minor-pentatonic trichord seems to suggest unstated, ulterior motives from below whereas the ultra-bright major triads of the bridge illuminate the twist party "where the bright moon shines." The melody of the verse beginning at 1:26 rises to high falsetto to ask Sherry to reassure her mother that "everything is all right" in the exposed open air, but we suspect from the wordless I—♭III—IV trichord that immediately follows (1:38) that any worries are not unfounded. Otherwise, the lead vocal soars with hope, rising with the ascending arpeggio, 5—1—3, that calls Sherry, and then falling from 8 to 1 for a 3—2—1 conclusory gesture in the low register for a heartfelt inner-voice plea, "won't you come out tonight?"

The Crystals' "He's a Rebel" features bold, absolutely mutinous harmonic relationships to get its point across. The form is conventional enough: intro, two verses, chorus, sax break going into the end of the third verse, chorus, and coda. And for the most part, the harmony and melody are also quite standard, opening with four bars of I for the intro, the first verse establishing another four bars of I (in support of a major-scale melody ornamenting the fifth with its upper neighbor, 1—2—3—4—5—5—6—5, repeated) before a startling, swirling melodic sequence in falling thirds, 3—2—1—7, 1—7—6—5, 6—5—6—5…, also ends up sitting on 5 with its upper neighbor over the basic vi—IV—V—V progression dropping in thirds to prepare a half cadence. The second verse, suggesting marked behavior in the swirling sequence ("My baby, always the one to try the things they've never done…"), however, moves from IV to II, a bold chromatic shift to tonicize V. The chorus, in turn, also begins simply, satisfied with diatonic chords until IV slides down to a shocking major III chord ("he doesn't do what everybody else does," in stop-time unison vocals, indeed!), and then the next IV (at 0:59) goes directly to II, which instead of leading to the tonicized V, substitutes for it, leading straightway back to I for a diatonic close ("he's no rebel to me").

Strangest of all, though, is the unprepared truck driver's modulation up a minor second that takes the second verse to the first chorus ("they say–a–hey, 'He's a Rebel…'"), with a half-bar of V interrupted by a half-bar of ♭VI (artificial V of ♭II). Occurring before the first chorus and only once in the song (less than a third of the way through, at 0:41), the truck driver's modulation does not have one of its usual jobs of bringing new perspective to what's already been conveyed or taking the song to a finish of heightened intensity; it clearly is needed to express the rebel's unexpected earthquake-strong moves early in the character exposition. The coda, consisting of a nonfunctional I—vi—I—vi—I alternation that recalls the verses' several 5—6—5—6—5 neighbor motions, shows—as do many of the song's passages—that the singer is quite comfortable with the ride, perhaps not as rough as it looks from the outside.

The Beatles' "I Want to Hold Your Hand" introduces contrast in melodic design and harmonic strength to portray the unleashing of power. This and "Ticket to Ride" are the only true examples of AABA form among this sample of twenty-five songs ("Come Together" is close, but its strong opening tattoo overshadows the recurrences of the verses). As a quintessential example, the song presents a verse-refrain section (beginning at 0:08), repeats it with new lyrics (0:29+), and goes to a contrasting bridge (0:51+) that retransitions to a following verse-refrain pair (1:11+) before repeating once more bridge and verse-extended refrain. Following an energetic intro, the song begins unassumingly, with tentative descending melodic sequences (6—5—4—3, 5—4—3—2), before it falls from a reciting tone ("[3] I think you'll under-[down to 7] -stand"). This is repeated, with the leap instead going *up,* from 3 up a full octave to the higher falsetto 3 as John and Paul state the title for the first time. Although the singer believes the intended will "understand," he expresses his desires meekly, first with the descending 3—7 drop, and then, trying harder, with the ascending octave. But this ardor is largely undercut by arcane harmony, void of any energy, that can be intellectually but not passionately understood, when vi moves to the weak iii. So the singer bucks up, and presents his case in a much more energetic refrain (0:22+) that moves in double time harmonically (changing chords twice per bar as opposed to the foregoing once), with more powerful, goal-directed chords: IV—V—I—vi, IV—V—I, as the melody falls in a broken scale: 8—7—6—5—4, 5—4—3—2, 3—2—1, the portions of the descent coming faster and faster all the time.

The song's most dynamic moment, however, is the bridge's retransition. The bridge opens (0:51) with a relaxed tonicization of IV (made even softer the second time around, 1:34–1:45, by the addition of Paul's upper descant vocal), recoiling for a better jump forward, as it goes twice through the offset progression, ii^{m7}—V^{m7}—I—vi. Then a syncopated cadence interrupts (1:03+) with power chords on IV^5—V^5, IV^5—V^5, IV^5—V^5 as Lennon's vocal doubles the bass on 4—5 with Paul above for the climactic "I can't hide." As the song's emblem, these same syncopated power chords create the song's intro. From there on, it's a rollercoaster of energetic ups and downs with periodic bursts of harmonic power. The coda's surprising reharmonization of the refrain, where the meek iii suddenly appears as III^{m7}, provides a final burst, requiring a final pulling in of the reins (2:18+) with slow triplets and a plagal ending.

The Animals' "House of the Rising Sun" is a cover of Dylan's version, which was a remake of Joan Baez's 1960 recording of a nineteenth-century Appalachian folk tune. In most strophes of this one-part form, the tune itself is a slowly rising cry, gradually ascending the octave from 1 to 8 for a strongly accusatory "they call...," which leads to blues-trichord cadences, 8—♭7—5 (—8). (The four verses vary principally in which register, 1 or 8, the vocal melody uses as its starting point.) But it's a chromatic harmonic twist that carries the main point of the story. Each verse consists of an antecedent phrase of two motions: i—♭III—IV—♭VI, followed by the arpeggiation i—♭III—V, with one bar on each chord except for the half-cadential V, which receives two bars. The consequent phrase repeats the first gesture but then cadences i—V—i (with then a turnaround bar on V). It is the opening gesture's move from the major IV chord to the major ♭VI that compares the dorian's higher 6 to the minor mode's lower ♭6; the song is predominantly in minor, but the ever-present IV chord intrudes with its 6 to spice things up. The garish 6 might be heard as the whorehouse's siren call to ruin. It's as if the contrast is set perfectly with the line, "spend your life in sin and misery," with the IV chord portraying the too-pleasurable-to-be-natural "sin" and the following ♭VI portraying the misery that results. "Rising Sun" is the perfect name for the house that is always seen in a different light the morning after. And "garish" is indeed the perfect word for Alan Price's final jazz chord on the Continental, $i^{M9/m7}$.

Roy Orbison's "Oh Pretty Woman" seems to turn the truth on its head, if harmony can be taken for a lie detector. The listener is struck in the first verse (which opens each time with the titular refrain) by the odd metric and melodic handling of the cadential dominant; folowing a normal, single-bar-per-chord opening alternation I—vi—I—vi (0:14+), the next chord, IV, sustains for 1.5 bars before moving to the late-arriving eight full bars of V, which supports a strangely strong 6 in the vocal, resolving twice to 5: "[6] I can't believe [5] you, [4] you're [2] not [4] the [5] truth, [6] no one can look [5] as [4] good [2] as [5] you." This double-take is presented over the heavily textured ostinato, 5—5—7—2—4—6—5—4, from which the 6—5 idea derives. The 6—5, present in the song's ubiquitous ostinato and in the gawking prolongation of V (stretching every verse to an off-balance 13.5 bars), seems to indicate the singer's lack of trust in his good luck.

But, in turn, the gawker hides his own true self in the bridge (1:06+), where he tries to get his prey to "look my way" with a straining tonicization of ♭III and a look-at-me-I'm-safe-as-milk melodic sequence on a perfectly well-behaved one-chord-per-bar: 4—3—2 over ii—V, 3—2—1 over I—vi, 2—1—7—6—7—8 over ii—V—I—I, repeated. (These Roman numerals indicate the functions as heard in the tonicized area; in the home key, they require iv—♭VII, ♭III—I, iv—♭VII—♭III—III.) But, surprise!, the man behind the curtain is exposed, the singer's true self shows through at 1:34, when the final "I" in the repeat (really ♭III in the home key) is replaced by the true I for a jarring revelation of "me." Baring his soul ("'Cause I need you, I'll treat you right... be mine tonight," all more imploring than "look my way"), Orbison harmonizes his now less artifical vocal line in the home key, throwing in a soulful Italianate minor-mode iv chord at 1:38 to underline his desperation: the real I leads to vi—iv—V, repeated to a retransitional half-cadence: I—vi—iv—V. As in the verse, phrase lengths take on an odd off-balance rhythm, here 3 + 3 + 4 bars. Also, note that the double-tracked vocals, elsewhere always in parallel thirds, suddenly move in contrary motion, the rising 4—5 over the descending 1–7 at "...you right" and "tonight," a strong reminder of the singer's two voices (one true, the other less so?) presented throughout the song. As in "I Want to Hold Your Hand" and "Sherry," the singer of "Oh Pretty Woman" makes polite overtures and yet something in the music reveals his full desires. This song ends happily; the final verse leads to a coda (2:09+), in which a reappearance of the can't-believe-my-luck V^{M9} ostinato signals the singer's surprise when the desired woman walks not away but back to him, reinforcing his hope for the night.

In the Beatles' "Ticket to Ride," harmonically supported melody is the device that bursts through the singer's conservative comfort zone in search of freedom. The verses begin with arpeggiation from deep within Lennon's low register: 5—1—3—4—3—1—5. This low zone is where he, not she, is comfortable (after all, living with him is "bringing her *down*"), and the low arpeggiation is sung over a simple six bars of I moving to one bar each of ii and V. But his girl has much more variety and activity in mind, and she plans an escape upwards, as each chorus (0:23+, "She's got a ticket to ride") takes the tune upward, twice via 3—5—6, then pushing up a bit harder to 3—5—♭7 (♭7 was the scale degree by which she was "driving me mad" in the verse), and finally up to 8 in McCartney's vocal part in the cadence. The chorus's supporting chords, one bar each, indicate how far the girl is willing to go to break away: the determined vi moves to a dead-end IV^{M7}, then vi tries again, going to great lengths, to the highly unusual ♭VII^{M7}, and then vi finally breaks through to V^{m7} so she may resolve into I—freedom! This song exemplifies the AABA structure with verse-chorus pairings: A (Verse 1—Chorus, 0:07+), A (Verse 2—Chorus, 0:38+), B (Bridge, 1:09+), A (1:27+), B (1:58+), A (2:15+).

Lou Christie treats a familiar theme with unusual musical frankness in "Lightnin' Strikes," a cynical portrayal of domestic bliss as a fantasy in the face of real-life temptation and male dominance. The form consists of two progressions: the verse (0:07+, given new lyrics at 0:58+) as a wake-up call, followed by the depiction of the domestic fantasy (0:22+, 1:12+), leading to a prechorus warning (0:36+, 1:26+), with the resulting chorus (0:44+, 1:33+) illustrating an inevitable perfidy. Following the guitar solo (1:48+), the form becomes somewhat telescoped in recapitulation, moving from chorus (2:01+) to fantasy (2:16+, without need for a preparatory verse), and then fading out after the prechorus (2:30+) finds its chorus (2:37+). The verse itself is an aggressively accented double-plagal statement, I—♭VII—IV—I, heard four times as the singer demands attention ("Listen to me, baby") as he means to explain his version of the facts of life and demand adherence ("you're old enough to know the makings of a man"; "live by my rules"). This call to attention leads to the ingratiating recited fantasy, set in a tonicization of VI. Its distance from tonic sets the scene as false, as do the new instrumentation and vocal approach—a fairy land of rocking right-hand piano figuration, chapel-in-the-pines bells, and cloying melodic sequence: 6—♯5—♯4, 7—6—♯5. He sings here, "every boy wants a girl he can trust to the very end," despite the double standard by which he expects his own two-timing behavior to be accepted. Perhaps he would like to believe in the blissful fairy tale himself, but he knows too well what the real world holds—when aroused by another woman, "when I see lips," and "if she's put together fine," the prechorus brings us a bit closer to home with the tonicized VI becoming a long-extended V^{m7} of ii, the singer explaining why he cannot stop himself, with the prior sequence rising in desperation, unstoppable, 6̲—7—♯1, ♯1̲—2—3, 3̲—♯4—5. In the chorus, lightning strikes with a climactic half-cadence in the ii area (two bars of ii going to one of iii^{4-3sus} and two of VI^{m7}, repeated), and

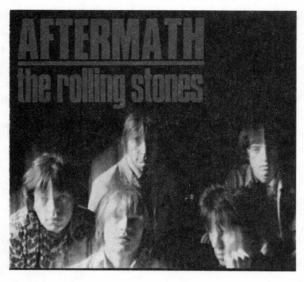

Photo 11.03. The Rolling Stones' first album of all-original compositions led off with "Paint It, Black."

we need not consider too long what anatomical analogy he is drawing with lightning bolts in rationalizing his infidelities, the bari sax thrusting away in the man's image as his falsetto vocal becomes buried within the women's backing parts.

The Rolling Stones' "Paint It, Black" has an uncomplicated two-part structure, with simple alternation of an eight-bar refrain and a six-bar verse:

```
0:00   0:14 0:27   0:39 0:51   1:04 1:15   1:27 1:40   1:52   2:04 2:16–3:45
Intro–Ref – Vs 1– Ref – Vs 2–Ref – Vs 3–Ref – Vs 4 – Ref 1– Vs 1–Ref – Coda
```

Each refrain has a different set of lyrics, as does what we're calling the verse; the refrain almost always includes the title, whereas the verse never does. Another anomaly is that each verse ends on V (normally the function of a bridge), but these verses, unlike bridges, do dwell on tonic: a half-bar each is heard of a progression suggestive of dorian and aeolian, i—♭VII—♭III—♭VII—two bars of i. This is repeated but with a minor-mode half-cadence, IV—V, one bar each, heard the second time around in place of the first phrase's final tonic. The progression is practically an octave doubling of the minor-pentatonic vocal tune, 8—♭7—♭3—4—5, which probably came first to the songwriters. The minor-mode refrain, by contrast, simply alternates two bars each of i—V—i—V while Mick Jagger sings the sitar's repetitive introductory melody, 1—2—♭3—4—♭3—2—1—7. Whether it was sitarist Brian Jones or usual music-writer Keith Richard who came up with this tune, we can't be certain, but only Jagger and Richard receive songwriting royalties. The lyrics are quasi-psychedelic, certainly melancholic, perhaps all things considered a bad trip.

The Lovin' Spoonful's "Summer in the City" mixes modes for deepest effect. The song's opening gesture, a thrice-heard ♭6—5 descent, establishes the minor mode in a way not heard in the body of the song. In fact, in the verse, the raised sixth degree is heard in *descent,* more a marker of dorian than minor procedure, as a descending voice above the minor tonic chord produces the repeated combination i—i^{m7}—i^{add6}—i—V; the vocal line in this phrase, ♭3—1—♭7—1—5, is squarely minor-pentatonic. But the vocal arpeggiation of the major V ("[5] all around, [7] people lookin' [2] half dead") confirms the mode as minor, only to shift abruptly to major, i moving directly to I, when John Sebastian's lone voice bursts into flames of vocal harmony (0:19), "hotter than a matchhead."

This leads directly to what ought to be called the bridge, because it begins with a tonicization of IV (in the major mode) and leads to V, even though it concludes with the song's only post-opening reference to the title. The early part of the bridge is "a different world," that of the major-mode cool summer night, in a fourfold hearing of IV—♭VII (half-bar each, sounding like a plagal I—IV in the tonicized IV area). This is then undercut by a move to a bridge-ending ii—V—ii—V progression (still a half-bar each, now sounding like a dorian i—IV alternation in a weakly tonicized ii area), in a highly unusual blend of retransitional and refrain functions. The bridge strongly highlights the raised 6 as third of the tonicized IV harmony, as fifth of the ii chord, and in the repeated 4—5—6—4 melody ("in the summer, in the city"), intensifying the suggested dorian quality of i^{add6} in the succeeding verse. The whole song alternates verse and bridge, with a second break (1:59+) leading into an instrumental coda that fades away on the major mode's carefree night dance.

In the face of the down-to-earth messages of our previously discussed songs, Bob Dylan's "Visions of Johanna" represents a ponderable turn to abstraction. The story tells us that Johanna has left the singer, but ghostly reminders of her constantly interrupt his less-than-satisfying new life with Louise. The seven-and-a-half-minute recording consists of five barely representational verses, each with refrain, plus coda. The construction of each verse is expressive in its blend of perfect balance and odd asymmetry. Each verse/refrain pair is a balanced period of two phrases, one antecedent and one consequent, but the two phrase lengths are an odd twenty answered by eight. Despite the disparity in phrase lengths, the first half of the consequent (we'll label this subphrase *a,* 1:05–1:15) has the same melodic and harmonic structure as the first four bars of the antecedent (*a,* as well, 0:13–0:23), creating a parallel construction overall. The last half of every consequent represents the refrain (*d*, 1:16–1:26), always rhyming with the just-completed *a* subphrase, and repeated with the title (and therefore providing the song's strongest linchpin), although each refrain presents with new words a different perspective on the lingering visions of Johanna. The construction of the antecedent presents interesting variations: its first four bars (*a*) are repeated, but then its remaining twelve contain two more subphrases, each one built of new, contrasting melodic and harmonic material. The *b* subphrase (0:34–0:44) rhymes with the *a*, and both end 4–3 melodically, whereas the various lines of *c* (0:45–1:04) all rhyme internally. The following, then, represents the thematic and harmonic structure of each subphrase of each verse; fractions indicate the portions of bars devoted to each chord that does not sustain for a full bar:

ANTECEDENT (20 bars):

| *a* | | *a* | | *b* | | *c* |

I–.5 IV–.5 V–I–I,   I–.5 IV–.5 V–I–I;   V^{m7}–V^{m7}–I–I,   IV–I–IV–I–IV–I–V–V

CONSEQUENT (8 bars):

| *a* | | *d* (refrain) |

I–.5 IV–.5 V–I–I,   IV–I/3–V^{m7}–I

Each consequent phrase is followed by an interlude, an instrumental hearing of subphrase *a*, which material also serves as the song's introduction. If 20 + 8 is not asymmetrical enough, the final verse is expanded to 26 + 8 bars when its *c* gesture (elsewhere always double the duration of every other subphrase) is given a seemingly improvised sixfold repetition of the IV—I succession. (It comes across as improvised—almost arbitrarily—not because of the expanded lyrics, which build forcefully in intensity to the point of cathartic explosion, but because the hapless bass player muffs the changes here (6:29), playing 5 for 4 in a karmic reversal of his previous wrong note, 4 played for 5, at 1:57.) Note the fact that in the refrain, the line's interior I chord is played over a light 3 in the bass, as the absent Johanna is no longer home, the place represented by I when its root is in the bass. (So, the bass player deserves *some* credit.)

The song is a confusion of images and voices; the narrator is split into multiple selves, expressed in second person ("you're tryin' to be so quiet," "temptin' you to defy it"), third person ("Louise and her lover"), first-person plural ("We sit here stranded," "We can hear the night-watchman") and first-person singular ("that conquer my mind"), so we're not surprised when visions themselves "have now taken my place." The blending of the lingering images of Johanna with the remnants of self, conquering the singer's mind, seem to be portrayed by the strong vocal nonresolutions of dissonant fourth scale degrees that sustain above the I at the conclusion of nearly every verse. The song is redolent of trickery, isolation, misery, hollowness, futility, and sterility, as if an overarching pessimism and denial have rendered the use of brightening agents such as chromaticism or superficial rhythmic complexity pointless and superfluous. The paradox of a long parade of specific images against a large-scale ambiguity seems to fit the song's arranged marriage of symmetries and imbalances.

The Beach Boys' "Good Vibrations" uses the minor mode not to express sadness or drudgery or anything at all negative. Combined with Brian Wilson's lilting, highly ornamented melody that moves across a broad range in skips then in stepwise fashion but with lots of twists and turns, the minor-key chords project an air of mystery. The verse, which opens the song without intro, is built of the repeated descending i—♭VII—♭VI—V progression in support of a tune that moves "[8—5] I [5] I love the [8] color- [♭3] -ful [4] clothes [♭7] she [♭7—♭6—5] wears, [4] and [5] the [♭6] way [♭7] the [4] sun- [5] -light [♭6] plays [5] up- [4] -on [♭3] her [4—♭3—2] hair. [5] I hear the sound [4] of [♭3] a [♭7] gen- [8] -tle [5—4—♭3] word...." One can easily "hear" perfume lifted by the wind in such prettily wafting waves of sound, first gently descending through a minor scale featuring the 5—♭6 minor second three times, and then, in its second freefall (second sentence), restricted instead to members of the major-pentatonic scale on ♭3 (♭3—4—5—♭7—8). This major-pentatonic scale subtly predicts a shift from the opening minor to a tonicization of the major *key* on ♭III, home of the chorus (0:25+), where Mike Love sings "I'm pickin' up good vibrations" in a comfortable confidence that breaks through all ambiguity, the tonicized ♭III now oscillating with its own crystal-clear plagal IV. The vibrations rise, as the repeating I—IV—I structure is transposed up a step to tonicize IV (0:38—0:44), and then another step to reach V (0:44—0:50). From this V, it's an easy return to i, the minor tonic, for a second verse (0:51+) and its chorus (1:16+).

The second chorus ends, however, with its tonicized V continuing with its own I—IV—I pattern through a digression (1:41+, "I don't know where but she sends me there..."), in an unexpected turn to a foreign area. Where are we, indeed? The dominant has a bipolar nature in this song; the V at the end of the first chorus retransitions back to i, but the V at the end of the second chorus has prepared itself as a continuing key area. Surely, this song is about the joy of unexpected pleasures, something perhaps the song's many interwoven backing vocal parts are able to express without direct words. A second digression (2:21) tonicizes II (eventually working as artificial V of V), and then the coda (2:57) that develops chorus material proves that the structural tonal center is as variable as the wind, with brief tonicizations that waft through V (2:57—3:03)—IV (3:03—3:09)—♭III (3:10—3:16)—IV

(3:16–3:19)—V (3:20–3:23)—IV (3:23+), areas that represent scale degrees common to both the minor and major-pentatonic tunes heard way back in both the first and second verses, never repeated again in their own right after the first digression.

The Doors' "Light My Fire" portrays frustration and ungratified desire as a constant state that must be transcended—"the time for hesitation's through." Harmonic values underline the status quo with the repetitive and aimless v^{m7}—iii^{m7} alternation through the verses (as at 0:10+). The long enervating jam featuring Vox Continental (1:06+) and Gibson SG (3:18–5:13) similarly takes place on the repeated alternation of an aimless pair, v^{m7}—vi^{m7}. In the choruses (0:38+), Jim Morrison implores his lover for action, and hints at absolute wildness with his suggestions of chromatic chords such as VI and II as phrase endings: "[IV] come on, baby [V^{add6}] light my [I] fire, [IV] come on, baby [V^{add6}] light my [I] fire [VI; IV] try to set the [I] night on [II] fire." The radiant II is brought back to dull reality as artificial V of the ensuing minor v beginning the verses and jam that follow it. This song opens and closes with one of rock's best-ever tattoos, Ray Manzarek's sequential baroque call on the organ that also serves as lead-in (5:33–5:43) from jam to verse, a wild string of garish relations among chromatic major triads that finds its way out of the dark depths of ♭III, ♭VI, and two steps beyond, to the demanding dominant: IV—I, ♭III—♭VI, ♭II—♭V (one half-bar each)—V (two bars). There the recording ends, its twisted demands unresolved.

The one-part form of Jimi Hendrix's "Little Wing" is the simplest of all large-scale structures in our twenty-five examples: a thirty-five second intro is followed by two verses and a guitar solo (1:40+), all four parts based on the same harmonic structure. The melody is also rather straightforward, falling an octave with swirls as fanciful as those in "Good Vibrations," especially in depicting "walkin' through the clouds," a melisma rolling through the smoky wisps of that last word. The harmonies and the two phrase lengths, however, are as imaginatively varied and psychedelic as can be: an opening phrase is simple, with one bar each of i—♭III—iv—i^{m7}. The motion from i to ♭III does suggest a move from a minor to a major tonic, befitting the change of mood given in the second verse, "when I'm [i] sad, she comes to [♭III] me," smiling freely. The second phrase is anything but simple, formed by a chain of chords in a descent of phrygian-related roots embellished by a chromatic passing ♭V chord: three beats of v pass through one of ♭V to a full bar of iv, then a bar is divided, half on ♭III and half on ♭II^{add9}, before cadencing with a bar on ♭VI and two on ♭VII, with ♭VI substituting for a passing i and then ♭VII substituting for V in a half-cadential gesture, each verse then an open phrase group. "Riding with the wind": Jimi's answer to Brian Wilson?

Cream's "White Room" sets music that is unique in many ways, common in others, to a lyric almost as oblique as that of "Visions of Johanna." Just as Eric Burdon, in "House of the Rising Sun," sings that he has "one foot on the platform, one foot on the train," Jack Bruce lives in two worlds that happen to join at a train platform. One world is white and black (curtains, roof, starlings), no gold pavement providing any promise, a shadowy land of hard and lonely crowds. But another world of fiery adventure was once glimpsed in the eyes of his lover, wherein "silver horses ran down moonbeams" and where "yellow tigers crouched in jungles." These images lie in the past; she has left him in his sterile environment—"no strings could secure [her] at the station." He contemplates leaving this realm himself to lie with her once again, but this plan remains in the undetermined future, and the song's refrain, "the shadows run from themselves," seems to tie together his lover's escape from him and his own hoped-for flight from his own everyday life, a bleak existence.

The song's monumentally oppressive opening tattoo is an impressive emblem for both a forbidding environment and the singer's ambivalence. The aeolian materials, iv—$^\flat$III—i—$^\flat$VII, iv—$^\flat$III—i—$^\flat$VII—v^{m7}, are aimless without a leading tone, goalless, as is the five-beat meter; each chord but the last is held for an unyielding five beats pounded by domineering timpani. The last bar is a four-beat transition to the meter of the coming verse, but on a very non-committal minor dominant. The verse (0:24+) seems very goal-oriented, but all travel returns to the source: a very directional progression, I—$^\flat$VII—IV/6—$^\flat$VI, is made more so by Bruce playing the third, not the root, of the IV chord on the bass, allowing for the descending line, 1—$^\flat$7—6—$^\flat$6, in the lowest voice. Chords then simply move back through $^\flat$VII to I, where the repeated cycle begins once again for eight uninterrupted hearings. Bruce repeatedly sings most of a tenth-long descending dorian scale, divided into sequential thirds, articulating the divided meter of the poetry: $^\flat\underline{3}$—2—1—1, $\underline{6}$—5—4—4, $^\flat\underline{3}$—2—1—1. The chorus ends with the verse's same $^\flat$VI—$^\flat$VII—I cadence, every time "the shadows run from themselves," although it moves at one fourth the speed, running in slow motion, never getting anywhere. Otherwise, the chorus (0:59+) makes one attempt to get away, breaking the song's overall major/dorian cast with a minor-mode $^\flat$VI—V half cadence (1:03–1:06) as one bar is heard of each chord: $^\flat$VII—IV—$^\flat$VI—V, $^\flat$VII—IV—$^\flat$VI—$^\flat$VII—I (this tonic held for two bars). The vocal melody of the chorus is related to that of the verse in that it is comprised of stepwise filled-in thirds, but now they are jumbled, descending and ascending, unsure as to where the underlying scale points: $\underline{2}$—$^\flat$3—4, $\underline{1}$—1—2—$^\flat$3, $\underline{4}$—$^\flat$3—2 (at the half cadence), $\underline{2}$—$^\flat$3—4, $\underline{1}$—1—2—$^\flat$3—3, $\underline{2}$—1—$^\flat$7, 1. If anything is able to break out of the white room's constraints and leave behind the conventions of the verse, it is Clapton's wah guitar, all silver horses and yellow tigers growing progressively restless throughout the song, working against the bound melody in the third verse (2:38+), and rebelling straight through the coda.

In "Remember a Day," Pink Floyd alternate straightforward rock verses with spaced-out piano interludes. The verses are wistful, each harking back to days spent playing children's games in the same spirit as the Rolling Stones' "Dandelion" (to which the coda's "blow away" seems a direct homage). The wistfulness is well expressed by the gentle double-plagal motion, with each verse simply repeating the line I—♭VII—IV (three bars each)—four bars of I, supporting a decorated vocal descent winding around the structure, 8—♭7—6—5—1. The song has two bridges (1:38+ and 3:09+), each with the distinctly dorian cadence, IV—♭III—♭VII—i, repeated, also with a (slower and now barely decorated) vocal descent, this time filling in the verse's 5—1 gap to concentrate on a darker region, 4—♭3—2—1. Note the opposition of the major-mode verse and the dorian bridge; the first piano interlude (and the similar intro) reverse this direction, moving from a loose, timeless first half in single notes that twice arpeggiate the fully dorian progression, i—ii—♭III—IV, to a strongly accented second half repeatedly blocking off bold major-mode I chords in three rising registers, an idea that continues underneath the verses, blending the two sections just as the verses die away over the dorian piano that has already appeared so as to lead the way into each interlude. A looser jam suggests the dorian. Altogether, the song follows the following format (d = dorian, M = major), with verses gradually appearing and disappearing over their varied accompaniments:

0:00	0:25	0:45	1:10	1:30	1:38	1:55	2:42	3:01	3:09	3:26
Intro	Vs 1	Interlude	Vs 2	Interlude	Bridge	Jam	Vs 3	Interlude	Bridge	Coda
d–M	M–d	d–M	M–d	d		d	d–M	M–d	d	d	d

The underlying melody of "I Heard It Through the Grapevine" is partly unobserved in Marvin Gaye's riveting performance, so often does he substitute his high-register howls of pain ("Losin' *you*," "you could have *told* me yourself") for the prescribed, underlying tune. This song has a dominant, but it melts into the much more pervasive IV before a whole bar can pass. The dorian verse begins as an SRDC pattern, with two bars of i and three beats of V followed by 1.25 bars of IV, all repeated. The Departure-gesture (0:38+) also moves to IV by repeating the progression vi^{m7}—IV^{m7}, Marvin painfully singing ♭3 against the major-mode's 3 in the vi chord in his most confrontational lines ("you could have *told* me yourself," "do you *plan* to let me go"), and then the chorus enters in place of the Conclusion-line, all in the alternation of i and its dorian neighbor IV. The chorus's interruption of the verse structure portrays the surprise by which Marvin has received the news.

The Who's "Overture" to *Tommy* is a harmonically rich piece, using fourteen different major or minor triads on all available diatonic and chromatic roots but one, with all manner of sevenths and dissonant suspension chords to fill out the tonicizations of eleven short-lived tonal centers or mode changes. This is all fitting for an overture, which is charged with foreshadowing much of the variety of the opera to come, and this is accomplished with grand contrasts of texture and meter, along with those of tonal centers and tunes. Following is a schematic diagram of the Overture's sections by timing, thematic material, and changes of key center:

0:00 0:17 0:33 0:37 0:59 1:07 1:33 1:48 1:56 2:04 2:19 2:56 3:00 3:04 3:36 3:45 4:06

a   *b*   *c*   *d*   *e*   *e–f b*   *g*   *e*   *f*   *h*   *e*   *e*   *d*   *d*   *i*   *j*

CM gm   GM   FM GM em EM   FM GM FM DM

Note that materials from four different sections, *b, d, e,* and *f,* return at various points, whereas other ideas are presented only once each. Lacking any sung lyrics, these themes cannot be thought of as verses or choruses, and they are mostly fragmentary, referring to full numbers (mostly from "Go to the Mirror") that occur later in the opera. None of the key centers can be thought of as tonic; they come and go, without relation to any gravitational center. So in these ways, this piece is fundamentally different from other tonal and formal structures we've investigated, even revolutionary in its way.

Each section is simple on its own, and very different from the others, but as we'll see, most are unified by conspicuous suspension figures that decorate cadences. The opening *a*-gesture is simply a slow bass descent, 8—♭7—6—♭6—5, at which point (0:09) the chord changes from I to V$^{sus6/sus4}$, which resolves to V$^{5/3}$ (0:12) for a dramatic half cadence. The tonal center changes as the *b*-gesture moves to a strummed-tremolo foreshadowing of the later "See me, feel me" line, on a slow-moving ♭VI^{M7}—♭III/5—i—V^{sus4}—V^3—i. The minor i (*c,* itself a mode change from the V goal of the opening phrase) gives way to I, appearing without mediation, announced by repeated notes, two per beat, on the horn, for a four-times heard double-plagal idea (*d*), I—IV—♭VII—IV, which then settles into a plagal I—IV^{add9}—I—IV^{add9} tag. The *e*-gesture (0:59+) always performs a transitional role. Consisting of two beats of I, followed by a beat of V dissolving into a beat of IV, this idea is heard four times and then (1:07+) twice more, but is transposed down a major second to prepare the way for the important *f* tune (1:11), introduced by the horn. This is the idea later given the words, "he seems to be completely unreceptive," supported four times by the *e* progression, before that gives way to a dramatic artificial dominant in III^{m7}—vi—IV^{M7}—V^{sus4}—V^3 (later, "His eyes react to light, the dials detect it..."), this big suspension and its resolution filling four bars from 1:25 to 1:33.

This dramatic point is answered, as it had been at 0:17, by the "See me, feel me" theme *b* beginning in major but leading to a large V with suspension (1:52–1:54) in a new minor area, which becomes major (1:56) for transition (through *e*) to the second half of *f* (2:04+, in a transposed replay of III^{m7}—vi—IV^{M7}—V^{sus4}—V^3). This large suspended dominant breaks open with the Hammond's appearance (2:19), for the "Listening to you I get the music" theme, *h*. Continuing in the just-won major mode, this phrase divided into four subphrases gives us the magisterial modal progression, IV—V—♭VI, IV—V—I, IV—V—♭VI, ♭III—♭VII—V^{sus4}—V^3, which is repeated. Our transition figure, *e,* then appears in this key and, in the manner of the "Good Vibrations" chorus, up a minor second (3:00) and then up again a major second to four playings of the *d* idea (3:04)—not heard since 0:37—now with a new horn figure, a repeated lipped glissando. The overture ends with a V^{sus4}—V^3 cadence transposed down a whole step (3:20 to 3:61) to prepare the solo acoustic guitar (3:45+) for its long intro to "Captain Walker" (4:06). Changes of key and mode, in tandem with varied thematic elements, are rampant; many of the Overture's colorful ideas, particularly the suspension figure (noted elsewhere as an important motive in both "Pinball Wizard" and "Cousin Kevin"), recur throughout the opera to follow.

The Beatles' "Come Together" consists of a repeated verse/refrain section. The song's only formal contrast comes with an introductory tattoo riff that recurs after all four verses, a break (2:02) preparing the fourth, and a coda (3:12+) following the last riff (3:00+). To establish room for growth, the refrain is withheld from the first verse. The verse has strongly bluesy materials, supporting a repeated vocal blues trichord, ♭3—1—♭7—1 with four bars of I$^{♯9/m7}$ to two each of V^{m7}—IV^{m7}. The refrain (1:10+), by contrast, descends 3—2—1 in the major mode, with major-mode chords vi—V—IV—V before we resolve into the bluesy I$^{♯9/m7}$ and the opening riff. This is a swampy boogie for Lennon's gibberish lyrics.

Creedence Clearwater Revival's "Down on the Corner" is part of the late-1960s revival of early rock 'n' roll. Nothing but I, V, and IV chords in its alternations of verses and choruses, with one interlude (1:43) based on the first four bars of the verse and a syncopated guitar tattoo heard as intro and then once again (1:17+) for balance. It's squarely in the major-mode, the vocal melody mostly triad arpeggiations (1—3—5—3—1—3—5—3, then 4—5—6—5—3—1—3—5—5—3—1), and yet as funky as any Booker T. and the M.G.'s number.

Photo 11.04. The Beatles had Sgt. Pepper's band; the more down-to-earth Creedence Clearwater Revival posed with washtub bass and washboard, as Willy and the Poor Boys, in "Down on the Corner."

Although the preceding pages should make it clear that we have already covered quite a bit of material and a number of techniques to help the listener build a deep and satisfying interpretation of songs from this era, there are still more topics to cover, and still more important techniques to add to the analyst's bag of tricks. It is hoped that the following three chapters will fully round out the reader's understanding of available approaches that may be brought to bear in such pursuits, further enriching the listening experience.

CHAPTER 12

Musical Time: Rhythm, Meter, and Tempo

"It's got a good beat—you can dance to it!" This was for a long time seemingly the first, foremost, and perhaps only consideration useful in judging the value of a pop song, if the frequency with which the phrase was uttered in late-1950s and early-1960s amateur record reviewing (a regular feature in television shows such as *American Bandstand* [U.S.] and *Juke Box Jury* [U.K.]) is any indication. "Beat" here most likely refers to a repeated rhythmic pattern in a particular meter at a certain tempo; the terminology may be universally abused by rock fans, but the most direct appeal of so many favorite songs is correctly understood by them as being related to their rhythmic properties. It is the goal of this chapter to clarify just what makes that "beat," and many other rhythmic events and relationships, so infectious, driving, and danceable. We'll see how various rhythmic patterns, heard against an unchanging grid of beats grouped into regular meters that proceed at a tempo that's fast, slow, or in between, can mark time at the surface level of a song. At deeper levels, we'll judge how many bars make a phrase, and how phrases of various lengths group together to make sections of various lengths, all producing rhythms against longer time spans. Each in their own way, these and other considerations (At what rates do chords change? What proportions relate one section of a song to the Whole? what position does a song take within the album that contains it?) concern the articulation of time in music. But we'll also come to appreciate that this is *all* that rhythm can accomplish, and that the world of pitch is crucial for bringing individuality to every song. Who, for instance, has ever noticed that the melodies sung in Cat Stevens's "Morning Has Broken" and John Denver's "Annie's Song" are practically identical in surface rhythm, meter, and tempo? The differences in pitch construction between the two songs are great enough to keep the rhythmic similarities from rising to most listeners' awareness. Add to this the fact that scale degrees—whether expressed in melodic or harmonic domains—carry differing accentual weights, as do changes in dynamic stress, instrumentation, and other textural markers, and as do changes in perceptions of formal function, and rhythm can be a far more nuanced domain than one that simply permits dancing to a repetitive beat.

Regular patterns

In nearly all music, time is marked by irregular surface articulations that interact with regular underlying pulses. In our discussion of the rhythmic properties of the drum kit in chapter 1, we found that one of the underlying levels, that of meter, groups regularly recurring beats into repetitive bars. Each bar has the same pattern of strong accented beats alternating with weaker beats, all acting as a backdrop, a grid,

> **Regular rhythmic patterns:** quadruple, triple, and duple meters; the backbeat and offbeat; the groove; simple and compound time; the tempo modulation; the shuffle, dotted, Bo Diddley, and Latin rhythms and grooves.

against which changeable surface rhythms are organized. We saw that most pop music is in quadruple meter, with beats organized four to the bar, ONE—two—Three—four—ONE—two—Three—four, with each downbeat (the first beat of each bar) given the strongest metrical accent and the backbeats given less (but that the third beat carries a bit more stress than the evenly numbered beats). (Recall Web audio examples 1.04 and 4.05, both quadruple-meter examples.) A fair amount of pop music is in triple meter, with three beats per bar. (For examples in triple meter, recall the middle section of Web audio example 4.21 and all of Web audio example 5.05.) Regardless of the meter, the last beat of the bar—the upbeat—is always metrically weakest.

One example of a rhythmic pattern working against the meter is the backbeat pattern, in which the drummer hits the snare on even-numbered beats, producing a (1)—two—(3)—four—(1)—two—(3)—four design. (Recall Web audio example 3.03.) This and all such patterns in which the articulated accents (here, even-numbered beats) work against the normally strong metric accents (on odd-numbered beats) produces a clash of foreground against background called syncopation. Another rhythmic term we covered in chapter 1 is offbeats, which fall in the spaces between beats: ONE—and—two—and—a—Three—and—a—four—and, for example. Note that here, each beat is divided by an offbeat on "and," and that the second halves of beats two and three are further subdivided on "a." (Recall different offbeat patterns in Web audio examples 1.12 and 3.04.)

Many pop and rock musics are composed of a rhythmic backdrop known as the groove, a regularly repeating pattern in drums, bass, rhythm guitar, keyboards, and backing vocals—the group's rhythm section—against which freer rhythms will be performed by lead guitar, winds, lead vocals, and any other soloing forces. The groove's pattern may be entirely regular (Donovan's "Mellow Yellow") or may be syncopated in some way (the Zombies' "She's Not There"), but its constant repetition and background status lend it a known regularity that keeps the less predictable soloists in the spotlight. Our path will begin with regular meters and rhythmic patterns that form background grooves, and will then move to irregular meters and asymmetrical rhythmic techniques, before covering tempo relationships and ending with larger-scale rhythm at the level of the phrase.

Quadruple meter is so strongly the norm in our repertoire that music in other meters that has been borrowed into pop from other genres is often converted to the four-beat structure. Consider the Toys' "A Lover's Concerto." As written by Bach, this tune was once a triple-meter dance, a minuet. In the hands of songwriters Linzer and Randell, it became a quadruple pop song: "HOW gentle is the RAIN that FALLS lightly on the MEAD-ow" (downbeats are capitalized; note the four beats per bar). But whether slow (The Platters' "Smoke Gets In Your Eyes"), moderate (Simon and Garfunkel's "Sounds of Silence"), or fast (the "nice and rough" section of Ike and Tina Turner's "Proud Mary"), four-beats-per bar is standard.

Quadruple meter falls into two categories, based on how the beat is divided. The beat is commonly bisected into two equal parts, with a single offbeat per beat (ONE—and—two—and—Three—and—four—and). (Recall the offbeat ride pattern in Web audio example 1.09.) This meter and beat division is referred to as *simple* quadruple meter. If, however, the beat is divided evenly into *three* equal parts (with two offbeats for every beat: ONE—trip—let—two—trip—let—Three—trip—let—four—trip—let, each syllable falling evenly), we have what is called *compound* quadruple meter. One example is Fats Domino's "Blueberry Hill," in which the ride cymbal is given three even taps per beat. The piano articulates the three parts per beat in Don Cherry's "Band of Gold," the Platters' "Only You (And You Alone)," Pat Boone's "Love Letters in the Sand," and many others. (Web audio example 3.05 is a piano illustration of compound time, each beat divided into three equal parts.) Although not nearly as common as the simple beat division, compound time is not at all rare—consider the triplet divisions in songs as different as the Beatles' "Norwegian Wood (This Bird Has Flown)" and Sly and the Family Stone's "Hot Fun in the Summertime." Compound quadruple meter is probably most usually heard at slow tempos, as in Elvis Presley's "One Night," Brenda Lee's "I'm Sorry," James Brown's "It's a Man's, Man's, Man's, Man's World," the Beach Boys' "In My Room," and Bob Dylan's "Just Like a Woman."

Songs are most often in either simple or compound meter, but occasionally there is mixture of the two. Often, a song in simple meter will borrow a bar or two of compound divisions, usually in a transitional or retransitional flurry on the drums, as in Herman's Hermits' "Can't You Hear My Heartbeat" (0:39–0:40), Donovan's "Mellow Yellow" (0:40–0:44), and the Turtles' "Happy Together" (0:38–0:39). (Listen to Web audio example 1.14.) In exceedingly unusual cases, a song may move from compound to simple division or vice versa, stretching or shrinking the value of the beat if the division durations remain equal as their number per beat changes. This occurs at a propitious point in the Beatles' "The End." Note how, following the extensive three-man guitar interlude, this song opens ("And in the end...") with three piano chords per beat; without warning, at the word "equal," the accompaniment slows down to group *four* chords per beat (the chords continuing at the same rate), greatly slowing the song into a broad tempo, to portray a verbal equation with an unusual musical one, a third of the initial beat equaling the duration of a fourth of the eventual beat. This change is roughly predicted at the warning, "Wait a minute! Watch what you're doing with your time" at 0:42 in the Grateful Dead's "Cream Puff War." (Web audio example 4.21 includes a similar tempo modulation: Note how towards the end of the triple-meter middle section (at 1:03), the piano begins to play two equal chords in the time of three, and then maintains these with offbeats, four equal notes per bar. The violin joins in the new duple division and at 1:16, returns with the first theme at a more stately, broader tempo, continuing in the new beat lengths created by the tempo modulation.)

Despite the great preponderance of quadruple meter, triple time is heard in a good deal of pop music. And this is nearly universally *simple triple meter* (with each of the three beats divided into two equal parts), as *compound triple meter* is virtually nonexistent (the Beatles' "Dig a Pony" being an uncommon exception). Songs in triple meter can be slow (Debbie Reynolds's "Tammy," Aretha Franklin's "A Natural Woman (You Make Me Feel Like)," Cream's "Pressed Rat and Warthog"), but are generally faster, at a waltz tempo ("A Wonderful Guy" from *South Pacific,* David Seville and the Chipmunks' "The Chipmunk Song (Christmas Don't Be Late)," Henry Mancini's "Moon River," and the Mothers of Invention's "Concentration Moon"). Triple meter often lilts with sentiment, as in Grace Kelly and Bing Crosby's "True Love," Elvis Presley's "Old Shep," the Everly Brothers' "Ebony Eyes," and "My Favorite Things" from *The Sound of Music*." In "The Lonesome Death of Hattie Carroll," Bob Dylan suggests an urbane social context with a waltz backdrop, making the song's thoughtless murder seem all the more barbaric.

Other meters exist as well. Some songs are in duple meter, with only two beats per bar. Occasionally, these may be in simple duple meter (Dusty Springfield's "Wishin' and Hopin'," Tommy Roe's "Dizzy," Blood, Sweat and Tears' "Meagan's Gypsy Eyes"), but much more prevalent is compound duple meter, with each of the two beats divided into three equal parts, as in the Platters' "The Great Pretender," Louis Armstrong's "What a Wonderful World," Bob Dylan's "A Hard Rain's a-Gonna Fall," Barbara Mason's "Yes, I'm Ready," and Tom Jones's "Delilah." The Beatles' "Being for the Benefit of Mr. Kite" shifts from duple to one section in triple meter in order to portray a horse's waltz steps. Other meters are irregular and will be discussed at a later point.

Before we get to those irregular meters, there are some regular patterns that occur in repetitive rhythmic designs, which help establish a song's groove, that we should cover first. One is the shuffle, the most common factor in compound meters. In the shuffle, each beat is evenly divided into three parts, but normally only the first and third part of each beat are sounded, leading to a swinging, uneven long-short, long-short ONE— (trip)—let—two— (trip)—let pattern, a lazy sort of beat division. Think of the piano introduction to the Monkees' "Daydream Believer." Jackie Brenston's "Rocket 88" sounded the shuffle, also heard in Johnny Burnett's "You're Sixteen," The Doors' "Roadhouse Blues," Canned Heat's "On the Road Again," and John Sebastian's "You're a Big Boy Now." In 1961, Kokomo gave us "Asia Minor," a shuffle version of a tune from Grieg's Piano Concerto in A Minor. Sometimes, as in Solomon Burke's "Got to Get You Off My Mind," the shuffle is carried in the bass, but it is much more frequently articulated by rhythm guitar (as in the intro to the long version of the Guess Who's "American Woman") or piano (Howlin' Wolf's "How Many More Years"). (Various shuffles were heard in Web audio example 3.06.)

Much less informal and lazy sounding is the more rigid "dotted" rhythm, so-named for its musical notation. In this division of pairs of beats into two uneven parts, the first part is *three* times longer than the second part: ONE— (+2)—and—Three—(+4)—and. (The bass has a dotted rhythm in Web audio example 2.07, as do the harpsichord's repeated-note bass line in the intro to Web audio example 3.24 and the keyboard's top part in Web audio example 8.03.) It was once a favorite rhythm of bassist Paul McCartney, who so divides every first half of the bar in the Beatles' "She Loves You" (verse, 0:13–0:25) and "I Want to Hold Your Hand" (verse, 0:08–0:18, and bridge, 0:51–1:01), each passage sounding ONE—(+2)—and—Three—(+4+).

The ONE—(2)—and—Three—four rhythm is associated with the Ronettes ("Be My Baby"), but it also was taken up by the Grass Roots for the verse of "The River Is Wide." The Easybeats' "Friday On My Mind" has beats that are anything but easy—the verse features a guitar dividing each beat into harsh equal halves, and the bass drum takes a solo in two bars of dotted rhythm between the second verse and coda. In the Cyrkle's "Red Rubber Ball," the verse is gentle enough, but the chorus ("I think it's gonna be all right, yes, the worst is over now…") introduces a new urgency with dotted rhythms pervading the ensemble; dancers to this recording could feel and express the loss of relaxation. The compulsive stress-every-beat groove in the bass drum, tambourine, and handclaps of Napoleon XIV's "They're Coming to Take Me Away, Ha-Haaa!," is made more tense by the dotted rhythm in the snare.

The dotted rhythm is also part of the famous Bo Diddley "beat": ONE—(2)—and—Three—four—(1)—and—two—Three—(4). (The Bo Diddley rhythm was the basis of Web audio example 9.15.) This is a well-used rhythm guitar figure in Bo's songs, whether original to him or covered by others (as in the Rolling Stones' "Mona (I Need You Baby)" and Quicksilver Messenger Service's "Who Do You Love"), in those of Buddy Holly ("Not Fade Away"), and in many others (Rick Nelson's "Be Bop Baby," the verse of Elvis Presley's "(Marie's the Name) His Latest Flame," Dick Dale and the Deltones' "Surfing Drums," the Strangeloves' "I Want Candy," and with an acoustic guitar in one album-only mix of Simon and Garfunkel's "Mrs. Robinson."

Another regular "background" rhythm is heard with compound divisions. This is the bolero, which divides the two weakest beats of quadruple meter into three parts each: ONE—two—trip—let—Three—four—trip—let. (Recall Web audio example 9.08.) Naturally, this is the basis of the Jeff Beck Group's "Bolero," but it is also the backbone of Roy Orbison's "Running Scared." The fourth beat is suppressed and the downbeat emphasized by a preceding offbeat in the tango rhythm: and—ONE—two—Three—(4)—and—ONE—two—Three, as in Hugo Winterhalter's "Blue Tango" Alternatively, another Latin rhythm will suppress the second beat, as in Buddy Holly's "Heartbeat" and the accompaniment to "Maria" from *West Side Story*: ONE—(2)—and—Three—four, also heard in a busier version, ONE—and—(2)—and—Three—and—four—and, in Caterina Valente's "The Breeze and I (Andalucia)" and Vaughn Monroe's "Ballerina." Another Latin pattern achieving popularity in the late '50s and early '60s was the cha-cha, ONE—two—Three—and—four (Dave "Baby" Cortez's "Rinky Tink," Brian Hyland's "Itsy Bitsy Teenie Weenie Yellow Polkadot Bikini"). (Recall Web audio example 2.40.) The samba (Paul Anka, "Eso Beso (That Kiss!)"), calypso (Arthur Lyman, "Yellow Bird"), mambo (Perez Prado, "Cherry Pink and Apple Blossom White"), and bossa nova (Stan Getz and Charlie Byrd,

"Desafinado") also made landfall in the United States. These Latin grooves are all marked by strong downbeats and strongly accented simple beat divisions.

Irregular patterns

Popular music includes a wealth of examples of irregular patterns at both the deeper metric level and that of surface rhythms. Irregular meters take two forms: those by which the measures have identical recurring numbers of beats but the numbers are not divisible by two or by three (making for an asymmetrical five or seven beats per measure), and those where meter is not

> **Irregular rhythmic patterns:** asymmetrical meters; mixed and changing meter; combined meters; stop time; the hocket; syncopation and cross-rhythms; rubato.

regularly maintained, but may change from bar to bar (so that several bars of quadruple meter might be followed by others in triple meter). Whereas either sort of asymmetrical pattern may recur with enough regularity to be predictable and fade into the background, they remain irregular at their core.

The former type, repetitive asymmetrical meters, are heard less often than the second type. Meters with five beats per measure, immortalized in Dave Brubeck's "Take Five," are also heard in the verse of the Turtles' "Grim Reaper of Love," the introductory tattoo of Cream's "White Room," and all of Lalo Schifrin's theme from "Mission Impossible" and Blind Faith's "Do What You Like." (Such a quintuple meter is heard in the ostinato of Web audio example 2.28 and in the song sketched in Web audio example 11.13.) A septuple meter, with seven beats per measure, is also used by Cream ("Passing the Time") and in other rock numbers such as the Mothers of Invention's "Dog Breath, In the Year of the Plague" and "Oh No," the interlude (3:27–3:49) and coda (4:29+) of the Grateful Dead's "Uncle John's Band," and the bridge of The Band's "Just Another Whistle Stop," but also in the opening (through 0:21) of the less progressive Monkees' "Love Is Only Sleeping." Ten beats per measure? Try Ginger Baker's Air Force's "Don't Care" (accented as 3 + 3 + 3 + 1). Eleven? The Grateful Dead's "The Eleven" is an obvious choice. Perhaps rock's most complex asymmetrical meter is heard in Soft Machine's "Box 25/4 Lid," in which a repeated twenty-five-beat pattern in the fuzz bass doubled by piano, heard five times running, is accented as 13 + 12. These last song titles make clear how self-conscious the artists are in creating and performing such longer irregular patterns.

Much more common is the phenomenon of mixed meter, whereby the number of beats can change from bar to bar. First, it should be explained that what we're *not* talking about here is *changing* meter, where one section of a song might be in quadruple meter and another section, in triple (as in Web audio example 4.21). This is fairly frequently heard, as when the bridge of the Beatles' "She Said She Said" leaves the quadruple-meter verse behind for a new triple meter passage to underscore the reference to a different "time," that of childhood, when the middle section (1:06–1:13) of The Mamas and the Papas' "Trip, Stumble and Fall" moves from quadruple to triple time to suggest the title, or when Crosby, Stills and Nash seem to introduce a new quadruple-meter song in the midst of "49 Bye-Byes," which had begun in triple meter. Like these cases, the Parade recomposes the meter of the verses of "Sunshine Girl," all of which are quadruple but the last, which appears in triple time. Stranger is the case of the Marvelettes' "He's a Good Guy (Yes He Is)," which abandons its quadruple-meter verse at 0:33–0:41 to quote the folk tune, "Did You Ever See a Lassie," in its own triple meter.

These and many other examples contrast some sections with others in different meters, but the sections themselves are in unchanging meters. More interesting are songs exhibiting mixed meter, where often-unpredictable changes of meter occur within the phrase. (Recall Web audio example 11.16.) Such techniques would prove quite challenging and rich for those dancing along. Usually, chord changes introduce new downbeats that might also be marked by vocal entries or rhythm-section patterns; otherwise, the irregularly spaced barlines would be impossible to detect. Sometimes, the meter is fundamentally regular except every so often, a beat seems to go missing; the verses of the Beatles' "All You Need Is Love" are basically in quadruple meter, but the second, fourth, and eighth bars all have three beats only, at nonvocal points where it seems that John Lennon is relieving the listener of "dead time." In Marvin Gaye's "Pretty Little Baby," each of the verses' four lines follows two triple-meter bars sung by Marvin with a single two-beat bar of backing vocals. Likewise, three quadruple bars are followed by single three-beat bars in the verses of the Dead's "Uncle John's Band." On other occasions, extra beats appear; this is true in the Beatles' "Across the Universe" (the fourth bar of which has an extra, fifth, beat) and Janis Joplin's "My Baby" (where three bars of triple meter are answered by a single bar of four beats).

But more often, meters change so often that no such underlying regularity-gone-amok can be suggested. Composer Burt Bacharach is widely known for this technique, as in his "(Theme From) Valley of the Dolls," as sung by Dionne Warwick, which features a woozy, all-questions-and-no-resolution attitude in the verse, underscored by waves of contracting and expanding bars containing four, then three, then two, then three, then five beats each, an irregular pattern that is then repeated. This is mimicked a bit in Rotary Connection's "Amuse." Highly irregular combinations of meters characterize the Beatles' "Good Morning Good Morning," Every Mothers' Son's "Come On Down to My Boat," and the Rascals' "Real Thing." The lack of rigid, predictable meter lends a gently free, weightless quality with no direction home to the Grateful Dead's "Easy Wind," Crosby, Stills and Nash's "Guinnevere," and Jimi Hendrix's "Drifting."

Much more experimental are the rare cases in which no barlines are recognized by the entire ensemble, which may consist of different people simultaneously playing in different meters. In one passage (1:47–2:02) of the Beatles' "Happiness Is a Warm Gun," the opening twenty-one bars of which had contained six *different* meters, Ringo drums out a *simple* quadruple pattern for 4.5 bars while everyone else agrees to a *compound* quadruple meter, completing three bars in the same amount of time. In the opening section of the Dead's "St. Stephen," Phil Lesh plays double stops in the bass in a compound duple meter at 88 beats per minute, while Jerry Garcia plays guitar in a simple triple meter exactly one-third slower, 132 beats per minute. Surely

Photo 12.01. First pressings of first albums. Shown are covers for the Mothers of Invention's *Cruising with Ruben & The Jets, Lumpy Gravy, Freak Out!, Absolutely Free, Uncle Meat,* and *We're Only in It For the Money* (a parody of *Pepper* thought so confusing to buyers it was folded inside out), and Zappa's first solo effort, *Hot Rats.* (Photo: Annie Eastman)

representing the extreme in meter combination is the Mothers of Invention's "Toads of the Short Forest," midway through which Frank Zappa announces that one drummer is playing in septuple meter; the organist is in quintuple meter; and a second drummer, tambourine, and bass are in triple time.

There are numerous techniques whereby the meter may be regular, but foreground rhythms may break out of a continuous regular pattern to provide contrast and emphasis. In fact, the continuing regularity of the underlying meter is crucial for the success of the foreground effect. We shall organize these approaches from large scale to small. By far, the most drastic and most commonly heard such technique is that known as stop time (noted in some 245 examples from our repertoire), where everything suddenly comes to a stop—while the meter continues, without articulation—for either a dramatic universal silence (interrupted by the returning lead singer following the bridge of the Hollies' "He Ain't Heavy, He's My Brother," from 2:26, or uninterrupted for a frozen silent moment of two beats at 1:57 in Crosby, Stills, Nash and Young's "Everybody I Love You"), for a single soloist to continue without backing (as for the bassist in Chuck Berry's "I'm Talking About You"), or for a drastic reduction in forces to feature a small group without the continuing support of its brethren (as in the horns' 1—3—5—♭7—9 arpeggiation at 0:18–0:20 in James Brown's "I Got You (I Feel Good)"). (Recall Web audio example 2.24, where the rhythm guitar gets out of the way of the lead's whammy, or Web audio example 5.01, where the guitar stops time for the vocal entry.)

Stop time often serves a word-painting function, clearing the decks for a lone sound effect that acts as an emblem. Thus, each verse of Buzz Clifford's "Baby Sittin' Boogie" ends with stop time for a baby's babbling. Stop time makes room for repeated exhalations in Jerry Lee Lewis's "Breathless," conga heartbeats and crickets in Tommy James and the Shondells' "I Think We're Alone Now," tambourine and tom tom in the Lemon Pipers' "Green Tambourine," rattling chains in the Classics IV's "Spooky," snare "knocks" in Eddie Floyd's "Knock on Wood" and ceiling knocks in Tony Orlando and Dawn's "Knock Three Times," a woodsaw in the Turtles' "Sound Asleep," and a referee's whistle in the Mothers' "Status Back Baby." The intention is a bit more metaphorical in the itch-scratching electric-guitar finger vibrato that ends each verse of the Coasters' "Poison Ivy." And the lead singer's text is appropriately surrounded by sudden silence at "as you *stop* to say hello" in Roy Orbison's "Crying," at "Excuse me!" in the Jimi Hendrix Experience's "Purple Haze," in the most vulnerable lines of the Animals' "We Gotta Get Outta This Place" and the Seekers' "Georgy Girl," and in the most suggestive unspoken imagery of the Troggs' "Wild Thing." Stop time allows a delicate nylon-string guitar the acoustic space to almost "break just like a little girl" in Bob Dylan's "Just Like a Woman." Very often, the stop time allows for a simple drum fill with no pretense to extramusical meaning—see, for instance, just before the bridge of Betty Everett's "Shoop Shoop Song (It's In His Kiss)" or the retransitions of the Chiffons' "He's So Fine" and Max Frost and the Troopers' "Shape of Things to Come."

Early in rock history, stop time allowed for the placement of a jokey interjection, sometimes from a bass singer. See Mel Blanc's lines in Pat Boone's "Speedy Gonzalez," the Popeye-like interruption in the Orlons' "Cross Fire!," the title appearing in the Champs' otherwise instrumental "Tequila," impersonations of various authority figures in Eddie Cochran's "Summertime Blues," and Will Jones's bass interjections in the Coasters' "Yakety Yak" ("don't talk back"), "Charlie Brown" ("why is everybody always pickin' on me?"), and "Along Came Jones" ("slow-talkin' Jones"). Given this tradition, it's hard to know if laughs are intended or not when Nick Massi places his bass-vocal texture-breakers in the Four Seasons' "Sherri" ("why don't you..."), "Big Girls Don't Cry" ("silly boy..."), and "Walk Like a Man" ("he said...").

Most appearances of stop time, however, can be heard for heavy musical drama, articulating points of tension in the form with sudden texture changes as if the musicians were hoping to capture a heart standing still. This is most effective in the retransition from the bridge, when the momentum has built to a big V chord crying out for resolution. In fact, the singer often cries alone at just this point, with one or two bars of stop time underneath, unleashing cascades of heartfelt melismas. Witness the ends of the bridges of Elvis Presley's "Love Me," Johnnie Ray's "You Don't Owe Me a Thing," Jackie Wilson's "Lonely Teardrops," Jimmy Jones's "Handy Man," Paul Anka's "Puppy Love," and the Beatles' "This Boy" and "Oh! Darling." Sometimes this point underlines belligerence, as "with my two fists of iron but I'm going nowhere" in Dion's "The Wanderer." Sometimes the stop time catches the singer asleep at the wheel, as with Ritchie Valens's late reentry in "La Bamba." Sometimes, the retransition is taken not by the voice, but by the lead guitar, leading then into the solo as does a forward-lurching Ted Nugent in the Amboy Dukes's "Journey to the Center of the Mind." Sometimes, stop time marks the ends of sections other than the bridge, as with the refrain of Dion's "A Teenager in Love" and Aretha Franklin's "I Never Loved a Man" and "Baby I Love You," the chorus-ending break in Buddy Holly's "That'll Be the Day," the verse-ending line in his "Think It Over," the ending of the prechorus in Gary Lewis and the Playboys' "She's Just My Style" and the Monkees' "I'm a Believer," and the coda of the Marvelettes' "Please Mr. Postman."

Stop time is inimically tied to the twelve-bar blues, occurring very often in either the first or the third, but not the second, of the three lines of that structure. The entire first line of four bars is often unaccompanied, except perhaps by downbeat stabs, with the instrumental ensemble entering in earnest only for the fifth bar and following. This is characteristic of Carl Perkins's "Blue Suede Shoes," Roy Orbison's "Ooby Dooby," Chuck Berry's

"Too Much Monkey Business," the third verse of Little Richard's "Lucille," the Shirelles' "Boys," the Regents' "Barbara-Ann," and Creedence Clearwater Revival's "Travelin' Band." The third line of the blues, bars 9–12, are interrupted by stop time at various junctures: bars 9–11 of Gary U.S. Bonds's "New Orleans," bars 9–10 of Elvis Presley's "I Got Stung" and the Cookies' "Don't Say Nothin' Bad (About My Baby)," bar 10 of Chubby Checker's "The Twist" (and its equivalent spot in the slow-grinding twenty-four bar blues of Wilson Pickett's "Mustang Sally"), and bars 11–12 of Joey Dee and the Starliters' "Peppermint Twist."

Somewhat related to the effect of stop time is the hocket. Here, one singer or instrumentalist has a brief break—often just a beat or even a half-beat—that is filled by someone else. (Web audio example 11.18 features a hocket in the bass line, with backbeats coming from the guitar heard to the left of center, and the remainder of the bass line assigned to the synth, heard right of center.) This can encompass just a single glimpse through the window, as when the bass drum takes the vacant second beat in the refrain of the Monotones' "Book of Love," or involve a complex set of relationships among performers, as in the ensemble of speakers in "Rock Island" from *The Music Man* or in the ecstatic, rapidly alternating backing vocals in the studio recording of The Who's "Christmas." Often, the accompanimental groove is marked by hockets (follow the syncopated drums, Stratocaster, and bass working with the backbeat tambourine and rhythm guitar through the verse of the Beatles' "Ticket to Ride" and the drums and bass in their "In My Life," and listen for the right-hand piano chords off the third and fourth beats in the verses of the 5th Dimension's "Stoned Soul Picnic"). Sometimes the hocket effect is reserved for special punctuation (as in the big finish, "New (!) Old- (!) Fashioned Way" in Brenda Lee's "Rockin' Around the Christmas Tree" or, in the far less gaudy piano octaves on 5 interjecting at 0:50 in Sam and Dave's "Soul Man"). The hocket-based groove is in fact intrinsic to funk; note how the bass is out during the brass stabs in James Brown's "Papa's Got a Brand New Bag" and "I Got You (I Feel Good)," perhaps suggesting the title food substance in "Mother Popcorn (You Got to Have a Mother for Me)." See also how the bass and snare share time in the verse of the Animals' "Don't Let Me Be Misunderstood," how the chimes interact with the clarinets and bass in the Beatles' "When I'm Sixty-Four" (0:57–1:07), and how the bass, fuzz guitar, and two volume-pedal-controlled lead guitars work against each other in the break, 1:19–1:47, of the Balloon Farm's "A Question of Temperature." Hocket-based grooves appear in the Drifters' "Under the Boardwalk" and Cher's "You Better Sit Down Kids," but nowhere as masterfully as in the Zombies' "Time of the Season," a study in texture. Its introduction joins the Fender Precision bass, hi-hat, a highly reverbed woodblock, and an unvoiced "kah" from the back of the throat, all in a weave of hockets; in the prechorus

(0:25–0:32), a chick guitar adds to the mix at two well-placed points per measure. Although it's not an example of hocket because the effect is on a larger scale, Janis Joplin's "Half Moon" has an interesting texture in that the piano and lead guitar stay out of each other's way, dividing their shared space in half.

Surface rhythmic effects include all sorts of syncopation, the accenting of normally weak beats or parts of beats. Sometimes these are irregular accents, sometimes they are recurring groups of accents that may offset the meter by half-beats or may thoroughly contradict the meter; occasionally, syncopation involves the accenting of irregular beat divisions. We'll take up each of these techniques in order. First, though, a negative example: it's a total *lack* of syncopation that thoroughly whitens Pat Boone's style in such songs as "Ain't That a Shame" and "Don't Forbid Me," making him just the wrong person to cover Little Richard. Irregular syncopation may be manifested in short drum patterns, as in Cream's "Sunshine of Your Love" (underneath the chorus) and retransitional lead-ins in Cream's "SWLABR" (1:15–1:17) and Steppenwolf's "Born to Be Wild" (2:06+), or in any number of Jerry Garcia's guitar solos with the Dead. In very rare cases, syncopation can impact the normal stresses of verbal language; this technique marks Donovan's early hits, as when normally weak second syllables of words fall on strong metric beats for "crystal" and "spectacles" in "Epistle to Dippy" (0:39–0:41).

Sometimes a pattern of syncopation may be repeated, bar after bar; the groove of Blood, Sweat and Tears' "God Bless the Child" divides the twelve divisions of a compound quadruple meter into groups of $3 + 2 + 4 + 3$ beat parts, obviously arriving at the third accent too early. A cool, swinging effect is achieved in the repeated (1)—two—Three—and—(4)—and groove of Bobby Darin's "Irresistible You," the Impressions' "You Must Believe Me," the Shirelles' "Love Is a Swinging Thing," Neil Sedaka's "Little Devil," and Etta James's "Something's Got a Hold on Me." A climax is reached in the pre-chorus of the Rascals' "Good Lovin'" by repeating the pattern, ONE—two—and—(3)—and—four, on shouted "yeah's," and following up with chromatic guitar chords articulating II, an emphatic artifical dominant, on all offbeats. A simpler repeated accent of the offbeat is heard in Simon and Garfunkel's "The Dangling Conversation," the second verse of which has Artie sing a half-beat behind Paul for the words "in syncopated time." (Recall the guitars moving in contrary motion in the second half of Web audio example 2.50.) Backbeats are brought out more violently by the second- and fourth-beat crash cymbals alternating with the word "Stop!" in the Hollies' "Stop Stop Stop," and a more ecstatic effect is the orgasmic culmination in offbeat backing vocalists' "wop wop wop" on the second halves of beats 1, 2, and 3 for the "fifteen minutes for blowin' my top" in the stop-time bridge retransition of the Dominoes' "Sixty Minute Man." A sneaky accenting of offbeats, heard before the true strong parts of beats has been established, leads to very off-center introductions in the Beatles' "I Want to Hold Your Hand" and "She's a Woman."

Syncopation that contradicts the meter occurs especially when repeated accent-marked groups are of a different length than the bars themselves. In the Four Lads' "Standing On the Corner," the sequenced phrase, "watchin' all the girls, watchin' all the girls, watchin' all the girls...," accents the first of every three beats, even though the song continues in four-beat bars. Such cross-rhythms also mark the stubborn refrain in Sammy Davis Jr.'s (and the McGuire Sisters' far less supple) "Something's Gotta Give," the chorus of Little Anthony and the Imperials' "Goin' Out of My Head," and the opening lines of verses in the Beatles' "Mean Mr. Mustard." These cross rhythms pit strong beats against weak in an irregular way; this can also happen at the half-beat level, as in the melody of Ernie Fields' "In the Mood," the instrumental passages (as at 0:14–0:18) of The Who's "Sensation," the repeated guitar figure in the solo (1:06–1:22) of Manfred Mann's Earth Band's "Blinded By the Light," and, at a much slower tempo, the repeated pairs of guitar notes (alternating bent and straight articulations) in the intro to the Rolling Stones' "Time Is On My Side."

Our final type of syncopation involves the accenting of parts of beats not normally articulated by combining mismatched divisions. One text-related example of six evenly spaced accents in the time of four underscores the line, "Robbin' people with a six-gun" in the Bobby Fuller Four's "I Fought the Law." This effect occurs most often in dramatically stubborn retransitions. Consider the line, "my smile is my makeup I wear since my breakup with you" (2:11–2:16) in Smokey Robinson's "The Tracks of My Tears," and similar climaxes in the chorus of the Righteous Brothers' "You've Lost That Lovin' Feeling" (0:30–0:32) and the end of the organ solo (just before the return of the tattoo lead-in) of The Doors' "Light My Fire." The same effect, six in the time of four, pulls back the reins to cap off the excitement in the coda of the Beatles' "I Want to Hold Your Hand" (2:18–2:20) and illustrates the crash-cymbal-enhanced "fussing and fighting" in the bridge of their "We Can Work It Out." (Both Web audio examples 3.22 and 3.23 end with six in the time of four.) A more unusual instance occurs in the Jefferson Airplane's "Embryonic Journey," where two finger-picked acoustic guitars often play the parts of six against four, once even articulating five against four.

All of the aforementioned rhythmic techniques are of easily measured, simple proportions. In other words, the ratios between durations we've thus far related would all involve fairly low numbers: 1:1, 2:1, 3:1, 3:2, 4:1, 4:3. Only just at the end of the preceding paragraph have we found a ratio as complex as 5:4. But there is a much more subtle sort of rhythmic displacement at work in most popular styles that can be so irregular that the ratios involved would be exceedingly complex, and in fact, there has never arisen a system to notate for performance the relationships involved. Such rhythmic shifts take place on the absolute surface of expression, usually improvised by the lead singer or soloist, but in some styles they may be adopted by the rhythm section. This involves articulating notes not exactly *on* the beat on which they function, but slightly *ahead of* or *behind* the beat. This sort of stretching of the beat in one part, while the other parts maintain a regular measurement of time, is referred to in classical performance as *rubato* (the time is borrowed or "robbed" from one part of a beat and shifted to another), but we might think of it as a sensitive placement that gives a soloist one more means of rendering their individuality. (The guitar plays behind the beat in Web audio example 9.20; note also the emphatic delay of the guitar's chord at 0:10 in Web audio example 2.15.)

It was in the light jazz-flavored world of adult-contemporary singers— Peggy Lee, Nancy Wilson—that this technique first appeared in our repertoire; one can just imagine a conductor watching every move of Sammy Davis Jr. singing the opening of "What Kind of Fool Am I," or Nina Simone in "I Put a Spell On You," trying to keep time. Barbra Streisand's "People" is sung with very free rhythm—sometimes eccentric, at other times regular and soaring. This is imitated by David Clayton-Thomas in Blood, Sweat and Tears numbers such as "Blues—Part II." There is also a strong bluegrass contribution, as captured by John Sebastian's flexible rhythm (along with flexible pitch and grammar) in the Lovin' Spoonful's "Nashville Cats." This train derails in such performances as those of Mrs. Miller, the soprano with the hideous vibrato who sang so totally without rhythmic control, inadvertently stretching and pulling as though she had momentarily forgotten the words or just forgotten to breathe, as in the lamest possible buildup to a climax (2:14–2:21) in "Downtown." But this is an extreme of singularity to which few aspire.

Nearly all stretching of the beat involves placement *behind* the beat, but Dusty Springfield, for example, anticipates the beat in the first verse of "The Windmills of Your Mind." And in "Just Like a Woman," the ever-unconventional Bob Dylan rushes in excited anticipation in such lines as "aw, you fake" (3:13–3:16) and "you make love just like a woman" (3:21–3:24). Singing behind the beat creates a relaxed, cool, laid-back atmosphere, and has a long heritage; one can recall how Bing Crosby would begin every phrase late in songs such as "Good Night, Sweetheart," and how Judy Garland milks every ounce of expression from "Over the Rainbow" by singing behind the beat. Patti Page suggests a lazy beach-hammock luxury with her vocal placement in "Old Cape Cod." Patsy Cline's vocal style is marked by singing far behind the beat, as in "Sweet Dreams (Of You)" and "She's Got You," a style seemingly copied by the Everly Brothers in the bridge of "Don't Blame Me."

Sam Cooke's "Cupid" and "You Send Me" have their uncontrolled moments, as in the latter's bridge, "at first, I thought it was innnnfatuation, but nooo, it's lasted soooo long." Some extreme examples from the '60s include the Shirelles' "Dedicated to the One I Love," Little Esther Phillips's "Release Me," and a half-asleep-sounding Ray Davies in the Kinks' "Tired of Waiting for You." Interesting are places where two performers or one double-tracked soloist must match their behind-the-beat performances, but this is achieved marvelously by the two trumpets in Mongo Santamaria's "Watermelon Man" and in Little Peggy March's twice-sung vocal for "I Will Follow Him" (as at 1:52–1:54).

Rhythm-section examples of *rubato* also tend to begin with the night-club circuit; note the sensitive rhythmic placement in the piano introduction to Johnny Mathis's "Chances Are." Jerry Wexler claims to have invented the late-arriving beat in the rhythm section in producing such tracks as Wilson Pickett's "Mustang Sally," but this technique was certainly practiced in the Chess studios before Wexler brought it to Stax. And note the sultry far-behind-the-beat snare in the Rolling Stones' "Honest I Do," or the appropriately nonchalant, slow-as-molasses tambourine in their ever-patient "Time Is On My Side."

Tempo

Slow dances, warp-speed rock and roll. The rate at which the beats go by, a concept referred to as tempo, has a great impact on a song's character and meaning. Such rates are normally represented as beats per minute. Table 12.01 shows all the tempos found in a sample of 570 songs from our period, indicates the relative rarity or commonness of each tempo by giving its percentage of the total sample, and lists representative songs for each. The table consists of two charts, one for songs in which beats are divided by two (in simple meters) and the other for songs in which beats are divided by three (in compound meters). It should be acknowledged that tempos are not always maintained metronomically without fluctuation, but the assignments in the table are certainly close enough for rock and roll.

> **Tempo:** slow and fast tempos; the slow introduction; the coda standstill, cadenza and grand pause; acceleration and other tempo changes; the half- and double-time close.

A few things become evident from studying tempo. The Mothers of Invention's album, *Cruising With Ruben and the Jets,* contains some of rock music's most glacially moving songs—"I'm Not Satisfied" (in simple meter) and "Anything" (compound), both among the slowest entries in table 12.01. Although the basic tempo of the Rolling Stones' "19th Nervous Breakdown" is a moderate 96 bpm, its frantic beat subdivisions make it seem twice as fast,

Table 12.01 Prevalence of various tempos in simple and compound meters in an unscientifically selected sample of 570 recordings, with representative examples

Given: Tempo in beats per minute (prevalence of that tempo in total sample expressed as a percentage); Selected examples at each tempo. For comparison, the mean prevalence of each tempo marking is (1.4%).

Simple Meters

38 (0.2%) Mothers of Invention, "I'm Not Satisfied"

50 (0.2%) The Originals, "Baby, I'm for Real"

56 (0.4%) Steppenwolf, "Hootchie Kootchie Man"; Jimi Hendrix Experience, "Voodoo Chile"

58 (0.7%) Platters, "Smoke Gets in Your Eyes"; N. Simone, "I Loves You, Porgy"; Blind Faith, "Presence of the Lord"

60 (0.4%) P. Boone, "I Almost Lost My Mind"; Casinos, "Then You Can Tell Me Goodbye"

63 (1.1%) D. Washington, "What a Diff'rence a Day Makes"; B. E. King, "I (Who Have Nothing)"; B. Dylan, "A Hard Rain's a-Gonna Fall"; Rolling Stones, "Heart of Stone"; A. Neville, "Tell It Like It Is"; The Band, "I Shall Be Released"

66 (0.4%) Beatles, "The Long and Winding Road," "Something"

69 (0.7%) C. Francis, "Mama"; Jimi Hendrix Experience, "1983...(A Merman I Should Turn to Be)"; Bee Gees, "I Started a Joke"; Crosby, Stills, Nash and Young, "Almost Cut My Hair"

72 (1.2%) McGuire Sisters, "He"; Impressions, "People Get Ready"; Procol Harum, "A Whiter Shade of Pale"; The Band, "The Weight," "Up on Cripple Creek"; Bee Gees, "Lonely Days"

76 (2.1%) P. Page, "Allegheny Moon"; Drifters, "Save the Last Dance for Me"; B. Dylan, "Ballad of a Thin Man"; Beatles, "Hey Jude," "Let It Be"; Hollies, "He Ain't Heavy, He's My Brother"; P. McCartney, "Maybe I'm Amazed"; Grateful Dead, "Black Peter"

80 (2.6%) Four Lads, "Moments to Remember"; Dion and the Belmonts, "A Teenager in Love"; Jimi Hendrix Experience, "The Wind Cries Mary"; Donovan, "Hurdy Gurdy Man"; Big Brother and the Holding Co., "Piece of My Heart"; Beatles, "Come Together"

84 (3.0%) B. Vaughn, "Melody of Love"; Dion and the Belmonts, "Runaround Sue"; B. Vinton, "Blue Velvet"; C. Adderly, "Mercy, Mercy, Mercy"; O. C. Smith, "Little Green Apples"; G. Campbell, "Wichita Lineman"; Simon and Garfunkel, "Bridge Over Troubled Water"

88 (2.8%) R. Charles, "Hit the Road Jack"; B. Darin, "Mack the Knife"; Beach Boys, "You Still Believe In Me"; Jimi Hendrix Experience, "Hey Joe"; Temptations, "I Wish It Would Rain"; Simon and Garfunkel, "The Boxer"; Sly and the Family Stone, "Everybody Is a Star"

92 (2.1%) S. Cooke, "You Send Me"; P. Boone, "April Love"; H. Mancini, "Moon River"; Righteous Brothers, "You've Lost That Lovin' Feelin'"; Doors, "The Crystal Ship"; A. Franklin, "Baby I Love You"; 5th Dimension, "Stoned Soul Picnic"; Turtles, "You Showed Me"; Oliver, "Jean"

96 (4.4%) Ruby and the Romantics, "Our Day Will Come"; B. Dylan, "Like a Rolling Stone"; Simon and Garfunkel, "Homeward Bound"; Rolling Stones, "19th Nervous Breakdown"; Buffalo Springfield, "For What It's Worth"; Lulu, "To Sir With Love"; Led Zeppelin, "Whole Lotta Love"

100 (1.1%)	B. Vinton, "Roses Are Red (My Love)"; B. Lewis, "Baby I'm Yours"; the Guess Who, "These Eyes"; S. Wonder, "My Cherie Amour"; Ike and Tina Turner, "Proud Mary" [nice and easy section]
104 (1.9%)	Everly Brothers, "All I Have to Do Is Dream"; Simon and Garfunkel, "Sounds of Silence"; Beatles, "We Can Work It Out"; B. J. Thomas, "Raindrops Keep Fallin' On My Head"; Creedence Clearwater Revival, "Lookin' Out My Back Door"
108 (5.4%)	G. Chandler, "Duke of Earl"; D. Troy, "Just One Look"; Temptations, "My Girl"; Mamas and the Papas, "Monday Monday"; Association, "Cherish"; Rolling Stones, "Ruby Tuesday"; Young Rascals, "Groovin' "; A. Franklin, "Respect"; Classics IV, "Traces"
112 (3.2%)	S. Fabares, "Johnny Angel"; Simon and Garfunkel, "I Am A Rock"; Lovin' Spoonful, "Summer in the City"; W. Pickett, "Mustang Sally"; Beatles, "Penny Lane"; J. Brown, "Cold Sweat"; Jimi Hendrix Experience, "Purple Haze"; D. Ruffin, "My Whole World Ended"
116 (3.5%)	C. Berry, "Maybelline"; Four Seasons, "Sherry"; Beatles, "And I Love Her"; Supremes, "Stop! In the Name of Love"; W. Pickett, "In the Midnight Hour"; Beach Boys, "California Girls"; A. Franklin, "A Natural Woman"; Cream, "Sunshine of Your Love"
120 (3.2%)	F. Avalon, "Venus"; Everly Brothers, "Cathy's Clown"; P. Clark, "Downtown"; Beatles, "Nowhere Man"; Temptations, "Ain't Too Proud to Beg"; Turtles, "Happy Together"; B. Gentry, "Ode to Billie Joe"; Creedence Clearwater Revival, "Proud Mary"
126 (7.0%)	B. Holly, "That'll Be the Day"; Coasters, "Yakety Yak"; Martha and the Vandellas, "Dancing in the Street"; Beatles, "Ticket to Ride"; J. Brown, "Papa's Got a Brand New Bag"; ? and the Mysterians, "96 Tears"; Doors, "Light My Fire"; Zombies, "Time of the Season"
132 (5.4%)	Miracles, "Shop Around"; Ronettes, "Be My Baby"; Beatles, "A Hard Day's Night"; R. Orbison, "Oh Pretty Woman"; S. Wonder, "Uptight"; Donovan, "Sunshine Superman"; Small Faces, "Itchycoo Park"; Grateful Dead, "Uncle John's Band"
138 (3.0%)	N. K.Cole, "Route 66"; Angels, "My Boyfriend's Back"; Supremes, "Baby Love"; Who, "I Can't Explain"; Rolling Stones, "(I Can't Get No) Satisfaction"; Beatles, "Day Tripper"; Box Tops, "The Letter"; T. James and the Shondells, "Mony Mony"; J. Cocker, "Delta Lady"
144 (3.0%)	B. Darin, "Splish Splash"; D. Shannon, "Runaway"; B. Lewis, "Tossin' and Turnin' "; Peter, Paul and Mary, "Puff (The Magic Dragon)"; J. Brown, "I Got You (I Feel Good)"; Association, "Along Comes Mary"; Steppenwolf, "Born to Be Wild"; Beatles, "Back in the U.S.S.R."
152 (2.3%)	B. Holly, "Peggy Sue"; Chiffons, "He's So Fine"; Peter, Paul and Mary, "Blowin' In the Wind"; Beatles, "She Loves You"; Beach Boys, "Fun, Fun, Fun"; Jimi Hendrix Experience, "Manic Depression"; Crosby, Stills and Nash, "Suite: Judy Blue Eyes" [Parts I and III]
160 (2.1%)	B. Freeman, "Do You Want to Dance"; Ventures, "Walk—Don't Run"; Beach Boys, "Surfin' U.S.A."; Martha and the Vandellas, "Heat Wave"; Beatles, "I Saw Her Standing There"; 5th Dimension, "Up-Up and Away"; Crosby, Stills, Nash and Young, "Teach Your Children"
168 (1.2%)	B. Vee, "Take Good Care of My Baby"; F. Cannon, "Palisades Park"; P. Clark, "My Love"; N. Sinatra, "These Boots Are Made For Walkin' "; Ventures, "Hawaii Five-O"; Creedence Clearwater Revival, "Travelin' Band"

(continued)

Table 12.01 Continued

176 (1.1%)	C. Francis, "Everybody's Somebody's Fool"; Supremes, "My World Is Empty Without You"; W. Pickett, "Land of 1000 Dances"; Creedence Clearwater Revival, "Bad Moon Rising"; Ike and Tina Turner, "Proud Mary" [nice and rough section]
184 (1.2%)	C. Berry, "Roll Over Beethoven"; Everly Brothers, "Wake Up Little Susie"; T. Jones, "It's Not Unusual"; Beatles, "Help!"; Who, "My Generation"; O'Kaysions, "Girl Watcher"; 5th Dimension, "Aquarius/Let the Sunshine In (The Flesh Failures)"
192 (1.1%)	Danny and the Juniors, "At the Hop"; Rolling Stones, "It's All Over Now"; Young Rascals, "Good Lovin'"; Supremes, "You Can't Hurry Love"; Monkees, "Last Train to Clarksville"
200 (0.4%)	Monotones, "Book of Love"; J. Dee and the Starliters, "Peppermint Twist"
208 (0.2%)	Crosby, Stills and Nash, "Marrakesh Express"
216 (0.2%)	K. Rogers and the First Edition, **"Ruby, Don't Take Your Love to Town"**
252 (0.2%)	Grateful Dead, **"Sitting On Top of the World"**

Compound Meters

40 (0.2%)	Friends of Distinction, "Going in Circles"
44 (0.5%)	K. Lester, "Love Letters"; Cream, "Sitting On Top of the World"; Jeff Beck Group, " Blues DeLuxe"
46 (0.4%)	B. Holloway, "Every Little Bit Hurts"; Mothers of Invention, "Anything"
48 (0.5%)	Shep and The Limelites, "Daddy's Home"; B. Hyland, "Let Me Belong to You"; Fleetwood Mac, "Need Your Love So Bad"
50 (0.5%)	O. Redding, "I've Been Loving You Too Long (To Stop Now)"; T. Jones, "I'll Never Fall in Love Again," "Without Love (There Is Nothing)"
52 (0.4%)	Demensions, "Over the Rainbow"; Led Zeppelin, "You Shook Me"
54 (1.1%)	B. Benton, "The Ties That Bind"; J. Brown, "It's a Man's, Man's, Man's, Man's World"; Moody Blues, "Nights in White Satin"; Big Brother and the Holding Co., "Ball and Chain"; V. Morrison, "Astral Weeks"; Chicago, "Colour My World"
56 (0.5%)	J. Ace, "Pledging My Love"; B. Vinton, "Mr. Lonely"; Blood, Sweat and Tears, "God Bless the Child"
58 (1.1%)	Teddy Bears, "To Know Him is to Love Him"; T. Yuro, "Hurt"; Paris Sisters, "I Love How You Love Me"; B. Dylan, "Sad-Eyed Lady of the Lowlands"; Brenda and the Tabulations, "Dry Your Eyes"; Dells, "Stay in My Corner"
60 (1.6%)	P. Cline, "She's Got You"; E. Grant, "The End"; L. Welch, "Since I Fell for You"; Impressions, "I'm So Proud"; Miracles, "Ooo Baby, Baby"; Beatles, "You've Got to Hide Your Love Away"; Big Brother and the Holding Co., "Summertime"; S. Davis Jr., "I've Gotta Be Me"
63 (2.1%)	McGuire Sisters, "It May Sound Silly"; Tune Weavers, "Happy Happy Birthday Baby"; B. Benton, "It's Just a Matter of Time"; Santo and Johnny, "Sleep Walk"; B. Dylan, "All I Really Want to Do"; L. Gore, "You Don't Owe Me"; P. Sledge, "When a Man Loves a Women"
66 (2.1%)	R. Charles, "Georgia On My Mind"; R. Valens, "Donna"; Rosie and the Originals, "Angel Baby"; Don and Juan, "What's Your Name"; E. Presley, "Can't Help Falling In Love"; Ray Charles Singers, "Love Me With All Your Heart"; E. Arnold, "Make the World Go Away"
69 (1.9%)	J. Mathis, "Misty"; F. Cramer, "Last Date"; Capris, "There's a Moon Out Tonight"; J. Brown, "Prisoner of Love"; Beach Boys, "Surfer Girl"; Shangri-Las, "Remember (Walkin' In the Sand)" [verses only]; Righteous Brothers, "Unchained Melody"

72 (3.3%)	Penguins, "Earth Angel"; E. Presley, "Love Me Tender"; Little Anthony and the Imperials, "Tears on My Pillow"; T. Edwards, "It's All in The Game"; Skyliners, "Since I Don't Have You"; B. Lee, "I'm Sorry"; Beatles, "This Boy"; Beach Boys, "The Warmth of the Sun"
76 (2.3%)	Platters, "The Great Pretender"; J. Mathis, "Chances Are"; P. Anka, "Put Your Head on My Shoulder"; The Miracles, "You've Really Got a Hold on Me"; Paul and Paula, "Hey Paula"; Rolling Stones, "Time Is On My Side"; B. Dylan, "Just Like a Woman"
80 (2.5%)	Four Aces, "Love is a Many-Splendored Thing"; E. Presley, "I Want You, I Need You, I Love You"; Shirelles, "Dedicated to the One I Love"; R. Charles, "I Can't Stop Loving You"; Animals, "The House of the Rising Sun"; H. Alpert, "This Guy's In Love With You"
84 (1.1%)	J. Weber, "Let Me Go Lover"; S. Turner, "Lavender Blue"; Islanders, "The Enchanted Sea"; P. Cline, "Sweet Dreams (Of You)"; C. Twitty, "It's Only Make Believe"; G. Pitney, "Only Love Can Break a Heart"
88 (0.5%)	C. Francis, "Who's Sorry Now"; P. Phillips, "Sea of Love"; B. B. King, "The Thrill is Gone"
92 (0.2%)	Beatles, "Revolution 1"
96 (0.5%)	F. Domino, "Blueberry Hill"; F. Avalon, "Why"; The Browns, "Scarlet Ribbons"
100 (0.7%)	E. Presley, "Heartbreak Hotel"; T. Hunter, "Young Love"; Fleetwoods, "Mr. Blue"
108 (0.5%)	F. Domino, "Blue Monday"; P. Cline, "I Fall to Pieces"; Impressions, "It's All Right"
112 (0.2%)	M. Gaye, "How Sweet It Is (To Be Loved By You)"
116 (0.5%)	W. Harrison, "Kansas City"; H. Dorman, "Mountain of Love"; Dion and the Belmonts, "The Wanderer"
120 (0.7%)	D. Seville and the Chipmunks, "Alvin's Harmonica"; Bill Black's Combo, "White Silver Sands"; Tokens, "The Lion Sleeps Tonight"; Beatles, "Revolution" [single version]
126 (0.5%)	F. Domino, "Ain't It a Shame"; N. Sedaka, "Calendar Girl"; F. Ifield, "I Remember You"
132 (0.4%)	B. Benton and D. Washington, "Baby (You've Got What It Takes)"; E. Presley, "Return to Sender"
138 (0.2%)	L. Price, "Stagger Lee"
144 (0.5%)	Crystals, "Da Doo Ron Ron (When He Walked Me Home)"; L. Van Dyke, "Walk On By"; Dion, "Abraham, Martin and John"
152 (0.5%)	E. Presley, "All Shook Up"; Jimmy Jones, "Handy Man"; Johnny Burnette, "You're Sixteen"
160 (0.5%)	J. L. Lewis, "Whole Lotta Shakin' Going On," "Great Balls of Fire"; R. Nelson, "Poor Little Fool"
168 (1.4%)	C. Perkins, "Blue Suede Shoes"; E. Presley, "Hound Dog," "Don't Be Cruel," "Jailhouse Rock"; C. Berry, "Sweet Little Sixteen," "Johnny B. Goode"; Everly Brothers, "Bye Bye Love"; Big Bopper, "Chantilly Lace"
176 (0.5%)	B. Knox, "Party Doll"; E Presley, "(Let Me Be Your) Teddy Bear"; B. Day, "Rockin' Robin"
184 (0.5%)	B. Haley, "(We're Gonna) Rock Around the Clock"; R. Nelson, "Stood Up"; Champs, "Tequila"
200 (0.2%)	R. Nelson, "Hello Mary Lou"

and 192 bpm is fast indeed. (The song's relationship to twelve-bar blues aids the listener in making the correct interpretation of the more moderate underlying tempo.) The rate of 126 bpm can almost be considered to be the official Motown tempo; many major hit songs by the Marvelettes, the Miracles, Marvin Gaye, Martha and the Vandellas, the Supremes, the Four Tops, and the Temptations are found at that measure. Nevertheless, Norman Whitfield's productions of "I Heard It Through the Grapevine" for Gladys Knight and the Pips and for Marvin Gaye both clock in a bit slower, at 112 bpm. The Supremes' "You Keep Me Hanging On" (126 bpm) was remade about one-third slower, at 88 bpm, by the Vanilla Fudge. Ike and Tina Turner's cover of "Proud Mary" lurches from a turning 100 ("nice and easy") to a burning 176 bpm ("nice and rough"). "Sitting on Top of the World" is the table's fastest simple-meter song when performed by the Grateful Dead (252 bpm), but it is also one of the slowest compound-meter examples when done by Cream (44 bpm). The Beatles' "Revolution" was first cut at 92 bpm, but when the group wanted to perform it faster as a single, it was executed about a third quicker, at 120 bpm. Nancy Sinatra is power-walking in "These Boots Are Made for Walkin'" (168 bpm), and the Everly Brothers sound truly urgent with a tempo of 184 bpm in "Wake Up Little Susie." Irony abounds in the Supremes' tempo for "You Can't Hurry Love" (192 bpm), and speeding locomotives set some of rock's fastest tempos in both the Monkees' "Last Train to Clarksville" and Crosby, Stills and Nash's "Marrakesh Express." A good number of the biggest early rock 'n' roll hits were played in compound time at 168 bpm.

Of course, what's really interesting is not the song that maintains its tempo, but the one in which tempo changes for one reason or another. A song's momentum can be given a great push when the stage is set by an introduction, one that may be simply slow or might be without tempo at all, proceeding freely. This approach is a holdover from Tin Pan Alley songs of the early part of the twentieth century; in fact, the original slow introductory verses are preserved if abbreviated in the Happenings' performances of "I Got Rhythm" and "My Mammy." Carole King's Tin Pan origins show in her slow intro to "It Might as Well Rain Until September." Slow intros are made more dramatic with imitations of tremolo mandolins, as in the Crystals' "Uptown," the Contours' "Do You Love Me," and the Four Seasons' "Let's Hang On," but full melodrama requires a timpani roll, as in Connie Francis's "Follow the Boys." Often, a song is justified by a slow introduction that frames the story that is about to unfold; this is the case in the Miracles' "Shop Around," Bobby Vee's "Take Good Care of My Baby," Barry Mann's "Who Put the Bomp," O. C. Smith's "Little Green Apples," the Beatles' "Honey Pie," and the Cowsills' "Hair." A major-mode song in a moderate tempo may seem fresher following a slow minor-mode intro, as in the Beatles' "Do You Want to Know a Secret." In "Little Star," the Elegants begin with one very slow line, and gain the proper tempo right away as if a thumb has been removed from the turntable, allowing it to come up to the proper speed. Ditto Crosby, Stills, Nash and Young's "Our House." The same effect is intensified in the Young Rascals' arrangement of "A Place in the Sun," which follows the simulation of a Renaissance-era two-part organ intro with Eddie Brigati's first vocal line, slow and without accompaniment of any kind; at the words "movin' on," the band enters and picks up the tempo.

Just as a song's opening is subject to an unstable tempo, so is its close. The final line of a song may be sung at a dramatically slower tempo than all that has preceded it; such is the case in Debbie Reynolds's "Tammy," Skeeter Davis's "The End of the World," and, appropriately, the Beatles' "Wait." The pedal steel guitar in Santo and Johnny's "Sleep Walk" finally drifts off this way. Sometimes the last line is sung at its regular tempo, then repeated for the slow effect, as in Patti Page's "Old Cape Cod" and the Vogues' "Turn Around, Look At Me." Most often, the last line is sung slowly, until the arrival of the final syllable, when the band kicks in again to finish with the original feel. This is characteristic of Jim Lowe's "Four Walls" and Bobby Vinton's "Blue Velvet." Similarly, time may come to a standstill in the final line, as in the Five Satins' "In the Still of the Nite," Elvis Presley's "It's Now or Never," the Beach Boys' "Surfer Girl," the Beatles' "She Loves You," "In My Life," and "Happiness Is a Warm Gun," and perhaps most majestically in Cream's March 10, 1968, Winterland 16'39" performance of "Spoonful," whose last line is set off by several instrumental vamps then sung very slowly, unaccompanied, until the instruments bring the track to a sustained close. The words, "Hold me," are sustained as time stops at the end of the Miracles' "You've Really Got a Hold On Me," before the original tempo resumes with the coda.

When time stops in the ending, it is often an opportunity for a flamboyant pouring forth from the soloist, in the manner of a concerto cadenza. Such outbursts are exhibited in the blues descent at the end of Pat Boone's "I Almost Lost My Mind," the humorous surprise from the lips of Johnny Cash in "A Boy Named Sue," the staggered entries of five singers in the Capris' "There's a Moon Out Tonight," Billy Stewart's lip-buzzing vocal acrobatics, coming up with "do————n't you br............cry" in "Summertime," and the floor-tom roll at the end of the Moody Blues' "Peak Hour." A humorless ametrical punch line, "And that's why you've never seen a unicorn to this very day," is thus emphasized in the Irish Rovers' "The Unicorn." Sometimes a story development requires the slow setting of the final verse, as when love is lost in Bill Hayes' "The Ballad of Davy Crockett," when death comes in Rolf Harris's "Tie Me Kangaroo Down, Sport" or Georgie Fame's

"The Ballad of Bonnie and Clyde," or when the shroud of gravitas descends, as in Zager and Evans's "In the Year 2525 (Exordium and Terminus)."

Time-stopping interruptions can come in the form of grand silent pauses or elaborate unaccompanied gestures in the body of a song as well. A most affected case occurs in Herb Alpert and the Tijuana Brass's hit version of "A Taste of Honey." Each chorus comes to its cadence at a standstill, dropping from 160 bpm to no tempo at all (as at 1:10–1:20) until a solo bass drum, pounding all beats for three bars, rouses a solo trombone (1:23+), which provides a two-bar alarm that gets everyone up and back on track until the same sleepy cadence returns with the next chorus. A more judicious pause is heard on breath-catching 4–3 suspensions on the V chord just before verses begin in Chicago Transit Authority's "Questions 67 and 68." Such form-articulating dominant harmonies are ripe for adding to the tension with a surprising pause—thus the coda-inducing two-bar silence following the tremulant-heavy end to the Hammond solo (1:37–1:58) in the Young Rascals' "Good Lovin'." With great effectiveness, a pause of unpredictable length stops the beginning of the last line of the verses of Eddie Fisher's "On the Street Where You Live." The pause can be triggered by the text; in the Four Seasons' version of "I've Got You Under My Skin," time dutifully stops as Valli sings, "stop! [2:04] before I begin . . ." And in the Shangri-Las' ultradramatic "I Can Never Go Home Anymore," the musical heartbeat stops at the command, "Don't!" Sometimes, a pause implies informal intimacy, as when Donovan waits for nearly a full bar between verses of his "Guinevere." Once in awhile, time seems to stop still with a long-sustained note, even though time continues to be marked beneath; when the bass singer of the Dells sings a note thirteen seconds long (beginning at 2:37) in the bridge of "I Can Sing a Rainbow/Love Is Blue," it seems as if resolution will never appear.

Tempos can change gradually, accelerating or slowing down for expressive purposes. The former change is more common; the tempo increases in order to bring the freight in both Lonnie Donegan's and Johnny Cash's recordings of "Rock Island Line." In the auto race of the Playmates' "Beep Beep," verses rise in turn from one at 69 bpm to a second increasing from 104 to 160, a third speeding up from 208 to 252, a fourth moving from 304 to 336, to a fifth verse boiling over at 368 bpm. In the Mothers of Invention's "Trouble Every Day," a rant on the Watts conflict of 1965 accelerates to a riotous finish. Musical portrayals of physiological accelerations include both Jim Morrison's fantasy of Oedipal orgasm achieved towards the end (9:30–10:30) of The Doors' "The End" and a mainline rush in the Velvet Underground's "Heroin." The Tijuana Brass's "Zorba the Greek" induces an infectiously gradual increase in the pleasures of the dance by accelerating from 66 to 184 bpm. The final chorus of the Four Seasons' "Will You Love Me Tomorrow" comes to a halt with a very high-register violin obbligato (at 38 bpm at

2:28–2:35) but somehow catches a spark from the harpsichord and accelerates from 104 to 126 for the full-band coda.

Examples of a gradual slowing of the tempo include the drop from 126 to 101 bpm at 1:33–1:58 in the Beach Boys' "Wouldn't It Be Nice," for a vulnerable, introspective suspension of the song proper over mandolins in strummed tremolo. Large-scale decreases of speed bring a tense halt to the ends of choruses in the Buckinghams' "Mercy Mercy Mercy," at the ends of verses in Phil Ochs's "Cross My Heart," and just before the coda in Badfinger's "Come and Get It." In the Grateful Dead's "Casey Jones," the chugging train comes to a slow, grinding stop in the song's repeated, spent, final line. A storyteller's suspense has each verse slow to a near stop only to bring the last line up to tempo in "Little" Jimmy Dickens's "May the Bird of Paradise Fly Up Your Nose." And melodrama is created with great slowings to a stop before the first verse (0:07–0:11), before the first chorus (1:03–1:10), and to usher in the coda (3:01–3:06) of Petula Clark's "This Is My Song." Most unusually, a song will proceed with irregular tempo. This is one way Bob Dylan evinces distress, as when he strums agitated, irregularly proceeding chords to suggest his difficulty accepting myths in "With God on Our Side" and when a plasticity of tempo portrays a fluidity of arbitrary justice as it heightens the dramatic tension in "The Lonesome Death of Hattie Carroll."

Finally, tempos can change directly, without any gradual transition from one speed to another, when one section is succeeded by another. Tempo changes suggest schizophrenia in Count Five's "Psychotic Reaction," contrast the dullness of waiting and the anticipation of a better life in Simon and Garfunkel's "Homeward Bound," illustrate the titular condition in Crosby, Stills, Nash and Young's "Déjà Vu," characterize the changing narrative points of view ranging from anger to sensitivity in the Moody Blues' "Question," and magnify the patchwork natures of the Dead's "St. Stephen," the Beach Boys' "Heroes and Villains," and the Mothers' "Cruising for Burgers." And two sudden song-ending changes of tempo, the half-time and double-time endings, are holdovers from the vaudeville circuit that remain alive in mid-century. The half-time ending, whereby a song closes with one or more lines twice as slow as the prevailing tempo, is heard in songs as diverse as Elvis Presley's "I Got a Woman," "Gee, Office Krupke!" from *West Side Story,* Peter, Paul and Mary's "Puff (The Magic Dragon)," Senator Everett McKinley Dirksen's "Gallant Men," Bob Dylan's "Peggy Day," and Creedence Clearwater Revival's "Lookin' Out My Back Door." The much rarer double-time ending is practiced in Elvis's "I'll Never Let You Go (Little Darlin')" and B. J. Thomas's "Raindrops Keep Fallin' On My Head." A similar effect is achieved in the coda (at 2:40) of the Association's "Windy," when a tambourine enters on every offbeat, doubling the surface activity. A sort of double-time change may be activated when the harmonic rhythm suddenly intensifies with chords changing twice as fast as they had been; note, in the verses of the Beatles' "I Want to Hold Your Hand," that chords initially change every four beats, but then change every *two* beats to underline urgency in the song's refrains. Conversely, when Gene Chandler boasts that "nothing can stop me," he becomes larger than life when his chords begin to change half as fast in the verses of "Duke of Earl." In "You Don't Own Me," Lesley Gore becomes more forceful in choruses ("Don't tell me what to do!"), where chords move four times more slowly than in verses. Another vaudeville technique was to introduce a song in one tempo and then double it for the bulk of the song; thus, Herman's Hermits' "Leaning On the Lamp Post" sets a false pace in its first verse that is thereafter normalized, twice as fast, implying an initial ruse much more than does the normal slow introduction using material not heard again.

Duration

Another time-related issue in our music is the question of overall length. The duration of a recording was primarily governed by two factors external to composition and performance. One was the

Duration: track length; market-based edits; larger-scale recordings.

medium of vinyl: 45-rpm singles, which when mastered at normal dynamic levels for an optimum signal-to-noise ratio, would typically run for two-and-a-half or three minutes. This standard was most popularly challenged in 1968 by lengths such as 7'20" with Richard Harris's "MacArthur Park" and then 7'11" with the Beatles' "Hey Jude." Album sides running at 33 1/3-rpm were limited for most programming to about twenty-five minutes. The second factor was dictated by radio programming, which regardless of format embraced the brief and dynamic, and avoided the long and static. Songs were practically never as short as the Beatles' "Her Majesty," offering a single verse and a truncated final chord for a playing time of 0'28", but through the mid-1960s they were rarely longer than three minutes outside the folk-music realm, where multiverse songs could extend to 5'54" as with Joan Baez's "Mary Hamilton" or 7'10" with Bob Dylan's "Chimes of Freedom." Bob Dylan's six-minute A-side of 1965, "Like a Rolling Stone," set the bar higher than anyone else would attempt for three more years. Much more typical of pop music was the 2'18" of the Beatles' power-packed "She Loves You." The Beach Boys' "Good Vibrations," at 3'35", was considered very long for AM radio's heavy-rotation hit formats in late 1966.

Many singles were edited versions of longer cuts appearing on albums, and some radio-only promotional mixes were further edits of those edited singles. Examples include Donovan's "Sunshine Superman" (the 3'15" single omits most of Jimmy Page's solo, preserved in the 4'31" mix), The Doors' "Light My Fire" (the 2'52" monophonic single omits the guitar and organ solos from the album's 7'08" stereo mix; a later third edit made in stereo for FM radio containing only the end of the break clocks in at 3'04"), and the Grateful Dead's "Feedback" (presented at 8'52" on the original vinyl but cut to 7'49" for the compact disc). Solo-omitting edits were common in the late-'60s era of hard rock, as the management of bands such as Vanilla Fudge, Big Brother and the Holding Company, Jimi Hendrix, Cream, the Chambers Brothers, Santana, Led Zeppelin, and Iron Butterfly struggled to market their long-jamming clients to the radio-friendly popular audience. Even Arlo Guthrie cut a single version of his 18'20" shaggy-dog epic, "Alice's Restaurant Massacree," removing the entire story and retitling the result, "Alice's Rock & Roll Restaurant." But just two minutes could at times seem an eternity, as when that length of an unperturbed groove appeared as a memorial to a miscarried fetus in John Lennon and Yoko Ono's John Cage-inspired "Two Minutes Silence."

As market forces and artistic aims both brought the album to new prominence among the ever-younger record-buying fans of popular music in the mid-1960s, ever-longer conceptions of the song appeared. Sometimes, these long recordings were made so by simply adding more and more verses in the folk tradition, as with Bob Dylan's "Desolation Row" (11'21") and "Sad-Eyed Lady of the Lowlands" (10'44"). But, in an emergence of grander suite-like structures that were to lead to the concept albums and progressive rock of the 1970s, groups began to link larger numbers of contrasting ideas into more-or-less unified compositions. Such works as the Mothers of Invention's "Help, I'm a Rock" (8'37") and "Brown Shoes Don't Make It" (7'26"), the Grateful Dead's "That's It for the Other One" (7'46"), The Who's "A Quick One While He's Away" (9'11"), the Small Faces' "Happiness Stan" (18'33"), the Incredible String Band's "Creation" (16'03"), and Crosby, Stills and Nash's "Suite: Judy Blue Eyes" (7'22") fulfill such aspirations. Deep Purple's *Concerto for Group and Orchestra,* recorded with the Royal Philharmonic Orchestra in London's Albert Hall, comprises three movements lasting 19'06", 19'01", and 15'24", respectively; the record must be turned over partway through the second movement.

And then, of course, the timeless worlds of the acid experience, spiritual search, jazz-like attempts at virtuosic jams (sometimes performed on a pair of alternating chords, at other times on a single unadorned harmony), and atonal experimentation could also be reflected in larger-scale recordings, as in John Lennon and Yoko Ono's "Cambridge 1969" (26'28"), Quicksilver Messenger Service's "Who Do You Love" (25'22"), the Grateful Dead's "Dark Star" (appearing at 23'15" on *Live/Dead*), the Mothers' "The Little House I Used to Live In" (18'41"), Isaac Hayes's "By the Time I Get to Phoenix" (18'40"),

Cream's "Toad" (17'35" from the Winterland performances of March 7–8, 1968), Chicago Transit Authority's "Liberation" (15'41"), Blind Faith's "Do What You Like" (15'16"), the Jimi Hendrix Experience's "Voodoo Chile" (15'00"), Pink Floyd's "A Saucerful of Secrets" (12'51"), King Crimson's "Moonchild" (12'15"), Ten Years After's "I'm Going Home" (9'20"), Soft Machine's "Joy of a Toy" (8'47"), Phil Ochs' "The Crucifixion" (8'45"), and the Beatles' relatively economical "Revolution 9" (8'12"). Some multiple LP sets, such as the Mothers of Invention's *Freak Out!*, the Rascals' *Freedom Suite,* and George Harrison's *All Things Must Pass,* included tight song-filled records along with side-filling free-form jams, perhaps in hopes of mollifying a wide range of customers with preferences for one genre or the other.

Phrase Rhythm

In between the temporal ratios among notes, chords, and beats on the surface, and the larger durational aspects of songs as entire entities, lies the question of phrase rhythm. Here, one can compare the proportions of phrases to each other

Phrase rhythm: regular and irregular phrase lengths; phrase expansion and contraction.

and sections to each other, bridging the notions of small-scale rhythm and formal structure. (See Web audio example 4.21, in which a four-bar intro is followed by an opening section with three phrases of five, seven, and five bars each.) Not only are the lengths of some units comparable to others appearing in the same song; they can also be measured against normal, prototypical lengths that exist as abstract standard models. In our chapter on form, we were able to relate structures of all sorts of lengths to the twelve-bar blues prototype; we may take the same approach with phrase lengths and relationships in other forms. As in all other domains, the Beatles were highly imaginative in their approach to phrase rhythm when the actual phrase lengths are measured against prototypical norms. Table 12.02 lists a number of songs by other artists that the reader may wish to investigate for their play with phrase rhythm, but we'll simply focus on the music of the Beatles for this introduction to the topic.

First, one should be aware of the relationship between phrase and meter. Most often, phrases are groupings of regular numbers of bars in powers of two—phrases are most often of four or sometimes eight bars, depending on tempo. This can be heard as a metric arrangement at a level higher than that of beats counted within a bar—one can often count hypermetric bars in a phrase the same way. (Grouping irregularities of the same sort can affect both levels, and it should be noted that occasionally, phrase beginnings and endings cross against the hypermetric levels—this large-scale cross-rhythm is what is alluded to in the suggestions below of "Sexy Sadie" and "Because.")

Table 12.02 Examples of representative songs with unusual phrase rhythm, listed in chronological order by chart-entry date

Ferlin Husky, "Gone"
Jerry Lee Lewis, "It'll Be Me"
Buddy Knox, "Hula Love"
Margie Rayburn, "I'm Available"
Jerry Lee Lewis, "Great Balls of Fire"
Silhouettes, "Get a Job"
Bobby Freeman, "Do You Want to Dance"
Chuck Berry, "Beautiful Delilah"
Clyde McPhatter, "A Lover's Question"
Impalas, "Sorry (I Ran All the Way Home)"
Everly Brothers, "Poor Jenny"
Carl Dobkins Jr., "My Heart Is An Open Book"
Bobby Darin, "Beyond the Sea"
Roy Orbison, "Only the Lonely"
Drifters, "Save the Last Dance for Me"
Bill Black's Combo, "Blue Tango"
Roy Orbison, "I'm Hurtin'"
Ben E. King, "Spanish Harlem"
Bobby Lewis, "Tossin' and Turnin'"
Dee Clark, "Raindrops"
Curtis Lee, "Pretty Little Angel Eyes"
Ray Charles, "You Be My Baby"
Bobby Edwards, "You're the Reason"
Don and Juan, "What's Your Name"
Bobby Vinton, "Roses Are Red (My Love)"
Dionne Warwick, "Don't Make Me Over"
Little Eva, "Let's Turkey Trot"
The Essex, "A Walkin' Miracle"
Bob Dylan, "A Hard Rain's a-Gonna Fall"
Singing Nun, "Dominique"
Ginny Arnell, "Dumb Head"
Dionne Warwick, "Anyone Who Had a Heart"
Andy Williams, "A Fool Never Learns"
Bob Dylan, "Only a Pawn in Their Game"
Elvis Presley, "Viva Las Vegas"
Earl-Jean, "I'm Into Something Good"
Jackie Ross, "Selfish One"
Jay and the Americans, "Come a Little Bit Closer"
Miracles, "That's What Love Is Made Of"
Joe Tex, "Hold What You've Got"
Dobie Gray, "The 'In' Crowd"
Bob Dylan, "Love Minus Zero/No Limit"
Bob Dylan, "Subterranean Homesick Blues"
Bob Dylan, "Like a Rolling Stone"
Sonny and Cher, "Baby Don't Go"
Ronnie Dove, "I'll Make All Your Dreams Come True"
Vogues, "You're the One"
Statler Brothers, "Flowers On the Wall"

(continued)

Table 12.02 Continued

Petula Clark, "My Love"
Young Rascals, "I Ain't Gonna Eat Out My Heart Anymore"
Turtles, "You Baby"
Peter and Gordon, "Woman"
Herb Alpert and the Tijuana Brass, "Spanish Flea"
Doctor Zhivago soundtrack, "Lara's Theme"
Cyrkle, "Red Rubber Ball"
Beach Boys, "You Still Believe In Me"
Grass Roots, "Where Were You When I Needed You"
Troggs, "Wild Thing"
Bob Dylan, "Most Likely You Go Your Way (And I'll Go Mine)"
Bob Dylan, "Visions of Johanna"
Jefferson Airplane, "Come Up the Years"
Mamas and the Papas, "Look Through My Window"
Bob Crewe Generation, "Music to Watch Girls By"
Monkees, "She"
Lovin' Spoonful, "Darling Be Home Soon"
Mothers of Invention, "Who Are the Brain Police?"
Who, "Happy Jack"
Tommy James and the Shondells, "Mirage"
Bee Gees, "New York Mining Disaster 1941 (Have You Seen My Wife Mr. Jones)"
Scott McKenzie, "San Francisco (Be Sure to Wear Some Flowers in Your Hair)"
Pink Floyd, "See Emily Play"
Monkees, "Words"
Brenton Wood, "Gimme Little Sign"
Petula Clark, "The Cat in the Window (The Bird in the Sky)"
Youngbloods, "Get Together"
Joe Tex, "Skinny Legs and All"
Henson Cargill, "Skip a Rope"
Leonard Cohen, "Suzanne"
Blood, Sweat and Tears, "Meagan's Gypsy Eyes"
Sergio Mendes and Brasil '66, "The Look of Love"
Friend and Lover, "Reach Out of the Darkness"
O. C. Smith, "Little Green Apples"
Four Jacks and a Jill, "Master Jack"
The Band, "The Weight"
Grass Roots, "Midnight Confessions"
Johnny Nash, "Hold Me Tight"
B. J. Thomas, "Hooked On a Feeling"
Mary Hopkin, "Goodbye"
Mothers of Invention, "Uncle Meat Main Title Theme"
Mama Cass, "It's Getting Better"
Kenny Rogers and the First Edition, "Ruby, Don't Take Your Love to Town"
Flying Machine, "Smile a Little Smile for Me"
Janis Joplin, "Kozmic Blues"
B. J. Thomas, "Raindrops Keep Fallin' On My Head"
Creedence Clearwater Revival, "The Midnight Special"
Grateful Dead, "Uncle John's Band"
Supremes, "Stoned Love"

Often, an instrumental arrangement emphasizes the relationship between strong and weak downbeats. Even in his early bass playing, Paul McCartney shows a sensitivity to the fact that some downbeats are stronger than others. Take, for instance, the Beatles' "Eight Days a Week." Note how in the four-bar phrases of the verse, the first three bars ("Ooh I need your love babe, guess you know it's...") have two rising arpeggiations followed by a reversal of direction in the fourth bar ("true"), which has a descent in the bass (8—6—5—3) to the deep downbeat beginning the following phrase on 1 ("Hope," at 0:14). McCartney recognizes that the deepest structural points call for the deepest bass register, and this governs his approach to large-scale rhythm.

The Beatles' phrases consist of four bars more than often enough to permit this hypermeter to be heard as the standard against which other lengths, both shorter and longer, are to be heard as irregular. We can examine a number of different sorts of manifestations of the Beatles' flexibility in phrase rhythm, often tied to poetic connotations of the lyrics. For instance, the verses in the song "Long Long Long" are each comprised of three lengthened phrases, the first two being six bars in length instead of the usual four, and the third lengthened by yet one more bar. Each bar is in simple triple meter (three beats per bar): Phrase one: bars 1–4: "long, long, long time"; bars 5–6: sitar and acoustic guitar. Phrase two: bars 1–4: "How could I ever have lost you"; bars 5–6: Hammond organ. Phrase three: bars 1–4: "when I loved you?"; bars 5–7 (!), extended by one beat: organ and pickup to next verse: "It took a...." Essentially, all four-bar phrases are lengthened by two or more "extra" instrumental bars, an unambiguous musical illustration of a "long, long, long time." In "Wait," *two* identical three-bar phrases form a verse treating the topic of delay. Note a similar approach in "All I've Got to Do": the solo singer begins a phrase with four quadruple-meter bars ("I...want you around yeah, all I've got to..."), and the backing singers lengthen the phrase by two more bars with the song's title, until Lennon answers with a second, five-bar phrase. Seven-bar phrases appear in verses of "Not a Second Time" and "Yesterday," and the verse of "Your Mother Should Know" follows one normal-length four-bar phrase with a second of seven bars.

Previously, we've seen how pauses can interrupt the musical flow for an indeterminable amount of time. Sometimes the Beatles expand a phrase by vocally pausing through a measured extra length. "You've Got to Hide Your Love Away" is basically in a compound quadruple meter (think of "Here I stand, head in hand" as a single four-beat bar, each beat divisible by three parts). Each verse consists of two phrases, the first of 4.5 bars (as a pause on "two foot *small*" continues an extra two beats) and the second of five bars (the pause on "hear them *say*" is extended a whole extra bar).

Unusual phrase lengths are not always the result of added material; sometimes, it seems as if material has been cut. Occasionally, expected hypothetical bars of music simply do not appear. The verses of "Any Time at All" contain four phrases, each based on a four-bar prototype. The first phrase ("If you need somebody to love, just look into my eyes") fulfills the function of the normal four-bar first phrase, but the answering second phrase is cut short, its second half interrupted by the early appearance of the third phrase ("If you're feeling sorry and sad..."), which is then answered by a normal four-bar consequent. In songs like "Any Time at All" and, for that matter, "It Won't Be Long," the regulation of time is the central concern musically as well as lyrically. In other songs, musical factors create interruptions; in "I Will," the opening antecedent phrase comes to an abrupt halt and dangles "still" at 3.5 bars when the roadblock of a nondirectional iii harmony (0:08) appears. The ensuing consequent phrase lasts for 5.5 bars (0:09–0:21) when going to another verse, but 4.5 if going to the bridge (0:30–0:40). The reader is left to puzzle out the strange phrase-rhythm relationships in "Sexy Sadie," "Because," and the middle section of "A Day in the Life."

This chapter has presented just a short introduction to the topic of rhythm, one that many listeners hold as the single most fundamental element of rock music, perhaps combining it with tone color as the top two elements. Despite its relative brevity as opposed to our chapters on harmony, we've been able here to outline all significant ways by which underlying patterns and surface rhythms may be measured, even though nearly every song has its own unique set of rhythmic devices. Hopefully, the interested reader would be able to use the techniques covered here to discover all manner of captivating rhythmic events in a song of interest. But it's important to bear in mind that when studying rhythm, one must always be conscious of just *what* is being measured. The beat is shared by all instruments and singers in an ensemble, but how do all forces relate to each other rhythmically? Similarly, all chords may adhere to the same governing tempo, but some will move more powerfully and some sit back more graciously based on their role in the circle of fifths, their degree of chromaticism, or their inherent dissonance, even if all are presented for the same numbers of beats or bars. So, in some ways, rhythmic relationships may be objectively measured by a timepiece, whereas in others, personal interpretation plays as large a role as it does in judging the interplay of relative loudness and softness, or the degree of distortion added to a guitar's signal. It is perhaps at these less concrete levels that the study of rhythm is among the most interesting of all musical considerations, while at the same time the least thoroughly explored.

CHAPTER 13

Engineering the Master

Once the artists, producer, and any session musicians have arranged their song as a composition to be performed, a studio's recording engineers, tape operators and disc cutters play a large role in creating the sound as heard on record. Their chief responsibility, of course, is to record what the artists play so it will sound its best when reproduced, but because every step in the recording process can affect the resulting sound, the final product may range from a relatively neutral reproduction of a song as performed in an ideal environment to a highly colored and even profoundly changed reading of what had been done in the studio. Aside from live concert performances, which make up a small percentage of our listening, virtually all music recorded for radio programming and home listening in the 1950s and '60s was produced in acoustically designed sound studios, with sound waves converted by microphones to analog electrical signals that would be routed through processors and controllers of various types (often laid out on a mixing board) and recorded on a multitrack magnetic working tape, to be manipulated still further in the creation of a monophonic or stereo master that would then be subject to dynamic alteration in the cutting of the proto-type for the making of the metal parts that would stamp the record's groove into thousands of vinyl consumer copies. Traditional music recordings, in the way of classical music, Broadway shows, jazz, and folk songs, tended to be transparent, relying on the studio's ideal neutrality as a way of preserving the original sound. After all, a violinist might have spent tens of thousands (today, millions) of dollars for an exquisitely crafted instrument because of its sonic properties, and moreover would have worked for decades developing a technique that would permit the control of every nuance of the resulting sound, and would then depend upon an engineer to reproduce as close a likeness to the original as the medium would permit. Rock musicians, by contrast, began to find an aesthetic potential in the manipulation of sound for its own sake, discovering that the studio would provide an ideal blank canvas upon which to work, and so the engineers who could develop and control circuits that would shape every imaginable facet of a sound became an artist's collaborator, often contributing much more than a final scrub and polish. Thus this chapter is devoted to engineering, which would not very likely find a place in a book structured like this on classical music but is crucial in our domain.

The final steps of the production process have an important effect on the resulting sound. These include the limiting of the master tape's dynamic peaks according to industry standards so that the signal could enjoy maximum volume against the record's surface noise without pushing the more sensitive lightweight stylus out of the groove, the microgroove cutting of

Photo 13.01. Ross Leavitt and Joe Girard on saxes; note the hinged wooden wall panels, which swing open to reveal felt lining, changing the room's quality of reverberation from very live to dead. (Photo: Annie Eastman)

the lacquers by a lathe operator so as to fit revolutions of the concentric groove for a quiet passage as closely together as possible to allow more room for the wider grooves that would be necessary for greater loudness, and the regular inspection for wear of both the metal parts so that later pressings would have as sharp a fidelity as the first, and of the vinyl copies for errors such as off-center pressing, bad seams, bubbles, and impurities. These processes, however, are nearly always more matters of excellence in meeting industry norms than of artistic vision, and so will not be discussed further. Conversely, most of the prior steps in the recording process may be accomplished along a wide range of available choices, so we shall investigate the many ways that decisions made in recording and in postproduction can influence the resulting music. Most of these decisions will have been made by staff engineers, employees of given studios but always under the general direction of record producers, the most successful of whom are listed in table 13.01.

Table 13.01 Prominent pop record producers of the 1950s and 1960s, listed by city of main association

Chicago: Leonard and Phil Chess, Willie Dixon, Henry Glover and Ralph Bass, Charles Stepney, Joe Wissert

Clovis, New Mexico: Norman Petty

Detroit: Nick Ashford and Valerie Simpson, Berry Gordy, Brian Holland / Lamont Dozier / Eddie Holland, Smokey Robinson, Norman Whitfield

London: Joe Boyd, John Burgess, Chas Chandler, Tony Clarke, Denny Cordell, Gus Dudgeon, Tony Hatch, Glyn Johns, Kit Lambert, Tony Macaulay, George Martin, Joe Meek, Hugh Mendl, Jimmy Miller, Mickie Most, Norman Newell, Andrew Loog Oldham, Larry Page, Norrie Paramor, Ron Richards, Dick Rowe, Norman Smith, Robert Stigwood, Peter Sullivan, Shel Talmy

Los Angeles/Hollywood: Lou Adler, Steve Barri and P. F. Sloan, Bruce Botnick, Jimmy Bowen, Chip Douglas, Snuff Garrett, Dick Glasser, James William Guercio, Dave Hassinger, Lee Hazelwood, Bones Howe, Quincy Jones, Stan Kesler, Larry Levine, Jerry Lieber and Mike Stoller, Terry Melcher, Hugo Piretti and Luigi Creatore, Mike Post, Stan Ross, Paul Rothchild, Phil Spector, Lenny Waronker, Brian Wilson

Memphis: Steve Cropper, Chips Moman, Sam Phillips

Muscle Shoals, Alabama: Rick Hall, Jerry Wexler

Nashville: Archie Bleyer, Owen Bradley, Don Law

New Orleans: Dale Hawkins, Allen Toussaint

New York: Jeff Barry and Ellie Greenwich, Bert Berns, Bob Crewe and Frank Slay, Tom Dowd, Neshui Ertegun, Wes Farrell, Roy Halee, John Hammond, Jac Holzman, Erik Jacobsen, Bob Johnston, Jerry Kasenetz and Jeff Katz, Teo Macero, Mitch Miller, Shadow Morton, Felix Pappalardi, Artie Ripp, John Simon, Tom Wilson

Philadelphia: Kenneth Gamble and Leon Huff

San Francisco: David Rubinson

Through the mid-1960s, major American and British record labels usually held record producers as salaried employees, but upon the emergence of original approaches, those most in demand were able to break from their employers to contract independently. (Some fully independent producers, such as Sam Phillips, Leonard Chess, Norman Petty, and Phil Spector, enjoyed more latitude even in rock's early years with their small labels.) Producers would often assign a song to an artist, unless the song was already a main feature of the artist's set list or was an original composition. The producer might have to reshape the composition, customizing the intro, coda, or ordering of sections for impact or to achieve a certain timing; perhaps decide to have the song transposed to a suitable key for a singer's range; hire (perhaps through a fixer) any necessary arranger and outside musicians, including conductor if necessary; book time in the appropriately sized and equipped studio; determine any necessary studio effects; oversee rehearsals and recording; and supervise editing and mixing. This chapter will take up the recording process beginning with the commitment of signal to tape.

Microphones

The engineers will choose microphones based on sensitivity (a mic placed in front of a singer will not need as strong and unyielding a diaphragm as would one placed in front of a bass amplifier cabi-

> The recording process: microphone choice and placement.

net) and directionality (a mic that must capture a number of instruments will have a different pickup pattern from one that must not pick up unwanted stray sounds). Often, large baffle screens ("gobos"—as in "go-betweens") are set up to keep the sounds of different performers separate; the drummer or singer may even have to work in an isolation booth to keep this sound from leaking onto the other tracks. In recording acoustic instruments, the engineer may wish to have the sonorities blend, as composers would often arrange parts so that the harmonics from bass instruments would draw enriched sound from those in higher registers. This is less often an ideal in rock recording.

If every instrument is captured by a separate microphone, that sound may reside on its own track of tape (or may be combined with others either during recording or later, during mixing) and thus may be subject to its own filtering, reverb, coloring, and balance. Generally, the more the instruments blend onto a smaller number of microphones, the more "live" the recording will appear but the less control one will later have over the individual constituents. The more each sound source is isolated, the more control can be gained in the later manipulation of that sound, but the more artificial the resulting mix may appear. Decisions about such preferences and needs must be made before recording begins; in psychedelic recordings, for instance, distance from anything sounding real is often the goal. One curious recording along the lines of these concerns is Moby Grape's "Just Like Gene Autry," which seems to have had a singer and an entire dance band (including saxes, banjo, ukulele, and trap set) recorded with a single microphone to simulate an acoustic horn recording of the 1920s. At the opposite extreme, engineers progressed in the late 1960s from recording a drum set with a single suspended microphone to miking each part of the kit separately, all of which individual sounds might be fed to different parts of the final stereo image. (In Web photo 1.06, note the different dynamic and condenser microphones; the dynamic mic on the bass drum is similar to one that would mic a guitar amplifier. A singer's more sensitive condenser mic, as in Web photo 5.02, is a cardioid, named for the heart-shape of its receptivity pattern.) Early examples of multiple drum miking include Blood, Sweat and Tears' "And When I Die," the Beatles' "The End," and Chicago Transit Authority's "Liberation." The drum solo in Steam's "Na Na Hey Hey Kiss Him Goodbye" shows the bass drum (heard center) to have been miked separately from the rest of the kit (heard right). And although the drums are not separated in the stereo image, particularly clear drum miking is heard in examples such as the Miracles' "My Girl Has Gone," "Going to a Go-Go," and "I Second That Emotion"; the Four Seasons' "Let's Hang On"; and the Rolling Stones' "Monkey Man." One might notice how clearly demarcated are the three guitars, entering one at a time over the pedaled hi-hat and bass drum in Stevie Wonder's "For Once in My Life"; compare these with the murky combined guitars of the Beach Boys' "Sloop John B" and "Wouldn't It Be Nice."

Another variable pertaining to microphones is their distance from the performer. Very close miking produces a hot result—one can hear the breathing of a singer, the pick against the string of a guitarist, and the clicking of keys on wind instruments. The "popping" of vocal P's should be eliminated by a mic's spitscreen, but this precaution is not taken in Ben E. King's "I (Who Have Nothing)," which was very closely miked, nor in Bob Dylan's "Visions of Johanna," wherein the passage from 0:46 to 0:57 includes popped P's in "opposite loft" and "plays soft," all sputtering as "the heat pipes just cough." More distant miking will capture the sound more like a listener might hear it in a concert hall, but the result will be less focused and more subject to room dynamics.

Earlier recordings tend to show more limitations in mic placement. In Al Hibbler's "After the Lights Go Down Low" (1956), for instance, the drums sound very muffled from distant miking, but the vocal is hot enough that at 1:20, the "T" sound of "teasin'" produces pronounced distortion. (Note also how "Pittsburgh" is blasted at 0:04–0:05 of Chuck Berry's "Sweet Little Sixteen.") Berry Gordy's first hit, Barrett Strong's "Money (That's What I Want)"

Photo 13.02. Engineer Kristin Fosdick adjusts mic placement on Noah Reitman's string bass; she aims the mic just above the bridge to best catch the highest harmonics. (Photo: Annie Eastman)

sounds like a very low-budget recording, perhaps a single-mic effort with the lead vocal and tambourine very hot and all other performers—backing singers, piano—very distant. Led Zeppelin albums show a variety of miking techniques just as wide as their stylistic range; mics for Jimmy Page's acoustic guitars in "Babe I'm Gonna Leave You," "Thank You," and "Gallows Pole" are quite distant from their sources, and John Bonham's drums are captured by a room mic in "Since I've Been Loving You" and "When the Levee Breaks." The distortion from the too-close vocal mic in Jimi Hendrix's "Belly Button Window," recorded in the month before his death, reveals that this take was probably initially intended only as an informal demo, never receiving its finished vocal. Close-miked distortion can add to the performer's expression; Little Richard's multiphonics overdrive the mic in the bridge of "Can't Believe You Wanna Leave" for a deliciously nasty sound. Close miking, though, can also work to compensate for a weak voice, as detectable in Gale Storm's "Memories Are Made of This," which very unnaturally has her way out in front of her accompaniment. And intimacy is the result of close miking, as one can hear every tricle of saliva lubricating Elvis's pipes in "Crying in the Chapel." A closely miked tenor saxophone produces just as much wind noise as musical tone for a sultry sound in Dusty Springfield's "The Look of Love." A recording's resulting loudness is not necessarily a function of close vs. distant miking; every sound source must be recorded at the highest level possible without distortion, regardless of its eventual loudness in relation to other sources (which can be adjusted later), to keep the level of tape hiss as low as possible.

Distant miking is not usually an acceptable practice; not only are there issues with signal strength and distortion, separation and leaking, and with stereo imaging, but phasing can occur, with parts of the waveform cancelled out if picked up by other mics as well at a similar loudness level. Nevertheless, distant miking is often useful to get the same effect as from an offstage instrument, as with the far-off, muted trumpets in Patti Page's "The Tennessee Waltz" and the DeCastro Sisters' "Teach Me Tonight." In "Banana Boat (Day-O)," Harry Belafonte begins singing off-mike. In "Déjà vu," Crosby, Stills, Nash and Young go off-mike for their mystical incantation, "we have all been here before" (at 3:07–3:13). Web audio example 4.13 opens with the trumpet miked at a distance and also given dense reverb to suggest an offstage distance.

Coloring the tracks

At various stages during the recording process, sounds may be altered. At a minimum, the relative presence, loudness, and tone of every incoming sound may require adjustment to provide focus and definition. At what stage this coloring takes place depends upon either the number of tracks available on the mixing board, each of which accepts one or more different inputs (which may be from either a microphone or a directly injected instrument that may bypass an amplifier), or the number of tracks available on tape. If several vocals or instruments, each miked separately, are fed into a single track on the board, or if several tracks on the board are bussed to a single track of tape, they are thereafter locked together as they are and can no longer be treated individually. Today, when there is virtually an infinite number of digital tracks at the producer's disposal, one might have difficulty appreciating the economy of resources that had to be practiced with two-, four-, and eight-track working tape. Once all tracks of a tape were filled up, they could be bounced down to a second generation—mixed together and dubbed onto a smaller number of tracks on a second reel to make room for additional recording; not only did this process forever mix tracks together that could never be accessed individually again, but every new generation of tape would double the level of tape hiss that could threaten to mask important parts of the signal. So the successful producer had to be skilled in planning, anticipating every step of recording. (See Web photo 13.01.)

Presence is a useful term for describing how a sound fits into its environment, which provides enough reflection of the original signal to define the surrounding space. Some recordings are made completely dry, without any reverberation at all (Aretha Franklin's "I Never Loved a Man (The Way I Love You)" could serve for comparison), whereas others are swamped, swimming in the stuff. (Compare the heavy reverb given horn and backing vocals in Web audio example 4.12

Color alterations: presence (reverb, echo and delay; the Leslie; flanging); loudness and balance; tone (filtering, phasing, and compression).

with the dry sound originally obtained in Web audio example 13.01.) Reverb places the source in a natural setting—the amount, speed, and length of tail of the reverb applied can simulate a small chamber, a bright or a carpeted room, a stairwell or long tunnel, a bath-like tiled space, or a large hall. (A cathedral's worth of reverb has been added to a dry recording in Web audio example 4.11.) In fact, reverb would often be produced by routing the signal to a loudspeaker at the end of one of these environments (EMI at Abbey Road, London, filled a basement with tile plumbing pipes for its reverb chamber, and their engineers sometimes used a long hallway instead), picking up the resulting sound from a microphone at the other end and routing the result to the board, where it would be added to the original input. Or, reverb could be produced artificially by sending the signal through springs (as in a guitar amp's reverb circuit), or through a huge metal plate attached to a speaker and fitted with pickups that would detect the lingering reverberation. These and other effects might be built into a mixing board or require an offboard or plug-in module.

Aside from suggesting a performing space, reverb fulfills many functions in pop records. Reverb on vocal and anvil tracks suggests the interior of a mine in Jimmy Dean's "Big Bad John." Reverb applied to violins opens a metaphorical space measured in hundreds of thousands of miles in Jonathan King's "Everyone's Gone to the Moon." The threatening Nancy Sinatra is made to appear larger than life with vocal reverb in "These Boots Are Made for Walkin'." Sandy Posey's reverberating inner thoughts penetrate to the listener as if spoken aloud in "I Take It Back," as do those of dirty-minded City Hall Fred in the Mothers of Invention's "Brown Shoes Don't Make It." Reverbed horns are made extra nostalgic in the Young Rascals' "I've Been Lonely Too Long" and extra mournful in the Association's "Requiem for the Massses." Chuck Berry's guitar is heated by a reverb chamber for "School

Days," backing singers are drenched in reverb in the Turtles' "You Baby," and in Led Zeppelin's "You Shook Me," Jimmy Page's vocal is married to his guitar by their matching reverb, particularly notable in their glissando duet at 0:28–0:31. The backbeat tambourine stands out through reverb in Jackie Wilson's "Lonely Teardrops," the Four Seasons' "Ronnie" opens quite unusually with reverb on ratchet, timpani, and traps, and Brian Wilson prefers reverb on only the timps in three *Pet Sounds* songs including "Wouldn't It Be Nice." Reverb is altered through the course of Ralph Marterie's "Shish-Kebab" (one can hear the reverb of the shawmlike sax quickly turned down as the lead guitar enters), an odd experimentation seems afoot in Ike and Tina Turner's "It's Gonna Work Out Fine" (where the two backing singers are wettest at 2:19–2:26 and dry immediately afterwards), and a sudden addition of reverb to the lead vocal at 2:10 in the Marvelettes' "Please Mr. Postman" suggests that a superimposed vocal might have been punched into a mismatched circuit. When the same degree of reverb is applied to all signals, the result implies a live performance, whereas sources given varying amounts of reverb lead the listener to identify a more artificially crafted process perhaps suggestive of an unreal experience.

An effect related to reverb is echo, whereby tape delay or some other electronic means produces reflections that can be heard as separate, unblending entries. Singers often used an echo box to magnify their presence against their bands in live performance, but the same effect could be created by a tape operator in the studio's control room. (Recall the echo effect on guitar in Web audio example 2.28.) Known as tape slap, such echo would be produced by the combination of the original signal and a copy routed through a loop of tape circling the playback head and record head on a slave machine other than the one making the master recording. By repositioning the distance between the playback and record heads and by switching the gears that control the tape-driving capstan, the speed of the echo could be adjusted along a wide range, often from as little as sixty milliseconds to as much as two seconds. (See Web photo 13.02.) Single delay without a repeating echo creates the effect of two guitars from a single instrument in the solo from the Jimi Hendrix Experience's studio version of "Red House" and also thickens the harp texture in the Beatles' "She's Leaving Home." (Listen to Web audio example 13.02.) Slap echo marks the radio announcer's break-in in Buchanan and Goodman's "Flying Saucer" and adds a spooky edge to the ends of phrases in Napoleon XIV's "They're Coming to Take Me Away, Ha-Haaa!" The speed of the tape echo is adjusted live for an unusual effect at the ends of refrains in the Beatles' "Paperback Writer" and the Lemon Pipers' "Green Tambourine." Echo gives the time-marking cowbell a sinister cast in the Chambers Brothers' "Time Has Come Today." But tape echo for its own sake is also one of the defining characteristics of a rockabilly vocal, as shown in Eddie Cochran's

"Twenty Flight Rock," Elvis Presley's "Tryin' to Get to You," and Jerry Lee Lewis's "Whole Lotta Shakin' Goin' On," and imitated as a style marker in Creedence Clearwater Revival's "Green River" and the Beatles' "Everybody's Trying to Be My Baby" and "The Ballad of John and Yoko." The rockabilly guitar and sometimes the country guitar as well were caught in the same quicksand: witness Duane Eddy's "Shazam!" and Don Gibson's "Oh Lonesome Me." Heavy tape echo is heard in the backing vocals of Jan and Dean's "Baby Talk," the piano of Bent Fabric's "Alley Cat," the xylophone in Lesley Gore's "You Don't Own Me," and the electric bass in the Beach Boys' "God Only Knows" (as in the high register at 0:21–0:24). One text-painting use is heard in Tommy James and the Shondells' "Mirage," selectively added to the second line, which is set in the reverberant "alleys and the hallways."

For the Beatles' "Tomorrow Never Knows," engineers found that the vocal could be given an unusual whirly sound if run through a Hammond's Leslie speaker; this became a favorite guitar coloring of George Harrison's, as heard in most of his late work with the group. (Recall Web audio example 2.27.) Leslied vocals are also heard in the Grateful Dead's "Rosemary," Brian Hyland's "Gypsy Woman," Cream's "As You Said," and the Moody Blues' "Dear Diary." Late in the '60s, engineers found that a low-speed oscillator could be applied to the vocal line, effecting a very wide tremolo reminiscent of slap echo; oscillators control the vocals in the Rolling Stones' "Please Go Home" and "In Another Land," the Hollies' "Dear Eloise," (backing vocals in) the First Edition's "Just Dropped In (To See What Condition My Condition Was In)," Donovan's "Hurdy Gurdy Man," Tommy James and the Shondells' "Crimson and Clover" and "Sweet Cherry Wine," and the Moody Blues' "Isn't Life Strange."

Similar to reverb, but less regular, is the chorus-like effect produced by unison double tracking (covered previously in chapter 5), or by artificial double-tracking (ADT), sometimes known as "flanging," which modulates the delay time in tape-derived reverb. This thickens the sound without the decay of reverb. ADT, invented by the Beatles' engineers, is noticeable in the lead guitar of "Here, There and Everywhere," which is also very wet with reverb, and in Paul McCartney's vocal in the chorus of "Eleanor Rigby" ("all the lonely people...," 0:31–0:44). (Listen to Web audio example 13.03.) Via ADT, Jerry Garcia's vocal is sent three separate ways in the Grateful Dead's disembodied "What's Become of the Baby," and the lead guitar shimmers with ADT in Iron Butterfly's "In-A-Gadda-Da-Vida."

In addition to presence, the loudness and tone of each source is typically controlled. It has already been mentioned that to keep noise at a minimum every source should be recorded at the loudest possible nominal level, but at whatever stage it is to be mixed with other sounds, the relative loudness of each is adjusted with knobs or faders on the board. Usually, a fine balance

Photo 13.03. Kristin Fosdick sets up bassist Erik Santos's personal mixer. All tracks from the drums, guitar, and bass, as well as floor microphones for the performers and a talk-back mic from the control room, can be set to any desired relative loudness in Erik's headphones. Each button along the bottom turns an incoming signal's channel (each labeled by Sharpie on masking tape) on or off. (Photo: Annie Eastman)

between all parties is achieved, but some unusual treatments exist. Lead vocals mixed lower than their accompaniments are heard in the Kingsmen's notoriously vague "Louie Louie," Jimi Hendrix's "Purple Haze," Martha and the Vandellas' "Jimmy Mack," the Supremes' "The Happening," Eric Clapton's part in Blind Faith's "Presence of the Lord," and Elvis Presley's "Burning Love." A low-in-the-mix vocal with very heavy reverb is characteristic of the Moody Blues, as in "Send Me No Wine" and "Gypsy." Instruments that seem unnaturally low include an alto sax in Connie Francis's "My Happiness," the trumpets in the Rolling Stones' "Have You Seen Your Mother, Baby, Standing in the Shadows," the piano in Donovan's "Skip-a-Long Sam," John Cale's viola in the Velvet Underground's "Sunday Morning," the strings in the Beatles' "Something," and the electric rhythm guitar in Gary Puckett and the Union Gap's first three hits. The lead singer is mixed way louder than necessary in Frankie Laine's "High Noon (Do Not Forsake Me)" and the Four Tops' "Ask the Lonely." The bass is too loud, like a pounding headache, in both Marvin Gaye's "Too Busy Thinking About My Baby" and, perhaps more appropriately, in the Everly Brothers' "Torture." The bass is similarly loud in the Guess Who's "These Eyes," but this seems a good foil for Burton

Cummings's strong tenor voice. The cello is much too obtrusive, spoiling the balance in Friend and Lover's "If Love Is In Your Heart." Drums are way out front in the Strangeloves' "I Want Candy," Bob Seger's "Ramblin' Gamblin' Man," and everything by the Dave Clark Five. Can a guitar be too loud? One candidate for consideration is Clarence Carter's in his "Slip Away."

It can be interesting to hear the faders at work, as the volumes of individual tracks are brought up or down in real time. At 0:25 in the Four Seasons' "Let's Hang On," the drums and guitar drop to highlight the entries of the bass and tambourine. Likewise, the introductory upright piano of Sly and the Family Stone's "Hot Fun in the Summertime" is suddenly mixed down when the strings, bass, and backbeat drums enter at 0:10. One of two electric twelve-string guitars is boosted for a solo (1:43–2:14) in Jefferson Airplane's "Let's Get Together," the Musitron is brought way up for its solo in Brenton Wood's "Gimme Little Sign" and so is the harpsichord in The Doors' "Love Me Two Times." Near the end of Jimi Hendrix's "1983 . . . (A Merman I Should Turn to Be)," the bass is boosted for a solo and then the remainder of the band is faded up for a jam on one final chord before the song's structure returns.

As for tone, a circuit for each track on the board will be fitted with high-pass, low-pass, and band-pass filters, each allowing a particular range of frequencies to be boosted or cut. The relative strength or equalization of different frequencies—the highs, middles, and lows—greatly affects the timbre of the signal, and is useful for defining sounds, particularly their attacks, primarily in order to give contrasting colors to several sounds that happen to share the same tonal range, such as two mid-range rhythm guitars playing similar patterns. (Listen to Web audio example 13.04.) Just as with reverb, the loudness and EQ of each track can be adjusted at any point in the recording process, typically when sources are combined. In Web audio example 5.05, the soprano's vocal is altered by a hi-cut filter beginning at 0:30, at first masking all frequencies above 3,100 cycles per second (for "But she also has a much darker side"), but gradually opening so that by 0:45 ("and then back she can glide") all frequencies below 20,000 cps are unaffected. Filtered vocals represent the singer's conscience in Lesley Gore's "Brink of Disaster," a read-aloud letter in Dale Ward's "A Letter From Sherry," and simple 1920s-style low-fidelity recordings in the New Vaudeville Band's "Winchester Cathedral," the Rolling Stones' "On With the Show," and the Mothers of Invention's "Bow Tie Daddy." Shadowing vocals are created when the vocal track is heard both straight and, overdubbed or through a split separate signal, filtered as well; this splits the singer in the refrain of Janis Ian's "Insanity Comes Quietly to the Structured Mind." In The Doors' "Strange Days," Morrison's shadowing vocal is given a ghostly tremolo as well as filtering. A guitar may be routed so that most of its signal is "straight," but part of it can be distorted and either blended back with the original signal or both may be sent to separate locations in the stereo image. (Listen to Web audio example 13.05.) Some guitar amplifiers permit the blending of two or more (clean and dirty, for instance) circuits, but this can be achieved after the fact at the engineer's desk if track space allows.

When tape delay is brought down to the millisecond range, another effect known as phasing is possible. The overlapping of a signal against itself (as by tape delay) by such a small amount that individual wavelengths are out of phase with each other causes them to cancel each other out, often with a cascading filtering effect upon upper partials. (Recall Web audio example 2.31.) Although apparently first discovered for the recording of Miss Toni Fisher's "The Big Hurt" in 1959, this effect became a mainstay of psychedelia; in representative songs charting between November 1967 and February 1969 alone, phasing is heard in vocals and drums in the bridges of the Small Faces' "Itchycoo Park," the vocal of Jimi Hendrix's "Little Wing," all instruments and vocals in Grapefruit's "Dear Delilah," the opening guitar lick of Eric Burdon and the Animals' "Sky Pilot," vocals and guitars in the Status Quo's "Pictures of Matchstick Men," the drums of Blue Cheer's "Just a Little Bit," the organ, guitars, and drums in Mike Bloomfield, Al Kooper, and Steve Stills' "You Don't Love Me," the vocal track at 0:43–1:03 in the Grateful Dead's "That's It for The Other One," and the vocals in the last verse of the Arbors' "The Letter."

Another important effect is compression. This boosts sounds at low volume and cuts those at high volume, in effect squeezing the volume range. Compressors make for a hard, solidly saturated quality when set with a low threshold (thus submitting all or nearly all parts of the signal to the effect) and high ratio (resulting in more extreme changes to the signal's gain). Vocals in Web audio examples 5.04 and 7.07 are given heavy compression; compare the quality with those of 5.02, 5.03 and 5.05, which have almost none. (Listen also to Web audio example 13.06.) With certain instruments, particularly drums and guitars, this effect can smooth out the sound, removing unwanted variations. When used at maximum settings, the compressor can virtually remove the natural attack and decay colorings of a sound; this is why the rhythm guitar sounds more like an electronic organ in the Beatles' "I Want to Hold Your Hand" and "Don't Bother Me." Drums are highly compressed in the Beatles' "You Won't See Me," as are the brass in "Got to Get You Into My Life" and "Good Morning Good Morning," and John Lennon's final muttering and dog howls in "Hey Bulldog." A banjo track is highly compressed in Herman's Hermits' "Mrs. Brown You've Got a Lovely Daughter" as are the tom-toms in King Crimson's "Moonchild" and Jim Morrison's vocal in The Doors' "Love Her Madly." Whereas the compressor can be applied to any individual track or any signal along the way, it is chiefly used to a small degree in the mixdown of the final working tape so as to give all aspects of the final master (no matter how sonically varied the individual songs on an album, for instance, might be) a uniform flattened or damped, well-stepped-on tonal quality.

Tape manipulation

Multitrack tape was useful not only for allowing the isolation of particular performances, but also for allowing the sound-on-sound superimposition of solo lines or other details on top of a previously recorded backing track. This opportunity led to

> **Tape manipulation:** sound-on-sound; sound effects; speed changes and reverse tape; editing.

the near-universal adoption of eight-track tape by the end of the 1960s and the jump to sixteen tracks within months after that. In the early 1950s, Les Paul and Mary Ford experimented with trick vocal overdubs, so that Mary sings duets with herself in "How High the Moon" and "Vaya Con Dios (May God Be With You)," and a self-trio in "The World Is Waiting for the Sunrise." Self-duets and -trios were taken up by Patti Page, Buddy Holly, Bobby Vee, Connie Francis, Neil Sedaka, Gene Pitney, and many other singers. As rock groups came to consist of performers who both played and sang simultaneously (a rare breed in prior styles), standard recording procedure changed to concentrate first on instrumental backing tracks (sometimes just the rhythm section), then the superimposition of vocals, lead guitar solos, and any other sweetening on top of that. In 1963 and thereafter, pop singers were often double-tracked at the unison, beefing up their own single-line vocals. This seems to have been practiced most often with young women; thus do we hear the lead singers of the Chiffons' "He's So Fine," the Angels' "My Boyfriend's Back," and the Crystals' "Then He Kissed Me," major hits by Little Peggy March and Lesley Gore. The technique was also adopted by males, as heard in Brian Wilson's perfectly matched vocal parts in many Beach Boys songs ("Be True to Your School," "Don't Talk (Put Your Head on My Shoulder)"), with Paul McCartney ("Can't Buy Me Love") and John Lennon ("I Should Have Known Better") bringing the Beatles onto the bandwagon as well. Overdubbed vocals are used for new artistic purposes in the Beatles' "Julia," so that John Lennon can overlap the end of one vocal phrase with the beginning of his next.

Guitar lines added after the recording of basic tracks can be detected in Fats Domino's "Bo Weevil," Chuck Berry's "Johnny B. Goode," the acoustic twelve-string solo in the Beatles' "I've Just Seen a Face," much of Jimi Hendrix's and Jimmy Page's work, and Eric Clapton's rhythm and lead parts in all of John Mayall's Blues Breakers and in much of Cream. In the *Wheels of Fire* version of "Politician," Clapton plays *three* simultaneous guitar solos at 2:04–3:21. In Fabian's "Tiger," two different, simultaneously competing solos survive, as if two attempts were recorded but the producer forgot to mute one of them in mastering. In "I Want to Hold Your Hand," the Beatles seem to celebrate their first taste of four-track recording with George Harrison's overdub of a one-bar bass line (0:10–0:12) that he was to play onstage always thereafter in preference to the guitar line he plays on the single's basic tracks. Many Doors records have two simultaneous solo keyboards, as with Ray Manzarek's electric organ and electric piano in "The Crystal Ship" or his two harpsichords in "Wintertime Love."

The freedom of overdubbing allowed other developments such as the creation of interesting bass lines, particularly those invented by Paul McCartney in counterpoint to previously completed Beatles tracks. Frank Zappa performs and arranges many overdubs in *Uncle Meat* and *Hot Rats,* and *McCartney* is basically performed by a multitracking one-man band. Not only would overdubbing involve the recording of complete new parts, but sometimes a singer or other soloist might need to replace one errant note or passage by punching in a correctly performed substitute. To do this, the tape operator would cue up the original tape, to which the performer(s) would listen with headphones, singing or playing along, and an engineer would engage the record control just for the passage that needed replacement. In one case, at 1:50 and 2:32 in the Beatles' "Day Tripper," engineers simply punched out bad guitar notes (along with the tambourine hits that came out with them) without replacing them, leaving a moment of blank space in their stead. Because of guitar doublings, it was likely thought that because the only projected release of "Day Tripper" at the time of recording was a monophonic single, the dropouts would not be noticed. They are easily heard in stereo mixes, in which the doubled guitars have been routed to different locations.

Once the producer has all the necessary work out of his artists, he may hire outside musicians to add orchestral instrumentation or may turn to the studio's tape library to add sound effects. Table 13.02 lists most of the common sound effects from this period with representative recordings making use of them. These effects range from the barely heard pop of a wine cork in the Beatles' "Lovely Rita" to entire compositions by the Beatles, the Mothers of Invention, Pink Floyd, and others, formed of tape loops and electronically produced sounds.

Final possibilities with tape manipulation include changing the speed of the performance and playing material in reverse. (Listen to Web audio example 13.07.) Les Paul made his guitar sound almost like another instrument when he would record it four times slower than normal so on playback at normal speed it would sound highly sped up, as in "Lover" (1948) and "Hummingbird" (1955). The result sounded not only four times faster than he played it, but also four octaves higher, in a very nonguitarlike register. Later examples of sped-up guitar include the flamenco take-off in the

Table 13.02 Selected examples of sound effects in recordings of 1955–70

Rain, thunder:

Priscilla Wright, "The Man in the Raincoat"
Dee Clark, "Raindrops"
Cascades, "Rhythm of the Rain"
Ronettes, "Walking in the Rain"
Four Seasons, "Tell It To the Rain"

Cowsills, "The Rain, the Park and Other Things"
Temptations, "I Wish It Would Rain"
Rascals, "A Rainy Day"
Grass Roots, "The River Is Wide"

Ocean surf, bubbles, fog horn, seagulls, ship's bell:

Frankie Ford, "Sea Cruise"
Islanders, "The Enchanted Sea"
Platters, "Harbor Lights"
Tymes, "So Much In Love"
Robin Ward, "Wonderful Summer"
Stevie Wonder, "Castles in the Sand"
Shangri-Las, "Remember (Walkin' In the Sand)"
Beatles, "Yellow Submarine"

The Doors, "Horse Latitudes"
Donovan, "Starfish-On-The-Toast"
Otis Redding, "(Sittin' On) The Dock of the Bay"
Pink Floyd, "Set the Controls for the Heart of the Sun"
Beatles, "Octopus' Garden"
Jefferson Airplane, "Wooden Ships"

Running brook:

Spirit, "Water Woman"

Airplane/jet engine:

Royal Guardsmen, "The Return of the Red Baron"

Box Tops, "The Letter"
Beatles, "Back in the U.S.S.R."

Car/bus/motorcycle engine:

Beach Boys, "409"
Jan and Dean, "Drag City"
Detergents, "Leader of the Laundromat"
Davie Allan and the Arrows, "Blue's Theme"

Arlo Guthrie, "The Motorcycle Song"
Beatles, "Magical Mystery Tour"
Simon and Garfunkel, "Baby Driver"

Car/bicycle horn/bell:

Bob McFadden, "The Mummy"
Eddie Hodges, "I'm Gonna Knock on Your Door"
Herb Alpert and the Tijuana Brass, "Tijuana Taxi"

Lovin' Spoonful, "Summer in the City"
Soul Survivors, "Expressway To Your Heart"
Rascals, "Dave and Eddie"
Rolling Stones, "Country Honk"

Sirens:

Napoleon XIV, "They're Coming to Take Me Away, Ha-Haaa!"

The Move, "Fire Brigade"

Car/motorcycle crash:

Nervous Norvous, "Transfusion"
Shangri-Las, "Leader of the Pack"

Moby Grape, "Motorcycle Irene"

Roller-coaster, calliope:

Freddie Cannon, "Palisades Park"

Beatles, "Being for the Benefit of Mr. Kite"

Insects, birds:

Screamin' Jay Hawkins, "Alligator Wine"
Martin Denny, "Quiet Village"

Blood, Sweat and Tears, "House in the Country"

Chubby Checker, "The Fly"
Tommy James and the Shondells, "I Think We're Alone Now"
The Parade, "Sunshine Girl"
Young Rascals, "Groovin'"
Donovan, "Voyage Into the Golden Screen"
Steppenwolf, "Disappointment Number (Unknown)"
Beatles, "Blackbird"
The Incredible String Band, "Greatest Friend"
Pink Floyd, "Grantchester Meadows"

Barking dogs, galloping horse, other animals:
Patti Page, "(How Much Is) That Doggie in the Window"
Chordettes, "Zorro"
Beach Boys, *Pet Sounds*
Beatles, "Good Morning Good Morning"
Deep Purple, "Hush"
Jeff Beck Group, "I Ain't Superstitious"
Beatles, "Piggies"

Newborn cry:
Donovan, "Song of the Naturalist's Wife"

Gunshots:
Olympics, "Western Movies"
David Seville and the Chipmunks, "Ragtime Cowboy Joe"
Jerry Landis, "The Lone Teen Ranger"
Coasters, "T'Ain't Nothin' to Me"
Jr. Walker and the All Stars, "Shotgun"
Lee Dorsey, "Ride Your Pony"
Royal Guardsmen, "Snoopy vs. the Red Baron"
Country Joe and the Fish, "I-Feel-Like-I'm-Fixin'-To-Die Rag"
Georgie Fame, "The Ballad of Bonnie and Clyde"

Explosion:
Soul Survivors, "Explosion In Your Soul"
Steve Miller Band, "Brave New World"

Smashed glass:
The Who, "Smash the Mirror"

Barroom, night club, audience noise:
Gary U.S. Bonds, "Quarter to Three"
Jack Ross, "Cinderella"
Gary U.S. Bonds, "Twist, Twist Senora"
Herb Alpert and the Tijuana Brass, "The Lonely Bull (El Solo Torro)"
Dixiebelles, "(Down At) Papa Joe's"
Kingsmen, "Money"
Bob Dylan, "Rainy Day Women #12 & 35"
"Cannonball" Adderly, "Mercy, Mercy, Mercy"
Byrds, "So You Want to Be a Rock 'N' Roll Star"
Beatles, "Sgt. Pepper's Lonely Hearts Club Band"
Mothers of Invention, "America Drinks and Goes Home"
Big Brother and the Holding Company, "Turtle Blues"
Ray Stevens, "Gitarzan"
Jimi Hendrix, "My Friend"

Typewriters/cash register/ticking clock:
The First Edition, "I Found a Reason"
Jefferson Airplane, "Lather"
Scaffold, "Thank U Very Much"

Bubbling beakers:
Bobby "Boris" Pickett and the Crypt-Kickers, "The Monster Mash"

Pop of champagne cork:
Beatles, "Lovely Rita"
Royal Guardsmen, "Snoopy's Christmas"

(continued)

Table 13.02 Continued

Lighting of a match:
Simon and Garfunkel, "Overs"

Boomerang:
Charlie Drake, "My Boomerang Won't
    Come Back"

Woodsaw:
Turtles, "Sound Asleep"

Pounding gavel:
Unifics, "Court of Love"

Telephone ring:
Big Bopper, "Chantilly Lace"   Garland Green, "Jealous Kind Of Fella"
Mothers of Invention, "Bow Tie Daddy"

Footsteps:
Bobby Vee, "Walkin' with My Angel"   Zombies, "The Way I Feel Inside"

Knocking/doorbell, opening/slamming door:
The Sopwith "Camel," "Postcard from   Rolling Stones, "We Love You"
    Jamaica"   Moody Blues, "House of Four Doors"
Simon and Garfunkel, "Fakin' It"   Temptations, "Psychedelic Shack"

78-rpm record surface noise:
Monkees, "Magnolia Simms"   Beatles, "Honey Pie"

Electronic effects, found sounds, tape loops:
Beatles, "Tomorrow Never Knows"   Grateful Dead, "Caution (Do Not Stop on
Mothers of Invention, "The Return of the   Tracks)"
    Son of Monster Magnet"   Jimi Hendrix Experience, "1983...
Beatles, "Inner Groove"   (A Merman I Should Turn to Be)"
Phil Ochs, "The Crucifixion"   Beatles, "Revolution 9"
Jefferson Airplane, "A Small Package of   Bonzo Dog Band, "We Are Normal"
    Value Will Come to You, Shortly"   Beatles, "You Never Give Me Your Money"
Buckinghams, "Have You Noticed You're   Pink Floyd, "Set the Controls for the Heart
    Alive"   of the Sun"
Mothers of Invention, "Are You Hung Up?"   Pink Floyd, "Sysyphus"
Mothers of Invention, "Nasal Retentive   Pink Floyd, "Several Species of Small Furry
    Calliope Music"   Animals Gathered Together in a Cave and
Frank Zappa, *Lumpy Gravy;*   Grooving With a Pict"
Grateful Dead, "That's It for The Other One"   Pink Floyd, "The Narrow Way"

Monkees' "Valleri" and many examples from Frank Zappa for the Mothers, including the resulting harpsichord-like guitar sound (at 1:21–2:05) in "Call Any Vegetable," the electric-guitar solo in "Nine Types of Industrial Pollution," and a nylon-string solo in "My Guitar Wants to Kill Your Mama." Aside from Les Paul, other early tape-speed tricks include the vocal imitations of chipmunks (David Seville and the Chipmunks' "Witch Doctor" and

"The Chipmunk Song") and aliens (Buchanan and Goodman's "The Flying Saucer," Sheb Wooley's "The Purple People Eater"). A less drastically altered speed would simply make singers sound much younger than they actually were (The Cowboy Church Sunday School's "Open Up Your Heart"). But although the Beatles also manipulated tape speed to make themselves sound younger (as did Paul McCartney in "When I'm Sixty-Four"), they discovered that slighter adjustments to tape speed altered their vocal timbre without such profound effects; note the different speeds of John Lennon's voice in "Strawberry Fields Forever" and "Lucy in the Sky With Diamonds." Ringo's voice, by contrast, sounds ridiculously high in the mono mix of "Don't Pass Me By." The Mothers record quite a bit of double-speed "chipmunk" vocals, as in "Take Your Clothes Off When You Dance" and "Electric Aunt Jemima"; Jimi Hendrix drops the speed of his voice by half for his alien imitation in "Third Stone From the Sun" and "EXP," and James Taylor and Peter Asher record double-speed backing vocals for the former's "Carolina in My Mind" in an apparent attempt to emulate female singers.

The piano, which sounds a good bit like a harpsichord when replayed at double speed, is probably treated this way more than any other instrument; this is heard in the Bach-like "harpsichord" solo in the Beatles' "In My Life," Herb Alpert's "Spanish Flea," the Cyrkle's "Turn-Down Day," the Mothers' "The Chrome Plated Megaphone of Destiny," and the Association's "Wasn't It a Bit Like Now." Zappa also sped up a celesta, harpsichord, organ, and mallet instruments, as well as woodwinds and other percussion throughout *Uncle Meat* and following albums. Tape-speed manipulation was used for purposes other than creating "new" instruments; sometimes, it worked unobtrusively to raise the pitch a minor second, as in Eddie Cochran's "Cut Across Shorty," Brian Wilson's "Caroline No," the Beatles' "She's Leaving Home," and the original monophonic single mix of The Doors' "Light My Fire." This slight speeding-up of the tape also might serve to tighten the ensemble, blending a bit better any rhythmic imprecision that might be audible at the recorded speed. But probably its most outlandish effect was for a full glissando, the speed changing as recording was taking place, as on the last chords of the Rascals' "It's Wonderful" and the Hollies' "Dear Eloise," the cadence of the Turtles' "Sound Asleep," or most ambitiously, through the lines of Napoleon XIV's "They're Coming to Take Me Away, Ha-Haaa!," in which the voice manages to keep a steady tempo while approaching lunacy with ever-higher cycling of the tape-speed effect.

Backward taping maintains the tone color of the original source but completely reverses its envelope of attack and decay (as well as any melodic, rhythmic, or harmonic progressions it may have contained). The only purpose served by such a technique is to create an otherworldly sound, clearly a goal in much rock music. Reversed vocals are heard in the Beatles' "Rain," the end of Side One of the Mothers' *We're Only In It For the Money,* and Moby

Grape's "Bitter Wind." Backward guitar is heard in the Beatles' "I'm Only Sleeping," the Electric Prunes' "I Had Too Much to Dream (Last Night)," The Who's "Armenia in the Sky," Jimi Hendrix's "Are You Experienced?," and (with acoustic guitar) the First Edition's "Just Dropped In (To See What Condition My Condition Was In)." Backward percussion is heard in the Beatles' "Strawberry Fields Forever," the Association's "On a Quiet Night," and Tommy James and the Shondells' "Mirage," backward piano is heard in the Rolling Stones' "2000 Light Years From Home," and other backward tapes are used in The Who's "Amazing Journey" and "Sparks." Entire singles are reversed to create their B-sides in the case of Napoleon XIV's "They're Coming To Take Me Away, Ha-Haaa!" and Yellow Balloon's "Yellow Balloon." It may be worth considering that visual analogs to such distortions are the time-warping fish-eye album covers for the Byrds' *Mr. Tambourine Man* and the Dead's *Anthem of the Sun* and the Beatles' otherwise distorted cover for *Rubber Soul,* and that the color-negative cover of the Mothers' *Freak Out!* is not too bad an analogue for reversed tapes.

Especially with such trick recording techniques as these, one is sometimes pushed to question how close to an ideal a recording may come in terms of production values. Universal agreement as to underproduced and overproduced records is somewhat rare, and often such judgments are made when considered at a great remove from the original style's popular context. This being said, it still seems odd that sopranos would wordlessly double the tenor sax for the intro and interludes of Paul Anka's "The Story of My Love." And whereas James William Guercio's interpolations of Varèse and other points of electronic collage within the Buckinghams' "Susan" may be very interesting, they aren't integrated well enough with the various parts of the love song to convince the listener that they may, for example, represent the singer's losing his mind, which he complains at one point is happening. More effective is the single's flip side, where "Foreign Policy" uses key lines from John F. Kennedy's celebrated American University commencement address on world peace and other unexpected additions to the Buckinghams' musical statement about the country's wrong-headed future. It is difficult, really, to decide that Tom Wilson went overboard in adding electric bass, electric guitar, and drums, all without the artist-composer's permission, to the simple two-voice and acoustic-guitar performance that had been Simon and Garfunkel's "Sounds of Silence." Most listeners, it seems, think he did fine, as he thereby produced a number-one record, but he never worked for them again. Some arrangements are fairly bad; the Tremeloes' "Even the Bad Times Are Good" is sung nearly all in unison—is this a bad choice of material or simply an underproduced recording? It's easier to spot out-and-out errors, like the false entry at 2:42–2:43 in The Mamas and the Papas' "I Saw Her Again," that would normally have been punched out. And there's plenty of sloppy play and a poor resulting balance in what was likely an underrehearsed production of Deep Purple's *Concerto for Group and Orchestra*. But there must have been mitigating circumstances resulting in such imperfect releases. Conversely, matters of interpretation are more interesting and subject to debate.

Following these tape techniques, one other step may be necessary before creating the master: there may be some editing required. Joining part of one performance to part of another or adding edit pieces that were specifically taped to insert into an otherwise complete recording is usually done before the final shading is added in the mixdown to the one- or two-channel master. (The final chord of the Beatles' "Roll Over Beethoven" can be identified as an edit piece because its level is louder than the previously heard guitar, and its EQ is different as well; in the case of Pat Boone's "Bernadine," the guitar's intro and final chord must be from edit pieces because their pitch is slightly higher than that of the remainder of the guitar playing.) In order to keep track of the whereabouts on one or more reels of all the different takes of a record-ing, its overdubs and edit pieces, a tape operator will typically keep a written log through a recording session, noting tape-counter numbers as an index, and will also announce the "slate" through a control-room microphone every time the tape begins rolling. The log will often note preliminary decisions about what take or what part of a take is the best of a series. The slate (named after the clapboard that marks the scene, take, camera, and sound-synchronization information in raw film outtakes) may consist of the song's working title, take number, overdub or edit-piece information. An edit piece may be a re-done interior passage, but is more often an ending of some sort to be tacked onto the body of the song. A slate for "Take 7A" from a vocal overdub session is heard with a bit of prerecording banter at the opening of the Monkees' "Daydream Believer." Usually, the slate information is trimmed from the start of a song along with any count-off or drumstick clicks that may have been necessary to achieve an ensemble entry. In the Monkees' case, however, the hijinks involv-ing singer Davy Jones's not catching the slate information and having to ask his mates about it was not only untrimmed, it was disingenuously spliced onto the opening of the track as an edit piece from somewhere else in the project, just to let listeners think they were getting a behind-the-scenes perspective.

Edits are made with splices, the joining of bits of recording tape that have been carefully marked by a grease pencil for cutting, the two bits of tape aligned and cut together with one swipe of a razor blade. Splices are usually most evident from subtle clues, such as the sudden appearance or disappear-ance of reverb, as in the Beach Boys' "And Your Dream Comes True" (as at 0:13 and 0:26), in the Four Seasons' "C'mon Marianne" (0:17), and through-out Senator Bobby's "Wild Thing." But sometimes they are not so clean; the sustain of Joe South's guitar is cut short in his intro to Aretha Franklin's "Chain of Fools," betraying the splice, and something similar happens to

John Lennon's vocal at 1:28 in "This Boy." In Diana Ross and the Supremes' "Reflections," the splice at 2:31 is unconvincing, as if composer-producers Holland, Dozier and Holland couldn't think of a good way to end the song and so just attached a repetitive coda recorded separately. It's tempting to guess that the intro to Donovan's "Happiness Runs" might have been composed after most of the song had been recorded, because the splice of the intro to the song proper is audible at 0:51. Apparently, the blistering guitar solo of Mitch Ryder and the Detroit Wheels' "Devil With a Blue Dress On and Good Golly Miss Molly" must have been cut short, as the solo returns very awkwardly to the vocals of "Devil." In the Beatles' "She's Leaving Home," all refrains run an irregular seven bars because the last, eighth, performed bar (comprising a less than satisfactory line from the solo cello) was excised each time. Splicing is part of the compositional process behind Frank Zappa's stratified "Help, I'm a Rock" and "Plastic People," both of which contain some sections of music joined to others. Brian Wilson worked the same way in 1966–67, as is evident in such sectional Beach Boys tracks as "Good Vibrations" and "Heroes and Villains."

In our chapter on rhythm, we touched on different final edits that might be released simultaneously for the radio and for the singles and album markets. But other anomalies exist between extant mixes that aren't easily accounted for—why does the stereo mix of Bobby Lewis's "Tossin' and Turnin'" have a slow introduction not appearing on the monophonic mix? Why does the stereo mix of the Buckinghams' "Kind of a Drag" restore the out-of-tune trumpets that were muted out of the organ break in the monophonic single mix? Crossfaded recordings, such as result when separately performed sections of Cream's "Passing the Time" fade into and out of one another, normally don't require remixes, but because the Moody Blues' album version of "Nights in White Satin" crossfades into orchestral material, it had to be remixed in order that the single maintain its integrity as a complete and independent work. It is quite understandable why the Grateful Dead's *Anthem of the Sun,* a complex weaving together of intricate concert and studio performances, was released in somewhat different forms for stereo and mono albums (and yet again for the digitally mixed compact disc); its editing and mixing had to be quite a messy operation!

Creating the Master

So, with all recording done, it is time to reduce all the desired material on the working tape to a master of two channels for stereo pressings, or just one channel for monophonic ones. 45-rpm singles were all in mono until early 1968, at which time stereo pressings first appeared and gradually became common. Album pressings were made in both mono and stereo versions throughout our period, but mono albums became quickly rare in 1969. The final mix, in the analog age, was a live dub from the working tape to another machine, all the time setting the final compression, working the EQ

> **Mastering:** stereo and mono mixing, track muting, fades, final coloring, soundstage and panning.

and volume faders to pass only the desired material and mute what may be on the tape but unusable (such as a click track for keeping a steady rhythm, a guide vocal later replaced by a finished performance, bleed-through from one loud track to its empty neighbor, or alternative solos; obviously, an eight-track tape was more liable to contain such detritus than was a more efficiently packed four-track tape). In addition, for a stereo master, balance knobs had to be set to send each source to the desired location in the stereo image. These settings may have had to be changed from one part of the song to another, especially when one tape track would include, for instance, a tambourine in the verses, backing vocals in the choruses, and a punched-in guitar solo in the break. The mix may be quite a complex procedure; all aspects of the mix may have to be written down, carefully rehearsed, and attempted in a number of takes before the final mix has been deemed acceptable. In today's world of digital mic and amp modeling, of digital recording and audio processing, all of these elements can be performed in any order during the post-production process—not so in the live, analog age. (See Web photo 13.03.)

Photo 13.04. The forty-channel API Vision desk in the University of Michigan Audio Studio control room, designed for 5.1 surround sound as well as for conventional mixing. (Photo: Annie Eastman)

Many recordings from the period were made hits only at the mixing stage. The Zombies' "Time of the Season," examined for its intricate texture in our chapter on rhythm, is most effective because of the stop time that thins out the originally recorded full instrumental texture for every hearing of the three-part choral refrain, as at 0:32–0:40. The mix for Steam's "Na Na Hey Hey Kiss Him Goodbye" is a complicated mess involving an immediate muting of pitch instruments at 1:44 to allow for a drum solo; superimposed vibraphone, tubular bells, and piano enter between 2:32 and 2:41, and then the basic track is restored at 2:49 before the Vox organ is added at 2:57. But the original backing track here, consisting of drums, bass, and guitar, continued to hammer away until muted out in the mix. Unusual fade-outs are given to Tommy James and the Shondells' "Sweet Cherry Wine," in which a piccolo is allowed to continue at full volume after everything else has faded out, and "Ball of Fire," in which drums and vocal are selected for outliving their colleagues. A minute-long coda for electric guitar lingers beyond the fading out of the rhythm section in Bloomfield, Kooper and Stills's "His Holy Modal Majesty," and a percussive mix of claves, cowbell, Chinese blocks, and maracas from the rhythm track outlasts the pitch instruments that fade out early in Chicago Transit Authority's "Beginnings." Basic tracks are muted out of the backward guitar solo (1:31–1:49) in the Jimi Hendrix Experience's "Castles Made of Sand," and there must have been some muted-out musical accompaniment to the Dead's a cappella song, "What's Become of the Baby," else Jerry Garcia surely would have strayed off pitch in his 8'14" vocal.

Two different mixes were made for single and album for The Doors' "Touch Me," even though both were pressed in stereo—the album mix retains the final "stronger than dirt" incantation from the Ajax detergent jingle, whereas this is muted out of the single mix. In The Doors' "The Crystal Ship," one is left to wonder what the electric piano might have been doing through the first verse, because it is only brought in after that is over, to be faded up over the guitar. In the Moody Blues' "The Best Way to Travel," if the middle section's multiple pans of the pitch-bending Mellotron don't manage it, then the listener is sure to get a surprise from the gradual fade-in of the next verse. The mix is the last chance to omit sins, as with wrong bass notes that are punched out of the Four Tops' "Loving You Is Sweeter Than Ever" (at 1:01 and 1:36), and handclaps that go astray in Archie Bell and the Drells' ironically titled "Tighten Up" are finally muted at 1:51, although the engineering remains sloppy as well: the vocal is suddenly unmuted mid-syllable at 2:51. And finally, muting can simply remove unwanted noise; note how the vocal track of the Beatles' "I Want to Hold Your Hand" (in the stereo mix appearing on CD) fades up late in the intro, just before the voices enter; this may have eliminated either pretake chat or unwanted bleed-through from monitor speakers in the vocal overdub session.

Unless a song was written with a cold finish, coming to a definite ending on a final chord, it had to be gradually faded out, typically after some repetitions of a never-ending coda. This would be done at the end of the mix, by carefully drawing down the master fader(s), one for each channel. The fade-out was not widespread in the 1950s, but was used then in many recordings by the Drifters. In the 1960s, only rare bands such as the Kinks preferred to use a concert ending in their recordings. Occasionally, a track would fade in, as with two processionals popular in 1959, Cyril Stapleton's Orchestra's "Nick Nack Paddy Whack (The Children's Marching Song)" and the Mormon Tabernacle Choir's "Battle Hymn of the Republic." The Beatles' "Eight Days a Week" fades in as a deliberate novelty. Other examples of fading in include the drums' opening of Creedence Clearwater Revival's "Suzie Q," the two very dirty guitars that bring in Steppenwolf's "Magic Carpet Ride," and the carefully matched drums and bass that fade in underneath the flute/alto flute duet, triangle tremolo, and violin harmonics to usher in a new age in the 5th Dimension's "Aquarius/Let the Sunshine In (The Flesh Failures)."

Sometimes a fade-out carries a cinematic quality. In the Monkees' "Pleasant Valley Sunday," the fade is very heavily distorted by massive reverb on the instrumental tracks, suggesting the permeation of the garage band's output through its suburban neighborhood. In Zager and Evans' "In the Year 2525 (Exordium and Terminus)," the fade-out accompanies a resumption of the first verse, making clear that in the coming millennia, we are doomed to repeat the same mistakes we have already made. Extra long fade-outs accompany the Beatles' "Hey Jude," Creedence's "I Heard It Through the Grapevine," and Blind Faith's "Do What You Like" (no doubt to preserve the late-appearing imitation of Edward G. Robinson). Fade-outs sometimes lead to a false ending, with the coda returning for a second finish. This comes as a shock in the Contours' "Do You Love Me," and then takes on different qualities in the Beatles' "Strawberry Fields Forever," the Rolling Stones' "Dandelion," the Jimi Hendrix Experience's "Are You Experienced?," the First Edition's "Just Dropped In," Led Zeppelin's "Thank You," and the Small Faces' "Afterglow." Three songs end neither with a concert ending nor a fade-out, coming rather to a sudden stop as the result of an arbitrary snip of an engineer's scissors: Deep Purple's "Chasing Shadows" and the ends of both sides of the Beatles' *Abbey Road* ("I Want You (She's So Heavy)" and "Her Majesty").

The overlapping crossfade, whereby one program fades in before the previous one fades out (analogous to the cinematographer's dissolve), was an old technique in sound recording, carried into the 1960s largely in comedy records; those by Bob Newhart and Bill Cosby were the decade's major chart-toppers whose work was arranged thus. Only occasionally was this used in popular music, and then not much until 1966–67, when traffic sounds thus infiltrated the Lovin' Spoonful's "Summer in the City" and the Soul Survivors' "Expressway to Your Heart." But new musical uses were also found at this time, as in the opening of the Association's "Wasn't It a Bit Like Now (Parallel 23)" (in which the rock riff, ♭VI—♭VII—I, is repeated for twenty-two seconds before melting into the vaudeville-like song proper), the ending of Simon and Garfunkel's "Fakin' It" (in which the ending fades into toms), and Cream's "Passing the Time" (which overlaps a number of separately recorded sections). In *Days of Future Passed*, Moody Blues' songs "Another Morning," "Tuesday Afternoon," "The Sun Set/Twilight Time," and "Nights in White Satin" each crossfade out of orchestral introductions and into orchestral endings. But, more important, suites like the Grateful Dead's "That's It For The Other One" and entire album sides were suddenly unified with this approach. Table 13.03 lists a number of projects in which the crossfade was used to join different songs; all date from the period beginning with the June 1967 appearance of *Sgt. Pepper* and continue through September 1970. Sometimes a patch covers the transition, as with the applause that joins the songs of the Hendrix example, or the finger cymbals and effects loops that join the Beatles' "You Never Give Me Your Money" and "Sun King." In the Moody Blues' *On*

Table 13.03 Crossfades from one song to the next

Beatles (*Sgt. Pepper's Lonely Hearts Club Band*), "Sgt. Pepper's Lonely Hearts Club Band" to "With a Little Help From My Friends"; "Sgt. Pepper's Lonely Hearts Club Band (Reprise)" to "A Day in the Life"

Beatles (*Abbey Road*), "You Never Give Me Your Money" to "Sun King"

Blood, Sweat and Tears (*Blood, Sweat and Tears*), "Blues—Part II" to "Variations on a Theme by Erik Satie"

Doors (*Morrison Hotel*), "Peace Frog" to "Blue Sunday"

Jimi Hendrix Experience (*Electric Ladyland*), "Crosstown Traffic" to "Voodoo Chile"

Jefferson Airplane (*After Bathing at Baxter's*), "The Ballad of You & Me & Pooneil" and "A Small Package of Value Will Come to You, Shortly" and "Young Girl Sunday Blues"

Moody Blues (*On the Threshold of a Dream*), "In the Beginning" to "Lovely to See You" to "Dear Diary"; "Send Me No Wine" to "To Share Our Love"; "Never Comes the Day" to "Lazy Day" to "Are You Sitting Comfortably" to "The Dream" to "Have You Heard—Part I" to "The Voyage" to "Have You Heard—Part II"

Moody Blues (*A Question of Balance*), "Question" to "How Is It (We Are Here)" to "And the Tide Rushes In" to "Don't You Feel Small" to "Tortoise and the Hare"; "It's Up to You" to "Minstrel's Song" to "Dawning Is the Day" to "Melancholy Man" to "The Balance"

Spirit (*The Family That Plays Together*), "I Got a Line On You" to "It Shall Be"

Steppenwolf (*Steppenwolf The Second*), "Disappointment Number (Unknown)" to "Lost and Found by Trial and Error"; "Resurrection" to "Reflections"

James Taylor (*James Taylor*), "Don't Talk Now" through "Greensleeves" to "Something's Wrong"

---

the Threshold of a Dream, what songs are not joined by crossfade are met by a hard edit with no space in between.

In mixing for mono and stereo, the producer had to bear in mind which mix was destined for AM radio, for this mix had to be treated particularly carefully for definition in the mid-range, the only part of the signal that would be broadcast. These recordings would also be more heavily compressed overall than others, because road noise would require a car radio to put out only a very limited dynamic range for a satisfying result. So a song's mono mix, usually the one destined for such a fate unless a special promotional mix was created specifically for the broadcast media, was rarely simply a reduction of a full-frequency, dynamically alive stereo mix down to a single channel. George Martin has always maintained that he, his engineers, and the Beatles devoted far more time to getting the mono mix right than they did the stereo. Phil Spector and Brian Wilson are both known for their tireless attention to the mono, rather than a stereo, result. For the former, this was always an obscured "wall of sound" of busy, inseparable instruments; note this quality in Spector's mixes of Darlene Love's "A Fine Fine Boy" and "(Today I Met) The Boy I'm Gonna Marry," and the Crystals' "Da Doo Ron Ron (When He Walked Me Home)," emulated in such tracks as Sonny and Cher's "But You're Mine."

Aspects of the stereo image make for our final topic. For live music, a natural image of a performing stage, with good spread for different instruments that bleed into each other, is desirable, particularly for jazz or blues, which demands creative interaction among players. B. B. King's *Live & Well* is a good example. Otherwise, strong separation between instruments is generally the goal, and each source is given a definite position in the stereo field. If 100 percent of a signal is routed to one channel or the other, it will sound extreme right or extreme left. Most signals, however, are sent partly to both channels. If both receive an equal amount of the signal, the result will sound in the center; if 25 percent of the signal is sent to the right channel and 75 percent to the left, the sound will come from the left-center of the image. Louder, drier sounds will seem to emerge from up front whereas wetter, quieter sounds will be more distant, a spatial illusion based on norms of aural perception. Early stereo demonstration albums, such as the *Persuasive* and *Provocative Percussion* albums of Enoch Light, are highly self-conscious arrangements made simply to show off spatial separation, much like the divided performing groups popular in Venice in the early 1600s. The extreme left—right divide is natural for such efforts as Lennon and Ono's "John and Yoko" (22'43" worth of both calling each others' first names), but most mixes tend to put the lead vocal in the center along with bass and drums, and divide other performers throughout the image. Other arrangements are common; the strong separation in Buddy Holly's "Learnin' the Game" has drums, bass, and backing vocals left, the lead vocal center, and both lead and rhythm guitars right.

Some arrangements add to the drama, as when backing vocals are heard on both sides and lead vocal is placed in the center in Paul Anka's "Put Your Head on My Shoulder."

Some mixes are strange, as when the lead guitar and its echo are sent to separate channels in the Jeff Beck Group's "Morning Dew." Sometimes extreme separation of like forces makes for a satisfying balance, as when the drummer alternates between two opposing cymbal bells in King Crimson's "Moonchild," trumpet and tenor sax join on the right but the bari sax is on the left in Janis Joplin's "Maybe," or when the two lead guitars playing in thirds are heard opposite each other in Crosby, Stills and Nash's "Marrakesh Express" or the nylon-string acoustic and fingerpicked twelve-string electric stand opposite in their "Guinnevere." This idea can be disconcerting when Janis Joplin's lead vocal is double-tracked in Big Brother and the Holding Company's "Bye Bye Baby," the two identical vocals sent to opposite corners (perhaps in an attempt to mask the fact that the fast vibratos cannot match).

Sometimes, a sound source will quickly jump from one place in the image to another, as with the different numbers in Felix Cavaliere's count-in (and with his later lead singing) for the Young Rascals' "Good Lovin'" and the lead guitar of their "Find Somebody" (both engineered by the pioneering Tom Dowd), each bar of the repeated-note guitar tattoo in the Supremes' "You Keep Me Hangin' On," and the vocal in the Mothers of Invention's "America Drinks and Goes Home." (This is also exemplified in the lead guitar part of Web audio example 7.11.) Much more often, a sound will gradually pan from one part of the image to another. (The term comes from the cinematographer's sideways swiveling of a camera across its panorama.) One early example of this effect, in the left-to-center tenor sax solo of Elvis Presley's "I Feel So Bad" (1961), was actually the result of Boots Randolph wandering from one mic to another, rather than having been created in a postproduction turning of the knobs. Generally, the moving pan in pop music dates from a 1964 effect, with a motorcycle crossing the field in the Shangri-Las' "Leader of the Pack." Musical pans seem to begin two years later with sounds criss-crossing the spectrum in the Beatles' "Tomorrow Never Knows." Their "Strawberry Fields Forever" (follow the svaramandal transitions) and "A Day in the Life" (Lennon's "aaah" moving left-to-right in the song's retransition from McCartney's bridge) are other early examples. The Monkees' "Star Collector" is adventurous both in panning and in its use of the Moog synthesizer. Other examples of 1968–69 songs with panning include the Beatles' "Oh! Darling," "Here Comes the Sun," and "Her Majesty"; the Moody Blues' "Dr. Livingstone, I Presume," "Legend of a Mind," and "Lovely to See You"; the Jimi Hendrix Experience's "Burning of the Midnight Lamp," "Rainy Day, Dream Away," and "Voodoo Child (Slight Return)"; Traffic's "Pearly Queen"; The Band's "I Shall Be Released"; Grand Funk Railroad's "Anybody's Answer"; and Led

Zeppelin's "Dazed and Confused," "What Is and What Should Never Be," and "Ramble On."

Web audio example 4.02 has the guitar pan from extreme left to extreme right and back again; a smooth pan like this is far easier to achieve with digital automation than it would have been in the mid-1960s, when the chicken-head knobs and linear faders had to be manipulated in real time! The panning in Web audio example 3.27 is more complex. Here, four tracks are devoted to the Theremin (backing-track guitar and synthesized vibraphone remain center). Two Theremin tracks are melodic, adding counterpoint to the guitar and keyboard. These pan slowly, right to left and back. The other two parts contain wild Theremin effects, and pan much more quickly, but with a simulation of orbiting by adding volume while decreasing reverb to suggest nearness, and reducing volume while adding extra reverb to suggest distance, all coordinated with the left-to-right panning; these wild tracks are also given a bit of tape delay mixed on top of the reverb.

Other than growing numbers of available tracks, customized boards and tape machines built for particular studios, producers, or artists, and improved mobile recording demanded by the fast-growing number of concert record-ings of rock music, the techniques of engineering and record production as advanced by 1970 remained little changed until the digital age rendered many prior difficulties of little consequence. Tape hiss and surface noise, once nuisances, are today's semiotic signs. But, hopefully, the reader will now find significance in dozens of other artifacts and colorings that make recording techniques of great interest in enjoying records made at any point from the preelectrical cylinder age to the computer era of sound files.

CHAPTER 14

Creating an Interpretation

Once a listener has a working knowledge of the basic properties of the musical languages within rock, one can begin to tie together relationships, and form a critical response a bit deeper than "it's a good song." When the listener can hear how rhythms, harmonies, melodic and contrapuntal ideas, tone colors, and formal schemes work with the ideas in the lyrics, he or she can begin to understand the song as a composition in a much more satisfying way than ever thought possible before, building a personal interpretation that makes that song more and more one's own. Part of the process involves listening to the lyrics themselves at a level beneath the surface, thinking about the characters who populate the song, their relationships, the situations and imagery by which character traits are amplified, remaining sensitive to possible references to other texts, to the ways in which language is poetically manipulated to suggest meanings beyond the words themselves, to the ordering of presentation, to the attitude of the narrator, and to possible thematic meanings of social or cultural interest. All of these poetic components can be compared to their songs' musical settings to see whether all is mutually supportive, or whether a new level of commentary is revealed by examining apparent contradictions.

In this chapter, we'll look at our music of the 1950s and '60s in an effort to suggest ways in which an interpretation and a critical stance can be created from a deeper understanding of all of the music's and lyrics' elements, and then address qualities of the rock artist and the musical text from perspectives that may help the reader shape different sorts of critical questions. The chapter will conclude with examinations of two songs, one from each end of our historical period.

Let's start with an example, the Zombies' "She's Not There," to see what one might make from a set of lyrics. The opening line, "Well, no one told me about her," raises a number of potential questions in the listener's mind: Why should the singer have been told about her? Was she unknown to him even though she was potentially his perfect match? Was she, instead, unmentionable? More insidious, was she close to him but representing a problem that was being concealed by conspiracy? The open question immediately heightens interest and goes along with the mysterious quality of the musical introduction. We find right away that the worst is true, that she has lied and has left a trail of many broken hearts. This is an age-old story, but told with interest. In fact, it might be compared with Marvin Gaye's "I Heard It Through the Grapevine," where the singer learns the same bad news not from his own experienced pain nor from the perpetrator but indeed from a third party—a reversed flow of information from that working in the Zombies track. Both songs have a mysterious introduction, because the Motown number still begins with an open question in the listener's mind—"I bet you're wonderin' how I knew." (Knew *what?*)

Back to the Zombies. Following a stanza of static minor-tonic harmony supporting the singer's consideration of his friends' silence, all musical qualities change suddenly: harmonies and rhythms build in intensity, as the singer quits ruminating about "her" and addresses her in second person—"it's too late to say you're sorry." He seems to confront her, telling her he doesn't care about her treatment of others. But suddenly, mid-stanza, he addresses others instead, out of her presence: "Please don't bother tryin' to find her—she's not there." It seems that the second-person address was imaginary, perhaps a rehearsal, and that he didn't confront her after all. When he says she's not there, he's talking about her being gone, history—she's nowhere around. But the chorus, sung in still more desperate tones than any prior section, tells a different story still—"Well, let me tell you 'bout the way she looked," painting her actions, her hair, her voice, her eyes, all presumably those of a seductress. But now, when he sings "she's not there," we know he's referring to the lack of a human quality in her lack of caring for others. She's not there for others, in other words; she exists for herself. Chords changing mode through these lines vividly portray the difference between the woman's actions and her reality. The final change of tonic chord from minor to major suggests a sudden enlightenment, as if the singer's increased perturbation has reached a boil, and he finally explains the unmentioned problem.

All good songs relate story, voice, and mode of telling with musical factors, and one need only become aware of available literary and musical techniques to begin to understand the artwork as a whole. When one recognizes aspects of lyric construction, one can compare lyrics of related songs and reach new insights. It's as if every song has its own composite psychology, reflecting both the meanings intended by the writer and those inferred by the analyst. In this chapter, we'll outline some of the ways to think about lyrics, leaving it to the reader to put it all together by drawing from the musical ideas already covered. Such approaches are not only different with every recording, but also reflective of varying interests from one listener to another.

Topics and approaches in lyrics

In examining a song's lyrics, it's important to consider the wider context established in all approaches to rock lyrics during our period. Some songs tell stories. The folk tradition brings such wide-ranging stories as those told of race relations in Washington, D.C., in Huddie Ledbetter's "The Bourgeois Blues" (1938), the civil war in Joan Baez's "The Night They Drove Old Dixie Down," the Vietnam draft in Arlo Guthrie's "Alice's Restaurant Massacree," autobiography in The Mamas and the Papas' "Creeque Alley," and mythical animals in the Irish Rovers' "The Unicorn." It's easy to trace this tradition in mainstream pop, where narrative stories of various kinds are told in Johnny Horton's "North to Alaska," the Animals' "Monterey," Bobbie Gentry's "Ode to Billie Joe," and even the Royal Guardsmen's "Snoopy Vs. the Red Baron." Quasi-religious paeans are popular: Nashville alone has been so glorified in Eddie Cochran's "Two Blue Singin' Stars," Carl Perkins's "Tennessee," Tex Ritter's "I Dreamed of Hillbilly Heaven," the Lovin' Spoonful's "Nashville Cats," and many others; odes to singing stars range from Tommy Dee's "Three Stars" to Bob Dylan's "Song to Woody." Some stories are organized by formulaic litany: a chorus will present the general thrust, whereas the verses will enumerate instances: American cities, for instance, are listed in Chuck Berry's "Sweet Little Sixteen" and "Back in the U.S.A.," Bobby Rydell's "Kissin' Time," James Brown's "Night Train," and many more. Hours of the day are noted in Bill Haley's "(We're Gonna) Rock Around the Clock" and Chuck Berry's "Reelin' and Rockin'," days of the week are sounded out in Fats Domino's "Blue Monday" and the Shirelles' "I Met Him on a Sunday," months of the year are

> Lyrics: stories, litanies, and topics; social perspective and intertextual references; cleverness, humor, and parody; rhyme, assonance, and onomatopoeia; metaphor and simile.

the stuff of Neil Sedaka's "Calendar Girl," years themselves are counted in the Beach Boys' "When I Grow Up (To Be a Man)," and millennia are ticked off in Zager and Evans' "In the Year 2525 (Exordium and Terminus)." Other songs go through the alphabet or a rainbow of colors or vegetables from the garden or they may count chapters of books, flights of stairs, lucky talismans, sources of itches, school subjects, dance steps, or steps to heaven. When such parallelisms of words occur, look for musical parallels—repeated rhythms, melodic or harmonic sequences, truck-driver's modulations, and the like.

Lyrics can cover a myriad of topics, often related to romance but many times not: nostalgia for the past is treated variously in the Shangri-Las' "Remember (Walkin' In the Sand)," the Beatles' "In My Life," Tom Jones's "Green, Green Grass of Home," and Classics IV's "Traces." Different perspectives of armed service are presented in Chuck Berry's "Too Much Monkey Business," Johnny Horton's "The Battle of New Orleans," and Kenny Rogers and the First Edition's "Ruby, Don't Take Your Love to Town." Hard labor is the subject of Bobby Scott's "Chain Gang," Tennessee Ernie Ford's "Sixteen Tons," the Vogues' "Five O'Clock World," and Lee Dorsey's "Working in the Coal Mine," whereas recreational pleasure is the object of Little Richard's "Rip It Up," Sam Cooke's "Another Saturday Night," and the Beach Boys' "409." Macho men are celebrated in Bill Hayes' "The Ballad of Davy Crockett," Johnny Cash's "A Boy Named Sue," and Billy Grammer's "Gotta Travel On." Authority of all sorts is fought in Eddie Cochran's "Summertime Blues," Bob Dylan's "Masters of War," The Who's "Anyway, Anyhow, Anywhere," the Beatles' "She's Leaving Home," Jimi Hendrix's "If 6 Was 9," Creedence Clearwater Revival's "Fortunate Son," and Spirit's "1984." Mothers offer advice in the Supremes' "You Can't Hurry Love," Percy Sledge's "Take Time to Know Her," and Jerry Butler's "Only the Strong Survive"; Frank Zappa declares that what you need is "Motherly Love." Spiritual life is central to the McGuire Sisters' "He," Pat Boone's "There's a Gold Mine in the Sky," Ferlin Husky's "Wings of a Dove," the Browns' "The Three Bells," Wink Martindale's "Deck of Cards," Gene McDaniels' "A Hundred Pounds of Clay," and also the Beatles' "Tomorrow Never Knows" and The Doors' "The Soft Parade." Love, or perhaps just a jukebox, is the medicine a doctor can't prescribe in Carl Perkins' "Boppin' the Blues," Johnny Burnette's "Rock Therapy," Keith's "98.6," the Young Rascals' "Good Lovin,'" and the Balloon Farm's "A Question of Temperature."

A lyric often needs to be considered as to the tenor of its voice on social issues. Most listeners today have much greater awareness of expressed insensitivities than did those in an age when discrimination on the basis of race, gender, sexual preference, and physical handicaps was deemed acceptable by many. Although no longer subjected to the incredibly offensive "coon" songs highly popular in recordings from the 1890s through 1920 or so, listeners in the 1960s still heard their share of ethnically insulting records, such as Ray Stevens' "Ahab the Arab." Homophobia was presented as normal in Johnny Cash's "A Boy Named Sue." Bob Dylan shone a light on racial bigotry in such songs as "Blowin' in the Wind" and "Only a Pawn in Their Game." But in the years before women's liberation, countless sexist songs affirmed the domestic role of women (Glen Campbell's "Dreams of the Everyday Housewife," James Brown's "It's a Man's, Man's, Man's, Man's World"), treated them as sex objects ("There Is Nothin' Like a Dame" from *South Pacific,* Eddie Hodges's "(Girls, Girls, Girls Were) Made to Love") and as creatures of lesser prowess (Kathy Linden's "Billy," the Rolling Stones' "Stupid Girl") if not slaves (the Rolling Stones' "Under My Thumb"), and perpetuated a "boys will be boys" tolerance for male but not female infidelity (The Chiffons' "One Fine Day," Lesley Gore's "That's the Way Boys Are" and "Maybe I Know," Lou Christie's "Lightnin' Strikes," the Stones' "Backstreet Girl"). Mistreatment because of gender, now a controversial topic in stagings of *Carousel,* is desired by Joanie Sommers in "Johnny Get Angry" and complained about by Sandy Posey in "Born a Woman" (who ultimately yields to her man: "no price is too great to pay"). Only Frank Zappa, in "Harry, You're a Beast" (1968), was decrying the subjugation of American womanhood before John Lennon sang "Woman is the Nigger of the World" and Helen Reddy sang "I Am Woman," both in 1972.

Messages, often wrapped in stories but sometimes not, abound as social complacency is lambasted in the Monkees' "Pleasant Valley Sunday" and the Mothers' "Hungry Freaks, Daddy" and "Uncle Bernie's Farm"; class division is criticized in Simon and Garfunkel's "Richard Cory" and Johnny Rivers' "Poor Side of Town"; racism is decried in Janis Ian's "Society's Child (Baby I've Been Thinking)" and Sly and the Family Stone's "Everyday People." The futility and tragedy of war are a frequent topic both because of the Cold War (Bob Dylan's "A Hard Rain's a-Gonna Fall") and Vietnam (the Monitors' "Greetings (This Is Uncle Sam)," Eric Burdon and the Animals' "Sky Pilot," the Buckinghams' "Foreign Policy," Donovan's "To Susan on the West Coast Waiting," The Doors' "The Unknown Soldier," Jimi Hendrix's rocket-filled version of "The Star Spangled Banner" and "Machine Gun," and Edwin Starr's "War"), but jingoism carried the airwaves in Senator Everett McKinley Dirksen's "Gallant Men," Ssgt. Barry Sadler's "The Ballad of the Green Berets," and Victor Lundberg's "An Open Letter to My Teenage Son." Songs about altered states of consciousness ran the gamut of social acceptability from dream imagery (the Rascals' "See," Soft Machine's "Why Are We Sleeping?"), booze odes by Roger Miller ("Chug-A-Lug"), Ray Charles ("Let's Go Get Stoned"), and The Doors ("Alabama Song (Whisky Bar)") to the ubiquity of tranquilizers (the Stones' "Mother's Little Helper"), pot and psychedelics (Donovan's "The Fat Angel," the Jimi Hendrix Experience's

"Are You Experienced?," the Small Faces' "Itchycoo Park," Cream's "Strange Brew"), and opiates (the Velvet Underground's "I'm Waiting for the Man" and "Heroin" and Steppenwolf's "The Pusher"). The Young Rascals, however, needed no chemical means to find "ecstasy" in "I've Been Lonely Too Long," "Groovin'," and "A Girl Like You."

Hip literary references, both classical and modern, appear in pop-rock music: The myth of Oedipus lies at the core of The Doors' "The End." Homer's *The Odyssey* is basic to Cream's "Tales of Brave Ulysses," whereas Joyce's *Ulysses* is at the core of Jefferson Airplane's "rejoyce." George Harrison took entire stanzas from sixth-century B.C. poet Lao-Tzu for "The Inner Light" and "All Things Must Pass." Tolkien's *Lord of the Rings* is a cult favorite, popping up in Jack Bruce's "To Isengard" and Led Zeppelin's "Ramble On." Steppenwolf takes its name from a novel by Hermann Hesse and the Steve Miller Band borrowed a book title from Aldous Huxley for their album, *Brave New World*. Film achieves literary status in this realm, as *Rosemary's Baby* is responded to in Deep Purple's "Why Didn't Rosemary?" One rock song will reference the lyrics of another, as when the "Goo goo ga-joob" of the Beatles' "I Am the Walrus" resurfaces a few months later in Simon and Garfunkel's "Mrs. Robinson," or when Lennon refers to "Dylan's Mr. Jones" in order to shade the suicidal notions of "Yer Blues" as darkly as are those in "Ballad of a Thin Man." Some lines have an extremely rich set of intertextual references; the military marching-cadence-inspired verse, "I don't know but I been told, the streets of heaven are paved with gold," appears in Peter, Paul and Mary's "Morning Train," the Seekers' "You Can Tell the World," and Bob Dylan's "I Shall Be Free No. 10" before it is given a whole new meaning for an outlaw in the Grateful Dead's "New Speedway Boogie": "Now I don't know but I been told it's hard to run with the weight of gold; other hand I heard it said, it's just as hard with the weight of lead."

Clever lyrics can be expansive, leading the mind in many directions beyond the literal text. The double entendre, in such songs as Big Joe Turner's "Shake, Rattle and Roll" ("like a one-eyed cat peepin' in the seafood store"), Elvis Presley's "A Big Hunk O' Love" ("I got a wishbone in my pocket"), and Bob Dylan's "Country Pie," make for an added layer of humor. But such cleverness need not be sexual in nature; Chuck Berry was the master at referring to multiple unspoken layerings in such lines as "Venus de Milo had the world in the palm of her hand" ("Brown-Eyed Handsome Man")—we can certainly anticipate what was to happen to *her*. Humor may take other forms, ranging from the cartooney voices in Pat Boone's "Speedy Gonzales," Bob McFadden's "The Mummy," and the Ivy Three's "Yogi," through silly word play, as when Jack Ross tells "a story about Cinderella, who lived in a big hark douse with her mean ol' mepstother and her two sisty uglers" in "Cinderella," to more sophisticated constructions, such as the puns on Ray Charles's "Georgia" and

Photo 14.01. Carl Perkins, seen here in the cover of a 1986 compact-disc compilation.

Chuck Berry's "Back in the U.S.A." in the Beatles' "Back in the U.S.S.R.," or the litotes by which the singer exaggerates the opposite of intended meaning, as when Della Resse sings, "I'll only love you as long as the sun shines" in "Not One Minute More." Sometimes, we just smile at a clever juxtaposition of sounds, as when Mick Jagger tosses off "two's a crowd on my cloud" in the Rolling Stones' "Get Off Of My Cloud." Cleverness, of course, need not be funny; little is more serious than the intriguing poetry of the Beatles' "A Day in the Life."

Humor often takes the form of parody; Phil McLean's "Small Sad Sam" answers Jimmy Dean's "Big Bad John." "The Battle of New Orleans" was targeted in Homer and Jethro's "The Battle of Kookamonga." The Beatles' "Lucy in the Sky With Diamonds" was satirized by John Fred and His Playboy Band in "Judy in Disguise (With Glasses)." Many songs are parodied in the Four Preps' "More Money for You and Me." Sometimes the parody is of a style rather than of a particular song, as when the Beatles invoke the civility of the eighteenth-century parlor with the string and harpsichord writing in "Piggies," or when Simon and Garfunkel blast Dylan's brand of folk-rock in "A Simple Desultory Philippic (Or How I Was Robert Macnamara'd Into Submission)." The Who mock radio jingles and station IDs in songs like "Odorono" and "Medak" and the inter-song bits of *The Who Sell Out*. Even this technique, though, has its earnest application, as when the Spokesmen's "The Dawn of Correction" responds to Barry McGuire's "Eve of Destruction." And, of course, an unfortunate unintentional humor can be the result of an overdone maudlin approach, as in Elvis Presley's "Old Shep," Ray Peterson's "Tell Laura I Love Her," the Barbarians' "Moulty," or Bobby Goldsboro's "Honey." In such humorless examples, the more determined the musical setting, the more hilarious the result. This effect is twisted yet one level further in the Bonzo Dog Band's ironic "Death Cab for Cutie."

Literary devices dominate the best lyric writing. End rhyme is the rule. Some end rhymes are truly inspired ("ocean" and "lotion" in the Coasters' "Poison Ivy," "party" and "hearty" in the Miracles' "The Tracks of My Tears," "frantic" and "Atlantic" in the Beatles' "Honey Pie," "physique," "peek," "critique" and "cheek" in the limericks of Ray Stevens's "The Streak"). Internal rhyme allows words within lines to resonate with line endings, as in Bob Dylan's "Just Like a Woman": "Everybody *knows* baby's got new *clothes*; lately I've seen her ribbons and her *bows* have fallen from her curls," the word "curls" rhyming only with the very end of the following chorus. Both internal rhyme and alliteration—words beginning with the same sound—bring out the sentimental meaning in Lulu's "To Sir With Love," when "the time has come for closing books and long last looks must end." Alliteration is explored differently in each verse of Crosby, Stills and Nash's "Helplessly Hoping." Assonant sounds cross-connect many of the words in lines such as "the gassed and flaccid kids are flung across the stars" in the Association's sensation-focused "Along Comes Mary." James Taylor is unstoppable in comparing himself to a "Steamroller": "a churnin' urn of burnin' funk, . . . a hefty hunk of steamin' junk." Onomatopoeia, by which sounds within words refer to other real sounds, brings to life the crying and sneezing going on as the protagonist enters the "KITCHen, CluTCHing her handKerCHief" in the Beatles' "She's Leaving Home." In the same song's next phrase, one can hear the latch clacking as the "baCKDoor Key" turns.

Metaphor and simile bring life to many lyrics, sometimes adding specific dimension, at other times freeing the imagination to explore multivalent symbols. Simon and Garfunkel revel in these devices in "Sounds of Silence," "I Am a Rock," and "The Boxer." In "Love Hurts," Roy Orbison explains through imagery, "love is like a cloud, holds a lot of rain." Tommy James and the Shondells portray the sun as a "Ball of Fire," whereas for the Cyrkle it is simply a "Red Rubber Ball." Jim Morrison conveys the rage of his torment through wild beasts in "Horse Latitudes." Metaphor may be subtle, as in the portrait of the civil rights struggle in the Beatles' "Blackbird." Simile can be rich and playful, as when Bob Dylan sings of a "Leopard-Skin Pill-Box Hat" that "You know it balances on your head just like a mattress balances on a bottle of wine." Conversely, what specific meaning does Dylan get across when he sings, "I got a bird that whistles, I got a bird that sings," in "Corrina, Corrina"? Procol Harum's "Whiter Shade of Pale" and Richard Harris's "MacArthur Park" carry many symbol-rich meanings that cannot be expressed in conventional words and thoughts.

Overinterpretation can be a source of humor; Johnny Cash meant something rather heart-related when he sang "Love is a burning thing and it makes a fiery ring" in "Ring of Fire," but Frank Zappa only heard a cry for hemorrhoid relief when referring to this song in *The Best Band You Never Heard in Your Life*. Musical metaphor also exists, as when a repeated backing-vocal rhythm, not quite onomatopoeia, evokes windshield wipers at "together, together..." in Lou Christie's "Rhapsody in the Rain." Sometimes literal meaning is intentionally unclear. The writer may pose puzzles for which there are no solutions, but still the words evoke haunting auras; consider Bob Dylan's "The Mighty Quinn (Quinn the Eskimo)", Donovan's "Mellow Yellow," the Beatles' "Dig a Pony," and the Beach Boys' "Heroes and Villains." And in "My Back Pages," Dylan tells us, anyway, that we're just not *supposed* to understand things in black and white; experience teaches us to be secure with doubt: "Ah, but I was so much older then; I'm younger than that now."

A complex example

Heading toward the parsing of an ambiguous lyric, let's look at a particularly thorny example, the Grateful Dead's "China Cat Sunflower." First appearing on the 1969 album *Aoxomoxoa* (a September 1971 remix has replaced the original master), this song became a

> Parsing the lyrics and music of the Grateful Dead's "China Cat Sunflower."

frequent second-set opener, always leading directly into the traditional wanderer's song, "I Know You Rider." Perennial Dead lyricist Robert Hunter supplied the "China Cat" poem around which Jerry Garcia wrote the tune, an up-tempo number that alternates three Hunter verses with a "na na na"-scatted lilting dance of a two-part vocal chorus (0:38–0:47). (In live performances, the vocalists are mute in the chorus jams, their melodic lines played by Bob Weir's second guitar and various keyboardists.) The verse lyrics are opaque; as if an extension of beat poetry, they present a string of vivid images redolent of colors and sounds that don't seem to relate to each other on the surface at all, in the dreamlike psychedelic manner of the Beatles' "Lucy in the Sky With Diamonds."

The first verse begins with the line, "Look for a while at the China cat sunflower, proud walking jingle in the midnight sun." The "China cat" may be a reference to the Maneki Neko, a porcelain cat figurine that serves as a common good-luck token in Japan. (Any confusion between porcelain and the country of China is only exacerbated by considering the Dead's two other songs to include "China" in the title: "China Doll" and "Chinatown

Shuffle.") There is also a nod to the phallic "one-eyed cat" of "Shake, Rattle and Roll" in the second verse's "one-eyed Cheshire," simultaneously a reference to the feline in Lewis Carroll's *Alice in Wonderland*. The image of a one-eyed cat persists in the opening of the second verse, "Crazy cat peekin' through a lace bandana," words that link to the alliterative sound of "crazy quilt," the words ending the first verse, just as it might recall George Herriman's frequently dancing "Krazy Kat," central figure in a groundbreaking comic strip of the early twentieth century.

The Maneki Neko is a proud, beckoning figure, and in "China Cat," the protagonist is a proud dancer, walking to a jingle. The swaying yet similarly proud eight-foot sunflower may in turn be seen as a one-eyed creation, a large single seed-bed surrounded by golden petals, the eye dark as a midnight sun. The album's cover painting, at first glance, might look like a bright multi-rayed sun in a cloudless sky, overlooking a groundcover of trees, flowers, and mushrooms. (See Web photo 14.01.) On second thought, the central object looks more like a sunflower, the "rays" actually dozens of petals surrounding the large seedbed. But a third look reveals the center to be a human ovum surrounded by dozens of hopeful sperm, freshly ejected from a penis-shaped death's head below; the other images in the illustration seem to derive from an acid-dream mixture of human reproductive organs and botanical fruit in a tableau of mythical proportion celebrating birth and death. The sexual fantasy might reverberate with symbols in the last line of "China Cat": "I rang a silent bell beneath a shower of pearls in the eagle winged palace of the Queen Chinee." (The top margin of the LP's painting is marked by fully spread eagle wings.) The two parts of the sunflower, the large eye and the surrounding petals, can be heard as represented in various images throughout the song: a "copper dome body" and "silent bell" as the central eye, and the "kimono," "stargown," "waterfall," and "shower of pearls" as the petals. The image of the "midnight sun" is reminiscent of "Dark Star," a contemporaneous Dead song based on Hunter lyrics that includes the line, "Shall we go...through the transitive nightfall of diamonds," itself recalling the petal images of "China Cat Sunflower." An aural image of the sun also underlies the "China" retransition (2:12–2:19) and coda, which feature backing vocals seemingly baked in the Beatles' "Good Day Sunshine."

But, aural appearances aside, it is not a copper dome "*body*"; the text as published reads "copper dome bodhi," the possible pun circling the Sanskrit word for enlightenment, a notion later central to Steely Dan's "Bodhisattva." The concept of a pun, whereby one meaning switches for another, is related to a host of inverted switches in "China Cat." The third verse refers to "Leonardo words," which could be a reference to da Vinci's mirror writing, most obviously reflected in the palindrome of the album's title. But note also the melodic structure of the "na na na" chorus, which alternates descents of scale degrees 3—2—1 (0:39) with ascents of 1—2—3 (0:41–0:42), a neat and obvious palindrome. (In the studio version, these lines are played by Pigpen on Hammond organ through the song's intro and the first verse; this part is not present on the song's prior demo recording, suggesting that Garcia chose to emphasize this core motive in one of the final phases of composition.) The markedly all-major chords by which the song moves to and from its bridge also create an inverted figure: the transition to the bridge takes place on the motion, IV (1:37)—V (1:38)—VI (1:40), a pattern inverted for the return to the third verse on III (2:16)—II (2:18)—I (2:20). The dark-star "midnight sun" is a different sort of inversion, as is the "diamond-eyed jack" of the second verse. The jack of diamonds is not in fact a one-eyed jack, but is still related to the palindromic mirror image in comparing the upper and lower halves of the playing card. And the surface of the sunflower itself is a perfectly symmetrical object.

The song's last words, by the way, are taken from the ending of a poem, Dame Edith Sitwell's "Trio for Two Cats and a Trombone": "When the phoca has the pica/In the palace of the Queen Chinee." These words tie our cat to the "silk trombone" mentioned in the third verse of Hunter's lyric. The *Aoxomoxoa* cover also manages to contain two symbols—the cobra and the scarab—that are certainly neither Chinese nor Japanese, but are far more suggestive of the East than of the West. As a final allusion, a later song by one-time Dead sideman Bruce Hornsby, "Sunflower Cat," opens with the line, "One eye is open, the other eye is shut," seemingly a nod to our much earlier song. While the lyrics of "China Cat Sunflower" remain intangible, some nonrepresentational meaning—highly musical—is contained in the numerous cross-referential suggestions of sun, conception, and enlightenment, all primal thoughts worthy of hallucinogenic development. Deep myth blends well with other psychedelia; Cream's "Tales of Brave Ulysses" might be approached with similar tools as those applied here.

Final thoughts on lyrics

Irony, as suggested by a singer, may encompass lyrics that intentionally lead a listener to a mistaken conclusion (the Ames Brothers' "The Naughty Lady of Shady Lane," we finally learn, is about an infant, and the "Two Lovers" of which Mary Wells sings are—surprise!—two sides of the same man) or that mean the opposite of what they say ("Don't Think Twice, It's All Right," Dylan sings through his tears; "heaven knows you're not to blame," Ray Stevens sings in "Mr. Businessman"). Lyrics may simply suggest that the performer is commenting upon his or her own performance with a hint of sarcasm: "This is a song about vegetables, they keep you regular, they're real good for ya," Frank Zappa tells us so as to introduce the Mothers of Invention's "Call Any Vegetable." "Who's that banging on the piano?," someone wants to know in the opening and closing of the Detergents' "Leader of the Laundromat," itself a parody of the Shangri-Las' "Leader of the Pack." False earnestness rings through much of the Mothers' work; note Roy Estrada's pleading, "I gave you my high-school ring at the root beer stand" in their "Go Cry On Somebody Else's Shoulder"—one never knows what Zappa takes seriously. But irony can also be musical. Thus the incongruous glorious major-mode celebration of a killing in Tom Jones' "Delilah." Thus the happy-go-lucky ragtime artificial dominants that go by more quickly than one can comprehend as Country Joe and the Fish thrill Moms and Dads with the prospect that they can "be the first one on your block to have your boy come home in a box" in "I-Feel-Like-I'm-Fixin'-To-Die Rag." Tack-piano, cowbell, brushed-drum, and pizzicato string-bass whimsy is similarly the musical setting for the upbeat tale of the light-of-day New York murder of Kitty Genovese in Phil Ochs's "Outside of a Small Circle of Friends."

Other thoughts on lyrics: irony, nonsense syllables, and non-English texts.

Great music can also have lyrics that mean little or nothing—nonsense syllables and scatted vocals populate enough rock songs to fill the charts many times over. Once a vehicle for bass singers (for instance, "bum bum bum" repeated underneath Eileen Rodgers's "Miracle of Love") and backing vocalists ("yip yip whip op di boom diddy boom diddy" sung alongside Johnnie Ray's lead in "Yes Tonight, Josephine" and "shop-shop-shoo-bop" in the Shirelles' "Boys"), this technique was taken over by lead singers in chants (Cannibal and the Headhunters' "Land of 1000 Dances," the Beatles' "Flying," Donovan's "Hurdy Gurdy Man"), in visceral outbursts that bypass the intellect entirely (for joyful exuberance in Oliver's "Good Morning Starshine," excitement in Perry Como's "Hot Diggity (Dog Ziggity Boom)" and Gene Vincent's "Be Bop a Lula," frenzy in Little Richard's "Tutti-Frutti," and perhaps forgetfulness in Frank Sinatra's last "doo be doo be doo" verse of "Strangers in the Night"), and simply as a means to mimic other sounds (as in imitations of instruments in Julius LaRosa's "Eh Cumpari," of a baby in Buzz Clifford's "Baby Sittin' Boogie," and of a Morse-code "dit dit" in the Five Americans' "Western Union").

Languages other than English were once heard often in pop songs; top-ten hits from our period were sung at least partially in Italian (most famously in Domenico Modugno's "Nel Blu Dipinto di Blu (Volare)"), Spanish (the Sandpipers' "Guantanamera"), German (Joe Dowell's "Wooden Heart (Muss I Denn)"), French (The Singing Nun's "Dominique"), Latin (Andy Williams's "The Village of St. Bernadette"), Zulu (the Tokens' "The Lion

Sleeps Tonight"), Portuguese (Stan Getz and Astrud Gilberto's "The Girl From Ipanema"), Japanese (Kyu Sakamoto's "Sukiyaki"), and other recordings featured Xhosa (Miriam Makeba's "Pata Pata"), Creole (the Dixie Cups' "Iko Iko"), Sanskrit (the Beatles' "Across the Universe"), Hawaiian (Andy Williams's "The Hawaiian Wedding Song (Ke Kali Nei Au)"), Swahili (the Temptations' "Ungena Za Ulimwengu (Unite the World)"), Twi (Ginder Baker's Air Force's "Aiko Biaye"), Hebrew (Spirit's "Jewish"), and Welsh (Mary Hopkin's "Y Blodyn Gwyn"). Italian and German singing was most universally popular in the 1950s and not much afterwards, but one number-two record from as late as 1966 began with the shouted intro, "Achtung! Jetzt wir singen zusammen die Geschichte über den Schweinkomischen Hund und dem lieben Red Baron"!

Style and influence

This is hardly the place for an accounting of the styles of rock music of our period—many entire books have been written to make clear the stylistic domains of blues, R and B, C and W, bluegrass, jump blues, doo-wop, rockabilly, rock 'n' roll, gospel, Tin Pan Alley, folk, pop, surf, soul, rock, garage bands, funk, acid rock, fusion, hard rock, prog, and later genres. And this list ignores the countless styles and genres of antiquity and the Medieval, Renaissance, Baroque, Classical, Romantic, and Modernist periods from which pop musicians at times draw inspiration. Regardless, an important part of critical listening is having an awareness of the influences that an aspect of one style might have upon another, or catching the references to one style in a song that belongs to another. Reference to a style is typically made in very general terms, as when medieval times are suggested by musical and lyrical setting in Donovan's "Guinevere" (with its concerns of the troubador), and a neo-Elizabethan ballad is the sense achieved in the Rolling Stones' "Lady Jane" ("I must take my leave, for promised I am," set with harpsichord) and "She's a Rainbow" ("have you seen a lady fairer?"). But musical references are often far more specific, embodying tropes of all types, ranging from brief quotations to fully rewritten songs.

A deeper look at intertextualities.

Brief musical quotations can bring added support to a song's meaning, as when a snippet of the Battle Hymn of the Republic appears in the Rascals' "A Ray of Hope" or, less earnestly, when the Scaffold cite "God Save the Queen" in "Thank U Very Much." The opening of Mendelssohn's *Wedding March* says more than could words when it is cited in Bill Haley and His Comets' "Burn That Candle," Rufus Thomas's "Walking the Dog," and the Brooklyn Bridge's "Worst That Could Happen." Brief warped quotes on piano from "Misty," "Smoke Gets in Your Eyes," and "Strangers in the Night"

Photo 14.02. Aretha Franklin's first album for Atlantic Records, *I Never Loved a Man the Way I Love You*, revolutionized soul music with a major style shift from her Columbia efforts.

set the cocktail-imbibing atmosphere in Phil Ochs's "The Party." References became more contemporaneous when the orchestral climax of the Beatles' "A Day in the Life" was suggested at the mention of jukebox fodder in Johnny Rivers's "Summer Rain," and then the Beatles went one better by quoting musical snippets of "The Fool on the Hill," "Fixing a Hole," and "Strawberry Fields Forever" in "Glass Onion." Sly and the Family Stone nodded to this trick in referring to three of their own hits in "Thank You (Falettinme Be Mice Elf Agin)." Blood, Sweat and Tears weave uncredited quotations of the central guitar riff of "Sunshine of Your Love," a guitar line from "Spoonful," and one melodic contour from "Try a Little Tenderness" into their "Blues—Part II," and in "South California Purples," Chicago Transit Authority use a heavy filter in quoting the opening vocal line from the Beatles' "I Am the Walrus." Frank Zappa fills the pastiches of the Mothers of Invention with quotations of "Havana Moon," "Louie, Louie," "Baby Love," and "Little Deuce Coupe," right along with others from Stravinsky, Holst, Rossini, and Varèse in *Absolutely Free*. Zappa reworks his own materials as much as he does those of others; many of his tunes appear under multiple titles ("Oh No" appearing in *Lumpy Gravy,* or "Dog Breath, In the Year of the Plague" turning up in "A Pound for a Brown on the Bus"), just as many of his album titles and covers are loaded with reflexive references so that his career output has something of a Balzac- or Roth-like interrelated core to it.

A different order, however, is at work in Jimi Hendrix's performances of "The Star Spangled Banner," in which his Fuzzface, Univibe, feedback, wrist vibrato, trills, string bends, wah, whammy bar, and other guitar pyrotechnics serve to illustrate "rockets' red glare" and "bombs bursting in air"; these are his own musical thoughts appearing as tropes within a traditional melody. He does include a quotation as well, when he plays a bit of Taps for further commentary. Then there's the self-deprecating silliness whereby an improviser will undercut his or her own work with a nursery-school tune, as when "Mary Had a Little Lamb" invades a solo for comic effect in songs such as Little Stevie Wonder's "Fingertips," Jeff Beck of the Yardbirds' "Jeff's Boogie," and ? (Question Mark) and the Mysterians' "I Need Somebody." Hendrix mocks the owner of his American label by riffing on Frank Sinatra's "Strangers in the Night" during his Monterey performance of "Wild Thing."

Sometimes, the borrowing is of lyrics only, as when Spirit takes the line "you can find peace of mind [is] waiting there" from the Beatles' "Within You Without You" for their "Uncle Jack," or Ray Stevens takes "carry moonbeams home in a jar" from "Swinging on a Star" for his "Gitarzan." The refrain line of Martha and the Vandellas' "Dancing in the Street," a strong cultural marker, was adapted in the Rolling Stones' "Street Fighting Man" before Bruce Springsteen used it in "Racing in the Street." And sampling has a history that precedes hip-hop, as when a loop of Charlie Parker and Dizzy Gillespie appears in Paul Jones' "When I Was Six Years Old" (at 1:43–1:53 and from 2:43 to the fade). Serial references to other songs establish stylistic placement in such records as Larry Williams's "Short Fat Fannie" and Bobby Darin's "Splish Splash," and serial quotations/impersonations lead to almost-medleys in Sheb Wooley's "The Purple People Eater," Spyder Turner's "Stand By Me," Arthur Conley's "Sweet Soul Music," Peter, Paul and Mary's "I Dig Rock and Roll Music," and Cat Mother and the All Night News Boys' "Good Old Rock 'n Roll."

Such musical references are so brief that even when the borrowed material is protected by copyright, there is no sense of plagiarism (as there is in such wholesale rip-offs as the Beach Boys' "Surfin' U.S.A.," credited by court decision to Chuck Berry for its similarity to his "Sweet Little Sixteen"). All of these short references highlight sources so as to enrich the cultural world of the newly composed song. This does not seem to be the case in many other examples where the borrowing of a prior riff or chord progression does not seem to have been a conscious decision, and only adds to a song's meaning through an arbitrary sharing of material. Sometimes this is the case with accompanying material, as when the Impalas fill "Sorry (I Ran All the Way Home)" with the backing-vocal parts of the Cadillacs' "Speedo" or when Skeeter Davis' "I Can't Stay Mad at You" takes both the backing vocals and transitional drum pattern from Neil Sedaka's "Calendar Girl." In "A Beautiful Morning," the Rascals reprise the same transitional guitar chords, ii—iii—

IV—V, in the same rhythm and key as they first appeared in the Marvelettes' "The Hunter Gets Captured by the Game." Sometimes it's a very characteristic melody from a lead-vocal phrase placed in a new context, so that a listener might not recall where the line "the things she likes to do" from Jay and the Americans' 1969 record, "Walkin' in the Rain," had been heard before, unless the line, "never let her go" from "Some Enchanted Evening" (a 1965 cover hit for the same group) was fresh in the mind. A listener might be forgiven for hearing the Buckinghams' "Don't You Care" in a hit of six months later, Strawberry Alarm Clock's "Incense and Peppermints," because of several harmonic borrowings including the alternation of $\flat\mathrm{VII}^{M7}$—I^{M7} in both the verse of the former and the coda of the latter.

Sometimes, the borrowing in question is fairly obvious, as when the guitar solo from "Love Is Strange" reappears in the Diamonds' "Words of Love" or when the entire musical matter of Fleetwood Mac's "Albatross" forms the basis of the Beatles' "Sun King," but when the reference remains part of the backing texture, these examples seem to make no referential statements beyond stylistic influence. This may also be true in cases such as the Mothers' "Love of My Life," which is a remake of "Eddie My Love" but, then again, this reprises countless other doo-wop melodic-harmonic examples as well. Finally, there's the curiously derivative case of Ronnie Dove: the verse of his "Right or Wrong" is a rewrite of Elvis Presley's "One Night" and the chorus of his "Hello Pretty Girl" comes straight from the Drifters' "Save the Last Dance for Me." The melody of the verse of his "Happy Summer Days," however, was itself stolen for Keith's "98.6," so perhaps some six-degrees-of-separation linkage is inevitable in such commercially "safe" pop music.

A curious phenomenon in the early 1960s was the answer song, whereby one hit might generate a response, with new lyrics responding to those of the original, the music of which was copied lock, stock, and barrel in the manner of the satirist Allan Sherman ("Hello Muddah, Hello Faddah (A Letter From Camp)"). Thus, Jim Reeves's "He'll Have to Go" was answered by Jeanne Black's "He'll Have to Stay," Shep and the Limelites' "Daddy's Home" responded to the Heartbeats' "A Thousand Miles Away," Sam Cooke's "Bring It On Home to Me" engendered Carla Thomas's identically arranged "I'll Bring It Home to You," and Roger Miller's "King of the Road" led to Jody Miller's "Queen of the House." Damita Jo's "I'll Save the Last Dance for You" answers the Drifters, and her "I'll Be There" repeats the music of "Stand By Me." In a related manner, but possibly more in the vein of an uncredited cover recording, the Trashmen's "Surfin' Bird" came directly from both the Rivingtons' "The Bird's The Word" and their "Papa Oom Mow Mow." In a category of its own, Bobby "Boris" Pickett's "Monster Mash" was based rather closely on Dee Dee Sharp's "Mashed Potato Time," which in turn seems a rather shameless remake of the Marvelettes' "Please Mr. Postman."

The artist and the text

The relationship of the artist and the song is a complex and interesting one. The degree to which a singer might represent the persona represented in the lyric is one of the most important measures of connection between rock stars and their fans. The question of authorship has perhaps never been as deep and simple at the same time as in the case of John Lennon and Yoko Ono's "Two Minutes Silence," a memorial to a miscarriage that sounds exactly as entitled. In the spirit of John Cage's 4'33," this track is incomplete without the full conceptual and musical involvement, indeed compositional skills, of the listener, and thus appears on one of two albums the artists labeled "Unfinished Music." The open-ended question of what constitutes the musical text, however, can be far more pervasive than in such extreme examples. In a cover version, for instance, how much of what aspects of the original composition must be present to "be" the same song? One might take the Underground Sunshine's cover of the Beatles' "Birthday" as a problematic example—the lyrics and tune are all there, but the signature guitar / bass riff has different notes. Are they *wrong* notes or just *different* notes? The question of what constitutes a text can be treated cynically, as when Quicksilver Messenger Service divides a single performance—a live jam on Bo Diddley's "Who Do You Love"—into several distinct titles, the divisions coming in between the soloing of different band members, obviously for the purposes of copyright royalties distribution pertaining to a musical experience they did not even actually compose.

Occasionally, the artist will "break the fourth wall" by commenting directly to the listener within a text that supposedly cloaks them in another identity. Bob Dylan almost clownishly steps out from behind the microphone at the end of "I Shall Be Free No. 10" by admitting to the baffling quality of the cadential guitar tag appending every verse. Such an attitude was likely not intended during Blood, Sweat and Tears' recording of "Spinning Wheel," which ended with general laughter and the comment, "that wasn't too good, was it?," but when this self-deprecating moment was retained for consumption, the band were relating to their recording in an ironic way, and to their audience in a rather direct way, as if offering a backstage pass, or at least sharing coveted inside information. The classical pretensions in string writing for Blood, Sweat and Tears' "Overture" are self-consciously undercut by the constant reverbed laughter in the distance. (Similarly, the Monkees' "Gonna Buy Me a Dog" and the Buckinghams' "The Married Life" both have an outtake quality in that both sets of vocals contain

> The song, the artist, and the audience; authenticity.

unmuted tracks of improvised commentary and laughter.) The Beatles reversed this communion with their audience by imagining themselves as a completely different band as they worked their way through *Sgt. Pepper's Lonely Hearts Club Band*, building an extra layer of identity between themselves and their fans. But there are layers of meaning in the newly electronic "1—2—3—4" count-in that announces *Revolver* to be a totally new and different experience from *Please Please Me*, which had previously opened with the count-in; the Beatles are announcing to their audience that they have an updated product, but in a subtle, purely musical way. Perhaps the late-1960s drive to break this fourth wall was a reaction to the artists who held themselves too precious, whose humor-less Vegas-bound performances went excessively beyond the accepted pale; this extreme continued into the early 1970s in such recordings as Tom Jones's "[o-whoa-whoa] She's a Lady" and Brook Benton's "Rainy Night [rainin' rainin' rainin'] in Georgia."

One obvious strain on the artist-audience connection is caused by the recording process, which erects boundaries as much as it does bridges. Most studio records of the 1950s and '60s have an antiseptic quality intended to separate the product from those who produce it. Additionally, because our repertoire is practiced by musicians who (particularly in the 1960s and beyond) do not work from musical notation, studio recordings tend to be formally composed and regarded as a definitive text, as opposed to the usually freely improvisatory nature of evanescent concert performances. There are a few ways in which an improvisatory quality may invade the studio (and, indeed, mobile facilities may capture for reproduction actual concert programs). At its most informal, a party atmosphere may be created in the studio, inviting the listener into an intimate setting. Thus, muffed lyrics, laughter, and a "pass the ashtray" request in the break of the Beach Boys' "Barbara Ann" (outdone by a "where's that joint?" query in the Stones' "Sing This All Together") bring everyone home together. Such devices color Jimmy Soul's "If You Wanna Be Happy," the Swingin' Medallions' "Double Shot (Of My Baby's Love)," the Beatles' "Yellow Submarine" and Donovan's "Mellow Yellow," the Tremeloes' "Here Comes My Baby," the Bar-Kays' "Soul Finger," and Janis Ian's "Younger Generation Blues."

Somewhat of a more formal setting, although not that of a staged concert, is intended in such nightclub performances as basic to nearly all comedy routines (as with Bob Newhart and Bill Cosby) and as suggested in Johnny Rivers' "Memphis" and "Secret Agent Man," the Ramsey Lewis Trio's "The 'In' Crowd" and "Hang On Sloopy," Jr. Walker and the All Stars' "How Sweet It Is (To Be Loved By You)," Joe Tex's "Skinny Legs and All," and Arlo Guthrie's "Alice's Restaurant Massacree." Here, audience participation can be requested, as in the "Say yeah! (Yeah!)" responses in Little Stevie Wonder's "Fingertips." In a similar vein, the live recording of the Plastic Ono Band's "Give Peace a Chance" preserved the choral chanting of all who happened to be in the

Photo 14.03. Graham Nash, Stephen Stills, and David Crosby: all accomplished songwriters ("Carrie Anne," "For What It's Worth," and "Eight Miles High," respectively) as well as vocal harmonists and guitarists when they left their former groups (the Hollies, Buffalo Springfield, and the Byrds) to create a new self-named trio. Evidently finding themselves in need of a fourth singer/songwriter/guitarist, CS&N recruited Buffalo Springfield founder Neil Young for their second album.

hotel room in which it was taped, a musical embodiment of the concept expressed in the print ad that superimposed the legend, "You are the Plastic Ono Band," on a "Jones" page of the London telephone directory.

But live concerts were to be the crowning achievement of hard rock; albums recorded on stage by the Grateful Dead, Pink Floyd, Cream, Jimi Hendrix, and others brought concert-hall improvisation into the living room. Don't believe everything you hear, though; a separate tape of club ambiance is added to a studio recording of Big Brother and the Holding Company's "Turtle Blues" to counterfeit a "live" feel. And "live" is not necessarily better . . . the Albert Hall recording of Deep Purple and the Royal Philharmonic Orchestra's *Concerto for Group and Orchestra* sometimes comes off as an underrehearsed, underproduced study in sloppy playing and poor balance. For most other music, some listeners prefer a live recording, in which an audience might bring out an artist's best performance, whereas others prefer a studio recording, in which all players have been carefully coached through multiple takes and punch-ins, and all engineering is subject to refined practice.

An artist's connection to the material is also measured in the degree to which they have participated in its composition. Popular recordings of our selected era range from flat-out traditional nineteenth-century songs (such as the Olympics' "By the Light of the Moon," the Highwaymen's "Michael," and Solomon Burke's "Down in the Valley") through blues that are handed down in an oral folk tradition from one player to another (Fleetwood Mac's "Rambling Pony" being exactly the same song as Cream's and then Bob Dylan's "Rollin' and Tumblin'," this a remake of Willie Dixon's "Down in the Bottom," each with different copyright information) to songs provided by contract composers (some teams, such as Jerry Lieber and Mike Stoller, Jay Livingston and Ray Evans, Doc Pomus and Mort Shuman, Gerry Goffin and Carole King, Hugo Piretti and Luigi Creatore, Jeff Barry and Ellie Greenwich, Barry Mann and Cynthia Weil, Tommy Boyce and Bobby Hart, Burt Bacharach and Hal David, and Eddie Holland, Lamont Dozier and Brian Holland, highly sought-after) to music created by the artists themselves (Chuck Berry and Buddy Holly being the rare early examples before the Beach Boys and the Beatles made this de rigueur).

Before the 1950s was over, a rift developed between the critical reception of folk music (which had for some an aura of authenticity about it because it derived from a gut-produced expression of true values without either the commercial potential that comes with writing credit or the chintz of artificial overproduction) and the sales-minded pop recording, a flash-in-the-pan, here-today-gone-tomorrow ditty trumped up with enough sugar added to have great appeal before its empty calories were to give out. This rift led to the reaction against Bob Dylan's adoption of rock-music instrumentation, as if he'd thereby sold out his folk roots for monetary gain. But well before that, in 1962, the liner notes of Peter, Paul and Mary's LP, *Moving*, declare, "Recording [is] a serious business. No one has been able to sell these three on kettle drums and chimes." This can only be taken as a slap at the Mitch Miller or even Snuff Garrett brand of recording, and ultimately at the artistic aims of Phil Spector's Wrecking Crew. Interestingly, the folkies were not above taking copyright ownership of folk tunes, as when the Kingston Trio rewrote "Midnight Special" as "The Tijuana Jail," Bob Dylan reset Woody Guthrie's "1913 Massacre" as "Song to Woody," or when Peter, Paul and Mary took the public-domain "Skewbald" for their "Stewball" and then "It's Almost Tomorrow" for "Puff (The Magic Dragon)." To be sure, many such arrangements were the province of managers and other agents who "protected" artists from having to make their own business decisions, which if made poorly might not have led to as much as possible in royalties.

In the 1970s, most progressive rock was vilified by critics as pretentious; its classical aesthetic of depth, complexity, instrumental virtuosity, and thematic development, and even the arrangement of complete movements from the masters of the eighteenth and nineteenth centuries were seen as reaching for things other than what visceral, simple, and direct rock 'n' roll was meant to embody. But roots for such pretensions lie much deeper than the topsoil of 1970s rock; previous decades had seen tunes by Chopin, Tchaikovsky, and Rachmaninoff turned into popular songs. This was not common in the 1950s, when the nearest example to such reaching back might have been the Applejacks' "Mexican Hat Rock," which was a medley of the "Mexican Hat Dance," "Oh Dem Golden Slippers," and "Mary Had a Little Lamb." But perhaps Elvis Presley deserves some credit for resurrecting a nod to the (quasi-)classics beginning in 1960, as his taking of "It's Now Or Never" from "O Sole Mio" and of "Surrender" from "Torna A Sorrento" seems to have led directly to Jackie Wilson's "Night" coming from Saint-Saëns, "Alone At Last" from Tchaikovsky, and "My Empty Arms" from Verdi. Sources from the nineteenth century continued to dominate, with Kokomo's "Asia Minor" taken from Grieg, but successively earlier inspiration came from Mozart for the Tymes' "Somewhere," from Bach for Procol Harum's "Repent Walpurgis" and Phil Ochs' "I've Had Her," and from Pachelbel for Los Pop Tops' "Oh Lord, Why Lord." Brian Auger and the Trinity's "Pavane" arranged a Fauré composition two years before Emerson, Lake and Palmer and Yes took such liberties with the likes of Mussorgsky, Janáček, and Brahms.

Artists, both those respected for their "authentic" approach and those derided for writing to formulas with the greatest hit potential, are sometimes guilty of cannibalizing their own work, repeating what sells. Sometimes, as in the case of the early Beatles (all of whose titles for their first twelve single sides used the prounouns I, Me, You, or She—except for the slightly wider-ranging "This Boy"—to connect directly with the listener), such repetitious writing is over-shadowed by enough imagination in musical areas to cover up the formula. But then there are cases such as Chuck Berry's "Let It Rock," a shameless remake of "Johnny B. Goode," and Roy Orbison's "I'm Hurtin,'" based on "Only the Lonely (Know How I Feel)." Less often forgiven are the "less authentic" artists such as Frankie Valli, whose "I Make a Fool of Myself" is a rehash of "Can't Take My Eyes Off You," and Gary Puckett and the Union Gap, who never found success outside of a "Woman Woman"/"Young Girl"/"Lady Willpower" rut of para-phrased and remixed ideas. It is here that, despite any value an individual song might have, commercial commodification is clearly a force overtaking artistic creativity. Regardless of their reputation, an artist's relationship with the material at hand is always a prime consideration in evaluating expressive merit.

Many aspects of interpretation-building have been anticipated in our second run-through of our twenty-five selected rock examples as presented at the conclusion of chapter 11. Ultimately, the reader will soon be on his or her own to practice any or all of the ideas covered in this book, but I will offer encouragement to per-haps begin with any favorite singles and albums that may appear on the lists given in tables 14.01 and 14.02. These titles are just as rich as the twenty-five songs discussed in chapters 3 and 11, and so should make for accessible and rewarding analytical projects. From there, it would be only a short hop to any song of our foundational era, or indeed, to any song from the decades that have followed.

Table 14.01 Selected singles for future study, listed in order of chart success for each year, 1955–69

1955:
"Cherry Pink and Apple Blossom White," Perez Prado
"Love is a Many-Splendored Thing," The Four Aces
"Dance With Me Henry (Wallflower)," Georgia Gibbs
"Unchained Melody," Les Baxter
"Only You (And You Alone)," The Platters
"Maybeline," Chuck Berry
"Heart," Eddie Fisher
"Whatever Lola Wants," Sarah Vaughan
"Cry Me a River," Julie London
"Man in the Raincoat," Priscilla Wright

1956:
"Don't Be Cruel," Elvis Presley
"The Great Pretender," The Platters
"I Want You, I Need You, I Love You," Elvis Presley
"Whatever Will Be Will Be (Que Sera, Sera)," Doris Day
"Standing on the Corner," The Four Lads
"Why Do Fools Fall in Love," The Teen-Agers
"Tutti-Frutti," Little Richard
"On the Street Where You Live," Eddie Fisher

1957:
"All Shook Up," Elvis Presley
"Tammy," Debbie Reynolds
"You Send Me," Sam Cooke
"Chances Are," Johnny Mathis
"Don't Forbid Me," Pat Boone
"Blueberry Hill," Fats Domino
"Kisses Sweeter than Wine," Jimmie Rodgers
"School Days," Chuck Berry
"Silhouettes," The Rays
"I'm Walkin'," Fats Domino
"Young Blood," The Coasters
"Lucille," Little Richard

1958:
"It's All in the Game," Tommy Edwards
"All I Have to Do is Dream," The Everly Brothers
"Don't," Elvis Presley
"Nel Blu Dipinto Di Blu (Volare)," Domenico Modugno
"To Know Him is to Love Him," The Teddy Bears
"Get a Job," The Silhouettes
"Problems," The Everly Brothers
"Beep Beep," The Playmates
"Tears On My Pillow," Little Anthony and the Imperials
"Rebel-'Rouser," D. Eddy
"Summertime Blues," Eddie Cochran

(continued)

Table 14.01 Continued

"I Beg of You," Elvis Presley
"Oh, Boy!," The Crickets
"Devoted to You," The Everly Brothers
"Maybe Baby," The Crickets
"Nothin' Shakin'," Eddie Fontaine
"Dizzy Miss Lizzy," Larry Williams

1959:
"What'd I Say," Ray Charles
"A Lover's Question," Clyde McPhatter
"Lonely Teardrops," Jackie Wilson
"What a Diff'rence a Day Makes," Dinah Washington
"It's Late," Ricky Nelson
"Since I Don't Have You," The Skyliners
"Poor Jenny," The Everly Brothers
"Love Potion No. 9," The Clovers
"Heartbeat," Buddy Holly

1960:
"Cathy's Clown," The Everly Brothers
"El Paso," Marty Robbins
"Georgia On My Mind," Ray Charles
"Handy Man," Jimmy Jones
"Only the Lonely (Know How I Feel)," Roy Orbison
"Night," Jackie Wilson
"Beyond the Sea," Bobby Darin

1961:
"Tossin' and Turnin'," Bobby Lewis
"Runaway," Del Shannon
"Travelin' Man," Ricky Nelson
"Will You Love Me Tomorrow," The Shirelles
"Shop Around," The Miracles
"Dedicated to the One I Love," The Shirelles
"(Marie's the Name) His Latest Flame," Elvis Presley
"Spanish Harlem," Ben E. King
"I Fall to Pieces," Patsy Cline

1962:
"Big Girls Don't Cry," The Four Seasons
"Johnny Angel," Shelley Fabares
"Ramblin' Rose," Nat King Cole
"Can't Help Falling in Love," Elvis Presley
"Town Without Pity," Gene Pitney
"Bring It On Home to Me," Sam Cooke
"I Left My Heart In San Francisco," Tony Bennett

1963:
"She Loves You," The Beatles
"My Boyfriend's Back," The Angels
"Blue Velvet," Bobby Vinton
"Walk Like a Man," The Four Seasons

"Be My Baby," The Ronettes
"It's Up to You," Rick Nelson
"In My Room," The Beach Boys

1964:
"A Hard Day's Night," The Beatles
"You Don't Own Me," Lesley Gore
"Remember (Walkin' in the Sand)," The Shangri-Las
"People," Barbra Streisand
"The Girl From Ipanema," Getz/Gilberto
"Time Is On My Side," The Rolling Stones
"Wishin' and Hopin'," Dusty Springfield
"Don't Worry Baby," The Beach Boys
"You Can't Do That," The Beatles

1965:
"(I Can't Get No) Satisfaction," The Rolling Stones
"Yesterday," The Beatles
"I Got You Babe," Sonny & Cher
"Help!," The Beatles
"You've Lost That Lovin' Feelin'," The Righteous Brothers
"Downtown," Petula Clark
"This Diamond Ring," Gary Lewis and The Playboys
"My Girl," The Temptations
"Let's Hang On!," The Four Seasons
"All Day and All of the Night," The Kinks
"Papa's Got a Brand New Bag," James Brown
"Goldfinger," Shirley Bassey
"Go Now!," The Moody Blues
"Don't Let Me Be Misunderstood," The Animals
"The Tracks of My Tears," The Miracles

1966:
"We Can Work It Out," The Beatles
"Cherish," The Association
"You Can't Hurry Love," The Supremes
"Reach Out I'll Be There," The Four Tops
"When a Man Loves a Woman," Percy Sledge
"You Keep Me Hangin' On," The Supremes
"Lil' Red Riding Hood," Sam the Sham and the Pharaohs
"I Am a Rock," Simon and Garfunkel
"Day Tripper," The Beatles
"What Becomes of the Brokenhearted," Jimmy Ruffin
"Mother's Little Helper," The Rolling Stones
"Wouldn't It Be Nice," The Beach Boys
"Eight Miles High," The Byrds
"Mr. Diengly Sad," The Critters
"Just Like a Woman," Bob Dylan
"God Only Knows," The Beach Boys

1967:
"To Sir With Love," Lulu
"Ode to Billie Joe," Bobbie Gentry

(*continued*)

Table 14.01 Continued

"Somethin' Stupid," Frank and Nancy Sinatra
"The Letter," The Box Tops
"Happy Together," The Turtles
"Respect," Aretha Franklin
"Incense and Peppermints," Strawberry Alarm Clock
"Love Is Here and Now You're Gone," The Supremes
"Penny Lane," The Beatles
"Reflections," Diana Ross and the Supremes
"There's a Kind of Hush," Herman's Hermits
"How Can I Be Sure," The Young Rascals
"Baby I Love You," Aretha Franklin
"A Natural Woman (You Make Me Feel Like)," Aretha Franklin
"Strawberry Fields Forever," The Beatles
"I Can See For Miles," The Who
"People Are Strange," The Doors
"She's My Girl," The Turtles
"Alfie," Dionne Warwick
"Happy Jack," The Who
"I Am the Walrus," The Beatles

1968:
"Hey Jude," The Beatles
"(Sittin' On) The Dock of the Bay," Otis Redding
"This Guy's In Love With You," Herb Alpert
"(Theme From) Valley of the Dolls," Dionne Warwick
"Those Were the Days," Mary Hopkin
"Born to Be Wild," Steppenwolf
"For Once In My Life," Stevie Wonder
"Classical Gas," Mason Williams
"Stoned Soul Picnic," 5th Dimension
"I Wish It Would Rain," The Temptations
"The Look of Love," Sergio Mendes and Brasil '66
"Angel of the Morning," Merrilee Rush
"Both Sides Now," Judy Collins
"Piece of My Heart," Big Brother and the Holding Company
"It's Wonderful," The Young Rascals

1969:
"Dizzy," Tommy Roe
"Proud Mary," Creedence Clearwater Revival
"Worst That Could Happen," The Brooklyn Bridge
"Time of the Season," The Zombies
"Something," The Beatles
"Touch Me," The Doors
"My Cherie Amour," Stevie Wonder
"Is That All There Is," Peggy Lee
"Stand!," Sly and The Family Stone
"A Ray of Hope," The Rascals

Table 14.02 Selected albums for further study, listed in order of chart success for each year, 1955–69

1955:
Oklahoma!, soundtrack

1956:
My Fair Lady, original cast
Elvis Presley, Elvis Presley
Elvis, Elvis Presley

1957:
Loving You, Elvis Presley
Love is the Thing, Nat King Cole

1958:
South Pacific, soundtrack
The Music Man, original cast
Come Fly with Me, Frank Sinatra

1959:
Sound of Music, original cast
At Large, The Kingston Trio
Music from Peter Gunn, Henry Mancini
Here We Go Again, The Kingston Trio
Have Twangy Guitar Will Travel, Duane Eddy

1960:
Sold Out, The Kingston Trio
String Along, The Kingston Trio

1961:
West Side Story, soundtrack

1962:
Modern Sounds in Country and Western Music, Ray Charles
In Concert, Joan Baez
Joan Baez, Joan Baez

1963:
In the Wind, Peter, Paul and Mary
Moving, Peter, Paul and Mary
Live at the Apollo, James Brown
Washington Square, The Village Stompers
Freewheelin' Bob Dylan, Bob Dylan

1964:
A Hard Day's Night, The Beatles
Mary Poppins, soundtrack
Peter, Paul & Mary, Peter, Paul and Mary
Concert, The Beach Boys
At PJ's, Trini Lopez

(continued)

Table 14.02 Continued

All Summer Long, The Beach Boys
The Times They are A-Changin', Bob Dylan
Another Side of Bob Dylan, Bob Dylan

1965:
Help!, The Beatles
Whipped Cream and Other Delights, Herb Alpert and the Tijuana Brass
Going Places, Herb Alpert and the Tijuana Brass
People, Barbra Streisand
Highway 61 Revisited, Bob Dylan
Bringing It All Back Home, Bob Dylan
Mr. Tambourine Man, The Byrds
Impressions: Keep on Pushing, The Impressions

1966:
Rubber Soul, The Beatles
Revolver, The Beatles
Parsley, Sage, Rosemary & Thyme, Simon and Garfunkel
Got Live if You Want It, The Rolling Stones
Blonde on Blonde, Bob Dylan
Pet Sounds, The Beach Boys
Wednesday Morning, 3 A.M., Simon and Garfunkel
Freak Out!, The Mothers of Invention

1967:
Sgt. Pepper's Lonely Hearts Club Band, The Beatles
I Never Loved a Man, Aretha Franklin
The Doors, The Doors
John Wesley Harding, Bob Dylan
Strange Days, The Doors
Surrealistic Pillow, Jefferson Airplane
Disraeli Gears, Cream
Are You Experienced, The Jimi Hendrix Experience
After Bathing at Baxter's, Jefferson Airplane
Absolutely Free, The Mothers of Invention
Velvet Underground with Nico, Velvet Underground
Piper at the Gates of Dawn, Pink Floyd

1968:
Hair, original cast
The Beatles, The Beatles
Cheap Thrills, Big Brother and the Holding Company
Bookends, Simon and Garfunkel
Wheels of Fire, Cream
Electric Ladyland, The Jimi Hendrix Experience
Axis: Bold as Love, The Jimi Hendrix Experience
Days of Future Passed, The Moody Blues
Beggar's Banquet, The Rolling Stones
Music From Big Pink, The Band
We're Only in It for the Money, The Mothers of Invention

Anthem of the Sun, The Grateful Dead
Lumpy Gravy, Frank Zappa
Ogden's Nut Gone Flake, The Small Faces
The Soft Machine, The Soft Machine
The Hangman's Beautiful Daughter, The Incredible String Band
A Saucerful of Secrets, Pink Floyd

1969:
Abbey Road, The Beatles
Led Zeppelin II, Led Zeppelin
Blood, Sweat & Tears, Blood, Sweat and Tears
Green River, Creedence Clearwater Revival
Blind Faith, Blind Faith
Nashville Skyline, Bob Dylan
Let It Bleed, The Rolling Stones
Tommy, The Who
I Got Dem Ol' Kozmic Blues Again Mama, Janis Joplin
Crosby, Stills & Nash, Crosby, Stills and Nash
Hot Buttered Soul, Isaac Hayes
The Band, The Band
Led Zeppelin, Led Zeppelin
Stand Up, Jethro Tull
Uncle Meat, The Mothers of Invention
Clear Spirit, Spirit
Aoxomoxoa, The Grateful Dead
Odessey & Oracle, The Zombies
The Stooges, The Stooges
Bread, Bread
Hot Rats, Frank Zappa

From "Blue Suede Shoes" to "Suite: Judy Blue Eyes"

To bring this study to a close, let's examine from the many perspectives employed in this book songs produced at both the beginning and the end of our period, 1955–1969, in order to see what they're about and whether they have interesting points in common or in opposition. The two selections were made rather arbitrarily, mostly because their titles make sweet bookends: "Blue Suede Shoes" and "Suite: Judy Blue Eyes." Several stark differences between the two are quite apparent on their surfaces: the Carl Perkins number is a two-minute throwaway by a band of post-juvenile Tennessean hillbilly brothers that brought a new musical exuberance to the national consciousness, whereas the Crosby, Stills and Nash record is a seven-minute poetic statement from three self-aware folk-rock superstars whose formative years had been spent at such far removes as southern California, Florida, and northern England. The Perkins song was taped live for a mono mix in the primitive confines of Sam Phillips's Sun Records studio in Memphis in December 1955, the month after Elvis Presley had cut his last sides there. It peaked with four weeks ranked at #2 in national juke-box plays the following May and June, barred from the top spot only by Presley's first pop hit, "Heartbreak Hotel." The "Suite," in contrast, was recorded in February 1969 by Los Angeles engineering visionary Wally Heider, who was to replace his studios' eight-track desks with twenty-four-track equipment after witnessing the overdubbing talents of Stephen Stills in the making of *Crosby, Stills & Nash*. "Suite: Judy Blue Eyes" was made into a 4'35" single that never entered *Billboard*'s top twenty, but it was a major hit on FM radio as a full-length album track and suggested whole new styles that were realized by the top album-selling groups of the '70s, the Eagles and Fleetwood Mac.

Peeling away these obvious layers of difference reveals some unexpected similarities. Both songs use lyrics expressively, each in their own way. Although the instruments sound very different from one track to the next, and although a greater number of sung as well as played parts appear in the later song, each performance accompanies the voice with drums, bass, and both acoustic and electric guitars. Both songs employ syncopation in supporting bluesy vocal tunes with a predominantly major-mode accompaniment. Both define their sonic envelopes with reverberation or echo for the soloist. Let's look more closely at each recording.

"Don't step on my blue suede shoes" is supposed to have been a phrase Carl Perkins had heard in two contexts a short time apart, leading him to borrow it as the motto-refrain of a flexible twelve-bar verse. He might also have been drawn to the phrase because of his penchant for introducing "blue" elements, including that blues structure, into his country style. Perkins presents three different verses (the third flanked by two lead-guitar solos), with the song's overall structure rounded by a repeat of the first verse and then a coda. The performers have the same instrumentation as Elvis Presley's rockabilly combo: Carl Perkins (vocal and electric guitar), Clayton Perkins (upright bass), Jay Perkins (acoustic rhythm guitar), and W. S. Holland (drums). Two early-1956 televised performances by the Perkins band are typically available through YouTube.

The song features some formal variation. Its first verse (built on a counting litany, as was "(We're Gonna) Rock Around the Clock" a half-year before) gets off to a halting start, as each of its first two stop-time bars ("one for the money, two for the show") is stalled by two extra beats that act as barriers before the starting gates open with "go, cat, go!" This opening-frame effect only need occur once, though, so later verses, including the repeat of this first one, keep the motion hopping with a regular four beats to the bar. Whereas both of these verses, the two guitar solos, and the coda are all in a regular twelve bars (if initially extended by two extra pairs of beats), the litanies of grievances in the second and third verses ("well, you can knock me down, step in my face..." and "well you can burn my house, steal my car...") require an extra four bars of initial I chords each time. The coda opens with repeated vamping on the conclusory line, "blue, blue—blue suede shoes," but ends with the regular final refrain.

At 168 bpm, "Blue Suede Shoes" is faster than 95% of its pop-rock peers. Its strong backbeat is marked on the snare, while percussive snaps of bass strings mark every half-beat, normally with chordal roots and fifths. The rhythm section blends very tightly; only with its 1—2—♯2—3—4 lead-in to the second line of each verse does the bass stand out; the ride cymbal is probably played but is inaudible due to poor microphone set-up. The rhythm guitar carries only major triads, all played in "cowboy" positions. Jay muffles his chords during the stop-time phrases, but they ring just a touch at 0:19 and 1:37; Carl doesn't play in these stop-time lines on his Les Paul but gestures here to his live audience instead before he must play in the refrains.

In contrast to the bland rhythm section, both the vocal and the lead guitar stand out with personality. For their era, the lyrics are audaciously informal ("lay hoffa dem shoes") and straight from the hills ("drink my liquor from a old fruit jar"). Extra syllables in each statement of the title combine with the syncopation created by the anticipation of third beats in each third line ("you can do any*thang* but lay hoffa my *ba*-loo suede shoes") to heighten the sense of threat felt by the singer and the warning he conveys; this antisocial quality is made strongest in the triplet that stomps against the beat of "step on my" at 0:09, bending the rhythm just as blue notes bend the pitch. And whereas the bass and acoustic guitar play strictly from the major scale, Perkins sings plenty of blue pitches, mixing ♭3 against natural 3 (" [♭7] well it's [1] one for the [♭3] money, [1] two for the [♭3] show, [1] three to get [3!] ready, [5] now [♭7] go [5] cat, [♭3] go!") and ending both the last verse and coda with descending minor-pentatonic cascades. The only sung pitch not taken from the minor-pentatonic scale (other than that unstable 3) is 2, which gives the threatening cadences something of a minor-mode pall: "[5] but [♭7] lay [1] offa [2] my [♭3] blue [1] suede shoes." A strong tape-slap echo on the vocal signal also helps the leader break through the rhythm texture. But the vocal microphone has a weak capture; one can hear Carl closing in on and then backing away from the mic in the lines, "well you can burn my house,...old fruit jar" (0:57–1:03).

The lead guitar finds corners to fill with minor-pentatonic interjections (♭3—1—♭7—8—5—♭7—8 at 0:10–0:13; ♭3—1—5—♭7—8 at 0:51–0:55), adds minor sevenths and even a lowered third (0:47–0:49) to the IV chord whereas the acoustic guitar is restricted to pure triads, and is replete with double stops, one characteristic example (0:41–0:46) sounding a constant first scale degree above a repeated hammered-on ♯4—5. The country-favored sixth scale degree creates a rockabilly version of the blues boogie in the repeated 1—♭3—[hammered up to 3]—5—6 ostinato at 1:54+, and the song ends with Carl's signature added-sixth chord. "Blue Suede Shoes" became an instant legend—not only was it widely covered, Elvis Presley and Boyd Bennett also taking it into the charts in 1956, but its title was mentioned in songs by Chuck Berry, Buddy Holly, Larry Williams, and many others for years to come.

Stephen Stills's 1968 departure from Buffalo Springfield and his new musical partnership with David Crosby and Graham Nash coincided with the dissolution of his romantic relationship with Judy Collins. No listener to "Suite: Judy Blue Eyes" can miss hearing how the perfect harmonies of Nash and Crosby offer Stills the balm that can soothe his anguish, as each of his blues-laden solo expressions of pain is replaced by confident, hopeful, and even joyous vocal exaltations in the major mode. The film *Woodstock* features Crosby, Stills and Nash's fine performance of this song with just two acoustic guitars (Stills's six-string and Crosby's twelve-string), but the studio recording is far more intricate.

The only litany apparent in "Suite" is in the form of an alliteration that focuses attention on the song's central concern, the loss of a lady: "lacy, lilting lyric, losing love lamenting." (To match the counting conceit of "Blue Suede Shoes," one has to listen to another Stills track on *Crosby, Stills & Nash*, "Helplessly Hoping," which follows one line sung by Stills alone, "they are *one* person," with another to which Nash adds a descant part, "they are *two* alone," and then with Crosby adding a third, lower, part for "they are *three* together, they are *for* each other.") This last play on words (resembling the same pun, "for" for "four," in the chorus of Country Joe and the Fish's "I-Feel-Like-I'm-Fixin'-to-Die Rag") reverberates with the suggestion of "*Sweet* Judy Blue Eyes." Another striking aspect of Stills's poetry is the Spanish-sung final stanza, an ode to the beauty of Cuba.

"Suite" is a song with four distinct sections, three of which incorporate contrasting sections within them, as outlined in Table 14.03. Although this suite is often said to be a collection of disparate songs joined without a break, it has more integrity as a whole than might first greet the ear. It seems to change tempo radically several times, but note the relationships: Part I has the beat moving at 152 bpm; Part II slows this down exactly by half, shifting instantly to 76 bpm; Part III keeps the 76 bpm rate, but strongly accents the offbeats, to prepare a return to 152 bpm for Part IV. The tempo is never really altered at all—Stills merely tempers and then reignites the level of dynamic accent from section to section, always to signify the vacillating frustration, contemplation, thrill, and release true to the song's four main parts.

"Suite" presents a narrative arc, as the singer admits the newly open acknowledgement of his pain in the first two verses, exhibits that pain at

Table 14.03 Structure of "Suite: Judy Blue Eyes"

Part I:	
0:00	Guitar Introduction
0:11	Harmonized Verse 1 ("It's getting to the point...")
0:36	Harmonized Refrain ("I am yours...")
0:46	Harmonized Verse 2 ("Remember what we said...")
1:11	Harmonized Refrain ("I am yours...")
1:18	Repeated Introduction
1:29	Solo Bridge 1 ("Tearing yourself...")
1:53	Harmonized Refrain ("I am yours...")
2:04	Harmonized Verse 3 ("Something inside...")
2:29	Extended Harmonized Refrain ("I am yours...")
Part II:	
2:48	Harmonized Verse 4 ("Friday evening...")
3:38	Solo/Backing-vocal Bridge 2 ("Can I tell it like it is?...")
3:58	Harmonized Verse 5 ("I've Got an Answer...")
4:41	Guitar/Bass Interlude
Part III:	
5:09	Solo/Harmonized Verse 6 ("Chestnut brown canary...")
5:22	Guitar/Bass Break
5:37	Solo/Harmonized Verse 7 ("Voices of the angels...")
5:51	Guitar/Bass Break
6:05	Solo/Harmonized Verse 8 ("Lacy, lilting lyric...")
6:19	Guitar/Bass Transition
Part IV:	
6:31	Scatted "Do do do" Harmonies for Stills's Spanish "Cuba" Lyric

Judy's leaving him in the first bridge, and reaffirms his love and offers himself to her in Verse 3. In Part II, Stills releases Judy in Verse 4, bares his soul more deeply still in Bridge 2, and resolves to release himself, "fly away," in Verse 5. In Part III, the singer goes against his own second-verse advice by reliving once again his past thrill at Judy's bird-like singing but also recalls how she had told him metaphorically that she would not be possessed ("How can you catch the sparrow?"). Part IV shows that the singer has liberated himself in an imagined flight to the beautiful Cuba. This narrative, particularly in juxtaposing the singer's vacillating states of mind, is supported by qualities in the vocal and instrumental arrangements as well as by the rhythmic and formal qualities already mentioned.

Vocals are divided between that of the lead singer, Stephen Stills, and those of the harmonizers, Graham Nash and David Crosby. But all parts are divided in other ways as well. One such division occurs in the stereo image; all vocals are center throughout the song until Part IV, in which Stills has physically taken leave of his dilemma through the left-side placement of his "Cuba" fantasy. Stills' voice is heard as a single recording through the first verse, but is thereafter double-tracked at the unison for growing emphasis of the song's motivation—her leaving him, his resulting pain and continuing love. (It would not have made sense in Verse 1 to sing "I am lonely" through two unison vocals.) The part reverts to a single vocal for the highly individualistic solo in Bridge 2, in which Stills's lonely, suffering heart leaps an octave at 3:46 into the empty space of suddenly added reverb. The double-tracked texture returns in Part III as the singer's confidence is boosted, but the extreme-left Cuban dream (with a softer, delayed signal from this track also appearing center) is from a once-again solitary voice.

Pitchwork is closely tied to expression. All of Stills's pitches in the first two verses map completely onto the major scale, except in the solo lines "I am sorry," "I am lonely," and "I am not dreaming," all of which descend ♭3—2—1 over IV. All of his harmonized singing is restricted to major-mode scale degrees except for Part III's pushy ♭7 in the demanding lines "sing a song...," "asking me...," and "change my life...." Stephen's own solo lines, by contrast, can be outbursts of melismatic, minor-pentatonic truth in complex rhythms ("[♭7] Can [8] I [♭3] tell [4] it like [♭3] it [4—♭3—1] is? [4] Lis-[♭3] -ten [4] to [5] me [♭3—1] ba- [1—♭7—5] -by; [♭7] it's [1] my [8] heart [♭7] that's a [4] suf- [♭3] -f'rin, it's [1] a [♭7—1] dy- [1] -in' and [♭3] that's what [♭3—4—♭3—2] I [1] have [5] to [♭7—8] lose"). The minor-pentatonic scale is even more pronounced in the solo lines as improvised live. The Cuban dream is all in the soothing and soaring major-mode scale degrees of 3, 4, 5, and 6, never again touching down on 1.

Although Stills is the composer and lead vocalist, Nash's voice, the highest, is the focus of passages wherein all three sing in the same rhythm. Nash does more than his mates to attempt to keep the song firmly planted in the major mode, especially with his frequent minor seconds in 4—3 and 1—7 (both intervals featured in the line, "[3] where [4] I'm no [3] fun [2] a- [1] -ny [7] more" (0:14–0:18), for instance), and also in his goal-fulfilling descents (as at "[1] what have you got [5] to [5—4—3—2—1] lose?" (3:08–3:12)). He does lament for the sparrow, however, through ♭7 ("[6] ruby throat- [8] -ed [8—♭7] spar- [♭7] -row"). Otherwise, his and Crosby's singing is entirely major-mode diatonicism except for one spot: Stills's soul-baring in 3:40–3:53 is accompanied by striking parallel fifths from Nash and Crosby: "[Nash's 4 over Crosby's ♭7] help [1 over 4] me I'm [♭7 over ♭3] suf- [1 over 4] -fering, [4 over ♭7] help [1 over 4] me I'm [♭7 over ♭3] dy- [1 over 4] -ing, [3 over 1] oooh," the only lines that are performed in rhythms that disagree with those in Stills's part, altogether creating the song's harshest vocal clash.

Crosby and Nash are often highlighted as a pair for two-part harmonies—in "Guinnevere," they seem to emulate Simon and Garfunkel—but in this song, most of the part-singing features Nash and Stills with Crosby hidden in between, all three in close harmony. Nash and Stills usually move in flowing parallel sixths (as in "the point where I'm no fun any-" 0:12–0:17 and "Friday evening," 2:55–3:00) and tenths ("are what you are," 0:39–0:40), but they change to harsher parallel fifths in the extended and demanding line, "sing a song, don't be long, thrill me to the marrow" (5:15–5:22, reminiscent of the fifths bounding the three Beatle vocal parts at "some are dead and some are living" in "In My Life") as well as in the soul-baring passage cited above. The recurring scatted line in the coda ties together these approaches in an affirming parallel unity, following the binding parallel fifths (6:31–6:33) with looser sixths (6:33–6:34), emblematizing in a wordless moment Stills's emancipation from shackles. (The song's conclusion in a joyous scatting "do do do do do" rhymes with the celebration of our earlier song's coda, "blue, blue—blue suede shoes.") The reverb applied to the vocal lines that would otherwise have ended cold at "sparrow" and "marrow," all their harmonies' overtones firmly locked-in, suggests a frisson brought on by the sparrow song that tingles to the bone; this also connects with the song's ending, where vocal-harmony reverb trails off following the last cold chord, the song taking leave of the listener amid resonant memories of this strong thrill. Contrary motion is restricted to the refrain's falsehood (0:36–0:37), "I am yours," where Nash rises, 4—5—8, against Stills' descent, 8—6—5. Most singing is heavily syncopated to suggest the underlying agitation (and sometimes the song's birdlike lilt), but Part II is marked by languid, regularized rhythms.

Four guitars, bass, organ, tambourine, and drums make intermittent appearances in "Suite." The tambourine, shaken so as to articulate every half beat, is heard only in Part I, and is out for both statements of the introduction. It is heard much higher in the mix in the 1994 remastering than it had been in the 1969 LP release. Drums were played by Dallas Taylor. They are silent through Part I (although they may have been played there and muted in the mix), but enter as replacement for the tambourine for Part II. Through Part II, the crash cymbal is struck on two, and the drums are busy otherwise, marking half-beats at the new slower tempo. Tension runs high behind Stills's emotive outburst in Bridge 2 (3:38–3:50), where the hi-hat is treated distinctively, being hit on the ands of 2 and of 4, and closed on the strong parts of each of the next beats. The drums are silent for the interlude and Part III, returning at 6:31 to provide a backbeat for Part IV.

Stills plays three of the guitars (we'll label them Guitars I, III, and IV), bass, and organ; Guitar II is Crosby's. Guitar I is Stills' acoustic Martin D-28 heard left; this and Crosby's Gibson twelve-string acoustic, drums, and (probably) Nash's tambourine were likely recorded as the basic track, with the composer adding the four other instruments (plus his final vocal overdub) after the group vocals were taped. Stills's electronic organ, with a heavy tremulant, is heard only in Part IV; this was mixed center for the LP but is heard to the right in the digital remaster. We'll examine, in turn, Stills's two acoustic guitars (the basic instrument, Guitar I, and an overdub, Guitar IV), Crosby's twelve-string (Guitar II), Stills's electric lead guitar (Guitar III), and the bass line.

In Guitar I, Stills uses an unusual tuning, E B E E B E (once suggested by Buffalo Springfield bassist, Bruce Palmer). This gives voice to open, ringing doublings of roots and fifths, appropriate for the song's tamboura-like drone and also reminiscent of a twelve-string's doublings as heard in both the old blues records of Skip James and the jug-band sound of Country Joe and the Fish. (The same tuning, but a major second lower, forms the bed of "Carry On," the suite that would open the group's second album. Friend Joni Mitchell was a fan of alternate tunings, and a different one was used by Crosby on "Guinnevere.") All tonic chords are played open, or with one or two of the highest-sounding strings stopped with root, third, and/or fifth above the drone strings, or (as at 1:55) barred all the way across on the twelfth fret for a bright solidity.

The intro highlights the drone: all strings are strummed (no pick) with a descending chromatic line, 5—#4—4—3 (0:01–0:02) played on the first string, answered by a 6—5 pull-off on the second string (0:04) while 3 is held above. The song's second-most used chord after I is IV, but this is usually voiced with two open B strings to create a $IV^{M9/5}$ without third (as at "point," 0:13). More interesting and disturbing is the $IV^{11/m7/5}$ without third (spelled, from the bass up, with scale degrees 4—1—1—1—$\flat$7—$\flat$3), heard in several contexts that either pass quickly (0:22, 0:35) or sustain (0:41–0:43, 1:53–1:54, 3:07–3:08), tying Judy ("what you are") to the "sorry" and "lonely" hearings of the chord in Verse 1 and also helping connect all of the song's first four minutes structurally through its restatements. (Chords like this seem far more complex than Carl Perkins's added-sixth chord, but it should be remembered that George Martin had cautioned the Beatles against using such a rich sonority to end "She Loves You" in 1963. Less than a year after that, the mystical opening sound of "A Hard Day's Night" displayed a new spirit of adventure at work.) The odd tuning of Guitar I also affects other functions: V is probably played 5—5—5—1 from the bass up, lacking third and fifth but including a suspended first scale degree, making for almost no harmonic drive. The wailing $\flat VII^{M9/add6}$ chord ("it's my heart that's a sufferin'," 3:44) is played with roots, two added sixths, and two ninths, but no fifths or thirds (spelled, from the bass up, with scale degrees $\flat$7—5—$\flat$7—1—5—1). Later ("chestnut brown canary," 5:09–5:20), a $\flat VII$ triad moves to I over an unchanging 1/5 drone, sonically linking Parts I, II, and III. The final guitar/bass retransition (6:19–6:31) introduces a hopeful new sonority that is full and rich, with a high-register neighbor ♭VII chord resolving down repeatedly to vi over an unmoving 1 pedal. Otherwise, pitch from Guitar I is largely obtuse and its unusual tuning is of almost no use in the harmonically straightforward coda, where Stills has to muffle his backbeat chords. In most rock contexts, guitar chording makes chord membership clear. In this song, it only muddies the waters so that the listener must rely on the bass part, which clarifies function, and on vocal parts, which articulate the triads.

Stills's playing, while not technically virtuosic, is loaded with variety beyond the novelty of his unusual chord voicings. At 1:12 and more clearly at 2:30, Guitar I introduces harmonics derived from all strings across the twelfth fret. Beginning at 2:49, this sound marks all second beats in the tonic at the new halved tempo through Verses 4 and 5 of Part II. Whereas the core minor-second conflict in Part I had been generated by the clash between ♭3 and 3 in contrasting ♭VII$^{M9/add6}$ against tonic, Part II features the diatonic major second 4—3 against tonic on all fourth beats, beginning at 2:51. The stable repeated harmonics and the 4—3 resolution are foiled by the return of the ♭VII$^{M9/add6}$ chord (3:07–3:08), which rings out like a question mark, fragmenting into a descending minor-pentatonic cascade in stop-time (3:09–3:10) at "what have you got to lose?" Elsewhere, Stills has an interlude very much like a sitar over tamboura at 4:41+, with a melodic line in mixolydian except for an accented lydian #4 at 4:53, all with a strong left-hand vibrato and featuring hammer-ons: 5—6—5—4—5—3—4—2—3—1 (4:44–4:46), a line seemingly taken from the Beatles' Bombay-recorded "The Inner Light."

This passage, the transition to Part III, features a tonic drone on the bass and a dynamic, rhythmic, reverb-laden hand-slapping of Stills's second acoustic, Guitar IV (right, 4:42+), which replaces the percussion of drums and tambourine. The slapping of the guitar's side sounds tabla-inspired here but drifts into more of a suggestion of Cuban percussion when continued at 6:31 (immediately thereafter replaced, following an apparent splice, by right-side handclaps marking every beat). Other than the slapping, Guitar IV has a few fingerpicked lead lines, as in its solo moment, a cadential 8—5—4—3—1 descent that ushers in the interlude between Parts II and III at 4:39–4:41.

In Guitar II (heard center in the original stereo mix but moving right to center in the remaster), Crosby demonstrates the same open tuning as does Guitar I, its twelve strings ringing in open fifths at 0:08 with even more brilliance than the sound produced by Stills. Crosby sustains tonic harmony even under Stills's chord changes, as at 0:22–0:24, amplifying the tamboura effect. In the released mixes, the guitar is muted or set to very low gain for much of the song, but has occasional shimmering tonic outbursts, as at 1:26 and, fainter, at 2:01. The guitar has only isolated tonic bursts in Part II, as at 2:52, 3:10 (answering the "questioning" chord from Guitar I at 3:07), and elsewhere, but takes strong, reverberant strums reminiscent of a sitar's sympathetic strings during the interlude (4:55+, 4:58+), continuing with these alongside more subdued strumming through Part III. I do not hear Guitar II in the edit-piece recording that became Part IV. Whereas the percussive body-slapping of Guitar IV was done as a Stills overdub for the studio version, Crosby would slap his twelve-string in live performance.

Guitar III is Stills's mid-register electric lead, played through the neck pickup, processed with a phase-shifter, and routed hard to the right side. The part starts unobtrusively with backbeat comping at 0:12, but grows intensely busy as the narrative progresses. The rough timbre gives the low open E string, our first scale degree, a strong buzz (as at 0:16), an effect that is to become a transcendental drone throughout Part II. It is Guitar III that cries out loud with a hammered-on ♭3—3—5—3 (0:31–0:36, also emphasizing the 4 and ♭7 of the IV^{11} chord in more stinging double stops, 0:54–0:59) in its first break from its backbeat-chord role, stepping out before Stills opens up his vocal solo full throttle. Guitar III lays out for the repeated introduction but returns with its chords and isolated licks in Bridge 1, building in outspokenness as its soloistic nature comes increasingly to the fore in bluesy bent notes, also sharing at 1:59–2:03 the ringing eleventh chord of Guitar I. In Verse 3, the part is simply wild, bringing out "something inside" with a high-register wail (2:09+); by 2:38, we figure that the guitar is bringing to life the singer's frustration as he repeats, "and you make it hard." As we enter the softer Part II, it seems for a moment that the rough timbre is to be replaced by the clean acoustic sound of Guitar IV, but the electric drone appears at 2:55 to tell us that the frustration is not gone, only grounded, and then foregrounded in strong support of the double-plagal ♭VII—IV—♭VII—IV—I of Stills's great outburst of 3:38–3:53. This ends the work of Guitar III, which disappears for the interlude that prepares Part III and does not return.

Stills introduces the bass on a repeated first scale degree at 0:06; it's always mixed to center. This part is also quite busy, but disciplined, as it finds its root on 1, 4, 5, or ♭7 on every downbeat, clarifying the tonal function that is often vague in the guitars. In fact, the bass is almost responsible for creating the V—IV—I harmony at 0:17–0:24 and elsewhere, seemingly a reference to the blues slogan that does not even appear in "Blue Suede Shoes," a song born before V—I in the third line of the blues would routinely be softened by IV, as it is in most later blues-rock. A nearly unmoving repeated 1 in the bass underlies the entire guitar interlude at 4:41+ and the breaks in Part III. The bass has many melodic descents in the song's inner sections; in Part II, it takes a page from the Beatles' "Rain" in arpeggiating I^{m7} with 1—8—5—♭7—8—5—1 (2:52+), fairly close to McCartney's 1—8—4—5—♭7—5, and much later it drops 8—♭7—5—4—1 (5:21–5:23). The very different line, 4—5—2—♭7—1, marks the roots in Part IV in such a way as to throw the major mode aside for the mixolydian.

The reader may have noticed a number of Beatles references cropping up in this discussion of "Suite: Judy Blue Eyes." In many ways, the song nestles in somewhere between *Rubber Soul* and *Revolver*. And this provides yet another link to Carl Perkins, whose "Blue Suede Shoes" was the Beatles' pabulum, one of the very first rock 'n' roll numbers covered by the Quarry Men and the song chosen by John Lennon to be performed without rehearsal with Eric Clapton and others in the always-changing Plastic Ono Band as the opener for a rock 'n' roll revival concert in Toronto in September 1969. It's a long way from "Blue Suede Shoes" to "Suite: Judy Blue Eyes," but there are still many connections, direct and indirect, between them. Like so much rock, they both find ways to connect joy and pain through music. Perkins and Stills worked with materials at far removes from each other, but as is true of these and thousands of other songs from the period, it's quite possible to find varied enrichments in them by examining each by the same principles, those developed and illustrated throughout our study.

Appendix: Lexicon of Chord Symbols

The symbols and spellings of the 120 chords encountered in this book are given here. The twenty-three sonorities used most often are represented in bold face.

Uppercase Roman numerals indicate chords with major thirds; lowercase Roman numerals indicate minor thirds

° sign indicates diminished fifth, + sign indicates augmented fifth; otherwise, fifth is perfect

M7 indicates major seventh, m7 indicates minor seventh, °7 indicates both diminished fifth and diminished seventh

+9 indicates augmented ninth, M9 indicates major ninth, m9 indicates minor ninth

NB: Grouped by common roots, collections of scale degrees in the second column are sequenced with bass pitch first then other members in rising order from the root, regardless of typical voicings. Spellings in the second column are as functioning except in cases where parenthesized respellings are given for simplification (e.g., 6 may stand in for $\flat\flat$7); pitches in the third column are tacitly spelled as given in the second column.

Symbol for chord	Scale degrees present	Pitches in the Key of C
i$^{\text{susM9}}$	1—2—$\flat$3—5	C—D—E$\flat$—G
i$^{\text{M9/m7}}$	1—2—$\flat$3—5—$\flat$7	C—D—E$\flat$—G—B$\flat$
I$^{+11\text{/M9/M7}}$	1—2—3—#4—5—7	C—D—E—F#—G—B
I$^{\text{M13/M9/m7}}$	1—2—3—5—6—$\flat$7	C—D—E—G—A—B$\flat$
I$^{\text{M9/m7}}$	1—2—3—5—$\flat$7	C—D—E—G—B$\flat$
I$^{\text{M9/M7}}$	1—2—3—5—7	C—D—E—G—B
I$^{+9\text{/m7}}$	1—#2—3—5—$\flat$7	C—D#—E—G—B$\flat$
i^{o7}	1—$\flat$3—$\flat$5—(6)	C—E$\flat$—G$\flat$—A
i	**1—$\flat$3—5**	**C—E$\flat$—G**
i$^{\text{m6}}$	1—$\flat$3—5—$\flat$6	C—E$\flat$—G—A$\flat$
i$^{\text{add6}}$	1—$\flat$3—5—6	C—E$\flat$—G—A
I	**1—3—5**	**C—E—G**
I$^{\text{m6}}$	1—3—5—$\flat$6	C—E—G—A$\flat$
I$^{\text{add6}}$	**1—3—5—6**	**C—E—G—A**
I$^{\text{m7}}$	**1—3—5—$\flat$7**	**C—E—G—B$\flat$**
I$^{\text{M7}}$	**1—3—5—7**	**C—E—G—B**
I^{+}	1—3—#5	C—E—G#
I^{5}	1—5	C—G
I/$\flat$3	$\flat$3—5—1	E$\flat$—G—C
I/3	3—5—1	E—G—C
#i^{o7}	#1—3—5—$\flat$7	C#—E—G—B$\flat$
#i	#1—3—#5	C#—E—G#
$\flat$II	$\flat$2—4—$\flat$6	D$\flat$—F—A$\flat$
$\flat$II$^{\text{add6}}$	$\flat$2—4—$\flat$6—7	D$\flat$—F—A$\flat$—B$\flat$
$\flat$II$^{\text{m7}}$	$\flat$2—4—$\flat$6—(7)	D$\flat$—F—A$\flat$—B
$\flat$II$^{+9\text{/m7}}$	$\flat$2—4—$\flat$6—(7)—(3)	D$\flat$—F—A$\flat$—B—E
$\flat$II$^{\text{M7}}$	$\flat$2—4—$\flat$6—8	D$\flat$—F—A$\flat$—C
II$^{\text{M9}}$/1	1—2—3—#4—6	C—D—E—F#—A
II/1	1—2—#4—6	C—D—F#—A
II$^{\text{m9/m7}}$	2—$\flat$3—#4—6—1	D—E$\flat$—F#—A—C
II$^{\text{M9/m7}}$	2—3—#4—6—1	D—E—F#—A—C
ii^{o}	2—4—$\flat$6	D—F—A$\flat$
ii$^{\text{m7/o}}$	2—4—$\flat$6—1	D—F—A$\flat$—C
ii	**2—4—6**	**D—F—A**
ii$^{\text{m7}}$	**2—4—6—1**	**D—F—A—C**
II$^{\text{m7/o}}$	2—#4—$\flat$6—1	D—F#—A$\flat$—C

II	**2—#4—6**	**D—F#—A**
II^{m7}	**2—#4—6—1**	**D—F#—A—C**
ii$^{m7/sus4}$	2—5—6—1	D—G—A—C
II^5	2—6	D—A
♭iii^{o7}	♭3—♭5—(6)—(1)	E♭—G♭—A—C
♭iii^{m7}	♭3—♭5—♭7—♭2	E♭—G♭—B♭—D♭
♭III	**♭3—5—♭7**	**E♭—G—B♭**
♭III^{M7}	♭3—5—♭7—2	E♭—G—B♭—D
♭III^5	♭3—♭7	E♭—B♭
III$^{M9/m7}$	3—#4—#5—7—2	E—F#—G#—B—D
iii^{o7}	3—5—♭7—♭2	E—G—B♭—D♭
iii	**3—5—7**	**E—G—B**
iii^{m7}	**3—5—7—2**	**E—G—B—D**
III	3—#5—7	E—G#—B
III^{m7}	3—#5—7—2	E—G#—B—D
III$^+$	3—#5—(1)	E—G#—C
III^5	3—7	E—B
iv/1	1—4—♭6	C—F—A♭
IV^5	4—1	F—C
iv$^{M9/m7}$	4—5—♭6—1—♭3	F—G —A♭—C—E♭
IV$^{M9/m7}$	4—5—6—1—♭3	F—G —A—C—E♭
IV$^{M9/5}$	4—5—1	F—G —C
IV$^{+9/m7}$	4—#5—6—1—♭3	F—G#—A—C—E♭
iv^{o7}	4—♭6—(7)—(2)	F—A♭—B—D
iv$^{m7/o}$	4—♭6—(7) —♭3	F—A♭—B—E♭
iv	**4—♭6—1**	**F—A♭—C**
iv^{m7}	4—♭6—1—♭3	F—A♭—C—E♭
IV	**4—6—1**	**F—A—C**
IV^{m7}	**4—6—1—♭3**	**F—A—C—E♭**
IV^{M7}	**4—6—1—3**	**F—A—C—E**
IV$^{11/m7/5}$	4—♭7—1—♭3	F—B♭—C—E♭
#iv^{o7}	#4—6—1—♭3	F#—A—C—E♭
#iv$^{m7/o}$	#4—6—1—3	F#—A—C—E
#iv	#4—6—#1	F#—A—C#
V$^{m9/m7}$	5—♭6—7—2—4	G—A♭ —B—D—F
v$^{M9/m7}$	5—6—♭7—2—4	G—A—B♭—D—F

V^M13/M9/m7	5—6—7—2—3—4	G—A —B—D—E —F
V^M9/m7	5—6—7—2—4	G—A —B—D—F
V^M9/m7/+	5—6—7—#2—4	G—A —B—D#—F
V^M9/sus4	5—6—1—2—4	G—A —C—D—F
V^M13/+9/m7	5—#6—7—2—3—4	G—A#—B—D—E —F
V^+9/m7	5—#6—7—2—4	G—A#—B—D—F
V^+9/m7/+	5—#6—7—#2—4	G—A#—B—D#—F
v	5—♭7—2	G—B♭—D
v^m7	5—♭7—2—4	G—B♭—D—F
V^5	5—2	G—D
V^m7/o	5—7—♭2—4	G—B—D♭—F
V	**5—7—2**	**G—B—D**
V^add6	5—7—2—3	G—B—D—E
V^m7/add6	5—7—2—3—4	G—B—D—E—F
V^m7	**5—7—2—4**	**G—B—D—F**
V^M7	5—7—2—#4	G—B—D—F#
V^+	**5—7—#2**	**G—B—D#**
V^m7/+	5—7—#2—4	G—B—D#—F
V^sus4	5—1—2	G—C—D
♭VI	♭6—1—♭3	A♭—C—E♭
♭VI^m7	**♭6—1—♭3—♭5**	**A♭—C—E♭—G♭**
♭VI^+9/m7	♭6—1—♭3—♭5—7	A♭—C—E♭—G♭—B
♭VI^M7	♭6—1—♭3—5	A♭—C—E♭—G
♭VI^5	♭6—♭3	A♭—E♭
vi^m7/o/1	1—♭3—5—6	C—E♭—G—A
VI^M9/m7	6—7—#1—3—5	A—B —C#—E—G
VI^+9/m7	6—(1)—#1—3—5	A—C —C#—E—G
vi	**6—1—3**	**A—C—E**
vi^m7	6—1—3—5	A—C—E—G
VI	**6—#1—3**	**A—C#—E**
VI^m7	6—#1—3—5	A—C#—E—G
VI^M7	6—#1—3—#5	A—C#—E—G#
VI^M7/+	6—#1—#3—5	A—C#—E#—G
VI^5	6—3	A—E
♭VII^M9/M7	♭7—1—2—4—6	B♭—C —D—F—A
♭VII^M9/add6	♭7—1—5	B♭—C —G
♭vii	♭7—♭2—4	B♭—D♭—F
♭VII	**♭7—2—4**	**B♭—D—F**

♭VII^add6	♭7—2—4—5	B♭—D—F—G
♭VII^m7	♭7—2—4—♭6	B♭—D—F—A♭
♭VII^M7	♭7—2—4—6	B♭—D—F—A
♭VII^5	♭7—4	B♭—F
vii°	7—2—4	B—D—F
vii°7	7—2—4—♭6	B—D—F—A♭
vii	7—2—#4	B—D—F#
vii^m7	7—2—#4—6	B—D—F#—A
VII	7—#2—#4	B—D#—F#
VII^m7	7—#2—#4—6	B—D#—F#—A

Further Print Resources in Pop-Rock
Music of the 1950s–60s

NB: Whereas many fine resources including essays, catalogs, video, and audio collections, auctions, newsgroups, critics' blogs, participatory sites, and ency-clopedic resources such as AllMusic (http://www.allmusic.com) and YouTube (http://www.youtube.com) are available via the Internet, there has been no effort here to compile any sort of listing of these more ephemeral sources, other than the inclusion of one item from the journal *Music Theory Online*. Additionally, many video resources such as the fine *Classic Albums* DVD series marketed by Eagle Rock Entertainment could be recommended.

Reference volumes

Babiuk, Andy. 2001. *Beatles Gear*. Balafon.
DeCurtis, Anthony, et al., eds. 1992. *The Rolling Stone Album Guide*. Random House.
Jorgensen, Ernst. 1998. *Elvis Presley: A Life in Music*. St. Martin's Press.
Lewisohn, Mark. 1988. *The Beatles Recording Sessions*. Harmony Books.
Moorefield, Virgil. 2005. *The Producer as Composer: Shaping the Sounds of Popular Music*. Massachusetts Institute of Technology.
Rees, Dafydd, and Luke Crampton. 1999. *VH1 Rock Stars Encyclopedia*. DK Publishing, Inc.

Suskin, Steven. 2000. *Show Tunes: The Songs, Shows, and Careers of Broadway's Major Composers*, 3rd ed. Oxford University Press.

Whitburn, Joel. 1990. *Joel Whitburn Presents the Billboard Pop Charts: The Sixties*. Record Research, Inc.

———. 1992. *Joel Whitburn Presents the Billboard Pop Charts: 1955–1959*. Record Research, Inc.

———. 1993. *Joel Whitburn Presents Billboard Pop Album Charts: 1965–1969*. Record Research, Inc.

———. 1996. *Joel Whitburn's Top R&B Singles 1942–1995*. Record Research, Inc.

———. 2000. *Joel Whitburn's Pop Annual: 1955–1999*. Record Research, Inc.

———. 2001. *Joel Whitburn's Top Pop Albums: 1955–2001*. Record Research, Inc.

———. 2003. *Joel Whitburn's Top Pop Singles 1955–2002*. Record Research, Inc.

———. 2005. *Joel Whitburn's Top Country Songs: 1944 to 2005*. Record Research, Inc.

Histories, style surveys

Bowman, Rob. 1997. *Soulsville, U.S.A.: The Story of Stax Records*. Schirmer.

Covach, John. 2006. *What's That Sound? An Introduction to Rock and Its History*. W. W. Norton & Co.

Kennedy, Rick, and Randy McNutt. 1999. *Little Labels—Big Sound*. Indiana University Press.

Starr, Larry, and Christopher Waterman. 2003. *American Popular Music From Minstrelsy to MTV*. Oxford University Press.

Stuessy, Joe, and Scott Lipscomb. 1999. *Rock and Roll*, 3rd ed. Prentice Hall.

Thompson, Gordon. 2008. *Please Please Me: Change and Sixties British Pop*. Oxford University Press.

Rudiments in music theory, voice leading, and harmony

Aldwell, Edward, and Carl Schachter. 2003. *Harmony & Voice Leading*. Thomson/Schirmer.

Clendinning, Jane Piper, and Elizabeth West Marvin. 2004. *The Musician's Guide to Theory and Analysis*. W. W. Norton & Sons.

Roig-Francoli, Miguel. 2003. *Harmony in Context*. McGraw-Hill.

Straus, Joseph N. 2002. *Elements of Music*. Prentice Hall.

Analytical and interpretive readings (those marked * are deeply technical)

Baur, Steven. 2002. "Ringo Round *Revolver*: Rhythm, Timbre, and Tempo in Rock Drumming." In *Every Sound There Is: The Beatles' Revolver and the Transformation of Rock and Roll*. Ashgate.

Bernard, Jonathan W. 2000. "Listening to Zappa." *Contemporary Music Review* 18/4.

———. 2008. "The Musical World(s?) of Frank Zappa: Some Observations of His 'Crossover' Pieces." In *Expression in Pop-Rock Music: Critical and Analytical Essays*, 2nd ed., ed. Walter Everett. Routledge.

*Berry, David Carson. 2000. "The Popular Songwriter as Composer: Mannerisms and Design in the Music of Jimmy Van Heusen." *Indiana Theory Review* 21.

Boone, Graeme M. 1997. "Tonal and Expressive Ambiguity in 'Dark Star.'" In *Understanding Rock: Essays in Musical Analysis*, ed. John Covach and Graeme M. Boone. Oxford University Press.

Bradby, Barbara, and Brian Torode. 2000. "Pity Peggy Sue." In *Reading Pop: Approaches to Textual Analysis in Popular Music*, ed. Richard Middleton. Oxford University Press.

Brackett, David. 2000. *Interpreting Popular Music*. University of California Press.

*Brown, Matthew. 1997. "'Little Wing': A Study in Musical Cognition." In *Understanding Rock: Essays in Musical Analysis*, ed. John Covach and Graeme M. Boone. Oxford University Press.

Covach, John. 1997. "Progressive Rock, 'Close to the Edge,' and the Boundaries of Style." In *Understanding Rock: Essays in Musical Analysis*, ed. John Covach and Graeme M. Boone. Oxford University Press.

———. 1997. "We Won't Get Fooled Again: Rock Music and Musical Analysis." In *Keeping Score: Music, Disciplinarity, Culture*, ed. David Schwarz et al. University of Virginia Press.

———. 2006. "From 'Craft' to 'Art': Formal Structure in the Music of the Beatles." In *Reading the Beatles: Cultural Studies, Literary Criticism, and the Fab Four*, ed. Kenneth Womack and Todd F. Davis. State University of New York Press.

*Everett, Walter. 1997. "Swallowed by a Song: Paul Simon's Crisis of Chromaticism." In *Understanding Rock: Essays in Musical Analysis*, ed. John Covach and Graeme M. Boone. Oxford University Press.

———. 1999. "'High Time' and Ambiguous Harmonic Function." In *Perspectives on the Grateful Dead: Critical Writings*, ed. Robert G. Weiner. Greenwood Press.

*———. 1999. *The Beatles as Musicians:* Revolver *through* The Anthology. Oxford University Press.

*———. 2001. *The Beatles as Musicians: The Quarry Men through* Rubber Soul. Oxford University Press.

———. 2002. "Detroit and Memphis: The Soul of *Revolver*." In *Every Sound There Is: The Beatles'* Revolver *and the Transformation of Rock and Roll*. Ashgate.

*———. 2004. "Making Sense of Rock's Tonal Systems." *Music Theory Online* 10/4.

———. 2006. "Painting Their Room in a Colorful Way: The Beatles' Exploration of Timbre." In *Reading the Beatles: Cultural Studies, Literary Criticism, and the Fab Four*, ed. Kenneth Womack and Todd F. Davis. State University of New York Press.

*———. 2008. "Pitch Down the Middle." In *Expression in Pop-Rock Music: Critical and Analytical Essays*, 2nd ed., ed. Walter Everett. Routledge.

Griffiths, Dai. 1993. "The High Analysis of Low Music." *Music Analysis* 18/3.

Harrison, Daniel. 1997. "After Sundown: The Beach Boys' Experimental Music." In *Understanding Rock: Essays in Musical Analysis*, ed. John Covach and Graeme M. Boone. Oxford University Press.

Headlam, Dave. 1997. "Blues Transformations in the Music of Cream." In *Understanding Rock: Essays in Musical Analysis*, ed. John Covach and Graeme M. Boone. Oxford University Press.

———. 1995. "Does the Song Remain the Same? Questions of Authorship and Identification in the Music of Led Zeppelin." In *Concert Music, Rock, and Jazz since 1945: Essays and Analytical Studies*, ed. Elizabeth West Marvin and Richard Hermann. University of Rochester Press.

Krims, Adam. 2003. "What Does It Mean to Analyse Popular Music?" *Music Analysis* 22/1–2.

Middleton, Richard. 1990. *Studying Popular Music*. Open University Press.

Moore, Allan F. 1992. "Patterns of Harmony." *Popular Music* 11/1.

————. 1993. *Rock: The Primary Text*. Open University Press.

————. 1997. *The Beatles: Sgt. Pepper's Lonely Hearts Club Band*. Cambridge University Press.

————. 2003. *Analyzing Popular Music*. Cambridge University Press.

O'Donnell, Shaugn. 1999. "Space, Motion, and Other Musical Metaphors." In *Perspectives on the Grateful Dead: Critical Writings*, ed. Robert G. Weiner. Greenwood Press.

Riley, Tim. 1988. *Tell Me Why: The Beatles: Album by Album, Song By Song, the Sixties and After*. Alfred A. Knopf.

————. 1992. *Hard Rain: A Dylan Commentary*. Alfred A. Knopf.

Schwarz, David. 1997. "Scatting, the Acoustic Mirror, and the Real in the Beatles' "I Want You (She's So Heavy).'" In *Listening Subjects*, ed. David Schwarz. Duke.

Tagg, Philip. 1982. "Analysing Popular Music: Theory, Method, and Practice." *Popular Music 7*.

————. 2000. "Analysing Popular Music: Theory, Method, and Practice." In *Reading Pop: Approaches to Textual Analysis in Popular Music*, ed. Richard Middleton. Oxford University Press.

Taylor, Timothy D. 2000. "His Name Was in Lights: Chuck Berry's 'Johnny B. Goode.'" In *Reading Pop: Approaches to Textual Analysis in Popular Music*, ed. Richard Middleton. Oxford University Press.

Temperley, David. 2007. "The Melodic-Harmonic 'Divorce' in Rock." *Popular Music* 26/2.

Tillekens, Ger. "Words and Chords: The Semantic Shifts of the Beatles' Chords." *Beatlestudies* 3.

Van der Bliek, Rob. 2007. "The Hendrix Chord: Blues, Flexible Pitch Relationships, and Self-Standing Harmony." *Popular Music* 26/2.

*Wagner, Naphtali. 2001. "Tonal Oscillation in the Beatles' Songs." *Beatlestudies* 3.

*————. 2003. "'Domestication' of Blue Notes in the Beatles' Songs." *Music Theory Spectrum* 25/2.

*————. 2004. "Fixing a Hole in the Scale: Suppressed Notes in the Beatles' Songs." *Popular Music* 23/3.

Zak, Albin J., III. 2001. *The Poetics of Rock: Cutting Tracks, Making Records*. University of California Press.

Index of Topics

An Index of Names and Index of Titles are provided at the link "Supplemental Indexes" at the book's Web site.